S0-AOK-664

FAIR PLAY : DIVERSITY AND CONFLICTS
IN EARLY CHRISTIANITY

SUPPLEMENTS TO
NOVUM TESTAMENTUM

VOLUME CIII

Professor Heikki Räisänen

FAIR PLAY: DIVERSITY AND CONFLICTS IN EARLY CHRISTIANITY

Essays in Honour of Heikki Räisänen

BY

ISMO DUNDERBERG, CHRISTOPHER TUCKETT

AND

KARI SYREENI

BRILL
LEIDEN · BOSTON · KÖLN
2002

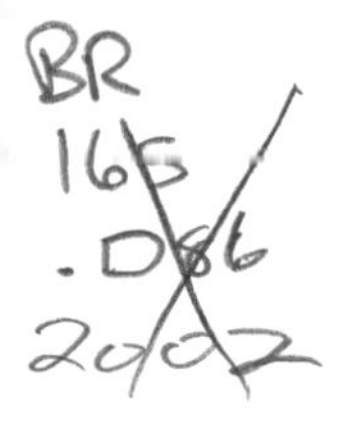

This book is printed on acid-free paper.

Library of Congress Cataloging-in-Publication Data

Fair play : pluralism and conflicts in early Christianity : essays in honour of Heikki Räisänen / by Ismo Dunderberg, Christopher Tuckett, and Kari Syreeni.
p. cm. — (Supplements to Novum Testamentum, ISSN 0167-9732 ; v. 103)
Includes bibliographical references and indexes.
ISBN 9004123598 (alk. paper)
1. Church history—Primitive and early church, ca. 30-600. 2. Bible. N.T.—Criticism, interpretation, etc. 3. Religious pluralism–Christianitty—History. I. Räisänen, Heikki. II. Dunderberg, Ismo. III. Tuckett, C.M. (Christopher Mark) IV. Syreeni, Kari. V. Series.

BR165 .F24 2001
270.1—dc21 2001046477
CIP

Die Deutsche Bibliothek – CIP-Einheitsaufnahme

Fair play : pluralism amd conflicts in early Christianity : essays in honour of Heikki Räisänen / by Ismo Dunderberg ; Christopher Tuckett and Kari Syreeni. – Leiden ; Boston; Köln : Brill, 2001
(Supplements to Novum testamentum ; Vol. 103)
ISBN 90–04–112359–8

ISSN 0167-9732
ISBN 90 04 12359 8

PRINTED IN THE NETHERLANDS

CONTENTS

PART THREE

PAUL IN CONFLICT

PART FOUR

THE PROBLEM OF DIVERSITY IN OTHER EARLY CHRISTIAN LITERATURE

PART FIVE

HERMENEUTICAL ISSUES

FOREWORD

The scholarly production of Heikki Räisänen extends over many fields in New Testament, early Christian literature, early patristic studies, and comparative religion. What is characteristic of his research in all these areas is methodological awareness combined with a keen interest in basic ethical issues. Both aspects of Heikki Räisänen's work are included in what he often has called "fair play". It is both a scholarly and moral attitude, a call for intellectual honesty and moral integrity. It is a serious, engaging form of "play" that presupposes some basic rules accepted by all players. But the players are not all alike, nor should they be; what makes the "play" so morally serious is precisely the fact that biblical interpretation is the business of so many different people, in history and now.

For Räisänen, "fair play" means above all an honest dialogue, a real encounter, as well as recognition of diverging opinions. Räisänen has recently pointed out the connection of these aspects with historical research as follows: "Whatever little I understand about dialogue, encounter, diversity and pluralism, I have learnt in critical historical work" (*Reading Bible in Global Village*, SBL, Atlanta, 2000, p. 23). Anyone familiar with Räisänen's work must acknowledge that it is these aspects of "dialogue, encounter, diversity and pluralism", and the spirit of fair play, that pervade all that he does, both academic and non-academic. (On the other hand, anyone familiar with Heikki's way of playing soccer, which is his favourite hobby, knows that his idea of fair play certainly does not exclude unyielding and tough defence nor even hard tackles, if necessary.)

Thus, the theme for this collection of essays in honour of Heikki Räisänen's 60th birthday came quite easily: the decision was made to invite his international colleagues and his students in Helsinki to contribute essays on issues related to pluralism and conflicts in early Christianity and to their challenge for biblical interpretation. The large number of Heikki Räisänen's students involved in this project demonstrates, in addition, his dedication not only to his own research but also to the stimulation, guidance and encouragement he has given to his doctoral students; more than 20 dissertations in New Testament have been brought to completion in Helsinki during his career as New Testament professor in the University of Helsinki since 1975 and as Research Professor of the Academy of Finland for a number of terms during this period.

The editors wish to thank, in particular, Dr Jarmo Kiilunen, who set the whole project in motion, the other members of the "editorial board" meeting in the Department of Biblical Studies of the University of Helsinki, Dr Petri Luomanen, Prof Antti Marjanen, Dr Matti Myllykoski, and Dr Risto Uro, for their indispensable help in laying out the contents of the present volume with us, M.Th. Tuomas Rasimus for his assistance in technical editing of the articles in this book, and M.Th. Arto Järvinen for compiling the indexes. We are also grateful to Professor David Moessner for accepting this book in the Novum Testamentum Supplements series, and the staff of Brill for their assistance in bringing this volume to completion.

The editors

PART ONE

JESUS

JESUS' GALILEE

E.P. SANDERS

The topic "Jesus' Galilee" indicates an effort to describe Jesus' environment or context—what New Testament scholars often call his "background." Since context is essential to understanding, this is part of the "quest for the historical Jesus." If we have a saying or an event and do not know the context, our fertile minds will make one up. The context that our brain supplies may be quite inaccurate, and the result may be misleading, but we automatically try to fit new information into what we already know. The historian, of course, ought to base the context on research. This paper is about a few basic aspects of the context in which Jesus lived and worked, with emphasis on Galilee. It will provide some examples of imaginary contexts that have been supplied even when historical knowledge is not difficult to attain, but my principal aim is description and clarification rather than the assessment of recent scholarship.

We know a lot more about Galilee than we did twenty years ago. A new era in research on Galilee was signaled by two books that appeared in the early 1980s: a large work by Seán Freyne that was based largely on literary evidence (1980) and a relatively brief book by Eric Meyers and James Strange that was based largely on archaeology (1981).[1] (The latter work dealt with Jewish Palestine in general, but it paid special attention to Galilee.) During the 1980s new archaeological work at several Galilean sites began to be published.

[1] Seán Freyne, *Galilee from Alexander the Great to Hadrian. 323 BCE to 135 CE* (Wilmington DE: Michael Glazier; Notre Dame: University of Notre Dame, 1980); Eric M. Meyers and James F. Strange, *Archaeology, the Rabbis and Early Christianity* (Nashville: Abingdon, 1981). A very valuable study on Sepphoris also predates the recent spate of archaeological publications: Stuart S. Miller, *Studies in the History and Traditions of Sepphoris* (SLJLA 37; Leiden: Brill, 1984). The work is based on a doctoral thesis completed in 1980, but it provides a thorough discussion of the information that was then available, with heavy emphasis on rabbinic literature. See also Miller's historical surveys, "Hellenistic and Roman Sepphoris: The Historical Evidence" and "Jewish Sepphoris: A Great City of Scholars and Scribes", in Rebecca Martin Nagy, Eric M. Meyers, Carol L. Meyers, and Zeev Weiss (eds.), *Sepphoris in Galilee. Crosscurrents of Culture* (North Carolina Museum of Art, 1996) 21–27, 59–65.

So as not to turn this essay into a bibliographical report, I shall mention only Capernaum[2] and Sepphoris.[3] The archaeology of Sepphoris in particular has touched off an enormous quantity of publications.[4] These finds, more than any other factor, have led to revised views of Galilee, especially as presented by scholars interested in Jesus of Nazareth.[5] Conferences, substantial books and doctoral dissertations attest to the recent burst of enthusiastic interest in Galilee during approximately the period of Jesus.[6]

1. *Purpose of the present essay; relationship to recent discussions*

The title of this essay should be "Jesus' Galilee part I." I have been working on this topic off and on for several years, and this essay deals with only the first of the topics that I presently have in hand or in mind. I shall give a fairly full list of topics in order to put the present essay in context. Several of these have been discussed briefly

---

[2] See Vassilios Tzaferis, *Excavations at Capernaum: 1978–1982* (Winona Lake IN: Eisenbrauns, 1989).

[3] For an early report, see Eric Meyers, Ehud Netzer and Carol Meyers, "Sepphoris (Sippori), *IEJ* 35 (1985) 295–97; more recently Ehud Netzer and Zeev Weiss, *Zippori* (Jerusalem: Israel Exploration Society, 1994).

[4] It is useful to compare M. Avi-Yonah's article on "Sepphoris", in Michael Avi-Yonah and Ephraim Stern (eds.), *Encyclopedia of Archaeological Excavations in the Holy Land*, vol. 4 (Oxford: OUP; Jerusalem: Massada, 1978) 1051–55 with Zeev Weiss' article "Sepphoris", in Ephraim Stern (ed.), *The New Encyclopedia of Archaeological Excavations in the Holy Land*, vol. 4 (Jerusalem: The Israel Exploration Society and Carta; New York: Simon and Schuster, 1993) 1324–28. On the important topic of the theater, however, Weiss' position had changed since this publication; see below, p. 30.

[5] See below at nn. 10–14 and nn. 75–76.

[6] Lee I. Levine (ed.), *The Galilee in Late Antiquity* (New York and Jerusalem: Jewish Theological Seminary, 1992; papers from the First International Conference on Galilean Studies in Late Antiquity); Eric M. Meyers (ed.), *Galilee through the Centuries* (Winona Lake, IN: Eisenbrauns, 1999; papers from the Second International Conference); Seán Freyne, *Galilee, Jesus and the Gospels. Literary Approaches and Historical Investigations* (Philadephia: Fortress, 1988); Richard A. Horsley, *Galilee: History, Politics, People* (Valley Forge, PA: Trinity, 1995); idem, *Archaeology, History and Society in Galilee. The Social Context of Jesus and the Rabbis* (Harrisburg PA: Trinity, 1996); Marianne Sawicki, *Crossing Galilee: Architectures of Contact in the Occupied Land of Jesus* (Harrisburg PA: Trinity, 2000); Mark Chancey, *The Myth of a Gentile Galilee: The Population of Galilee and New Testament Studies* (unpubl. dissertation, Duke University, 1999). One should also mention an important study of second-century Galilee that has implications for first-century Galilee: Martin Goodman, *State and Society in Roman Galilee, AD 132–212* (Totawa, N.J.: Rowman & Allanheld, 1983).

in an earlier essay,[7] but they all require reconsideration, especially in light of recent scholarship on Galilee and on Jesus.

- Government in Jewish Palestine in general and Galilee in particular; Roman imperial policy; the presence or absence of the Roman army; governmental distinctions between Jewish and non-Jewish areas, including policy on Hellenization or Romanization; the presence of non-Jews, in particular Gentile colonists, in Galilee; land ownership. All the items in this category are important in one way or another for the question of "Hellenization," though that question requires study of additional topics.
- Galilean loyalty or lack thereof to common Judaism and especially to the Judaism of Jerusalem: the temple, the priesthood, tithes, offerings, pilgrimage, synagogues, immersion pools.
- Other aspects of Hellenization: language, education, drama, athletics, games; the question of whether or not Hellenization corroded loyalty to the law.
- Money, taxes, class divisions, poverty, oppression, leisure, travel, the role of building programs.
- Class divisions; relations between rural and urban areas.
- Revolutionaries; Galilee compared to Judea.
- The role of the Pharisees.
- Legal observance in Galilee compared to Judea.
- The Galilee of the gospels compared to the Galilee of other sources.

Because of the limited subject matter of the present essay (the topics in the first category above, beginning "Government") I shall not offer here a general dicussion of the "state of the question," except for the following brief comments, which merely indicate that opinions about Galilee are now very diverse. Richard Horsley seems to me to be correct on many topics under the heading "government," such as the role of the Roman army and the supposed policy of Hellenization, but in error on taxes, economic conditions, and the degree to which Galileans were loyal to the Judaism of Judea. My disagreement with Horsley on economic conditions will also put me in opposition to Dominic Crossan, while my agreement with Horsley on the Roman army and Roman officials in Galilee leads to

[7] Sanders, "Jesus in Historical Context", *Theology Today* 50 (1993) 429–48.

disagreement with Richard Batey, Howard Kee, and others. A few specific examples of scholarly disagreements will appear in the substantive discussion.[8]

2. *Government, the Roman army, geographical distinctions, governmental policy on Jewish and Gentile areas (including "Hellenization"), colonization, land ownership*

2.1 Many scholars, including some who know better, refer to Jewish Palestine as having been "annexed" and "occupied" by Rome.[9] From time to time scholars take these words literally and suppose that Palestine became "Roman" and that Rome directly governed on a day-to-day basis, which involved bringing in Roman bureaucrats, magistrates, and the army. This perception leads to the view that there was a large Gentile population, pagan temples and numerous pig farms.[10] According to Howard Kee, in Jesus' day Sepphoris was "one of the four major centers of Greco-Roman culture and Roman administration for all of the Galilee"; it contained "a theater, hippodrome, and temples"; it was an "important Roman cultural and administrative center."[11] The view shared by Kee and Batey (n. 10), that in Jesus' day there were pagan temples in Sepphoris, is a logical inference from a more widely-held view, that there was a substantial Gentile population in Galilee in general and in Sepphoris in particular, and that among these Gentiles were important Roman officials. The first sign of a pagan temple in Sepphoris, however, is

[8] I gave three very brief sketches of scholarly positions on some of these topics in "Jesus in Historical Context", 429–32. There are references to the works by Batey, Crossan and Kee below.

[9] Marcus J. Borg, *Jesus: A New Vision*, 83 (Palestine was annexed in 63 BCE), 137 (Gentile occupiers); Dominic Crossan, *Revolutionary Biography*, 89 ("occupied"); Sawicki, *Crossing Galilee* (the subtitle of the book includes the phrase "the Occupied Land of Jesus"). Even non-New Testament scholars can fall into this error: according to Alan Segal, the Roman "occupation" of the land of Israel began in 63 BCE (*Rebecca's Children* [Cambridge MA: Harvard, 1986] 35).

[10] Richard Batey, *Jesus and the Forgotten City. New Light on Sepphoris and the Urban World of Jesus* (Grand Rapids 1991) 140. Some responses are Stuart S. Miller, "Sepphoris, the Well-Remembered City", *Biblical Archaeologist* 55 (1992) 74–83; Lawrence Schiffman, *ibid.* 105f., with appended remarks by Eric Meyers, pp. 106f.

[11] Howard Kee, "Early Christianity in the Galilee: Reassessing the Evidence from the Gospels", in Levine (ed.), *The Galilee in Late Antiquity*, 15; so also Batey, *Forgotten City*, 56.

a coin of Caracalla, who ruled the empire *c.* 211–216.[12] As will become clear in the course of the argument, it is not possible that pagan temples existed in Sepphoris during Jesus' day but disappeared without leaving any evidence. The mere fact that there were no pagan temples should have led numerous scholars to doubt the theory of a large Gentile population.

Batey cites the coin of Caracalla as supporting some of his views, but Kee's only "evidence" of Roman administration and temples is a sentence in Josephus to the effect that in the period 57–55 BCE, shortly after Pompey the Great conquered Palestine (63 BCE), the Roman general Gabinius established five administrative districts (*AJ* 14.91; *BJ* 1.170). Kee imagines that these districts were staffed by Romans and furthermore that this form of government continued for at least the next 90 years.[13] In fact, the five districts were governed by Jews, and the arrangement was changed after only one or two years. Under the new arrangment the high priest Hyrcanus II was ethnarch and the Idumean Antipater was second in command.[14] There were to be several other re-arrangements of the governmental structure before Jesus' day, but none of them placed Romans in Galilee (see below, pp. 9–12, 14–18, 34f.).

If it is not true that Roman administrators governed Palestine, what was the system? The answer is quite clear in all the sources and should never have been in dispute. I shall begin by noting that Rome governed its empire in diverse ways. Shortly after he came to power in 31 BCE, Augustus proposed to the Senate, and the Senate accepted, a plan that distinguished between Senatorial provinces

---

[12] Batey, *Forgotten City*, 56; ch. 1 n. 34.

[13] Kee cites the two passages in "Early Christianity", 15 n. 40. In a letter to the author, he made it clear that he thought that the "Roman" administrative districts still existed in Jesus' day.

[14] Correctly Horsley, *Galilee*, 113f. Josephus describes Gabinius' actions as creating a government by an "aristocracy" (*BJ* 1.169f.), by which he means a Jewish aristocracy. Roman Senators did not govern these little Palestinian districts. Peitholaus, who was second in command at Jerusalem (probably under Hyrcanus II), was Jewish: *BJ* 1.172, 180; *AJ* 14.84. Before he left Syria, Gabinius changed the government to accord "with Antipater's wishes" (*BJ* 1.178). Antipater, of course, wished Hyrcanus II to be ethnarch with himself as second in command—as Pompey had previously arranged—and this system was soon restored. A few years after Gabinius' rearrangements of the government, Hyrcanus II and Antipater were in charge (e.g. *BJ* 1.187; *AJ* 14.127–32; *c.* 48–47 BCE).

and Imperial provinces.[15] The Senatorial provinces, such as Macedonia, Achaia and Asia (western Asia Minor), were the more "civilized" areas, while the Imperial provinces, such as Syria and Egypt, were not as easily adapted to Greco-Roman society and government.

Geographically, Palestine lay in the region of Imperial provinces. Rome, however, had two ways of governing the territories that were not Senatorial provinces. Method A was use of a king who was the "friend and ally" of Rome, that is, a client king; in this case the territory was not a Roman province, but an allied kingdom (so, for example, Cappadocia). A reliable client king was highly desirable, since he kept his country at peace and defended his borders without costing Rome either money or men; Rome had built a large empire on a small base, and the problem of manpower was a substantial one.[16] When Octavian (who became Augustus) came to power, Herod already occupied this position in Palestine, and Augustus kept him; subsequently the emperor even increased Herod's kingdom.[17] After Herod's death in 4 BCE, Augustus redistributed his domain (*BJ* 2.94–101). Much of it was divided among three of his sons (Archelaus, Antipas and Philip) and his sister, Salome, while other parts were assigned to the province of Syria. For our purposes, we can largely ignore the areas that went to Philip, Salome and Syria.[18] Antipas received Galilee and Perea, while Archelaus received Samaria, Judea, and Idumea.

Antipas was a success, and he ruled Galilee as "tetrarch" (a lesser title than "king") until 39 CE. Archelaus, however, soon proved to be unsatisfactory, and he was deposed in 6 CE. Augustus then went to method B for the southern part of Jewish Palestine plus Samaria: rule by a Roman governor, supported by a few troops. In 6 CE

[15] H.S. Jones, "The *Princeps*", in S.A. Cook and others (eds.), *The Cambridge Ancient History*, vol. 10: *The Augustine Empire 44 BC–AD 70* (third impression; Cambridge: University Press, 1963), 128. [Hereafter this volume is cited as *CAH* 10.]

[16] On the problem of manpower, see e.g. Tacitus, *Annals* 4.4. On the advantages of client kings, see e.g. W.W. Tarn, "Antony in the East", *CAH* 10.34; F.E. Adcock, "The Achievement of Augustus", *CAH* 10.600f. Note also Augustus' very favorable treatment of his client kings and their families, which indicates their importance: H.S. Jones, "*Senatus Populusque Romanus*", *CAH* 10.174f.

[17] On Augustus' dealings with the client kings in the East, whom he "inherited" from Antony, see W.W. Tarn, "Octavian in the East", *CAH* 10.113f.

[18] Most of these areas, however, are listed on the table below, p. 15, and briefly discussed.

Augustus sent a minor Roman aristocrat to Judea as prefect. As is abundantly clear in the gospels, Acts and Josephus, the Roman prefect did not govern Judea on a day-to-day basis. Presumably smaller towns and villages were governed by elders, but Jerusalem was assigned to the high priest, who governed with the aid of a council.[19] This form of government was in accord with ancient Jewish tradition (going back to the sixth century BCE).[20]

Thus during Jesus' adulthood, Galilee was an allied tetrarchy, while Judea was an Imperial province; the prefect of Judea, however, governed indirectly: the high priest was the *de facto* ruler of Jerusalem.

2.2 What about the Roman army? To secure stability and peace, Rome stationed legions at strategic points. The legions that were ultimately responsible for good order in Palestine were stationed in Syria, not in Palestine. Rome did not impose "good order" by occupying every small area that it conquered, and the Roman army was not spread throughout the eastern provinces and allied kingdoms. Since the army was the empire's greatest expense, resources were concentrated in the areas that were either the most dangerous or the most vital. For example, eight legions in the north guarded Italy against the Celts and Germans (the main military threats to the empire); three were in Spain, two in Egypt, and two in the rest of Africa. In the period of Jesus' adulthood, the East—the vast territory from Syria to the Euphrates (apart from Egypt)—"was kept in restraint by four legions" stationed in Syria.[21] The "restraint" was the threat of retaliation by the legions. As Richard Horsley has

[19] I take the history recounted in this paragraph to be common knowledge, and so do not give notes for all details. One may readily consult Emil Schürer, *The History of the Jewish People in the Age of Jesus Christ (175 BC–AD 135)* (rvsd. and ed. by Geza Vermes, Fergus Millar and others; 3 vols. in 4 parts; Edinburgh: T & T Clark 1973–87) 1.287–398. [Hereafter this work is cited as Schürer/Vermes/Millar, *HJP*]. For the history of the period, see further below, pp. 14–18.

[20] The high priest became the ruler of Judea sometime after Zerubbabel dropped out of history. High priestly rule over Jerusalem was interrupted by Herod and Archelaus. In 6 CE the Romans simply restored the ancient tradition (though they also assumed the right to appoint the high priest, a practice begun by Herod).

[21] Tacitus, *Annals* 4.5, referring to the period 23–28 CE. During Tiberius' reign, the arrangement of legions was stable (G.H. Stevenson, "The Army and Navy", *CAH* 10.224). For the precise locations of the legions in Syria, see Yann le Bohec, *The Imperial Roman Army* (E.t. New York: Hippocrene; London: Batsford, 1994) 172. (*L'Armée Romaine, sous le Haut-Empire*, 1989.)

emphasized, Rome ruled by terror, not by military occupation.[22] Because of the slowness of communication and transportation, retaliation against disloyal or rebellious rulers or cities sometimes took a long time, but it was inevitable and the result was catastrophic. The events of the first Jewish revolt exemplify the situation: the small force available to the procurator, Gessius Florus, could manage no more than a minor massacre in response to Jewish unrest (*BJ* 2.305f.). This allowed time for the revolt to progress. It took from the spring of 66 CE until the autumn for the first legion to arrive from Syria. This force was ineffective, and it withdrew with losses; the new commander, Vespasian, did not have his army ready to move until the next spring—twelve months after the revolt began.[23] Three years later Jerusalem fell and the inhabitants were severely punished for their rebellion.

Except for the slowness of Roman military response, the Soviet empire in eastern Europe provides a good parallel to the way in which Rome controlled its empire in the East. The governments of Poland, Czechoslovakia and Hungary were local and "independent," but when things did not go well (from Moscow's point of view), the Soviet army intervened. While the Soviets could arrive more quickly than the Romans, they were much gentler in their treatment of rebellious "allies." In 1968, for example, Prague was not burned, and the citizens were not sold into slavery.

Rome did not station armies in the client kingdoms, and thus there were no Roman soldiers in Herod's kingdom (after he gained full control of it), or in the tetrarchies of Archelaus and Antipas.[24] Troops did, however, support Roman governors who were in charge of the imperial provinces. When Augustus deposed Archelaus and sent a prefect to govern Judea, the prefect was supported by a small "Roman" force: about 3,000 infantry and a few cavalry. The prefect dwelt in Herod's palace in the great port, Caesarea (about two

[22] Horsley, *Galilee* 115f.

[23] Schürer/Vermes/Millar, *HJP* 1.485–92.

[24] For what follows, see Zeev Safrai, "The Roman Army in the Galilee", in Lee Levine (ed.), *The Galilee in Late Antiquity*, 103–14; there is a summary on pp. 104f. There are numerous discussions of the movements of Roman legions, but no Roman historian ever places a legion in Palestine during Jesus' lifetime: that is the practice only of a few New Testament scholars. Knowledge of the legions can conveniently be found in *CAH* 10, index *s.v.* "Legions."

days' march from Jerusalem), surrounded by his troops. This very small army was not actually Roman: it was recruited from local Gentiles, especially from the cities Sebaste (formerly Samaria) and Caesarea.[25] The prefect was from Rome; we do not know the national origin of the military officers, but the senior officers may have been from Italy.[26]

It need only be added that in Jesus' day there was a small permanent garrison of Roman troops (raised locally) in the Antonia fortress in Jerusalem (*BJ* 5.244). Roman soldiers were rather like the cavalry in western movies: they stayed behind walls (the Antonia fortress) or in a friendly city (Caesarea), away from the hostile natives.

After the failure of the first revolt (70 CE), a substantial Roman army (the tenth legion) was stationed in Judea; from *c.* 120 CE there were two legions in Palestine, one of which was stationed in Galilee.[27]

Thus during the lifetime of Jesus, there was no Roman army in Galilee; there was a small force in Caesarea and a few troops in the fortress in Jerusalem.

Richard Horsley comments that "one frequently encounters the misapprehension that Galilee at the time of Jesus was not just controlled by Roman power but occupied by Roman troops."[28] This continues. Quite remarkably a recent book that shows signs of being

---

[25] According to *BJ* 2.268, the soldiers in Caesarea were mostly from Syria; according to *AJ* 20.176, most of them were from Caesarea and Sebaste. This evidence is not necessarily conflicting, since the "Greeks" in Caesarea were Syrians (as these two passages also show), and the same is probably true of the Gentiles in Sebaste. See further Schürer/Vermes/Millar, *HJP* 1.362–7.

[26] An army of 3,000 infantry is about 3/5ths of a legion. Under the prefect, who was in command, there would have been tribunes (in Greek, *chiliarchs*), who commanded approximately 1,000 men each (two cohorts, Greek *speira*). Under each tribune there would have been several centurions. In a legion, one would expect that the tribunes were Roman, but we cannot assume this in the case of a small auxiliary force in a province governed by a member of the equestrian order, since ordinarily a tribune was himself of this order. It is noteworthy that, according to Acts, a tribune stationed in Judea had bought his Roman citizenship (Acts 22:28). This at least shows that late in the first century not all tribunes were Romans. On the organization of legions and the various ranks, which I have greatly simplified, see le Bohec, *Roman Army*, 1–59; on the national origins of centurions in the legions, see pp. 74–6.

[27] In addition to Safrai (n. 24 above), see also le Bohec, *Roman Army*, 173: in Palestine, "for the most part there were two legions, the *X Fretensis* in Jerusalem from the time of Vespasian and the *VI Ferrata* at Caparcotna in the north from Hadrian's time."

[28] Horsley, *Galilee*, 115.

influenced by aspects of Horsley's work on Galilee nevertheless steadfastly ignores his discussion of the supposed Roman rule and occupation. It is based on the theory of a full Roman takeover: during the Hasmonean period the Romans had built aqueducts, to which Jewish immersion pools were the counter; Rome colonized Palestine; the cities were rebuilt with streets laid out in grids.[29] It is hard to know why New Testament scholars persist in holding views that are entirely opposed to the evidence. Those who write about Roman occupation can cite no evidence; they never say which legion occupied Galilee in Jesus' day. In the past, the view that Rome occupied Palestine was probably based simply on naive reading: the centurion whom Jesus healed (Matt 8:5–13; Luke 7:1–10) must have been a Roman (Horsley's example). In part, I suppose, the theory of the Hellenization or Romanization of Galilee is based on wishful thinking: it is much better, in the eyes of some, for Jesus to have been a cultured Hellene, or even an ignorant but nevertheless Greek-style teacher, rather than a Jewish prophet. A third factor may be the unconscious assumption that "conquest" means "occupation," an equation readily explained by recent history, when after the second world war the victorious nations did in fact establish large armies of occupation in the defeated nations.

Whatever the explanations of the view that Rome governed and occupied Galilee in Jesus' day, and that Roman troops were spread around all of Jewish Palestine, it has no basis in historical fact. As far as we know for certain, the only Roman in Jewish Palestine in Jesus' day was Pilate, though conceivably the tribunes were Roman

[29] Sawicki, *Crossing Galilee.* Horsley's influence seems evident in the sharp distinction between the "Judeans" and the "Galileans" (e.g. pp. 83, 133). On immersion pools as a response to Roman aqueducts, see pp. 83 ("indigenous cultural resistance" to "Roman aqueducts"), 99 (the Hasmonean immerision pools); cf. 99, bot. (immersion pools in Sepphoris were a response to "the municipal baths", which had been built as part of "Roman water architecture"). On streets, 83: "Roman imperial intrusions" are seen in "the rectilinear design imposed upon cities to implement Roman urbanization policies." Rome "colonized" Galilee or Jewish Palestine: 82, 85, 88 and frequently. Sawicki's book is supposedly about Jesus (p. 1), but she allows herself a considerable latitude in defining Jesus' day by including "the Roman period", which she dates from 37 BCE through "the middle of the fourth century CE" (82). For the most part she declines to date the developments that she discusses. When she does mention dates or periods (e.g. the Hasmonean and Sepphorite immersion pools in relation to Roman aqueducts and bathhouses), she is wildly inaccurate. Similarly her view of colonization is completely wrong (n. 88 below).

(n. 26 above). There may also have been Roman merchants in the port cities, especially Caesarea.

2.3 We now note that both the Romans and the Herodians distinguished between the Jewish and the non-Jewish parts of Palestine, either separating them or treating them differently, and that neither tried to gentilize or paganize them. We begin with the basic facts of government. The following table, which spans the period from Alexander Jannaeus (103–76 BCE) to Herod's heirs and the Roman prefects (indicated by "Pilate"), shows who governed what. The concluding date is 39 CE, when Antipas was deposed; Pilate had been dismissed in 36 CE. The table distinguishes the following categories:

a) Traditionally Jewish areas: Judea, plus areas incorporated, converted, or substantially repopulated by the Hasmoneans: Joppa (since Simon, 142–135 BCE),[30] Galilee, Perea and Idumea.[31] These areas are in bold type.
b) "Greek" cities:[32] (i) the cities of the Decapolis (including Scythopolis, which is west of the Jordan river); (ii) the coastal cities: Raphia,

---

[30] Schürer/Vermes/Millar, *HJP* 2.110–14.

[31] See Schürer/Vermes/Millar, *HJP* 2.1–14; on Galilee, see *HJP* 1.142, 164f., 217f. Galilee and Perea seem to have been more clearly "Jewish" than Idumea (cf. Freyne, *Galilee*, p. 44). Recently Horsley has paralleled Galilee with Idumea and has argued that even by the time of Jesus Galilee was not fully Jewish in the Judean sense (loyal to the temple and the Torah): *Galilee* and *Archaeology*, e.g. *Galilee*, 39–61. I shall have to leave this topic for another occasion, but I shall briefly make two comments: (a) it is quite correct to grant that we do not know just how or when Galilee became fully "Jewish"; (b) with regard to Galilee I agree with Freyne far more often than with Horsley (esp. Freyne, *Galilee*, 41–56).

[32] "Greek" in this context refers to a town or city that was primarily inhabited by Gentiles who spoke Greek. In many of these cases it would be accurate to use the term *polis* (on which, see n. 52 below), and sometimes I shall use it. The phrase "a 'Greek' city" is intentionally vague as to whether or not the place was a *polis*, and in the case of traditionally Gentile cities it is usually not necessary to decide. Another consideration also makes the word *polis* inappropriate as a replacement for "a 'Greek' city": *polis* could refer to a predominantly Jewish city that had been refounded and had received the constitution of a *polis*. See the discussions of Tiberias and Sepphoris below; further, Victor Tcherikover, *Hellenistic Civilization and the Jews* (E.t. S. Applebaum; Philadelphia: Jewish Publication Society, 1961; Jerusalem: Magnes, 5722) 31: "a 'Greek city,' as it is mentioned in the sources, means a city organized in the form of a Greek *polis*, not a city whose inhabitants were racial Greeks." "Greeks" could mean Orientals "who had learned Greek and acquired Greek culture"—at least to some degree; see at n. 94 below. Whereas Tcherikover used "a 'Greek' city" to mean a *polis*, I find it clearer to distinguish the terms. "Greek city" means populated primarily by Gentiles, while *polis* refers to the constitution.

Gaza, Ascalon, Caesarea (Strato's Tower),[33] Dora, and Ptolemais and points north; (iii) The city Samaria, which had been Hellenized by Alexander the Great, who settled Macedonians there. Herod refounded it and named it Sebaste.[34] It appears in the table as Seb.
c) Samaria (the geographical region), which was neither Jewish nor traditionally "Greek."

The simplest way of seeing who governed what area during what period is to look at the maps in *The Macmillan Bible Atlas*. For the issues with which we deal, the maps in the second edition are clearer than those in the third.[35] These are the map numbers in the second edition: Alexander Jannaeus, 213; Pompey, 216; Julius Caesar, 217; Herod, 220; Antipas, Archelaus, Philip, Salome, 222; Antipas and Pilate, 229. For numbers in the third edition, add 1 or 2. In the table, "y" means "yes" (this area was governed by a Jewish ruler); "n" means "no" (it was not under Jewish control). The exception is the last name on the table, "Pilate": in this case, "y" means that the area was in Pilate's jurisdiction.

In brief: Alexander Jannaeus conquered many Gentile areas; Pompey drastically reduced the area controlled by Jews; Caesar returned Joppa to Jewish control; Herod received several Gentile areas; most of these areas were segregated from the Jewish areas and given to Philip or Syria after Herod's death. Thus they were ruled by neither Antipas, Archelaus nor Pilate.

At the time of Antipas and Pilate, the following territories were in the province of Judea (Pilate) or in Galilee/Perea (Antipas): Idumea,

---

[33] Here and throughout I consider Caesarea predominantly Gentile, following Josephus, *BJ* 3.409. At the time of the revolt, however, the Jewish residents claimed that the city was theirs, since it was founded by Herod. The Gentiles proposed that it was Gentile, since it had previously been Strato's Tower, which was Gentile, and Herod would not have placed pagan statues and temples there if the city had been Jewish: *BJ* 2.266–70; *AJ* 20.173–8. It seems to me that the Gentiles had the better argument, especially since it was supported by the presence of the prefect and his army. There was, however, an important Jewish minority; according to *BJ* 2.457 20,000 Jewish residents were massacred at the time of the revolt, which actually began because of a dispute about the synagogue in Caesarea (*BJ* 2.285–92). On Caesarea, see further Schürer/Vermes/Millar, *HJP* 2.115–18.

[34] On the city Samaria, see Schürer/Vermes/Millar, *HJP* 2.160–64.

[35] Yohanan Aharoni and Michael Avi-Yonah, *The Macmillan Bible Atlas* (rvsd. ed.; New York: Macmillan; London: Collier Macmillan; prepared by Carta, Jerusalem, 1977); Yohanan Aharoni, Michael Avi-Yonah, Anson Rainey, Ze'ev Safrai, *ibid.* (New York: Macmillan, prepared by Carta, Jerusalem, 1993).

	IJ[2]	Sam[3]	**Gal**	**Perea**	AD[4]	SD[5]	Scy[6]	Seb[7]	Gaul[8]	Raphia	Gaza	Asca	**Joppa**	Caes	Dora	Ptol & n.[9]
Alex. Jan.	y	y	y	y	y	y	y	y	y	y	y	n	y	y	y	n
After Pompey	y	n	y	y	n	n	n	n	n	n	n	n	n	n	n	n
After J. Caesar	y	n	y	y	n	n	n	n	n	n	n	n	y	n	n	n
Herod	y	y	y	y	n	y	n	y	y	n	y	n	y	y	n	n
A, A, P, S[1]	y	y	y	y	n	n	n	y	y	n	n	n	y	y	n	n
Archelaus	y	y	n	n	n	n	n	y	n	n	n	n	y	y	n	n
Antipas	n	n	y	y	n	n	n	n	n	n	n	n	n	n	n	n
Pilate	y	y	n	n	n	n	n	y	n	n	n	n	y	y	n	n

[1] Archelaus, Antipas, Philip and Salome combined
[2] Idumea and Judea
[3] The region Samaria
[4] All of the Decapolis
[5] Some of the Decapolis
[6] Scythopolis
[7] The city Samaria, refounded and named Sebaste by Herod
[8] Gaulanitis, which here is intended to include Trachonitis, Batanea and Aurantis
[9] Ptolemais and points north

Judea, Joppa, Samaria, Galilee, and Perea. All of these, except Samaria and two Greek cities in Judea, were traditionally Jewish (at least since the time of the Hasmoneans). Antipas governed only traditionally Jewish areas (Galilee and Perea). The only territories governed by Pilate that were traditionally "Greek" were the cities Caesarea and Sebaste (formerly Samaria). Moreover, Pilate governed the region Samaria, which was non-Jewish but not traditionally Greek. There were, however, no traditionally Jewish areas that were governed by Gentiles other than Pilate. Some Jews lived in traditionally "Greek" cities, such as Caesarea and Scythopolis, and we may assume that there were a few Gentiles in the Jewish cities, especially Tiberias (where Antipas probably employed some Gentiles, such as military officers and construction engineers). But on the whole, Jewish and Gentile areas were separated by government. Herod was the exception to the rule.

I shall give a slightly fuller but nevertheless brief account of the history that is revealed by the table above; this partial history focuses on rearrangements of territories.[36] Alexander Jannaeus (d. 76 BCE) crowned the Hasmonean conquests by bringing many "Greek" cities (which were also *poleis*) under Jewish control: both the Decapolis and the cities of the Mediterranean coast as far north as Dora. Pompey (63 BCE) reduced the areas governed by Jews to those that were traditionally Jewish, except that he deprived the Jewish government (Hyrcanus II, supported by Antipater) of Joppa, which included a port, and the "villages of the great plain," usually considered to be the plain of Esdraelon (Jezreel), but more likely some of the coastal plain near Joppa.[37] Julius Caesar (d. 44 BCE) restored Joppa and

[36] With the exception of the "the great plain" (on which see the next note), I agree entirely with the history that is presupposed in the *Macmillan Bible Atlas*, and that can be found in Schürer/Vermes/Millar, *HJP*. I leave most points unannotated because they are uncontroversial "common knowledge."

[37] This is the one point where I suspect that the maps on which I am relying may be inaccurate. The phrase "the villages of the great plain" comes from *AJ* 14.207, which is in a lengthy section containing decrees of Caesar and the Roman Senate that reflect Caesar's desire to improve the lot of the Jews, after Pompey had deprived them of much valuable land and many valuable cities. From this passage of restoration ("it is the pleasure of the Senate" to restore to "Hyrcanus and the Jews" "the villages in the great plain, which Hyrcanus and his forefathers before him possessed") we derive the information that Pompey had removed this area from Jewish control. "The great plain" is usually taken to be Esdraelon, but it is equally likely, or even more likely, that it refers to part of the coastal plain near Joppa. I

"the villages of the great plain" to Hyrcanus II. *The actions of Pompey and Caesar reveal with great clarity the fact that there were Jewish areas and Gentile areas,*[38] and they also point to the common desire that these areas be kept separate. In particular, the Gentile cities did not want to be governed by Jews, and many celebrated their liberation by Pompey by instituting a new calendar that began with Pompey's conquest.[39] Pompey's reduction of the Jewish territory to an area smaller than the traditionally Jewish regions may have been punitive, in which case Caesar's restoration of Joppa and "the villages of the great plain" to Jewish control redressed the balance; Caesar, of course, was motivated by gratitude to Hyrcanus II and Antipater for their support in his struggle with Pompey.

After Caesar's modifications, Hyrcanus II (backed by Herod's father, Antipater) governed the Jewish areas until he was overthrown by his nephew Antigonus II, who was supported by the Parthians. This ultimately resulted in the Roman appointment of Herod as king of the Jews (40 BCE). Herod, supported by Roman troops, gained control of his kingdom in 37 BCE.

In the years after Herod came to power, Augustus gave him increasing territories to govern: Samaria, most of the rest of the coast from Gaza to just north of Caesarea, some of the cities of the Decapolis (though not Scythopolis), and land north and east of Galilee (Gaulanitis, Batanaea, Trachonitis and Aurantis). All of these were traditionally non-Jewish, and the grants of these areas reveal Augustus' confidence in Herod. According to Josephus, Augustus gave Herod Trachonitis, Batanea and Aurantis "to prevent [Trachonitis] from again being used by the brigands as a base for raids upon Damascus." Later the emperor added "all the territory between Trachonitis and Galilee" (*BJ* 1.398–400). In the chart above I used "Gaulanitis," which is the closest to Galilee, to indicate all of these territories north and east of Galilee.

After Herod's death (4 BCE), Augustus removed some of the Gentile areas from Jewish control: Hippus, Gadara, Esbus and Gaza,

am following here the work of Fabian Udoh, *Tribute and Taxes in Early Roman Palestine (63 BCE–70 CE): the Evidence from Josephus* (unpubl. doctoral dissertation, Duke University, 1996), 113–37. If this argument from Udoh's work (which has been accepted for publication) prevails, the maps will need to be revised.

[38] Cf. Freyne, *Galilee*, 44, 61.

[39] Schürer/Vermes/Millar, *HJP* 2.92.

with their surrounding territories, were attached to the province of Syria. Most of the other Hellenistic areas were segregated from the Jewish territory by being given to Philip: that is, Philip became tetrarch of much of Herod's non-Jewish domain. Only the Hellenistic cities Caesarea and Sebaste, and the region Samaria, were governed by the same man who governed Jewish areas.

These rearrangements of territories reveal that the Romans—Pompey, Julius Caesar and Augustus—recognized the differences between Jews and others, and on the whole they kept them under different governments. Augustus' grants to Herod constitute an exception to the rule, but it is noteworthy that even Herod did not receive all of the cities of the Decapolis, not even Scythopolis, which was on "his" side of the Jordan.

2.4 It is also very important to note that Herod distinguished between the Jewish and the non-Jewish parts of his territory and treated them quite differently. This can be seen clearly in his buildings.[40]

I should begin by noting that it is very probable that Josephus provides virtually complete information about Herod's principal buildings. The reason for this confidence is that his lists are drawn from at least two different sources. a) One of these praises Herod for his "works of piety" (*BJ* 1.400), which included the Jerusalem temple (1.401) but also the pagan temple at Panias; *gymnasia* in Tripolis, Damascus and Ptolemais; and temples in Berytus and Tyre (1.422). This source also notes that Herod endowed the Olympic games (1.427). Source (a) is presumably Herod's Gentile courtier, Nicolaus of Damascus, who put the construction of both the Jewish temple and pagan temples in the same category, "works of piety."

AJ 16.136–49 also comes from Nicolaus (or conceivably from another source friendly to pagan customs). It celebrates the completion of Caesarea, which was marked by "music and athletic exercises," including gladiators and wild beasts, as well as horse races (16.136f.). This implies the existence of an amphitheater and a hippodrome. The tone of the passage is indicated by the following comment: "they say that Caesar himself [Augustus] and Agrippa often

[40] See the discussion in Peter Richardson, *Herod: King of the Jews and Friend of the Romans* (Columbia, SC: University of South Carolina, 1996), 174–96, and the comprehensive list on pp. 197–202. I disagree with Richardson on a few points; see the next note.

remarked that the extent of Herod's realm was not equal to his magnanimity, for he deserved to be king of all Syria and of Egypt" (16.141). The passage continues by listing the cities that Herod founded (16.142–5) and some of the buildings that he constructed outside his realm: the Pythian temple at Rhodes, public buildings in Nicopolis, and colonnades on either side of the long street in Antioch (16.146–8). Finally the source mentions his endowment of the Olympic games (16.149).

b) A second source condemns Herod for departing from native (Jewish) customs, as a result of which "we [the Jews] suffered considerable harm," since Herod's establishments were opposed to "piety"—that is, Jewish piety (*AJ* 15.267). This source lists, among other things, athletic contests, a theater in Jerusalem, and an amphitheater "in the plain" (15.268–76), which here probably refers to the plain of Sharon (the coastal plain) and thus to the amphitheater in Caesarea.[41]

[41] Many scholars read *AJ* 15.268 as saying that Herod built an amphitheater in Jerusalem. Josephus states that Herod built "a theater in Jerusalem, and after that a very large amphiteater in the plain." They fail to see the distinction between "Jerusalem" and "the plain." For references see my "Jesus in Historical Context", 434 n. 29; the discussion is on pp. 434–6. "The plain" where Herod built the amphitheater of *AJ* 15.268 is probably the plain of Sharon (the coastal plain); that is, the reference is to the amphitheater at Caesarea, which was the site of the quadrennial games (*BJ* 1.415); these games are discussed in the paragraphs following 15.268 (15.269–75). (It is conceivable that "the plain" is the Jordan valley, since Herod also built an amphitheater at Jericho; see below). Since my article was published, but independently of it, Peter Richardson has noticed the phrase "in the plain" (*Herod*, 187 n. 41); he suggests that this is the "Rephaim Plain, southwest of the city proper." This refers to what is now a section of Jerusalem called Emek Rephaim (the Valley of the Giants). It is to Richardson's credit that he noticed the phrase "the plain", but the low spot that he proposes does not correspond to Josephus' use of "plain." I shall quote briefly from my earlier work: "A plain, in Josephus' terminology, was a large area, not a low spot in the midst of hills.... *Antiq.* 13.89–91 is typical of Josephus' usage: he contrasts Jerusalem 'in the mountains' with Joppa 'in the plain,' which here is the plain of Sharon" ("Jesus in Historical Context", 435). My study of the word "plain" in Josephus has been both corrected and expanded by Fabian Udoh, *Tribute and Taxes*, 113–137. Neither Udoh nor myself can find an instance in which Josephus used "the plain" to refer to a small depression surrounded by hills.

Scholars who have thought that Herod built an amphitheater in or near Jerusalem either have not noted the indisputable fact that the activities housed by an amphitheater took place in Caesarea (*BJ* 1.415; *AJ* 16.136f.), or they have supposed that Herod put on quadrennial games in both Caesarea and Jerusalem, which is intrinsically unlikely, given the vast expense and the offensiveness to most Jews. Had foreign gladiators (*AJ* 15.269) come to Jerusalem to fight one another and wild animals

Source (b) is from a Jewish pietist—who, of course, might be Josephus himself.

This or a similar source has also supplied *AJ* 15.326–41, which notes how Herod governed his Jewish and Gentile territories: he kept his subjects (Jews) submissive by both fear and generosity; he was "inexorable in punishment," but he showed himself "greathearted in his care . . . when a crisis arose" (15.326). He treated the cities (*poleis*, obviously the "Greek" cities) "skilfully and humanely, and he cultivated their local rulers" (15.327). *This source thus explicitly recognizes the distinction between Herod's Jewish subjcts and the residents of the "Greek" cities within his kingdom.*[42] It continues by criticizing Herod for departing from "the customs"—that is, Jewish customs—by honoring Augustus too much and by founding *poleis* and erecting temples; the author quickly adds, "not in Jewish territory, for the Jews would not have put up with this, since we are forbidden such things." The *poleis* and (pagan) temples, rather, were "built in foreign and surrounding territory" (15.328f.; cf. *BJ* 2.266: Herod would not have built a pagan temple in a Jewish city). This section continues by giving an exten-

(*AJ* 15.273), the outcry against this activity would appear in Josephus. One might ask, where, in Jerusalem, were the foreign gladiators and wild animals housed? Where were the Roman religious rites conducted? We must contrast silence about such heinous activities with the uproar caused by Pilate's relatively innocuous introduction of Roman standards into Jerusalem (*AJ* 18.55–9). I should finally note that Josephus or his source combines a reference to the theater near Jerusalem with a description of the amphitheater and games at Caesarea, which has fostored scholarly confusion. The amphitheater is mentioned in *AJ* 15.268 along with the theater in Jerusalem; 15.269–75 deals entirely with the amphitheater and its contests; *AJ* 15.276–279 refers to the theater in Jerusalem ("theater" 15.278), though the passage may be somewhat confused. There is no clear break between the games ("throwing men to wild beasts," 15.275) and the "trophies," which are described as "images surrounded by arms" (15.276) and which apparently were in the theater (cf. "images of men," 15.279). *AJ* 15.276–9 indicates that Herod was strongly criticized for these apparent images, but he demonstrated that the ornaments covered only bare wood. We should note a parallel story in which Agrippa I asks a pious Jewish critic what activities in a theater were contrary to the law (*AJ* 19.332f.).

[42] From the point of view of the pious Jewish critic, Herod treated the "Greek" territories in his domain "humanely and skilfully", but the Gentiles themselves would not all have agreed. Thus the Gadarenes brought charges against him (*AJ* 15.351). As Jones suggests, this probably shows that Gadara in theory "enjoyed local self-government" and that Herod was transgressing against the rights of the citizens: A.H.M. Jones, *The Cities of the Eastern Roman Provinces* (2nd ed., rvsd. by various scholars; Oxford: OUP, 1971; repr. Amsterdam, 1983) 271 [hereafter *CERP*].

sive summary of the development of Strato's Tower into the new city Caesarea (15.331–41). The author notes that Caesarea included a temple to Rome and to Augustus, a theater and an amphitheater (*AJ* 15.339–41; cf. *BJ* 1.413–15).

It is most unlikely that both the source friendly to paganism and the one hostile to paganism omitted pagan constructions in the Jewish parts of Herod's domain. Josephus and his sources may not provide us with an absolutely complete list of Herod's buildings and endowments, but they allow us to rule some things out: Herod did not build pagan temples in Jewish areas such as Sepphoris; he did not build an amphitheater in Jersusalem (n. 41 above); he did not build gymnasia anywhere in his realm. One source would have praised him for such constructions, while the other would have blamed him. We may note the extensive discussion of whether or not the theater in (or near) Jerusalem, which was foreign to Jewish custom, contained "images of people": it did not (*AJ* 15.277–9). Had there been an amphitheater in Jerusalem, with gladiatorial contests, it would have caused a great commotion and left some sign in our sources (n. 41 above). The theater at Jerusalem, which did not contain idols or images of people, was as far as Herod went in putting Gentile/pagan institutions in the Jewish part of his domain.

The previous paragraphs do not contain all the buildings that are important in our present discussion, and so I shall offer a summary of Herod's most important Gentile/pagan buildings. In Gentile and predominantly Gentile cities, both within and without his domain, Herod provided for Greco-Roman culture and entertainment. (1) In Tripolis, Ptolemais and Damascus he built *gymnasia* (*BJ* 1.422), but these were cities outside his realm. (2) In Jericho, which was crown land,[43] he built a hippodrome (*BJ* 1.659; *AJ* 17.175; 17.178, 193, 233) and an amphitheater (*BJ* 1.666; *AJ* 17.194). (3) In Caesarea he built a temple in honor of Rome and Augustus (*BJ* 4.414), an amphitheater, a theater and an agora; there were quadrennial games

[43] Antony gave Jericho to Cleopatra (*BJ* 1.361). It passed from her to Augustus and from him to Herod. See Schürer/Vermes/Millar, *HJP* 1.298–302. Archaeology reveals that Herod simply developed an area that had previously served as a royal estate for the Hasmoneans: Ehud Netzer, "Roman Jericho", *ABD* 3.737–9.

(*BJ* 1.415; in ancient terminology, the games were called "quinquinnial").[44] (4) He refounded the city Samaria, naming it Sebaste, which is Greek for "Augustus". The city contained an enormous temple dedicated to the emperor (*BJ* 1.403). (5) He also built a temple in honor of Augustus at Panias (*BJ* 1.404f.), later called Caesarea Philippi, a Gentile city north of the sea of Galilee.

These buildings and the activities of those who used them were potentially very hateful to the vast majority of the Jewish populace, but Herod placed them in places that were Gentile or largely Gentile (Caesarea, Sebaste and Panias, as well as foreign countries), or in a place that he treated as his private estate (Jericho).

2.5 There are other indications of Herod's reluctance to offend his Jewish subjects by publically transgressing against the law and Jewish tradition. This reluctance is especially clear in a study of his coins, the most publically visible symbol of his reign. During the years when he was conquering his realm (40–37 BCE), his mint in the Hellenistic city Samaria struck coins that were "imitations of designs that appeared on the Roman republican coins struck in Rome between 44 BCE and 40 BCE." After he conquered Jerusalem, however, and became in fact "king of the Jews," the symbols on his coins "can be related to Jewish art and to the temple."[45] To comply with new pious views of purity, during the construction of the Jerusalem temple he had priests trained as masons so that laypeople would never step into the most sacred areas (*AJ* 15.390). In all of his palaces, he installed Jewish immersion pools so that he, his family and his staff could be pure by Jewish law.[46] He defended Jewish rights in the Diaspora, which shows that he thought that *even in Gentile lands* Jews did not have to become like Gentiles. They could remain partially separate; they could keep the sabbath, assemble in synagogues, and eat kosher food.[47]

---

[44] It seems that there was already a hippodrome at Caesarea, and at some time or other a stadium was also built. Apparently all the main types of games and entertainment were offered in Caesarea. See *AJ* 16.136–41; Schürer/Vermes/Millar, *HJP* 2.46f.

[45] Ya'akov Meshorer, *Ancient Jewish Coinage* (2 vols.; New York: Amphora, 1982) 2, 5–30; quotations from pp. 19, 23.

[46] Sanders, *Jewish Law from Jesus to the Mishnah* (London: SCM; Philadelphia: Trinity, 1990) 220f.

[47] *AJ* 16.29–58, on Ionia.

2.6 Herod also founded new cities, and these raise the question of whether or not he was inserting Gentile colonists into Jewish areas.[48] We have already noted that Herod's two major foundations were in non-Jewish areas. (a) Caesarea was previously Strato's Tower. It fell into the hands of Alexander Jannaeus, but Jannaeus did not expel the Gentile residents and turn the town Jewish (as Simon had done in the case of Joppa). Pompey liberated it from Jewish control, but Augustus awarded it to Herod, along with most of the coastal plain (excluding Ascalon). Herod kept it as a basically Gentile city, complete with a Roman temple, though with a substantial Jewish population.[49] (b) Sebaste was Herod's refoundation of Samaria. As we noted above (at n. 34), the city was originally Hellenized by Alexander the Great, and thereafter it was never Samaritan or Jewish. We also noted above that during the period 40–37 Herod struck Roman-style coins there, and when he refounded it he presumably settled more Gentiles there. It was the site of one of his temples in honor of Augustus. Both Caesarea and Sebaste supplied troops for Roman armies (n. 25 above).

We shall glance briefly at some of Herod's other foundations:

AJ 16.142f.: Antipatris was a new city (not a refoundation), which Herod established in the plain of Sharon (the coastal plain), slightly northeast of Joppa. There is no specific information about the ethnic identity of the residents.

AJ 16.143: Cypros, north of Jericho, was apparently only a fortress, not a city or even a town.[50]

AJ 16.145: Phasaelis, in the Jordan valley north of Jericho, was in a general area that was traditionally Jewish, but this particular spot seems to have been previously uninhabited. Herod planted palm trees, and the dates were famous. Phasaelis remained "crown land": it was inherited by Salome and after her death passed to Livia (Julia), Augustus' wife.[51]

---

[48] On Herod's cities, see the complete list and evaluation in Jones, *CERP*, 274f.; Schürer/Vermes/Millar, *HJP* 1.306–8; and the paragraphs on individual cities in *HJP* 2.85–183.

[49] See above, n. 33.

[50] See Schürer/Vermes/Millar, *HJP* 1.306.

[51] Schürer/Vermes/Millar, *HJP* 1.161f. For the inheritance, see *AJ* 18.31, where Josephus writes "Julia", though he sometimes refers to Augustus' wife as "Livia" (e.g. *BJ* 1.566), which was her original name. Under Augustus' will, "she was adopted into the Julian *gens* and renamed Julia Augusta" (*OCD*[2], 614; cf. *OCD*[3], 876).

The survey of some of Herod's political foundations leads to the same conclusion as the study of his building program: Herod respected the Jewish character of most of his kingdom and did not create Gentile settlements in areas that were traditionally Jewish.

With regard to the question of his fostering Hellenism, we should note that not only did he not place Gentile cities in Jewish areas, or pagan temples in Jewish cities, he also did not encourage the autonomy that one associates with the term *polis*.[52] Moreover, on at least one occasion a *polis* (Gadara) brought charges against him, probably for trampling on its rights (*AJ* 15.351; see n. 42 above). Although I wish to avoid an overly technical discussion of the word *polis*, it should be said that Herod's new foundations were not full *poleis* (though he may have given them the title) and that he did what he could to reduce the autonomy of the previously existing *poleis* in the territories that Augustus assigned to him.[53] It is worth quoting the evaluation of A.H.M. Jones:

> [Herod] took good care . . . that these spectacular foundations should interfere as little as possible with the highly centralized system of administration of his kingdom; he was no lover of local autonomy and had no intention of allowing any devolution of power in his kingdom. . . .
>
> Herod's foundations thus hardly modified the administrative scheme of his kingdom. Sebaste and Gabae may have received accessions of territory; there is, however, no evidence that the lots of land which Herod's settlers received were attached to the city territory. One toparchy must presumably have been suppressed to form the territory of Antipatris; even this, however, is not certain, since some of the cities founded by the Herodian dynasty possessed no territory. . . . '[T]he

[52] The clearest definition of a *polis*, especially as it applies to cities in Palestine, is in Tcherikover, *Hellenistic Civilization*, 21–33; 90–112. Some main items: (1) independence, that is, "liberty" and "autonomy" (often modified by alliance with a king); (2) a city wall; (3) a distinctive name (that of the founder, his ancestor, a Greek or Macedonian place, etc.); (4) "municipal educational institutions—the *gymnasion* and the *ephebeion*" (p. 27); (5) "public life revolved within the framework of Greek religion" (p. 28); (6) at least some use of the Greek language. To this we should add (7) the right to issue its own coinage and (8) possession of a defined territory (see e.g. Schürer/Vermes/Millar, *HJP* 2.182). It is important to note that one does not find all of these indicators in each town that was established as a *polis*.

[53] See Schürer/Vermes/Millar, *HJP* 2.182f.; 196–98 ("It must . . . be presumed that, in the proper Graeco-Roman sense of the word, none of the places in question was a *polis*", p. 196). This refers to the toparchic capitals in Judea, Galilee and Perea (listed on pp. 192–4). I leave aside Schürer's view, refuted by subsequent research, that Jerusalem may have been the exception to the rule (197f.).

general tendency of Herod's policy would have been rather to reduce local autonomy than to increase it.'[54]

2.7 We must look at the behavior of Herod's heirs much more briefly, since the evidence is relatively slight. The wealth of information that Nicolaus of Damascus (via Josephus) provides us on Herod is not available for his heirs. What evidence there is, however, indicates that they followed in their father's footsteps.[55]

2.7.1. Philip, who governed Gentile territory, behaved appropriately. He refounded Panias, where Herod had previously built a temple, naming it Caesarea (it was subsequently called Caesarea Philippi or Caesarea Panias).[56] Philip also struck Roman-style coins, featuring the head of the emperor, his own head, or a portrait of a temple, probably the temple to Augustus built by his father.[57] We recall that Herod had imitated Roman coins prior to his conquest of Jerusalem: like father, like son.

2.7.2. Archelaus, who ruled Idumea, Judea and Samaria from 4 BCE to 6 CE, struck coins that were continuous with coins issued by Herod or by the Hasmoneans, except for three, which were equally innocuous in Jewish eyes.[58] He founded one new town or city, Archelais, which was located in the Jordan valley, probably a little south of Herod's Phasaelis (*AJ* 17.340; map 222).[59] In the absence of information, I assume that this new town, like Phasaelis, was in previously uninhabited territory. Archelaus planted palm trees, whose dates were famous (like those of Phasaelis), and to water them he diverted part of the water that supplied Neara. This implies that the area was not previously cultivated.[60] Archelais (again like Phasaelis) was "crown land": Salome seems to have acquired it after Archelaus was deposed, since it passed from her to Julia (Livia)[61] (*AJ* 18.31).[62]

[54] Jones, *CERP*, 274, 275.

[55] Immediately after the paragraph just quoted, Jones observes that "Herod's sons carried on the same policy" (*CERP*, 275). This is true in more respects than just the establishment of quasi-cities, to which Jones refers.

[56] Jones, *CERP*, 282; Schürer/Vermes/Millar, *HJP* 2.169–71. I leave aside Philip's other foundation, Julias.

[57] Meshorer, *Coinage* 2.42–49.

[58] Meshorer, *Coinage* 2.31–34.

[59] Schürer/Vermes/Millar, *HJP* 1.355 and n. 12.

[60] Josephus calls Archelais a "village" (*AJ* 17.340). It may have been populated only by the families that tended the palm trees.

[61] On the change of name from "Livia" to "Julia", see n. 51 above.

[62] Salome died during the prefecture of Marcus Ambivulus (*AJ* 18.31), which ran from 9 to 12 CE. Schürer/Vermes/Millar (*HJP* 1.335) propose *c.* 10.

2.7.3. Antipas, who received Galilee and Perea, both traditionally Jewish areas, also followed in his father's footsteps and engaged in extensive building activity. Sepphoris was the natural capital of Galilee, but it had been partially destroyed by Roman troops led by Varus during the uprisings that followed Herod's death. Antipas rebuilt it, making it (in a famous phrase) "the ornament of all Galilee" (*AJ* 18.27). Some years later (the date is not certain, but it was approximately 17–22 CE)[63] Antipas founded a new city, on previously uninhabited land, and named it Tiberias after Augustus' successor.[64]

Were these two Jewish cities "Greek" in their constitutions? And did they involve bringing in a significant number of Gentile colonists? It is important to note that these two questions can receive different answers; many scholars proceed on the assumption that a city with the constitution of a *polis* must have included a good number of Gentile colonists, but this is not the case (see n. 32 above; on colonization, see section 2.8 below). With regard to Tiberias, the answers to these two questions seem to be "sort of" and "no": Tiberias was founded as a *polis* or semi-*polis*, but it was a Jewish city.

We take up first the question of its constitution (on the characteristics of a *polis*, see nn. 52, 53 above). Josephus' extensive account of Tiberias at the time of the revolt includes many of the terms that characterize a *polis*: "we hear of an ἄρχων (*Life* 271.278.294), ten leading men (πρῶτοι; *War* 2:639), a βουλή of 600 citizens (*War* 2:641) and an assembly of the citizens (*War* 2:618, the δῆμος of the classical *polis*)."[65] Even more decisive is the fact that in the second cen-

[63] The date has been often discussed. I follow Meshorer in thinking that Avi-Yonah's analysis of second-century coins from Tiberius provides the earliest possible date. For example: "'the coins of Hadrian, struck in the year 100 of Tiberias, could not have been dated before the accession of Hadrian in 117; it follows that Tiberias was not founded before AD 17'" (Meshorer, *Coinage* 2.35, quoting M. Avi-Yonah, "The Foundation of Tiberias", *IEJ* 1 [1950] 160–69, here 168).

[64] For general treatments of Tiberias and Sepphoris, see Freyne, *Galilee*, 122–34; Schürer/Vermes/Millar, *HJP* 2.172–76, 178–82; Chancey, *Myth*, 101–24, 131–43. On Sepphoris, see also Miller, *Sepphoris*, 1–4 and the articles by Miller cited in n. 1 above. After the present article was completed, there appeared an entire issue of *Biblical Archaeology Review* dedicated to Sepphoris: vol. 26, no. 4, July–August 2000. One of the articles contains a history of the city and a description of archaeological discoveries: Mark Chancey and Eric M. Meyers, "How Jewish was Sepphoris in Jesus' Time?", pp. 18–33. I simultaneously learned that an article by Mark Chancey has been accepted for publication in *New Testament Studies*: "The Cultural Milieu of Ancient Sepphoris", *NTS* 47 (2001) 127–45.

[65] Freyne, *Galilee*, 129, relying on Schürer/Vermes/Millar, *HJP* 2.179f.

tury it minted coins that were dated from the year of its foundation ("the year 100 of Tiberias").[66] We must, however, doubt that it had anything like full autonomy. The degree of autonomy implied in Josephus' account of the revolt is probably misleading with regard to the lifetime of Jesus. At the time of the revolt, Tiberias and its district had been assigned to Agrippa II, but it was not his capital and he did not live there.[67] During the reign of Antipas, we must assume that the tetrarch governed as he liked, whatever the discussions of the council. That is, Antipas was probably no more supportive of autonomy than his father had been. This also has implications for the administration of the land around the city. In a true *polis* the farmers in the lands belonging to the city were citizens of the city, and the citizens elected the city government: the farmers could vote. Was this the case in Tiberias? I shall again quote Jones:

> [Antipas'] foundations made no difference to the administrative structure of Galilee. Josephus expressly states that Tiberias with its toparchy was given by Nero to Agrippa II. The city thus had a merely municipal autonomy, and the surrounding country was administered by royal officials resident in it.[68]

At the time of the revolt, two of the leading citizens were named "Herod," which probably indicates long-standing allegiance to the royal family, while another (Compsus son of Compsus) was the brother of the prefect of Agrippa I (*Vita* 33). This makes it highly probable that some of the land surrounding Tiberias had been given to royal officials, which supports Jones' view: Antipas and his appointees governed, and his officials probably also had the choicest land. That is, the *polis* Tiberias was very much like a toparchic capital putting on a show of being a *polis*.[69] Finally, we note another telling point from Jones: Justus' speech to the Tiberians (*Vita* 38) shows resentment of the fact that Nero gave Tiberias to Agrippa II, not because this act

[66] N. 63 above.

[67] Agrippa II presumably considered Caesarea Philippi his capital (he enlarged it, renaming it Neronias), but he actually treated Berytus (modern Beruth) as if it were his capital (*AJ* 20.211f.). We should also note that Tarichaea and Tiberias, though ordered to submit to Agrippa II, were in some respects not actually in his kingdom, which was basically the previous tetrarchy of Philip (*BJ* 3.56f.).

[68] *CERP*, 276.

[69] On toparchic capitals (the principal town/city of a region governed by a *toparch*), see e.g. *BJ* 2.252, where Tiberias is classed together with Abila, Julias and Taricheae. Many details in *CERP*, 274 and nn. 63–65, p. 462.

enslaved a free city under a king, but because the royal bank and the archives moved to Sepphoris, which became *de facto* the capital of Galilee again. If the Tiberians were not principally concerned with their "autonomy" and "freedom," one may doubt that Tiberias had been a *polis* in the fullest sense.

The conclusion of this part of the discussion of the cities of Galilee is that Tiberias was formally a *polis*, but it was a *polis* of a modified Herodian sort that made it not much different from a toparchic capital, controlled by a ruler or his appointees. It lacked many of the features of a true *polis*.

In terms of the buildings that are typical of a *polis* during the Roman era, one can mention only a *stadion* and a palace that was decorated with the images of animals.[70] The Galileans destroyed the latter during the revolt—which surely says something about the "Hellenization" of the populace. The stadium, which was used in foot races, did not do much to promote Greco-Roman culture; Antipas did not treat Tiberias the way Herod treated Caesarea, embellishing it with many of the constructions desired by Hellenized or Romanized Gentiles; there seems to have been no theater, no amphitheater and no hippodrome—and, of course, no *gymnasion* or pagan temples: civic life did not revolve around the Greek religion. If at the time of the revolt the Galileans burned Antipas' palace because of its pagan decoration, what would they have done to a temple dedicated to Tiberius, after whom the city was named?

In any case, it seems that Antipas settled his new city principally with Jews, many of whom would have disliked such buildings. The story of the need to coerce settlers to live there, since part of the city was built over a graveyard (*AJ* 18.36–8), implies a Jewish population. Josephus also writes, however, that Antipas accepted "even those who came from anywhere" (*pantachothen*) (18.37); this sentence may well refer to the acceptance of some Gentiles. Schürer regards Antipas' difficulties in settling the city as evidence that the population was "of a very mixed character."[71] Elsewhere he states that "the population of Tiberias was very mixed," but he grants that the residents "were mainly Jewish."[72] Above I indicated that it seems prob-

[70] The *stadion: BJ* 2.618; 3.539; *Vita* 92, 331 (it served as a place of common assembly); the palace: *Vita* 65f.
[71] Schürer/Vermes/Millar, *HJP* 1.342.
[72] Schürer/Vermes/Millar, *HJP* 2.179.

able that Antipas employed Gentiles in various capacities, especially in the military and in connection with his buildings (p. 16). The statement in *AJ* 18.37 seems to imply admission of a few low-class Gentile immigrants.[73] Thus we may assume that some Gentiles lived in Antipas' Tiberias. At the time of the revolt there was a small Gentile (Josephus: "Greek") population, which was massacred (*Vita* 67).[74]

It is on Sepphoris, however, that the advocates of a Hellenistic Galilee have pinned their hopes. Dominic Crossan offers a convenient catena of statements from publications by various scholars: "life in lower Galilee in the first century was as urbanized and urbane as anywhere else in the empire"; the urban areas were "Greek oriented"; Nazareth was located near "the very administrative center of the Roman provincial government"; in Galilee life was affected "by the all-pervasive presence of the Roman city."[75] We may also note Robert Funk's claim that a "pagan environment" surrounded Jesus "in Galilee, especially in Sepphoris, a hellenistic city."[76] We shall again address our two questions: Was Sepphoris legally a *polis*? Did Antipas resettle it by bringing in a substantial number of Gentile colonists?

We cannot be certain whether or not Antipas founded Sepphoris as a *polis*. Jones regarded this as probable, since the city had this status during Nero's reign, when it struck coins under its new (and not long-lasting) name, Neronias Irenopolis.[77] These coins, which are the earliest known to have been struck in Sepphoris, come from the year 68, Nero's last year as emperor, and were minted under the authority of Vespasian.[78] The coins might mark either a first foundation

[73] Jones (*CERP* 275f.) apparently construed "from anywhere" to mean "poor immigrants from abroad." He also wrote that "the few 'Greeks' seem to have belonged to the lower stratum of the population."

[74] As noted above, "Greek" in our sources refers to people who were Gentiles and who spoke Greek. Thus, for example, "Greek" sometimes interchanges with "Syrian" in Josephus (e.g. *BJ* 2.266; cf. Mark 7.26). See further Tcherikover, *Hellenistic Civilization*, 30f.; nn. 25, 32 above.

[75] Crossan, *Historical Jesus*, 19; the quotations are from Andrew Overman, Douglas Edwards, Eric Meyers, and Thomas Longstaff. Further study of the archaeology, however, has led Meyers to view Sepphoris as a Jewish city: see Chancey and Meyers, "How Jewish was Sepphoris?", n. 64 above.

[76] Robert Funk, *Honest to Jesus: Jesus for a New Millennium* (San Francisco: HarperSanFrancisco, 1996) 34. For further remarks on the supposed Hellenization/Romanization of Sepphoris, see pp. 6–7 above. And see now Chancey's article, "Cultural Milieu", above, n. 64.

[77] *CERP*, 276.

[78] Ya'akov Meshorer, "Coins of Sepphoris", in Nagy and others (eds.), *Sepphoris in Galilee*, 195–98.

or a refoundation. The theory of a refoundation (which would imply that Antipas had given Sepphoris the status of a *polis*) gains a little support from the fact that Antipas had earlier renamed the city Sepphoris Autocratoris and had also built a city wall (*AJ* 18.27). Possibly these two points indicate that in Jesus' day Sepphoris was a Jewish *polis* of the Herodian sort—that is, lacking many of the traditional features, such as a *gymnasion* and a pagan temple.

It may be that a theater stood in Sepphoris in Jesus' day, which would be another possible sign of Hellenistic influence and the status of a *polis*. The literature on the large and impressive theater is itself large and sometimes impressive. The question of the theater's date can be settled only by extensive soundings under its floor to observe pottery and coins, which can establish the latest possible date of construction. The problem is, of course, that the entire theater cannot be dug up in order to conduct a comprehensive search. To illustrate the difficulty of the question of date, I shall quote three successive statements by the same author. In an article on Sepphoris published in 1993, Zeev Weiss wrote that "the theater apparently was built in the early first century CE, possibly in the reign of Antipas"; in a booklet published in 1994 he and Ehud Netzer wrote that "archaeological soundings conducted at the core of the theater and its foundations fix the date of its construction at no earlier than the second half of the first century CE. It was probably erected some time after the first revolt or even at the beginning of the second century . . ."; and in a short article that appeared in 1996 the same two authors wrote that the archaeological evidence "suggests that this large edifice was not erected before the end of the first century CE."[79] It appears from this that archaeological work is now tending towards a date after the time of Antipas, but I do not regard this issue, interesting though it is, as being crucially important for the present questions concerning the constitutional status of Sepphoris, its population, and signs of Hellenism. It would be perfectly reasonable to think that Antipas built a theater as part of his first major construction project, since his father had built a theater at Jerusalem.

[79] See Weiss in *New Encyclopedia* (n. 4 above), 1325; Ehud Netzer and Zeev Weiss, *Zippori* (n. 3 above), 19; Netzer and Weiss, "Hellenistic and Roman Sepphoris, the Archaeological Evidence", in Nagy and others (eds.), *Sepphoris in Galilee* 29–49, here p. 32.

We must note, in this case, that there seems to have been no theater in Tiberias, since meetings of large numbers of people were held in the stadium (*Vita* 331) or the synagogue ("house of prayer," *Vita* 277). The absence of a theater in Tiberias counts somewhat against the view that Antipas built a theater in Sepphoris.

Whether a *polis* or not, the evidence of the literature is that Sepphoris had a Jewish population.[80] Josephus states that at the time of the revolt, the city, which was pro-Roman, admitted a Roman garrison, promising to give it active support against "their countrymen" (*homophylōn; BJ* 3.32), that is, against other Jews. Josephus also accused the Sepphorites of refusing to help defend the temple, "which was common to us all" (*Vita* 348).[81] Throughout Josephus' accounts of Sepphoris during the revolt he never has occasion to refer to even a Gentile minority. It was the decision of the Sepphorite Jews to side with Rome, and that was their long-term and consistent policy.[82] A striking story makes clear the traditionally Jewish character of the city: at the beginning of the revolt two Gentile nobles from Trachonitis sought refuge in Sepphoris, but the Sepphorities wished to circumcise them as a condition of letting them reside in the city. Josephus defended their right not to be forced to Judaize (*Vita* 112f.).

A review of the archaeology of Sepphoris leads to the same conclusion, though we should not come to a completely firm judgment, since archaeological work is continuing. But if one canvasses the reports thus far, one does not find any firm evidence of pagan practices in Sepphoris before or during the lifetime of Jesus. The absence of signs of Gentile habitation in Jewish Galilee in general and in Sepphoris in particular, prior to the first revolt, is crucial to the argument of this essay, but here I rely on the work of Mark Chancey, which is now supported by Eric Meyers.[83] I am not an expert in this area, and I shall not repeat their detailed arguments. I should say, however, that a lot of the evidence that scholars cite as proving that Sepphoris was a Hellenistic or Roman city comes from the

[80] Thus, quite correctly, Freyne, *Galilee*, 123, 133; earlier Jones, *CERP*, 276. More recent views to the contrary generally ignore the literary evidence and are based on misdating the city's pagan archeological remains.

[81] Freyne, *Galilee*, 123.

[82] Cf. Freyne, *Galilee*, 124f.

[83] Chancey, *Myth*; on Sepphoris, see pp. 101–124, especially 113f., 123f.; Chancey and Meyers, "How Jewish was Sepphoris in Jesus' Time?", n. 64 above.

second and third centuries, after a Roman legion was stationed in Galilee.[84] With regard to the Sepphoris of Jesus' day, there are lots of signs of Jewish habitation and no or virtually no signs of pagan habitation. Since the recent doctoral dissertation of Mark Chancey is not yet available in print, I shall quote his comment on the proposal by James Strange that Rome had established an "urban overlay" that is visible in architecture.[85]

> Strange's model is useful for understanding the interplay of Roman urban culture and indigenous culture in Palestine, but it is more applicable to later periods, not to the first century CE, and to cities in the regions surrounding Galilee, not to Sepphoris (or Tiberias, for that matter). Sepphoris did have some type of public water works in the Early Roman era and possibly a theater, if the disputed earlier dating is accepted. Some buildings' interiors were decorated with frescoes. As of yet, however, none of the other [architectural] features [that] Strange highlights as part of the Roman 'urban overlay' have been discovered in Sepphoris from the first century CE or later. Neither hippodromes, amphitheaters, odeons, nymphaea, statues, nor monumental architecture have been found, and the presence of temples in the second century CE and later must be inferred from their depictions on coins. Most conspicuously absent of all is the gymnasium, the most important agent of Hellenistic education and socialization. For these architectural features, one must look to the gentile cities on the coast (Caesarea), in the Decapolis (Scythopolis, for example), and in Samaria (Sebaste).[86]

Above we noted claims that that there were pagan temples in Sepphoris (at nn. 10, 11). It is evident that there were not. There were no Roman soldiers or Roman administrators there to require them. Herod did not build pagan temples in the Jewish parts of his kingdom (p. 21 above). Antipas certainly did not build one; it is dubious even to claim that he built a theater. The Sepphorites wanted to circumcise would-be Gentile residents. Thus no one built a pagan temple, and no one there would worship in one.

We conclude that there were no cities in Antipas' Galilee that were, in population and culture, "Hellenistic" or "Greco-Roman." I

---

[84] See above, p. 11.

[85] James F. Strange, "Some Implications of Archaeology for New Testament Studies", in James Charlesworth and Walter Weaver (eds.), *What has Archaeology to Do with Faith?* (Philadelphia: Trinity, 1992) 23–59.

[86] Chancey, *Myth*, 113f.

should, however, offer the following caveat: to some degree the entire Roman empire was "Hellenized." Nevertheless, Jewish Palestine was one of the least Hellenistic areas, for the good and simple reason that the Jews did not want to be Hellenized, and all rulers, from Pompey to Antipas, accepted this fact. (See section 3.4 below.)

I wish to comment further on the absence of *gymnasia* from Jewish Palestine. The Greek *gymnasion* was "the place where boys and youths were educated—educated in the Greek language, in literature, in religion, philosophy, and in politics. There, too, they exercised in the nude. The *gymnasion* was the prime instrument of the spread of Greek culture. A city that received an amphitheater but not a *gymnasion*, as did Caesarea and Jericho, did not get much Greco-Roman culture."[87]

While motives are hard to reconstruct, I shall offer two explanations of the absence of *gymnasia* from the domains of Herod and Antipas. The first is fear of uprisings. Herod, ruthless though he was, like any other good king did not want to provoke actual rebellion. The building of a *gymnasion* in Jerusalem had been a significant factor in provoking the Hasmonean revolt, since it involved not only education in Greek, but more importantly obscuring circumcision by an operation called "epiplasm." The youths "abandoned the holy covenant" (1 Macc 1:14f.). The Hasmonean revolt decisively rejected such extreme forms of Hellenization, and they did not resurface until the time of Hadrian—at which time the Jews bitterly resisted them.

The second suggestion is that Herod did not have a deep commitment to Greco-Roman culture; that is, he was not motivated by evangelistic zeal to Hellenize the Jews in his kingdom. He was interested in *appearing* as a model Greco-Roman king, and so in various places he put on appropriate public displays. But his policies did not promote a substantial Hellenization of his Jewish subjects. Besides the absence of *gymnasia*, we must also recall that Herod's newly founded cities were not actually governed as were *poleis*: a despotic form of government prevailed. These points appear to be true of Antipas as well: no educational institution to promote Hellenism, no truly Greek form of government, only a very small surface "show" (the stadium in Tiberias, the [dubious] theater in Sepphoris). We might compare the Hellenism fostered by Antipas to the Europeanism

[87] Quoted from my "Jesus in Historical Context", 436f.

fostered in the Arab Emirates by the presence of football (soccer) teams. Western sports do not Europeanize or Americanize all the aeras where they are accepted. Similarly the theaters, whatever plays they put on, could not conceivably have influenced the populace to the same extent as do movies and television programs, and even the latter create a very shallow "westernization" in non-western nations. And it must always be remembered that many Palestinian Jews deeply disliked the small amount of Hellenism to which they were exposed.

2.8 We need to discuss colonization, since occasionally a scholar will say that Palestine was a "colony."[88] Dominic Crossan, very well known for his work on the historical Jesus, has a colonial image of first-century Palestine, and he parallels it with Ireland under the British empire.[89] "Colonization" should mean that there were "colonials" or "colonists," people whom the imperial country settled in a foreign land. This was, of course, true of Ireland. The English made Dublin a partially English city, with English institutions (e.g. Trinity College, established by Elizabeth I, probably in imitation of her father's establishment of Trinity College, Cambridge). In the countryside, many of the large landowners were Englishmen who received their land from the British crown. They displaced the former aristocracy (as the illustration given by Crossan indicates).

Colonies were very well known in the ancient world, as is much of the history of colonization.[90] Colonies required the foundation of a new city, which might be merely an old city that the founder

[88] E.g. Crossan, *Revolutionary Biography*, p. xii; similarly Sawicki, *Crossing Galilee*, 92 ("the colonial context of Hasmonean and Herodian Galilee"); 133 ("Jesus was born precisely on what might be termed the historical fault line between the Hasmonean expansion and the Herodian takeover, when the former colonizers of Galilee were undergoing colonization by Rome"); see also pp. 82, 85, 88. The sentence quoted from p. 133 is a good example of Sawicki's chronological statements. The "former colonizers of Galilee" were the Hasmoneans, and Jesus was born on the "fault line" between the Hasmoneans and Herod, i.e. about 40–37 BCE.

[89] Crossan illustrates the situation in Jewish Palestine by telling a story about Ireland (*Revolutionary Biography*, p. 105). Personal conversations have persuaded me that the analogy with Ireland is very important in Prof. Crossan's view of first-century Palestine.

[90] The classic study of cities that includes a discussion of colonies is Jones, *CERP*. One can obtain good general knowledge from Jones' shorter book, *The Greek City From Alexander to Justinian* (Oxford: OUP 1940; repr. 1998) passim. The definitive study of Roman colonization is Fergus Millar, "The Roman *Coloniae* of the Near East: a Study of Cultural Relations", in Heikki Solin and Mika Kajava (eds.), *Roman Eastern Policy and Other Studies in Roman History* (Commentationes Humanarum Litterarum 91; Helsinki: Societas Scientiarum Fennica, 1990) 7–58. Brief accounts may be found

renamed, partially repopulated, and to which he gave a Greek (or Hellenistic) mode of government (an *ekklesia*, a *boulē* that was elected by popular vote, etc.); that is, it became a *polis*. A *polis* also had to be endowed with outlying farmland, which it governed. Some, a lot or all of this farmland would be given to new residents. This often meant that native landowners were dispossessed. We should note that, while a town could become a *polis* without repopulation, a colonial *polis* required repopulation—otherwise it was a *polis* but not a colony!

Neither Alexander, his successors, nor the Roman emperors established colonies in Jewish Palestine. They established them all around.[91] As we saw above (at n. 34) Alexander the Great established the city Samaria as a Hellenistic city; it is probable that at least some of the cities of the Decapolis were originally established by Alexander's successors (to provide land for retiring soldiers); Augustus colonized Berytus (modern Beruth), where he gave land to veterans; after Jesus' time Claudius "elevated Ptolemais to the level of *colonia* and settled veterans from his Syrian legions there."[92] And so on. But prior to the first revolt there were no foreign colonies in Jewish Palestine. We have already seen that Herod and his heirs did not establish Gentile cities in Jewish areas.

2.9 In the absence of colonies, we must assume that the farmland belonged to Jews. Neither Augustus nor Tiberius would have rewarded individual loyal Romans by giving them farmland in Herod's or Antipas' Galilee: no colony, no farmland. The only references to Gentiles in Jewish Palestine place them in the cities, and there are few such references (above we noted that there was a small population of Gentiles in Tiberias). In short, there were not many Gentiles in Jewish Palestine.

in *OCD*[2] and *OCD*[3], *s.vv.* "Colonization, Greek"; "Colonization, Hellenistic"; "Colonization, Roman." See also Benjamin Isaac, "Roman Colonies", *ABD* 5, 798–801.

[91] Alexander and his successors were prodigious colonizers. Often the place-name tells the story. Alexander established several Alexandrias, the most famous of which is in Egypt; his successors in Syria established sixteen Antiochs and nine Seleucias (Jones, *Greek City*, 7; cf. Tcherikover, *Hellenistic Civilization*, 21f.). Early in the second century BCE some of the aristocrats in Jerusalem wanted to open a *gymnasion* and be registered as "the Antiochenes in Jerusalem" (2 Macc 4:9), which would have made Jerusalem a sort of colony, but the Hasmonean revolt destroyed these efforts, and they did not reappear.

[92] Chancey, *Myth*, 78.

3. *Conclusions*

3.1 I summarized evidence about the government of Jewish Palestine that all New Testament scholars ought to know, though a few do not: in Jesus' day Galilee was a Jewish state governed by Antipas, who was a client ruler (a "friend and ally" of Rome); Judea was an Imperial province administered by Pilate, a Roman prefect. In Jerusalem, however, power on a day-to-day basis was wielded by the high priest and his council.

3.2 A second point that everyone should know but does not is that the Roman army did not actually "occupy" Judea until after the first revolt; Galilee was first occupied in the second century CE. The first Roman troops to be stationed anywhere in Palestine appeared in 6 CE, but for the most part they stayed in the largely Gentile city, Caesarea, and played no role in the daily life of Jews in Judea. There were only a few of them: *c.* 3,000. In Jesus' day there were no Roman troops in Galilee.

3.3 More importantly, I have tried to show that both the Romans and Herod and his heirs distinguished between the Jewish parts of Palestine and the Gentile parts. The clearest indication of what was Jewish is seen in the arrangements made by Pompey and Julius Caesar (above, p. 17): Galilee, Perea, Idumea and Judea (including Joppa and its port, probably with surrounding villages) were Jewish. When the same person governed both (as did Herod), Gentile institutions and culture were established or fostered in the Gentile areas (see especially *AJ* 15.327–9; *BJ* 2.266, above, pp. 20f.), though Herod also built a theater near Jerusalem. After the reign of Herod, most of the Gentile areas were governed separately from the Jewish areas.

In Antipas' Galilee, we find very minor aspects of Hellenistic culture. Antipas may have called Sepphoris a *polis*, but it was a Jewish city. Tiberias was a predominantly Jewish *polis*, with a small Gentile population. In both cases, it is highly unlikely that Antipas accorded these cities the freedom and independence that were central to the idea of a *polis*. As far as we know, he built only a few Gentile buildings: a stadium and a decorated palace at Tiberias, conceivably a theater at Sepphoris.

Neither Augustus, Tiberius, Herod, Archelaus, Antipas, nor the Roman prefects made any substantial effort to Hellenize or Romanize the Jewish areas. One may contrast the efforts of some of the Jewish aristocrats prior to the Hasmonean revolt, who established a *gymnasion* and wanted to be registered as "the Antiochenes in Jerusalem" (2 Macc. 4:9, n. 91 above). There is no parallel in the first century CE. Moreover, while the Jews doubtless absorbed a certain amount of Hellenism, they opposed the Hellenistic attributes and institutions that seemed to them to threaten their separate identity: see for example the "Jewish pietist" source above (pp. 19–21), the burning of Antipas' palace (p. 28), and the Sepphorites' desire to circumcise Gentile refugees (p. 31). One could add the objections of the Jerusalemites to Pilate's introduction of Roman standards into the city (*BJ* 2.169–74; *AJ* 18.55–9), as well as many other points from Josephus' history, which show that the Jews resisted gentilization.

There were not many Gentiles in the Jewish cities, and either very few or none in the Jewish countryside. In fact, the evidence is that there was hostility towards Gentiles in the areas of the country that the Jews regarded as their own (e.g. *Vita* 67), just as there was towards Jews who lived in the Hellenistic cities that surrounded their country (*BJ* 2.285–92; cf. also the accounts of massacres, *BJ* 2.477–80; 2.457; 2.558–61). If, despite the absence of Gentile colonies, one wishes to assume the presence of a large number of individual Gentiles in Jewish areas, one must offer some kind of rationale. Why would an individual Gentile family settle in Sepphoris? The family would be cut off from its customary worship; it would not have access to Greek-style schools; for entertainment and festivals it would have to travel to Caesarea; and it would be surrounded by people who resented its presence and who thought that the males should be circumcised. The promise of free property drew some Gentiles to Tiberias, but apart from this incentive it is hard to imagine why a sizable number of Gentiles would wish to live in the interior of Galilee. They could just as well find land and housing in the cities of the Decapolis or the coast. Most humans prefer to live among their own kind. Just as Gentile cities did not want to be governed by Jews (p. 17 above), individual Gentiles would also find Jewish areas inhospitable to many of their pursuits.

3.4 I shall add a few comments about Hellenization to clarify the statement that to some degree Palestinian Jews were Hellenized (above, p. 33). I have just proposed that the Jews resisted the obvious signs of Hellenization, but of course it is impossible to escape the influence of a dominant culture entirely. The problem with making this perfectly true statement is that in the present state of New Testament studies admitting the word "Hellenization" is like inviting your camel to stick its nose into your tent: the rest of the camel may follow. Thus beginning with the word "Hellenization," many scholars then allow their imaginations to soar: Roman administrators in Antipas' Galilee, athletes wrestling and running in the nude, Roman soldiers in the streets and marketplaces, fluency in Greek, commitment to Greek philosophy and culture, and the presence of a large corps of construction engineers to construct aqueducts, erect temples, and rebuild the cities on a grid. Scholars sometimes cite Tcherikover's *Hellenistic Civilization and the Jews* as proving that the Jews were fairly thoroughly Hellenized.[93] Tcherikover, however, was aware of how thin the veneer of Hellenization often was, and he remarked that "the Greek towns could not Hellenize the East, but the East was strong enough to 'barbarize' them."[94] Since there were no gentile cities in the Jewish parts of Palestine, even this small cultural influence was lacking.

One suspects that one of the factors that leads scholars to think that Galilee was thoroughly Hellenized is the misperception that proximity equals influence. In fact, places that are close physically may be very remote socially and mentally. Since Scythopolis was near Nazareth, it is easy, especially to a modern American, unaccustomed to cultural borders, to suppose that the Nazarenes regularly went to Scythopolis to see the pagan sights and soak up Greek.[95] In real life, the peasants worked from dawn to dusk six days a week and rested on the sabbath. For holidays they went to Jerusalem. Paganism up close would have scared or offended them. The desire for cosmopolitanism that modern scholars have should not be attributed to ancient Jews below the elite. And even the elite were not entirely keen to acquire it. As one of this group, Josephus, remarked,

[93] Richardson (*Herod*, 92), while acknowledging that Hellenism in the coastal cities was stronger than "in any of the major cities of Judea", nevertheless maintains that "Greek ideas and institutions, not to mention Greek language and literature, had long influenced the Jewish heartland", citing Tcherikover.

[94] Tcherikover, *Hellenistic Civilization*, 35.

[95] White Americans can, however, experience cultural shock by visiting black or Latino ghettos. English speakers also do not feel entirely at home in all parts of Québec, and their presence is sometimes resented.

he and his countrymen did not wish to acquire foreign languages and culture (*AJ* 20.263–6).[96]

I suspect that there is also a misperception of time. As we look back at antiquity, the third and fourth centuries seem to be close to and thus similar to the first century. As a consequence, the Hellenization and Romanization of Galilee, including both architecture and knowledge of Greek, which undoubtedly took place from the second to the fifth century,[97] are attributed to the first half of the first century.[98] We do not make this mistake in more recent periods; no one uses nineteenth century evidence when writing about the sixteenth century. We should always bear in mind that great changes took place in Jewish Palestine after the first revolt and that the pace of change increased after the second revolt, when Jerusalem became a Hellenistic city and a Roman legion was stationed in Galilee.

Once we dismiss the fantasy of the thorough sort of Hellenization that many scholars now accept, we must immediately admit that it is hard to define *precisely* what "Hellenization" meant in the Jewish Palestine of Jesus' day. The prevalence of unwarranted assumptions (e.g. that knowledge of merchant's Greek implies immersion in Greek literature and culture) has seriously hindered the quest. Although this paper makes only a minor contribution towards answering the question of Hellenization—a question that requires the study of numerous additional topics—, I wish to conclude it with a comparison that I find helpful.

If one reads all of Jewish literature from Alexander the Great to the early Rabbis, one finds remarkably few signs of Hellenistic influence in Judaism. Yes, I have read Philo and Joseph and Aseneth—as well as Erwin Goodenough. Nevertheless, one finds only a few modifications of basic Jewish belief and practice under Hellenistic

---

[96] The archaeology of the Jerusalem's upper city provides further evidence for the study of the Jewish elite, but this lies outside the bounds of the present essay.

[97] The earliest specific example that Lieberman cites to show rabbinic knowledge of Greek is a passage in the Palestinian Talmud about R. Eliezer and R. Joshua, who flourished at the beginning of the second century: Saul Lieberman, *Greek in Jewish Palestine: Studies in the Life and Manners of Jewish Palestine in the II–IV Centuries CE* (2nd ed.; New York: Philipp Feldheim, 1965) 15–19; cf. p. 1: "an academy of Greek wisdom existed in Jewish Palestine under the auspices of the Patriarch. It was established in the beginning of the second century for the purpose of facilitating the relations between the House of the Patriarch and the Roman government."

[98] Cf. the comment on Sawicki, n. 29 above.

influence. One may see this by comparing the influence of Babylon and Persia, which was very substantial. Sabbath law changed dramatically after the exile, and tithing was entirely redefined. For example, the prohibition of warfare on the sabbath troubled the kings of Judah and Israel not it all; it first appears in the Hellenistic period (1 Macc 2:29–41). Subsequent stories in Josephus show that this was regarded as a firm law, though it was modified by allowing the Jews to fire if first fired upon (e.g. *BJ* 1.145–7).[99] The requirement to give ten percent of produce to the temple is also exilic or post-exilic (it appears in Leviticus, Numbers, Nehemiah and Malachi). Both changes were important modifications of basic religious practice, and they came as the result of Babylonian influence.[100] From the Persians the Jews acquired belief in a final judgment and in the resurrection.[101] Hellenism, relatively speaking, made a very small impact on Judaism. The Greek idea of an immortal soul crops up here and there in Jewish literature, but there was no Hellenistic ingredient in Judaism that was the equivalent of sabbath, tithing, resurrection and final judgment. Hellenistic influence was not very deep.

3.5 A review of everything that we now know about Galilee—of which I have discussed only a fraction—generally supports the impression given by the gospels. The gospels *allow* readers to supply erroneous contexts—such as that Roman soldiers were thick on the ground. But if we read them carefully, we see that they do not *require* an erroneous context on any of the subjects I have discussed and that they fit into our other evidence about Galilee perfectly well. With regard to society and population in Galilee, the governmental structure of Jewish Palestine, and several other subjects, I find that

---

[99] Further details in Sanders, *Jewish Law from Jesus to the Mishnah*, 7f.

[100] On tithing in Babylonia in the 6th–4th centuries BCE, see M.A. Dandamayev, "State and Temple in Babylonia in the First Millennium BC", *State and Temple Economy in the Ancient Near East* (2 vols., OLA 5 and 6, Leuven: Peeters 1979) 2.589–96. For further details, see M.A. Dandamajew, "Der Tempelzehnte in Babylonien während des 6.–4. Jh. v. u. Z.", *Beiträge zur alten Geschichte und deren Nachleben: Festschrift für Franz Altheim* I, Berlin, 1969; Erkki Salonen, "Über den Zehnten im alten Mesopotamien. Ein Beitrag zur Geschichte der Besteuerung" (Studia Orientalia Edidit Societas Orientalis Fennica XLIII:4, Helsinki, 1972).

[101] Mary Boyce, "Persian religion in the Achemenid Age", in W.D. Davies and Louis Finkelstein (eds.), *The Cambridge History of Judaism* (3 vols.; Cambridge: University Press, 1984ff.) 1.279–307, here 300f. One could add the dualism of the DSS and numerous other points that reveal Persian influence.

the gospels are quite accurate. According to the gospels, Jesus encountered one Gentile centurion (presumably Antipas' centurion) in Capernaum (Matt 8:5–10). He also met Gentiles when he walked west towards Tyre and Sidon (Mark 7:24–30) or sailed east across the Sea of Galilee and walked to the territory of one of the cities of the Decapolis (Mark 5:1–20). This seems to me to be correct. I would not wish to construct a picture of life in Jewish Palestine on the basis of the gospels, but it is interesting to note that their depictions of that life harmonize perfectly well with Josephus and archaeology.

WHAT HAPPENED TO THE BODY OF JESUS?

Matti Myllykoski

1. *The Traditional Christian View and Its Alternatives*

> The name of Joseph of Arimathea and, with it, the account of the burial of Jesus must be historical; they cannot be simply discarded. But if the primitive community had any kind of information, based on fact, about the burial of Jesus, the investigations on the subject of the tomb must have begun, certainly, very early. What was actually shown was, in all probability, an empty tomb, and, unless we are prepared to explain everything, with the Jews, as a fraud and a subsequent fabrication, it is hard to see why the discovery should not have happened in the way, by the persons and at the time stated by the most ancient tradition. Any other explanation is unverifiable. Anyone who likes to hold that there was a substitution or some kind of mischance can, of course, let his imagination run as he pleases—anything is possible, in that case, and nothing demonstrable. But this has nothing to do with critical investigation. If we test what is capable of being tested, we cannot, in my opinion, shake the story of the empty tomb and its early discovery. There is much that tells in its favour, and nothing definite or significant against it. It is, therefore, probably historical.

This view expressed by Hans Freiherr von Campenhausen[1] represents the communis opinio among Biblical scholars. Even Rudolf Bultmann considered the story of Jesus' burial in Mark 15:42–47 to be a historically reliable account, although he separated it from the Easter narratives.[2] There are no legendary traits at all, merely a statement of a simple burial given to Jesus by Joseph of Arimathea, a respected member of the council—a man who himself was a sympathizer of Jesus, but not his disciple or follower. Both the tomb of Jesus and the identity of the man who buried him were known as well among his followers as among his executors. Mary of Magdala and some other women were known to have found his tomb empty.

---

[1] H. Freiherr von Campenhausen, *Tradition and Life in the Church: Essays and Lectures in Church History* (ET; London: Collins, 1968) 76–77.

[2] R. Bultmann, *The History of the Synoptic Tradition* (ET; Oxford: Blackwell, 1972) 274.

They were also said to have encountered an angel; possibly they had met the Lord in person as well. Among the first members of the new community in Jerusalem, this confirmed the reality of the appearances of Jesus to his male disciples and other converts.[3]

This basic theory is quite reasonable and it is quite often meant to provide suitable scientific backing for the resurrection of Jesus,

---

[3] For the defence of the historicity of the burial account, see particularly J. Blinzler, "Die Grablegung Jesu in historischer Sicht", in *Resurrexit: Actes du symposium international sur la résurrection de Jésus (Rome 1970)* (Città del Vaticano: Libreria editrice Vaticana, 1974) 56–107; G. Ghiberti, *La sepoltura di Gesù: I Vangeli e la Sindone* (Roma: Marietti, 1982); R.E. Brown, "The Burial of Jesus (Mark 15:42–47)", *CBQ* 50 (1988) 233–45; B.R. McCane, "'Where No One Had Yet Been Laid': The Shame of Jesus' Burial", in *SBL 1993 Seminar Papers* (Atlanta: Scholars Press, 1993) 473–84.

L. Schenke, *Auferstehungsverkündigung und das leere Grab: Eine traditionsgeschichtliche Untersuchung von Mark 16,1–8* (SBS 33; Stuttgart: Katholisches Bibelwerk, 1968) 93–103, assumes that the first Christians knew the tomb of Jesus and celebrated his resurrection there.

General works on passion and Easter narratives that defend the traditional Christian view: P. Benoit, *Passion et résurrection du Seigneur* (Paris: Cerf, 1966); T.A. Mohr, *Markus- und Johannespassion: Redaktions- und traditionsgeschichtliche Untersuchung der Markinischen und Johanneischen Passionstradition* (AThANT 70; Zürich: Theologischer Verlag, 1982); H. Hendrickx, *The Passion Narratives of the Synoptic Gospels* (London: Chapman, 1984); idem, *The Resurrection Narratives of the Synoptic Gospels* (London: Chapman, 1984); R.E. Brown, *The Death of the Messiah: From Gethsemane to the Grave* (2 vols.; New York: Doubleday, 1994).

For commentaries on Mark that argue for historical reliability of the passion and resurrection traditions, see particularly R. Pesch, *Das Markusevangelium* (2 vols.; HTK 2I; Freiburg: Herder, 1976–77), and R. Gundry, *Mark: A Commentary on His Apology for the Cross* (Grand Rapids: Eerdmans, 1993). The knowledge of the tomb of Jesus among the first Christians and the historicity of Mary Magdalene's experiences at the tomb are also presupposed e.g. by E. Schweizer, *Das Evangelium nach Markus* (7th ed.; NTD 1; Göttingen: Vandenhoeck & Ruprecht, 1989) 199–200, 203–5; J. Gnilka, *Das Evangelium nach Markus* (2 vols.; 3rd ed.; EKKNT 1; Neukirchen-Vluyn: Neukirchener, 1989) 2.336, 345–47.

Scientifically oriented apologetical works that wish to demonstrate that the tomb of Jesus was empty and that he really was risen from the dead: W.L. Craig, "The Empty Tomb of Jesus", in R.T. France (ed.), *Studies of History and Tradition in the Gospels* (Gospel Perspectives 2; Sheffield: JSOT Press, 1981), 173–200; idem, "The Historicity of the Empty Tomb of Jesus", *NTS* 31 (1985) 39–67; idem, *Assessing the New Testament Evidence for the Historicity of the Resurrection of Jesus* (Lewinston, NY: Mellen, 1989); H. Hempelmann, *Die Auferstehung Jesu—eine historische Tatsache?: Eine engagierte Analyse* (Wuppertal: Brockhaus, 1982); S.T. Davis, *Risen Indeed: Making Sense of the Resurrection* (Grand Rapids: Eerdmans, 1993); idem, "Was the Tomb Empty?", in E. Stump & T.P. Flint (eds.), *Hermes and Athena: Biblical Exegesis and Philosphical Theology* (Notre Dame: University of Notre Dame Press, 1993) 77–100.

The importance of the empty tomb is evident also in a recent public debate that is now published as a book: P. Cohan & R.K. Tacelli (eds.), *Jesus' Resurrection—Fact or Figment?: A Debate Between William Lane Graig & Gerd Lüdemann* (Downers Grove, IL: InterVarsity, 2000).

which is beyond doubt the most important article of faith among Christian theologians. Scholarly defence of the historicity of the empty tomb is in most cases quite obviously related to the religious conviction of the scholar. Correspondingly, it is not astonishing that opposing views are experienced as attacks against the foundations of Christianity itself. Christianity seems to stand and fall with the resurrection of Jesus and the most important events related to it.[4]

For the traditional Christian view as represented by several Biblical scholars, it is essential that the stories in the earliest Gospel about the burial (Mark 15:42–47) and of the women at the tomb (16:1–8) are historically reliable. (The appearance and announcement of the young man or the angel to the women can be interpreted at least in terms of deep and original religious experience.) This view presupposes that these and related Markan passion stories belong to a coherent unity that cannot be dissected into diverse traditions. It is further presupposed that this traditional narrative unity used by Mark can be traced back to the earliest tradition. The author of the earliest Gospel may have learned all these stories from Peter,[5] or from reliable oral tradition in general.[6] If this was not the case, he may have used a very old and historically reliable passion narrative as the source of his presentation.[7]

Among those scholars who think that the development of the Gospel stories was much more complicated, three alternative historical reconstructions have been presented:

1) Jesus was buried by Joseph and/or other Jewish authorities, but we cannot be sure whether the first Christians knew where and how he was buried.[8]

---

[4] Thus e.g. J. Moltmann, *The Theology of Hope: On the Ground and the Implications of the Christian Eschatology* (ET; London: SCM Press, 1967) 165–66. The dilemma of faith, scholarship and the resurrection of Jesus has been recently treated in a stimulating way by G. Lüdemann and A.J.M. Wedderburn. See G. Lüdemann, "Zwischen Karfreitag und Ostern", in H. Verweyen (ed.), *Osterglaube ohne Auferstehung?: Diskussion mit Gerd Lüdemann* (QD 155; Freiburg: Herder, 1995) 13–46, esp. 13–21; and A.J.M. Wedderburn, *Beyond Resurrection* (London: SCM Press, 1999) 3–23.

[5] Thus Gundry, *Mark*, 1026–45.

[6] The role of reliable, informal and controlled oral tradition among the first Christians is emphasized by N.T. Wright, *Jesus and the Victory of God* (Minneapolis: Fortress, 1996) 131–37.

[7] Pesch, *Das Markusevangelium*, 15–26.

[8] Broer, *Die Urgemeinde und das Grab Jesu: Eine Analyse der Grablegungsgeschichte im Neuen Testament* (München: Kösel, 1972) 293–94 remains undecided. His literary analysis of the Gospels leads to a historically negative result, while he maintains

2) Jesus was buried by Jewish authorities in a common graveyard reserved for executed criminals.[9]

3) As a criminal crucified by the Romans, Jesus was not properly buried or not buried at all.[10]

Since nothing in the early Christian tradition indicates that something like this happened, these hypotheses are for the most rejected out of hand as futile and unfounded speculation.

However, I think that there are some serious questions and observations that make the traditional view so vulnerable that alternative hypotheses deserve to be considered. If both the disciples and executors of Jesus knew where the respected Joseph of Arimathea had buried the body of Jesus, and acknowledged the testimony of the women who found this tomb empty on Sunday morning, then we have surprisingly few traces left of this major evidence for the resurrection of Jesus. Early traditions do not indicate the need for a proof of an empty tomb. Paul who on the basis of Jesus' resurrection argues at length for faith in resurrection of the dead (1 Cor 15) pays careful attention to the male witnesses of the risen Jesus, but does not even mention the empty tomb. In this respect, the tradition preserved by Paul consists of two basic elements. The fact that Jesus was buried simply meant that Jesus really had died on the cross. The appearances, in turn, demonstrated that he was risen from the dead.

---

that the first Christians probably sometime and somehow learned to know where and how Jesus was buried. G. Lüdemann, *The Resurrection of Jesus: History, Experience, Theology* (ET; London: SCM Press, 1994) 44–45 is more sceptical (p. 45): "We can no longer say where Joseph (or Jews unknown to us) put the body." See also G. Lüdemann, *Jesus after Two Thousand Years: What he really said and did* (ET; London: SCM Press, 2000) 110–11. W. Reinbold, *Der älteste Bericht über den Tod Jesu: Literarische Analyse und historische Kritik der Passionsdarstellungen der Evangelien* (BZNW 69; Berlin: de Gruyter, 1994) 279–80 finds it quite plausible that Joseph buried Jesus in a private tomb, but doubts whether the early Christian community really knew where the tomb was.

[9] This option is sometimes suggested as a possible or most probable way to solve the enigmas of the tomb stories and the historical circumstances behind them: H. Grass, *Ostergeschehen und Osterberichte* (Göttingen: Vandenhoeck & Ruprecht, 1956) 180; H. Braun, *Jesus: Der Mann aus Nazareth und seine Zeit* (Berlin: Kreuz-Verlag, 1969) 51; M. Myllykoski, *Die letzten Tage Jesu: Markus und Johannes, ihre traditionen und die historische Frage* (2 vols.; AASF/B 256 & 272; Helsinki: The Finnish Academy of Science and Letters, 1991–94) 2.104; M. Sawicki, *Seeing the Lord: Resurrection and Early Christian Practices* (Minneapolis: Fortress, 1994) 257 ("possibly"). See also Wedderburn, *Beyond Resurrection* 65.

[10] Crossan, *Who Killed Jesus? Exposing the Roots of Anti-Semitism in the Gospel Story of the Death of Jesus* (San Francisco: HarperCollins, 1995) 160–88, especially 187–88.

Furthermore, we can gather valuable information about the earliest Christian community in Jerusalem, but we learn nothing about the empty tomb. If they had known the place, which was essentially related to the greatest miracle of all, they probably would have paid at least some attention to it and we could follow the traces of this interest back to the earliest stage of the tradition. Instead, our sources only reveal a mosaic. Joseph of Arimathea, the key witness of the tomb, has nothing to do with earliest testimonies to the resurrection of Jesus. Excluding the burial tradition, we learn nothing about him. For James the Just, Peter, Stephen, Paul and others, the empty tomb was no argument for the miracle of resurrection, nor did they feel pressed by outsiders to defend such a piece of evidence. In Acts Luke merely tells us that the Jewish leaders took Jesus down from the cross and put him in a tomb (Acts 13:29).[11] Polemic against the story of the empty tomb belongs only to a later time (Matt 27:62–66; 28:2–4, 11–15), and the concrete identification of the tomb of Jesus in Jerusalem stems from the early 4th century.[12]

---

[11] Lüdemann, *Jesus after Two Thousand Years*, 110, sees both here and in John 19:31–37 a reliable reference to "a burial by (hostile) Jews". Davis, "Was the Tomb Empty?" 86 regards Acts 2:27–29 (and 13:29–37) as evidence for knowledge of Jesus' tomb among early Christians in Jerusalem: ". . . Jesus, who because of his resurrection 'was not abandoned to Hades, nor did his flesh see corruption,' is contrasted to King David, whose tomb 'is with us to this day'. The implication seems to be that Jesus' tomb is empty while David's is not." However, Luke allows Peter talk about David's tomb in order to argue that in Psalm 15:8–11 (LXX) David does not prophecy about himself. The main point about Jesus is that God did not abandon him to Hades (Acts 2:31). Luke's Peter does not refer even vaguely to the tomb of Jesus.

If Luke would have written about the burial and the empty tomb in the narrative or speeches of Acts, scholars probably would not agree on historical reliability of these traditions. Those inclined to support it would treat such texts as old traditions, while those who have problems in embracing this position would most likely consider such passages as Lukan creations.

[12] Tourists who visit the Church of the Holy Sepulchre in Jerusalem are well informed about the site where Jesus was crucified, buried, and rose again. Historians and Biblical scholars who are unconvinced of the historical value of many other holy places in the holy city, are often less uncomfortable about the authenticity of this site. Located outside the ancient city walls, but within a suitable distance of them, the Holy Sepulchre is often regarded as most probably the place where Jesus was buried. There is also a relatively old tradition of the history of the site. The Church Fathers of the fourth and fifth centuries passed on the tradition that Hadrian built on this site a temple to Aphrodite/Venus in order to defile the holy place of the Christians and deprive them from believing in Jesus' passion and resurrection.

Joan E. Taylor has examined the archaeological and literary evidence twice. In her book *Christians and the Holy Places: The Myth of Jewish-Christian Origins* (Oxford:

Considering this silence of the earliest traditions, we have remarkable evidence of apologetics that was occupied with quite other kinds of problems. To legitimate their faith in Jesus' resurrection, the early Christians referred to the testimony of those who had seen the risen One (1 Cor 15:3–7; Luke 24:34) as well as to passages of the Scriptures indicating that the Messiah must suffer and die (John 12:27 cf. Psalm 6:4–5; Mark 14:65 cf. Is 50:6; Mark 15:24 cf. Psalm 22:19; Mark 15:29–30 cf. Psalm 22:8; 109:25; Mark 15:34 cf. Psalm 22:2; Mark 15:36 cf. Psalm 69:22). Correspondingly, one of the basic ideas in passion narratives is that Jesus was crucified as the king of the Jews. Questions concerning the resurrection of Jesus were not related to his tomb but to his person: how can a troublemaker from Nazareth, crucified by Pontius Pilate, be the Messiah? For the chief priests and the members of the Sanhedrin Jesus was one troublemaker and

Clarendon, 1993) 113–42 she has argued that the tomb of Jesus is of later origin and was not primarily related to the tomb, but to the cross. They were blended together when the place uncovered by Constantine the Great became venerated. For the Christians of the first century, Golgate was not a particular spot, but a large area. This seems to be already indicated by the author of the Fourth Gospel who mentions that "in the place where he was crucified" there was a garden with tombs (John 19:41). Melito of Sardis locates the spot of Jesus' crucifixion "in the middle of the city" and at a colonnated street (*Paschal Homily* 93–94) without referring at all to the temple of Venus. The basilica that replaced this temple was not built to venerate the tomb, but the cross (*Laus Const.* 9.16). The Constantinian workmen found tombs that had been cleared of corpses as Agrippa included this area in the city. Eusebius writes that the discovery of an empty tomb here was "contrary to all expectations" (*Vita Const.* 3.28).

In a more recent article ("Golgotha: A Reconsideration of the Evidence for the Sites of Jesus' Crucifixion and Burial", *NTS* 44 [1998] 180–203), Taylor has revised her thesis concerning the historical value of the traditional identification of the tomb. Now she thinks that (pp. 200–1) "Christians in Jerusalem remembered the site, and may have visited it from time to time to show visitors. Hadrian indeed covered up the tomb on purpose and placed a statue of Jupiter on the exact spot, as the focus of one of the shrines within a larger Temple of Venus, and this was remembered by the Jerusalem church and communicated in due course to Constantine, who saw fit to remove the Temple entirely and build his new Christian edifice instead. In this case, the authenticity of the tomb was self-evident because of its placement right under the statue of Jupiter." She now claims that the tomb found under the *temenos* of the Temple of Venus was self-evidently held as the the tomb of Jesus, because it was in precisely the right place and because it was of the arcosolium type, which corresponds to the description of the empty tomb in Mark 16:5 (cf. John 20:12). However, it is doubtful whether the tomb of Jesus was always considered to be of the arcosolium type. There is some weighty evidence for the assumption that the burial story was originally independent of the empty tomb tradition and that the simplicity of the burial tradition rather refers to a quite simple tomb (see below pp. 60–66).

impostor among many. Most likely they thought that people like this suffered their just punishment in Sheol.[13]

Silence about the tomb challenges all attempts to present a convincing theory about the fate of Jesus' body. We can never find out what really happened. All a scholar can do is read the texts, make observations, present arguments, draw conclusions and let the discussion go on. This may be called scientific imagination, shared by both defenders and critics of the historical reliability of the empty tomb tradition. All general arguments and counter-arguments that are related to the silence of earliest traditions can never be proved or confuted. Those who follow the traditional arguments may ask with Stephen T. Davis: "If the story [of the empty tomb] is an apologetic legend invented by later Christians, why is it that the story is made to hang so crucially on the testimony of women, whose evidence was not legally admissible in Jewish proceedings?"[14] It is not difficult to imagine a quite plausible, but equally unverifiable counter-argument: women might have been looking for the body of Jesus, and their quest and personal experiences became the starting point for the legendary tradition of the empty tomb. It is not necessary to imagine here an intention to convince anybody in terms of legal proceedings.

Another general argument presented by Davis is this: "It is that early Christian proclamation of the resurrection of Jesus in Jerusalem would have been psychologically and apologetically impossible without safe evidence of an empty tomb."[15] If this is correct, we have to imagine one single pattern of exaltation or resurrection shared by both Christians and their opponents. Then we also have to imagine that with the tradition in Mark 16:1–8 it was meant to prove that the tomb was empty, while the story itself implies no more than Jesus' translation to heaven.[16] Secondly, meaningful debates about

[13] On judgement in Sheol in the Hebrew Bible, see R. Rosenberg, *The Concept of Biblical Sheol Within the Context of Ancient Near Eastern Beliefs* (Ph.D. thesis, Cambridge, MA: Department of Near Eastern Languages and Civilizations, Harvard University, 1981) 174–75, cited by J. Davies, *Death, Burial and Rebirth in the Religions of Antiquity* (London: Routledge, 1999) 92.

[14] Davis, "Was the Tomb Empty?", 87.

[15] Davis, "Was the Tomb Empty?", 93.

[16] The classical article on this question is E. Bickermann, "Das leere Grab", *ZNW* 23 (1924) 281–92. See also A. Yarbro Collins, "The Empty Tomb in the Gospel According to Mark", in E. Stump and T.P. Flint (eds.), *Hermes and Athena: Biblical*

the empty tomb must have taken place soon after the burial, because the body that the Jewish leaders possibly could have produced would have become unidentifiable in less than about eight weeks. If the fate of Jesus' body ever became a problem for them, it is not certain whether they then knew any longer where they had laid the body or whether they would have found it meaningful to try searching and possibly identifying it.[17] In turn, for later Christians it was certainly not difficult to imagine that in the same afternoon as Jesus died the tombs opened, many bodies of saints were raised, "entered the holy city and appeared to many" (Mt 27:52–53). Those who developed this tradition had no need to debate with anybody or prove that these tombs were empty. On the whole, it is possible that the first Christians had the safe evidence of the empty tomb on their side and that the mysterious disappearance of the body of Jesus supported their proclamation, but the silence of the earliest sources does not necessitate such a scenario.

In the following analysis (section 2), the examination of Mark 15:42–47 leads to the theory that there once was an independent burial tradition that was not related to the story of the empty tomb. In section 3, observations about the pre-Pauline tradition in 1 Cor 15:3–5 and the earliest, oral stage of the burial story suggest an alternative historical reconstruction about the fate of Jesus' body.

2. *The Markan Burial Story and the Pre-Markan Tradition*

The Markan story of the burial of Jesus is generally considered as a piece of tradition utilized by Mark, although some scholars are

---

Exegesis and Philosophical Theology (Notre Dame: University of Notre Dame Press, 1993), 107–40, esp. 130.

B. Lindars, "The Apocalyptic Myth and the Death of Christ", *BJRL* 57 (1975) 366–87, traces the origins of the early Christian exaltation myth (Acts 3:20–21) back to the Jewish idea of the ascension of particular persons—like Henoch and Elijah—and to the earliest apocalyptic Son of Man traditions (pp. 375–80). He assumes that there once was an idea of the exalted Jesus who was "revealed to be the person who is to fulfill the role of God's agent in the final judgement" (p. 377). He concludes that "the idea of the exaltation of Jesus could have been reached [. . .] without the experience of the resurrection as an historical event" (p. 380).

[17] R.H. Gundry ("Trimming the Debate", in P. Cohan & R.K. Tacelli (ed.), *Jesus' Resurrection—Fact or Figment?*, 114) assumes that the Jewish leaders who buried Jesus would in such case have been able to show "something, at least the skeleton". However, this argumentation is circular, because it presupposes a clearly identifiable tomb for the body of Jesus.

inclined to regard it as a Markan creation.[18] However, the internal tensions of the story and its primitive character in comparison to the story of the empty tomb speak for the theory of a pre-Markan burial tradition.

2.1. *The Time of the Burial*

According to the Markan time indication in 15:42 the evening had already come, but it was still the day of Preparation. If this information is read harmonistially, ὀψία must be located between the ninth hour (15:34) and the sunset. "Since" it was the day of Preparation and because the evening had "already" come, Joseph had to hasten in order to get Jesus buried before the sunset. His actions described by Mark (going to Pilate who would call the centurion, buying a linen cloth, taking the body down, tying it up, and putting it in the tomb) must have taken some two hours. This seems to be confirmed by the fact that Mark can specify the coming of the evening with the notion of the sunset (1:32). Accordingly, in 15:42 he must indicate that Joseph buried Jesus before the beginning of Sabbath.[19]

This scenario is possible, but some weighty observations about Mark's redaction speak against it. Since Mark imagined the coming of the evening in terms of the third, sixth and ninth hour of the crucifixion narrative (15:25,34,37), I find it most natural to relate the coming of the evening to the twelveth hour and sunset. The typical Markan expression ἤδη ὀψίας γενομένης is at least in notable tension with the obviously traditional time indication "since it was the day of Preparation".[20] If the former time indication is indeed added by Mark, the idea that the evening had "already" come does not necessarily imply that Joseph was in a hurry to bury Jesus. On the other hand, there are no indications for the assumption that Mark would have wanted to label the sabbath observation as "night" by adding this emphatic time indication.[21]

---

[18] For the latter view, see B. Mack, *A Myth of Innocence* (Philadelphia: Fortress, 1988) 308–9 and Crossan, *Who Killed Jesus?* 172–77.

[19] This theory is supported by R.E. Brown, *The Death of the Messiah*, 2.1211–13. See also Blinzler, "Die Grablegung Christi", 60.

[20] Broer, *Die Urgemeinde und das Grab Jesu* 139–52 and others.

[21] *Pace* J. Schreiber, *Theologie des Vertrauens: Eine redaktionsgeschichtliche Untersuchung des Markusevangeliums* (Hamburg: Furche, 1967) 87–89. For criticism of this theory, see Broer, *Die Urgemeinde und das Grab Jesu* 152–56.

There is another way to explain why Mark added the time indication ἤδη ὀψίας γενομένης to the burial tradition. He is eager to present Jesus as a miracle-worker who is active even after the sunset (1:32) and very early next morning wakes up for prayer. Mark is not bothered about the practical side of the mass healing activity, since he wants to magnify Jesus' miraculous powers and highlight the events in which those powers break through. This is evident also in Mark 4:35–41, where Jesus demonstrates his powers (that hint at his true identity) on the way to the other side of the sea after the evening has come. Then Mark allows Jesus and his disciples to come to the other side in order to make Jesus heal the Gerasene demoniac and "cross again in the boat to the other side" to meet Jairus (5:21). Here Mark does not consider it necessary to mention the sunrise. A similar arrangement accompanies later in the story of Jesus walking on the sea. Mark again utilizes darkness and night as the context in which Jesus' divine qualities become apparent. Before the miraculous feeding of the five thousand men the hour was already late (6:35), and after that, when the disciples were in the boat and Jesus was praying alone on the mountain, the evening had come (6:46–47). "And about the fourth watch of the night" Jesus comes to his discples, walking on the sea (6:48). At the last supper Jesus foretells the dramatic events of that night and prays perseveringly in Gethsemane before he is arrested (14:17–42).

I think that the motifs of these passages can bring to light the redactional aspects of the time indication in Mark 15:42. The time scheme related to the miraculous darkness in 15:34, 37 prepares for Jesus' burial in the evening. For Mark, it is not a problem to have the sun set before Jesus is buried. He likes to cross the limits of the day as he portrays the final events of his Gospel. The coming of the evening also creates a suitable link to the scene at the empty tomb, which takes place "very early" in the following morning (16:1; cf. 1:35!). The greatest of all miracles, Jesus' resurrection, takes place in the middle of the night, just as some earlier miracles that have already hinted at his divine identity. The time indications are here even more important, because Mark does not portray the miracle itself—a taboo that was broken only later, in the resurrection tradition preserved in the *Gospel of Peter* 34–42.[22]

[22] There are some weighty arguments for the assumption that Matthew was famil-

This view presupposes that Mark wished to create the impression that the burial of Jesus took place in the evening even at the cost of the traditional notice that it was still the day of Preparation, i.e. the sun had not set and Sabbath not yet begun. There is indeed some evidence that Mark did not take into consideration or did not care about the fact that for the Jews Sabbath and other days started at sunset. Instead he tended to follow the Roman order and counted the days from daybreak to daybreak.[23] This seems to be the case in 1:21, where Jesus "immediately when the sabbath came" enters the synagogue and teaches, and later "that evening, at sundown" heals "all who were sick or possessed with demons" (1:32). In 6:2 Jesus begins to teach in the synagogue when Sabbath had come (γενομένου σαββάτου) and—after a conflict with people of "his own country"—goes around teaching in the villages (6:6). In 16:1 Mark mentions explicitly that Sabbath was past, when the women "bought spices, so that they might go and anoint" Jesus. This action can be better imagined as taking place in the morning. In this respect it is notable that Mark complements the traditional time indication "very early" with the delaying notion "when the sun had risen". Thus Mary Magdalene and her friends had time to buy the spices the same morning.

These observations are in accord with the uneasiness with which Matthew and Luke have treated the Markan time indications. Matthew removes the reference to the day of Preparation from the beginning of the burial story (27:57) and avoids awkwardly mentioning the sabbath in his time indication to the story of the guard at the tomb (27:62): "Next day, that is, after the day of Preparation . . ."[24] Luke solves the problem differently. He leaves aside all time indications from the beginning of the burial story and mentions only later that

iar with a more primitive form of this tradition; see particularly J. Denker, *Die theologiegeschichtliche Stellung des Petrusevangeliums* (Europäische Hochschulschriften, Series 23, 36; Bern: Lang, 1975) 43–47. For the priority of the Matthean story, see Brown, *The Death of the Messiah* 2.1305–9.

[23] See also Lührmann, *Das Markusevangelium* (HNT 3; Tübingen: Mohr, 1987) 267 and Myllykoski, *Die letzten Tage Jesu* 2.108.

[24] Another kind of explanation is offered by D. Senior, "Matthew's Account of the Burial of Jesus", in F. van Segbroeck et alii (eds.), *The Four Gospels 1992: Festschrift Frans Neirynck* (3 vols.; BETL 100; Leuven: Leuven University Press, 1992) 2.1433–48, esp. 1443: ". . . here irony may be at work since the Jewish leaders consort with Pilate on the Sabbath day itself although Matthew does not seem to draw particular attention to this point." Furthermore, "Matthew . . . continuously looks forward to the 'third day', the day of resurrection."

"it was the day of Preparation, and the sabbath was beginning" (23:54). John who according to a number of scholars was dependent on Luke ends up with a similar arrangement of his text (19:42).

If these considerations are on a right track, the time indication of the pre-Markan burial story was simply ἐπεὶ ἦν παρασκευή, "since it was the day of Preparation".[25] The explanatory note ὅ ἐστιν προσάββατον stems from the Evangelist who felt necessary to explain the meaning of the term παρασκευή for his Gentile audience. As "the day before the sabbath" this term was known also to Josephus (*Ant.* 16,6,2 [163]).

In the light of arguments presented above I find it understandable that the Gentile Evangelist Mark did not take into consideration the commandment of Deut 21:22–23: "When someone is convicted of a crime punishable by death and is executed, and you hang him on a tree, his corpse must not remain all night upon the tree; you shall bury him that same day, for anyone hung on a tree is under God's curse. You must not defile the land that the Lord your God is giving you for possession." Mark was not worried about the sunset, but preoccupied with his hour scheme and its connection to the miracle of resurrection.

It is also remarkable that the pre-Markan passion tradition did not indicate any problem with the late hour of the burial, but instead explained the actions of Joseph with the coming of the sabbath. The time scheme was all that mattered: Jesus was risen on the third day, and the tomb was empty on the Sunday morning.

However, if there once was a burial story that was not familiar with the women who went to the tomb early on Sunday morning (see below), it is reasonable to assume that in the pre-Markan passion tradition the time indication παρασκευή was added in order to connect these stories to each other.

2.2. *Joseph of Arimathea*

Mark portrays Joseph of Arimathea as "a respected member of the council, who was also himself looking for the kingdom of God"

[25] With Broer, *Die Urgemeinde und das Grab Jesu*, 152–56; Gnilka, *Das Evangelium nach Markus* 2.331; Lührmann, *Das Markusevangelium*, 267; Brown, *The Death of the Messiah*, 2.1238–9 and many others.

(14:43). The first item in this information has puzzled not only modern scholars, but also Matthew and Luke. In his report on the trial of Jesus Mark emphasizes that "the chief priests and the whole council sought testimony against Jesus to put him to death" (14:55) and that "they all condemned him as deserving death" (14:64). Some scholars have assumed that Joseph was a member in the council of Arimathea,[26] but the relevance of such information in the burial story is difficult to explain. It is most natural to assume that Joseph was a member in the council of Jerusalem. The term used for his membership, βουλευτής, corresponds to the usage of Josephus (*War* 2.17.1 [405]), and it is clear from the contemporary evidence that βουλή and συνέδριον were interchangeable terms used for the council of Jerusalem. Mark's use of the term συνέδριον in the trial scene actually confirms that the stories of trial and burial stem from different traditions. Particularly if the evidence for heavy Markan redaction in the trial scene is convincing,[27] one can assume that he passed on the traditional information about Joseph without paying too much attention to the problem. He may have taken the term βουλευτής as reference to membership in some other coucil. Anyway, with his episodes about the mockery at the cross (15:27–32a) and the following ominous signs accompanying Jesus' death (15:33–39) Mark makes his final remarks about the Jewish leaders.

The discrepancy in the text of Mark was noticed by Matthew, Luke, and John. Matthew ignores Joseph's membership in the council and makes him instead a rich man and a disciple of Jesus (27:57).[28] In turn, Luke presents Joseph as a member of the council, but stresses that he was "a good and righteous man who had not consented to their purpose and deed" (23:50–51). John probably also knew the traditional characterization of Joseph, but introduced him as "a disciple of Jesus, but secretely, for fear of the Jews" (19:38).

The second piece of information given by Mark about Joseph, that Joseph was looking for the kingdom of God, is taken up by Luke, but rejected by Matthew. This characterization was naturally also unsuitable for Joseph's portrayal in John. It is obvious that for Mark and Luke Joseph was not a disciple of Jesus, but a pious Jew who took care of the burial. If they had known that Joseph later

[26] Lührmann, *Das Markusevangelium*, 267.
[27] Myllykoski, *Die letzten Tage Jesu*, 1.53–66.
[28] Senior, "Matthew's Account of the Burial of Jesus", 2.1443–45.

became a Christian or a sympathizer of the Jesus movement they would have mentioned it—particularly because of their problems with the trial scene. In Mark, Joseph's characterization as a "respected" member of the council implies a certain distance from his figure. For Matthew and John, all this was obviously too obscure and unbelievable to motivate the action of Joseph. If somebody gave Jesus such a burial, he had to be a disciple.

The idea that Joseph was looking for the kingdom of God is somewhat problematic. It simultaneously brings this "respected member of the council" closer to the followers of Jesus and distances him from them. His religious identity is not expressed in independent terms, but only in a general reference to the idea of the kingdom of God that was proclaimed by Jesus and his followers. He seems to be a sort of "would-be" Christian, an outsider with a positive characterization.[29] For Mark, who in the beginning of his Gospel allows Jesus to exclude the outsiders from the kingdom and its mysteries (4:10–12), there seems to be, after all, such a category. The scribe who agrees with Jesus on the great commandments is "not far from the kingdom of God" (12:34). The Markan Jesus also advocates the possibility of entering the kingdom, as his sayings on the children (10:14) and the rich (10:23) reveal. As women who witnessed the crucifixion and the burial, and many other minor characters in Mark, Joseph was "also himself" looking for God's rule. Moreover, this is the only category into which Mark could possibly have placed those traditional characters who were positive about the cause of Jesus before the time of the Gospel. Therefore it is quite plausible that Mark himself extended the traditional characterization of Joseph with the remark that he was looking for the kingdom of God.[30]

According to all the burial stories, Joseph went to Pilate to ask specifically for the body of Jesus. This presupposes that Joseph knew

[29] Cf. Wedderburn, *Beyond Resurrection*, 62: "That Joseph was in fact no follower of Jesus, probably not even a sympathizer, would also explain why the women took no part in Jesus' burial, but merely observed it (Mark 15:47)." In principle, this argument surely makes sense, but I find it hardly likely that the women were there at all (see below).

[30] With Broer, *Die Urgemeinde und das Grab Jesu*, 159–61; J. Marcus, *The Way of the Lord: Christological Exegesis of the Old Testament in the Gospel of Mark* (Edinburgh: T & T Clark, 1992) 182, and Lüdemann, *Jesus after Two Thousand Years*, 109. Against this view argues e.g. Mohr, *Markus- und Johannespassion*, 353–54, who sees here an early Jewish-Christian piece of information.

Jesus was already dead and that he naturally assumed that Jesus' relatives and followers would not come and ask for his body or that their request would be denied. Joseph does not seem to care about the burial of the other criminals crucified with Jesus. Both Mark and the tradition used by him presupposed that burying a crucified criminal was a matter of private initiative.[31] If Joseph had not asked for the body of Jesus, nobody would have buried him. Since the story focuses on the body of Jesus, Joseph is not thought of as a council member who would have been ex officio responsible for the burial of all crucified criminals.

The curious detail, omitted or ignored by other evangelists, that Joseph had to "take courage" before going to Pilate, underlines his private initiative. The expression is strong and refers most naturally to the setting of the passion story as a whole. It can be imagined that Joseph, even as a respected member of the council, could have been worried about Pilate's reaction, because the crime of Jesus was particularly serious ("king of the Jews").[32] However, the neutral reaction of Pilate—with or without Mark 15:44–45—does not point at this direction. Correspondingly, among those who were crucified by the Romans, Jesus was less harmful than zealots who encouraged people to armed rebellion or bandits who instigated violence. If Joseph used to bury all kinds of people who had been crucified, it is not conceivable that he should have needed particular courage to ask for the body of Jesus or that Mark would have wanted to emphasize this.

I find it more likely that "taking courage" is related to Joseph's personal sympathies with Jesus and his cause, which is introduced in the text by the idea that he was "also himself looking for the kingdom of God". Motivated by such a conviction, his action is in tension with his position as a Jewish leader. Therefore I find it likely that it was Mark who added that Joseph was "looking for the kingdom of God" and that he had to "take courage" for asking Jesus'

[31] Craig, *Assessing the New Testament Evidence*, 176, speculates that Joseph, being both a member of the Sanhedrin and a disciple of Jesus, obtained all three bodies, but placed the bodies of the bandits in a common grave. Brown, *The Death of the Messiah*, 2.1216 n. 28, assumes that "the story in the Synoptics has been narrowed down in its focus to Jesus, ignoring the two others who were no longer theologically or dramatically important."

[32] Brown, *The Death of the Messiah*, 2.1217.

body.[33] In spite of these additions, I find the pre-Markan burial story as positively disposed towards Joseph, as it characterized him as a respected member of the council. It was important to stress that he who buried Jesus was respected by everybody.

2.3. *Pilate's Hesitation*

Pilate's inquiry of the centurion into the death of Jesus in Mark 15:44–45 can with good reason be considered a Markan addition to the traditional burial account.[34] The centurion is the same who witnessed the death of Jesus and the accompanying ominous events, which made him conclude that this man was the Son of God (15:39). Particularly the centurion's "confession" is with good reasons regarded as a detail introduced into the text by the Evangelist himself.[35] The centurion episode in the burial story is connected with the dramatic death of Jesus. Its basic function is to convince the reader that Jesus really died as soon as the crucifixion narrative suggests (εἰ ἤδη τέθνηκεν). As Mark tells us, Jesus was crucified at the third hour (15:25) and died at the ninth hour (15:34–37). This hour scheme makes a secondary impression in the framework of the crucifixion narrative. I think that it belongs together with the motif of judgement (15:38), the confession of the centurion (15:39) and the request of Pilate, all of which can be attributed to Mark's redaction of his passion tradition.[36] Pilate's desire to know whether it was long since Jesus died (εἰ πάλαι ἀπέθανεν) and the centurion's report confirm the narrow chronology of the events that have been described above. That Joseph

---

[33] These positive characterizations are in tension with the Markan idea of hardening of the outsiders (4:10–12) and with its relation to the Markan development of the kingdom theme. Marcus, *The Way of the Lord*, 182, solves the problem by seeing both here as in the case of the good scribe (12:28–34) a similar ironic point: "Joseph should no longer be waiting, since the kingdom of God has now been revealed with the revelation of the kingship of the crucified Jesus." I am inclined to think that Mark did not try to adjust the figure of Joseph to his theological schemes. I assume that he rather tried to motivate the noble action of Joseph towards Jesus with a positive characterization that implies certain distance to the kingdom—just as in the case of the good scribe. People like them would become good soil for the preaching of the Gospel in the time of the Church.

[34] Particularly Broer, *Die Urgemeinde und das Grab Jesu*, 165–69, with emphasis on Markan expressions in these verses; see also Mohr, *Markus- und Johannespassion* 354–56.

[35] Thus also e.g. Schreiber, *Theologie des Vertrauens*, 26; Schweizer, *Das Evangelium nach Markus*; 193–94; Gnilka, *Das Evangelium nach Markus*, 2.313; Lührmann, *Das Markusevangelium*, 264.

[36] Myllykoski, *Die letzten Tage Jesu*, 1.124–30.

asks for Jesus' body (σῶμα), but receives his corpse (πτῶμα), also stresses that Jesus was really dead.[37] The Markan presentation does not presuppose that Joseph was present when Jesus died. That he starts acting only after the evening had already come rather creates the impression that he learned about Jesus' sudden death from others and decided to act as soon as possible.

The centurion episode, missing from the burial stories of Matthew and Luke, is one of the tricky minor agreements between Matthew and Luke against Mark. Some scholars have indeed regarded Mark 15:44–45 as a post-Markan addition.[38] However, the parallel omissions can be explained as indepedent redactional changes on the part of Matthew and Luke. They both consider the episode unnecessary, because in their presentations of the events there are enough "outsider" witnesses for the death of Jesus. Matthew indicates this by reporting about the Jewish leaders who recognize Jesus' death by asking for a guard at the tomb (27:62–66), while Luke introduces the crowd who had assembled for the spectacle and went home after seeing what had happened (23:48). Because of their independent emphasis on the Jewish witnesses, they did not need to tell how the Roman prefect doubted whether Jesus was already dead.[39] Possibly both Matthew and Luke knew that Mark 15:44–45 was a separate episode.

Joseph's request for the body of Jesus and Pilate's positive response belonged without doubt to the pre-Markan burial story. Although the story does not disclose why Joseph had to turn to Pilate instead of asking directly the soldiers at the cross for the body of Jesus, this action implies that his request was considered a delicate matter. In spite of this, there is nothing dramatic or unusual about permitting Joseph to take the body. All that mattered was the encounter between these two men, the idea that the highest representative of Roman power handed over the body of Jesus to Joseph of Arimathea, a respected council member who also buried it. The traditional

[37] Daube, *The New Testament and Rabbinic Judaism* (London: Athlone, 1956) 309–10, assumes that πτῶμα "was particularly suitable for describing a mutilated corpse, and thus a corpse mutilated in the course of an execution" and that this also was the case with the corpse of Jesus.

[38] See e.g. Bultmann, *History of the Synoptic Tradition*, 274; Grass, *Ostergeschehen und Osterberichte*, 174, and more recently, in a study arguing for the "Deutero-Markus" hypothesis, A. Ennulat, *Die "Minor Agreements": Untersuchung zu einer offenen Frage des synoptischen Problems* (WUNT 2/62; Tübingen: Mohr) 406.

[39] Cf. Brown, *The Death of the Messiah*, 2.1222.

burial story served to present Pilate as witness for the death and burial of Jesus.

The pre-Markan statement as well as the redactional Pilate episode imply that Joseph either knew or took it for granted that the family and followers of Jesus could not bury him or ask for permission to do it. However, he is presented as having no contact at all with them.

2.4. *The Simple Burial*

According to Mark Joseph bought a linen cloth, took Jesus down from the cross, wrapped him in the cloth, laid him in a tomb hewn out of rock, and rolled a stone against the opening of the tomb. Even though the buying of the linen cloth is mentioned separately, the description of the burial is rather scanty. There is no mention that Joseph would have washed (cf. Acts 9:37) or anointed the body, which in the Jewish tradition belonged to an honourable burial. Some scholars have suggested that these details are implied but not mentioned, because there was no need to give a detailed description of all the actions. If one imagines the scene as a historical event, there is nothing complicated about the missing details. For washing of the body Joseph needed a water jar and for anointing a bottle of oil. As he bought the linen cloth he could as well have bought a small amount of oil.[40]

However, the fact that the missing anointing is treated as a problem in the passion tradition contradicts this interpretation. The anointing of Jesus in Bethany is secondarily explained as anointing for his burial (14:8).[41] This interpretation is likely to stem already from the pre-Markan tradition, since the Evangelist himself interprets the anointing quite differently, viz. in terms of the world-wide Christian mission: wherever in all the world the Gospel is proclaimed, the deed of this woman will be told in memory of her (14:9).[42] Furthermore, Mark has utilized the anointing motif of the burial story by associating it with the visit of the women at the tomb (16:1). They must

[40] Thus Blinzler, "Die Grablegung Christi", 63, and Gundry, *Mark*, 982.

[41] Thus already Bultmann, *The History of the Synoptic Tradition* 263. See also Daube, *The New Testament and Rabbinic Judaism*, 315–317; Mack, *A Myth of Innocence*, 199–202.

[42] Thus also e.g. Gnilka, *Das Evangelium nach Markus*, 2.222, and Mohr, *Markus- und Johannespassion*, 140–41.

see the actions of Joseph in order to realize that they should complement them by anointing Jesus.[43] The Evangelist does not bother about their intention to anoint a corpse that is already rotting as he gives a motive for their visit at the tomb.

Because of this double use of the anointing for burial that was lacking in the burial story itself, it seems likely that its use in the Bethany story belonged already to a pre-Markan passion narrative. I find it most likely that the motif of anointing was introduced into the pre-Markan passion narrative as both pericopes, the anointing in Bethany and the burial of Jesus, were joined into the passion narrative.[44] As soon as the independent burial tradition was brought together with other passion material, the simplicity of Joseph's actions became a problem. However, both Mark and the passion tradition that preceded him left the account of the simple burial in this respect untouched. Only John introduced the anointing in the burial story, by using Nicodemus, another Jewish leader, whom he had introduced in the beginning of his gospel (19:39–40).[45]

These considerations favour the conclusion that it was the purpose of the traditional story to describe a simple burial. However, nothing reveals a tendency to characterize the burial as hasty, incomplete or unsatisfactory.[46] The idea that Joseph bought the linen cloth, which is hardly a redactional feature, stresses the completeness of his action. The strong verb ἐνελίσσειν, which is used of fettering prisoners, putting children in swaddling by hand and feet, and holding people fast in the net, is probably used to imply that the body of Jesus was tightly wrapped. This indicates more likely a complete than an incomplete action.

Once the simplicity of the burial is acknowledged, the connection of the burial story to the story of the empty tomb becomes a problem. The story about the empty tomb implies that Jesus was buried in an expensive tomb of arcosolium type—rather than a more modest

---

[43] Mack, *A Myth of Innocence*, 309, connects this with the lateness of hour as an explanation for the incomplete burial. He regards the whole narrative plot as a Markan invention.

[44] Myllykoski, *Die letzten Tage Jesu*, 2.100–1.

[45] John 12:7 indicates that for the fourth Evangelist the anointing in Bethany was not really an anointing for burial. In this verse John tried to reconcile this traditional anointing with the one that he himself introduced to the burial story. See Myllykoski, *Die letzten Tage Jesu*, 1.190–91.

[46] Pace Brown, *The Death of the Messiah*, 2.1245–46.

tomb of loculi type. Only in such a tomb it is natural to imagine the young man sitting "on the right side" (16:5) on the bench of the arcosolium (cf. John 20:12) or in an antechamber.[47] Furthermore, we must imagine the three women coming inside the tomb and inspecting the spot where Jesus' body was placed. In addition, the name lists of these women and the account of their actions indicate that these two stories were originally independent.

2.5. *The Women as Witnesses*

There are three divergent lists of female witnesses of the crucifixion, burial and empty tomb presented by Mark in 15:40–41, 15:47 and 16:1:

> There were also women looking on from a distance, among them were Mary Magdalene, and Mary the mother of James the younger and of Joses, and Salome. These used to follow him and provided for him when he was in Galilee; and there were many other women who had come up with him to Jerusalem (15:40–41).
>
> Mary Magdalene and Mary of Joses saw where he was laid (15:47).
>
> And when the sabbath was over, Mary Magdalene, and Mary of James, and Salome, bought spices, so that they might go and anoint him (16:1).

There is one much-debated difficulty in these lists. Following the ordinary practice of identification, Mary of Joses (15:47) and Mary of James (16:1) must be understood as wives (or daughters) of these two men, but in the crucifixion scene the second Mary is mentioned as the mother of Joses and James the younger. Mark quite obviously wanted to have the reader understand that this was the case also in 15:47 and 16:1. Some scholars find it reasonable to assume that all these lists stem from an old passion tradition and refer to three eye-witnesses.[48] Others assume that Mark used a traditional list and that differences in these lists "may be explained perfectly well as stylistic variations that avoid monotonous repetition".[49] Neither of these assumptions can be excluded, but I think that they are not able to

---

[47] For the latter alternative, see Brown, *The Death of the Messiah*, 2.1248–50.

[48] Pesch, *Das Markusevangelium*, 2.503–9; Mohr, *Markus- und Johannespassion*, 331–35; Gundry, *Mark*, 989.

[49] Yarbro Collins, "The Empty Tomb", 116.

explain the unnecessary and clumsy repetition of the list in 16:1 immediately after 15:47. Why did not Mark or an earlier narrator simply repeat the list in 15:47 and refer to these women as "they" in 16:1? If he wanted to avoid repetition or tell the story as simply as possible, why did he not just refer to the second Mary as "the other Mary"—as Matthew does in 27:61 and 28:1? I find it more reasonable to assume that Mark simply transmitted both lists as he combined the burial and the empty tomb story as originally independent traditions and combined these lists secondarily in Mark 15:40–41.[50] However, the thorny problem in this solution is that the presence of the female eye-witnesses at the end of the burial story also presupposes a narrative that spoke about their presence at the empty tomb. I find it hardly likely that the list in 15:47 would once have belonged to an independent burial tradition.

In spite of this difficulty, I suppose with many others that Mark wanted to make Mary of James and Mary of Joses one and the same person by introducing Mary the mother of James and Joses in the list of women watching the crucifixion. Because of the curious problem with the names, the list in 15:47 may have originally belonged to the crucifixion narrative. In that case, Mark replaced this original list and placed it at the only location left in his arrangement—after the burial story. By making this harmonistic list appear first in his presentation Mark led his audience to harmonize the diverging lists which these Christians possibly knew from their traditions.[51]

This arrangement is related to other redactional motifs in the narrative. The Markan female witnesses who have seen the burial wish to complement it by anointing the body of Jesus. As they are still on their way to the tomb they ask among themselves who will roll away the stone for them. Of course, Mark does not wish to emphasize that they have forgotten to ask anybody to help them, but instead prepares them for their encounter with the supernatural young man. I find it reasonable to regard 15:47 and 16:3–4a as Markan redaction

[50] Thus Schenke, *Auferstehungsverkündigung*, 20–30, and Broer, *Die Urgemeinde und das Grab Jesu*, 135—a conclusion drawn by both after a careful and exhaustive analysis.

[51] I think that Mark's real or assumed knowledge of two diverging lists among his readers and his subsequent need to present both of these lists as well as the harmonized list explain why he did not show any interest in harmonizing 15:47 and 16:1—an objection presented by Crossan, "Mark and the Relatives of Jesus", *NovT* 15 (1973) 81–113, esp. 106.

and that these notes demonstrate how the Evangelist combined the two originally independent stories. I assume that the traditional account of the empty tomb mentioned three female witnesses, while the originally independent burial story did not know about the presence of any women at the tomb.

If this reasoning is correct, the account of the empty tomb in 16:1–8 is a later legend that is dependent on the burial tradition.[52] Taken as a whole, this legend does not presuppose that the tomb of Jesus was known in Jerusalem. Instead it indicates that Jesus was translated to heaven from the very spot where his body was laid: the women as witnesses must go inside the tomb to see clearly this spot and then, seized by terror and amazement, go out and flee from the tomb—and say nothing to anyone.[53] However, I find it questionable to assume that in the pre-Markan tradition the women would have discarded the divine and salvation-historically important message of the young man or that Mark would have created *ex nihilo* a story that emphasizes such a failure. I do not think that Mark wanted both male and female disciples to end up with a lack of understanding about the resurrection and appearance of Jesus—simply because in Mark Jesus never fails; at least in 14:28 it is Jesus himself who foresees the reunion with his disciples in Galilee. Therefore I imagine that Mark added the message of the young man to the women (16:6–7) to an enigmatic original story, in which the young man appears as a symbolic figure (cf. 14:51–52).[54] This might have been a veiled reference to an earlier tradition, which told how the women saw the risen Jesus himself. If this is correct, it is not difficult

[52] Because of numerous redactional traits in Mark 16:1–8, some scholars have doubted whether there ever was a pre-Markan tradition of the empty tomb; see Crossan, "Empty Tomb and Absent Lord", in W. Kelber (ed.), *The Passion in Mark: Studies on Mark 14–16* (Philadelphia: Fortress, 1976) 135–52; Mack, *A Myth of Innocence*, 308–09; Collins, "The Empty Tomb", 128–31. According to Lüdemann, *The Resurrection of Jesus*, 109–118 there was "a small unit which Mark worked in at this point" (p. 115). My own view on the pre-Markan tradition is more optimistic; see Myllykoski, *Die letzten Tage Jesu*, 2.106–21.

[53] In his old and important article, Bickermann ("Das leere Grab", 286–90) emphasized that the empty tomb traditions of antiquity generally do not presuppose any appearance of the translated hero. He therefore assumes that the Markan story of the empty tomb was also originally unrelated to the appearance traditions. This theory has more recently been applied to Q: D. Zeller, "Entrückung zur Ankunft als Menschensohn (Lk 13, 34f.; 11, 29f.)", in *À Cause de l'Évangile: Études sur les Synoptiques et les Actes* (FS J. Dupont; Lectio Divina, 123; Paris: Cerf, 1985) 513–30.

[54] Myllykoski, *Die letzten Tage Jesu*, 2.111–5, 169–71.

to imagine why their experiences had been suppressed. On the other hand, it is striking that the story ends with the note that the women "said nothing to anyone, for they were afraid". Long ago Bousset and Bultmann read this as an explanation of the fact that this account had remain unknown for so long.[55] I assume that there is something right in this assumption. However, the late age of the tradition might be related to the idea that the experience of the women had to be related to the tomb of Jesus, because they were known to have lamented for him.[56] Mark, in turn seems to have used their frightened reaction—and the whole story—in order to indicate that Jesus did not appear in Jerusalem. According to him, the gospel message of his resurrection was spread from Galilee, where "his disciples and Peter" saw him.

To sum up: With the redactional time indication ἤδη ὀψίας γενομένης as well as the redactional addition of the women in 15:47 Mark tied the burial story closer to its context in the traditional passion narrative. Furthermore, the story was originally an independent unit in the oral passion tradition. I assume that the references to the day of preparation and the rolling of the stone against the door of the tomb were added to the oral tradition as it was articulated in the pre-Markan passion narrative. The original independence of the burial tradition can be seen particularly in the presentation of the simple burial, which does not match with the idea of the spacious,

---

[55] Bousset, *Kyrios Christos: Geschichte des Christusglaubens von den Anfängen des Christentums bis Irenaeus* (4th ed.; Göttingen: Vandenhoeck & Ruprecht, 1926) 7, n. 1; Bultmann, *The History of the Synoptic Tradition*, 285. Lüdemann, *Jesus after two Thousand Years*, 114 sees a redactional connection between the young men in Mark 14:51–52 and 16:5. He assumes that "Mark implicitly identifies himself as the first one to tell the story of the empty tomb".

[56] K.E. Corley, "Women and the Crucifixion and Burial of Jesus", *Forum New Series* 1 (1998) 181–225. She pays attention to the suppression of the female lament traditions in favour of the masculine and heroic noble death tradition in Greek, Roman and Jewish burial customs. She suggests that this trend also explains the suppression of the women's lament in the traditions about the burial, tomb and resurrection of Jesus. This suppression resulted in the fictional tradition of the empty tomb, which followed a common Hellenistic model (pp. 203–9). This, of course, included also the suppression of their position as witnesses for the risen Jesus (p. 203–4): "The overall effect of the empty tomb tradition, which featured women in this stereotypical role of tomb visitation, functioned to marginalize women followers of Jesus more than men thus weakening their claim to having seen (ὁράω) the risen Christ." See also Sawicki, *Seeing the Lord*, 257 who connects the grief of the women to the loss of the body of Jesus. This, in turn, was "the starting point of the reflection that culminates in a 'finding' of the empty tomb and 'seeing' of Jesus as already risen from the dead."

probably arcosolium type tomb in Mark 16:5. The tradition behind 16:1–8 is later and dependent on the burial story; it is possibly based on the fact that Jesus appeared to these women as well. I assume that the earliest, oral stage of the passion tradition was not articulated in terms of exact dates and that Jesus was crucified and buried before the Passover festival.

3. *The Origins of the Burial Tradition*

There are some good arguments for the assumption that in 1 Cor 15:3–5 Paul gives some evidence of a particular stage of oral tradition concerning the death, burial and resurrection of Jesus. Furthermore, even the original, orally transmitted pre-Markan burial story is not quite easy to read as a straightforward testimony of what really happened to the body of Jesus. What really happened must remain obscure, but alternative reconstructions are worth consideration.

3.1. *The Tradition Received by Paul (1 Cor 15:3–5)*

In 1 Cor 15 Paul argues against those who deny the resurrection of the dead. As an introduction to his argument he reminds the Corinthian Christians of the traditions that he had transmitted them (vv. 3–7). However we read the rest of the chapter, Paul wishes to emphasize with these traditions that Christ died and was risen, in order to demonstrate that all the dead will also rise in the eschatological resurrection. The reference to the burial of Jesus emphasizes that he was really dead. By naming a great number of witnesses to the resurrection of Jesus Paul wants to prepare his case in vv. 12–58: one cannot be a follower of all these very first Christians without believing in the resurrection of the dead.

The use technical terms παραλαμβάνειν and παραδιδόναι in 1 Cor 15:1 makes it clear that Paul cites old tradition, but there is no agreement as to which pieces belonged to it and how Paul presented it. In vv. 3b–5 Paul lists four points that he marks with *hoti recitativum*. He has extended these key points with an additional list of witnesses to the resurrection of Jesus in vv. 6–7. Most scholars have regarded vv. 3b–5 as an old traditional unit.[57] Joachim Jeremias has

[57] Extensive studies on this passage: J. Kremer, *Das älteste Zeugnis von der Auferstehung*

listed non-Pauline semitisms and argued that the tradition must be traced back to the earliest Christian community in Jerusalem.[58] However, the key expressions Χριστός as the subject at the start of the sentence, as well as κατὰ τὰς γραφάς, do not favour the assumption of an Aramaic original. Furthermore, there are no compelling reasons to relate ὑπὲρ τῶν ἁμαρτιῶν ἡμῶν specifically to the MT of Is 53:5, 12 rather than to the LXX version. The expression τῇ ἡμέρᾳ τῇ τρέτῃ may or may not be derived from the Hos 6:2 (LXX), but the expression itself is not necessarily based on an Aramaic original. It is therefore not necessary to assume that Paul knew the contents of 1 Cor 15:3b–5 as a formula that was taught to him soon after his conversion.[59]

Furthermore, there are some difficulties in seeing vv. 3b–5 as a traditional whole. The short statement ὅτι ἐτάφη is related to the preceding statement about the death of Christ, while the appearance to Peter and the twelve belongs to the latter statement about his resurrection. Because of the similarities between the fuller statements about the death and resurrection of Jesus (parallelismus membrorum, κατὰ τὰς γραφάς), the short statement ὅτι ἐτάφη rather looks like a link between these major statements. Furthermore, it does not refer to direct divine action as the major statements do.[60] The fourfold ὅτι supports the assumption that Paul wished to remind Corinthians about four separate traditional items that he brought together here.[61] It is less likely that he had a concise formula which he resolved into its component parts by adding the fourfold *hoti recitativum*.[62] If this reasoning is correct, it is not necessary to assume that ὅτι ἐτάφη belonged to a pre-Pauline confessional formula.

Christi: Eine bibeltheologische Studie zur Aussage und Bedeutung von 1 Kor 15,1–11 (3rd ed.; SBS 17; Stuttgart: Katholisches Bibelwerk, 1970); K. Lehmann, *Auferweckt am dritten Tag nach der Schrift* (QD 38; Freiburg: Herder, 1968); Lüdemann, *The Resurrection of Jesus*, 33–109.

[58] J. Jeremias, *Die Abendmahlsworte Jesu* (4th ed.; Göttingen: Vandenhoeck & Ruprecht, 1967) 95–97. On the discussion of this theory, see Lehmann, *Auferweckt am dritten Tag*, 87–115.

[59] Pace Kremer, *Das älteste Zeugnis*, 30 and others.

[60] K.H. Rengstorf, *Die Auferstehung Jesu: Form, Art und Sinn der urchristlichen Osterbotschaft* (Witten/Ruhr: Luther-Verlag, 1967) 54.

[61] With U. Wilckens, *Die Missionsreden der Apostelgeschichte: Form- und traditionsgeschichtliche Untersuchungen* (3rd ed.; WMANT 5; Neukirchen-Vluyn: Neukirchener, 1973) 76, n. 1. Wilckens emphasizes correctly that there is no evidence of the repetitious use of *hoti recitativum* in confessional formulas.

[62] Thus Lehmann, *Auferweckt am dritten Tag*, 73–77.

I find it reasonable to assume that Paul had taught the Corinthians the essentials of the passion and resurrection tradition, also that Jesus was buried. He surely knew that Jesus was buried by the Jewish leaders, and possibly he had heard of Joseph of Arimathea. Following the imagery that he uses later in this chapter, it can be assumed that he considered the dead body of Jesus like a dead and bare seed sown in the ground (1 Cor 15:35–37). That Jesus was buried meant that his perishable, physical body was sown in dishonour and weakness before his imperishable, spiritual body was raised in glory and power (cf. vv. 42–44).[63] I think that this interpretation does not presuppose any interest in the tomb of Jesus or its location in Jerusalem: it is just fitting to think that Jesus' perishable body was buried in weakness, by his enemies. I think that Paul does not mention the empty tomb because he did not know about it.[64] He surely could have made use of such knowledge, but his manner of arguing for the resurrection of Jesus was completely different. Paul was eager to mention all the appearances known to him, not least because these finally lead to himself, "the least of apostles"—who in any case had "worked harder" than any of these other witnesses (vv. 8–11). Thus Paul's way of using the passion and resurrection traditions seems to speak for a general background of the burial story and a later origin of the story of the women in the empty tomb.

The reference to the third day is often traced back to Hos 6:2 (LXX), but the absence of this passage elsewhere in the New Testament as well as its late reception among later Christian writers is puzzling.[65] A suggestion has been made that both Paul and his tradition made in v. 4b two separate statements that are meant to express the scriptural basis of the third day: 1) that Christ was raised from the dead in accordance with the scripture and that 2) his resurrec-

[63] See also e.g. Wedderburn, *Beyond Resurrection*, 70–75.

[64] With e.g. Grass, *Ostergeschehen und Osterberichte*, 173, and A.Y. Collins, *The Beginning of the Gospel: Probings of Mark in Context* (Minneapolis: Fortress, 1992) 124–27. Grass also refers to the Pauline resurrection faith in 2 Cor 5:1–11. Against this view argues e.g. Kremer, *Das älteste Zeugnis*, 37–38, with particular reference to burials of great Old Testament figures whose tombs were claimed to be known.

[65] The earliest church father we know to have referred to Hos 6:2 in the context of Jesus' resurrection is Tertullian (*Adv. Marc.* 4.43). Curiously enough, he takes this passage as prophecy about the restoration of the faith of the women who come to the tomb. Hos 6:2 indeed "clearly refers to revival and restoration of more than one person" (Wedderburn, *Beyond Resurrection*, 50–51).

tion took place on the third day.[66] However, it is difficult to assume that an early statement about the resurrection of Christ was based on such a complicated idea. The statement about the death of Christ in v. 3b is easier to understand in the light of a particular passage in the scriptures, Is 53 (vv. 5, 12), which is used by Paul himself as he refers to the death of Jesus (Rom 4:25). Here the idea of scriptural fulfilment is most probably traditional.

Because of these problems it makes sense to assume that Paul himself took the notion κατὰ τὰς γραφάς from v. 3b and added it to the resurrection statement in v. 4b. It is remarkable that he did not respond to the serious denial of the resurrection of the dead (v. 12) with a scriptural passage and that he did not cite the Scriptures in order to prove that there will be a resurrection of the dead. Instead he opened his case by reminding the Corinthians of the traditions which they had received and approved (vv. 1–11). They knew that Christ had died for their sins in accordance with the Scriptures. As Paul reminded them of the old tradition that Christ was raised on the third day, he added the note about Scriptures here as well. By doing this he meant to emphasize that the resurrection of Jesus from the dead was prophesied in the Scriptures, which is particularly important for the starting point of his argumentation in v. 12. Therefore he quite naturally did not take into consideration the reference to the third day in the traditional statement.

Although the statement that Jesus was raised on the third day must be a quite old tradition, I assume that the earliest community did not memorize the exact date of the death, burial and resurrection of Jesus.[67] The appearances, which took place soon after the death of Jesus, became the starting point of reflection. Following a familiar scriptural expression indicating a short period of time in which a significant divine action takes place,[68] the tradition fixed these events,

[66] Thus B.M. Metzger, "A Suggestion Concerning the Meaning of 1 Cor xv,4b", *JTS* 8 (1957) 126–32. He refers to 1 Macc 7:16–17 as a similar case.

[67] It seems to be a popular view that the first visions of the risen Jesus must be dated to the third day after his death. Even Wedderburn, *Beyond Resurrection*, 65, can still after his critical remarks hold that "something did indeed happen on that first day of the week".

[68] K. Lehmann, *Auferweckt am dritten Tag*, 180–81, has listed almost 30 Old Testament passages using the time indication of the third day in order to mark a significant event or decisive turning point in the narrative. In some of these passages the third day indicates God's salvific action. Lehmann also points out the role

which took place on various days after the death of Jesus, to the third day after his death. The importance of the third day in the Jewish lament tradition may also have played a role here, if we assume that the Easter experiences of Mary Magdalene and other women were related to their lament for Jesus.[69] Furthermore, since the deceased person was often not considered properly dead within three days of death (cf. John 11:39), it was natural to locate the appearances of the risen Jesus after this period.[70] All these deep-rooted traditional conceptions may have contributed to the fact that Jesus' resurrection was proclaimed to have happened on the third day.

I assume that only after these developments the scheme of three days was articulated in the events of crucifixion, burial and empty tomb. Locating the first and the third day around the sabbath was quite natural: this explained why Mary Magdalene and other women had to come to the tomb only on the third day. Their relation to the tomb of Jesus may be originally related to the motif of lament. Curiously enough, no empty tomb story of the canonical Gospels mentions that these women came to the tomb in order to lament the death of Jesus.[71] Mark has added the artificial motif of anointing to the traditional story and Luke follows him, while Matthew says that the women "came to see the tomb" (28:1) and John gives no explanation at all. All this hints at the lateness of the empty tomb tradition: as it was created, the motif of lament was already history. The sole focus of the story was on the women's encounter with the young man or angel(s) very early on the third day morning.

---

of the third day in the Rabbinic literature (ibid. 262–90). Against this evidence, Craig ("The Empty Tomb of Jesus", 45–50) emphasizes the late dates of various Rabbinic writings cited by Lehmann. He maintains that in the apocalyptic texts of the first century CE it was not number three, but number seven that was used in connection with the eschatological resurrection. He also hints at the minimal reception of the corresponding third day passages in the New Testament.

[69] Corley, "Women", 203.

[70] See e.g. Metzger, "A Suggestion", 123. Cf. also Brown, *The Death of the Messiah*, 2.1309, n. 55: "In the Gos. Pet. storyline the wish to safeguard the burial place 'for three days' (8:30) need imply only that after such a period the imposter would surely be dead".

[71] This theme comes up again in the later Gospel tradition (*Gos. Pet.* 52). Most likely it stems from the weeping of Mary Magdalene in John 20:11, 13. For Johannine themes in the empty tomb story *Gos. Pet.* 50–57, see Crossan, *The Cross that Spoke: The Origins of the Passion Narrative* (San Francisco: Harper, 1988) 285–88, and Corley, "Women", 210–11.

3.2. *Tendencies in the Oral Burial Tradition*

In a stimulating and thought-provoking article from 1981, Johannes Schreiber has presented sharply the contradictions of the character of Joseph in the Markan burial story.[72] Joseph belonged to the Sanhedrin, whose members all heard the divine revelation of Jesus (Mark 14:62), but both violated the law and rejected the Son of God by condemning Jesus to death during the Passover. Furthermore, Joseph bought the linen cloth and buried Jesus on sabbath (Mark 15:42: "when evening had come") and excluded himself from the feast of Passover by visiting a Gentile and touching a corpse. He buried Jesus after the sunset and therefore violated also the commandment expressed in Deut 21:23.

These violations of the law make the characterization of Joseph as a respected member of the council and his pious expectation of the kingdom of God look deeply ironical. Schreiber concludes that the Markan burial story is a gnostically coloured allegory of distorted obedience to the law among Jews and Jewish Christians.[73] All these features are indeed striking, but the description of the burial itself bears no traces of irony or implicit accusations.

Most of the contradictions pointed out by Schreiber are due to the redactional date (Passover) and time (after the sunset) of the burial. If the analysis above is correct, the pre-Markan burial tradition at its original, oral stage did not specify that Jesus was buried during the Passover festival. Assuming that Schreiber is wrong, I take two particular features of the tradition to indicate that Joseph was not thought to have buried Jesus then. Since early Christian storytellers must have been Jewish Christians or at least well aware of Jewish traditions, they most probably did not think that the respected Joseph bought the linen cloth during the festival.[74] And although

[72] J. Schreiber, "Die Bestattung Jesu: Redaktionsgeschichtliche Beobachtungen zu Mark 15:42–47 par.", *ZNW* 72 (1981) 141–71, esp. pp. 141–57. According to him, Mark wished to present Joseph as one of the hardened outsiders who look and do not perceive. Schreiber relates his interpretation of the burial story to the theme of Messianic secret in Mark.

[73] Schreiber ("Die Bestattung Jesu", 173–77) characterizes the pre-Markan tradition as Jewish Christian and holds that Joseph of Arimathea was a Jewish Christian who buried Jesus.

[74] Daube (*The New Testament and Rabbinic Judaism*, 312) assumes that "Mark, or his source, when introducing the point as to the quality of the burial clothes, went too far and, by some oversight, spoke of a purchase on the first day of Passover".

there was nothing wrong with corpse-impurity itself, it seems likely that they did not imagine him defiling himself in those days. However, it does not seem likely that they bothered to imagine how Joseph remained impure for seven days after he had buried Jesus (cf. Num 19:16).

These observations are related to a wider problem concerning the dating of the crucifixion at the oral phase of the tradition. I have elsewhere argued that both the synoptic and the Johannine datings are based on secondary theological reflections.[75] Furthermore, some positive signals in the passion tradition suggest that the arrest and crucifixion of Jesus were originally taken to have happened before the festival. In its original form, the Barabbas story (Mark 15:6–15) seems to presuppose that Barabbas was released in order to celebrate the Passover with his people. The successful plan of the chief priests to arrest Jesus as soon as possible, but "not during the festival" (Mark 14:2) also supports such a chronology. To be sure, Paul refers to Christ as "our paschal lamb" who has been sacrificed (1 Cor 5:7), but this does not necessarily hint at the Johannine chronology of Jesus' crucifixion.[76] I am inclined to regard it as a theological reflection of the fact that Jesus died in the context of a Passover festival.

The burial story thus stems from a relatively early stage of the oral passion tradition, but it was hardly a historically reliable description of the events after Jesus' death on the cross. To put it quite simply: the story suggests that Joseph acted alone. It is he alone who takes courage, goes to Pilate, asks for the body of Jesus and takes it down from the cross. This is, of course, an idealized presentation of something that really happened or what the first Christians imagined to have happened. It is difficult to imagine that Joseph the member of the Sanhedrin went to the abominable place of crucifixion and personally took care of the body of Jesus. His role as a historical figure was more likely much less concrete than the Markan burial story suggests.

There is another question closely related to this. The traditional burial story presupposes that Joseph did not go to Pilate in order to bury all the crucified criminals, but only Jesus. He was not inter-

[75] Myllykoski, *Die letzten Tage Jesu*, 2.35–37, 153–54.

[76] *Pace* M. Lang, *Johannes und die Synoptiker: Eine redaktionsgeschichtliche Analyse von Joh 18–20 vor dem markinischen und lukanischen Hintergrund* (FRLANT 182; Göttingen: Vandenhoeck & Ruprecht, 1999) 48.

ested in the two others crucified with him or anybody else crucified at the time of the feast. The story implies that he or his trusted men followed the final struggle of Jesus in order to take care of his burial immediately after his death.[77] This makes him look like a particular sympathizer of the cause of Jesus, although the story itself is very reticent in this respect. If he was commonly known as such a notably exceptional member of the Sanhedrin—to say the least—why is his sympathy expressed only in a very general and obscure way, i.e. by mentioning that he was looking for the kingdom of God? If this is a Markan way of interpreting the tradition—as I assume—then the difficulty is even more serious. I do not think that Joseph originally was known as a member of the council who took pains to bury only and exclusively the body of Jesus. As the tradition was passed on, this well-respected outsider became in the imagination of the early Christians first someone who was looking for the kingdom of God—whatever that meant—and finally a disciple.

It is reasonable to assume that the burial of Jesus was not honourable and that Joseph buried Jesus like any other crucified criminal. But can it be demonstrated that the tradition preserved by Mark was meant to serve this purpose? Is his story, then, historically reliable? Byron R. McCane has attempted to prove this by reading the Markan burial story against the background of Jewish burial practices.[78] Honourable Jewish burial included washing, anointing and careful wrapping of the corpse on the day of death. "Thus prepared, the corpse was placed on a bier or in a coffin and carried out of town in a procession to the family tomb, usually a small rock-cut cave entered through a narrow opening that could be covered with a stone."[79] Eulogies were spoken and the corpse was placed in the tomb with some valuable objects that belonged to him. Mourning continued in the family home; the ritual at the tomb usually took

[77] Crossan (*Who Killed Jesus?*, 173) correctly objects the idea that the Markan Joseph would have been a member of the Sanhedrin who buried Jesus just because he was following pious Jewish customs. This latter view is supported by Brown, *The Death of the Messiah*, 2.1216–19.

[78] B.R. McCane, "'Where No One Had Yet Been Laid'", 473–84. Regarding the later developments of the burial story (particularly in the *Gospel of Peter*), he emphasizes that (p. 482) "the early stages of the tradition do not deny that Jesus' burial was shameful". This interpretation of the Markan burial story has been put forward also by Daube, *The New Testament and Rabbinic Judaism*, 310–12, and R.E. Brown, "The Burial of Jesus (Mark 15:42–47)", *CBQ* 50 (1988) 233–45.

[79] McCane, "'Where No One Had Yet Been Laid'", 474.

place before sunset. McCane emphasizes that "Jewish death rituals were closely linked to ties of kinship and family" and that they "also addressed the social impact of death".[80] The time of mourning continued to the second burial after about a year from the first burial. Then the bones of the deceased were collected and placed in an ossuary.

McCane points out that the essential features of an honourable burial are lacking in the Markan burial story as well as in Acts 13:29b, where Paul says that Jewish leaders took Jesus "down from the tree and laid him in a tomb". McCane concludes that according to the earliest Christian tradition "Jesus was buried in shame, i.e. laid in the criminals' tomb without any public rites of mourning".[81] That Jesus was buried in a new tomb—as Matthew, Luke and John tell us—also reflects historically plausible circumstances, because it may be assumed that the deceased criminals were buried in new tombs in order to separate them from their people.[82]

I think that this reasoning makes sense to some extent. It is indeed not convincing to assume that Mark 15:46 indicates a hastily performed and provisorial burial. It is also unlikely that this short description was meant to imply the washing and anointing of the corpse as so self-evident actions that they did not have to be mentioned. If the description was intended to be as short as possible, then the buying of the linen cloth could as well have been left unmentioned. Furthermore, it is obvious that the actions of Joseph are related to his role as a non-member of the family, because he is said to have acted alone and without performing any mourning rites. The simplicity of the burial is most convincingly related to the official role of Joseph as a member of the Sanhedrin.

However, it is another question whether the burial is presented as shameful. Several features of the text indicate that Joseph acts out of respect towards Jesus. He is "a respected member of the council" whose motivation to bury Jesus is pious ("who was also himself waiting for the kingdom of God"). He demonstrates particular courage ("went boldly to Pilate") as he asks for the body of Jesus. He is said to have taken care of the whole burial by himself and bought a

[80] McCane, "'Where No One Had Yet Been Laid'", 477.
[81] McCane, "'Where No One Had Yet Been Laid'", 480–82, esp. 481.
[82] See also Benoit, *Passion et résurrection du Seigneur*, 259–60.

linen cloth for this purpose. All these features underline the dignity of Jesus' burial,[83] even though the piety and courage of Joseph may be traced back to Markan redaction.

I cannot escape the conclusion that there is a double motivation to describe the actions of Joseph. He is a member of the council who was known to have belonged to the enemy camp, but he is also a pious and powerful man who buried Jesus on his own initiative. It is quite natural that Joseph is not said to have washed and anointed the corpse or organized mourning rituals. This might be a matter of taste, but I think that his actions do not indicate any shameful treatment the body of Jesus, but rather his unavoidable lack of intimacy with the deceased. Even if Mark had understood Jesus' burial as shameful, all other evangelists surely did not. They were willing to multiply the positive features of Joseph and his actions, and I find it rather unlikely that they mentioned the newness of the tomb in order to point in the opposite direction.[84]

The motivation to portray Joseph as a "friendly enemy" does not favour the assumption that the role of Joseph in the burial of Jesus was completely invented by later Christians.[85] I think that there was a strong need to ensure that Jesus' body was treated with dignity and by an honourable person even if he was known to have been buried by his enemies. And so this Joseph, a distant, respected man was thought to have buried Jesus. If he was not known as a Jewish

---

[83] Cf. Gundry, *Mark*, 980–81, who argues for the historical reliability of Mark's narrative.

[84] Crossan (*Who Killed Jesus?*, 174) offers a more plausible explanation: "The newness answers an obvious problem: What if the body of Jesus got mixed up with other bodies in the tomb?" For a more theological explanation, see J. Davies, *Death, Burial and Rebirth*, 8: "The tomb marks territory, dynasty, tribe. Jesus' new and empty tomb marks the real beginning of a new religion."

[85] *Pace* Crossan (*Who Killed Jesus?*, 172–73) who draws from the dual character of Joseph exactly such a conclusion: "I consider Joseph of Arimathea to be a total Markan creation in name, in place, and in function. Mark's problem is clear: those with power were against Jesus; those for him had no power. No power: not power to do, not power to request, not power to beg, not even power to bribe. What is needed is an in-between character, one somehow on the side of power and somehow on the side of Jesus. What is needed, in fact, is a never-never person." Crossan further argues for awide-spread tendency to create names in the gospel tradition. He assumes that Mark invented the events concerning Barabbas, Simon of Cyrene, and Joseph (pp. 176–77). Brown (*The Death of the Messiah*, 2.1240) argues against this view that "a Christian fictional creation from nothing of a Jewish Sanhedrist who does what is right is almost inexplicable, granted the hostility in early Christian writings towards the Jewish authorities responsible for the death of Jesus".

Christian or as a sympathizer of the cause of Jesus—which I think was the case—there must have been some later Christians who were puzzled by the fact or common assumption that the body of Jesus ended up in the hands of the Jewish authorities.

There may have been two further reasons to think that Joseph was there and that he buried Jesus in a proper way, even though he could not have treated his body with same care as his relatives and friends would have done. It was important to emphasize that Jesus was not buried naked, since nakedness of a corpse was abhorred by the Jews (cf. Acts 5:6).[86] Furthermore, in popular imagination those who had suffered a violent death and had not been properly buried were easily imagined as restless ghosts who would wander between the world of the living and the realm of the dead.[87] For the first Christians, it was necessary to resist such an idea. If Jesus was decently buried, it was sure that he did not just wander around like a ghost as he appeared to his disciples. It is obvious that both Pilate and the members of the Sanhedrin held belief in ghosts merely as superstition, but among the common people it had to be taken seriously.

I assume that the first Christians knew the name, positition and reputation of Joseph. They may also have learned about his involvement with the burials of crucified criminals. They seem to have neither known Joseph personally nor been familiar with his activities, and they did not have the need or opportunity to consult him about what happened to the body of Jesus.

3.3. *Death-Without-Burial or Burial of the Criminal?*

John Dominic Crossan has made a case for the theory that Jesus was not buried at all. He has argued that the narratives about the burial and the empty tomb are completely fictitious and created by Mark. Crossan thinks that the oldest passion narrative can be found in a source that he has reconstructed behind the apocryphal *Gospel of Peter*. This original stratum, which he calls the Cross Gospel, had only the guards at the tomb and nothing about the burial of Jesus or the women at the tomb. Crossan observes notable literary prob-

[86] Lüdemann, *Jesus after Two Thousand Years*, 110.

[87] For this motif in ancient Greece, see particularly S.I. Johnston, *Restless Dead: Encounters between the Living and the Dead in Ancient Greece* (Berkeley: University of California Press, 1999) 127–60.

lems in the narrative of the *Gospel of Peter.* The request for burial (*Gos. Pet.* 3a–5) interrupts the trial scene and is presented as preparation for the burial itself (*Gos. Pet.* 23–24). The actions of disciples in *Gos. Pet.* 26–27 and 58–59 (mourning and hiding from the Jewish authorities) prepare the reader for the appearance scene in 60. Thirdly, the descent of the angelic young man to the tomb in *Gos. Pet.* 43–44 is a preparation for the scene at the empty tomb in 50–57. According to Crossan, the main units (burial in 23–24, women at the empty tomb in 50–57, and appearance to the disciples in 60) originated in the canonical Gospels and were included in the Cross Gospel by a redactor. This is the intracanonical stratum. A later redactor included preparatory passages in order to soften the contradictions created by the addition of the intracanonical passages (the redactional stratum). Crossan's main argument against the presence of the burial story in the Cross Gospel is that in the rest of the narrative the Jews and their elders control both the deposition of the body of Jesus (*Gos. Pet.* 15: "the Jews drew the nails from the hands of the Lord and laid him on the earth") and the tomb (*Gos. Pet.* 29–33: elders and scribes are told to have guarded the tomb together with the soldiers).[88]

In spite of some insightful observations of Crossan, it is difficult to exclude the passages related to the burial from the text without damaging its narrative logic. In *Gos. Pet.* 15, the Jews become "anxious and uneasy lest the sun had already set, since he was still alive", which refers back to *Gos. Pet.* 3a–5, where Herod expresses in advance his desire to have Jesus buried before sunset (Deut 21:22–23). As Crossan excludes *Gos. Pet.* 3a–5 from the original text, the anxiety of the Jews in *Gos. Pet.* 15 remains all too poorly introduced. Similarly Crossan excludes their rejoicing (23) at the return of sunlight (22). These narrative elements belong together, even though the Jews have to begin with their lament soon after this episode of rejoicing in *Gos. Pet.* 25. The motif of darkness in *Gos. Pet.* 15, 17 and 22 simply hangs in the air without 23–24 and 26.

There are some further difficulties with the exclusion of the burial scene. The Jewish elders and other leaders do indeed take part in the crucifixion, deposition of the body of Jesus, and his burial, but it is not quite plausible to claim that they control the situation. Although Herod is in charge of the crucifixion, it is Pilate who controls

[88] J.D. Crossan, *The Cross That Spoke*, 16–23.

the guard. Furthermore, without *Gos. Pet.* 23–24 it remains totally obscure who buried Jesus, although the tomb itself is vitally important for the Cross Gospel. These and similar problems make it difficult to reconstruct an early source behind the *Gospel of Peter.* If this apocryphal Gospel does not betray earlier sources, it is much more likely that it represents a late creative composition based on the canonical passion narratives. If this is correct, all Gospels known to us knew Joseph of Arimathea as the man who buried Jesus.

Crossan has also argued that the body of Jesus was treated according to the usual Roman practice.[89] Like all crucified criminals, he was left unburied. We learn that Brutus' companions were left after their execution as food for carrion-birds and beasts (Suetonius, *Aug.* 13.1–2) and that many of those who plotted against Tiberius preferred to commit suicide rather than face execution and the fate of being left unburied (Tacitus, *Ann.* 6.29). Disobedient slaves were often crucified and left on their crosses to feed crows (Horace, *Epist.* 1.16.46–48). Crucified victims were guarded even after death so that nobody could take them down and bury them (Petronius, *Satyr.* 111–12; a parody of this practice). The bodies of the crucified Christian martyrs of Lyons were displayed for six days and then burned, and their ashes were scattered in the Rhone (Eusebius, *Hist. eccl.* 5.1.61–62). However, there is also some evidence for special permissions to bury the bodies of those crucified. Philo (*Flacc.* 83–85) tells that he knows instances of men who had been crucified at the time of festivals and whose bodies had been taken down and given up to their relatives for a worthy burial. Writing in the early 40's against Flaccus, the governor of Egypt, he emphasizes that this man never gave such orders but instead tortured the Alexandrian Jews condemned by him even before their crucifixion.

The bones of a crucified man found in 1968 in an ossuary located in one of the four tombs at Giv'at ha-Mivtar demonstrate that bodies of some crucified people could have been buried in a family tomb. The tomb can be dated back to the first century CE. However, it is notable that only these remains of one crucified person have been found among all the bones that have been discovered from

[89] For a survey of the Roman practice, see Crossan, *Who Killed Jesus?*, 160–63, 167–68.

those times. Crossan assumes that the relatives might have got the body for the burial through bribery, mercy, or indifference.[90]

Crossan further argues that the Roman practice was followed also in Judaea. He rejects the idea that those who were crucified by the Romans would have been buried before sunset, because Deut 21:22–23 presupposes crucifixion after death and because exposure of the body must end by nightfall as in Josh 8:23,29 and 10:5,26–27. Crossan points out that Alexander Jannaeus did not care about this commandment of the Torah as he crucified hundreds of Pharisees and others who had fought against him (*Bell.* 1.97 par. *Ant.* 13.380). Crossan further pays attention to the fact that according to *11QTemple* the Essenes of the Dead Sea equated dead and live crucifixions and kept both under the removal-by-sunset law of Deuteronomy. He thinks that this interpretation suggests an ideal of the Qumran community to accomplish what the Jewish establishment in Jerusalem did not do. His conclusion: Deut 21:22–23 was not followed after Roman crucifixions in Jerusalem.[91] I do not find this reasoning compelling. The Qumran text is focused on the interpretation of hanging on the tree as Jewish punishment and does not betray any attitudes about Roman crucifixion and the burial of those crucified in Jerusalem.

Crossan next cites a text of Josephus, which contradicts his theory that the Jews did not apply Deut 21:22–23 to Roman live crucifixions. When Josephus describes the terror of the peasant Zealots in Jerusalem during the Jewish War, he reveals knowledge of this practice and is proud to enlighten his Roman readers about it (*Bell.* 4.5.2 [317]):

> They actually went so far in their impiety as to cast out the corpses without burial, although the Jews are so careful about funeral rites that even malefactors who have been sentenced to crucifixion are taken down and buried before sunset.

Crossan does not take this as the practice, but merely as the theory, which was well known to Josephus and which he found useful

[90] Crossan, *Who Killed Jesus?*, 168. About the archaeological evidence, see V. Tsaferis, "Jewish Tombs at and near Giv'at ha-Mivtar, Jerusalem", *IEJ* 20 (1970) 18–32, and N. Haas, "Anthropological Observations on the Skeletal Remains fro Giv'at ha-Mivtar", *IEJ* 20 (1970) 38–59.

[91] Crossan, *Who Killed Jesus?*, 163–66.

to cite against the Zealots.[92] Crossan refers to the mass crucifixions by Varus in 4 BCE, by Gessius Florus in 66 CE, and by Titus in 70 CE and states that in these instancies "Josephus never mentions anything about removal by sunset". However, there may be a difference between mass crucifixions and other situations. If Josephus is merely talking about the theory in the text cited above, how can he point to a practice that did not exist at all? Maybe it would be rather appropriate to ask, to what extent such a practice was reality. Presumably Josephus knew that it was customary to bury individual victims of crucifixion before the sunset, if it was not a question of mass punishments. Furthermore, the statement of Josephus quite obviously refers to the practice before the war, and this includes the periods of the particularly ill-reputed governors like Albinus (62–64 CE) and Gessius Florus (64–66 CE). If crucified criminals were under their rule buried before sunset, how much more can we assume such a practice for the time of Pilate and Tiberius?

Most scholars point out that we have no evidence of graveyards for Jewish criminals executed by Romans in the 1st century CE. The Mishnaic tradition in *m. Sanh.* 6:5–6 from the 2nd or 3rd century CE offers no direct evidence either, but supports the view presented by Josephus that the Jews found it very important to bury even criminals:

> And they did not bury [the felon] in the burial grounds of his ancestors. But there were two graveyards made ready for the use of the court, one for those who were beheaded or strangled, and one for those who were stoned or burned. When the flesh had rotted, they [then do] collect the bones and bury them in the appropriate place. And the relatives [of the felon] come and inquire after the welfare of the judges and of the witnesses, as if to say: "We have nothing against you, for you judged honestly." And they did not go into mourning. But they observe a private grief, for grief is only in the heart. (trans. J. Neusner)

This text hints at a practice that may have been followed also in Jerusalem during the Roman occupation.[93] I find it unlikely that the Jewish leaders would have left the bodies of crucified people and other outcasts lie around unburied—particularly when the Passover

---

[92] Crossan, *Who Killed Jesus?*, 166–67.
[93] See also Sawicki, *Seeing the Lord*, 257.

festival was at hand. For Romans who respected politically harmless Jewish customs this must have been an acceptable practice. Otherwise we could expect to find some evidence of conflicts around this issue. If this suggestion is correct, it is natural to assume that close to the place of crucifixion there were simple rock-hewn tombs or a burial ground prepared for those crucified. Since we know of only one crucified person whose bones have been found in a rock-hewn family tomb, it is most natural to assume that in Roman Palestine relatives and friends in practice rarely asked for the body of the executed for burial or his bones for a second burial.

This lack of evidence favours the assumption that fields were used as graveyards for executed criminals. At least the Gospel of Matthew informs us of the existence of fields that were used as graveyards for strangers (27:7). Although there was a lot of rock in Jerusalem and although it was relatively easy to hew, there certainly was a need for simple graveyards for those who died in masses: poor people, strangers, and particularly victims of epidemics and massacres. Josephus mentions with deep indignation that the Zealots did not let anybody bury the victims of their massacres (*Bell.* 4.6.3 [382]):

> . . . as though they had covenated to annul the laws of nature along with those of their country, and to their outrages upon humanity to add pollution of Heaven itself, they left the dead putrefying in the sun.

In the case of such slaughter it is not thinkable that most relatives of the dead could have buried their deceased beloved ones in rock-hewn family tombs. A decent and realistic solution would have been to bury most of the victims in graveyards of the poor, i.e. in common ditches. Josephus also sums up his interpretation of the orders for burial of criminals and enemies in Deut 21:22 as follows (*Ant.* 4.8.24 [265]): "Let burial be given even to your enemies; and let not a corpse be left without its portion of earth, paying more than its just penalty."

4. *Conclusion*

I find it likely that the Jewish high priests, powerful men and other members of the Sanhedrin followed this maxim and buried Jesus, like many others who had been crucified routinely in a graveyard of crucified criminals close to the place where he was crucified. The grieving women, who had followed him, went to the area where they knew that he was buried in order to be close to him and lament his death. The male disciples had fled. But soon Mary Magdalene, Peter and others "saw" Jesus—whatever that means.

The arguments presented in this article have lead to the conclusion that the burial story in Mark 15:42–47 was originally independent of the crucifixion narrative and the empty tomb story. The oral tradition emphasized that Jesus was buried by a respected member of the Sanhedrin, and that his burial was simple but honourable. It is reasonable to assume that Joseph of Arimathea had something to do with the burial of those crucified so that later Christians could imagine that he took care of the body of Jesus. Since there is some evidence of burial of the criminals crucified by the Romans, Jesus may have been buried like any one of them.

JESUS THE JEW: DILEMMAS OF INTERPRETATION

Halvor Moxnes

Was Jesus a Jew?[1] I suppose that Heikki Räisänen would respond with an univocal "yes". After all, he has shown how Jesus of history in important matters stayed within the boundaries of the first century CE Judaism.[2] At the same time, he is also very well aware that the interpretation of Jesus goes well beyond the boundaries of Judaism and Christianity. As early as 30 years ago, Räisänen investigated the picture of Jesus in the Qur'an, a question that recently has become important within the Muslim-Christian dialogue. In his recent book, *Marcion, Muhammad and the Mahatma* (1997), Räisänen shows how images of Jesus participate in a broad spectrum of religious traditions and innovations. The present study is also inspired by another interest of Räisänen's, viz. the history of interpretation of biblical texts and the effect that the Bible has had through centuries of use. It is with gratitude for many years of challenging inspiration and friendship that I offer these reflections on the interpretation of the Jewishness of Jesus.[3]

In one sense the question: "Was Jesus a Jew?" is very simple. The Gospels leave no doubt that he was born to Jewish parents. Matthew and Luke even give his family tree (Matt 1:1–17; Luke 3:23–38), that, although they are different and most likely an example of creative reconstruction, place Jesus within a long Jewish tradition. But why is it that even so the question is not so simple? Is it because it combines two words that are difficult to define and identify, "Jesus" and "Jew"? This question combines two names that have served an important function to define European identity, positively and negatively. "Jesus" has historically been a positive symbol for European

[1] This is an English, revised version of a study published in Norwegian as "Jøden Jesus" in H. Moxnes (ed.), *Jesus: 2000 år etter Kristus* (Oslo: Universitetsforlaget, 2000) 57–83.

[2] "Jesus and the Food Laws. Reflections on Mark 7:15", *JSNT* 6 (1982) 79–100.

[3] My approach is inspired by cultural studies; for a more systematic, historical-critical review of this discussion, see Hans Dieter Betz, "Wellhausen's Dictum 'Jesus was not a Christian, but a Jew' in Light of Present Scholarship", *ST* 45 (1991) 83–110.

identity, and even in recent times, with the influx of Muslim immigrants, this name has served to identify who "we" are as opposed to "them". Jesus as an ideal, as a figure in history, is a person whom many Europeans will identify with as a part of their history and culture. This identification has found many and varied expressions. Works of art is a typical example, in European figurative art Jesus has as a matter of fact been portrayed as a European.[4]

If Jesus was a sign of positive identification for many Europeans, "Jew" has served as an anti-type to this identity. Since the Middle Ages "Jew" has been an important part of European identity, but as "the other", that which represented the opposite of a European, implicitly Christian identity. The history of anti-Semitism shows the fateful outcome of this negative combination of identities. The negative image of Jews in anti-Semitism was a result of many myths and ideas that were central to the identity of Christian Europe. The very epitome of this negative image was reached in the accusation that "the Jews killed Christ". This accusation shows how the term "Jews" was used in an a-historical sense, or rather, in an all inclusive sense, spanning both past, present and future. Even if the intention was to say that a group of Jews in the first century were to blame for the execution of Jesus (in itself a doubtful historical reconstruction), we hear something totally different, the saying takes on the meaning of "all Jews at all times are guilty in the death of Christ". Christianity was not the only source for anti-Semitism, however. In many instances "Jew" represented the negative mirror image of the national identity that was consciously constructed in many European nations, both newly created and old ones, in the 19th century.[5] The most famous example was the Dreyfus affair, in which the Jewish officer Henri Dreyfus was made a scapegoat in a matter of espionage against France.[6]

Consequently, "Was Jesus a Jew?" is not an innocent question. In the longest period of European history Jews have served as "the oth-

---

[4] See for instance *The Image of Christ* (London: National Gallery, 2000) catalogue for the exhibition "Seeing salvation" at The National Gallery in London in the spring of 2000, with only Western art being represented.

[5] See especially on Germany, R. Brubaker, *Citizenship and nationhood in France and Germany* (Cambridge, MA: Harvard University, 1992) 134–36, 166–68.

[6] A.S. Lindemann, *The Jew Accused: Three Anti-Semitic Affairs: Dreyfus, Beilis, Frank, 1894–1915* (Cambridge: Cambridge University, 1991), esp. pp. 57–128.

ers", somebody with whom one did not have a common identity. I think that it was this circumstance that made the historical question about the identity of Jesus so difficult. It was often solved by softening the Jewish heritage of Jesus, and by portraying him in strong contrast to the Jewish milieu of his time. This attitude influenced Christian biblical scholarship and resulted in a picture of the Jews at the time of Jesus that was wholly negative. If we shall look at the discussion of "Jesus the Jew", we must therefore ask what was the image of the Jew held by various interpreters, what was it meant to identify, or to present as the opposite of?

Jesus in German Nationalism

German universities and German scholars dominated the development of the modern, historical-critical Bible study and Jesus research in the 19th century. This development in the academic world happened at the same time and was partly a parallel movement to the development of German nationalism and the unification process in (Northern) Germany. In the mainly Northern Protestant part of Germany this political unification was manifested through the war against France in 1870 and with the establishment of the German Empire under the leadership of Prussia. From the end of the 18th century philosophers, authors and theologians had developed a philosophy of German identity, of characteristics of a German nation and a German people. This influenced the pictures of Jesus in the early phases of historical Jesus research. Friedrich Schleiermacher gave the first lectures on the historical Jesus at a German university in Berlin 1818 onwards.[7] Schleiermacher was an active participant in the protest against French occupation and influence, and was active in the early stage of German nationalism and in the effort to create the idea of a German nation.[8] In his lectures Schleiermacher drew a picture of Palestina with great similarities to Germany at his time: divided into political structures that were irrelevant to the divisions into natural regions with their respective "tribes" or groups,

[7] They were not published till 1864, see the English translation: Friedrich Schleiermacher, *The Life of Jesus* (ed. J.C. Verheyden; Philadelphia: Fortress, 1975).

[8] Jerry F. Dawson, *Friedrich Schleiermacher: The Evolution of a Nationalist* (Austin: University of Texas, 1966).

that nevertheless represented a unified people. Against this background Schleiermacher portrays Jesus as a teacher concerned with national unity. From this reason Schleiermacher downplays any conflicts between Jesus and the Jewish leaders in Jerusalem, after all, the concern for national unity served as a common ground.

David Friedrich Strauss was (the second) founder of the historical Jesus research, although his *Das Leben Jesu* (1835) actually proved that it was impossible to write a biography of Jesus. The book made Strauss immediately famous, and created strong negative reactions from the church. In 1864 Strauss published a new version, "revised for the German people".[9] Strauss argued that the critical attitude in the historical Jesus research was in direct continuation with the Reformation as a characteristic representation of the Protestant German people. Strauss did not explicitly discuss whether Jesus was a Jew. The issue was raised implicitly in his presentation of Jesus' relations to the Jewish leaders in Jerusalem and his attitude to Jewish law and traditions. Strauss put up Jesus in contrast to the Jewish leaders and Jewish traditions; he described Jesus as a typical Galilean, and introduced a conflict between Galilee and Jerusalem. Hermeneutically, the result was a picture of Jesus the Galilean that modern, Protestant Europeans could identify with. Judeans and Jerusalem on the other hand represented that which was backwards and fanatical, for instance the conservative leadership of the church.

The so-called German cultural Protestantism after Strauss followed him in stripping Jesus of his Jewishness, emphasising instead ethical aspects that made it easier to integrate Jesus in modern culture. Albrecht Ritschl was a prominent representative for his tendency. He wanted to develop a Protestant culture in support of a German Protestant national state. His interpretation of Jesus' proclamation of the Kingdom of God was central to this project. For Ritschl the Kingdom of God was a moral category that was closely associated with human cultural activities. It was his attempt to integrate Jesus and the Kingdom of God in his concept of modern culture that Albert Schweitzer challenged so vigorously in his *Die Geschichte der Leben Jesu Forschung* (1906/13). Central to Schweitzer's picture of Jesus

[9] *Das Leben Jesu für das deutsche Volk bearbeitet* (Bonn: Emil Strauss, 1864). The title of the English translation does not convey this reference "to the German people", it was simply called *A New Life of Jesus* (London: Williams and Norgate, 1879).

was his "consistent eschatology." Schweitzer held that Jesus shared the contemporary Jewish eschatological views of a near end, and that these views coloured all his activities. Historically it was impossible to understand Jesus apart from this Jewish eschatology, but at the same time this picture of Jesus resisted an easy integration into a modern, non-eschatological culture.

With his picture of the eschatological, Jewish Jesus put up as criticism of modern, cultural Protestantism of his time, Schweitzer chose another direction than that which became the dominant one within German Protestantism, viz. the dialectical theology. The dialectical theology also represented a radical criticism of contemporary culture, but from the point of view of the risen and proclaimed Jesus Christ as the "totally other" from modern culture. The result was a diminished interest in the historical Jesus, and consequently in the question of the Jewishness of Jesus.

However, the attempt to integrate Jesus in a national German culture did not totally disappear. Within a German national ideology that wanted to draw a line against Jews, but still was eager to retain a Christian identity, there was a peculiar discussion of Jesus' Jewishness. That Jesus was a Jew, was felt to be a problem, and attempts were made to remove him from his Jewish background. Paul de Lagarde (1827–91) was instrumental in starting and inspiring this movement. He was a well known philologist in Oriental languages and cultural ideologue who argued for a "Germanised" religion.[10] He wanted to cleanse Christianity of its Jewish aspects, which he meant were introduced by Paul, and argued for a return to Jesus. Since Jesus grew up in Galilee, far from the centre of Judaism, was Lagarde's argument, his mentality was formed in opposition to Judaism of his time. A central piece in this argument was that Galilee in fact was not Jewish, this region distinguished itself not only by geographical and religious distance from Jerusalem, but also by a different ethnic composition. This last proposition was part of a discussion of what happened after the capture of Galilee in 732 BCE when the region became an Assyrian province. Did the Assyrians settle other ethnic groups in Galilee at that time? This discussion was well known among historians and Biblical scholars, but it got a new importance when

[10] See especially *Deutsche Schriften* (Göttingen, 1878).

the question of the ethnic composition of Galilee was made into a matter of national identity.

The English-born historian H.S. Chamberlain, the son-in-law of Richard Wagner, was influenced by Lagarde and continued his arguments about Galilee. When he wrote his massive cultural history, *Die Grundlagen des Neunzehnten Jahrhunderts* (1899) it was under the influence of the new interest in biology that had important consequences for the discussion of *race*. According to these racial theories, incorporating social Darwinism, race according to biology was the determining factor in national characteristics.[11] Thus, Chamberlain argued that even if Galileans were Jews in terms of religious observation, they were not Jews when it came to ethnic origin. Religion was different from race! Chamberlain insisted that being a Galilean Jesus did not have one drop of Jewish blood. Even if he had a Jewish upbringing he had nothing in common with Judaism. Chamberlain even claimed that the Jews had no sense of religion, they possessed will power and rationality, but lacked emotions that were the source of religion. The Germans, of course, possessed these emotions.

We find a similar type of ideological argument in the writings of a number of theologians in Nazi-Germany. A prominent representative was the New Testament scholar Walter Grundmann who wrote a book called *Jesus der Galiläer und das Judentum* (1941). In the introduction to the book he writes that because of the "Jewish danger" which the German nation needed to defend itself against, it was of great interest to study the relationship between Jesus and Judaism. One could not deny that Jesus had his origin in Palestine. Consequently, it was important for Grundmann to associate Jesus with a region in Palestine that could not be identified with Judaism. Galilee filled this need. Grundmann uses the well-known historical argument about the mixed population of Galilee, and claims that Jesus most likely did not belong to the Jewish population but to one of the other ethnic groups. Since Jesus was not a Jew in terms of his religious sensitivity, most likely he was also not a Jew "by blood". Here "blood" comes into play as an important factor when it comes to definitions of ethnic identity. In addition to "blood", also "culture" played an important part to define identity. Therefore it was important for

[11] G. Mosse, *The Crisis of German Ideology* (New York: Grosset & Dunlap, 1964) 92–93.

Grundmann that there was a strong Hellenistic, that is, a non-Jewish, influence in Galilee. Grundmann concludes his discussion of the ethnic origin of Jesus by saying that one cannot reach a definitive verdict, but there were in Galilee both "Aryan" and "non-Aryan" groups. In this way Galilee has become that part of Palestine with which Germans can identify, and there were enough Aryans so that Jesus might be plausibly presented as a non-Jew.

Jesus in Jewish Nationalism

It was not only among German historians and theologians that nationalism became the leading ideology. At the end of the 19th century there was in Jewish groups a rise of a type of nationalism that became a strong ideological factor in the form of Zionism. It was a result of hard work, above all by the Hungarian writer Theodor Herzl (*Der Judenstaat*, 1896) at the end of the 19th century. This was a form of nationalism that was inspired by the German form of nationalism, based on the idea that people of the same descent or who spoke the same language formed a nation, and also ought to form a state of their own.[12] It was this idea of a separate state for Jews that was the new idea of Herzl. He saw that as a solution to the problems of many Jews in Europe: partly anti-Semitism, partly that many secularised Jews had lost contact with their Jewish roots.

Initially the idea of the Jews as a separate nation and the suggestion to establish a Jewish state received a less than enthusiastic response in the main Jewish groups in Western Europe. The last part of the 19th century was by and large a period with growing political tolerance vis-à-vis Jews in many European countries, and this strengthened those who wanted an assimilation of Jews in their home country. Claude C. Montefiori was a prominent representative for this attitude. He was a strong defender of integration of Jews in their home countries, and accordingly an equally strong opponent of Zionism. He belonged to one of the leading Jewish families in England, and spoke of himself as "an Englishman of Jewish faith". His studies of Jesus and the Gospel may possibly be regarded as expressions of a general cultural interest and as a result of assimilation among liberal Jewish scholars in Western Europe. Montefiori

[12] Brubaker, *Citizenship*, 114–37.

regarded Jesus as a Jew, not a Christian, and he held Jesus and the Gospels in high esteem.[13] Zionists, however, accused him of being too positive towards Jesus in his judgement of Jesus' importance for Judaism, and likewise that his picture of Judaism was skewed, it did not carry enough communal and nationalist elements.[14]

The first large study of Jesus by a Jewish scholar in the 20th century did not come from Montefiori, however, but from a totally different and unexpected quarter. It was a book by Joseph Klausner, who was born in Lithuania, but became an eager Zionist and moved to Palestine, at that time a British protectorate. The book was written in Hebrew in 1922 and translated to several languages; the title of the English translation is *Jesus of Nazareth: His Life, Times and Teaching* (1925). Many of the positions that Klausner held became standard among many Jewish studies of Jesus. He claims that Jesus was fully part of Judaism of his time, and has a description of his background in Galilee that is totally different from that of Grundmann. Klausner grants that there were many non-Jews in Galilee, but he claims that Jesus was not in the least influenced by them. Galilee was a centre of Jewish observance of the Law, and Jesus represented the Pharisaic Judaism of his time that was loyal to the holy Scriptures. Klausner claimed that Jesus obeyed the Torah until the end of his life, also the ritual laws. However, he probably opened up for the possibility of breaking the law, a possibility that was later realised by Paul and his followers in early Christianity.

Klausner placed Jesus squarely within a Pharisaic type of Judaism of his time. However, he nevertheless found such conflicts between Jesus and Judaism that he claimed that the teaching of Jesus "brought Judaism to such an extreme that it became, in a sense, *non-Judaism*" (376). In reaching this judgement, Klausner measured Jesus against his own definition of Judaism, based on his Zionist ideology. His main point of criticism was what he regarded as the *individualism* on the part of Jesus. In this Jesus parted from what Klausner regarded as the most important side of Judaism: it was a religion not for individuals, but for a people, a nation. Klausner found Jesus lacking in the integration of the individual in the nation, and in a political per-

[13] *The Synoptic Gospels* (2 vols. London: MacMillan, 1909).

[14] Joseph Klausner, *Jesus of Nazareth* (With a new Foreword by S.B. Hoenig. New York: Bloch, 1989) 114.

spective. It is in his portrayal of the Scribes and the Pharisees that Klausner most clearly expresses his nationalism. He portrayed them as carriers of the idea of a Jewish state. Their symbiosis of religion and culture presupposed "a nation not minded to be only a religious community, but a real nation, possessed of a land, a state and authority in every sense" (373). Jesus destroyed all of this, the most flagrant example was his saying in Mark 12:17: "Render to Caesar the things that are Caesar's, and to God the things that are God's". It represented a breach with the authority of political power. His words in the Sermon on the Mount not to resist evil (Matt 5:39–41) would destroy justice and efforts from the state to bring an end to social evils. For a disciple of Jesus, who had praised eunuchs and prohibited divorce (Matt 19:1–12), even family life must collapse. And Jesus who said "consider the lilies in the field" did not show any interest in labour, in culture and economic and political progress.

Klausner recognised that Jesus was Jewish in his statements, but it was an exaggerated form of Judaism that would ruin a national culture, a national state and a national life. There was nothing in his teaching that could serve to support order in the real world. Klausner found the same fault in Jesus' teaching about God. If God did not make distinctions between sinners and righteous, God was only merciful, but he was not just, not a judge, and consequently not the God of history. However, despite Klausner's extremely harsh criticism of Jesus, that he destroyed society, he concluded in a totally different vein: "But in his ethical code there is a sublimity, distinctiveness and originality in form unparalleled in any other Hebrew ethical code; neither is there any parallel to the remarkable art of his parables" (414). Klausner responded to the question of what Jesus meant for the Jewish nation by saying that he was "a great teacher of morality and an artist in parable" (414). We might say that according to Klausner, the ethics of Jesus was not meant for nations and social structures to-day, but it was nevertheless an ideal for the future, for the messianic period.

It is this double, contradictory picture of Jesus that is so remarkable in Klausner's presentation of Jesus. On the one hand there is a very positive side, Klausner focuses on everything that made Jesus a Jew. On the other hand comes his very negative criticism when Klausner makes nationalistic Zionism the criterion for true Judaism. Jewish studies of Jesus after Klausner have followed up on the first aspect, a positive evaluation of Jesus as a Jew, and they have often emphasised the creative aspect of his ethics. However, Klausner's ideal picture of Judaism, determined by Zionism, has not stood the test of time. It has given way for other, more nuanced positions based on recent historical studies and on other concepts about what was central to Judaism.

Jesus after Holocaust

What happened to the question "Was Jesus a Jew?" in the last part of the 20th century? Have the contexts for the two terms in question, "Jesus" and "Jew" changed? It may be that the issue is no longer part of a discussion of national identities, it has become more limited, a part of the relations between Christian churches and Jewish synagogues. As part of the process of secularisation the public interest in the figure of Jesus has dwindled. And Jews no longer play the role of "the other" for Western identity. One contributing factor has been the importance that Holocaust has played in later decades, recognised as the most cruel expression of the attempt to construct Jews as "the other", and at the same time used to strengthen Jewish identity.[15] It is much to be hoped that it will not any longer be possible in the Western mind or politics to reinstate the Jews as "the other". At the same time the need for a contrasting figure of "the other" to support one's own identity continues to be strong. It has been suggested, not without justification, that the Islamic world, particularly the so-called fundamentalist Islam, now plays that role.[16] And new examples of cruelty towards groups that are depicted as "the other" multiply, for instance in the form of "ethnic cleansing" against Tutsies, Muslim Bosnians and Kosovo Albanians.

The establishment of the state of Israel in 1948 may have contributed to a change in Western attitude towards Jews in general. To become a state might demystify a group and make it seem less particular. We might think of how after 1948 it was the Palestinians who in a change of roles became a people without land and were looked upon as a possible danger, within the Middle East and also

[15] See Eva Hoffmann, "The Holocaust in American Life", *New York Review* 47:4 (2000) 19–23.

[16] John Esposito, *The Islamic Threat: Myth or Reality?* (New York: Oxford University, 1993).

outside. The new Israeli state has also resulted in a strong activity to develop a national identity and not least to establish a historical past. The finds of the Dead Sea Scrolls and many archaeological excavations have documented and brought to life ancient cultures and traditions that were earlier unknown, or only known from ancient texts. This has made it possible to present the areas of Israel and its occupied territories as central to the rise of Western culture, and may have created a sense of a common history in the minds of Europeans and North-Americans. For many Christians the creation of the state of Israel led to a strong positive interest in Jewish history and in the Bible. On the other hand, a specific Christian identity in religious terms continued to be based on a negative image of Judaism. Judaism was everything which Christianity was not: it built on law, not gospel, on works, not faith, etc. And Jesus was the core example of this contrast between the two religions.

Strangely enough it seems that the Second World War and Holocaust initially had little effect on historical Jesus research. The question "how can we talk of God after Auschwitz" became important in discussions of theology and played a part also among many ordinary church members, but it did not seem to challenge New Testament scholars. In Germany no measures of censoring or public criticism seem to have been taken towards the Nazi-inspired New Testament scholarship. There may have been more of an attempt to forget that period. For instance Walter Grundmann continued to participate in New Testament academic life and to publish about Jesus, but without referring to his publications from the 1930s and –40s.[17] German theology and also New Testament scholarship was dominated by the dialectical theology and its concentration on Christ, not Jesus. This situation did not provide an opening for a dialogue with Jewish scholars about Jesus. The American Jewish scholar Samuel Sandmel, who wrote extensively on the New Testament and Jesus,[18] had a negative view of the situation in the early 1960s. Because of the dominant position of dialectical theology, Jews and Christians

[17] See e.g. "Verkündigung und Geschichte in dem Bericht vom Eingang der Geschichte Jesu im Johannes-Evangelium", in Helmut Ristow und Karl Matthiae (eds.), *Der historische Jesus und der kerygmatische Christus: Beiträge zum Christusverständnis in Forschung und Verkündigung* (2nd ed.; Berlin: Evangelische Verlagsanstalt, 1961) 289–309.

[18] Samuel Sandmel, *We Jews and Jesus* (New York: Oxford University, 1965).

were further apart in their understanding of Jesus than in the preceding hundred years!

This situation did not substantially change when the "New quest for the Historical Jesus" arose in Europe in the 1950s. It was launched at the same time in the Nordic countries by the Norwegian scholar Nils A. Dahl,[19] and in Germany by Ernst Käsemann.[20] Käsemann set up criteria to judge the historicity of words of Jesus. One of the most important criteria was that of "dissimilarity", that identified true words of Jesus by their distinctiveness from Judaism of his time or later Christian traditions. Since the image of Jesus was overwhelmingly positive, it followed from the use of this criterion a negative image of Judaism and especially of Jewish leaders. One characteristic example of that is *Jesus von Nazareth* (1956) by Günther Bornkamm. Despite its title there is little attempt to put Jesus within the context of his own milieu. The book is a Christian theological evaluation of Judaism that can hardly be described as historical. Bornkamm claims that at the time of Jesus the Jewish people lived in a vacuum. They looked back upon a past when God had given the people its life and its character, and forward, towards the future, when God would do the same once more. The result is a negative picture of "the present", Judaism at time of Jesus, as simply a void that Jesus came in to fill. It is noticeable that Bornkamm was a pupil of Bultmann, who was little concerned with the historical Jesus, but more with the message about Jesus. In Bornkamm's presentation the message of Jesus is put in focus. He is not much interested in what Jesus did, the miracles do not play any role. Existentialism, the concern with the impact of the word upon the individual, still is the dominant presupposition.

We find the same concentration upon the word and the individual in Jewish philosophers and theologians with a background in German cultural traditions. In contrast to Klausner's Zionism with its emphasis upon the national aspect of Judaism, they focus on the individual. In *Zwei Glaubensweisen* (1950) Martin Buber distinguishes between two types of faith. The Hebrew *amuna* expresses the absolute trust and confidence in God, and represents a surrender into the

[19] N.A. Dahl, "Problemet 'den historiske Jesus'" in idem, *Rett lære og kjetterske meninger* (Oslo: Land og kirke, 1953) 156–202, now as "The Problem of the Historical Jesus" in idem, *Jesus the Christ* (ed. D.H. Juel; Minneapolis: Fortress, 1991) 81–111.

[20] "Das Problem des historischen Jesus", *ZTK* 51 (1954) 125–53.

hands of God. The Greek *pistis*, on the other hand, is more intellectual, a faith "that" something is in a certain way. Buber sees in Jesus the most typical example of *amuna*, while Paul represents *pistis*. It is in this book we find Buber's famous words about "my brother Jesus":

> Jesus habe ich von Jugend auf als meinen grossen Bruder empfunden. Dass die Christenheit ihn als Gott und Erlöser angesehen hat und ansieht, ist mir immer als eine Tatsache von höchstem Ernst erschienen, die ich um seinet- und meinetwillen zu begreifen suchen muss. . . . Mein eigenes bruderlich aufgeschlossenes Verhältnis zu ihm ist immer stärker und reiner geworden, und ich sehe ihn heute mit stärkerem und reinerem Blick als je. Gewisser als je ist mir, dass ihm ein grosser Platz in der Glaubensgeschichte Israels zukommt und dass dieser Platz durch keine der üblichen Kategorien umschrieben werden kann.[21]

We find a similar attitude to Jesus as brother in Schalom Ben-Chorin, *Bruder Jesus* (1967). Ben-Chorin says:

> Jesus ist für mich der ewige Bruder, nicht nur der Menschenbruder, sondern mein JÜDISCHER BRUDER. Ich spüre seine brüderliche Hand, die mich fasst, damit ich ihm nachfolge. Es ist NICHT die Hand des Messias, diese mit den Wundmalen gezeichnete Hand. Es ist bestimmt keine GÖTTLICHE, sondern eine MENSCHLICHE Hand, in deren Linien das tiefste Leid eingegraben ist.[22]

To recognise the suffering in the hand of Jesus is important for a Jewish identification with him, that becomes visible also in works of the painter Marc Chagall. In several of his paintings the sufferings of Jesus, especially the crucifixion, becomes a symbol of the sufferings of Jews throughout history.

Do Buber, Ben-Chorin and Chagall reflect a philosophical, almost mystical approach, an intuitive identification with Jesus that may be part of a common European culture? We find a totally different approach in the American Jewish scholar Samuel Sandmel. For Sandmel, Jesus does not represent an existential issue, he keeps his distance from Montefiori and Klausner, and says that Jesus does not touch him in a religious way. Sandmel does not recognise in Judaism an unfilled "need" that a person like Jesus could fill. Since it is difficult to see Jesus without the Christian claims about him, it is

---

[21] Martin Buber, *Zwei Glaubensweisen* (Zürich: Manesse Verlag, Conzett & Huber, 1950) 11.

[22] Schalom Ben-Chorin, *Bruder Jesus: Der Nazarener in jüdischer Sicht* (München: List Verlag, 1972) 12.

Jesus as a part of Western culture that Jews will have to relate to. Maybe Sandmel here reflects the position of intellectual Judaism in the US, keeping its identity and at the same time integrated into modernism, represented by for instance the Protestant reformation, the French revolution, Darwin and Freud. Jesus as a part of Western tradition that Jews also will have to relate to because they also belong to the same tradition, that is a far cry from Klausner's Zionism, and Sandmel consequently rejects Klausner's goal "to bring Jesus home".

A New Perspective on Judaism among Christian Scholars

When the quest for the historical Jesus was reopened from the 1950s onwards, there was among Nordic New Testament scholars, in distinct difference from the German discussion, much more emphasis upon seeing Jesus in his Jewish milieu.[23] Nils A. Dahl pointed the way in 1953 by saying that the more we know about Judaism at the time of Jesus, the more we know about Jesus. Developments after that has proved him to be right. We now have a much broader knowledge of Palestine in the first century CE in terms of archaeology, and the social, economic and religious situation. But new information in itself was not sufficient, it was more important to change the conceptual framework, the understanding of Judaism as a system held by Christian scholars. A central piece of this construction was based on the Gospels and their picture of the conflict between Jesus and the Jewish leaders. Paul gave a theological expression to this by describing Judaism as a legally oriented religion in contrast to the "faith" of Christian beliefs. This was more than just a historical description. Words like "Pharisaic" or "legalistic" have become part of a common vocabulary of negative characteristics. Moreover, this was not just individual words, it became a pattern with universal application that has been transferred to internal Christian conflicts. This vocabulary was for instance much used in Protestant polemics against the Roman Catholic Church.

Within New Testament of the last generation there has been a definitive break with this paradigm of conflict. It started with a dis-

[23] See especially the works by Gøsta Lindeskog, *Die Jesusfrage im neuzeitlichen Judentum: ein Beitrag zur Geschichte der Leben-Jesu-Forschung* (Leipzig, 1938, repr. Darmstadt: Wissenschaftliche Buchgesellschaft, 1973); idem, *Das jüdisch-christliche Problem: Randglossen zu einer Forschungsepoche* (Stockholm: Almquist & Wiksell, 1986).

cussion over Paul and the interpretation of him, especially in a German Protestant tradition, within this conflict pattern. I remember one of the first public controversies over this issue, at an SNTS meeting at Duke University in 1976, where Ernst Käsemann protested vehemently against Heikki Räisänen's interpretation of Paul and the law.[24] Räisänen has been in the forefront of this reinterpretation of Paul, which does not take his picture of the law in Judaism at face value.[25] In this task, Räisänen has had a colleague in E.P. Sanders. With his magisterial *Paul and Palestinian Judaism* (1977) Sanders coined a new term, "covenant nominalism", to explain Jewish attitudes to the Law in positive, not negative terms.

Later Sanders attempted a similar turn in the interpretation of Jesus and his relations to the Jewish milieu in *Jesus and Judaism* (1985). The predominant ideology in Judaism at the time of Jesus, Sanders says, was "restoration eschatology", i.e. the restoration of Israel, and also Jesus shared this view. But how can Sanders justify that Jesus shared this view on the history of Israel? Sanders makes a decisive shift in the evaluation of what sources to use in a reconstruction of the historical Jesus from the teaching of Jesus to a collection of his deeds and activities. The speeches of Jesus were largely applied to individuals. Sanders instead focused on the acts of Jesus, that were more oriented towards the community and the nation. Here Sanders combined the miracles of Jesus and his tablefellowship with sinners with his proclamation of the Kingdom. Jesus shared the eschatological expectation that the Kingdom was close at hand. He expected the restoration of Israel, in which everybody were secured their place, even the sinners, and where Jesus and his disciples had a prominent place. Sanders challenged the view that Jesus broke with the Mosaic Law when it came to rules for the Sabbath, for food and purity. The most important proof was that there is no sign that his disciples left the observance of the law after the death of Jesus. What was extraordinary about Jesus was not to be found in his opinions, Sanders claims, but rather in the results of his life, in the form of (the belief in) his resurrection and the establishing of a movement that continued after his death.

---

[24] I think that the discussion took place in the SNTS Seminar group on "The Function of Nomos in the Ethics of Paul".

[25] See especially Heikki Räisänen, *Paul and the Law* (WUNT 29; Tübingen: Mohr & Siebeck, 1986); idem, *The Torah and Christ* (PFES 45; Helsinki, 1986).

This shift in the paradigm of interpretation, from seeing Jesus in conflict with Judaism to seeing him in basic continuity with it, has great consequences also for contemporary relations between Jews and Christians. Although Sanders speaks primarily as an historian, we have seen that history plays an important part in constructions of present images as well. Sanders' picture of Jesus in basic continuity with Judaism of his time makes it impossible to claim that he belongs exclusively to the Christians. Moreover, it challenges Christian interpreters of early Christianity to redraw their picture of Judaism in light of the ecumenical discussion between Jewish and Christian scholars.

The New Jesus the Jew

The result of this paradigm shift and of the larger knowledge of Jesus' historical context, has resulted in a blurring of the dividing lines between Jewish and Christian research on Jesus. To name only two significant participants on the Jewish side, it does not seem adequate to speak of David Flusser and Geza Vermes primarily as "Jewish scholars" on Jesus, but as scholars who combine their knowledge of Judaism with their studies on the historical Jesus. David Flusser is the Israeli scholar of religion who most extensively has studied the New Testament and Jesus in light of Rabbinic literature, while Geza Vermes has topped his scholarship of Jewish Studies in Oxford with three books on the historical Jesus. In order to put their view of Judaism at the time of Jesus into perspective, we may compare them with Klausner's criticism that Jesus rejected Judaism as a communal system that was concerned with the nation. With his proclamation of God's love towards sinners he parted from the communal basis for a morality based on the justice of God.

Flusser shares the view that belief in God's justice, that rewards the just and punishes the unjust, is an important part of Jewish religion.[26] But Flusser is much less dogmatic about this than Klausner. He will not make this division into an absolute, unchangeable position and maintains that these simple categories were problematised in Jewish literature at the time of Jesus. Is it possible to divide peo-

[26] David Flusser, "Jesus, His Ancestry, and the Commandment of Love", in J.H. Charlesworth (ed.), *Jesus' Jewishness* (New York: Crossroad, 1996) 153–76.

ple so easily into "righteous" and "evil", since good and evil are combating each other in all human beings? And what is the limit for the grace of God and his love towards humans? Flusser speaks about a "new sensitivity" in these issues among Jews in the period before Jesus. He finds the best expression for this new ethics in *The Wisdom of Jesus the Son of Sirach* (2.c. BCE). Here we find the idea of love towards neighbour as a requirement for reconciliation with God. If one asks for forgiveness, one must be willing to forgive (*Sir* 27:30–28:7). There are many similar statements in Rabbinic literature, best known is that by Hillel, a variation of the Golden Rule. Also the commandment from Lev 19:18, to love one's neighbour as one self, was frequently quoted and interpreted, and combined with the commandment to love God above all else. Thus, Flusser argues, many of Jesus' statements about love of neighbour are part of this "new sensitivity" in Judaism and have parallels in Jewish scriptures.

However, Flusser holds that Jesus is unique when it comes to extending love of neighbour even to enemies, in the saying "love your enemies and pray for those who persecute you" (Matt 5:44). This commandment, Flusser says, can only be understood in light of the totality of Jesus' understanding of himself and his task, especially of being sent to sinners. And the commandment to love one's enemies is so unique for Jesus that this is the only place where it is found even in the New Testament. Flusser concludes that it was this commandment, not his criticism of the Law, that was most revolutionary about Jesus. In his view there is in our time a better basis to understand Jesus at this point, because we once more find a "new sensitivity" with an anxiety for the future. Thus, in contrast to Klausner, it seems that Flusser will award the ethics of Jesus an important function in society as well, not only towards individuals.

Geza Vermes makes direct references to Klausner's characterisation of the ethical teaching of Jesus as unique, original and elevated above other Jewish teachers. But Vermes differs from Klausner in his description of Judaism at the time of Jesus. In his three books on Jesus,[27] Vermes portrays Jesus as an Hasidic prophet and miracle worker. This was a figure that was well known from Galilee,

[27] Geza Vermes, *Jesus the Jew: A Historian's Reading of the Gospels* (London: Fontana/Collins, 1973); idem, *Jesus and the World of Judaism* (London: SCM Press, 1983); idem, *The Religion of Jesus the Jew* (London: SCM Press, 1993).

especially from the descriptions by Josephus. It is in a comparison with these prophetic figures that Vermes quotes the positive evaluation by Klausner. But Vermes draws a very different picture of Judaism at the time of Jesus. Above all, it is not so monolithic, he sees Judaism in the first century as much more varied, characterised by different tendencies, than Klausner held. Especially the Qumran documents are important in proving that there were strong eschatological groups in Palestine at the time. Consequently, what Klausner speaks of simply as "Judaism", is in Vermes' picture just one of several groups or tendencies. He speaks of it as that "mainstream Judaism" that later developed into Rabbinic Judaism. The eschatological strands were a parallel development, and Vermes finds that Jesus was closer to this type of Judaism. Apart from the difference in historical reconstruction, Klausner and Vermes also seem to represent very different types of modern Judaism. Klausner was part of a movement fighting for a Zionist programme, while Vermes shows sympathies for a more individually oriented Judaism.

Vermes presents Judaism and the Jewish faith of Jesus in a way that is immediately recognisable to modern readers. The faith of Jesus, Vermes claims, can be summed up as an attempt to follow God as a model for life, it is a constant attempt at *imitatio Dei*. Vermes finds this most clearly expressed in the words of Jesus in their Lukan version: "be merciful, even as your Father is merciful" (Luke 6:36). The purpose of this imitation of God is a dedication to one's brothers and sisters, following the ideal of a merciful, heavenly father. Moreover, Jesus showed this attitude not only towards the sick and the helpless, about whom the prophets spoke, but also towards the morally and religiously outcasts, even enemies. Vermes concludes that Jesus gave himself up unconditionally to save, not a communality, but individuals in despair. This represents a direct challenge to the position of Klausner. Both Vermes and Klausner recognise that Jesus represented an ethical challenge. Klausner regards it, however, as a perverted form of Judaism since it broke away from Judaism understood in communal and national terms. Vermes, on his side, regards this very concentration upon the individual as an expression of what is central to Judaism.

Vermes claims that Jesus represented an authentic Judaism, but that did not mean that it did not have its own characteristics. There is a surprising agreement between scholars, both Christian and Jewish, about these characteristics: Jesus spoke prophetically, without attempts to support his authority with scriptural proofs. In contrast to the rabbis, who were concerned with questions of what was allowed or not, Jesus was concerned with the ultimate purpose of the law. And the central message of the parables was forgiveness and trust in God. The main difference between scholars becomes visible in the evaluation of these characteristics and how to understand them. Christian scholars typically have regarded these elements as a transformation of Judaism, as the beginning of a movement that finally parted ways with its origin. Vermes, on the other hand, views these characteristics as individual traits in Jesus that did not break the boundaries of Judaism.

Both Jewish and Christian scholars alike now want to portray a Jewish historical Jesus, we can no longer speak of two distinct pictures, one Christian and another Jewish. This will not, however, bring to an end the plurality of images of Jesus since there will still be many ideas of what type of Judaism Jesus represented.

Is Jesus a Jew?

The historical question "Was Jesus a Jew" is easier to answer than the hermeneutical question: what are the implications of the new consensus between Jews and Christians in Jesus research, what does it mean for the way Jesus is spoken of today? One of the important results is in fact the dialogue itself, that matters of controversy have been discussed between scholars of different backgrounds. Another result is the awareness of how interpretation is determined by cultural presuppositions. Here I would particularly want to single out the role of ethnic identity, both its importance for the identity of the interpreter of Christian texts, as well as the role it attributes to the objects of interpretation.[28] It was this role of ethnic identification that resulted in the accusation against Jews as a group that they were murderers of Christ. Here an ethnic, group oriented way of thinking determined the hermeneutical application of the Jesus story, and especially when the ethnic was determined by "race" this ideology proved

[28] For a discussion of ethnicity and hermeneutics, see several of the essays in Mark G. Brett, *Ethnicity and the Bible* (Biblical Interpretation Series 19, Leiden: Brill, 1996), especially Brett, "Interpreting Ethnicity: Method, Hermeneutics, Ethics", ibid. 3–22.

to be fatal. It is now high time to realise that it is within European and Western Christian cultures that the tradition of Jesus has been "at home" for 2000 years. Thus, it is within this culture that we should look for rejection and misuse of this tradition, not among Jews.

An ethnic identification of Jesus had a positive function and was important as a balance against a discrimination of Jews on ethnic and racial grounds. However, such an ethnocentrism must be ethically defensible, as a protection of the weaker part.[29]

The problem of an ethnic logic is illustrated in a special way by a small group of Christians who live in the "homeland" of Jesus, for instance in Bethlehem or Nazareth. I am of course thinking of the Palestinian Christians, who have largely been forgotten and overlooked by the Western, Protestant churches. In an area in which the Jews in Israel are the rulers and the Palestinians remain oppressed, it would be hermeneutically irresponsible to say that Jesus was a Jew in contrast to being a Palestinian. Palestinian Christians on their side point towards a non-ethnocentric interpretation of the history of Jesus. A Palestinian priest, E. Chacour, speaks of Galilee as a land that does not uniquely belong to Palestinians, but as a land that represents a type of space with which all can identify.[30] He speaks of Galilee as a land of resurrection and hope, as a meeting place between human beings and between humans and God. For Palestinian Christians their history on the very places in which the history of Jesus was played out, has meant a special identification, in which *place* has played an important part. This points to another aspect of identity that has often been overlooked. *Time* and *place* are the two main pillars of human identity. Time, in terms of history, also genealogy and thereby ethnic continuity, has often been the predominant factor. The importance of place has often not been recognised. It is time to consider the relevance of place, also in a cultural interpretation of Jesus. The places where he lived and his activities there were also part of his identity. Therefore, the Gospel narratives about his birth in poverty and his flight to Egypt as a refugee, although not historical, are important interpretations of Jesus' identity from

[29] Brett, "Interpreting Ethnicity", 19–21.

[30] In N.S. Ateek, M.C. Ellis, R.R. Ruether (eds.), *Faith and the Intifada. Palestinian Christian Voices*. Maryknoll (New York: Orbis, 1992) 85.

the earliest Christian period. And his choice of place among the poor, the socially marginalised is also an expression of an identity that may take precedence over ethnicity. It is this similarity in place that have formed the basis for an immediate identification with Jesus from many poor Christians all over the world. In many instances this identity of place is more ethically motivated than an identity of ethnicity.

Thus, I suppose, it is in line with the universal and cross-cultural interests in Biblical interpretation that Räisänen has defended, to conclude by saying that the question "Is Jesus a Jew?" is not so easy to answer as the question "Was he a Jew?"

PART TWO

THE GOSPELS

THE "SOCIOLOGY OF SECTARIANISM" IN MATTHEW: MODELING THE GENESIS OF EARLY JEWISH AND CHRISTIAN COMMUNITIES

Petri Luomanen

1. *Introduction*

During the 1990s, three studies were published on Matthew's gospel where the genesis and social situation of Matthew's community were interpreted in the light of sect analysis. J. Andrew Overman argued in his *Matthew's Gospel and Formative Judaism* that Matthew's community was a sectarian minority group in struggle with formative Judaism. The criticism of the Jewish leaders shows that the members of Matthew's group were underdogs in the battle.[1] In a similar vein Anthony J. Saldarini argued in his *Matthew's Christian-Jewish Community* that Matthew's gospel testifies to a conflict within Judaism. Matthew wrote as a Jew to other Jews, and his Christian-Jewish community is to be regarded as a sect within Judaism.[2] A few years earlier Graham N. Stanton had published his *A Gospel for a New People*, which included an article that compared Matthew's gospel with the Damascus Document. In Stanton's view both documents were written in order to sustain the separate identity of sectarian communities.[3]

---

[1] J.A. Overman, *Matthew's Gospel and Formative Judaism: The Social World of the Matthean Community* (Minneapolis: Fortress, 1990) 8, 154. Overman's definition of a sect is based on J. Blenkinsopp, "Interpretation and the Tendency to Sectarianism: An Aspect of Second Temple History", in E.P. Sanders (ed.), *Jewish and Christian Self-Definition* (3 vols.; Philadelphia: Fortress, 1981) 2.1–26 and B. Wilson, *Magic and the Millennium: A Sociological Study of Religious Movements of Protest among Tribal and Third World Peoples* (London: Heinemann, 1973) 16–26.

[2] A.J. Saldarini, *Matthew's Christian-Jewish Community* (Chicago Studies in the History of Judaism; Chicago/London: University of Chicago Press, 1994) 114–15. In this context Saldarini follows Wilson's definition of a sect (see above, n. 1).

[3] G.N. Stanton, *A Gospel for a New People: Studies in Matthew* (Edinburgh: T & T Clark, 1992) 98, 104–7. Stanton has argued that Matthew was writing "in the wake of the parting of the ways;" just after Matthew's group had parted company with the Jewish community. See, for instance, Stanton, *Gospel*, 113–42; idem, "Revisiting Matthew's Communities", *SBLSP* 33 (1994) 13–18. In contrast, Saldarini (*Matthew's Christian-Jewish Community*, 109–10) emphasizes that Matthew's community is still within Judaism. As regards Overman's view, Stanton finds him sometimes suggest-

The above studies are part of a larger current of New Testament studies which seeks to draw on social-scientific models originally developed for the analysis of minority movements within contemporary societies.[4] They have helped us to see Matthew's gospel in a new light but they also show some inconsistencies which call for closer attention to the basic assumptions of a "sociology of sectarianism."[5]

The following discussion consists of two parts. In the first part I shall discuss the appropriate *concepts* to be used in describing the social setting of Matthew's community. The assessment of the above mentioned studies will show that the popular idea about multiple Judaisms does not cohere with the basic assumptions of sect analysis. The discussion will also show that instead of paying attention to a sect's "response to the world" (Wilson), a more traditional definition of a sect as a religious deviant group is preferable. An assessment of E.P. Sanders' concept of "common Judaism" concludes the first part. In the second part the discussion proceeds on the level of *modeling* by tracing typical causes and responses effective in the formation of early Jewish and Christian movements. Drawing on Stark and Bainbridge's theory of religion I will sketch a model for describ-

ing a view similar to his while some other parts of the book seem to claim just the opposite (Stanton, *Gospel*, 123 n. 2). In my view Matthew's relation to Judaism is characterized by *social separation* and *ideological affinity* that, nevertheless, breaks the pattern of traditional Judaism. See P. Luomanen, *Entering the Kingdom of Heaven: A Study on the Structure of Matthew's View of Salvation* (WUNT 2/101; Tübingen: Mohr, 1998) 164. Therefore, Matthew's community is best understood as a cult movement, as I shall argue below.

[4] A "New Wave" in sociological studies started in the mid-1970s. Among the first studies to apply sect analysis were John Gager, *Kingdom and Community: The Social World of Early Christianity* (Prentice-Hall Studies in Religion; Englewood Cliffs, NJ: Prentice-Hall, 1975), which compared earliest Christianity to modern millenarian movements, and Robin Scroggs, "The Earliest Christian Communities as Sectarian Movement", in J. Neusner (ed.), *Christianity, Judaism and other Greco-Roman Cults: Studies for Morton Smith at Sixty* (4 vols. Studies in Judaism in Late Antiquity 12; Leiden: Brill, 1975) 2.1–23, which described earliest Palestinian Christianity with the help of Werner Stark's list of seven characteristics typical of sects. In the wake of these sweeping studies there followed in the 1980s a number of analyses of the epistles of the New Testament. Philip F. Esler, *Community and Gospel in Luke-Acts: The Social and Political Motivations of Lucan Theology* (SNTSMS 57; Cambridge: Cambridge University Press, 1987) is the first to apply sectarian approach to one of the synoptic gospels.

[5] The term "sociology of sectarianism" is borrowed from P.F. Esler, "Introduction: Models, Context and Kerygma in New Testament Interpretation", in P.F. Esler (ed.), *Modelling Early Christianity: Social-Scientific Studies of the New Testament in its Context* (London/New York: Routledge, 1995) 1–20, esp. p. 4.

ing the development of these communities in the post-70 CE situation, suggesting that Matthew's community is best understood as a cult movement. The present study—an attempt to understand the formation of an early Christian group from a sociological point of view and in terms of a general theory of religion—also seeks for its part to move "beyond New Testament theology" by breaking the pattern of explaining the genesis of Christianity in theological terms.[6]

2. *Conceptualizing the Social Setting*

2.1. *Sects within Judaisms?*

Sect as a sociological concept is rooted in Ernst Troeltsch's classic study in the early 20th century on two radically opposed organizational forms of Christianity. In Troeltsch's study, national protestant churches or the Catholic Church represented the mainstream church. Thus the cultural and historical limitations of the original church-sect distinction were obvious. When social scientists later wanted to apply the concept of sect to the analysis of religious minorities in different cultural contexts, it became necessary to redefine its content so as to line up with the data at hand.[7] In recent New Testament studies the concept has usually been applied in redefined forms.

Bryan Wilson's re-conceptualization focuses on a sect's "response to the world," that is, the way it tries to overcome evil. According

[6] Heikki Räisänen published his program questioning the theology-centered explanation of Christianity in the early 1990s (H. Räisänen, *Beyond New Testament Theology: A Story and a Program* [London: SCM, 1990]). Voices to the same effect were also raised in the SBL Myths and Modern Theories of Christian Origins Consultation in 1995, where Burton L. Mack, for instance, argued that instead of a naively assumed theory of religion where Christianity provides the categories for naming and explaining the early Christian phenomena, "we need a theory of religion firmly anchored in a social and cultural anthropology, capable of sustaining a conversation with the humanities." (B.L. Mack, "On Redescribing Christian Origins", *Method & Theory in the Study of Religion* 8 [1996] 251–52, 254). Gerd Theissen, who started to work towards a similar goal at the same time as, and independently of, Räisänen, published in 1999 his description of primitive Christian religion, which puts aside theological categories and describes religion as a cultural sign system paying attention to the religion's psychological and sociological functions in life (G. Theissen, *The Religion of the Earliest Churches: Creating a Symbolic World* [Minneapolis: Fortress, 1999] xiii–xiv, 2–12).

[7] On the reasons for redefinition, see B. Wilson, *Religion in Sociological Perspective* (Oxford: Oxford University Press, 1982) 100–5.

to Wilson there are seven types of sects: conversionist, revolutionist, introversionist, manipulationist, thaumaturigal, reformist, and utopian.[8] Another redefinition of the church-sect distinction is Benton Johnson's re-conceptualization of a church as "a religious group that accepts the social environment in which it exists" and a sect as "a religious group that rejects the social environment in which it exists."[9] These re-definitions are often welcomed as a means of overcoming the culturally bound restrictions of the classic distinction: What is most important is not a group's relation to the religious church-like parent body but its relation to the social setting in general.[10] Both Saldarini and Overman make use of Wilson's redefinition,[11] and this raises the question of how they would describe the "world outside" to which Matthew's community is responding.

Overman views the whole period between 165 BCE and 100 CE as sectarian in character. Those who were in power and those who felt alienated changed often. The Pharisees are a prime example of a sect that experienced both favour and alienation. Overman solves the problem of locating the parent body by assuming that the parent body was not a fixed group. The religio-sociological powers with which the "sects" might have been at odds could have been "the priests in the temple in Jerusalem or the local *boule*, or authorities who exercised power because they enjoyed the favor of a ruler or Roman client."[12] As for Matthew's gospel, the most important parent body would have been "formative Judaism," which was emerging as a dominant group within Palestinian Judaism.[13] On the other hand, when Overman discusses Matthew's relation to the civil realm,

[8] Wilson, *Magic*, 22–26. Typologies are always constructed from a certain point of view and Wilson's typology—focusing on the means of overcoming evil—is openly soteriological in its approach.

[9] B. Johnson, "On Church and Sect", *American Sociological Review* 28 (1963) 539–49. Saldarini, *Matthew's Christian-Jewish Community*, 108–9, cites Johnson's definition followed by Stark and Bainbridge's definition of a religious institution and a religious movement. On the basis of Saldarini's quotation one may get the impression that the distinction between religious institutions and religious movements are to replace the church-sect distinction. However, in Stark and Bainbridge's general theory of religion sect movements are only one sub-category of religious movements (cf. below).

[10] For instance, Saldarini, *Matthew's Christian-Jewish Community*, 108–9 and J.H. Elliott, "The Jewish Messianic Movement: From Faction to Sect", in Esler, *Modelling Early Christianity*, 75–95, esp. p. 76.

[11] Cf. above, n. 1, 2, 9.

[12] Overman, *Matthew's Gospel*, 8–16.

[13] Overman, *Matthew's Gospel*, 23, 141–49.

it is the civil realm that appears as the parent body.[14] Nevertheless, in the last analysis Overman seems to give the priority to formative Judaism as the parent body, admitting that the analysis of the relationship of formative Judaism and the Roman empire goes beyond the bounds of his study.[15]

I find Overman's view dubious in that the position of the Pharisees oscillates between "a parent" and "a sect." Overman may too easily identify the political fortunes of the party of the Pharisees with their position in Israelite religion. Bengt Holmberg has well criticized Christopher Rowland's similar interpretation about the "sectarian" character of pre-70 Judaism: "This use of the term robs it of any sociological significance."[16] I will also argue below that, in contrast to the Essenes, the Pharisees were not a sect.

In Saldarini's view the social context of Matthew's group is to be found "somewhere in Syria or Coele Syria" and Matthew's "setting and set of social and intellectual relationships will have to be sought within the *Judaisms* of the Roman Empire in the late first century."[17]

Using Wilson's categories Saldarini labels Matthew's group as a "reformist movement or sect" within Judaism.[18] He also thinks that

---

[14] Overman, *Matthew's Gospel*, 106–13.

[15] Overman, *Matthew's Gospel*, 154–55.

[16] B. Holmberg, *Sociology and the New Testament: An Appraisal* (Minneapolis: Fortress, 1990) 99. However, Holmberg, too, can be criticized for accepting too easily the idea that before 70 CE there was not a parent body available in Judaism and therefore sect analysis can be only applied to the post 70 CE situation (*Sociology*, 91).

[17] Saldarini, *Matthew's Christian-Jewish Community*, 26 (italics mine). See also p. 15: "Thus, the late first-, and second-century Judaism was less a finished product or a coherent community and tradition and more a group of communities within a varied and changing tradition that was developing toward the comprehensive, unified, and relatively stable Talmudic system of later centuries. . . . Similarly, the many Jewish communities scattered around the Roman Empire varied greatly from one another and had adapted significantly to local conditions."

[18] Saldarini, *Matthew's Christian-Jewish Community*, 114. Saldarini (ibid., 112–13) also applies a typology of deviant associations that distinguishes four types: 1) conformative 2) alienative 3) expressive 4) instrumental. In Saldarini's view Matthew's community is alienative-instrumental. That means that it is separated from the dominant Jewish assembly but still struggles to gain power within it. On the whole Saldarini's study makes use of a large collection of different sociological theories. In addition to deviance theory and sect analysis, he uses realistic conflict theory and social identity theory in order to describe the formation of Matthew's group. However, the actual social processes these theories seek to describe do not get much attention in Saldarini's presentation, which hurries from concept to concept and from theory to theory with such speed that it is sometimes impossible to keep up

Matthew's group had been expelled from the local synagogue and it formed an assembly of its own with a different name (ekklesia). Matthew's group also found their "core identity and 'master status' in being believers-in-Jesus."[19]

How does Saldarini picture the parent body that lends Matthew's group its sectarian position "within Judaisms?" At least three different characterizations can be found: "leadership of the Jewish community" influenced by a rabbinic group, "Jewish society as a whole," and/or the "majority of Jews."[20] Thus Saldarini does not describe Matthew's conflict only as a local incident between two competing "Judaisms," but assumes a larger body of "Judaism" against which Matthew's sectarianism is defined. Since this is in contradiction with the starting point of his book, which emphasizes the multiplicity of Judaisms, it can be asked if the *hostile majority* that appears in the characterizations is generated by the concept of a sect as a minority-group. In any case, Saldarini's argumentation indicates that the concept of a sect works better if a hostile, unified majority is assumed.

The idea of multiple Judaisms is also ignored elsewhere in Saldarini's book. When Saldarini argues that despite the cleavage Matthew's gospel should still be regarded as a Jewish document, an idealistic picture of an *all-embracing majority* Judaism surfaces:

> Community [as a term] implies the presence of a strong sense of identity and a common set of deeply held values and perceptions, which result in close, supportive, loving contact. The Jewish community fits this description because of its history, literature, strong social organization, and rich cultural life. . . . Though Matthew's group is in some

with the shifting viewpoints. See, for instance, pp. 88–89, where Saldarini starts with realistic conflict theory but suddenly seems to shift his focus to Stark and Bainbridge's theory of religion that is based on exchange theory.

[19] Saldarini, *Matthew's Christian-Jewish Community*, 112–13.

[20] According to Saldarini, "within Judaism, Matthew's smaller group is viewed by the majority as deviant" and "Matthew's group had enough fundamental disputes with the majority of Jews to be classified as deviant in a deeper sense than many other Jewish movements" (*Matthew's Christian-Jewish Community*, 109, 111). "His quarrel is with the leadership of the Jewish community and the emerging rabbinic group, which is influencing that leadership" (115). "From the viewpoint of *society at large*, they were a deviant group, a reformist sect with millenarian tendencies, seeking to change *Jewish society*" (italics mine). . . . "Matthew's group has deviated from the majority position through its devotion to Jesus as a risen apocalyptic figure who is divinely sent emissary. Unlike the rabbinic group it is in serious conflict with the society as whole" (121–22).

> sense a community, we will argue that it is first part of the larger Jewish community.[21]

In addition, Saldarini thinks that Matthew's gospel should be regarded as Jewish because of its self-understanding.[22] This remark raises the important question of how much emphasis one should place on the self-designation of communities when discussing the definition of Judaism. I will come back to this question later in this article.

On the whole it seems that although both Overman and Saldarini use the definition of a sect in its wider cultural meaning, Matthew's sectarianism is, nevertheless, mainly defined against the religious parent body of formative Judaism or an ideal, abstract majority-Judaism. Overman in particular seems to have difficulty deciding what kind of role the civil realm played in the formation of Matthew's sectarianism.[23] In the last analysis this is not surprising since the actual conflict we meet in the narrative of the gospel is between Jesus' movement and the representatives of Judaism.

2.2. *The Pros and Cons of a More Traditional Approach*

Stanton's description manages to avoid the kind of inconsistencies found in Overman's and Saldarini's analysis by staying closer to the traditional understanding of a sect. Aware of the shortcomings of the Troeltschian approach, Stanton finds L.M. White's definition a good starting point for cross-cultural "distant comparisons:" a sect is a "deviant or separatist movement within a *cohesive and religiously defined dominant culture*."[24] Stanton also finds helpful Blenkinsopp's comments about the tendency of sects to claim to be what the parent body

---

[21] Saldarini, *Matthew's Christian-Jewish Community*, 87. The quote is from a context where Saldarini explains why he uses the term "Matthew group" instead of "Matthew's community." At the end of the book (*Matthew's Christian-Jewish Community*, 199), Saldarini notes that the term "Jewish community" refers to the Jewish community as a whole, including the full variety of Jewish groups and sub-traditions in Israel and the diaspora during the first century.

[22] "The Gospel of Matthew cannot be compared or contrasted with Judaism because the gospel is in a real sense a Jewish document, written within what the author and his opponents understood as Judaism. They were debating the shape of Judaism and forging competing identities in contrast to one another. But they did this within the Jewish tradition, in Jewish categories, concerning Jewish questions" (Saldarini, *Matthew's Christian-Jewish Community*, 110).

[23] See above.

[24] Stanton, *Gospel*, 90 (italics mine) referring to L.M. White, "Shifting Sectarian Boundaries in Early Christianity", *BJRL* 70 (1988) 7–24, esp. p. 14.

claims to be (legitimation). Stanton uses the singular term "Judaism" but manages to avoid a sweeping description by focusing his analysis mainly on the local level: Matthew wrote his gospel for a cluster of Christian communities, "minority groups still living in the shadow of thriving local Jewish communities." In Stanton's view, the separation was most probably part of the process whereby post-70 Judaism began to draw boundaries.[25]

Stanton's more traditional approach results in a less inconsistent picture; but at the same time it raises the question about the limits of the approach. For instance, his comparison with the Damascus Document (CD) shows the similar sectarian character of the communities, yet falls short in explaining the differences. Why did the Qumran sectarians remain Jewish while Matthew's sectarian community—as a result of the parting of the ways—became Christian?[26] Furthermore, the character of Judaism at the time of the writing of CD as compared to the Judaism contemporary with Matthew remains an open question in Stanton's analysis. A more comprehensive picture of the process of the parting of the ways and the formation of new communities would obviously require a model that allows for different modes of separation and development as well as a more thorough discussion about Judaism as a parent body.

2.3. *Common Judaism, Complex Judaism or All Kinds of Judaisms?*

The above discussion has shown that if the concept of a sect is to be useful at all in New Testament studies, it can only be applied if a reasonable amount of cohesion and centralized power can be shown to have existed among different "Judaisms." In contemporary research E.P. Sanders is considered the scholar who has presented the most detailed description of the unity of Jewish belief and practice around

---

[25] Stanton, *Gospel*, 3, 145.

[26] In a footnote (*Gospel*, 107 n. 1) Stanton deals with similar criticism given by Ernest Best after the first presentation of the paper in Oxford. In his answer Stanton notes that in his view Matthew's community did not link up with a larger Christian group immediately following the parting with Israel, and thus retained an independent character similar to the Qumran community. I agree with Stanton that Matthew did not yet necessarily see his community as part of larger Christian "church." Nevertheless, it seems to me that Matthew's "parting of ways" was caused by new "Christian" ideas whereas the Qumran community departed because it wanted to stick to more traditional Jewish ideas. Cf. below the distinction between cult movement (Matthew) and sect movement (Essenes and the Qumran community).

the beginning of the Common Era. His description, however, has not escaped some criticism.[27]

In the concept *common Judaism*, Sanders uses the word "common" in two of its most obvious senses. He refers to the broad agreement of practice and belief he finds between different Jewish groups, and he also aims at describing what the ordinary people did in religion and what they thought about it. According to Sanders, "within Palestine, 'normal' or 'common' Judaism was what the priests and the people agreed on" and "normal Judaism was, to a limited degree, also 'normative:' it established a standard by which loyalty to Israel and to the God of Israel was measured."[28] If Sanders is right, then it was primarily the priests in cooperation with the ordinary people who ran the religion before the destruction of the temple. Sanders also argues—against the traditional view—that when not occupied in the temple service the priests and Levites who lived outside Jerusalem served their communities as legal experts and scribes. Accordingly, synagogues would not have been predominated solely by the Pharisees who were laymen.[29]

Martin Hengel and Roland Deines view Sanders' attempt to focus on "common Judaism" as a welcome correction to the prevailing tendency to make too much of the differences among the Jewish groups. Hengel also values highly Sanders' description of the temple cult and the Essenes.[30] However, on the whole he finds Sanders' description too harmonistic. It only describes Judaism as it appeared to the outsiders. For the people who looked at the religion from the

[27] E.P. Sanders started his series of epoch-making studies on Judaism and Christianity with *Paul and Palestinian Judaism: A Comparison of Patterns of Religion* (London: SCM, 1977). There he introduced the concept of "covenantal nomism," which was meant to characterize the "pattern" of Palestinian Judaism between 200 BCE and 200 CE. Sanders set himself the task of holistic "comparison of patterns of religion," and he was not so much concerned with the daily activities of the adherents. What Sanders did came quite close to an analysis of "soteriology" or the "pattern of salvation" although he himself preferred not to use the term "soteriology." Sanders thinks that the "common denominator" of Jewish theology, "covenantal nomism," is an essential part of a broader "common Judaism" that he describes in *Judaism: Practice and Belief 63 BCE–66 CE* (London: SCM, 1994). See Sanders, *Judaism*, ix.

[28] Sanders, *Judaism*, 47.

[29] Sanders, *Judaism*, 170–82. For an opposite view, see M. Hengel and R. Deines, "E.P. Sanders' 'Common Judaism', Jesus, and the Pharisees: Review Article of Jewish Law from Jesus to Mishnah and Judaism: Practice and Belief by E.P. Sanders", *JTS* 46 (1995) 60–67.

[30] Hengel and Deines, "E.P. Sanders' 'Common Judaism'", 67–68.

inside, for the Jews themselves, things were much more complicated. Therefore, instead of "common Judaism," Hengel would rather speak of "complex Judaism."[31]

In Jacob Neusner's (and Bruce Chilton's) view[32] Sanders' "common-denominator Judaism yields little that is more than simply banal," it reaches "so stratospheric a level of generalization that all precise vision of real people practicing a vivid religion is lost."[33] Neusner's own program goes still further than Hengel's "complex Judaism." Instead of analyzing one "common-denominator Judaism" within a particular time span, Neusner wants to study individual *Judaisms* on their own as they can be observed in different documents or a canon of writings.[34] As for Judaism, in Neusner's view everything that lays claim to Scripture and Torah qualifies. Thus it is logical, that for Neusner and Chilton, Christianity is one Judaism among others.[35] They intentionally turn their attention to the self-understanding of the documents: "We replicate the very perspectives of the documents and their authors themselves. For they held that they formed Israel, and, in our categories, theirs was a Judaism (that is, the Torah)."[36]

In my opinion it is good to keep in mind the scale of what in Sanders' analysis is a *complete religion* that—at least in Palestine—was largely equivalent with the Jewish nation. A group of this size can never be harmonious. Due to the nature of the Temple worship, people were able to socialize only with their own circle of friends, and most likely this is what they did, as Sanders aptly demonstrates.[37]

---

[31] Hengel and Deines, "E.P. Sanders' 'Common Judaism'", 53. Hengel is also very critical of Sanders' description of the Pharisees. In Hengel's view the Pharisees never completely lost the relatively central position in Jewish religion and politics which they attained during the reign on Salome Alexandra (Hengel and Deines, "E.P. Sanders' 'Common Judaism'", 62–67).

[32] Jacob Neusner has often criticized Sanders' interpretation of Judaism. In the following I shall deal with the points presented in a book that Neusner has written together with Bruce Chilton: B. Chilton and J. Neusner, *Judaism in the New Testament: Practices and Beliefs* (London/New York: Routledge, 1995). The title of the book recalls Sanders' heading on purpose, setting forth Neusner's (and Chilton's) own program for the study of Judaisms. Neusner wrote the drafts for the pages to be discussed below but the authors state that the book speaks for both of them at every point (xix).

[33] Chilton and Neusner, *Judaism*, 12, 15.

[34] Chilton and Neusner, *Judaism*, 16–18.

[35] Chilton and Neusner, *Judaism*, 4–8.

[36] Chilton and Neusner, *Judaism*, 9.

[37] Sanders, *Judaism*, 440–43.

In doing so they did not necessarily agree with the people partying next door, but by coming to the festivals they kept the temple institution alive. The same applies to the synagogue services, although it is clear that it is not so easy to enter the same synagogue with one's enemy as was the Temple. However, it probably was possible to attend the one next door.

Although Neusner is critical of the degree of abstraction in Sanders' study, at an earlier stage he himself described Judaism in a similar vein:

> Before the destruction, there was common 'Judaism' in the Land of Israel, and it was by no means identical to what we now understand as rabbinic Judaism. The common religion consisted of three main elements, first, the Hebrew Scriptures, second, the Temple, and third, the common and accepted practices of the ordinary folk—their calendar, their mode of living, their everyday practices and rites, based on these two.[38]

For me, this description seems to come pretty close to what Sanders means by common Judaism.[39]

Neusner's and Chilton's program for the study of Judaisms raises the same question as one of the arguments Saldarini presented in favour of Matthew's Jewish character: how much attention should a student of antiquity give to the self-understanding of a particular group? For the sake of modern dialogue between religions it may be relevant to emphasize the common roots of religions we have thus far called Judaism, Christianity and Islam (obviously Islam should be included, too).[40] However, to call all of them different forms of

---

[38] Neusner, "The Formation of Rabbinic Judaism: Yavneh (Jamnia) from AD 70 to 100", *ANRW* II 19.2, 21.

[39] On the whole Neusner's criticism repeats similar arguments he earlier presented against Sanders' covenantal nomism. It seems that Neusner does not pay very much attention to how "covenantal nomism" or "common-denominator Judaism" is related to "common Judaism" (cf. above, n. 27). Because "covenantal nomism" deals with the "theology," one could perhaps see it as "lifeless, dull, hopelessly abstract, lacking all social relevance" (Chilton and Neusner, *Judaism*, 11–12). However, I do not find this as an apt characterization of "common Judaism," which describes how ordinary people led their lives in religion. In the last analysis, Sanders' common Judaism stands or falls with the question of whether there really were such people and customs that Sanders describes and to that extent he argues, and not because he would present assertions that are too abstract and have nothing to do with real life.

[40] In this regard I find the common undertaking of Chilton and Neusner, "an Anglican/Episcopalian priest and a rabbi," valuable. In the preface to *God in the*

Judaism violates the ordinary use of language. More importantly, to do so would be to assume that religious groups can be defined mainly on the basis of the traditions they hold to or the scriptures they claim. It completely ignores the social barriers that exist between the groups.

Observations based on the sociology of knowledge and legitimation, as well as sociological studies of sects, have revealed that it is customary for emerging religious groups to lay claim to traditions they share with the parent group.[41] Therefore, a proper description of dissenting religious groups will not pay attention only to their self-understanding. Groups also have to be compared with each other, tracing the items that separate or unite them both socially and ideologically. For this end we need terms and concepts that bridge the gap between our modern analytical point of view and the language of insiders. The concept of "Judaisms" does not do that reasonably since it places too much emphasis on the language of insiders.[42]

For the most part it seems to me that criticism presented against "common Judaism" concerns the focus of Sanders' study. The critics would like to see more emphasis on the differences between the self-understandings of the Jewish groups. Neusner, in particular, seems to challenge the meaningfulness of the whole undertaking, preferring instead his own program. In the last analysis, however, this line of criticism does not question Sanders' common Judaism as a valid generalization from the etic point of view. In any case, even if one should disagree with Sanders on some points (the role of the Pharisees, for instance), for sect analysis his description provides a critically argued and testable theory of Jewish "majority," which is much better than implied or hastily sketched "majority views" that seem to come into play when sect analysis is applied. In the following we shall also see that in the case of a classic Jewish sect—the Essenes—

World (Judaism and Christianity—The Formative Categories; Harrisburg, Pennsylvania: Trinity Press International, 1997) vii, reference is made to Islam as a conversation partner. For an overview of the undertaking's publications, see B. Chilton and J. Neusner, *Types of Authority in Formative Christianity and Judaism* (London/New York: Routledge, 1999) viii–xiii.

[41] R. Stark and W.S. Bainbridge, *A Theory of Religion* (Toronto Studies in Religion 2; New York: P. Lang, 1987) 132. For legitimation in Matthew's gospel, see Stanton, *Gospel*, 101–7 and Luomanen, *Entering*, 264–65.

[42] For a healthy discussion about the role of analysis from emic and etic points of view, see P.F. Esler, "Introduction", 4–8.

the temple Judaism which forms the core of Sanders' description did actually play the role of the parent body.

3. *Modeling the Social Setting*

3.1. *Typologies and Modeling*

Among those who use some idea of sect in studying the New Testament documents, there is a tendency to get rid of mere classifications by using models that allow for change in the nature of groups in the course of their development.[43] Philip F. Esler has proposed a "model of sectarianism" which focuses on the genesis and development of a reform movement into a sect,[44] and John Elliot has introduced a related model which analyzes the shift from a faction to a sect.[45] Since models assume causal relationships and describe developments, they obviously have more explanatory value than pure conceptualizations or typologies that, while perhaps providing a starting point for comparison, are not very well suited for explaining development—unless supplemented with other theories.[46] Since Esler's and Elliot's models both focus on one line of development, their usability is still limited, although not so narrowly as in the case of pure typologies.

Rodney Stark has criticized New Testament scholars (and some social scientists) for mistaking concepts for explanations. Stark emphasizes that concepts are unable to give explanations unless they are

[43] The sociology of sectarianism has often been criticized for its polarly assumptions. See, for instance, S.C. Barton, "Early Christianity and the Sociology of the Sect", in F. Watson (ed.), *The Open Text: New Directions for Biblical Studies?* (London: SCM, 1993) 156, and Holmberg, *Sociology*, 110–12, who also provides further references (n. 87). It is to be noted, however, that at some points Holmberg's criticism misses the target. For instance, he criticizes the concept of sect for the reason that Philip Esler and Rodney Stark use it differently. We cannot assume that all scholars use a term exactly the same way although we can expect that a scholar's use of a particular central term is consistent throughout the study. Thus we cannot discard sect analysis by putting Esler's sect against Stark's sect.

[44] Esler, *Community*, 46–70; idem, *The First Christians in their Social Worlds: Social-scientific approaches to New Testament interpretation* (London/New York: Routledge, 1994) 13–17. A version of the model was also used by F. Watson, *Paul, Judaism and the Gentiles: A Sociological Approach* (SNTSMS 56; Cambridge: Cambridge University Press, 1986) 19, 38–41.

[45] J.H. Elliott, "Jewish", 76–80.

[46] For instance, Stanton, *Gospel*, 98–104, supplements his analysis with Lewis Coser's conflict theory.

connected to theories of "*why* and *how* some phenomena are linked."[47] Stark's distinction is helpful. Unfortunately, not all theorizing and conceptualizing make such clear-cut distinctions between definitions and propositions as does Stark and Bainbridge's theory of religion (cf. below). In my view, this applies especially to concepts such as sect, which seem inherently to contain some relational and genetic aspects. Various definitions of a sect, especially the "simple" ones,[48] do not just list features that allow one to identify a group as a sect, but also often suggest the way *how* the sect was born. A good example of this is Wilson's "responses to the world" as the basis of sect typology. Wilson's typology does not just describe different kinds of sects, but also explains the variations as different responses to the experience of evil. When a genetic-descriptive concept like this is introduced into New Testament studies, the question should be raised about whether this concept is to be taken as a description or as an explanation, or perhaps both. Although the question is usually ignored, the concept nevertheless carries with it all the explanatory potential, competing with other explanations and creating confusion as to how one should understand the causes of a sect's genesis.

The above considerations suggest that Wilson's re-conceptualization of the term sect may not be so useful to New Testament studies after all. It was created for the study of third world religious movements and also proved useful in the analysis of religious minorities of modern secularized society.[49] In the final analysis, the religious situation in early 20th century Europe, where the churches still had a dominant position in the culture, may actually have been structurally parallel to the situation when emerging Christian movements struggled to legitimize their existence against the powerful traditions of Judaism. In New Testament studies, the cross-cultural potential of Wilson's "responses to the world"—approach cannot be fully utilized because of our limited information about the overall social context of the writings. Thus a more "traditional" definition of a sect should be preferred. Nevertheless, Wilson's approach has some heuristic value for the study of Matthew's gospel and the New

[47] R. Stark, *The Rise of Christianity: A Sociologist Reconsiders History* (Princeton, New Jersey: Princeton University Press, 1996) 23–27.

[48] Cf. Overman's use of two "simple" definitions of a sect by Blenkinsopp and Wilson (Overman, *Matthew's Gospel*, 8).

[49] See Wilson, *Religion*, 100–5.

Testament in general by raising the question of Matthew's relation to the society as a whole.

As regards sect analysis, my suggestion is that Stark and Bainbridge's distinction between sect movements and cult movements is more helpful than a broader cultural definition of a sect. Stark and Bainbridge define religious movements "traditionally" on the basis of their relation to religion. Yet, instead of providing a closed typology of sects, they think more in terms of axes of tension. On the basis of their model, which includes also propositions explaining the genesis of different kinds of movements, it is possible to do justice to the sectarian features that Matthew shared with Jewish movements, as well as to new Christian elements in the gospel.[50] However, before the different modes of dissent can be discussed in more detail, the role of the Jewish parent body must be outlined. I shall start by discussing the role of the "world outside" in the formation of Jewish movements, a question raised by Wilson's approach.

3.2. *The Romans as the "World Outside"*

From the viewpoint of a modern historian, the time after Pompey's conquest of Judea in 63 BCE when Rome controlled Palestine in cooperation with Jewish vassal kings, high priests and aristocrats (or the Pharisees if one wishes) could be defined by observing how Roman "secular" politics and military action influenced Judaism. However, in ancient societies there was no clear distinction between secular and religious spheres as there is nowadays in most Western countries. This applies especially to Judaism, since Jews tended to view reality more from a religious point of view than the average members of Hellenistic-Roman society, for whom religion was one dimension of the virtuous life.[51] A question that for a modern historian appears to be purely political or military in nature (etic point of view) soon turns out to be a religious problem of great significance if viewed from the point of view of Jewish self-understanding (emic point of view).

Furthermore, apart from any direct military action by the Romans, which sometimes aroused the nationalistic feelings of Jews, I suspect that many of the questions that were dealt with in inner-Jewish or

[50] For Stark and Bainbridge's theory and definitions, see below.

[51] Cf. Sanders, *Judaism*, 50–51.

Jewish-Christian debates were of a nature that hardly aroused the interest of the Romans, so long as their subjects remained relatively peaceful. For the Romans it probably was quite inconsequential how strictly the Sabbath was obeyed, what kind of food and purity rules were regarded as binding, or how the sacrifices were offered in the Temple. But for Jews and Christians these were burning issues that created social and ideological boundaries.

The above considerations are confirmed by the genesis of the main Jewish parties under the earlier Hellenistic rule. The Hellenization policy of Antiokhus IV culminated in the defilement of the Temple in 167 BCE, causing an uprising that was led by Mattatias. In the course of the insurrection, the high priesthood was granted to his non-Zadokite descendants, known as Hasmoneans, and the foundation was laid for their rule. However, the traditional Zadokite priesthood still had its supporters, and the disputes about the high priesthood became a watershed among the Jews that took their first steps on the road to full autonomy.

Most scholars agree that the party of the Essenes mainly comprised Zadokite priests critical of the Hasmonean priesthood. Some of them withdrew to the Dead Sea, founding their monastery at Qumran. It is also possible that the party of the Sadducees consisted of former Zadokite priests and aristocrats who, however, were not so critical of the Hasmoneans as the Essenes.[52] The inception of the party of the Pharisees probably did not have much to do with the disputes over the priesthood, although they undoubtedly had their views on it.[53] Thus the impulse came from the "world outside;" Hellenization put pressure on Jews and different groups took different positions. Nevertheless, all the groups were motivated by their desire to stick to their ancestral religion, which they each interpreted in their own way and therefore each can best be characterized by their different *religious* opinions. Occasionally, the changes in military and political reality affected the relative position and power of the par-

[52] Sanders, *Judaism*, 25–26; B. Chilton and J. Neusner, *Trading Places: The Intersecting Histories of Judaism and Christianity* (Cleveland, Ohio: Pilgrim, 1996) 42–50.

[53] Sanders, *Judaism*, 13–29. However, Sanders notes that in 1 Maccabees, a pious group of Hasideans appears that quickly joined the uprising instigated by Mattatias. These are characterized by their strict adherence to the Law and are called scribes (1 Macc 2:29–38; 7:12). Thus, the origin of the Pharisees might be traced to them. However, this remains purely a hypothesis since at the time of the revolt there may have been several groups that were zealous for the Law.

ties within Jewish society, as happened, for instance, during the reign of Salome Alexandra who favoured the Pharisees. In the final analysis, however, incidents like this did not have much effect on the factors that distinguished the Jewish groups from each other.

3.3. *Judaism as Institutional Religion*

At this juncture it is important to note a distinction between religious institutions and parties. In order to function, second temple Judaism needed the Temple and the priests and the Levites. In broader terms, Jewish society, as with all other ancient societies, also needed scribes to keep records and to run legal affairs. Since biblical law seeks to cover the whole range of human life, it is clear that in Jewish society the scribes also had to be learned in religious law.[54] It also appears that, in the first century, the synagogue had established its position as a place of learning and worship. All these can be called institutions. By institutions I mean—following Stark and Bainbridge—"a stable sector of the social structure, a cluster of roles, norms, values, and activities associated with the performance of key social function or functions."[55]

We know that many of the priests probably were Sadducees, but not all. Accordingly, many of the scribes may have been Pharisees, but not all.[56] The names of the Jewish parties were labels given to a group of people that held similar views about how best to be obedient to God's law. Thus, for Judaism as a religion, it was of secondary importance whether the Sadducees or the Pharisees had the upper hand so long as they both were able to take part in the same temple worship. In doing so they both kept the temple institution alive. In this regard a key issue was that both parties held similar views of the festal calendar. On this point the Essenes disagreed with the majority of the population, and that is why they became a group with distinct boundaries towards the outsiders. They disagreed with

---

[54] Sanders, *Judaism*, 179–82; J. Neusner, "Formation", 37–41.

[55] Stark and Bainbridge, *Theory*, 126. Stark and Bainbridge also use the concept of church in the meaning of "conventional religious organization" (124). However, I do not find it an appropriate term for the characterization of second temple Judaism. Not so much because of the Christian connotations of the word as because I think that Judaism is better understood as closely interwoven network of key religious institutions.

[56] Neusner, "The Formation", 39; Sanders, *Judaism*, 179–89.

the Temple institution. They became a sect movement. There were probably also some other pietist groups that could be characterized as sects, and most likely on similar grounds; they were a minority in opposition to the "normal" or "common Judaism" in which the Temple played the central role. The parties of the Pharisees and the Sadducees were not like these groups, and it is misleading to emphasize the disparity within Judaism to such a degree as to label everything as "sectarian."[57]

3.4. *The Power of Tradition*

When the post 70 CE situation is discussed, it is difficult to proceed on the assumption of a contemporary, powerful parent body that would have controlled the social scene to such a degree as to have been able to lend a sectarian self-understanding to other opposing groups within the same Jewish tradition. Neither can we assume that there would have been a corresponding "Christian" parent body. Nevertheless, keeping in mind all the problems, I dare to suggest that the concept of common Judaism provides the best starting point for sect analysis after 70 CE as well. The reasons for this are as follows:

1) Ideologically, temple Judaism seems to play the role of a parent body both for rabbinic Judaism and for the mainstream Christianity documented in the NT writings. The Temple had such a central role in Judaism that splinter groups could not avoid dealing with it, that is, with its loss after 70 CE.
2) Something of the basic power structures, or hopes for their restoration, must have survived for quite a while after 70 CE, at least until the second revolt in 132–135. Jacob Neusner, for instance, explains the emergence of rabbinic Judaism on the basis of pre-70 scribalism and Pharisaism.[58] Furthermore, we have no indication that the destruction of the Temple seriously harmed the instruction and cult in synagogues.[59] Judaism lost one of its central institutions but another one,

[57] In contrast to Overman, *Matthew's Gospel*, 6–16. See also Neusner, "The Formation", 21–22, who calls the Pharisees a sect. However, Neusner does not give any definition for the term sect and the overall impression is that the term is used loosely to refer to a "peculiar group."
[58] Neusner, "Formation", 21–22. Overman, *Matthew's Gospel*, 38, gives the impression that after 70 CE Judaism had to start virtually from scratch.
[59] Cf. Sanders, *Judaism*, 198–202.

the synagogue, continued and priests probably had a role there as well. Furthermore, it is not plausible that ordinary people would have lost their confidence in the priestly lineage overnight. At least up until the second revolt there must have been hope that the Temple would be rebuilt.[60] Had this been possible, who would have been best positioned to occupy the offices?[61]

3) If sociological theory to be used is not based on a static typology but rather gives room for social change and development, then its power to explain extends beyond the limits of where the original parent body has lost its coercive power or where it has had to give up some of its central social functions. New religious movements are seldom spun out of thin air. Although there is something distinctively new in some religious movements, there usually are also many traditional features.[62]

Heikki Räisänen has aptly described the development of early Christian *thought* in terms of interplay with tradition, experience and interpretation.[63] Räisänen's model crystallizes the basic factors that contribute to the development of religious traditions. Everyday experiences are understood in the framework of inherited religious tradition, but when the dissonance between experience and tradition becomes unbearable, a new interpretation of the tradition emerges.

[60] Eliezer ben Hyrcanus, for instance, clearly hoped for the rebuilding of the Temple (Neusner, "The Formation", 34–35).

[61] It is possible that one indication of the continuing role of the (Sadducaic) priests in Judaism can be found in Matthew's gospel. Within Matthean studies it has been customary (I include myself) to refer to Matthew's lumping together of Sadducees and Pharisees in several places (3:7; 16:1, 6, 11, 12) as one indication of the author's historical distance from the real life of the Judaism before 70 CE. Since it was possible for the author to present the Pharisees and the Sadducees as one uniform coalition, it has been thought that in practice the Sadducees had disappeared from the scene and that the editor wrote some time after 70 CE when the disagreements between the Pharisees and the Sadducees were of no concern. See, for instance, D.E. Garland, *The Intention of Matthew 23* (NovTSup 52; Leiden: Brill, 1979) 44, n. 32. However, in the face of the obvious knowledge that the author has about the real life of his Jewish contemporaries, this is not a totally convincing line of argumentation. What if Matthew knew better? What if during his time the Pharisees and the Sadducees did work together? In my view it is not at all unbelievable that at least the lower ranks of priests with Sadducaic views and their descendants, who never received their total income from the temple service, could have worked in cooperation with the Pharisees in local synagogues.

[62] Cf. Stark and Bainbridge, *Theory*, 126–27.

[63] For Räisänen's model see, Räisänen, *Beyond*, 122–41; idem, *Marcion, Muhammad and the Mahatma: Exegetical Perspectives on the Encounter of Cultures and Faiths* (London: SCM, 1997) 195.

If Räisänen's model is transposed to describe the development of religions in their entirety, including both theology and practice, the concept of tradition should also include religious institutions, which also cannot be changed overnight. Religious traditions are anchored not only in material remains like papyrus scrolls and public buildings, but also in the network of human bonds and collective memory. Although the physical temple was destroyed, it still continued its existence in the traditions of the Mishnah, which records discussion about temple service although it was clearly written after the destruction of the temple in 70 CE.[64] Also, several scriptures within the Christian canon, Hebrews in particular, drew imagery from temple worship.

3.5. *A Model Based on Stark and Bainbridge's Theory of Religion*

In contrast to many other descriptions of Matthew's "sectarianism" the present study does not draw on several sociological theories but focuses on one: the general theory of religion by Stark and Bainbridge. Stark and Bainbridge's theory is a deductive theory with seven basic axioms and hundreds of propositions about religious behaviour. It combines a highly developed logical form with two distinguished scholars' mastery of the research done in their field. After a short discussion about their basic concepts I will in the following deal mainly with the section that describes the emergence of religious groups.

Stark and Bainbridge's theory is characteristically an exchange theory. Their second axiom expresses the basic idea: "Humans seek what they perceive to be rewards and avoid what they perceive to be costs."[65] The key to their theory of religion is the concept of compensators: when people cannot obtain the rewards they desire, they may accept compensators that "are postulations of reward according to explanations that are not readily susceptible to unambiguous evaluation." Consequently, religion "refers to systems of general compensators based on supernatural assumptions."[66] Conventional reli-

---

[64] Eliezer ben Hyrcanus, for instance, discussed temple worship probably with the hope of its restoration (Neusner, "The Formation", 34–35).

[65] Stark and Bainbridge, *Theory*, 27.

[66] Stark and Bainbridge, *Theory*, 38–39. R. Collins, review of *A Theory of Religion*, by Rodney Stark and William Sims Bainbridge, *JSSR* 32 (1993) 402–6, has criti-

gious movements are called *churches*. Churches, as well as religious institutions, which were already discussed above, are in low tension with their sociocultural environment.[67]

A basic distinction that Stark and Bainbridge make is the one between religious institutions and religious movements. In contrast to religious institutions, which accept the social environment in which they exist and adapt to its changes, *religious movements* "wish to cause or prevent change in a system of supernaturally-based general compensators" (i.e. in religion). Institutions and movements are the two opposite poles of one axis that permits different degrees of institutionalization. The benefit of this kind of conceptualization is that it allows for degrees of tension instead of adopting a predetermined number of types, which seldom match perfectly the case under examination, resulting in the proliferation of new terms and categories.[68]

Stark and Bainbridge postulate two basic avenues by which new

---

cized Stark and Bainbridge's theory for its unsatisfactory treatment of the traditional monastic religions. According to Stark and Bainbridge's theory, monks would have been greatly in need of compensators. However, Collins thinks that monasteries grew, not because of an increasing need of compensators, but because—being only extra-familial organizations at the time—they provided opportunities to expand rewards (p. 403).

In my opinion, this line of criticism does not challenge the theory itself but rather only challenges the way in which it is applied to monastic religions. More important is Collins' second line of criticism; he makes notice of Stark and Bainbridge's rejection of Durkheimian model, which would find the core of religion in social membership or solidarity. In Collins' view, Stark and Bainbridge's theory should be supplemented by Durkheimian theory of ritual and morality so that morality and social status might be viewed as real social emotions and sources for real rewards, not compensators. Nevertheless, Collins thinks that the views also presented in this second line of criticism can be fitted in the theory (pp. 404–6).

Interestingly, it seems that Collins' criticism does not really challenge the basics of Stark and Bainbridge's theory. Stark and Bainbridge do take into account the fact that in many cases religious organizations provide real rewards (*Theory*, 42–51). Since their theory also assumes that "compensators are treated by humans as if they were rewards" (p. 15), the line between real rewards and compensators is not very clear, especially if viewed from the vantage point of an individual's personal experience. Also, W. Davis, review of *A Theory of Religion*, by Rodney Stark and William Sims Bainbridge, *JR* 69 (1989) 287–88, thinks that Stark and Bainbridge's theory devalues morality. In my view these judgements can be traced back to the fact that an exchange theory is not to everyone's taste, especially if applied to religion. Nevertheless, Stark and Bainbridge's theory—as with all social scientific theories—does not try to say anything about the existence of the supernatural (*Theory*, 22–23); it only explains human behavior.

[67] Stark and Bainbridge, *Theory*, 124–26.

[68] See, Stark and Bainbridge, *Theory*, 16–17. For instance, Elliot, "Jewish", 80–89, lists twenty-one salient sectarian features and nine sectarian strategies.

religious movements emerge. *Sects* come into existence through schisms with existing religious organizations.[69] *Cults*, for their part, come into existence when invented new religious ideas gain social acceptance.[70] Consequently, Stark and Bainbridge define *sect movements* as deviant religious organizations holding traditional beliefs and practices, contrasting these to *cult movements*, which are deviant religious organizations with novel beliefs and practices.[71] The theory of Stark and Bainbridge implies that, just as religious institutions and religious movements represent the two opposite ends of one axis, there is also a continuous spectrum of degrees of novelty between sect movements and cult movements.

Stark and Bainbridge think that religious movements can also be classified according to the direction of their development. It is understandable that *sect movements*, deviating from religious institutions and churches that are in low tension with sociocultural environment, move toward the high tension pole. However, there may at times also be opposite developments. When religious movements move toward less tension with their sociocultural environment they are called *church movements*.[72]

The concepts presented above allow much more variation in Matthew's social surrounding than does the classic church-sect distinction. The following picture presents a theoretical model of a post-70 CE situation. It is not an exhaustive description of the situation nor does it imply that all the groups presented by it existed. Rather, it sets forth a set of concepts predicted by Stark and Bainbridge's model. It also includes arrows reminding of the fact that societies and cultures usually interact with outsiders (foreign impulses) and change in the course of time (velocity of cultural change).[73] Since churches and religious institutions adapt to change, the direction and speed of their development matches the velocity of cultural change. Dotted lines leading to cult movement indicate that even new cults usually draw on tradition to some extent. In the next section, some of the concepts of the model are identified with Matthew's movement and its contemporaries.

---

[69] Stark and Bainbridge, *Theory*, 128.
[70] Stark and Bainbridge, *Theory*, 156.
[71] Stark and Bainbridge, *Theory*, 124.
[72] Stark and Bainbridge, *Theory*, 126.
[73] Cf. Stark and Bainbridge, *Theory*, 60–66.

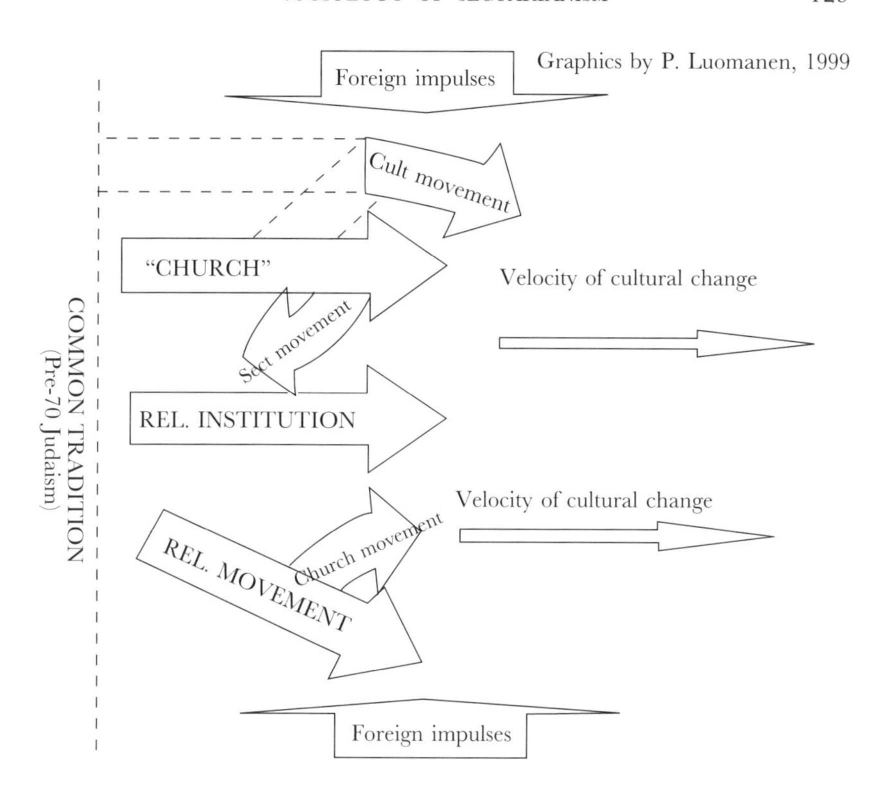

3.6. *Matthew's Community as a Cult Movement*

The role Matthew gives to Jesus marks the boundary between Matthew's group and his Jewish contemporaries. Within Matthew's narrative the disciples, obviously standing paradigmatically for the Christians of Matthew's time, acknowledge Jesus' position as Kyrios. Jewish leaders, however, never address Jesus with this name. For them he is only a teacher. This new "Jesus cult," connected with a liberal interpretation of the law, characterizes Matthew's community and distinguishes it from contemporary Jewish groups.[74] Although Jesus' role can be partly traced back to Jewish messianic expectations there is so much new to it that it can be regarded as a religious innovation. On the axis between sect and cult movements, Matthew's

[74] I have argued for this in Luomanen, *Entering*, 263–65, 278–84.

community finds its place closer to the cult end of the axis and can thus be characterized as a *cult movement.*[75]

The Pharisaic-scribal communities for their part can be best understood as the backbone of the synagogue *institution*, which continued its existence after the destruction of the Temple and managed to *adapt to change.*[76] In the Pharisaic-scribal communities there was also development, but this concerned the means of compensation: the temple cult was replaced with the study of the Torah.[77] This, however, happened within traditional Jewish modes of compensation. Thus the Pharisaic-scribal community can be understood as an institution within the Jewish subculture, but the relationships between Jews and local Roman authorities must have varied in the different parts of the Roman society.

In spite of everything new, there are also many traditional beliefs in Matthew's community. Especially on the level of symbolic universe, Matthew lays claim to the Jewish heritage of his community and legitimates the existence of his group in the same way as many sect movements do. Nevertheless, due the new elements the term *cult movement* characterizes the community better. In the long run it is clear that the form of Christianity which took over Matthew's gospel became *institutionalized* within the structures of the Roman empire.[78]

[75] R. Stark, "The Class Basis of Early Christianity: Inferences from a Sociological Model", *Sociological Analysis* 47 (1986) 223–24, has himself described the early church (i.e. Pauline Christianity) as a cult movement.

[76] It is to be kept in mind that there is always change in societies. Thus, in order to keep their positions, even institutions have to change; they adapt to their social surrounding (cf. Stark and Bainbridge's definition of institution cited above).

[77] See, Neusner, "Formation", 35–41.

[78] Cf. Proposition 300 in Stark and Bainbridge's theory (*Theory*, 270): Successful sects and cults tend to move toward lower tension. On this see also Holmberg, *Sociology*, 104–5.

THE DISCIPLES AND THE MESSIANIC SECRET IN MARK

Christopher Tuckett

It would be difficult to underestimate the significance of Heikki Räisänen's book *The "Messianic Secret" in Mark's Gospel.*[1] Although dealing primarily with the theme of the so-called "messianic secret" in Mark, Räisänen ranged far and wide over a large number of important broader issues relating to the interpretation of a text such as Mark's gospel. Above all, Räisänen pointed to the problematic nature of interpretations of Mark which assume too high a level of sophistication on the part of the author. In relation to the messianic secret, Räisänen's brilliant analysis made clearly visible the fault lines inherent in many previous interpretations of the secret in Mark. He also showed convincingly that "the" secret in Mark, i.e. the collection of different motifs considers together as part of "the" messianic secret ever since Wrede's epoch-making book of 1901,[2] should really be split up and seen as a conglomeration of different motifs, each serving a potentially different purpose. By no means the least impressive part of the analysis in the book is Räisänen's willingness to enter into critical dialogue with some of his own earlier views, to question some of his own previous results and to think through afresh many of the key issues in the debates concerned.[3]

[1] H. Räisänen, *The "Messianic Secret" in Mark's Gospel* (Edinburgh: T & T Clark, 1990).

[2] W. Wrede, *Das Messiasgeheimnis in den Evangelien* (Göttingen: Vandenhoeck & Ruprecht, 1901); ET *The Messianic Secret* (Cambridge: James Clarke, 1971).

[3] Räisänen's 1990 book represents the combining of two previous studies: *Die Parabletheorie im Markusevangelium* (PFES 26; Helsinki, 1973) and *Das "Messiasgeheimnis" im Markusevangelium. Ein redaktionskritischer Versuch* (PFES 28; Helsinki, 1976). However, the 1990 book was no mere straight translation into English of the earlier works; rather, the later book represented at a number of points a radical rewriting of many of the arguments of the earlier studies, and reached in some cases very different conclusions, at times arguing directly against Räisänen's own earlier claims. This was especially the case in relation to the analysis of the "parable theory" in Mark 4. Räisänen also rewrote the conclusion of his *Messiasgeheimnis* book; and it is part of that rewritten conclusion that is the focus of the present essay.

Heikki Räisänen has built up a formidable reputation as an international scholar in his own right; he has also nurtured and developed an impressive group of younger Finnish scholars in NT studies and related disciplines. Yet Räisänen has never apparently (or at least so it appears to an outsider!) encouraged any kind of cult following among his students or admirers. Rather, he has actively encouraged others to pursue their own ideas, rigorously and honestly, wherever that may lead them. Certainly it would appear that he has never regarded his own theories as sacrosanct and incapable of being re-evaluated, as his own rewriting of his book on the messianic secret makes clear. It is in that spirit that the present essay is offered to a good friend and a fine scholar, with thanks for many personal kindnesses as well as gratitude for the stimulation and interest which his work has aroused.

In this essay I would like to pursue further some of Räisänen's suggestions about the origin of the secrecy theme in Mark. And if I question some of the individual details of his suggestions, it is I believe only to press more positively the implications of other aspects many of his overall claims about the secrecy texts in Mark.

One of the most intriguing parts of Räisänen's latest book on the messianic secret concerns his claim that there might be a link between some of the secrecy elements in Mark and the Christians responsible for collecting and preserving the Q material in the gospels. Räisänen refers in this context to some aspects of the picture painted by Mark of the disciples in the gospel. Mark is well known for presenting the disciples in a poor light. In particular, the disciples are shown as failing to understand at many points in the narrative. As is well known, Wrede argued that this theme of the incomprehension of the disciples is to be regarded as part of the complex of secrecy texts in Mark, including commands to silence (to the demons, as well as to the disciples as in 8:30 and 9:9).

According to Räisänen (e.g. pp. 217–18),[4] the incomprehension of the disciples can be seen as focused in three areas. First, the disciples fail to recognise Jesus' true identity (as the divine Son of God) on the basis of the miracles they witness (cf. 4:41; 6:52; 8:17–21). Second, they fail to understand the fact that Jesus' teaching means the abrogation of the Jewish food laws (cf. 7:18, a "context which

[4] Page references in the body of the text refer to Räisänen, *Messianic Secret*.

hints at the Gentile mission": cf. the link between 7:14–23 and 7:24–30 [p. 218]). Third, they regularly show lack of understanding in relation to Jesus' teaching about the importance of the passion and the resurrection (cf. the well-known three-fold pattern in Mark where Jesus' prediction of his passion and resurrection in chs. 8, 9, 10 is followed by an indication that the disciples have failed to understand the implications of what Jesus has just said.)[5] However, in relation to the first of these categories, it is probable that in Mark the disciples *do* suddenly understand who Jesus is in 8:29: Peter confesses Jesus to be "the Christ" in a scene which Räisänen argues must be interpreted positively in Mark's view—Peter is expressing the valid *truth* about Jesus (p. 179: see below). However this confession is immediately silenced by Jesus (8:30). Similarly the (four) disciples see the unveiled glory of Jesus in the transfiguration, but they too are told not to tell anyone what they have seen until after the resurrection (9:9).

All this, Räisänen argues, shows a remarkable negative correlation with the Q material in the gospels (pp. 218–19). First, Q has a rather different perspective on the miracles: they are perhaps "signs of the inbreaking kingdom, (but) not indications of Jesus' divine nature of sonship" (p. 218); and indeed the Q temptation narrative seems to reject such a miracle-worker Christology. Second, "the Q tradition is by and large strictly Jewish in its orthopraxy (cf. Lk 16:17 par. Mt 5:18)" (p. 218), and Q "holds fast to traditional piety in relation to the Law, apart from a few disputed and late hints" (p. 252). Third, Q has no passion narrative and no accounts of resurrection appearances. Whilst no doubt Q Christians did not deny the resurrection, and did not ignore the passion completely, the emphasis lies elsewhere. In Q, "Jesus' fate is seen as part of the chain of prophetic deaths of which Israel is guilty according to the deuteronomistic view of things" (p. 252), in contrast to Mark's emphasis on the divine plan of Jesus' suffering. Further, Q has no idea of the vicarious nature

[5] After the first passion prediction in Mark 8:31, Peter rebukes Jesus in v. 32, only to provoke Jesus' stern reproof in v. 33. The second passion prediction in Mark 9:31 is immediately followed by the note that the disciples are discussing among themselves who is the greatest, again clearly failing to grasp the significance and relevance of Jesus' suffering. The third prediction in Mark 10:32–34 is immediately followed by the story of James and John asking for the chief seats in the kingdom, yet again showing their failure to grasp the significance of what Jesus has been telling them.

of Jesus' suffering as in Mark 10:45; 14:24. (Although this is not explicitly related to the disciples' failure to understand, 10:45 at least occurs within a broader context [8:31–10:52] where the disciples' incomprehension in relation to Jesus' suffering is a very much to the fore.) Finally, Q is totally silent about Jesus' "messiahship". The term "Christ" does not occur at all in Q. And although Jesus is occasionally called "Son (of God)", this is only in "later strands" of Q (p. 252) and in any case not as a divine being.

All this, Räisänen suggests, could be accounted for if Mark were engaged in some kind of critical dialogue with another group of Christians similar to, if not the same as, the group of Christians responsible for Q. Such Christians may have appealed to the teachings of the pre-Easter Jesus to support their case. In order to confront them, Mark had to meet them on their own ground. It was insufficient to argue on the basis of post-Easter developments or claims. Thus Mark ascribes the viewpoint he wishes to counter to the disciples who are shown in these respects to be uncomprehending. In one respect (but only in one respect) Räisänen thus aligns himself with the theories of those such as Weeden, Tyson and others who see Mark as engaged in critical debate with a contemporary group in his own situation, with the disciples as the representatives of this opposition group.[6] However, Räisänen also shows very clearly that such a theory cannot explain all that Mark says about the disciples in the narrative of the gospel and he provides a powerful critique of Weeden in this respect (pp. 211–14).[7] Räisänen therefore

[6] Cf. T.J. Weeden, "The Heresy that necessitated Mark's Gospel", *ZNW* 59 (1968) 145–58; repr. in W.R. Telford (ed.), *The Interpretation of Mark* (2nd ed.; Edinburgh: T & T Clark, 1995) 64–77; idem, *Mark: Traditions in Conflict* (Philadelphia: Fortress, 1971); J.B. Tyson, "The Blindness of the Disciples in Mark", *JBL* 80 (1961) 261–68; repr. in C.M. Tuckett (ed.), *The Messianic Secret* (London: SPCK, 1983) 35–43. Cf. too E. Trocmé, *The Formation of the Gospel of Mark* (London: SPCK, 1975); J.D. Crossan, "Mark and the Relatives of Jesus", *NovT* 15 (1973) 81–113.

[7] Weeden's theory fails to explain adequately the positive portrayal of the disciples in the earlier parts of the gospel (cf. Mark 1:16–20; 3:13–19; 6:7–13, where the disciples are called by Jesus and respond positively). Nor does it fully explain why the *disciples* are the ones who are warned about the dangers of the coming false people in Mark 13, allegedly (in Weeden's theory) the counterparts of the disciples themselves in the narrative. For other critiques of Weeden's theory about the presentation of the disciples in Mark, see especially R.C. Tannehill, "The Disciples in Mark: The Function of a Narrative Role", *JR* 57 (1977) 386–405; repr. in Telford (ed.), *Interpretation*, 169–95; E. Best, "The Role of the Disciples in Mark", *NTS* 23 (1977) 377–401; repr. in idem, *Disciples and Discipleship: Studies in the Gospel according to Mark* (Edinburgh: T & T Clark, 1986) 98–130; also E. Struthers Malbon, "Text and Contexts: Interpreting the Disciples in Mark", *Semeia* 62 (1993) 81–102.

does *not* argue that Mark's polemic is directed against the disciples in the story as such. For the disciples in the story *do* come to realise who Jesus is (Mk 8:29). Thus the true significance of Jesus is perceived by the disciples, though not by all since the disciples are silenced! The disciples themselves thus represent the Markan viewpoint; and it is the *earlier* view of the disciples that is the real focus of any critique by Mark.

> The disciples are not seen as representing Mark's opponents; rather they are the vehicles for Mark's *own* point of view. They did comprehend, although neither very soon nor very well. The 'opponents', however, have preserved the early and limited view of the disciples, whereas the disciples' mature perception lives on in the tradition of Mark himself. (p. 222)

> With the aid of the secrecy theme, Mark tries to reject the claims of people like the bearers of the Q-tradition who appealed to the authority of the historical Jesus. Mark defends (unjustifiably at the historical level) his Hellenistic viewpoint by showing that the disputed points go back to Jesus himself. However, not everyone knew about it. Palestinian wandering preachers still put forward a defective Christology, misunderstand the importance of the resurrection, misunderstand the meaning of the passion, hold fast to the old attitude to the Law, and are suspicious about the Gentile mission. They are re-presenting the obsolete viewpoint of the disciples at the time of their failure to understand; however, the disciples gave this up, partly during the lifetime of Jesus, but definitively after Easter. (p. 254)

In all this there is much to agree with and much that is very persuasive. That Mark may be engaged in an element of polemic, speaking *to* other Christians quite as much as speaking *for* them, seems to me entirely credible. The possibility that Mark is seeking to *address* other Christians in his own situation and *challenge* their views, rather than (as in the classic form-critical model) simply reflect their already existing situation, seems to me very plausible. Certainly the extended teaching by Jesus in Mark 8:31–10:52 on the importance of suffering—his own as well as potentially that of any would-be disciple—seems to make much better sense if it is addressed to a community that is not yet suffering than the older, traditional view that Mark is (simply) reflecting a situation of a community that is already suffering.

Further, the theory that the object of any "polemic", or any "targeted address", is *not* the counterpart of the disciples themselves in the story is also convincing. The full-blown theory of Weeden and others, that Mark is engaged in a sustained polemic against a group of "heretics" in his community, represented by the disciples in the story, is probably untenable. Talk of "heresy" is almost certainly somewhat anachronistic in this context; and, as already noted, the view that the disciples tout court represent Mark's "opposition group" is not really sustainable. As Räisänen himself and others have argued, there is enough that is positive about the disciples, whether explicit or implicit, to suggest that a Weeden-type theory of a sustained polemic against the disciples is not true to the text of Mark as a whole.[8] Nevertheless, Räisänen's explanation of the origin of this part of the secrecy complex may provoke some questions in relation to some of the other details concerned.

Mark and Q?

Some questions might arise in relation to Q. In one way this might not matter at all in relation to Räisänen's theory. As he himself says, "In the final analysis, it does not matter whether Mark was in debate with precisely the bearers of the Q tradition. It could be a question of quite *different* people who *were appealing to the historical Jesus*." (p. 251: his stress). Nevertheless, an appeal to Q could serve to anchor the alleged opposition group proposed within history by relating such a group to a more concrete historical reality "known" to exist.[9]

An implied negative attitude to miracles, or at least a not sufficiently positive attitude to miracles and a failure to relate miracles to Jesus' identity as a divine Son of God, is not necessarily easy to relate to Q. It is true that Q does not (apparently) record many miracles. Yet Q does quite clearly regard the miracles of Jesus as important and as indicating at least something of significance about Jesus' identity. Thus the saying in Q 11:20 ("If I by the spirit/finger of God cast about demons, then the kingdom of God has come upon you") asserts

[8] See n. 7 above. One should also note that the reference in Mark 16:7 almost certainly implies (though it does not explicitly relate) the rehabilitation of the disciples after Easter: on this see especially N. Petersen, "When is the End not the End? Literary Reflections on the Ending of Mark's Narrative", *Int* 34 (1980) 151–66.

[9] Provided of course one accepts that Q, and Q Christians, are "known" to exist! I myself would be more than happy to accept this, but one must remember that others would dispute the existence of Q, and/or the existence of a specific group of Q Christians, very vigorously.

that with the exorcisms of Jesus, the kingdom of God has in some sense arrived already. By implication at least, Jesus' exorcistic activity implies something of great significance about his own person. So too, in the account of the messengers of John the Baptist coming to Jesus (Q 7:18–23), Jesus is asked whether he is the "coming one". The reply (in Q 7:22) is at least in part focused on Jesus' *miracles* of making the blind see, the lame walk, of cleansing lepers, and raising the dead. Further, in context the reply is evidently taken as an affirmative response to the question of the Baptist. Clearly then the miracles *do* attest to Jesus' identity. Any reference to a lack of explicit stories of detailed miracles should perhaps be treated with some caution: any (relative) silence in Q should not be assumed to indicate a more positive lack of interest too hastily.[10] And even the temptation narrative in Q may need a little more care. There may be an element of polemic against demands for a particular kind of miracle, e.g. a very "showy" demonstration of divine power for the sake of it. But in this Q may be no different from Mark (cf. Mark 8:11–12).[11]

Whether Q's miracles indicate a rather "lower" Christology than Mark is also debatable. Q 7:18–23 indicates that the miracles of Jesus imply that he is indeed the "coming one", who in Q is probably to be equated with the "Son of Man" figure and also as such will be involved in the final judgment (cf. Q 12:8; 12:40; 17:23–30).[12] It is true that Q does not relate the miracles explicitly to Jesus' status as a "Son of God". But whether Mark means by this that Jesus is a fully divine being must also remain debatable. The references to Jesus as Son of Man in Q certainly imply some transcendent features!

Q's attitude to the Law may fit Räisänen's suggested reconstruction better in one way. Q does indeed seem to have a rather conservative attitude to the Law: Q 16:17 appears to assert the abiding validity of the Law; and Q 11:42d also goes out of the way to assert

---

[10] Cf. J.S. Kloppenborg, "The Sayings Gospel Q and the Quest of the Historical Jesus", *HTR* 89 (1996) 307–44, esp. pp. 320–22 on the miracles in Q. More generally on the dangers of reading too much into the silence of Q, see M. Frenschkowski, "Welche biographischen Kenntnisse von Jesus setzt die Logienquelle voraus?", in Jon Ma. Asgeirsson et al. (eds.), *From Quest to Q: Festschrift James M. Robinson* (BETL 146; Leuven: Leuven University Press & Peeters, 2000) 3–42.

[11] On the temptation narrative in Q, see my "The Temptation Narrative in Q", in F. Van Segbroek et al. (eds.), *The Four Gospels 1992* (FS Frans Neirynck; 3 vols.; BETL 100; Leuven: Leuven University Press & Peeters, 1992) 1.479–507.

[12] Cf. D.R. Catchpole, *The Quest for Q* (Edinburgh: T & T Clark, 1993) 60–78.

that the smaller details of the Law (here on tithing) should not be abrogated even by reference to broader general principles of love, mercy etc. Further, it is arguable that both the sayings represent secondary, editorial glosses on earlier traditions to ensure Torah observance by Christians: thus Q 16:17 may be guarding against a possible interpretation of Q 16:16 ("the Law and the prophets were until John") which might be taken as implying that the Law belonged to an the old era and had now lost some of its validity. So too Q 11:42d looks like a correction to an earlier tradition which might have called into question the value of the practice of tithing.[13] On the other hand, one should not forget that it is Q that preserves the radical statement of Jesus "Let the dead bury their dead" (Q 9:60) which seems at first (and second!) sight to question important OT laws about family obligations.[14]

Q's attitude to the passion and death of Jesus and the resurrection is also not so clear, partly again because of the partial silence in Q. Yet, as before, silence may be dangerous if over-interpreted. In any case, as Räisänen himself says, Q is not completely silent about Jesus' death (at least by implication), probably seeing it as in a line of continuity with the violence suffered by all God's prophets in the past (cf. Q 6:22; 11:49–51; 13:34–35).[15] Moreover, any would-be disciple must be prepared to suffer the same fate by "taking up the cross" (Q 14:27). The overall scheme of may be different from Mark's, but it is no less real for that.

It is thus not entirely easy to equate Mark's "opponents" as reconstructed by Räisänen specifically with the Q tradents although, as already noted, that may not be important. (On the other hand, some such historical anchor would do no harm to the theory! A group of

---

[13] On Q and the Law, see the discussion in my *Q and the History of Early Christianity* (Edinburgh: T & T Clark, 1996) 404–24, with reference to other literature and previous discussions.

[14] Räisänen also relates the issue of food laws to that of the Gentile mission, suggesting that a conservative attitude to the food laws may be connected with a negative attitude to the Gentile missions (cf. above). The question of Q's attitude to the Gentile mission is uncertain: cf. my *Q and the History*, 393–404 for a full discussion. There is little that tells positively in favour of a Gentile mission in Q, but equally no sign of clear opposition to such a mission. Perhaps then Q was aware of the Gentile mission, but Q Christians were not actively engaged in it: their prime concern was to address their fellow-Jews.

[15] Cf. J.S. Kloppenborg, "'Easter Faith' and the Sayings Gospel Q", *Semeia* 49 (1990) 71–99.

"Christians" who cannot discern that the proper (or perhaps any) significance of Jesus' miracles, who see little if any significance in his death and resurrection, and who remain firmly wedded to obedience to the Jewish Law does begin to look more like a group of Jewish opponents of Jesus and/or the Christian movement than of any Christian followers of Jesus!) What though of the theory in relation to the interpretation of Mark's gospel itself?

The Disciples in Mark

Räisänen's theory succeeds brilliantly in combining aspects of the disciples' incomprehension in Mark and some of the secrecy charges in one overall explanation. Nevertheless, the individual parts of the theory fit together slightly unevenly. In relation to the miracles and the identity of Jesus, Räisänen's theory makes the opposition view correlate with the *earlier*, "uncorrected" view of the disciples: the disciples early on failed to grasp who Jesus was, but later come to see (and are silenced). However, in relation to the food laws, and to the passion and resurrection, there is no such progression from incomprehension to enlightenment clearly visible. The disciples remain unable to accept the necessity of Jesus to suffer almost right to the end (certainly they all desert Jesus in the end and Peter denies him).[16]

So too there is no "Damascus road experience" in relation to the food laws. If the disciples are not "seeing the light" in the debate in Mark 7, they do not see any light on this issue any more clearly later in the story. (Unless of course Jesus' explanation himself in Mark 7:19 implies that the disciples have now moved from a position of incomprehension to one of understanding: see below.) If though one extends the issue to consider Law observance more widely, it is noticeable that the disciples *earlier* in the story are portrayed as behaving without any apparent constraint in relation to another key contemporary legal issue, viz. Sabbath observance. In Mark 2:23–28, it is the disciples who are doing things which (apparently) break the Law[17] and Jesus defends *their* actions, not his own.

---

[16] As noted earlier (n. 8), Mark 16:7 may well *imply* a rehabilitation for the disciples, but it is at best only implicit!

[17] There has been debate about what exactly the disciples were doing here that was regarded as illegal. Clearly there is scope for debate at the historical level.

Similarly at the start of Mark 7, the disciples apparently show no qualms about eating with unwashed hands, an action which (whatever the historical difficulties) Mark appears to assume runs counter to universally held Jewish legal traditions (cf. v. 3). One could perhaps argue that the disciples of Mark 2 act as the Markan counterbalance to the disciples of Mark 7:17, similar to the way in which the insight of the Peter of Mark 8:29 counterbalances the disciples' earlier ignorance. But in the case of Law observance, the relative order seems a little difficult since the "Law-free" disciples come before the disciples showing scruples (or ignorance) about the food laws.

In any case it is not certain how far the words of Jesus' response to the disciples in Mark 7:18 ("Do you also fail to understand? Do you not see that whatever goes into a person from outside . . .") are to be seen as on a par with some of the other elements in Mark illustrating the disciples' failure to understand (e.g. 4:13; 6:52; 8:17–21). The language here is probably redactional, and hence probably one can justifiably see the Mark's hand at work.[18] Yet one must say that any rebuke of the disciples here seems relatively mild. Others have argued in any case that many of the rebukes of the disciples in Mark are rather milder than the language of, say, 4:11–12. The words of Mark 8:17–21, similar in one way to the language of 4:11–12 and apparently equating the disciples with "those outside", are probably to be punctuated as questions and there is no definitive statement of the impossibility of any future repentance and forgiveness.[19]

However, for Mark himself, there seems to be no question that the disciples have broken Sabbath law. The only point at issue is how that is to be explained and justified.

[18] Räisänen, *Messianic Secret*, 196. Cf. also R. Pesch, *Das Markusevangelium* (2 vols.; HTKNT II; Freiburg: Herder, 1984) 1.380; R.A. Guelich, *Mark 1–8:26* (WBC 34A; Dallas: Word Books, 1989) 377.

[19] Cf. A.M. Ambrozic, *The Hidden Kingdom* (CBQMS 2; Washington: Catholic Biblical Association, 1972) 69; J. Marcus, *The Mystery of the Kingdom of God* (SBLDS 90; Atlanta: Scholars Press, 1986) 101; also my "Mark's Concerns in the Parables Chapter (Mark 4,1–34)", *Biblica* 69 (1988) 1–25, on p. 12.

Räisänen also seeks to correlate broader aspects of the rebuke of Mark 7:18 with the rebuke in Mark 4:13 by saying that both occur in contexts relating to the Gentile mission: Mark 7:14–32 is connected with 7:24–30, and 4:13 is "in a context devoted to mission problems" (p. 218). However, while Räisänen has argued very persuasively that many of the broad concerns in Mark 4:1–34 are about mission, it is not easy to relay 4:13 is particular to such concerns directly. Mark 4:13 itself is about the ability/inability to understand the *parables* themselves.

The words of Mark 7:18 are in one sense even milder. They are clearly formulated as questions rather than as a condemnatory statements. Further, while the question in the first part of the verse ("Are you too ἀσύνετοι?") stands on its own grammatically, the words in the second half ("do you not understand?") is not presented so absolutely: rather it is couched in the form of an expanded sentence, "do you not understand *that*...", with the clear implication that, immediately after the rhetorical question has been uttered, they *will* understand![20] Indeed this may then provide the immediate answer to the question in the first part of the verse about their being ἀσύνετοι: although their initial question implied they do not understand, Jesus' reply immediately places them in a position where they do. The words of Mark 7:18 may therefore be functioning more as simply an enabling device to move the dialogue on so that Jesus can give the clear explanation of the (possibly) enigmatic saying in 7:15.[21]

As already noted, all this could in one way fit Räisänen's theory well. The uncomprehending disciples of Mark 7:17 *are* now enlightened by Jesus in v. 18 and hence no longer lack understanding. However, one wonders if this is pressing the details of v. 17 a little too far. Certainly within the pericope Mark 7:1–23 as a whole, and even within that this section of the pericope in 7:15–23, the note about the disciples occupies a very small role: the bulk of the space is devoted to the substance of Jesus' teaching, the statement in v. 15 and its subsequent elaboration in vv. 18–23. Any rebuke of the disciples here seems to be a very subsidiary motif that receives virtually no emphasis at all in the structuring of the narrative. It may therefore be better to see the note about the disciples' intervention as simply a (redactional!) device to enable the Markan Jesus to move on and to spell out the full implications of the saying in v. Mark 7:15 (as perhaps also in 10:10–12, though there without any explicit rebuke).

[20] This is then in quite striking contrast to e.g. Mark 8:17 οὔπω νοεῖτε οὐδὲ συνίετε; Here the two verbs are used absolutely; and nothing in the story at that point seems to imply that they do understand even by the end of the incident in the boat.

[21] Cf. J. Gnilka, *Die Verstockung Israels: Isaias 6.9–10 in der Theologie der Synoptiker* (SANT 3; München: Kösel, 1961) 33; idem, *Das Evangelium nach Markus* (2 vols.; EKKNT 2; Neukirchen: Neukirchener, 1978–79) 1.285. For similarities in this respect between Mark and other Greco-Roman literature, see V.K. Robbins, *Jesus the Teacher: A Socio-Rhetorical Interpretation of Mark* (Philadelphia: Fortress, 1984) 65 (with particular reference to Xenophon's *Memorabilia*).

What then of the situation of the disciples in relation to the miracles? Räisänen places much emphasis on the role of Peter's confession in the story as the point at which the disciples move from a situation of total incomprehension to one of full understanding about the identity of Jesus. Thus Räisänen says:

> After the first half of the gospel, there is no more uncertainty amongst the disciples in relation to their Master. In this respect Peter's confession really does mark a turning point. Questions like 4.41 do not occur any more. Yet the disciples' lack of understanding is not set aside. It is simply its nature which is different.... The disciples do not understand Jesus' talk about his *suffering* and his *resurrection*. (pp. 204–5)

Further, Räisänen makes a very strong case (against, for example, Weeden) for the view that Mark regards Peter's confession in positive terms, or at least not in negative terms (p. 179). The structure of the pericope *contrasts* Peter's confession with the views of the "others"; the latter are clearly inadequate from Mark's point of view—hence Peter's words are by implication more adequate. So too the words of Peter are silenced by Jesus (Mark 8:30) in a way similar to the cries of the demons being silenced (e.g. Mark 3:11–12); in the latter case, the words of the demons themselves express things of which Mark approves—hence the same probably applies in the case of Peter's confession.[22] There is thus no justification for the theory that Peter has expressed a view about Jesus of which Mark disapproves (e.g. Jesus as the "Christ" means Jesus as the wonder-working "divine man", a Christology which Mark allegedly rejects).[23]

Nevertheless, it may still be the case that Mark implies an element of reserve about Peter's confession. Mark does not think that Peter's confession is completely wrong. But that does not necessarily mean that Mark thinks that Peter's confession is completely right! Räisänen has argued strongly that Mark should not be seen as too sophisti-

[22] Cf. too M.D. Hooker, *The Message of Mark* (London: Epworth, 1983) 54; D.R. Catchpole, "The 'Triumphal' Entry", in E. Bammel & C.F.D. Moule (eds.), *Jesus and the Politics of His Day* (Cambridge: Cambridge University Press, 1985) 319–34, on p. 326.

[23] See e.g. Weeden, *Traditions in Conflict*, 51–69, esp. pp. 64–65. More recently, cf. the similar view (at least in relation to the evaluation of Mark's attitude to Peter's confession) in W.R. Telford, *The Theology of the Gospel of Mark* (Cambridge: Cambridge University Press, 1999) 40 ("Christ" represents a Jewish-Christian Davidic messiahship which Mark rejects).

cated a writer, and that it is time for the pendulum to swing back.[24] Yet as Räisänen himself has said (in relation to a slightly different context), "the pendulum will have to swing back to the older position, perhaps to stop half-way".[25] Mark may not be as sophisticated as John, but equally he may not be totally unsophisticated (hence the value of the suggestion that any pendulum should perhaps only swing back "half-way"!); and any single issue may not be answerable in very simple either-or, black-and-white terms. Thus the way is still open I believe for Peter's confession being regarded by Mark as certainly not wrong, but perhaps not completely right either.

Certainly it is the case that Mark implies an element of reserve about Peter himself, as is clear from Mark 8:33. As Räisänen himself recognises too, the incomprehension of the disciples continues on after Mark 8:29, even if (as Räisänen argues) it is of a different form: from uncertainty about Jesus' identity to incomprehension about the necessity of the passion. Yet even in relation to the miracles, it is not so clear that very much changes with Mark 8:29. It is true that questions after miracles such as the "Who is this?" of Mark 4:41 no longer reappear as such in the second half of the gospel. On the other hand, for whatever reason, very few miracles appear at all after Mark 8:29. But in so far as the question of Mark 4:41 is put in slightly more explicit terms in relation to what Peter and others *lack*, it is in relation to their lack of "*faith*" (cf. Jesus' rebuke in 4:40: "do you not yet have faith?"). And in one of the two miracles which do occur in the second half of the gospel, the story of the epileptic child in Mark 9:14–29, it is striking that the disciples cannot heal the child and Jesus upbraids all concerned (including by implication the disciples) for being "faithless" (cf. 9:19: "O faithless generation", also 9:22 and the discussion between Jesus and the child's father about "believing"/showing faith). It is then not so clear, even in relation to the miracles, that the disciples are in a very different position after Mark 8:29 to what they were before. They

[24] This is the main thrust of Räisänen, *Messianic Secret*, ch. 1.

[25] The translation of the conclusion of Räisänen's earlier *Messiasgeheimnis*, 167–68, in Tuckett (ed.), *Messianic Secret*, 139. The contrast there was between the picture of Mark as a collector of traditions (as the older form critics postulated) and the picture of Mark as an original thinker with his own theology (as more recent redaction criticism has proposed).

still show the lack of "faith" which earlier prevented them from seeing who Jesus is.

A similar, slightly more ambivalent attitude to Peter's confession might be shown by the use of Χριστός here and elsewhere in Mark. Mark's attitude to Χριστός is not at all clear. Räisänen argues against the view that there is any sharp contrast between "Christ" and "Son of Man" here; rather, "for Mark, it does not seem to be decisive which title he uses, although 'Son of God' seems to be the most congenial" (p. 180). In any case, Son of Man cannot be seen as correcting Son of God, e.g. in the transfiguration story, since "Son of God" is the term used by God Himself. The last point is undoubtedly true and must tell powerfully against the (by now older) view that Mark is giving a "corrective Christology", "correcting" the allegedly defective term Son of God, with his own preferred term Son of Man.[26] Nevertheless, it is still not clear how Χριστός fits into all this.[27]

A case certainly can be made for Mark regarding Χριστός in thoroughly positive terms.[28] It is after all present in the opening "title" verse of the gospel (Mark 1:1: "The beginning of the gospel of Jesus *Christ*") which clearly announces to the reader the terms which Mark wishes to present as the true categories in which Jesus is to be seen. So too the question of the high priest at the Sanhedrin trial (Mark 14:61: "Are you with the Christ, the Son of the Blessed?") seems to place "Christ" and "Son of God/the Blessed" in parallel as virtually synonymous. Nevertheless, one wonders if the two can be equated completely. "Christ" is still relatively rare in Mark's gospel and sometimes the noun loses its definite article completely, becoming virtu-

[26] In addition to Weeden, cf. e.g. N. Perrin, "The Christology of Mark. A Study in Methodology", *JR* 51 (1971) 173–187; repr. in Telford (ed.), *Interpretation*, 125–40; N.R. Petersen, *Literary Criticism for New Testament Critics* (Philadelphia: Fortress, 1978) 62–68; P.J. Achtemeier, *Mark* (2nd ed.; Philadelphia: Fortress, 1986) 53–65. For a full discussion and critique of the idea of Mark as offering a "corrective Christology", see J.D. Kingsbury, *The Christology of Mark's Gospel* (Philadelphia: Fortress, 1983) 25–45.

[27] In any case the fact that "Son of Man" does not correct "Son of God" need not say anything about the relationship between "Christ" and "Son of Man" in Mark (unless "Christ" and "Son of God" are regarded as synonymous: see below).

[28] See e.g. J.R. Donahue, "Temple, Trial and Royal Christology. Mark 14:53–65", in W. Kelber (ed.), *The Passion in Mark: Studies in Mark 14–16* (Philadelphia: Fortress, 1976) 61–79; D.H. Juel, "The Origin of Mark's Christology", in J.H. Charlesworth (ed.), *The Messiah: Developments in Judaism and Early Christianity* (Minneapolis: Fortress, 1992) 449–60; also Kingsbury, *Christology*, passim.

ally just another proper name for Jesus (as in 1:1; 9:41).[29] Further, the key climactic moments in the gospel of the revelation of who Jesus is, *apart* from Mark 8:30, are more in terms of Jesus as Son of God. Hence God Himself speaks at the baptism and the transfiguration to declare that Jesus is His Son (Mark 1:11; 9:7); and the centurion at the moment of Jesus' death declares that he is a/the son/Son of God (Mark 15:39).[30]

Further, what Mark wishes apparently to claim about Jesus in his capacity as Son of God seems to go considerably further than the category of Jewish messiahship. It is for example arguable that the centurion's confession of Jesus as Son of God shows Jesus as the revelation of God Himself.[31] The confession comes immediately after the note about the torn veil; and if the "veil" concerned is the thought of as the veil within the Holy of Holies,[32] preventing human beings from seeing God, then the tearing of the veil implies that God Himself has become visible. For Mark this however happens precisely in the moment of Jesus' death on the cross: God becomes visible in the crucified one. This provides an extraordinarily powerful narrative of Christology and theology; and it is far removed from any ideas of Jewish messiahship. Thus Mark has no wish to deny that Jesus can be seen as a Χριστός figure. But it may be that this

---

[29] Hence despite the presence of the word Χριστός in 1:1, one wonders how important that term really is for Mark there since it lacks the article and appears almost just as a proper name for Jesus. Cf. M. de Jonge, "The Earliest Christian Use of *Christos*: Some Suggestions", *NTS* 32 (1986) 321–43, on p. 325: Mark "does not want to emphasize Jesus' messiahship [in 1:1], but uses the double expression 'Jesus Christ' as many Christians before and after him without any titular overtones. The emphasis is on 'the Son of God'." Cf. too Telford, *Theology*, 39, for some distinction between "Christ" and "Son of God" for Mark; I am however not persuaded by Telford's apparent view that Mark disapproves or rejects the Christ title for Jesus: Mark 8:29 in its context would seem to tell decisively against that (see above).

[30] I remain convinced, despite the long-standing debate, that Mark at least thinks that the centurion is confessing Jesus to be the Son of God (not just a son of a god). However, cf. the recent article of W.T. Shiner, "The Ambiguous Pronouncement of the Centurion and the Shrouding of Meaning in Mark", *JSNT* 78 (2000) 3–22, who argues that the centurion's words may be deliberately ambiguous: nevertheless, Shiner still argues that, for the audience of Mark, the meaning of the words is clear.

[31] See H.L. Chronis, "The Torn Veil: Cultus and Christology in Mark 15:37–39", *JBL* 101 (1982) 97–114. Cf. also R.H. Lightfoot, *The Gospel Message of St. Mark* (Oxford: Oxford University Press, 1950) 56; M.D. Hooker, *The Gospel according to St Mark* (London: A. & C. Black, 1991) 378.

[32] I am fully aware that this is debatable!

does *not* express the most profound truth about Jesus. For that, Mark uses the category Son of God. I remain therefore unpersuaded that Mark's christological terms are almost interchangeable (cf. above: "it does not seem decisive which title he [Mark] uses").

There may therefore be a case for reviving the view that Peter's confession represents a *partial* insight into the true nature of Jesus is identity. There has been a firm tradition of interpretation of Mark that relates Peter's confession to the immediately preceding story of the healing of the blind man at Bethsaida (8:22–26).[33] Further, the fact that the man is healed in stages has sometimes been related to Peter's personal odyssey, with the intermediate stage of half-seeing corresponding to the insight represented by Peter's confession here.[34] Räisänen questions such a view, saying that the disciples do not come to see who Jesus is gradually. "They see suddenly and unprepared, clearly and correctly" (p. 204). That they see suddenly and unprepared is undoubtedly correct.[35] That they see clearly and correctly may however be more questionable. As Räisänen himself goes on to say, "Looked at from another point of view, they see all the time only dimly (8:32–33!)". Maybe then that is the point. They do see suddenly, but that sight remains only dim and as yet unclear.

In any case, for Mark Jesus' identity is not just to be equated with any titles or words which human beings use. Or rather, Jesus' identity is not exhausted by such titles, as if the words alone are enough. Indeed there may be a real sense in which the reason why Mark writes his gospel story is precisely to put what he regards as the "true" meaning into the words/titles which may on their own be a little ambiguous.[36] Thus Mark announces, at least to the reader, right at the start of the gospel the terms of the story that is to follow.

---

[33] Cf. e.g. Gnilka, *Markusevangelium*, 1.314–5; E. Best, *Following Jesus: Discipleship in the Gospel of Mark* (Sheffield: JSOT Press, 1981) 134; D. Lührmann, *Das Markusevangelium* (HNT 3; Tübingen: Mohr, 1987) 140; Guelich, *Mark 1–8:26*, 430; Hooker, *Mark*, 200. Others cited in Räisänen, *Messianic Secret*, 203–4.

[34] See Best, *Following Jesus*, 135; E.S. Johnson, "Mark VIII.22–26: the Blind Man from Bethsaida", *NTS* 25 (1979) 370–383, esp. pp. 381–3; Guelich, *Mark 1–8:26*, 436; Hooker, ibid.

[35] Hence there is no question of any gradually dawning realisation on the part of the disciples, and hence too it is extremely unlikely that we see here anything historically factual about the original disciples themselves.

[36] Similarly (though in slightly different vein) Kingsbury, *Christology*, 100–1: "Destiny and identity are inextricably bound together. One cannot comprehend who Jesus is without at the same time comprehending what it is that God accomplishes in him." Cf. too Achtemeier, *Mark*, 59.

The story is about Jesus who is "Christ" and "Son of God" (Mark 1:1).[37] The correctness of a latter term is confirmed by no less a figure than God Himself in the story of the baptism.[38] Yet what these words really mean when ascribed to Jesus remains to be seen. And it is in a sense the rest of the story—and the whole of the rest of the story—that supply the relevant "filling out" of the term: Jesus is seen most clearly as the Son of God in the moment of his death.[39]

In all this the scene at Caesarea Philippi plays a part. One aspect—but perhaps only one aspect—of Jesus' identity is his ability to perform miracles. This Mark does not deny and certainly does not reject.[40] It may then be that it is this aspect that is implicitly affirmed by Peter in his confession.[41] But one cannot necessarily leave things are there—and indeed Mark does not leave things there! This is after all only half the story Mark chooses to tell! Mark then immediately follows the confession with Jesus' talk of his suffering (as Son of Man) and Peter's evident unwillingness/inability to accept any of this, thus revealing Peter's lack of understanding of this aspect of Jesus' role and/or identity. Mark's arrangement may thus imply at least a modification of Peter's confession. Peter may not be wrong in what he says and implies; but perhaps Peter is not fully right—yet!

This then may be the reason for the silencing command in Mark 8:30. Jesus' identity cannot be fully grasped until the end of the story at the cross, and hence Peter is silenced. Räisänen rightly points to

---

[37] Despite the variation in the manuscripts, I remain convinced that the words υἱοῦ θεοῦ should be read in Mark 1:1 as a genuine part of the text of Mark.

[38] See Kingsbury, *Christology*, 66. Hence any theory that Mark is in any way negative about the category "Son of God" applied to Jesus (and e.g. wants to correct it by "Son of Man") seems unconvincing.

[39] See F.J. Matera, "The Prologue as the Interpretative Key to Mark's Gospel", *JSNT* 34 (1988) 3–20; repr. in Telford (ed.), *Interpretation*, 289–306.

[40] Hence contra Weeden: see Räisänen, *Messianic Secret*, 204; cf. too Telford, *Theology*, 50.

[41] However, it must then also be conceded that this also goes far beyond what is normally predicated of a "messianic" figure within Judaism. Though cf. de Jonge, "Earliest Christian Use", who seeks to exploit the (admittedly limited) evidence that David was occasionally seen as a prophet and exorcist, and hence the Davidic Messiah would be so regarded as well. See his most recent exposition of this view (though relating it more to the historical Jesus than to Mark) in his *God's Final Envoy: Early Christology and Jesus' Own View of His Mission* (Grand Rapids: Eerdmans, 1998) 98–106, responding to the critique of W.A. Meeks, "Asking Back to Jesus' Identity", in M.C. de Boer (ed.), *From Jesus to John: Essays on Jesus and New Testament Christology in Honour of Marinus de Jonge* (JSNTSup 84; Sheffield: Sheffield Academic Press, 1993) 38–50, on pp. 46–47.

the fact that Mark's gospel and this section in the gospel, would still present a powerful statement of the importance of the cross and a *theologia crucis* without the silencing command of v. Mark 8:30: the *theologia crucis* comes through in vv. 31ff. and vv. 34ff., almost irrespective of v. 30 (p. 180). This is true. Yet perhaps the silencing command can still reinforce what is present elsewhere in Mark's text. (On their own, without any such reinforcing elements, the silencing commands would be almost unintelligible!) And as Räisänen himself says, the messianic secret is not the only thing which is present in Mark but is rather one motif among many others (p. 258).

Conclusion

The motif of the incomprehension of the disciples may therefore not be quite as unitary as has been suggested. One of the great achievements of Räisänen's book was to show clearly that the whole complex of secrecy texts assembled by Wrede and explained as part of a single "messianic secret" (singular!) has to be split up into different elements with perhaps separate explanations for each. Thus the "parable theory" (Mark 4:11–12), or the silencing commands after some of the miracles which are disobeyed (Mark 1:44; 7:36, as opposed to the silencing commands after the exorcisms or to the disciples, which are generally obeyed) are to be explained differently from the "real" messianic secret. But then exactly the same may apply to the motif of the incomprehension of the disciples. Different aspects of the disciples' incomprehension may function in different ways in the story. Räisänen is in my view convincing in his suggestion that an element of polemic—or at least a "speaking *to*" rather than just a "speaking *for*"—underlies at least part of this material in Mark. Where I would raise a query is over the question whether it underlies as much of the material in Mark about the disciples' failure to understand as Räisänen suggests. In particular, the note about the disciples' question in Mark 7:17 and the (semi?) rebuke by Jesus in 7:18 may be functioning rather differently in the narrative, i.e. simply as a device to enable the teaching of Jesus to be clarified and developed.

The other motifs of the disciples' lack of understanding may indeed belong more closely together and may indeed be part of what Räisänen calls the "real" messianic secret. They do concern Jesus' identity and how and where that identity can or should be perceived.

So too it is clear that part of the issue focuses on the significance of Jesus' identity in relation to his miracles. Yet it may be that Mark is trying to say not so much that the miracles clearly testify to who Jesus is, but rather that the miracles *in part* testify to who Jesus is; however, there is more to Jesus than (just) being a miracle-worker.

In part then this essay is an attempt to plead for a revival of theories such as Weeden's, though in a much less extreme form. Weeden is almost certainly mistaken in regarding the disciples as complete villains in the story. Räisänen and other have shown that all too clearly. So too Mark is not opposed to the view that Jesus is to be seen as (primarily) a miracle-worker. There is simply too much material in Mark supporting that kind of a Christology to make such a theory tenable. Again Räisänen and others are right to point to this as a fundamental weakness in Weeden's reconstruction. Nevertheless, the possibility that Mark might still be wanting to imply an element of reserve about such a view of Jesus should not be ruled out of consideration too quickly. Weeden's overall theory may have some elements of truth in it, elements of a "baby" which should not be thrown out with the rest of the less convincing "bath water" too quickly. Mark does portray the disciples coming to see who Jesus is, and Mark guides his readers through that odyssey. It is a journey that takes on board positively the miracle-working activity of Jesus; but, as the gospel as a whole indicates, that part of the journey only takes one half way. The rest of the journey of discovery about who Jesus is, or rather about what is means to call Jesus by the various terms and "titles", is filled in by the second half of the gospel, climaxing in the account of Jesus' life and death.[42]

Few would doubt that Mark does present a powerful "theology of the cross" in his gospel. Perhaps then the part played by the disciples and their lack of understanding in the narrative should indeed be seen as an integral part of that overall guiding theological theme in Mark's presentation of the "gospel" which he presents to his readers.

[42] Such a view is of course by no means very original in the history of scholarship: cf. for example U. Luz, "The Secrecy Motif and the Marcan Christology", in Tuckett (ed.), *Messianic Secret*, 75–96, esp. pp. 86–88 (German original: *ZNW* 56 [1965] 9–30); H.D. Betz, "Jesus as Divine Man", in F.T. Trotter (ed.), *Jesus and the Historian* (FS Ernest Cadman Colwell; Philadelphia: Westminster Press, 1963) 114–33. Others in Kingsbury, *Christology*, 29–30; Räisänen, *Messianic Secret*, 63–64.

CONFLICTING VOICES, IRONY AND REITERATION: AN EXPLORATION OF THE NARRATIONAL STRUCTURE OF LUKE 24:1–35 AND ITS THEOLOGICAL IMPLICATIONS

Turid Karlsen Seim

The story about the discovery of the empty tomb in Luke 24:1–12 is, despite its apparent clarity, marked by ambiguities. It conveys conflicting options and it ends by leading nowhere. The story also represents a transition from women's visibility in the gospel story to their subsumption under the leading male cast in Acts.[1] This happens by means of ironical devices.

The women at the tomb are approached by the angelic messengers in a manner that confirms their role as disciples. As they yet again receive words from God, they are reminded of how they had listened to the teaching of the Lord while he was still in Galilee. The women are told to remember, but according to Luke they are not commissioned with a message. Some see this lack of a charge as another Lukan attempt at silencing women.[2] However, it rather means that the female followers of Jesus are not cast in an intermediary, interim role which is exhausted when the message is delivered. They are not just "errand girls" sent with a message to the assumed target group for divine appointment, namely Peter and his fellow disciples. They are recognized in their own right as members of the group of followers from Galilee and asserted as bearers of the

---

[1] This is extensively argued in my book *The Double Message: Patterns of Gender in Luke-Acts* (T & T Clark/Abingdon Press: Edinburgh/Nashville, 1994) 147–63, and more briefly in "The Gospel of Luke", in E. Schüssler Fiorenza (ed.), *Searching the Scriptures. A Feminist Commentary* (New York: Crossroad, 1994) 728–62, esp. pp. 748–52.

[2] E. Schüssler Fiorenza speaks about "the Lukan silence" and throughout her writings she insists that Luke-Acts represents a programmatic androcentrism that intentionally excludes womeen or curtails their role. As a typical example cf. E. Schüssler Fiorenza, *In Memory of Her: A Feminist Reconstruction of Christian Origins* (New York: Crossroad, 1983) 49–50, 161, 167. Among those who share her view, are E.M. Tetlow, *Women and Ministry in the New Testament: Called to Serve* (Lanhan/New York/London, 1980) 101–9; and B.E. Reid, *Choosing the Better Part? Women in the Gospel of Luke* (Collegeville, Minnesota: The Liturgical Press, 1996).

traditio implied by the memory of the words of the Lord. Also in Luke's version the women do in fact act as messengers when they return from the tomb. But this happens at their own initiative, and it is not an act of obedience to a mandate.

However, albeit the women are recognized by the divine messengers as long standing followers entrusted with the word of the Lord, they are effectively rejected by the male disciples who are unwilling to receive their message and believe them. Not only do the men dismiss the women's word as idle talk, they simply do not have faith in women.[3] The irony of this is obvious to the readers who, informed by the omniscient author, know perfectly well that the women are trustworthy, their story true and the male disciples therefore mistaken in their mistrust and disbelief.

In Luke 24:9–11 a divide is described in the group of disciples and it follows a gender line: Together with the eleven "all the rest (of the men)" do not believe the three women named and "the other (women) with them". The wording is peculiar and imply a confrontation between the entire group of women and the entire group of men.[4] It is the lack of faith in women on the men's part which creates the suspension in the resurrection stories between the early faith and witness of the women and the delayed acceptance by the men and thereby the whole community.

It is maintained by some that this suspension serves a strategy whereby the women disciples are bypassed and the male apostles established as primary witnesses to the resurrection so that Luke also supports the priority of a Petrine tradition (cf. Luke 24:12, 34).[5] The women's witness is being disparaged or at least neutralized so that the significance of Peter's role as a resurrection witness is not preempted by them. However, the role of Peter in Luke 24 is remark-

[3] For the significance of the dual construction in 24.11, cf. Seim, *Double Message*, 156. Whether this reflects a social convention and legal ruling that women were not trusted as witnesses is possible, but debatable, cf. Reid, *The Better Part*, 200ff.

[4] This pattern of gender specific groupings in Luke-Acts is reflected also to the summary description of the whole community as ἄνδρες τε καὶ γυναῖκες, and it further corresponds to the organisation of epic material in gender pairs, cf. Seim, *Double Message*, 11–24.

[5] Schüssler Fiorenza and Reid both have this as a significant element in their very critical appraisal of the portrayal of women in Luke-Acts, see n. 2. For a broader survey of the discussion, see K.E. Corley, *Private Women, Public Meals: Social Conflict and Women in the Synoptic Tradition* (Peabody, Mass.: Hendrickson Publishers, 1993).

able vague and indirect. He is not referred to by the two disciples in Luke 24:24, and the report of his visit to the empty tomb in Luke 24:12 hardly supports a claim to priority either in faith or in witness. It leads in fact nowhere further towards restored faith. In his amazement Peter simply returns home.

Both stories about the disciples at the empty tomb are thus aborted accounts in the sense that they lead nowhere further. This introduces an element of suspension which may serve a narrative purpose as it keeps the reader in pursuit of a solution in what follows. But the primary interest among interpreters has often been the theological implications one might draw from it about the origin and nature of resurrection faith. The empty tomb is ambiguous and even dubious and may cause various speculations but does not necessarily lead to faith in the resurrected Christ—that happens only as the risen Lord himself is revealed.[6] In other words, there is no final proof to the resurrection of Jesus, the source of faith is the witness of those to whom the risen Christ appeared. This has stirred a debate as to the clarity of the kerygmatic formula in Luke 24:5 on the one hand, and on the other hand whether the women's remembrance and reaction to the empty tomb and to the proclamation of the resurrection by the divine messenger, in any sense, is an expression of faith.[7]

There is some text critical uncertainty about Luke 24:12 as the verse is missing in D, and this could be seen to represent a lectio difficilior. However, the majority of the best manuscripts include it, and most commentators leave it in. Since the apostle's name varies in Luke 24:12 (Peter) and 24:34 (Simon), they may stem from different sources. Since Luke 24:12 shows no trace of an appearance story, it is hardly introduced by Luke to support the claim in Luke 24:34 or for that sake v. 24a, as is suggested by P. Schubert, "The Structure and Significance of Luke 24", in *Neutestamentliche Studien für Rudolf Bultmann* (BZNW 21; Berlin: Alfred Töpelmann, 1954) 165–86, p. 172. He also explores the relationship to the tradition referred to by Paul in 1 Cor 15.5–7.

[6] R.J. Dillon's interpretation of Lk 24, *From Eye-Witnesses to Ministers of the Word: Tradition and Composition in Luke 24* (AnBib 82; Roma: Editrice Pontificia Iustituto Biblica, 1978), has this almost as its hermeneutical key, and it is characteristic that he has recourse to German theological terminology and speaks of "the transition from Ostererfahrung to Osterglaube", (p. 18). Already Schubert, "Structure", 167–68, insisted that Luke differed from Mark and Matthew in diminishing the interest in the empty tomb as providing by itself direct or even inferential evidence for the resurrection of Jesus. The living should not be sought among the dead.

[7] Dillon, *Eye-witnesses*, 26, 51–52, uses the term "cryptic designation". The assumption that the women do not understand and believe, is opposed i.a. by P. Perkins, *Resurrection: New Testament Witness and Contemporary Reflection* (Geoffrey Chapman: London, 1984–85) 155.

There is no doubt that the stories of the empty tomb in Luke 24 come to a deadlock. The conflict which arises between the men and the women is not resolved by Peter's visit to the tomb, and the outcome of his visit is simply amazement as he returns home.

The Lukan account continues by the Emmaus story which provides a transition from the account about the empty tomb to the first appearance story in the full gathering of disciples. It is a remarkably long story which by its very length dominates the whole of Luke 24,[8] and it has no parallel in Mark or Matthew. It therefore seems to come from a tradition particular to Luke but has also been substantially reedited by the evangelist to catch and comment Lukan phraseology and themes.[9]

In the present context several connecting strings have been introduced. Most strikingly, Luke 24 maintains a strict unity of place and time. It all happens within the chronological framework of one day only (see v. 13 ἐν αὐτῇ τῇ ἡμέρᾳ and v. 33 αὐτῇ τῇ ὥρᾳ, and v. 36, "while they were still talking"). The events also take place in or near Jerusalem in a manner that marks Jerusalem as the geographical focus. The estimation of the distance from Jerusalem to Emmaus, "about seven miles", indicates this and means that the two disciples can return to Jerusalem before night falls.[10] It is also made clear that the two walking the road to Emmaus belong to the group mentioned above v. 9; they are "two of them" v. 13, and in v. 22 and v. 24 they speak about "some women of our group (lit. from among us)"; v. 24: "some of those with us").[11] One of the two is called Cleopas, while the other remains unnamed.[12] All we ever learn about them is through this story; they are not among the apostolic celebrities.

---

[8] Schubert, "Structure", 168.

[9] For the discussion on tradition and redaction, see J.A. Fitzmyer, *The Gospel According to Luke* (2 vols.; AB 28; Doubleday: Garden City, New York, 1981–85), 2.1554–57. Fitzmyer supports V. Taylor's judgment in saying "Luke has embellished an existing tradition with unusual freedom".

[10] J. Wanke, "'. . . wie sie ihn beim Brotbrechen erkannten': Zur Auslegung der Emmauserzählung Lk 24.13–35", *BZ* 18 (1974) 180–92, pp. 186–87. Wanke, however, assumes that this implies a submission to the "Elferkreis wie ein kathedraresidierendes und lehrendes Kollegium". Not as strongly, but yet making the same point in relation to Luke 24:34, is Dillon, *Eye-witnesses*, 98ff. Also J. Lieu, *The Gospel of Luke*, (Epworth Commentaries; Peterborough: Epworth Press, 1997) 205, comes close to this.

[11] To the significance of this language, cf. H.D. Betz, "The Origin and Nature of Christian Faith According to the Emmaus Legend (Luke 24.13–32)", *Interpretation* 23 (1969) 32–46, p. 45.

[12] There are many attempts at identifying both Cleopas and especially the second

Despite the unity of place, the Emmaus story is presented as a journey. Cleopas and his fellow disciple are on their way home to their village, Emmaus. The narrative language of mobility, of walking, of moving along, of proceeding on one's way, of learning on the road, reflects a fundamental theme of Luke's writings. "The Emmaus disciples are being caused to recapitulate the path already charted by the evangelist".[13] This journey thus echoes other travel stories in Luke-Acts, yes the whole outline is one of moving from one place to another. In Acts, ἡ ὁδός, "the Way" is a designation for the self-understanding of the early Christian community (9:2; 19:9, 23; 22:4; 24:14, 22).[14]

However, the direction of the journey is not at any time insignificant. In the Emmaus episode the two disciples are on the road. But they are not moving on; they are leaving Jerusalem to return to where they came from like Peter who went back home after his visit to the tomb. They are disillusioned and sad with heavy hearts and minds struggling to come to terms with what has happened in Jerusalem as it means nothing to them but frustrated bewilderment and disappointment.

Their expectations of the prophet they had chosen to follow had been high. They had eagerly waited for the redeeming moment of victory, they had looked forward to seeing the enemies of their people slain and humiliated, they had hoped for their day of glory, the ultimate manifestation of God's preferential option for them, God's people. But reality had defeated them; their hero of promises had lost his case, and if hope was to survive they would have to look elsewhere. They are leaving Jerusalem, the place of power and glory now turned to misery; they are going home to Emmaus. This is the scream of their return, the hurt of misplaced trust, of faith no longer knowing what to believe. The Emmaus story begins by making the deadlock of the previous story exceedingly explicit.

There is an emphasis on the exchange going on between the two,

anonymous disciple either as one of the eleven or even as Cleopas' wife. Such conjectures may be tempting, but they remain speculative. For this, see Fitzmyer, *Gospel of Luke*, 2.1563–64.

[13] Dillon, *Eye-witnesses*, 145.

[14] B.P. Robinson, "The Place of the Emmaus Story in Luke-Acts", *NTS* 30 (1984) 481–97, esp. pp. 481–82, interprets this spiritually as an image of the Christian life following Christ.

on their dialogue as a common struggle for meaning.[15] They welcome even a stranger into their conversation as he overtakes them on the road. Initially he asks innocent questions, an outsider's questions, making them tell their story. They do so, assuming they possess a knowledge he does not have.

The story they have to tell, conveys their disappointment. It is intriguing to see how the three elements of their story all start by hopeful statements. These statements are in fact a christological summary and reflect traditional material which elsewhere in the New Testament constitutes positive affirmations of Christian faith.[16] But here they lead to expressions of utter frustration. The wonderful life of Jesus is punctured by his tragic death; their hope that he was the one to redeem Israel, is replaced by disillusion; the talk of some women that his grave is empty and angels had proclaimed that he is alive, is undermined by the fact that Jesus himself they did not see.

The report of the two reiterates meticulously the morning's events of that very same day, already reported in full just before. Yet it constitutes a major part of the dialogue in the Emmaus episode. It has been suggested that the last part of their response (Luke 24:21b–24) is a secondary, but pre-Lukan insertion that interrupts an original and better correspondence between the account of the disciples and Jesus' response.[17]

In terms of tradition history this may well be true, but why does it still make excellent sense as it is? Luke demonstrates here one of his most remarkable narrative skills, that of gathering a number of disparate stories into a single narrative.[18] And among four major features of Lukan style, H.J. Cadbury named "repetition and variation" the purpose of which should be "to demonstrate the divinely guided continuity of his story".[19] In Luke 24 collection and reiteration are uniquely combined into a mimnetic pattern which actualizes the emphasis on remembering in Luke.[20]

---

[15] On dialogue as an educational method in Luke, cf. Reid, *The Better Part*, 153–54.

[16] This is well covered by most commentaries. It appears as a blend of traditional material and Lucan redaction, cf. Fitzmyer, *The Gospel according to Luke*, 2.1555–57.

[17] Betz, "Origin", 34, in agreement with P. Schubert and F. Hahn.

[18] L.T. Johnson, *The Gospel of Luke* (Sacra Pagina Series, 3; Collegeville, Minnesota: The Liturgical Press, 1991) 398.

[19] Dillon, *Eye-Witnesses*, 109 n. 114.

[20] On the usage of μιμνῄσκομαι, cf. Seim, *Double Message*, 151–55.

Luke repeats stories also elsewhere. This happens most prominently in Acts, especially in the threefold recital of Paul's conversion. Further examples are: The decisions reached at the council in Jerusalem in Acts 15 are immediately repeated in the full quote of the letter to be sent to Antioch. Also Claudius Lysias' letter to Felix in Acts 23:26–30 serves as a summary of the events already told. The story about the baptism of Cornelius and his house is perhaps a closer parallel to Luke 24 as the event is first reported by the narrator's voice before being retold by Peter who is one of the narrated characters. These instances contain remarkable differences some of which are not easily reconciled.

In the Emmaus story there are no major inconcistencies as the events in Luke 24:1–12 are retold by the two disciples, even though some interpreters have pointed to the discrepancy between the verses 12 and 24. In v. 12 only Peter goes to the grave, while the report in v. 24 says "some of those who were with us".[21] But apart from this, it is, as R.J. Dillon has shown, a faithful rendering. Cleopas is made to rehearse Luke's own rendition.[22] So "Luke tells a story of men on the road, who tell what happened in the city, who relate what was related to them by the women, who have further experience of Jesus' words and actions, and who then report this to the assembled community, which tells them in turn of further such events. Beneath the calm . . . simplicity of the story, a complex process of narration is in process".[23]

However, the report of the two may be faithful, but it reveals a confusion and a hesitation on their part as to what and whom to believe beyond what they have experienced themselves and seen with their own eyes. Women may spread the word that he is no longer to be found among the dead but should be sought among the living—but isn't that the fanciful imagination and loose tongues of women who never really are trustworthy? The reiteration thus reflects the dissociation of the eleven and all the other men in v. 11. What they have been told may make them wonder, but it has not restored their faith and hope. Their retelling brings out the irony of the previous story; they still doubt what the readers know has truly happened.

---

[21] Betz, "Origin", 35, who also underscores that v. 12 is a dubious reading. Cf. also the brief, but good presentation in Lieu, *The Gospel of Luke*, 205.

[22] Dillon, *Eye-witnesses*, 108–10.

[23] Johnson, *The Gospel of Luke*, 399.

The story told by the two to their unknown companion shows how they struggle to transcend their own experience by trusting the stories of others whose credibility was not readily accepted. They ask for more, and in the end it seems that only the recognition of the Lord himself brings restoration; he is the one verifiable teacher. But the Emmaus story implies that by his appearance he lends credibility to those whom they had been reluctant to trust. The retelling of the many stories within this one story is a way of bringing them together, of having them receiving each other's stories, of reconciling the multiple witnesses into the one witness of a restored and reunited community.

As mentioned above, the language of the Emmaus story again and again subtly indicates that both the two on the road and the persons to which they refer, are all part of the same larger group, together they constitute a "we". They are still characterized according to this shared belonging, but they are about to move apart—each opting for their own destination. The two have left the others in Jerusalem. When they reach their village they want the stranger to stay with them. But what happens is that he makes them move. They have hardly settled when their recognition of him as Jesus makes them return to Jerusalem.

The road to Emmaus is no longer their walking away. In fact, the title given to the story in most translations is misleading. It is not a walk to Emmaus; it is a journey from Jerusalem and back again. On their return to Jerusalem the very same night, the two are reunited with the group from which they had walked away. Immediately and rather abruptly they learn that the risen Lord has appeared in Jerusalem as well — to Simon. They respond by telling their story[24] so that once again what has happened is being reiterated in a summarizing manner. Such a combination of a concluding account of an event with the return from it, can be found in Luke-Acts also elsewhere (Acts 4:23; 9:27; 10:8; 12:17).[25] But a par-

[24] This means that the reading λέγοντας is to be preferred—due to the strength of the witnesses and also because it represents the lectio difficilior. D's version λέγοντες eases the flow of the narrative in assuming the two from Emmaus as the speakers. I here agree with Dillon, *Eye-witnesses*, 96–97, in making a conceptual connection between ἠθροισμένους and λέγοντας.

[25] Dillon, *Eye-witnesses*, 103–4, draws on Wanke and calls it a distinctive feature of Lk's narrative style.

ticular feature in Luke 24:35 is the manner in which the different stories are shared, as the two meet with the group already gathered in Jerusalem—each with their own story to tell. The content of the disciples' common experience and confession constitutes the basis of their reconvention.

In this manner the Jerusalem story of the Lord's appearance to the prominent Simon Peter and the Emmaus story of Jesus' walk and meal with two otherwise unknown disciples, are merged with the story of the women into a shared recognition of the resurrection and presence of the crucified Lord. The deadlock is broken and the conflict is overcome. There is no further competition and no indication of the previous arguments among the disciples over which one of them is the greatest—as it happened after Jesus had foretold his death in Luke 9:44–48 and in a similar fashion at the last meal in Luke 22:24ff. The disciples are mutually giving account, and they mutually receive each other's story. For what remain of events in the gospel narrative of Luke, the appearances of the Lord happen to the entire community with none of its members in a privileged position.[26]

There is a certain proximity between the Lukan and Johannine resurrection narratives. In different ways they coincide in the attempt to reconcile witnesses that might have appeared to be competing or could threaten to become so. In an almost entertaining manner the narration of the story of the finding of the empty tomb in John 20:1–18 makes sure that none of the persons involved becomes the winner of the search for Jesus. The reduction in John's version of the number of women at the empty tomb as well as the introduction of Peter and the disciple whom Jesus loved, does not imply that the role of women is overruled and priority and authority transferred to male apostles. Rather it includes the witness of Mary Magdalene prominently in the cluster of witnesses. Each of the three, Mary of Magdala, Peter, and the disciple Jesus loved, is given some priority. But only when their various pieces are gathered, does the picture become complete and a full account is possible.

---

[26] Against among others Wanke, "Brotbrechen", 187, who sees Luke 24:34 as a clear indication that "Das Erlebnis der Emmausjünger soll mit dem Credo der Kirche in Verbindung gebracht werden *und vom diesem her seine Legitimation erhalten. Die durch V.34 angedeutete zeitliche Priorität der Petruserscheinung bringt eine sachliche Priorität zum Ausdruck.*" (my ital.)

An element of suspended recognition and, in some cases, of doubt or even of disbelief is common to several of the appearance stories. There are few signs of epiphany in these stories and they are remarkably devoid of apocalyptic stage props. There is neither smoke nor fire, not a hint of an earthquake, no breathtaking and bright transfiguration. Instead they tend to underscore ordinariness—perhaps in order to substantiate the reality of the resurrection.

In the Emmaus story this element is reinforced into an irony which is as obvious as the conjunct reiteration of potentially conflicting stories. The two disciples are on their way to Emmaus, and they respond to the curiosity of an unknown companion as they in their conversation grope for the meaning of what they have experienced. But they cannot possibly understand,—not yet. We are told that their eyes "were being kept" from recognizing that the stranger is Jesus himself. The gospels often display the blindness of people, including the disciples, their failure to understand Jesus and his teaching. But it is never expressed like this; this language is unique. It is also highly ironical: when Jesus himself does appear, the one whom the women and others from their group, despite all the circumstantial evidence, had not seen, they see someone whom they do not recognize as Jesus.[27] Not until their eyes are opened by the same initiative that closed them, do they know him for whom he is.

In the tradition of interpretation the blinding of the disciples has been a puzzle with which many have struggled: Why are their eyes being kept and by whom? Why does Jesus need to teach his disciples without them recognizing who their teacher is? Attempts at explaining this are multiple varying from assumptions about the disciples being blinded by grief to them being spiritual blind to the transformed nature of the resurrected body of the Christ. Jesus' reproach: "Oh, how foolish you are and how slow of heart to believe all that the prophets have declared", is therefore taken to refer to their closed eyes. But in this story their blindness does not seem to be their inability to get the message right. When the unknown traveller instructs them, there is no indication that they did not listen and learn. Indeed, they later say that their hearts were burning. The blindness affects only their recognition of who he is, and in his reproach Jesus is not holding something against them which is hardly

[27] Both in Luke 24:15 and 24:24, αὐτός/αὐτόν is intensive.

their fault. The passive constructions make clear that their recognition is meant to be suspended, Jesus' identity is being concealed.[28]

The appearance stories and the stories of the empty tomb respond to slightly different questions which it is important to keep apart. The story of the empty tomb is open to a variety of explanations, as the stories themselves reveal and interpreters and theologians repeatedly insist. More importantly, however, the Emmaus story also addresses a further question. The disciples might accept that Jesus' grave is empty, and also that he is risen, but where is he then? The question of his "whereabouts", of his presence remains—"but they did not see him".

By the irony of their eyes "being kept", the Emmaus story calls off this search for the resurrected, living Christ. He is the one who finds them. The language of the story is undergirded by Luke's understanding of divine necessity (the divine δεῖ). It is also consistent with the language of the appearance stories: The risen Lord comes to them, he shows himself to them. They are not finders of his presence: they are receivers. In the Emmaus story this is further reinforced by a pattern of role reversal: the questioner becomes/is the teacher, and the guest becomes/is the host.[29]

The deliberately delayed recognition in the Emmaus story illuminates a similar theme as the Thomas incident in the Gospel of John which concludes that "Blessed are those who have not not seen, and yet have come to believe" (John 20:29). The two who complain that the messengers from the empty tomb had not seen Jesus himself, are themselves deliberately kept from recognizing him when he is there. When in the end their eyes are opened to know him, he vanishes in the very same moment from their sight.

The readers are already in the beginning told what the two disciples cannot see and keep waiting for the moment when the disciples

---

[28] Cf. Dillon, *Eye-witnesses*, 146–47. Referring back to an observation by C.H. Dodd, "The appearances of the Risen Christ: a study in form-criticism of the Gospels.", in idem, *More New Testament Studies* (Manchester: Manchester University Press, 1968) 102–33, pp. 107–8, it has become common to assume this as an example of the anagnorisis device in Greek dramaturgy: delayed recognition, remembrance process, then recognition at a point coinciding with the completion of the argument of the author. Cf. Dillon, *Eye-witnesses*, 75–76. Betz, "Origin", 37, however, rejects that this is a case of anagnorisis.

[29] Betz, "Origin", 11–12; Dillon, *Eye-witnesses*, 111. Robinson, "The Emmaus Story", 486, insists that this makes the meal at Emmaus an eikon of the kingdom—the disciples are now feasting at the Lord's table.

will discover what the readers already know. The disciples in the story are allowed an innocence the readers cannot claim, but this innocence entails confusion and despair and must in the end stand corrected. The consolation is in this correction, in the indication of new configurations of familiar knowledge and material. The greater knowledge given to listeners/readers, no longer dealing with the raw facts but with a "connected account" compensates for their later role.

The discrepancy between the disciples in the story and the readers as the narrator's confidants, upon which St. John of Damascus was among the first to reflect, is more than a clever technical device of narrative suspension. It is more than the wisdom of hindsight. It entails a hermeneutical and theological challenge as it maintains within the tradition itself a permanent struggle for meaning. It admits that multiple interpretations are possible, even reasonable while insisting that certain events are at the core of the hermeneutical struggle. Their meaning is not neccessarily the obvious one, and it is not readily received and believed.

Accordingly, most interpreters identify as the irony of this story the counterpoint between the totality of facts which the two disciples recount and their total incomprehension with regard to the meaning of these events,—or, christologically speaking, the skandalon that the messianic access to glory is through humiliation. But this is far too simple.

There are two subtly connected hide-and-seek strategies in the Emmaus story. The identity of their fellow traveller is hidden from the disciples in the story, while, as mentioned above, the readers have no excuse for not recognizing him from the beginning. But what is kept from the readers is a full and precise account of what the two disciples learned from Jesus. The story shows a subtle connection between the unrecognized appearance of Jesus and the hidden meaning of texts.

Later interpreters have constantly tried to help the author out by providing the assumably implied list of proof-texts. The summary style of Luke 24:27 may be an invitation to do so, but there is no way of deciding whether the suggestions are correct or not. The importance of what the scriptural text withholds should be recognized as should the artistry of suggestion and implication that deliberately refrains from stating a definitive and exhaustive meaning.

It is remarkable how comprehensive and therefore vague the reference to Moses and all the prophets is. The point is not the particulars of the evidence as the repeated "all" ("all the prophets and all the scriptures") emphatically conveys. The point is the conviction that in the suffering of Jesus Messiah the witness of scripture is fulfilled and not contradicted. When Jesus' speech at this point is curtailed and no longer direct, this may be an indication that there is no fixed resolution to the particulars of interpretative efforts. The freedom to explore cannot be contained.

The insistence on God keeping the promises God has given, constitutes a fundamental pattern of promise and fulfilment in the writings of Luke.[30] This is not primarily a matter of proving exact correspondence, and therefore the term "proof from prophecy" may be inadequate in the case of Luke. Fulfilment is portrayed as something at the same time substantially old and new, predicted and yet unpredictable. Interpretative struggle and argument are needed, and the acceptance of fulfilment involves elements of surprise and of overcoming opposition and misinformed expectations, human objections and prejudices. In the process of reception experience blends with the reading of scripture, present history encounters past. The undergirding purpose in the Lukan effort to make scripture and history meet, is theological—in the specific sense of the term. It concerns the understanding of God, of how God remains faithful to God self. The pattern of promise and fulfilment is not a matter of logical exercise, it is a groping for consistency in God's words and acts. Ultimately, it represents an insistence on God's unswerving authority beyond all human manipulation.

The attraction of the Emmaus story has often been its seemingly simple conclusion: faith is restored when in the end the presence of the Lord is revealed in the breaking of the bread—stated in almost liturgical eucharistic language.[31] But the moment of revelation is not

---

[30] This is often called "proof from prophecy theology" and Schubert sees it to be at the heart of Luke 24 ("Structure", 173–77). Cf. also D.L. Bock, *Proclamation from Prophecy and Pattern*, (JSNT Sup, 12; Sheffield: Sheffield Academic Press, 1987) and my discussion in *Double Message*, 167–69.

[31] This is taken as a reinstitution by the resurrected Lord of the eucharistic meal as it looks forwards to the liturgical life of the church. Betz, "Origin", 37; Fitzmyer, *The Gospel according to Luke*, 2.1559–60. The majority of interpreters see this as a major point of the story, which reflects the assumption that the meal in Luke 24:28–31 is the core of the tradition to which verses 13 and 15b were added, cf. Dillon, *Eye-witnesses*, 76–77; Wanke, "Brotbrechen", 180 and 184: "Lk 24.28ff. scheint eine neue Erfahrung zu reflektieren: Der Kurios gibt sich gegenwärtig in dem Mahl, das die Gemeinde arrangiert." Different from Just who sees it as intimately associated

the conclusion of the story: The risen Christ does not remain with them beyond this moment. But as he vanishes, they move to join the others, to reaffirm a community about to fall apart. Luke 24:1–35 represents a negotiation of corporate witness and embodies a delicate balancing of several versions of the Easter events. As the historiographer Luke tries to come to terms with his sources, he reconciles what might seem to be contradictory and competing stories. This happens by means of irony and reiteration. The diverse stories and conflicting voices still speak but within the framework of one continuous narrative embracing them all. The cost involved is later to be paid on Acts' public arena where some are silenced as others continue to speak.

---

with the earlier mealscenes in the gospel. Robinson, however, finds it unlikely that the Emmaus meal is intended to be or symbolise the Eucharist, but rather manifests the kingship of Christ (*Emmaus Story*, 487–94).

"MINOR AGREEMENTS" UND DIE HYPOTHESE VON LUKAS' KENNTNIS DES MATTHÄUSEVANGELIUMS

JARMO KIILUNEN

Im einleitenden Kapitel seiner Untersuchung über 'Minor Agreements' schreibt Andreas Ennulat, die 'kleinen Übereinstimmungen' stellten ein Problem dar, welches es "vom Grunderklärungsmuster der Zwei-Quellen Hypothese her *gar nicht geben dürfte*" (Hervorhebung vom Verf.).[1] Wie liesse sich diese in ihrer Globalität überraschende, im Interesse einer vor-mtlk Bearbeitung des Mk gemachte Feststellung verifizieren? Wäre nicht eher die entgegengesetzte These aufzustellen: Wenn es keine 'minor agreements' gäbe, wäre die Zweiquellentheorie im Ansatz anzuzweifeln?

Tatsächlich bedeutet die Existenz der 'minor agreements' (MAs) für sich genommen für die Zweiquellentheorie (2QTh) kein Problem, sondern ist hypothesengemäss vorauszusetzen. Auch die Anzahl der Übereinstimmungen, auch wenn sie gross ist, stellt im Grunde kein Problem dar. Was entscheidet, ist die Art der MAs. Wenn ein alltäglicher Ausdruck hier und da gestrichen oder durch einen stilistisch gehobenen ersetzt wird, so ist das eben etwas dem Grunderklärungsmuster der 2QTh Gemässes. Sollte aber ein MA aus mehreren gemeinsamen Worten in gleicher Anordnung bestehen, drängt sich die Frage auf, ob es hypothesengemäss solch einen Fall überhaupt geben kann bzw. darf.

Zur Erklärung des Phänomens von MAs sind als Herausforderer der 2QTh in der gegenwärtigen Diskussion—sieht man von den französichen Mehrstadientheorien ab—besonders zwei Hypothesen aktiv vertreten worden. Es sind die Annahme einer nachmk Redaktion des Mk ("Deuteromarkushypothese") sowie die Annahme einer Benutzung des Mt durch Lukas ("Farrer—Goulder—Hypothese"; FGH), welche beide ihre Wurzel in der älteren Forschung haben. Während die erste vor allem mit dem Namen Albert Fuchs verknüpft ist, hat die zweite in Michael Goulder ihren prominenten Exponenten.

---

[1] A. Ennulat, *Die "Minor Agreements": Untersuchungen zu einer offenen Frage des synoptischen Problems* (WUNT 62; Tübingen: Mohr (Paul Siebeck) 1.

Im Jahre 1978 erschien Goulder's Aufsatz "On Putting Q to the Test", wo er zwölf MAs zur Diskussion stellte, die seiner Meinung nach entschieden ("conclusively") die Abhängigkeit des Lukas von Mt zeigten.[2] Der Aufsatz rief im Jahre 1984 die kritische Stellungnahme von Christopher M. Tuckett hervor.[3] Sieben Jahre später, im Jahre 1991, trat Goulder in dem in Göttingen veranstalteten Symposion über MAs mit der These auf, neun von den ursprünglich zwölf MAs seien in ihrer Beweiskraft nach wie vor gültig.[4] Methodisch geht er beide Male davon aus, dass ein MA, welches für Mt Typisches, für Lk aber Untypisches darstellt, ein Indiz für die Abhängigkeit des Lk von Mt ist.

Da Goulder in dem Göttinger Vortrag seine Argumentation bei manchen Übereinstimmungen erweiterte, präzisierte und vertiefte, hat es allen Grund, die neun MAs noch einmal genauer in Augenschein zu nehmen. Ausgegangen wird jeweils hypothesengemäss, d.h. die grundlegenden Annahmen der beiden Hypothesen als gegeben vorausgesetzt, ohne sie jeweils für sich in Frage zu stellen. Es wird hier der Versuch unternommen, zu überprüfen, ob die FGH in allen neun Fällen wirklich das Schwarze trifft oder ob sich die Anzahl—gerade im Interesse des von Goulder selbst betonten Prinzips des Ockhamschen Messers, d.h., möglichst aufgrund des Mk allein—verringern lässt.[5]

1. *Ναζαρά als lokaler Hintergrund der einsetzenden Mission Jesu*

Der Fall gilt den lk Bericht vom Beginn des Wirkens Jesu in Nazareth (Lk 4:14–30). Goulder verweist auf drei Probleme: Wie kommt Lukas dazu, Nazareth als Schauplatz des Auftretens Jesu vorzubringen? Woher erhält er den Gedanken, Jesu Predigt werde dort trotz eines

---

[2] M.D. Goulder, "On Putting Q to the Test", *NTS* 24 (1978) 218–34.

[3] C.M. Tuckett, "On the Relationship Between Matthew and Luke", *NTS* 30 (1984) 130–42.

[4] M.D. Goulder, "Luke's Knowledge of Matthew", in G. Strecker (hg.), *Die Minor Agreements: Symposium Göttingen 1991* (GTA 50; Göttingen: Vandenhoeck & Ruprecht, 1993) 143–62. Von den ursprünglichen zwölf Fällen wurden ausgelassen, weil ohne "probative force", Mk 6:7 Parr. Mt 10:1; Lk 9:1 und Mk 9:7 Parr. Mt 17:5; Lk 9:34 samt Mk 15:1 Parr. Mt 27:1; Lk 22:66.

[5] Zur Textgrundlage dient Nestle Aland, 27. revidierte Auflage vom 1993 (NA27). Wenn in einigen Fällen auch andere Editionen benutzt werden, wird das eigens erwähnt.

vielversprechenden Anfangs abgelehnt? Und wie ist das MA Ναζαρά zu verstehen?[6]

Mt 4:12–13
. . . ἀνεχώρησεν εἰς τὴν Γαλιλαίαν. καὶ καταλιπὼν τὴν Ναζαρὰ . . .
Mk 1:14
. . . ἦλθεν ὁ Ἰησοῦς εἰς τὴν Γαλιλαίαν . . .
Lk 4:14, 16
Καὶ ὑπέστρεψεν ὁ Ἰησοῦς . . . εἰς τὴν Γαλιλαίαν . . . καὶ ἦλθεν εἰς Ναζαρὰ . . .

Nach Goulder habe Lukas den geographischen Ort sowie dessen ungewöhnliche Form Ναζαρά aus Mt entnommen. Da Jesus nach Mt die Stadt verlässt, habe Lukas gemeint, der Besuch wäre ohne Erfolg geblieben, und stelle deswegen Mk 6:1–6a hierher, um das Verlassen der Heimat zu motivieren.

Die Gouldersche Lösung ist klug, wenngleich auch nicht einwandfrei. Um bei der letzten Frage zu beginnen, fällt es auf, dass an den drei Stellen, wo Jesu Heimat in Mt zur Sprache gebracht wird, jeweils eine unterschiedliche Form verwendet wird, und zwar:

Mt 2:23 Ναζαρέτ[7]
Mt 4:13 Ναζαρά[8]
Mt 21:11 Ναζαρέθ[9]

Angenommen, dass diese Ungleichheit wirklich ursprünglich ist, fragt sich, welchen Grund Matthäus haben sollte, bei 4:13 von dem Typus -ετ, -εθ abzuweichen. Nach Goulder sei Ναζαρά von dem Evangelisten aus dem Adjektiv Ναζαρηνός (welches in Mk 1:24 begegnet) abgeleitet, in Entsprechung mit etwa Μαγδαλά—Μαγδαληνός.[10] Mit dieser aus sprachlicher Sicht durchaus möglichen Auskunft wird allerdings zunächst nur eine technische Ermittlung der Herkunft von Ναζαρά gegeben, ohne dass erklärt wird, warum Matthäus unverhofft von seinem bisherigen Sprachgebrauch abkommen sollte.[11] Goulder meint,

[6] Goulder, "Knowledge", 144–48.
[7] Varianten: -ρεθ und -ρα (P[70] vid; Eusebius).
[8] Varianten: -ρετ, -ρεθ, -ραθ.
[9] Keine Varianten angegeben.
[10] Goulder, "Knowledge", 147–48. Genauer zum Problem vgl. den von Goulder genannten Aufsatz von H.P. Rüger, "ΝΑΖΑΡΕΘ/ΝΑΖΑΡΑ/ΝΑΖΑΡΗΝΟΣ/ΝΑΖΩΡΑΙΟΣ", *ZNW* 72 (1981) 257–63.
[11] Vgl. auch die Bemerkung von C.M. Tuckett, *Q and the History of Early Christianity: Studies on Q* (Edinburgh: T & T Clark, 1997) 228: ". . . it is not clear why Matthew should have changed the form of the place name to an -αρα ending here but never elsewhere."

"... Matthew may well have felt that the alternative feminine ending was suitable for the noun...." Doch zumindest für einen nichthebräisch sprechenden Leser des Mt wäre Ναζαρά überraschend, da ihm die hebräischen Voraussetzungen für das Zusammenspiel von Ναζαρέτ—Ναζαρά unbekannt sind. Übrigens kommt Ναζαρά auch deswegen für jeden Leser unerwartet, weil die Bezeichnung Jesu als Ναζωραῖος von dem Evangelisten in 2:23 ausdrücklich mit der Namensform Ναζαρέτ gekoppelt wird. Für die FGH spricht auch nicht gerade, dass Matthäus selber Ναζαρηνός nie benutzt—auch in 26:71 nicht, wo er gegen die von der Mk-Parallele (14:67) dargebotene Ναζαρηνός—im Einklang mit 2:23—Ναζωραῖος schreibt.

Über die Form Ναζαρά hinaus ist weiter zu fragen, weshalb Matthäus überhaupt auf Jesu Heimat zu sprechen kommt. Er war ja genauso wenig wie Lukas von Mk dazu veranlasst, und, was noch mehr auffällt, er weiss von dort nichts zu berichten. Auch die Erfüllung der Schrift in 4:14–16 hätte das nicht verlangt, weil der nach Galiläa ziehende Jesus direkt nach Kapharnaum hätte fahren können. Irgendwie ist der Satz wie überhastet niedergeschrieben: Jesus kehrt nach Galiläa zurück, und ohne sich zuerst nach Nazareth begeben zu haben, verlässt er schon die Stadt. Dies könnte ein Anzeichen dafür sein, dass Matthäus hier irgendwie von der Tradition beeinflusst ist.[12] Bedenkt man die Frage im Blick auf das Verhältnis von Mt und Lk, könnte man unschwer ebenfalls auf die Abhängigkeit des Mt von Lk schliessen: Matthäus will den in Lk breit geschilderten, unerwünschten Vorfall in Jesu Heimat möglichst übergehen, und erwähnt deshalb Nazareth bloss als eine Etappe bei Jesu Übersiedlung zum "Meergebiet", um später im Anschluss an die Akoluthie des Mk auf die Episode in Nazareth (Kap. 13) zurückzukommen.

Allerdings bildet die Bemerkung von Goulder eine konkurrenzfähige Alternative: "He [Matthew] has introduced Jesus' settlement in Nazareth into the gospel at 2.23, and now that he has Jesus to return to Galilee, he may be expected to say how the ministry came

[12] Einen anderen Fall, wo ein Stadtname in Mt in zweifacher Form überliefert wird, stellt "Jerusalem" dar, welches in Mt 11-mal mit Ἱεροσόλυμα und 2-mal (Mt 23:37) mit Ἰερουσαλήμ wiedergeben wird. Im Rahmen der FGH wäre zu erklären, weshalb Matthäus eben und nur in 23:37 von seinem normalen Gebrauch abweicht, während nach der 2QTh der Evangelist hier hypothesengemäss von Q (= Lk 13:34) abhängig ist. Angemerkt sei noch, dass Matthäus in 4:5 (Q) und 27:53 (S-Mt) statt "Jerusalem" von ἡ ἁγία πόλις spricht.

to begin in Capernaum. . . ."[13] Ohne Zweifel widerspricht es in keiner Weise der Erwartung des Lesers, dass einer, der laut prophetischem Wort seiner Heimat gemäss Ναζωραῖος genannt wird, zu Beginn seiner Mission, wenn auch nur beiläufig, in Zusammenhang mit seiner Vaterstadt gebracht wird—aber warum dann nicht eben die Form Ναζαρέτ?

Welche Gründe mag nun aber Lukas dafür gehabt haben, Jesu ersten Auftritt in Nazaret stattfinden zu lassen? Von entscheidender Bedeutung ist dabei die Frage, ob Ναζαρά die urspüngliche Lesart in Lk 4:16 bildet oder nicht. Wenn ja, dann dürfte zumindest feststehen, dass Lukas unmöglich von sich aus, ohne von einer Nebenquelle—von welcher auch immer—beeinflusst zu sein, jene Form geschrieben haben kann. Dann bliebe nur noch die Aufgabe, diese Quelle zu definieren zu versuchen.

Gleichzeitig ist jedoch die Alternative in Erwägung zu ziehen, dass Ναζαρά in Lk textkritisch sekundär ist.[14] Obwohl es sich um die schwierigere Lesart zu handeln scheint, kann die Möglichkeit einer frühen Angleichung nicht ausser Betracht bleiben, und zwar umso mehr, als die Lesart Ναζαρά in Lk auch sachlich-inhaltlich nicht ohne Probleme ist. Analog mit Mt 4:13 würde man als Leser bei Lk 4:16 naturgemäss erwarten, dass Lukas dieselbe Form verwendete, wie vorher schon viermal (1:26; 2:4; 2:39; 2:51).[15] Oder sollte man voraussetzen, dass der Verfasser sich in dem Mass an die ihm eventuell vorliegende Quelle gebunden sah, dass er auch bei einem ungewöhlichen Ausdruck nicht davon abweichen wollte bzw. im Gebrauch des abweichenden Ausdrucks kein Problem sah?

Auf alle Fälle ist es nicht unangebracht, die Frage anzuschneiden, wie die Lokalisierung der Auftrittsszene in Nazareth (und nicht etwa in Kapharnaum) erklärlich zu machen wäre, hätte in Lk 4:16 für Ναζαρά ursprünglich Ναζαρέθ gestanden. Es wurde schon auf die Bemerkung von Goulder hingewiesen, dass es die Intention des Matthäus war, Jesus als Nazarener von Nazareth nach Kapharnaum ziehen zu lassen. Im Vergleich mit Mt ist nun der lk Jesus in noch grösserem Mass ein Nazarener. Seine Eltern stammen von dort und kehren nach seiner Geburt dorthin zurück (Lk 2:4, 39). Dort wächst

[13] Goulder, "Knowledge", 147.

[14] Varianten: -εδ, -ετ, -εθ, -ατ.

[15] Von Nazareth ist im lk Doppelwerk nachher nur einmal die Rede, und zwar in der gleichen Form Ναζαρέθ (Apg 10:38).

er in Weisheit, Alter und Gnade (2:40, 52) heran. Es hat also guten Sinn, wenn Jesus sein Programm gerade in seiner Heimatstadt, wo er laut 2:52 ebenfalls unter den Menschen Beifall gefunden hatte, kundtut und nicht in Kapharnaum, mit dem er noch keine Verbindung gehabt hat. Über solche allgemeine Erwägungen hinaus ist die Bemerkung zu berücksichtigen, die Lukas der Nennung der Stadt beifügt: οὗ ἦν τεθραμμένος. Das ist natürlich ein Verweis auf Lk 2:39–40, 51–52, jedoch nicht nur das. Vielmehr klingen hier ebenso die Begründung und Erklärung dafür an, weshalb Jesu Wirksamkeit nach einer allgemeinen Mission in den galiläischen Synagogen gerade in Nazareth ihren konkreten Lauf nimmt: Weil er dort aufgewachsen war.

Auch funktionell und inhaltlich gliedert sich Lk 4:16–30 sinnvoll in seinen Kontext ein. Der Abschnitt enthält drei programmatische Motive. Erstens die prophetische Botschaft und Aufgabe Jesu (18–19), zweitens die Absage der Juden an das Evangelium sowie die Zuwendung zu den Heiden als deren Kehrseite (24–27), ein grundlegendes Thema der Apg, und drittens der Versuch, Jesus zu töten (29).[16] Auffallend ist—und zwar umso stärker, je grösser man den Anteil des Evangelisten bei der Gestaltung von 4:16–30 einstuft—die Entfaltung des dritten Motivs. Dazu bot der Text der Mk-Vorlage (ebenso wenig wie der des Mt) keinen Ansporn. Es ist Lukas selber, der hier, gerade in Nazareth, zum Beginn der Mission Jesu, die Ablehnung bis zum Äussersten treibt. Die Prophezeihung des Simeon über das Zeichen, dem widersprochen wird (2:34), wird in ihrer ersten Konkretisierung dargestellt. Die Dramatik der Szene wird dadurch gesteigert, dass die Verwerfung gerade von Seiten der Mitbürger geschieht. Nach dem Zwischenfall besucht der lk Jesus seine Heimat nie wieder.

Demnach scheint die Annahme, nach der Lukas Nazareth gleichermassen aus eigener Iniative zum Schauplatz der Programmerklärung Jesu hat wählen können, nicht aus der Luft gegriffen zu sein.[17] Das

---

[16] Vgl. hierzu J.T. Sanders, *The Jews in Luke-Acts* (Philadelphia: Fortress Press, 1987) 164–68, der u.a. auf thematische Zusammenhänge zwischen Lk und Apg verweist. Wie bei Jesus, so versucht auch im Fall des Paulus die Zuhörerschaft den Sprechenden zu töten, und bei Stephanos ist es tatsächlich gelungen; "and all three incidents follow statements either of God's intended salvation for the Gentiles (in the cases of Jesus and of Paul) or of the Jews' endemic refusal of God's salvation (in the case of Stephen)" (S. 167).

[17] Man könnte dazu freilich einwenden, dass Lukas damit gegen seinen eigenen

problematisiert die Hypothese einer Nebenquelle weiter. Freilich ist diese Annahme textkritisch verwundbar—doch unverwundbar ist keine. In dem Fall, dass man an der Lesart von NA27 festhält, können für die 2QTh zwei Möglichkeiten erwogen werden: Entweder deutet die von den beiden Evangelisten sonst nicht benutzte Benennung der Heimat Jesu auf die Tradition, und zwar am ehesten auf Q.[18] Oder aber, wenn Ναζαρά in Lk als sekundär zu betrachten wäre, wären die Lokalisierung sowie die Namensform der eigenständigen Redaktion des Lukas zuzuschreiben. Bei der intertextuellen Lösung der FGH bleiben wiederum die überhastete Erwähnung der Heimat sowie die spezielle Namensform Ναζαρά in Mt weiterhin problematisch.

2. *Die Berufung der ersten Jünger und der Tag in Kapharnaum*

Es handelt sich um die Divergenz der Erzählakoluthie zwischen Lk und Mk. Der lk Synagogenszene in Nazareth (4:16–30) folgt Jesu Auftreten in Kapharnaum und dessen Umgebung (4:31–44), dem sich die Berufung der ersten Jünger (5:1–11) anschliesst. Dagegen erscheint in Mk eine Abfolge, in der auf die Verkündigung des Gottesreiches (1:14–15) zuerst die Berufung der ersten Jünger (1:16–20) und dann das Wirken in Kapharnaum und Umgebung (1:21–39) folgen; also kommen die zwei letzten Etappen in Lk und Mk in umgekehrter Reihenfolge vor. Mt seinerseits schliesst sich grundsätzlich an

---

darstellerischen Grundsatz des καθεξῆς gehandelt hätte, s. Goulder, "Knowledge", 145. Was aber καθεξῆς für Lukas heisst, kann man in Lk 1:3 noch nicht wissen, sondern nur aus der tatsächlichen Erzählakoluthie seines Werkes herauslesen—und nicht unabhängig von der jeweiligen synoptischen Theorie interpretieren.

[18] Erwähnenswert ist die Vermutung, Ναζαρά habe in Q gar nicht zum Schauplatz eines Geschehnisses gedient, sondern einfach—zu Beginn der Quelle—ein "identification of Jesus as Jesus of Nazara" gebildet. So J.M. Robinson, "The Sayings Gospel Q", in F. Van Segbroeck, C.M. Tuckett, G. Van Belle and J. Verheyden (hgg.), *The Four Gospels 1992: Festschrift Frans Neirynck* (3 Bde; BETL 100; Leuven: Leuven University Press, 1992) 361–88, S. 377, s. auch S. 380.—Nach Fertigstellung des Aufsatzes wurde dem Verf. noch der Artikel von F. Neirynck, "NAZARA in Q: Pro and Con", in J.M. Asgeirsson, K. De Troyer, M.W. Meyer (hgg.), *From Quest to Q: Festschrift James M. Robinson* (BETL 146; Leuven: Leuven University Press, 2000) 159–69 bekannt. Neirynck geht von der Goulderschen Annahme eines Zusammenhangs von Mt 4:13 und Mk 1:24 aus und entwickelt und modifiziert diese zu der Hypothese, nach der der Einfluss des Ναζαρηνός in Mk dazu beigetragen habe, dass Matthäus und Lukas die Form Ναζαρά, wenn auch nicht "gebildet", so doch dem Ausdruck Ναζαρέθ vorgezogen haben (S. 169).

die mk Abfolge an: Nach der die Schrift erfüllenden Übersiedlung von Nazareth nach Kapharnaum (4:13–16) beginnt Jesus seine Predigt und beruft die ersten Jünger (4:17–22); daran knüpft sich seine Lehr- und Heilungstätigkeit in Galiläa an (4:23). Goulder zieht den Schluss, irgendetwas bringe Lukas dazu, von der Mk-Akoluthie abzuweichen.[19]

Dass Lukas die Veränderung vorgenommen hätte, um etwa die in Mk unvermittelt dargestellte Berufung "psychologisch" plausibler zu machen, reicht Goulder als Erklärung nicht aus.[20] Vielmehr findet er hier einen Fall, wo Lukas Mk anhand des Mt interpretiert. Goulder nimmt an, dass Lukas Mt 4:13–16 als eine Zusammenfassung von Mk 1:21–39 betrachtete, wobei Mt 4:17–22 und Lk 5:1–11 sich entsprechen, während Mt 4:23 für eine Zusammenfassung von Mk 1:40–3:6 zu halten war. Darüber hinaus verweist er darauf, dass Mt 4:17–18 im Horizont des Lukas als eine gedankliche Einheit verstanden werden konnte: Der Berufung des Simon ging Jesu Predigt voraus, genauer gesagt eine Predigt zur Umkehr. Die Busse des Simon ist dann eine folgerichtige Reaktion darauf. Goulder zieht den Schluss: "So Luke could well have drawn the seaside preaching and Peter's repentance from Matthew, as well as the change of order."[21]

Wie stringent ist die Gouldersche Argumentation? Was zunächst die Thematik von Umkehr und Busse angeht, kann man kaum einen prinzipiellen Unterschied darin sehen, ob Lukas den ihm ideologisch wichtigen Sachzusammenhang aus Mt 4:17→18–22 oder aus Mk 1:15→16–20 herausgelesen hat. Dass Jesu Busspredigt nach Mk unspezifischer in Galiläa, nach Mt genau in Kapharnaum zu hören war, ist sachlich dasselbe; nur hat Matthäus die Übersiedlung nach Kapharnaum, unter Aufnahme des Schriftbeweises, darstellerisch geschickter mit der Szene am See verknüpft.

Die Antwort auf die Frage, aus welchem Grund Lukas die Berufung des Simon nicht vor, sondern nach Jesu Wirken in Kapharnaum vorführt, kann man nur aus dem Duktus und der Logik des lk Berichts in Kap. 4 zu finden versuchen. Auszugehen ist von der Beobachtung, dass Lukas Jesus zunächst generell als einen in den Synagogen Lehrenden bzw. Predigenden auftreten lässt (4:14, 44),

---

[19] Goulder, "Knowledge", 149.

[20] Goulder, "Knowledge", 148, der als Beispiel für Vertreter solch einer Deutung J. Fitzmyer, *The Gospel According to Luke* (2 Bde; AncB 28; Garden City, NY: Doubleday 1981) 1.560 anführt.

[21] Goulder, "Knowledge", 148–49.

wie dieses Prinzip sich dann in den Synagogen von Nazareth und Kapharnaum (4:16; 4:31, 33) konkret realisiert. M.a.W., die Synagogen machen den Brückenkopf aus, von dem aus Jesus seine Mission ausrichtet. Diese Hervorhebung der jüdischen Institution als Schauplatz des Wirkens Jesu stammt nicht speziell aus Mt noch Mk, sondern ist als Lukas' eigene Intention zu bewerten.[22]

Mit diesem Sachverhalt würde es in Widerspruch stehen, wenn der lk Jesus sich bei seiner Ankunft in Kapharnaum zuerst zum Seeufer begeben hätte und in diesem "inoffiziellen" Kontext seine Predigt hätte beginnen wollen. Ganz natürlich ist es hingegen, dass er, nachdem er aus der Synagoge von Nazareth hinausgeworfen worden ist, ohne sein Programm in seiner Heimat in die Tat umsetzen zu können, eine andere Synagoge aufsucht, um von dort aus einen neuen Anfang zu machen. Die Intention des Verfassers ist klar: Was in Nazareth nicht möglich war, wird in Kapharnaum Wirklichkeit werden. Das ist daran zu erkennen, dass die in Lk 4:18–19 verkündigte prophetische Aufgabe im Rahmen von Lk 4:31–43 anhand von Mk 1:21–39 demonstriert wird. Dies kommt dadurch zum Ausdruck, dass in Lk 4:43 Formulierungen gebraucht werden, die deutlich auf Jesu Nazarether Programm zurückverweisen, wie ein Vergleich von Lk 4:43 mit der Mk-Parallele 1:38 zeigt:

Mk 1:38
Ἄγωμεν ἀλλαχοῦ εἰς τὰς ἐχομένας κωμοπόλεις, ἵνα καὶ ἐκεῖ κηρύξω. εἰς τοῦτο γὰρ ἐξῆλθον.
Lk 4:43
Καὶ ταῖς ἑτέραις πόλεσιν εὐαγγελίσασθαί με δεῖ τὴν βασιλείαν τοῦ θεοῦ, ὅτι ἐπὶ τοῦτο ἀπεστάλην.
Lk 4:18
Πνεῦμα κυρίου ἐπ' ἐμέ οὗ εἵνεκεν ἔχρισέν με εὐαγγελίσασθαι πτωχοῖς, ἀπέσταλκέν με κηρύξαι . . .

Sollte das Wirken Jesu in Kapharnaum (Lk 4:31–43) demnach ein direktes Gegenstück zu den Ereignissen in Nazareth (4:16–30) darstellen, so kann zwischen den beiden Abschnitten kein Platz für die Berufung des Petrus übrigbleiben. Dem ist eine weitere Überlegung hinzuzufügen, welche bei Lukas möglicherweise eine Rolle gespielt haben kann. Jesu Bemerkung: "Was wir alles gehört haben, das in

[22] Die gleiche Intention wird in Apg augenscheinlich, wo Paulus schematisch Synagogen aufsucht (Apg 9:19–20; 13:5, 14; 14:1, 17:1–2, 10, 17; 18:4, 19; 19:8; vgl. 16:13).

Kapharnaum geschehen ist, tue ebenfalls hier in deiner Heimat" (4:23)—wobei er doch bisher Kapharnaum nicht einmal besucht hat—wird als lk Bildung verständlicher, wenn es des Verfassers Absicht war, die verlangten Taten im weiteren Verlauf der Erzählung baldmöglichst ansichtig werden zu lassen.[23] Zur Demonstrierung von 4:18–19 und 4:23 würde der Abschnitt 5:1–11 nicht auf die beste Weise dienen, da der Berufungsbericht mit seinem Interesse für die Person des Simon allzu sehr auf das Private begrenzt ist, während hier eine breite Öffentlichkeit wie sie in Mk 1:21–39 zum Ausdruck kommt, vonnöten ist.

Im Lichte der obigen Auslegung hat Lukas in Kap. 4 nicht Mt 4:13–16, sondern Mk 1:21–39 im Blick. Wichtiger als die sofortige Berufung des Petrus ist dem Evangelisten das In-Gang-Bringen der Mission Jesu auf dem herkömmlichen Forum des jüdischen Glaubens.[24]

3. *Der ἐπὶ κλίνης getragene Gelähmte*

Zur Diskussion steht die Vokabel κλίνη (um welche Mt und Lk den Text des Mk ergänzen) für das Bett, auf dem der Gelähmte zu Jesus gebracht wird (Mk 2:1–12; Mt 9:2 8; Lk 5:17–26)

Mt 9:2
καὶ ἰδοὺ προσέφερον αὐτῷ παραλυτικὸν ἐπὶ κλίνης βεβλημένον
Mk 2:3
καὶ ἔρχονται φέροντες πρὸς αὐτὸν παραλυτικὸν αἰρόμενον ὑπὸ τεσσάρων
Lk 5:18
καὶ ἰδοὺ ἄνδρες φέροντες ἐπὶ κλίνης ἄνθρωπον

Nach Goulder heisse κλίνη in Mt 'Bahre', wobei zu fragen sei, ob diese Bedeutung dem Gebrauch bei Lukas entspricht. Wenn nämlich Lukas anderswo Bahre meint, verwende er κλινάριον und κράβαττος (Apg 5:15) sowie das im vorliegenden Abschnitt zweimal benutzte κλινίδιον (5:19,24). Dahingegen bedeute κλίνη in Lk Bett mit Füssen, eine Bedeutung, die in Lk 8:16 die einzig mögliche ist.[25]

[23] Insofern kann Lk 4:23 als eine Vorwegnahme von 4:31–44 verstanden werden.

[24] Das steht freilich in Widerspruch zu Goulders Betonung von καθεξῆς als der Leitlinie des Evangelisten für seine Darstellung. Da Lukas' Verfahren in 4:31–5:11 sonst jedoch ohne Einfluss von Mt erklärlich ist, vermag dieses Argument—jedenfalls nicht unumstritten—die Beweislast nicht allein zu tragen. S. auch Anm. 17.

[25] In Goulder, "Putting", 223, werden mehrere Beispiele vorgelegt, wo Lukas Deminutiva in einem von der Grundform abweichenden Sinn verwendet.

Das Fazit: "So his ἐπὶ κλίνης does not seem very natural, and looks like the influence of Mt 9.2."[26]

In der Tat, weshalb taugt das von Mk verwendete κράβαττος (2:4, 9, 11, 12; später noch 6:55) Lukas hier nicht, obwohl er das gleiche Wort in gleicher Bedeutung später in Apg aufnimmt? Wie kommt er zu κλίνη?

Zur Unterstützung von κλίνη als lk-red Bildung macht Tuckett zum einen auf die Verwendung von κλίνη in LXX aufmerksam und kommt zu dem Ergebnis, dass es meist unmöglich ist, einen Unterschied zwischen dem eigentlichen Bett und der Bahre zu machen. Die Bedeutung 'Bahre' sei jedenfalls im biblischen Spachgebrauch möglich und in Mt 9:2 von Matthäus auch deutlich so verstanden. Zweitens behauptet Tuckett, die Evidenz betreffs der von Lukas ausserhalb von Kap. 5 für Bahre gebrauchten Worte sei unzureichend, weshalb es nicht möglich sei zu bestimmen, welches Wort lk sei und welches nicht. Tuckett geht deshalb davon aus, dass Lukas das ihm von LXX bekannte κλίνη in 5:18 einsetzte und im weiteren Verlauf der Erzählung in der für ihn typischen Weise variierte: κλίνη (V. 18), κλινίδιον (VV. 19,24) und ἐφ' ὃ κατέκειτο (V. 25).[27] Gegen die Behauptung von Tuckett, dass nicht alle Deminutiva in Lk in abweichendem Sinn benutzt werden könnten, wendet Goulder ein, er kenne kein Stück in Lk, "where an important piece of furniture is spoken of in this varied kind of way", und verweist auf 5:1–11 als Beispiel für einen Fall, wo keine Variierung vorhanden ist: πλοῖον wird 5-mal, δίκτυα 3-mal, ἰχθύες 2-mal gebraucht.[28]

Angesichts dieses Dilemmas ist es am sichersten, das Problem in erster Linie als eine dem betreffenden Textabschnitt immanente Frage zu betrachten und nicht sosehr auf den generellen Gebrauch des Evangelisten zu berufen, der eben umstritten ist. Dabei kann im Ansatz festgehalten werden, dass der Verfasser zumindest bei der Wendung ἐφ' ὃ κατέκειτο (Lk 5:25), welche offensichtlich in Anlehnung an Mk 2:4 gebildet ist, auf Variation abzielt; doch das problematische Verhältnis von κλίνη und κλινίδιον ist damit nicht beseitigt. Zumindest kann Lk 8:16 den Sinn von κλίνη in 5:18 nicht entscheiden, da der Kontext verschieden ist.

[26] Goulder, "Knowledge", 150.
[27] Tuckett, "Relationship", 133.
[28] Goulder, "Knowledge", 150.

Um voranzukommen sei versucht, den Redaktionsprozess des Lukas tentativ nachzuvollziehen. Bei Mk 2:3 wäre der Evangelist zu dem Gedanken gekommen, er müsse den Text von Mk präzisieren und zum Ausdruck bringen, worauf der Gelähmte getragen wurde. Aus Mk, seiner primären Quelle, war κράβαττος, 'Bahre', zu entnehmen (Mk 2:4). Durch dieses Wort sowie im Hinblick auf den weiteren Erzählablauf war es Lukas natürlich klar, dass es sich um solch ein Bett handeln musste, das man mit sich tragen konnte (Mk 2:9, 11–12). Dasselbe muss genauso für den Fall gelten, dass Lukas auch Mt vor sich hatte, wobei er κλίνη nicht nur in V. 2, sondern auch in V. 6 (ἆρον σου τὴν κλίνην) las. Eben wegen V. 6 ist praktisch ausgeschlossen, dass Lukas die von Mt verwendete Vokabel im Sinn von 'Bett mit Füssen' verstanden haben könnte.

Immerhin stellt κλίνη nach wie vor ein MA dar, welches entweder auf eine Benutzung des Mt oder eine eigenständige Redaktion des Lukas zurückgeht. Lassen sich Gründe für die zweite Alternative vorbringen? Einmal ist zu beachten, dass κλίνη in Lk insgesamt dreimal begegnet, und zwar in verschiedenen Zusammenhängen (ausser 5:18 und 8:16 noch 17:34); Deminutive erscheinen ebenfalls dreimal (die schon erwähnten Stellen 5:19, 25; Apg 5:15).[29] In Mt kommt κλίνη nur hier (9:2, 6) vor; Deminutiva fehlen ganz. Darüber hinaus verwendet Lukas den Stamm κλιν- in verbaler Bedeutung weitaus öfter als Mt (κλίνω 1/4; ἀνακλίνω 2/3, κατακλίνω 0/5; insgesamt 3/12). Aus dieser Perspektive ist κλίνη in Lk 5:18 in der Tat leichter als in Mt 9:2 der Redaktion zuzuschreiben.

Freilich darf nicht ausser Acht bleiben, dass Mt 9:2–8 und Lk 5:17–26 viele weitere MAs aufweisen, die zu berücksichtigen hier jedoch nicht möglich ist. Allein was κλίνη anbelangt, muss es als schlagender Beweis für die Abhängigkeit des Lk von Mt entfallen.

4. *Die Stelle des Andreas in den Zwölferlisten*

Die Reihenfolge der vier erstgenannten Apostel ist in den drei Listen Mk 3:16–18, Mt 10:2 und Lk 6:14 verschieden. Während Andreas

[29] Übrigens ist zu beachten, dass κράβαττος in Apg 5:15 nicht selbständig, sondern als Glied eines Hendiadyoin, und zwar als das letztere, begegnet. Das könnte zusätzlich ein Hinweis darauf sein, dass Lukas den Stamm κλιν- bevorzugt und dass man daher bei Lk 5:18 nicht vorschnell voraussetzen darf, der Verfasser wäre ohne eine Nebenquelle in seiner Wortwahl Mk gefolgt.

in Mk als vierter angeführt wird, begegnet er in Mt und Lk als zweiter, gepaart mit seinem als erstem genannten Bruder Simon:

> Mt 10:2
> πρῶτος Σίμων ὁ λεγόμενος Πέτρος καὶ Ἀνδρέας ὁ ἀδελφὸς αὐτοῦ, καὶ Ἰάκωβος ὁ τοῦ Ζεβεδαίου καὶ Ἰωάννης ὁ ἀδελφὸς αὐτοῦ. . . .
> Mk 3:16–18
> καὶ ἐπέθηκεν ὄνομα τῷ Σίμωνι Πέτρον, καὶ Ἰάκωβον τὸν τοῦ Ζεβεδαίου καὶ Ἰωάννην τὸν ἀδελφὸν τοῦ Ἰακώβου καὶ ἐπέθηκεν αὐτοῖς ὀνόμα[τα] Βοανηργές, ὅ ἐστιν υἱοὶ βροντῆς· καὶ Ἀνδρέαν. . . .
> Lk 6:14
> Σίμωνα ὃν καὶ ὠνόμασεν Πέτρον, καὶ Ἀνδρέαν τὸν ἀδελφὸν αὐτοῦ, καὶ Ἰάκωβον καὶ Ἰωάννην. . . .
> Apg 1:13
> Πέτρος καὶ Ἰωάννης καὶ Ἰάκωβος καὶ Ἀνδρέας. . . .

Es kommt Goulder unwahrscheinlich vor, dass Lukas von sich aus Andreas mit Petrus zusammengebracht hätte, und zwar deshalb, weil der Evangelist ihn in dem Berufungsbericht seines Bruders (Lk 5:1–11) nicht nennt und weil sein Name in der Apostelliste Apg 1:13 wie in Mk 3:16–18 an vierter Stelle begegnet. Goulder macht dann noch auf die Anordnungsweise der Apostel aufmerksam: Während Mk die Apostel mit parataktischem καί verbindet, führt Matthäus sie paarweise auf, worin Lukas ebenfalls Mt folge. Daher die Schlussfolgerung: "So Matthean influence on both the pairing and promotion of Andrew seems the most plausible."[30]

Welche Gründe der Evangelist Markus letztlich dafür gehabt haben wird, dass er Andreas und dessen Bruder separat anführt, kann hier offen bleiben. Jedenfalls steht der Sachverhalt im Einklang mit dem Befund, dass in dem weiteren Verlauf des Evangeliums gerade Petrus, Jakobus und Johannes die Kerngruppe bilden, die in wichtigen Begebenheiten mit Jesus erscheint.[31] Eine Ausnahme bildet Mk 13:3, wo Andreas zu den vier zählt, die Jesus nach den Zeichen der Zeiten fragt; konsequenterweise wird er auch dann als letzter genannt.

---

[30] Goulder, "Knowledge", 151. Auf die Übereinstimmungen von Lk 6:14 mit Mt 10:2 gegen Mk 3:16–18 macht auch R.H. Gundry, "Matthean Foreign Bodies in Agreements with Luke to Matthew against Mark evidence that Luke knew Matthew", in Van Segbroeck etc. (hgg.), *The Four Gospels*, 1467–95, S. 1470 aufmerksam. Die Stelle ist eine von denen, auf deren Grund Gundry auf eine "subsiduäre" Abhängigkeit des Lk von Mt schliesst, ohne auf die Q-Hypothese zu verzichten.

[31] Mk 5:37; 9:2; 14:33.

Dass nun Lukas in Lk 5:1–11 über Andreas im Zusammenhang mit der Berufung seines Bruders kein Wort verliert, läuft tatsächlich der Erwartung eines Lesers zuwider, dem Mk 1:16–18 bekannt ist. Selbstverständlich hat auch der Evangelist das Stück gelesen, wie auch aus den in den VV. 4–7 gebrauchten Pluralformen zu schliessen ist.[32] Es wird zu vermuten sein, dass die Vorrangigkeit des Petrus unterstrichen werden soll. Damit verknüpft ist die folgende Erwägung: Wäre Andreas als Partner des Simon namhaft gemacht worden, hätte das zur Folge gehabt, dass Lukas auch von Andreas' Bekehrung hätte erzählen müssen, womit wiederum der Primat des Petrus angetastet worden wäre. Auf jeden Fall ist es schwer vorstellbar, dass Lukas grundsätzlich etwas gegen Andreas hätte, sonst wäre dieser in Kap. 6 kaum an auffallender Stelle neben seinem berühmten Bruder genannt. Auch deshalb war es leichter, ihn in Kap. 5 wie schon in 4:38 zu übergehen, weil er—trotz seines Status als Bruder des Petrus—im Rest des Evangeliums, anders als die drei namhaft gemachten, keine Rolle spielen wird. Andreas hat seinen Platz in der Zwölferliste als einer der vielen, deren Namen erwähnt werden, weil sie zu dem Apostelkreis gehören und ihre Funktion in diesem Rahmen haben, jedoch als Einzelpersonen nicht in Erscheinung treten.

Im Einklang damit steht die Tatsache, dass in der Liste der Apg diejenigen Apostel als erste angeführt werden—und zwar sind sie wieder Petrus, Johannes und Jakobus—, von denen der Verfasser noch später zu berichten weiss. Beachtenswert ist dabei, dass die Reihenfolge der Zebedäussöhne in Apg von der der synoptischen Listen, in denen Jakobus immer vor Johannes genannt wird, abweicht. Das wiederum entspricht der Sachlage, dass in Apg Johannes, weil Mitarbeiter des Petrus, eine wichtigere Rolle als Jakobus spielt.[33] Lukas scheint demnach die Apostel in Apg in ihrer "erzählstrategischen" Rangordnung vorzuführen. Dass Andreas auf dem vierten Platz und nicht etwa später wieder erscheint—um noch einmal diejenige Gruppe der Apostel anzuführen, von denen als Einzelpersonen

[32] Wahrscheinlich ist, wie Goulder, "Knowledge", 151, annimmt, mit dem Plural nur an Petrus und Andreas gedacht. Die zwei Boote, die erwähnt werden, können keinem anderen als Petrus und Andreas einerseits sowie Jakob und Johannes andererseits gehören. Tuckett, "Relationship", 134, meint zurecht, Lk 5:1–11 sei Substitution für Mk 1:16–20, doch ist er der Ansicht, die Parallelität braucht nicht unbedingt so weit gehen, dass die Teilnehmer ebenfalls identisch sein müssten.

[33] Apg 3:1ff., 4:1ff., 8:14ff.

nachher nichts gehört wird—ist durch seine Beziehung zu Petrus bedingt.

Nach alledem ist Lukas nicht ohne Bedacht mit den Aposteln umgegangen, was durchaus im Einklang mit der grundlegenden Bedeutung steht, die sie für ihn haben. Welche Stelle müsste er in seiner Liste dann bei seiner erwiesenen Umsicht Andreas geben? Sollte er etwa, lag ihm Mk als einzige Quelle vor, Andreas eben als den vierten Apostel anführen?

Lukas befand sich in einer widerspruchsvollen Lage. Gesetzt den Fall, er hatte ausschliesslich Mk vor sich, so brachte es in einer Stelle (Mk 3:16–18) die beiden Apostel getrennt vor, doch an einer anderen Stelle (Mk 1:16–18) gab Mk die Information, die Apostel seien Brüder gewesen und als solche beim gemeinsamen Fischzug berufen worden, nicht anders als Jakobus und Johannes. Wäre nun auch Mt Lukas vorgelegen, so wäre die Entscheidung für ihn leicht gewesen: Da die Quellen einstimmig die beiden Apostel als Brüder sowie als gleichzeitig Berufene darstellten, war es am natürlichsten, bei der Gestaltung der Apostelliste Mt zu folgen, der sie auch in seiner Liste ungezwungen einen nach dem anderen als Brüder aufführte. Hatte er dagegen Mk als seine einzige Quelle zur Verfügung, stand er vor einer Wahl: Auf der einen Seite wäre—mit Rücksicht auf die Rolle des Andreas im Rest des Doppelwerkes—konsequent gewesen, der Reihenfolge der Zwölferliste zu folgen. Auf der anderen Seite, da Jakobus und Johannes als Paar erscheinen, war es möglich, auch das andere Bruderpaar zusammen vorzustellen.

Darauf, dass Lukas in diesem Dilemma nicht einfach den Zufall bei seiner Lösung regieren liess, weist die Beobachtung hin, dass er in Lk 6:14, von seiner Mk-Vorlage abweichend, Jakobus und Johannes nur dem Namen nach nennt, ohne sie als Brüderpaar oder Zebedäussöhne vorzustellen. Das ist verständlich, denn die Vorstellung ist schon in 5:1–11 geschehen und erübrigt sich hier. Anders liegt es bei Andreas. Lukas führt eine bisher unbenannte Person auf und stellt sie als Bruder des Petrus vor, welche Information er, wie gesagt, aus Mk 1:16–18 erhält. Dabei müsste es sonderlich erschienen sein, den so beschriebenen Andreas, der laut Mk—und intentionsgemäss doch auch nach Lukas!—zur gleichen Zeit berufen war, von seinem Bruder zu trennen und in der Zwölferliste hinter die Zebedäussöhne zu rücken. M.a.W., mit der Beifügung des τὸν ἀδελφὸν αὐτοῦ begründet Lukas, gewissermassen sich selber und seinem Leser, weshalb er den bisher Ungenannten und sonst unbekannt Bleibenden sofort an der zweiten Stelle, vor den bedeutenderen Jakobus und Johannes erwähnt. Das zeigt, dass Lukas aufgrund von Mk 1:16–18, d.h., den natürlichen verwandtschaftlichen Verhältnissen seine Entscheidung trifft.[34] Darüber hinaus ist zu bemerken, dass die Berufungsgeschichten Mk 1:16–20 und Lk 5:1–11 dem Verfasser in Kap. 6 noch frisch in Erinnerung waren und so die Redaktionsarbeit beeinflussten.

Die verwandtschaftlichen Verhältnisse sind so stark im menschlichen Bewusstsein verankert, dass ein "sachliches" Argument, die vierte Stelle in der Liste von Mk, dem weichen muss. Es ist sehr bezeichnend, dass Markus, der Andreas von Petrus trennt, diesen eben nicht als seinen Bruder, sondern bloss dem Namen nach anführt. Man muss sich auch vergegenwärtigen, dass Matthäus seinerseits vor dem gleichen Problem stand und es in gleicher Weise und höchstwahrscheinlich aus gleichen Gründen löste: wie Lukas, so liess sich auch er bei der Gestaltung seiner Apostelliste von dem mk Berufungsbericht leiten. Damit erübrigt sich an dieser Stelle die Annahme einer Abhängigkeit des Lk von Mt.

5. *Das Mischzitat Mk 1:2b und seine Q-Parallele Mt 11:10/Lk 7:27*

Das Problem: Wie kann Mk 1:2b, eine Kombination von Mal 3:1 und Ex 23:20, in Mk und Q (Mt 11:10, Lk 7:27) in fast identischer Fassung vorkommen? Die fünf Modifizierungen, die in Mk unternommen sind—ἀποστέλλω, πρὸ προσώπου σου, ὅς, κατασκευάσει und letztes σου—können unmöglich in Q aus Zufall in gleicher Weise vorgenommen worden sein.[35] In ihrer in NA27 vorliegenden Form sind die Verse bis auf die mt Ergänzung ἐγώ und das MA ἔμπροσθέν σου identisch.

> Mt 11:10
> Ἰδοὺ ἐγὼ ἀποστέλλω τὸν ἄγγελόν μου πρὸ προσώπου σου,
> ὃς κατασκευάσει τὴν ὁδόν σου ἔμπροσθέν σου
> Mk 1:2b
> Ἰδοὺ ἀποστέλλω τὸν ἄγγελόν μου πρὸ προσώπου σου,
> ὃς κατασκευάσει τὴν ὁδόν σου

[34] Tuckett, "Relationship", 134, schliesst zwar die Möglichkeit einer gemeinsamen Quelle für Mt und Lk nicht aus, aber scheint eher zu dem gleichen Ergebnis wie oben zu neigen: ". . . independent redaction of Mark, pairing Peter and Andrew as brothers, is quite easy to envisage."

[35] S. Goulder, "Knowledge", 151–52.

Lk 7:27
Ἰδοὺ ἀποστέλλω τὸν ἄγγελόν μου πρὸ προσώπου σου
ὃς κατασκευάσει τὴν ὁδόν σου ἔμπροσθέν σου
Mal 3:1
Ἰδοὺ ἐγὼ ἐξαποστέλλω τὸν ἄγγελόν μου,
καὶ ἐπιβλέψεται ὁδὸν πρὸ προσώπου μου
Ex 23:20
Καὶ ἰδοὺ ἐγὼ ἀποστέλλω τὸν ἄγγελόν μου πρὸ προσώπου σου,
ἵνα φυλάξῃ σε ἐν τῇ ὁδῷ

Goulder kommt hier ganz zwanglos zu seiner konkreten Lösung: Matthäus wollte bei 3:3 das alttestamentliche Zitat von Mk 1:2b nicht mit aufnehmen, weil dieses nicht aus Jesaja stammt, benutzte es aber später in einem anderen Zusammenhang (11:10). Lukas seinerseits ist bei 3:4 dem Vorbild des Mt 3:3 gefolgt (allerdings unter Erweiterung des Jesaja-Zitats) und hat Mk 1:2b in Anlehnung an seine Vorlage an entsprechender Stelle vorgeführt.[36]

Verständlicherweise wird in der Forschung in der Regel—primär wohl aufgrund der Information von NA25, NA26 und NA27—davon ausgegangen, V. 2b sei ein ursprünglicher Bestandteil des Mk. Ein Blick in den Apparat der Greevenschen Synopse lehrt allerdings, dass die Beweislage nicht absolut widerspruchsfrei ist. Der Vers wird nämlich von Basileios, Epiphanius und Victorinus Pettau nicht zitiert.[37] Es ist gewiss durchaus mit der Möglichkeit zu rechnen, dass der Vers unterdrückt wird, weil er weder ein Jesaja-Zitat ausmacht noch in den Grossevangelien an dieser Stelle vorkommt; ausserdem könnte es prinzipiell unter den drei irgendwelche literarische Abhängigkeit (etwa Epiphanius von Victorinus) geben. Andererseits ist in Kauf zu nehmen, dass der auf lateinisch schreibende Victorinus (gest. um 304) als Westländer geographisch weit entfernt (Poetovio, Pannonia) von den beiden östlichen Schriftstellern gewirkt hat. Das gibt zu bedenken, dass zumindest einer von ihnen mit einer Tradition vertraut gewesen sein könnte, die das Zitat nicht aufführte. Auf jeden Fall wäre an und für sich leicht vorstellbar, dass Mk 1:3 später um ein

[36] Dazu s. Goulder, "Putting", 225.

[37] Genauer gesagt liegt ein Fall vor, wo es "hinreichend deutlich" ist, dass die drei Schriftsteller "aus einem bestimmten Evangelium zitieren wollen [(zB durch ausdrückliche Nennung des Evangelisten, durch den Kontext oder auch eine Variante, die ausschliesslich für das betreffende Ev. bezeugt ist)] ", wenngleich der Kontext die Variante nicht sichert. A. Huck – H. Greeven, *Synopse der drei ersten Evangelien mit Beigabe der johanneischen Parallelstellen* (13. Aufl.; Tübingen: Mohr (Paul Siebeck), 1981) XVI.

weiteres, thematisch zusammenhängendes Schriftzitat aus den Grossevangelien ergänzt wurde, zumal Mt 11:10/Lk 7:27 und Mk 1:2a durch das Stichwort γέγραπται zusammenklingen (οὗτός ἐστιν περὶ οὗ γέγραπται resp. καθὼς γέγραπται).

Bekanntlich ist die Ursprünglichkeit des Zitats Mk 1:2b, welches die Eröffnung VV. 2–4 überfrachtet, längst auch ohne textkritische Evidenz angezweifelt worden.[38] Hierbei ist eigens auf das Problem aufmerksam zu machen, welches der Angabe der Herkunft der beiden Zitate gilt. Wenn Mk 1:2b–3 in einem Stück als ein Jesaja-Zitat aufgeführt wird, so wird das öfters zu einem sachlichen Irrtum gestempelt. Aber *wessen* Irrtum? Des Evangelisten oder seiner Tradition? Diese Frage wird umso dringender, wenn die Zusammenstellung des Mischzitats mit Goulder dem Evangelisten zuzuschreiben wäre.[39] Es bleibt nämlich zu fragen, ob Markus, nachdem er Vers 2b aus Ex und Mal sorgsam verflochten hat, das Ganze von 1:2b–3 als *Jesaja*-Zitat dargestellt hätte. Wenn Mk1:2b ursprünglich wäre, würde man eine allgemeinere Formulierung wie καθὼς γέγραπται erwarten.

Würde man Mk 1:2b jedoch, trotz der vorgeführten Bedenken, als original ansehen, so wäre der Befund am ehesten dahingehend zu verstehen, dass der Evangelist das Zitat aus der Tradition bekam, entweder schon mit dem Jesaja-Zitat V. 3 kombiniert oder—wahrscheinlich ohne Angabe des Urhebers—aus einem anderen Zusammenhang herstammend. Im ersten Fall könnte die Herkunftsangabe ebenfalls traditionell sein, im zweiten hätte sich Markus bei der Herkunftsangabe an dem unbearbeitet aufgenommenen Jesaja-Zitat orientiert.[40] Ob die beiden Zitate Mk 1:2b und Mt 11:10/Lk 7:27

[38] U.a. G. Strecker, *Weg der Gerechtigkeit: Untersuchungen zur Theologie des Matthäus* (FRLANT 82; Göttingen: Vandenhoeck & Ruprecht, 1962) 63 Anm. 1. Neulich hat J.K. Elliott, "Mark 1.1–3—A Later Addition to the Gospel?", *NTS* 46 (2000) 584–88 die Hypothese vorgelegt, die ursprüngliche Einleitung des Evangeliums sei verlorengegangen und sogar Mk 1:1–3 als Ganzes sei ein späterer Zusatz.

[39] Als Vertreter der 2QTh vgl. A. Suhl, *Die Funktion der alttestamentlichen Zitate und Anspielungen im Markusevangelium* (Gütersloh, 1965) 134ff., S. 132: Mk 1:2–3 ginge "mit grosser Wahrscheinlichkeit" auf das Konto des Markus. Aber, wie Tuckett, "Relationship", 141 Anm. 22, dazu bemerkt, "this does not necessarily say anything about the ultimate origin of the individual parts which go to make the whole."

[40] Natürlich gibt es auch andere denkbare Alternativen. Bei einer traditionellen Kombination von 2b–3 etwa könnte die Herkunftsangabe wegen des "main part of the quotation" auch auf den Evangelisten zurückgehen. So I. Dunderberg, "Q and the Beginning of Mark", *NTS* 41 (1995) 501–11, S. 511. Nach E. Schweizer, *Das Evangelium nach Markus* (NTD 1; Göttingen: Vandenhoeck & Ruprecht, 1975) 11, wurde das Zitat Jesaja zugeschrieben, "vielleicht weil es in einer Sammlung von

dann entweder auf eine gemeinsame Tradition zurückzuführen sind[41] oder ob das eine von dem anderen abhängig ist und in welcher Richtung (Mk abhängig von Q[42] resp. Q abhängig von Mk),[43] sind Fragen, die vom Standpunkt des vorliegenden Aufsatzes aus nicht wesentlich sind, wohl aber innerhalb der 2QTh zu diskutieren sind.[44]

Bibelzitaten einmal hinter dem Jesajawort stand."—Gleichfalls der Tradition rechnet Tuckett, "Relationship" 135, Mk 1:2b–3 zu, allerdings ohne ausdrücklich auf das Problem der Jesaja-Angabe von V. 2a einzugehen.

Eigens ist an dieser Stelle H.T. Fleddermann, *Mark and Q* (BETL 122; Leuven: Leuven University Press, 1995) 30, zu nennen, dessen Schlussfolgerung hinsichtlich der Herkunftsangabe V. 2a sowie des Problems der Zusammenstellung von Ex- und Mal-Versen in die gleiche Richtung wie die oben vorgelegten Erwägungen geht: ". . . the combination of Exod 23,20 and Mal 3,1 is skillfully done. Mark could not have combined the texts and been ignorant of their sources. Attributing the quotation to Isaiah makes sense, though, if Mark found the quotation in Q which identified it as scripture but did not specify the exact place where it could be found." Als Markus dann das Zitat V. 2b mit dem Jesaja-Zitat V. 3 verband, liess er das Ganze irrtümlich auf das Konto des Jesaja gehen, da ihm nur dessen Herkunftsort bekannt war.

[41] So C.M. Tuckett, "Mark and Q", in C. Focant (hg.), *The Synoptic Gospels: Source Criticism and the New Literary Criticism* (BETL 110; Leuven: Leuven University Press, 1993) 149–75, SS. 167–68, und Dunderberg, "Q", 501ff.

[42] So Fleddermann, *Mark*, 25ff.

[43] Diese Alternative würde eine Spätdatierung von Q voraussetzen. In der Tat vertritt M. Myllykoski in seinem beachtenswerten Aufsatz "The Social History of Q and the Jewish War" in R. Uro (hg.), *Symbols and Strata: Essays on the Sayings Gospel Q* (PFES 65; Helsinki, Göttingen: The Finnish Exegetical Society, Vandenhoeck & Ruprecht, 1996) 143–99, SS. 185ff., die Hypothese—nicht etwa um eine literarische Abhängigkeit des Q von Mk zu verfechten, sondern von sozialhistorischen Gesichtspunkten aus—, dass Q am ehesten nach dem jüdischen Krieg, ca. 75, zu datieren sei. Der Verfasser von Q habe in grossem Mass Material benutzt, welches in den kritischen Jahren des Krieges entstanden sei; doch Lk 17, der friedliche Umstände voraussetzt, blickt schon auf die vergangene Krise zurück (199). An die Spätdatierung von Q schliesst sich auch A. Järvinen, "The Son of Man and His Followers: A Q Portrait of Jesus", in D. Rhoads & K. Syreeni (hgg.), *Characterization in the Gospels: Reconceiving Narrative Criticism* (JSNTSup 184; Sheffield: Sheffield Academic Press, 1999) 180–222, SS. 218–19 an, wenngleich die Situation in einigen Punkten etwas anders interpretierend.

[44] Natürlich ist prinzipiell auch mit der Möglichkeit zu rechnen, dass Mk und Q sich schon im Lauf ihres Werdegangs miteinander in Berührung kamen. So ist etwa der interessante Versuch von H. Räisänen, *The 'Messianic Secret' in Mark* (übers. von C.M. Tuckett; Edinburgh: T & T Clark, 1990) 217ff., SS. 250ff., zu berücksichtigen, das mk "Messiasgeheimnis" im Zusammenhang mit einer Auseinandersetzung mit Trägern der Q-Tradition, die u. a. eine "defektive" Christologie vertreten sowie die Bedeutung der Auferstehung und Passion missverstanden hätten, erklärlich zu machen. Eine Implikation der von Räisänen sorgsam und vorsichtig dargestellten Hypothese könnte darin bestehen, dass Markus den Schriftbeleg 1:2b in seiner Konfrontation mit der Q-Tradition aufnahm und in einem anderen Zusammenhang benutzte, um—wenn man so will—den Status des von der Q-Gemeinde "hochstilisierten"

Die Stärke der Goulderschen Lösung—die Herkunft von Mk 1:2b als einem mk-red Konglomerat vorausgesetzt—besteht darin, dass sich Buchstabe um Buchstabe verfolgen lässt, wie zuerst Matthäus den Vers Mt 11:10 aus Mk 1:2b etwas ergänzend übernimmt und wie Lukas dann Lk 7:27 aus Mt 11:10 bis auf ἐγώ abschreibt. Allerdings wird die Beantwortung der Frage, wie gravierend der von Goulder aufgenommene Fall letztlich ist, dadurch erschwert, dass es uns unbekannt ist, in welchem Mass die von den frühen Christen verwendeten LXX-Texte untereinander und mit den uns erhaltenen identisch waren. Wie die Maleachi- und Exodus-Zitate aussahen, aus denen Mk 1:2b zusammengestellt wurde, entzieht sich unserer Kenntnis. Folglich lässt sich nicht bestimmen, inwieweit der Bearbeiter des Verses einem ihm bekannten LXX-Text bzw.—Texten direkt folgt und inwieweit er ihn (resp. sie) modifiziert.[45]

Aufs Ganze gesehen ist die Situation bei Mk 1:2bparr. alles andere als eindeutig, wodurch auch die Relevanz des MA ἔμπροσθέν σου unklar bleibt.

6. *"Wer hat dich so geschlagen . . .?"*

Das MA ist im vorliegenden Fall besonders augenfällig: Hier geht es um fünf Worte in gleicher Anordnung.

> Mt 26:67–68
> Τότε ἐνέπτυσαν εἰς τὸ πρόσωπον αὐτοῦ καὶ ἐκολάφισαν αὐτόν, οἱ δὲ ἐράπισαν λέγοντες· προφήτευσον ἡμῖν, χριστέ, <u>τίς ἐστιν ὁ παίσας σε</u>;
> Mk 14:65
> Καὶ ἤρξαντό τινες ἐμπτύειν αὐτῷ καὶ περικαλύπτειν αὐτοῦ τὸ πρόσωπον καὶ κολαφίζειν αὐτὸν καὶ λέγειν αὐτῷ· προφήτευσον, καὶ οἱ ὑπηρέται ῥαπίσμασιν αὐτὸν ἔλαβον.
> Lk 22:63–64
> Καὶ οἱ ἄνδρες οἱ συνέχοντες αὐτὸν ἐνέπαιζον αὐτῷ δέροντες, καὶ περικαλύψαντες αὐτὸν ἐπηρώτων λέγοντες· προφήτευσον, <u>τίς ἐστιν ὁ παίσας σε</u>;

Bei diesem vielverfochtenen Fall führt Goulder drei Beobachtungen zur Begründung seiner Hypothese vor, mit denen erkennbar werden

---

Johannes zu relativieren (zum Status des Täufers in Mk und Q vgl. Goulder, "Knowledge", 152).

[45] Während Dunderberg, "Q", 510, etwa für κατασκευάζειν als möglich ansieht, dass das Verb aus einer LXX-Rezension stammen könnte, ist Fleddermann, *Mark*, 27, der Meinung, es handele sich am ehesten um eine freie Adaptation des LXX-Textes.

soll, wie Matthäus in der für ihn charakterischen Weise den Text des Mk verdeutlicht.

Erstens wird ἐμπτύειν αὐτῷ des Mk von Matthäus zu ἐνέπτυσαν εἰς τὸ πρόσωπον präzisiert entsprechend seiner Art in Mt 27:29, wo er seine Vorlage um die Bemerkung ergänzt, dass die Soldaten die Dornenkrone auf Jesu Haupt setzten und ihm ein Rohr in seine rechte Hand gaben. Zweitens ist durch versehentliches Weglassen von περικαλύπτειν αὐτοῦ τὸ πρόσωπον dem Verfasser wie etwa bei 14:3–12 ein Kurzschluss unterlaufen. Drittens ist die spöttische Frage τίς ἐστιν ὁ παίσας σε; eingeleitet mit dem sarkastischen χριστέ (wie auch die Einfügung des ebenfalls sarkastischen εἰ υἱὸς εἶ τοῦ θεοῦ in 27:40) sprachlich mt. Zwar ist παίειν, aus Mk 14:47 erhalten, in Mt hapax, doch Lukas gebraucht in Lk-Apg mehrere Synonyma für 'schlagen' (wie τύπτειν, πατάσσειν, δέρειν), und ausserdem standen ihm die mk κολαφίζειν und ῥαπίζειν zu Gebote. Dass er gerade παίειν verwendet, verrate seine Abhängigkeit von Mt.[46]

Verfechter der 2QTh haben die Schwierigkeit bekanntlich anhand der Annahme einer Interpolation in Mt zu umgehen versucht.[47] Goulder hält dem entgegen, dass für eine Interpolation kein Zeuge vorliegt und dass der Text des Mt als solcher verständlich sei.[48] Doch gerade dieser Punkt ist diskutabel.

Die Auslegung, dass es sich bei dem Vermissen des Gesichtsverhüllens um einen Lapsus des Verfassers handele, leuchtet deshalb schlecht ein, weil es unwahrscheinlich ist, dass Matthäus aus Versehen gerade das Motiv übergangen hätte, welches ihm den Anlass zu weiterer Interpretation des Mk-Textes gegeben hat.[49] Insbesondere aber die

---

[46] Goulder, "Knowledge", 153–54.

[47] Dazu s. C.M. Tuckett, "The Minor Agreements and Textual Criticism", in G. Strecker (hg.), *Die Minor Agreements*, 119–41, SS. 135ff.

[48] Goulder, "Knowledge", 155.

[49] Das Problem ist schon von B.H. Streeter, *The Four Gospels: A Study of Origins, Treating of the Manuscript Tradition, Sources, Authorship, & Dates* (London: Macmillan, 1924, repr. 1964). 326 scharf gesehen; seine diesbezügliche Bemerkung wird von F. Neirynck, "ΤΙΣ ΕΣΤΙΝ Ο ΠΑΙΣΑΣ ΣΕ", *ETL* 63 (1987) 5–47, S. 29, zitiert. S. auch Neirynck, "ΤΙΣ", 39.—Der vorliegende Fall ist nicht mit Mt 14:3–12 vergleichbar. Hier geht es um einen beim redaktionellen Kürzungsprozess entstandenen Lapsus, und nicht darum, dass der Verfasser auf eine bestimmte pointierte Aussage abzielt, s. auch F. Neirynck, "The Minor Agreements and the Two-Source Theory" in Strecker (hg.), *Minor Agreements*, 25–62, S. 50, und Tuckett,"Minor Agreements", 140 Anm. 72 (mit Verweis auf Neirynck). Mithin muss jede Stelle, da Matthäus des "Schlamperns" verdächtigt ist, für sich betrachtet werden, ohne vorschnell generalisierende Schlüsse zu ziehen.

Tatsache, dass der Evangelist—im Unterschied zu Mk—die Rollen bei der Misshandlung Jesu neu verteilt, spricht gegen ein Versehen. Während es in Mk dieselben Leute (τινές) sind, die Jesus anspeien, ihm das Gesicht verhüllen, schlagen und befehlen zu weissagen, teilt Matthäus sie in zwei Gruppen ein: Die einen speien ihm ins Gesicht und schlagen ihn mit Fäusten, wogegen die "anderen" (οἱ δέ)[50] ihn ohrfeigen und ihm befehlen zu prophezeien. Mit der neuen bzw. neu akzentuierten Rollenverteilung muss Matthäus auf etwas abzielen. Was immer das auch sein könnte, zumindest besteht zwischen Ohrfeigen und Prophezeihen kein logischer Zusammenhang, der in die Aufforderung, den jeweiligen Schläger nachher zu identifizieren, einmünden würde.

Vergleicht man die drei Synoptiker untereinander, ist Lk am klarsten. Mit verhülltem Gesicht soll Jesus prophezeihen, wer ihn geschlagen hat. In Mk wird das Motiv des Gesichtsverhüllens (wenn original) nicht weiter verarbeitet. In Mt entsteht der Eindruck, als ob in seinem Text etwas zu wenig oder etwas zu viel stünde.

Methodisch ist Mt 26:67–68 selbstverständlich zunächst für sich allein zu lesen, danach im Licht des Mk. Kein unbefangener Leser von V. 67, der von Lk nichts weiss, wird bei V. 68 erwarten, dass die Aufforderung προφήτευσον ἡμῖν, χριστέ dahingehend präzisiert würde, die Identität des Schlägers festzustellen. Ein Versehen des Verfassers könnte man noch in V. 67a erwägen, aber spätestens bei οἱ δέ in V. 67b ist vorauszusetzen, dass er sich seines Lapsus hätte bewusst werden müssen. Anstatt das Auslassen von περικαλύπτειν einem Versehen zuzuschreiben, wäre vielmehr zu folgern, dass Matthäus das Motiv gerade absichtlich strich, weil ins Gesicht speien das Verhüllen des Gesichts ausschliesst (womit im Einklang steht, dass das Ausspeien in Lk fehlt).[51]

Was die Aufforderung zur Prophezeihung sprachlich anbelangt, so ist auf die Beobachtung hinzuweisen, nach der der Satz τίς ἐστιν ὁ παίσας σε; eher dem lk als mt Gebrauch entspricht, ohne allerdings dem mt zuwider zu sein.[52] In Lk 20:2 formuliert Lukas analog mit 22:64 τίς ἐστιν ὁ δούς σοι τὴν ἐξουσίαν ταύτην, während

[50] Zum Problem der Interpretation von οἱ δέ s. Neirynck, "ΤΙΣ", 32–36.

[51] So R.E. Brown, *The Death of Messiah: From Gethsemane to the Grave—A Commentary on the Passion Narratives in the Four Gospels* (2 Bde; New York, London etc.: Doubleday, 1994) 1.578. Zur weiteren Interpretation vgl. jedoch unten.

[52] M.S. Goodacre, *Goulder and the Gospels: An Examination of a New Paradigm* (JSNTSup 133; Sheffield: Sheffield Academic Press, 1996) 105–7.—Wenn das in Mt und Lk

Matthäus Mk 11:28 direkt entnimmt: τίς σοι ἔδωκεν τὴν ἐξουσίαν ταύτην; (21:23). Weiter sind die lk-redaktionellen Formulierungen in Lk 8:45 τίς ὁ ἁψάμενός μου; sowie 20:17 τί οὖν ἐστιν τὸ γεγραμμένον τοῦτο zu beachten. Der Befund ist auffallend, denn Matthäus beginnt zwar mehrmals Fragen mit τίς/τί ἐστιν und gebraucht auch ὁ mit Partizip, doch begegnet nie beides zusammen in einer Konstruktion wie Mt 26:68. Der Befund lässt sich in die Frage kleiden: Wie ist zu erklären, dass Matthäus, als er zum ersten und einzigen Mal die fragliche Konstruktion benutzt, dies genau an der Stelle tut, wo Lukas die gleiche Konstruktion schon zum vierten Mal gebraucht? Die nächstliegende Antwort würde lauten: τίς ἐστιν ὁ παίσας σε; in Mt ist aus Lk übernommen.

Wenn der Sachverhalt von Goodacre dahingehend—nicht ohne Unterbewertung, wie es scheint[53]—interpretiert wird, dass es Lk desto leichter fiel, sich an Mt anzuschliessen, so geht es dabei um ein zwar angebrachtes aber hypothesengemässes Folgern, jedoch nicht länger um ein definitives Argument für die Abhängigkeit des Lukas von Mt. Im Sinn des Goulderschen Grundsatzes "typisch—untypisch" wäre hier sogar auf ein umgekehrtes Verhältnis der beiden Evangelien zu schliessen.

Ebenfalls kritisch hat man gegenüber der im Rahmen der 2QTh vorgelegten Vermutung zu verhalten, die fünf entscheidenden Worte seien von Matthäus aus der mündlichen Überlieferung, die auch Lukas zugänglich war, übernommen worden.[54] Sie stellten ein Signal dar, welches sich auf ein bekanntes spöttisches Spiel der Soldaten mit ihrem Opfer bezog und als solches den Lesern hinreichende Information gab, worum es ging.[55] Bei dieser Annahme würde der Text von Mt gewiss erklärlicher. Allerdings ist zu beachten, dass Lukas sich zumindest nicht imstande sah, das Verhüllen des Gesichts

nur einmal vorkommende παίειν in Mk 14:47 benutzt ist, ist es nicht verwunderlich, dass sowohl Matthäus wie Lukas die kontextgemässe Vokabel aufnehmen, trotz verschiedenen anderen Alternativen, die Lukas zur Verfügung gestanden hätten. Vgl. dazu auch Goodacre, *Goulder*, 105.

[53] Vgl. Goodacre, *Goulder*, 106: "The MA τίς ἐστιν ὁ παίσας σε; is then, if anything, a little [sic] more Lukan in style than it is Matthean." Im zusammenfasssenden Abschnitt (S. 107) sagt er alledings stärker: "Although the language is congenial to Matthew, it is also, if anything, more congenial to Luke."

[54] M.L. Soards, *The Passion according to Luke: The Special Material of Luke 22* (JSNTSup 14; Sheffield: Sheffield Academic Press, 1987) 102–3. Ähnlich Brown, *Death of Messiah*, 1.578–79.

[55] So Brown, *Death of Messiah*, 1.574–76.

auszulassen, und sowieso bleibt die Frage, woher es kommt, dass der Satz τίς ἐστιν ὁ παίσας σε; so sehr einer lk Redaktion ähnelt.

Wenn man die Gesamtlage, ohne den Druck eines synoptischen Problems zu verspüren, beurteilen könnte, so würde man sich mit Rücksicht auf die inhaltlichen Spannungen im Text des Mt sowie auf den sprachlichen Befund am ehesten für die Annahme einsetzen, dass Mt 26:67–68 uns nicht in seiner ursprünglichen Fassung vorliegt. Es würde sich dabei um eine Analogie mit Mk handeln, wo die Frage nach den Schlägern in einige Handschriften eingeschoben ist. In dem Fall aber, dass NA27 trotz allem den ursprünglichen Text überliefert, wäre die 2QTh in höchster Erklärungsnot, wohl aber hätte die FGH ihrerseits aus sprachlichen Gründen ein stringentes Argument eingebüsst.

7. *Die Reaktion des Petrus nach seinem Versagen*

Wie im vorigen Fall, besteht das MA aus einem längeren Satz:

Mt 26:75
καὶ ἐξελθὼν ἔξω ἔκλαυσεν πικρῶς.
Mk 14:72
καὶ ἐπιβαλὼν ἔκλαιεν.
Lk 22:62
καὶ ἐξελθὼν ἔξω ἔκλαυσεν πικρῶς.

Im Ansatz ist klar, dass eine Abhängigkeit irgendeiner Art zwischen Mt und Lk, ursprünglich oder sekundär, bestehen muss. Nach Goulder stelle Mt 26:75 eine mt-redaktionelle Bearbeitung der Mk-Parallele dar.[56] Der Annahme steht sprachlich nichts im Wege, doch aus denselben Gründen kann man den Satz genausogut Lukas zuschreiben. Sowohl ἐξέρχομαι als auch ἔξω kommen in Lk redaktionell vor, wenn auch nicht im gleichen Satz (etwa 5:8; 6:12; 8:46; 1:10; 4:29). Überdies begegnen beide reichlich in Apg, und zwar einmal auch im gleichen Atemzug (16:13).

Bekanntlich ist der textkritische Status von Lk 22:62 nicht gesichert, weil der Vers in einem Teil altlateinischer Zeugen[57] fehlt. Weshalb

[56] Goulder, "Knowledge", 155.

[57] Im Apparat von NA26 war dazu noch 0171 mit Bemerkung *vid* angeführt, in Greevens Synopse erscheint 0171 ohne Vorbehalt. NA27 gibt bloss "it" als Beweislage an. Hierzu vgl. Tuckett, "Minor Agreements", 133 Anm. 54.

der dramatische Satz übergangen worden wäre, ist nicht ohne weiteres ersichtlich, wenngleich der Einfluss der Joh-Parallele nicht ausgeschlossen werden kann.[58] Jedenfalls ist mit Goulder die Frage zu stellen, ob es sachlich und erzählerisch denkbar ist, dass Lukas—der doch Mk 14:72 vor sich hatte—von Petrus' Reaktion kein Wort gesagt hätte. Goulder betont, wie milde Lukas den Apostel behandelt: so ist Petrus etwa unter den in Getsemani schlafenden Jüngern nicht namentlich genannt, im Hofe des Hohenpriesters verflucht er nicht noch schwört (Mk und Mt beide Male anders). Wie hätte denn Lukas dem Versager Petrus die Tränen der Busse und Reu verweigern können?[59]

Im Blick auf die Rolle, welche Umkehr und Busse im Doppelwerk des Lukas insgesamt spielen, hat Goulder einen schwerwiegenden Punkt getroffen. Da jedoch der lk Passionsbericht einige Eigentümlichkeiten aufweist, die in diesem Zusammenhang relevant sein können, kann man das Argument nicht ohne Vorbehalt auf die gegenwärtige Stelle beziehen. Zum einen ist die erweiterte Vorhersage der Verleugnung Petri in Lk 22:31–34 in Betracht zu ziehen und besonders nach dem Sinn von 22:32 ἐγὼ δὲ ἐδεήθην περὶ σοῦ ἵνα μὴ ἐκλίπῃ ἡ πίστις σου· καὶ σύ ποτε ἐπιστρέψας στήρισον τοὺς ἀδελφούς σου zu fragen. Meint der Satz ἵνα μὴ ἐκλίπῃ ἡ πίστις σου, dass "Simon zwar mit seiner dreimaligen Leugnung feige versagte, nicht aber den Glauben aufgab"? Lässt sich im Hinblick auf Lk 22:54–62 sagen, dass man in dem "souveräne[n] Vorherwissen Jesu . . . den anstössigen Fall gewissermassen aufgehoben wusste"?[60] Wenn die Fragen zu bejahen wären, würde die folgende Frage naturgemäss lauten, ob die danach erfolgende, dramatisch betonte Busse überhaupt noch vonnöten ist.

---

[58] Vgl. hierzu die Auskunft in B.M. Metzger, *A Textual Commentary on the Greek New Testament: A Companion Volume to the United Bible Societies' Greek New Testament (3. Ed.)* (London: United Bible Societies, 1971) 178: "Although it is possible that the verse has come into the Lukan text from the parallel passage in Mt 26.75, a majority of the Committee regarded it as more probable that the words were accidentally omitted from several witnesses (0171^{vid} it$^{a.b.e.ff2.i.l*.r1}$) than added without substantial variation (only ὁ Πέτρος is added in several witnesses after ἔξω) in all other witnesses." Die Begründung "without substantial variation" fällt auf, da in Anbetracht der harmonisierenden Tendenz eher zu erwarten wäre, dass man Lk nach Mt ergänzte. Auf alle Fälle ist die in *The UBS Greek New Testament*, 3. Ed. gewählte (mit NA27 identische) Lesart mit dem Buchstaben C ("considerable degree of doubt") versehen.

[59] Goulder, "Knowledge", 155–56.

[60] So G. Schneider, *Das Evangelium nach Lukas* (2 Bde; ÖTK 3; Gütersloh: Gütersloher Verlagshaus Mohn, Würzburg: Echter-Verlag, 1977) 2.453.

Oder sogar unangemessen? Oder aber vom Standpunkt des Interesses, Petrus zu schonen, würde ein Tränenausbruch nicht das Versagen des Schützlings des Evangelisten nur noch hervorheben?

Zum zweiten ist zu beobachten, dass Lukas den Vorfall deutlicher als die anderen Evangelisten mit der Vorhersage Jesu verbindet, indem er den Herrn als an Ort und Stelle anwesend darstellt, und ihn seinen Blick auf Petrus werfen lässt (Lk 22:61). Diese Situation—nicht der Hahnenschrei—bringt Petrus das Wort des Herrn in Erinnerung. Die Frage ist, ob Petrus' Erinnern als Reaktion auf den Vorfall für Lukas sachlich hinreichend ist, um das Geschehene wettzumachen. Übrigens ist zu beachten, dass die Betonung der Busse bei Lukas sich auf die "christliche Existenz" begründende "Erstbekehrung" bezieht. Wie Lukas sich zum Problem der "christlichen Sünder"—als was der Fall des Petrus anzusehen wäre—verhält, ist ein Problem für sich.[61]

Derartige, durch die speziellen lk Züge in Lk 22:31–34 und 22:54–62 veranlassten Erörterungen lassen einen zu der Ansicht neigen—nicht ganz ohne Stütze der Textkritik—, dass der Bericht des Lukas von dem Versagen des Petrus ursprünglich mit 22:61 endete.[62] Bei gegenteiliger Meinung könnten sich die Vertreter der klassischen 2QTh etwa mit der Annahme einer mündlichen Tradition[63] bzw. mit der Notlösung einer Hypothese helfen, dass Lukas zwar eine Reaktion des Petrus überlieferte, diese aber in ihrem Wortlaut sekundär an Mt angeglichen worden sei. Im Sinn der FGH wäre das MA, weil die Richtung der Abhängigkeit sprachlich nicht bestimmt werden

[61] Vgl. Lk 17:3–4. Hätte Lukas diese Stelle beim Schreiben von Lk 22:61 im Sinn gehabt? Das lk Vorzugswort ἐπιστρέφειν, welches der Verfasser in Apg öfters (mit der Präzisierung ἐπὶ τὸν θεόν) in der Bedeutung "umkehren" gebraucht, ist in 22:32 wohl nicht sosehr auf die Reaktion des Petrus nach seinem Versagen (ὑπεμνήσθη) zu beziehen. Eher ist S. Légasse, "ἐπιστρέφω", *EWNT* 2.101–2, zuzustimmen, der meint, Petrus werde eingeladen, "nach seinem momentanen Versagen . . . aus der eigenen österlichen Erfahrung die Kraft zu schöpfen, die er seinen Brüdern mitteilen wird."

[62] Als Argument gegen die Ursprünglichkeit des Verses könnte ebenfalls die Überleitung von Lk 22:62 zu V. 63 dienen: in V. 62 ist Petrus das Subjekt, in V. 63 bezieht sich αὐτόν—gegen unmittelbare Erwartung des Lesers—jedoch auf den verhafteten Jesus. Mit Tuckett, "Minor Agreements", 134. Freilich, wie Goulder, "Knowledge", 156, zurecht bemerkt, bleibt das gleiche Problem auch ohne V. 62 bestehen, weil in V. 61 Petrus das tragende Subjekt ist. Doch der Übergang wird ohne V. 62 glatter.

[63] So Soards, *Passion* 101–2, und im Anschluss an ihn Brown, *Death of Messiah*, 1.609.

kann, zunächst hypothesengemäss zu bewerten, d.h., das MA findet seine Erklärung und wird zu einem schwerwiegenden positiven Argument, nachdem es sich aus anderen Gründen wahrscheinlich machen lässt, dass eher Lk von Mt als Mt von Lk abhängig ist.

Zuletzt ist kurz zu bemerken, dass die Szene von dem versagenden Petrus mit seiner beeindruckenden Reaktion in der christlichen Tradition so tief ins Bewusstsein der Menschen—die modernen Exegeten nicht ausgenommen—verankert sein wird, dass es einem psychologisch zunächst unwahrscheinlich vorkommt, die Episode könnte in einem Evangelium ursprünglich fehlen.[64] Doch zumindest der Verfasser des Joh (dessen Petrus-Bild sich zwar mit dem des Lk nicht deckt) hat sie verschwiegen. Ebensowenig ist von einem Anblick Jesu oder vom Erinnern des Petrus die Rede. Der Text wird lapidar mit der Bemerkung πάλιν οὖν ἠρνήσατο Πετρός, καὶ εὐθέως ἀλέκτωρ ἐφώνησεν (Joh 18:27) beendet. Damit tritt Petrus von der Bühne ab.

8. *Die Grablegung Jesu*

Im Bericht von Jesu Begräbnis zählt Goulder acht MAs.[65] Einzeln betrachtet sind sie von wechselnder Bedeutung. Was zählt, ist nicht die Quantität, sondern die Qualität der Übereinstimmungen:

> Mt 27:58–60
> οὗτος προσελθὼν τῷ Πιλάτῳ ᾐτήσατο τὸ σῶμα τοῦ Ἰησοῦ. τότε ὁ Πιλᾶτος ἐκέλευσεν ἀποδοθῆναι. καὶ λαβὼν τὸ σῶμα ὁ Ἰωσὴφ ἐνετύλιξεν αὐτὸ [ἐν] σινδόνι καθαρᾷ καὶ ἔθηκεν αὐτὸ ἐν τῷ καινῷ αὐτοῦ μνημείῳ . . .
> Mk 15:43–46
> ἐλθὼν Ἰωσὴφ . . . τολμήσας εἰσῆλθεν πρὸς τὸν Πιλᾶτον καὶ ᾐτήσατο τὸ σῶμα τοῦ Ἰησοῦ. ὁ δὲ Πιλᾶτος ἐθαύμασεν εἰ ἤδη τέθνηκεν . . . ἐδωρήσατο τὸ πτῶμα τῷ Ἰωσήφ. καὶ ἀγοράσας σινδόνα καθελὼν αὐτὸν ἐνείλησεν τῇ σινδόνι καὶ κατέθηκεν αὐτὸν ἐν μνημείῳ . . .

[64] Bezeichnenderweise hat J.S. Bach in seiner Johannespassion—gewiss auch um musikalisch-dramatische Motive willen—die Szene um einen Teil von Mt 26:75 ergänzt.

[65] Goulder, "Knowledge", 156–58. In "Putting", 230–31, führt Goulder sechs Fälle vor, von denen fünf auch in "Knowledge", 156–58, dargelegt werden. Den sechsten, mt-lk ἔθηκεν gegen mk κατέθηκεν, bringt er im letzteren Aufsatz nicht mehr vor, und zwar offensichtlich, weil, wie er in "Putting", 231, festhält, τιθέναι ein lk Vorzugswort bildet (5/12/18+23) und weder Mt noch Lk κατατιθέναι jemals im konkreten Sinn verwenden.—Es ist zu bemerken, dass in NA27 alle Synoptiker ἔθηκεν lesen, während in Greevens Synopse für Mk κατέθηκεν steht. Diese Lesart, der hier gefolgt ist, setzt auch Gundry, "Evidence", 1491, voraus, der weiter das Auslassen des Artikels vor σινδόνι als Übereinstimmung erwähnt.

Lk 23:50–53
Καὶ ἰδοὺ ἀνὴρ ὀνόματι Ἰωσὴφ βουλευτὴς ὑπάρχων [καὶ] ἀνὴρ ἀγαθὸς καὶ δίκαιος—οὗτος οὐκ ἦν συγκατατεθειμένος τῇ βουλῇ καὶ τῇ πράξει αὐτῶν—ἀπὸ Ἁριμαθαίας πόλεως τῶν Ἰουδαίων, ὃς προσεδέχετο τὴν βασιλείαν τοῦ θεοῦ, οὗτος προσελθὼν τῷ Πιλάτῳ ᾐτήσατο τὸ σῶμα τοῦ Ἰησοῦ καὶ καθελὼν ἐνετύλιξεν αὐτὸ σινδόνι καὶ ἔθηκεν αὐτὸν ἐν μνήματι λαξευτῷ οὗ οὐκ ἦν οὐδεὶς οὔπω κείμενος.

Wie Goulder meint, lässt sich der Text des Mt durchaus als redaktionelle Bearbeitung des Mk verstehen. Das Problem liegt darin, ob Lukas seinen Text ohne Einfluss des Mt so hätte gestalten können, ohne dass es zu acht (oder eher zehn) Übereinstimmungen gekommen wäre. Die MA's werden im Folgenden einzeln aufgeführt und kommentiert.

1) In Mt und Lk bleibt τολμήσας weg.
Vielleicht war der Verweis auf das Wagnis des Joseph dem Evangelisten deswegen unerwünscht, weil der römische Machthaber dadurch in ungünstigem Licht erscheint, als ob man generell—oder gar im Falle eines Mitglieds der jüdischen Obrigkeit, dazu noch eines Sympathisanten des Christentums—vor einem römischen Beamten Furcht zu haben müsste.

2) οὗτος προσελθὼν τῷ Πιλάτῳ
Zur Frage steht das "resumptive" οὗτος.[66] Goulder bemerkt, dass Lukas in seinen Vorstellungen neuer gerechten Gestalten—Zacharias, Simeon, Hanna, Cornelius—das Pronomen nicht verwendet, und nennt Apg 10:1ff als eine nahe Parallele, wo sich nach der viereinhalbzeiligen Vorstellung des Cornelius das Prädikat εἶδεν direkt anschliesst. Doch das entspricht der Gesamtlage nur zum Teil. In Apg finden sich einige weitere relevante Vergleichstellen:

Apg 4:9–10
εἰ ἡμεῖς σήμερον ἀνακρινόμεθα ἐπὶ εὐεργεσίᾳ ἀνθρώπου ἀσθενοῦς ἐν τίνι οὗτος σέσωται, γνωστὸν ἔστω πᾶσιν ὑμῖν καὶ παντὶ τῷ λαῷ Ἰσραὴλ ὅτι ἐν τῷ ὀνόματι Ἰησοῦ Χριστοῦ τοῦ Ναζωραίου ὃν ὑμεῖς ἐσταυρώσατε, ὃν ὁ θεὸς ἤγειρεν ἐκ νεκρῶν, ἐν τούτῳ οὗτος παρέστηκεν ἐνώπιον ὑμῶν ὑγιής.

Analog mit Lk 23:50–52 wird hier οὗτος nach einer längeren Zwischenbemerkung wiederholt. Zu beachten ist gleichfalls der Gebrauch eines

[66] Das Wort fehlt nach Aland, *Synopsis quattuor evangeliorum* (9. Aufl., 1976) in D*. In NA27 und Greevens Synopsis findet sich keine Erwähnung davon.

dritten οὗτος (ἐν τούτῳ) als Rückverweis auf ἐν τῷ ὀνόματι. Wie Lukas gerne die Vorstellung einer Person mit οὗτος weiterführt, zeigen auch die Fälle des Gelähmten in Lystra (καί τις ἀνὴρ . . . ὃς οὐδέποτε περιεπάτησεν. οὗτος ἤκουσεν . . .; Apg 14:8) und Jairos (καὶ . . . ἀνὴρ ᾧ ὄνομα Ἰάϊρος καὶ οὗτος . . . ὑπῆρχεν . . .; Lk 8:41). Die Satzkonstruktion ist beide Male die gleiche wie in Lk 23:50–52: Es wird zunächst jemand/einer vorgeführt (jeweils ein ἀνήρ), der dann in einem Relativsatz (ὅς/ᾧ) näher charakterisiert wird. In der dritten Phase wird die eigentliche Handlung in Gang gesetzt, wobei mit οὗτος die vorher aufgeführte Person als Subjekt wieder aufgenommen wird. Weitere Fälle, allerdings ohne einen Relativsatz, sind die Vorstellungen von Apollos (Apg 18:24–25; vgl. auch V. 26) und Hanna (Lk 2:36).

Demnach bildet Lk 23:50–52 ein typisches Beispiel für die lk-redaktionelle Manier. Der Evangelist beginnt seine redaktionelle Zwischenbemerkung, dass Joseph dem Beschluss des Synedrions nicht zugestimmt hatte, mit οὗτος (V. 51). Nachdem er dann die Herkunft von Joseph nennt und in einem Relativsatz ihn als einen auf das Gottesreich Wartenden bezeichnet, geht er zum eigentlichen Bericht über, indem er mit einem zweiten οὗτος den Hauptgedanken wieder aufnimmt (analog Apg 4:9–10). Im Vergleich mit der Vorstellung von Cornelius kommt es nicht nur auf die Länge—wobei Lk 23:50–51 übrigens eine Zeile länger ist—, sondern auch auf die Satzkonstruktion an. Diese ist in Lk 23:50–52, anders als in Apg 10:1–2, wo lauter Substantiva, Adjektiva und Partizipien im Nominativ aneinandergereiht sind, kompliziert, weswegen die Aufnahme von οὗτος gut motiviert ist. Aufs Ganze gesehen ist οὗτος in Lk 23:52 (wie in 23:51) dem lk Sprachgebrauch völlig gemäss und ohne Einfluss von Mt erklärlich.

3) προσελθών

προσέρχομαι ist ein Vorzugswort des Mt (51/5/10+10). Von den Vorkommen in Mt besteht die Hälfte (25) aus solchen Fällen, wo ein direkter Dativ folgt (öfters kommen die Jünger zu Jesus). Demgegenüber ist die einzige Belegstelle in Lk eben 23:52, wo eine Abhängigkeit von Mt vermutet ist. Doch ein Blick auf Apg zeigt, dass Lukas nach Ausweis der fünf Belegstellen die Vokabel (mit Dativ) auch autonom verwenden kann. Von grösstem Interesse in diesem Zusammenhang sind Apg 9:1–2 (ὁ δὲ Σαῦλος . . . προσελθὼν τῷ ἀρχιερεῖ), Apg 22:26 . . . ὁ ἑκατοντάρχης προσελθὼν τῷ χιλιάρχῳ und Apg 23:14 (. . . οἵτινες προσελθόντες τοῖς ἀρχιερεῦσιν καὶ τοῖς πρεσβυτέροις).

In allen drei Fällen handelt es sich um die Hinwendung zu einer Autorität.[67] Besonders erhellend ist der Vergleich von Apg 22:26 mit Lk 23:52, der zeigt, dass im Sprachgebrauch des Lukas προσέρχομαι hinsichtlich der Beziehung von Joseph und Pilatus eben der sachgemässe Ausdruck ist. Dass andere Verba, etwa ἐπ-/εἰσέρχομαι, im Zusammenhang mit dem Täufer, Jesus oder Maria von Lukas benutzt werden, spricht nicht dagegen, sondern bestätigt vielmehr, dass in Bezug auf die Obrigkeit προσέρχομαι mit Dativ eben das Angemessene ist.

4) ἐθαύμασεν εἰ ἤδη τέθνηκεν
Goulder meint, es sei nicht offenkundig, aus welchem Grund Lukas Mk 15:44–45 ausgelassen hätte, da er von Mk 15 sonst fast alles übernimmt. Tatsächlich streicht Lukas aber noch mehr als Matthäus—der die Verse mit der Bemerkung τότε ὁ Πιλᾶτος ἐκέλευσεν ἀποδοθῆναι immerhin zusammenfasst—und geht direkt zur Abnahme des Leichnams. Bei der Voraussetzung, Lukas behandle das Material von Mk 15 möglichst sparsam, sollte er bei einer Abhängigkeit von Mt sofort bei Mt 27:58b ankommen. Dass er das nicht tut, kann als Hinweis darauf gedeutet werden, dass er Mk 15:44–45 keine grosse Bedeutung beimass.[68]

5) ἀγοράσας σινδόνα
Weil Lukas sonst für Neues im biblischen Sinn positiv eingestellt ist (Lk 19:30, 23:53b), fragt Goulder, weshalb der Verfasser die Erwähnung vom Kaufen der Leinwand übergangen hätte, wenn nicht auch Matthäus dasselbe getan hätte.[69] Nun scheint aber klar, dass Matthäus den Ausdruck zwar gestrichen hat, aber sachlich—verkürzend—als καθαρός neu geschrieben hat (σινδόνι καθαρᾷ).[70] Damit geht das Argument in die umgekehrte Richtung: Wenn Lukas in Mk las, dass die Leinwand (neu) gekauft wurde, und in Mt, dass sie rein war, wie hätte er, da Neues ihm tatsächlich wichtig war, trotz des Zeugnisses der beiden Vorlagen diese Information ausgelassen?

---

[67] Apg 9:1 und 23:14 werden auch von Goulder erwähnt.

[68] Vgl. auch Tuckett, "Relationship", 139, nach dem die beiden Evangelisten die Bemerkung unschwer als "irrelevant" haben ansehen können.

[69] In "Putting", 231, meint Goulder zu Lukas' Verfahren: "It looks as if he was still thinking of Matthew at the beginning of the verse (no purchase), and of Mark at the end (no καθαρᾷ)."

[70] Vgl. auch Tuckett, "Relationship", 139: "Matthew's καθαρᾷ *may* (Hervorhebung von Tuckett) be a substitute for Mark's buying. . . ."

6) ἐνετύλιξεν

Tuckett hält fest, dass ἐνείλησεν für Matthäus und Lukas schlimme Assoziationen wecken konnte.[71] Goulder entgegnet darauf, u.a. Plutarchos, Dion Chrysostomos und Philostratos verwendeten das Verb neutral, und führt als Beispiel an, dass etwa ein Kind in Löwenhaut eingepackt werden konnte.[72] Ausserdem hätten Lukas laut Goulder mehrere Alternativen zu Gebote gestanden, wie ἐν-/περιελίσσειν/ἐν-/περικαλύπτειν.

Ohne Zweifel ist das MA auffällig. Seine Bewertung ist allerdings nicht leicht. Denn es kommt weniger darauf an, wie viele sprachliche Alternativen im Griechischen überhaupt möglich sind, sondern man müsste eben die Wendungen kennen, die im Sprachkontext des Matthäus und Lukas üblich und gebräuchlich waren, wenn von dem Verhüllen des Leichnams einer angesehenen Person gesprochen wird. Je mehr Alternativen es gab, desto stärker wird Goulders Einwand, je weniger, desto grösser wird die Möglichkeit einer Koinzidenz.

7) αὐτό

Nach Lukas nimmt Joseph zuerst Jesu Leichnam (αὐτό) ab und legt dann Jesus (αὐτόν) in das Grab. Läge Lukas ausschliesslich Mk vor, hätte er konsequenterweise entweder zweimal wie Mk αὐτόν oder zweimal αὐτό schreiben müssen. Die Schwerfälligkeit erkläre sich am besten als Übergang von Mt zu Mk.[73] In seiner Kritik an Goulder macht Tuckett geltend, αὐτό beziehe sich natürlicherweise auf σῶμα, während αὐτόν deshalb verständlich sei, weil Lukas eher den Menschen als den Leichnam begraben lässt (Apg 5:6,10).[74] Dem entgegnet Goulder, dass die Schwerfälligkeit nur umso eindrücklicher wird.[75]

Offenbar liegt hier ein Fall vor, der auf ein Patt hinausläuft. Die Frage ist, wieviel Folgerichtigkeit man hier von Lukas fordern darf. Der Gebrauch von αὐτό würde zumindest der Sachlage entsprechen,

---

[71] Tuckett, "Relationship", 139, auch Anm. 42, mit Verweis auf Taylor, *The Gospel according to St. Mark* (London: Macmillan, 1952) 601, bei dem es (wiederum auf Abbott bezogen) u.a. heisst: ". . . the verb is used of fettering prisoners, swathing children hand and foot, holding people fast in a net, entangling them in evil or in dept, and generally in a bad sense. In the papyri it is so used, but also colourlessly . . .").

[72] S.W. Bauer-K. und B. Aland, *Griechisch-deutsches Wörterbuch* (6. Aufl.; Berlin, New York: Walter de Gruyter, 1988) z. St.

[73] Goulder, "Knowledge", 157.

[74] Tuckett, "Relationship", 139.

[75] Goulder, "Knowledge", 157.

dass Lukas in 24:3 und 24:23 nicht von Jesus, sondern eben von seinem σῶμα spricht. Wenn noch nicht beim ersten, so hätte Markus ihn beim zweiten αὐτόν zur gleichen Form angeregt.

8) καινῷ//οὗ οὐκ ἦν οὐδεὶς οὔπω κείμενος
Goulder ist zuzustimmen, wenn er feststellt, dass Lukas sachlich dasselbe sagt wie Matthäus. Ihm ist ebenso beizupflichten, wenn er meint, Lukas formuliere an dem Modell von Mk 11:2, wo das Fohlen mit ἐφ' ὃν οὐδεὶς οὔπω ἀνθρώπων ἐκάθισεν bezeichnet wird.[76] (Die Darstellung in Lk 19:30 ist bis auf οὔπω identisch, wofür Lukas πώποτε schreibt.) Zu fragen ist aber, weshalb der Evangelist bei einer Abhängigkeit von Mt die Neuheit des Grabes nicht mit der gleichen Vokabel καινός bezeichnet, sondern sich eines aus Mk erhaltenen paraphrasierenden Ausdrucks bedient. Dass er bei dem Bericht von Jesu Reiten Mk 11:2 (und nicht Mt 21:2) folgt, zeigt, dass ihm die Idee der Neuheit des von Jesus Benutzten nicht ohne Belang war. Dass Lukas dann in 23:53 Jesu Grab eben mit einem gleich konstruierten Satz beschreibt, macht die alternative Erklärung möglich, dass sich der Evangelist—ohne Einfluss des Mt—die in 19:30 aus Mk 11:2 entnommene Idee des Neuen vergegenwärtigte und verwenden wollte. Auch sachlich und inhaltlich ist es etwas durchaus der Atmosphäre des lk Grablegungsberichts Gemässes (vgl. dazu unten), dass der gute und gerechte Joseph, "Halbchrist", Mitglied des Hohen Rats, den toten Jesus, den Märtyrer und Gerechten, mit einem neuen Grab ehrt.

Es hat sich aufs Ganze gesehen herausgestellt, dass den meisten MAs begründete alternative Erklärungen zur Seite gestellt werden können, welche eine Benutzung des Mt nicht voraussetzen. Einen möglicherweise gravierenden Fall für die 2QTh stellt ἐνετύλιξεν dar. Die Kehrseite der Medaille ist der Sachverhalt, dass die Übereinstimmung Nr. 5 eher gegen mt Einfluss spricht. Noch mehr aber wiegt, dass bei der Annahme einer Abhängigkeit von Mt aller Grund zur Erwartung bestünde, dass Lukas die Bemerkung von Mt 27:57, Joseph sei πλούσιος gewesen, mit Dankbarkeit aufgegriffen hätte!

---

[76] Goulder, "Putting", 231.

9. *Das Anbrechen (ἐπιφώσκειν) eines neuen Tages*

Das Mt und Lk gemeinsame ἐπιφώσκειν wird von Matthäus in der Einleitung zur Geschichte vom leeren Grab (28:1), von Lukas im Zusammenhang mit dem Bericht von Jesu Begräbnis (Lk 23:54) gebraucht:

> Mt 28:1
> Ὀψὲ δὲ σαββάτων, τῇ ἐπιφωσκούσῃ εἰς μίαν σαββάτων . . .
> Mk 15:42
> Καὶ ἤδη ὀψίας γενομένης, ἐπεὶ ἦν παρασκευὴ ὅ ἐστιν προσάββατον, ἐλθὼν Ἰωσὴφ . . .
> Lk 23:54
> καὶ ἡμέρα ἦν παρασκευῆς καὶ σάββατον ἐπέφωσκεν.

Goulder begründet seine These mit Verweis darauf, dass ἐπιφώσκειν im NT ausschliesslich in Mt und Lk begegnet und dass die Vokabel in Lk ungewöhnlich verwendet wird: Licht geht am Morgen, nicht am Abend auf. Diese Benutzung in übertragener Bedeutung der Vokabel erkläre sich daraus, dass Lukas ein Wort aufnahm, welches in einem engen parallelen Zusammenhang in Mt vorlag.[77]

Was in der Begräbnisgeschichte des Lk zunächst auffällt, ist die Tatsache, dass der Verfasser gegen Mk (und Mt) die Zeitbestimmung vom Anfang ans Ende des Berichts verlegt. Daraus folgt, dass Lukas' Bemerkung von dem Zeitpunkt in 23:54 die Szene einigermassen unterbricht, während in Mk und Mt das Auftreten des Joseph von Arimathia durch das Heranrücken des Sabbats gut motiviert wird, denn die Erwähnung der dem Begräbnis zuschauenden Frauen in Lk 23:55 würde sich am natürlichsten an V. 53 anschliessen. Trotzdem dürfte es sich um eine gut überlegte Massnahme des Redaktors handeln; denn damit hat Lukas gewonnen, dass Jesus ohne Eindruck von Eile, in aller Ruhe und Würdigkeit, zu Grabe gebracht wird. Erst nachdem dies unternommen ist, wird angemerkt, dass der Sabbat schon im Anbrechen war; und als Joseph nun sein Werk getan hat, kann der Fokus sich auf die Frauen richten, welche nach ihrer Rückkehr zwar noch Zeit haben, Salben und Öle zu bereiten, die aber nicht mehr imstande sind, zurückzukehren, um Jesu Leichnam zu salben.

[77] Goulder, "Knowledge", 158.

Wie kam nun Lukas dazu, in diesem Zusammenhang ausdrücklich das Verb ἐπιφώσκειν zu gebrauchen? Davor ist allerdings noch zu bemerken, dass sich keine letzte Sicherheit gewinnen lässt, in welcher Bedeutung Matthäus das wichtige Wort ὀψέ in 28:1 verwendet hat: in der von 'spät' oder—wie Goulder meint—in der von 'nach' (womit ἐπιφωσκούσῃ sich auf den frühen Morgen beziehe).[78] Wie man sich hier entscheidet, hängt davon ab, wie man den Sinn des Textes im Ganzen versteht.[79] Zwar schreibt Markus eindeutig ἀνατείλαντος τοῦ ἡλίου (16:2), aber Matthäus braucht nicht unbedingt Mk zu folgen, sondern kann den Aufbruch zum Grab absichtlich zeitlich vorverlegen, um Jesus möglichst bald, sofort nach dem Tageswechsel, auferstehen zu lassen. Mit ὀψὲ δὲ σαββάτων, τῇ ἐπιφωσκούσῃ εἰς μίαν σαββάτων könnte der Evangelist einfach an den Übergang vom Samstag zum Sonntag denken, als die ersten Sterne am Himmel zum Zeichen des Tageswechsels "anbrachen" i.S.v. erscheinen.[80] Damit wäre nicht erst der lk Gebrauch des Verbs aussergewöhnlich.

Doch wie auch immer Matthäus seinen Text gemeint hat, das lk Verständnis des Textes ist natürlich eine Sache für sich. Bei Lk 23:54 konnte Lukas sich zunächst nicht mit der allgemeinen Erwähnung seiner Quelle(n), dass es spät geworden war (Mk 15:42; Mt 27:57), zufriedenstellen. Es bedarf eigens einer Feststellung, dass der Sabbat unmittelbar vor der Tür stand, weil ja dadurch das Verhalten der Frauen, welches seinerseits den Gang der Ereignisse in der unmittelbaren Fortsetzung bestimmt, motiviert wurde. Wäre Lukas Mt vorgelegen, hätte er ὀψέ adverbiell verstanden und somit zu seinem Gebrauch von ἐπιφώσκειν in einem übertragenen Sinn gekommen.[81]

---

[78] Nach Goulder sei der adverbiale Gebrauch, dem Lukas folge, gewöhnlicher als der präpositionelle. M.D. Goulder, *Luke: A New Paradigm* (2 Bde; JSNTSup 20; Sheffield: Sheffield Academic Press, 1989) 772.

[79] Vgl. E. Schweizer, *Das Evangelium nach Matthäus* (NTD 2 Göttingen: Vandenhoeck & Ruprecht, 1981) 342–43, der das Problem des Zeitpunkts bespricht und zum Ergebnis kommt, Matthäus habe "den Gang zum Grab wahrscheinlich auf den Samstagabend und die Auferstehung Jesu in der Nacht zum Sonntag" datiert (S. 343).

[80] Vgl. hierzu Goulder, "Putting", 232, der für ἐπιφώσκειν ebenfalls die Alternative erwägt, das Verb "might be understood of the stars lighting up: but in any case Luke clearly means dusk on Friday." Zur früheren Diskussion um das Verb s. weiter Goulder, "Putting", 233.—Der mögliche rationalisierende Einwand, es hätte keinen Sinn gehabt, die Frauen zum Besehen des Grabes (θεωρῆσαι, Mt 28:1) in die Nacht zu schicken, bringt nicht weiter, wenn in der anderen Waagschale die gebotene Eile der Auferstehung dagegen wiegt. Übrigens begibt sich Maria von Magdala nach Joh 20:1 zum Grab, als es noch dunkel war (πρωῒ σκοτίας ἔτι οὔσης).

[81] Vgl. Goulder, *Luke*, 772.

Die entscheidende Frage an dieser Stelle lautet nun, welche sprachlichen Alternativen Lukas zur Verfügung standen, um den Tageswechsel zum Ausdruck zu bringen. Die Gewohnheiten seines Sprachmilieus sind uns unbekannt—genausogut wie die des Matthäus. Falls es sich um einen nicht-herkömmlichen Ausdruck der Alltagssprache der sprachlichen Umgebung des Verfassers handeln würde, wäre das MA als schwerwiegend zu betrachten. Je üblicher aber der Ausdruck war, desto wenigerwahrscheinlich wird die Benutzung des Mt.

Für Goulders These spricht der statistische Befund.[82] Insofern liegt die These einer Abhängigkeit des Lukas von Mt (oder grundsätzlich auch umgekehrt) recht nahe; doch naheliegend erscheint es zunächst nur deshalb, weil wir nicht alle relevanten Faktoren kennen. Überdies ist die Annahme, dass Lukas das Verb in einem anderen Sinn benutzt als Mt, insofern problematisch, weil eine verschiedene Bedeutung und ein etwas abweichender Kontext auch im Interesse der Selbstständigkeit des Evangelisten verstanden werden könnten. Doch das steht oder fällt mit der umstrittenen Frage, ob der übertragene Sinn bei Lukas in dem Masse ungewöhnlich ist, dass der Verfasser das Verb nicht ohne Mt aufgegriffen hätte.[83] Merkwürdig wäre jedenfalls die Voraussetzung, dass der dem hellenistischen Judentum nahestehende Autor zum ersten Mal in seinem Leben nur im Zusammenhang mit Jesu Begräbnis auf den Tageswechsel nach jüdischer Zeitrechnung zu sprechen gekommen wäre, ohne dabei eigenständige sprachliche Bereitschaft dafür zu haben.

Das zunächst überzeugend klingende MA zeigt sich bei näherer Betrachtung kompliziert und ist nicht eindeutig erklärbar. Die mit den MAs verknüpfte grundsätzliche Schwierigkeit tritt hier besonders deutlich hervor: die Relevanz einer Übereinstimmung im Einzelfall unzweideutig beurteilen zu können.

10. *Zusammenfassung*

Bei den besprochenen neun Fällen macht sich bemerkbar, dass es sich bei einem Drittel (die Fälle 1, 5, 7) um solche handelt, wo die

[82] Auch in LXX kommt ἐπιφώσκειν nur in der Lukian-Rezension für ἐπιφαύσκειν (Job 41:10) vor.
[83] S. dazu die Diskussion von Tuckett, "Relationship", 139–40 und Goulder, "Knowledge", 158.

Textbelege nicht völlig frei von Widersprüchen sind; dazu sind in einem Fall (6) schwere Bedenken gegen die Ursprünglichkeit des von NA27 bzw. von Greeven dargebotenen Textes anzumelden. Die dadurch bedingte Unsicherheit ist vom Standpunkt der Argumentation aus misslich. Um sinnvoll über die MAs diskutieren zu können, müsste den Forschern der absolut gesicherte "Urtext"[84] vorliegen. Mit wenigerem kommt man gerade im Fall der MAs nicht aus. Man kann nur versuchen, sich zu vorstellen, was es für die Kritik bedeuten würde, wenn mit hundertprozentiger Sicherheit davon ausgegangen werden könnte, dass etwa die NA27-Lesarten bei Lk 22:62 bzw. Mt 26:68 die wirklich ursprünglichen sind—oder eben nicht. Und weil es solche Sicherheit nirgends gibt, ist das synoptische Problem allein anhand von Textkritik unmöglich zu lösen, es müssen weitere exegetische Methoden, wie Literar- und Redaktionskritik, unbedingt zu Hilfe kommen.[85]

Worauf man heute in der synoptischen Diskussion mehr aufmerksam machen müsste, ist die Frage nach der textuellen Basis der synoptischen Evangelien und nach den Voraussetzungen der Möglichkeit einer sinnvollen Forschung des synoptischen Problems überhaupt. Es hat freilich den Anschein, als ob der Text der neuesten NA-Editionen in der Forschung praktisch an die Stelle eines Urtextes getreten sei.[86] In Wirklichkeit aber bedeutet das, dass die synoptische Diskussion, wie sie gegenwärtig geführt wird, eine Auseinandersetzung mit der synoptischen Frage darstellt, wie sie aufgrund einer Rezension, die, grob gesagt, hundert Jahre nach den Originaltexten unternommen wurde, am ehesten zu lösen wäre.[87]

---

[84] Der Inhalt des Begriffes "Urtext" würde jedoch von Fall zu Fall, und zwar gemäss der jeweiligen synoptischen Theorie, wechseln. Bei der 2QTh ginge es um den Text des Mk, den Matthäus und Lukas benutzt haben—und der natürlich nicht mit dem Original identisch zu sein braucht—sowie um die damit entstandenen "Urtexte" der beiden Evangelien, wie sie das Tageslicht erblickt haben. Dasselbe gilt mutatis mutandis für die FGH usw.

[85] S. Tuckett, "Minor Agreements", 135–38.

[86] Der psychologische Druck ist stark: Bei aller Relativität der Historie möchte auch der radikalste Forscher irgendwo ein Stück Fels unter den Füssen fühlen. Dazu soll der Text dienen. Der Text wird objektiviert, obwohl man weiss, dass er damit überstrapaziert wird.

[87] Vgl. hierzu die Bemerkungen von H. Köster, "The Text of the Synoptic Gospels in the Second Century", in W.L. Petersen (hg.), *Gospel Traditions in the Second Century: Origins, Recensions, Text, and Transmission* (CJAn 3; Notre Dame, London: University of Notre Dame Press, 1989) 19–37, S. 19: "The assumption that the reconstruction of the best archetype for the manuscript tradition is more or less identical with

Doch nicht genug damit: Hinzu kommt die gesamte Problematik der Geschichte der Textüberlieferung der synoptischen Evangelien im Laufe des zweiten Jahrhunderts mit ihrer Herausforderung der hunderten patristischen Zitaten.[88] Stimmt es, dass "the use of the Patristic evidence will . . . significantly alter the shape of the critical text,"[89] und trifft es zu, dass die synoptische Evangelienüberlieferung "was still evolving in the first part of the second century,"[90] so bleibt nur zu fragen, "how can one reconstruct a text 'as close to the original as possible,' if the 'original' *was not fixed* until at least 80 or 100 years *after* its 'composition'?" (Hervorhebungen im Original).[91] In einem Satz: Was kann auch der minuziöseste Textvergleich helfen, falls das "Original" sekundär entstanden ist? Kann die synoptische Frage auch nur approximativ gelöst werden, falls die Grundlage nicht gesichert ist?

Bei der Besprechung der neun von Michael Goulder präsentierten MAs, wie sie textkritisch aufgrund von NA27 und Greeven möglich ist, hat sich herausgestellt, dass sich die Anzahl der stringenten MAs verringern lässt. Relativ unschwer können die Fälle 2, 3, 4 geklärt werden, ohne dass man den Einfluss des Mt annehmen müsste. Der Fall 6 (τίς ἐστιν ὁ παίσας σε;) spricht, dessen ungeachtet, ob Mt 26:67–68 original überliefert ist oder nicht, wegen des sprachlichen Befundes eher für eine lk als mt Kreation. Der Fall 8 gibt bei den beiden Hypothesen zu bedenken (Unterlassen der Bemerkungen, dass das Leintuch neu und dass Joseph reich war gegenüber ἐνετύλιξεν), der Fall 9 (ἐπέφωσκεν) entzieht sich einer eindeutigen Beurteilung in die eine oder andere Richtung. Hätte man in den textkritisch unklaren Fällen (bes. 7) in der von NA27 vorgeschlagenen Weise zu lesen, wäre die 2QTh mit Lk 22:62 mit einer neuen Situation konfrontiert, wo die Textkritik nicht länger eine Zuflucht bieten würde.

the assumed autograph ist precarious. . . . Textual critics of classical text know that the first century of their transmission is the period in which the most corruptions occur. Textual critics of the New Testament writings have been surprising naïve in this respect."

[88] S. dazu W.L. Petersen, *Tatian's Diatessaron: Its Creation, Dissemination, Significance and History in Scholarship* (VCSup 25; Leiden, New York, Köln: E.J. Brill, 1994) 9ff.

[89] W.L. Petersen in seinem herausfordernden Aufsatz "What Text Can New Testament Textual Criticism Ultimately Reach?", in B. Aland & J. Delobel (hgg.), *New Testament Textual Criticism, Exegesis and Church History: A Discussion of Methods* (Kampen (the Netherlands): Kok/Pharos, 1994) 136–52, S. 151.

[90] Petersen, *Diatessaron*, 25. S. auch Köster, "Text", 37.

[91] Petersen, "Textual Criticism", 149.

Da unter den neun MAs die Beweiskraft der Pro- und Kontra-Argumente—nicht zuletzt aus textkritischen Gründen—von Fall zu Fall schwankt, ist ein eindeutiger Pauschalschluss verwehrt; oder dies zu tun, ist die Aufgabe des Lesers. Jedoch über Sieger und Verlierer entscheiden zu wollen, wäre auch nicht das Wesentlichste, solange nicht der gleiche Text zur Grundlage dient. Worum es zuvörderst gehen müsste, wäre die Erörterung der Frage, inwieweit *textkritische* Voraussetzungen gegeben sind, um die Diskussion über die synoptische Frage sinnvoll zu führen. Wie wäre etwa die argumentative Rolle der MAs in dem Fall zu bestimmen, dass sich die synoptische Überlieferung im ersten Teil des zweiten Jahrhunderts noch nicht stabilisiert hatte und der Text von NA27 aufgrund der patristischen Evidenz signifikant verändert werden müsste? Wäre es dann nicht methodisch sicherer, die Beweisführung auf einer anderen Grundlage, etwa auf der der kompositionellen Beobachtungen, aufzubauen?

DAS VIERTE EVANGELIUM UND DIE FRAGE NACH SEINEN EXTERNEN UND INTERNEN QUELLEN

Jürgen Becker

1. *Ein kurzer Blick auf die Geschichte des Problems*

Am Ausgang des zweiten Jahrhunderts festigte sich ein Konsens über das vierte Evangelium, der so aussah: Der Autor aller johanneischen Schriften ist der Lieblingsjünger (Joh 21:24). Er ist mit dem Apostel und Zebedäussohn Johannes identisch. Er schreibt nach den anderen kanonischen Evangelien als letzter sein Werk. Diesen Konsens bezeugen vor allem Irenäus (*haer.* 2,22,5; 3,1,1; 3,3,4) und der Kanon Muratori. Beide machen zu den Abhängigkeitsverhältnissen der Evangelien untereinander keine Angaben. Da Johannes qualifizierter Augenzeuge ist, ist seine geistgeleitete Autopsie die maßgebliche "Quelle" für die Wahrheit seines Evangeliums. Weil alle kanonischen Evangelien von dem einen Geist bewirkt wurden, sind die Unterschiede der Evangelien für den Glauben bedeutungslos (Kanon Muratori).[1] Clemens Alexandrinus (bei Euseb, *h.e.* 6,14,7), Euseb (*h.e.* 6,24,7–13) und Augustinus (*De cons. evang.* 4,11–20) fügen hinzu: Johannes benutzte die ihm bekannten kanonischen Evangelien und wollte sie ergänzen.

Diese Gesamtanschauung ruht auf dem Fundament einiger Entscheide und Überzeugungen der Kirchenväter:

1. Die Autoren der Evangelien sind vorkritisch Augenzeugen oder Schüler von solchen. Dies begründet ihre Autorität und Unmittelbarkeit zu den berichteten Ereignissen.
2. Die Argumentation wird nur zu den kanonischen Evangelien geführt. Die breite Evangelienproduktion der Frühzeit des Christentums bleibt ganz ausgeblendet. Man diskutiert nur innerhalb des Kanons.
3. Differenzen unter den Evangelien sind wegen der angenommenen übergeordneten Harmonie derselben domestiziert und in jedem

[1] Zur weiteren Diskussion über diese Unterschiede in der frühen Kirche vgl. H. Merkel, *Die Pluralität der Evangelien als theologisches und exegetisches Problem in der Alten Kirche* (TC 3; Bern/Frankfurt: Lang, 1978).

Fall für den Glauben ohne Belang. In allen vier Evangelien regiert ja der eine Geist. Widersprüche und Gegensätze kann es eigentlich nicht geben.

4. Das vierte Evangelium ist nicht darum das jüngste, weil man die Evangelien im Sinne des gegenwärtigen Methodenbewußtseins theologiegeschichtlich einordnet, sondern weil es eine kirchliche Tradition gibt, nach der man biographisch vom Apostel Johannes weiß, daß er als letzter aller Apostel in Ephesus starb. Diese Tradition zum Apostel Johannes ist allerdings weitgehend ein Kunstprodukt.[2]
5. Daß Johannes die Synoptiker ergänzt hat, ist ein Urteil, das dem damaligen Harmoniepostulat innerhalb der kanonischen Schriften entspricht. Es wird ebenso dem angenommenen Entstehungsdatum des vierten Evangeliums gerecht. Auch kann es wenigstens mit einigen seiner inneren Phänomene zur Begründung aufwarten.
6. Daß alle vier Evangelien auch eine literarische und traditionsgeschichtliche Diachronie besitzen könnten, liegt außerhalb des Horizonts der Kirchenväter. Die Evangelien sind nämlich als flächige Texte ohne diachronen Hintergrund eingeschätzt.

Dieser Konsens aus der frühen Kirche bestimmte mehr als 1600 Jahre die Auffassung von Kirche und Theologie. Erst mit D. Fr. Strauß und seinem "Leben Jesu" (1. Aufl. 1835/36) änderte sich diese Situation. Denn er stellte erstmals seine Leser vor die Entscheidung, aus theologischen und inhaltlichen Gründen ein Leben Jesu johanneisch oder nach den drei anderen kanonischen Evangelien zu schreiben. Das Harmoniepostulat der Kirchenväter war damit erschüttert. Zwar wählte Strauß innerhalb dieser Alternative den johanneischen Weg und erörterte die Sachlage nur unter dem begrenzten Gesichtspunkt, wie ein historisches Bild von Jesus gezeichnet werden könne, aber die erste Posaune zum Einsturz des ehrwürdigen Kirchenväterkonsenses war damit geblasen.

Als dann die Zwei-Quellen-Hypothese durch Chr. H. Weisse[3] und Chr. G. Wilke[4] aufgestellt wurde, ergab die nun literarisch beschreib-

[2] Vgl. J. Becker, "Geisterfahrung und Christologie", in B. Kollmann (hg.), *Antikes Judentum und Frühes Christentum* (FS H. Stegemann; BZNW 97; Berlin: de Gruyter, 1999) 428–42, S. 440f.

[3] Chr. H. Weisse, *Die evangelische Geschichte kritisch und philologisch bearbeitet* (2 Bde; Leipzig: Breitkopf u. Haertel, 1838).

[4] Chr. G. Wilke, *Der Urevangelist* (Dresden: Fleischer, 1838).

bare Nähe der Synoptiker untereinander zwangsläufig auch eine Sonderstellung des vierten Evangeliums im Rahmen der Frage nach der literarischen Entstehungsgeschichte der Evangelien und nicht nur unter dem Gesichtspunkt der theologischen Eigentümlichkeiten. Denn in dem Maße, in dem die literarische Verwandtschaft der Synoptiker präzisiert wurde, hoben sich davon die viel loseren und nur sporadischen Beziehungen des Johannesevangeliums zu den Synoptikern ab. Nun konnte man immer noch Johannes auf den Synoptikern fußen lassen, aber mußte dann zwangsläufig das Verhältnis zwischen Johannes und den Synoptikern in seiner Besonderheit überzeugend beschreiben und würdigen.[5] Für die andere Möglichkeit war jedoch nun auch die Tür einen ersten Spalt aufgetan: Johannes schreibt nicht im Angesicht der Synoptiker. Zugleich korrigierten die Entdecker der literarischen Synoptikerbeziehung untereinander eine inhaltliche Option von D. Fr. Strauß: Für ein historisches Jesusbild kann nicht Johannes, sondern müssen nun (vornehmlich) Markus und die Logienquelle dienen. Das Johannesevangelium gehört in die Spätphase der kanonischen Evangelienproduktion. Damit war eine anders begründete Kirchenväteraussage mit neuen Mitteln bestätigt und gleichzeitig die Verhältnisbestimmung der kanonischen Evangelien auf eine ganz neue methodische Basis gestellt.

Das hatte weitere Folgen. Die neu beschriebene Sonderstellung des vierten Evangeliums und seine späte Entstehung, aber auch die auf recht vager Quellenlage der frühen Kirche aufgebaute nur biographische Begründung der apostolischen Autorschaft ließ vermehrt an dem Apostel Johannes als Verfasser zweifeln.

Innerhalb dieser neuen Diskussionslage hielt man allerdings zunächst daran fest, daß der vierte Evangelist die Synoptiker "ergänzen" will. Die Meinung der Kirchenväter zeigte also weiterhin Wirkung. Solche Ergänzung beruhe jedoch—so lautete jetzt die neue Sprachregelung—auf einem sehr freien und souveränen Umgang mit den Synoptikern.[6]

[5] Auf diesen Problemstand hebe ich in J. Becker, *Das Evangelium nach Johannes* (2 Bde; 3. Aufl.; ÖTK 4; Gütersloh: Gütersloher Verlagshaus, 1991) 1.43 ab. Ich spreche von Schwierigkeiten und Folgeproblemen angesichts dieser Situation, wenn man Johannes Synoptikerabhängigkeit bescheinigen will. Daraus macht M. Lang, *Johannes und die Synoptiker* (FRLANT 182; Göttingen: Vanderhoeck & Ruprecht, 1999) 51, eine "fatale Alternative". Nun ist das Stichwort "Alternative" einfach eine Fehldeutung, aber was soll das Adjektiv "fatal" sagen?

[6] Zu diesem Konsens B.H. Streeter, *The Four Gospels* (London: Macmillan & Co., 1924), und H. Windisch, *Johannes und die Synoptiker* (UNT 12; Leipzig: Hinrichs, 1926) 43.

In diesem Urteil stecken allerdings zwei Probleme, die diese These als Formelkompromiß erkennen läßt: Der Einzelnachweis für die Verwendung jedes Synoptikers gelang nur recht unterschiedlich gut. Kannte Johannes wirklich alle drei Synoptiker? Auch das von den Kirchenvätern stammende und neu belebte Stichwort "Ergänzung" ließ sich hinterfragen: Johannes war zu eigenständig, widersprach sogar zum Teil den Synoptikern. Konnte solches komplexe und dialektische Verhältnis mit diesem Stichwort überhaupt angemessen beschrieben werden?

Nun konnte man die Zwei-Quellen-Hypothese als Vorbote literarkritischer Arbeit an allen vier Evangelien auffassen: Warum, wenn der Autor des jüngsten Evangeliums kein Augenzeuge war, sollte dann sein Evangelist nicht wie die Synoptiker Quellen verarbeitet haben? So verlagerte sich die Quellenfrage von den zu Johannes externen Synoptikern zu möglichen internen, also im vierten Evangelium verborgenen Quellen. Diese Frage stand ganz außerhalb des Horizontes, in dem die Kirchenväter dachten. Es war kein geringerer als J. Wellhausen, der wirkungsgeschichtlich nachhaltig (freilich nicht allein) die literarische Diachronie des Johannesevangeliums erkundete. Damit erreichte die Verhältnisbestimmung zu den Synoptikern ein neues, kompliziertes Stadium: Man konnte und mußte eigentlich nun auch die Frage für jede johanneische Schicht einzeln stellen und auch unterschiedlich beantworten. Der Variantenreichtum der Lösungsvorschläge stieg entsprechend an.

Der nächste wichtige Impuls ist mit dem Namen von P. Gardner-Smith[7] verbunden.[8] Der Beweis literarischer Synoptikerbenutzung hatte, bei Licht betrachtet, schon immer seine Tücken. Hatten nicht Lukas und Matthäus ihre Quellen wesentlich schonender behandelt, nämlich Sprache, Stoffe, ganze Sätze und vor allem die Akoluthie weitgehend bewahrt? Wie kann man das, was man die überall erkennbare johanneische Freiheit und Eigenständigkeit nannte, methodisch besser aufarbeiten? Die neue Forschungsrichtung der Form- und

[7] P. Gardner-Smith, *Saint John and the Synoptic Gospels* (Cambridge: University Press, 1938). Die Forschungsgeschichte von Gardner-Smith bis 1992 beschreibt D.M. Smith, *John among the Gospels* (Minneapolis: Fortress, 1992).

[8] Vor ihm hatte schon J. Schniewind, *Die Parallelperikopen bei Lukas und Johannes* (3. Aufl.; Leipzig: Brandstetter, 1914, Nachdruck 1970) denselben Weg beschritten. Doch fand diese Arbeit zunächst wenig Beachtung. Die Linie von Gardner-Smith setzte dann B. Noack, *Zur johanneischen Tradition* (Kopenhagen: Rosenkilde & Bagger, 1954) fort.

Traditionsgeschichte ließ Gardner-Smith jedenfalls das vierte Evangelium befragen, ob nicht statt einer literarischen Beziehung eine traditionsgeschichtliche Nähe zu den Synoptikern die Verhältnisse besser erklärte. Mit diesem Weg schrieb er Forschungsgeschichte. Seither gibt es viele Johannesforscher, die sich das komplexere johanneische Phänomen aus Nähe und Ferne zu den Synoptikern am besten traditionsgeschichtlich erklären können. Dies führte bald zu einem sehr breiten Konsens in dieser Frage, wie er sonst unter Johannesforschern eher eine Ausnahme ist. Große Johannesinterpreten wie R. Bultmann,[9] C.H. Dodd,[10] R.E. Brown[11] und R. Schnackenburg[12]—um nur einige Namen zu nennen—schlossen sich Gardner-Smith an.[13] Doch gab es auch angesichts des wachsenden Konsenses den damals etwas isolierten Widerspruch von C.K. Barrett.[14] Gleichzeitig wurde damit zwangsläufig innerhalb dieses Weges das Verhältnis zwischen Johannes und den Synoptikern noch lockerer als bisher eingeschätzt. Aus der kirchenväterlichen Ergänzungstheorie wird nun vom Ansatz her eine Unabhängigkeitstheorie. Außerdem hat es für dieses Erklärungsmodell in neuester Zeit eine Variation gegeben, die bei A. Dauers[15] Untersuchungen zum johanneischen Passionsbericht einsetzte und dann auch unter anderem durch verschiedene Untersuchungen zum Thomasevangelium neue Nahrung bekam: Es gibt nicht nur den Weg von mündlicher Tradition zur Verschriftlichung, sondern auch den entgegengesetzten Weg der Einflußnahme literarischer Werke auf mündliche Überlieferung, also sekundäre Mündlichkeit.

Neue Rahmenbedingungen für die Diskussion entstanden dann noch einmal, als der Strukturalismus und die breite Ausfächerung

---

[9] R. Bultmann, *Das Evangelium des Johannes* (20. Aufl.; KEK 2; Göttingen: Vanderhoeck & Ruprecht, 1978).

[10] C.-H. Dodd, *Historical Tradition in the Fourth Gospel* (Cambridge: Cambridge University Press, 1963).

[11] R.E. Brown, *The Gospel according to John* I–II (2 Bde; AB 29; Garden City, NY: Doubleday, 1966–1970) 1.15f.

[12] R. Schnackenburg, *Das Johannesevangelium* (4 Bde; HTKNT 4; Freiburg: Herder, 1975).

[13] Vgl. die Zusammenstellung bei W. Reinbold, *Der älteste Bericht über den Tod Jesu* (BZNW 69; Berlin: de Gruyter, 1994) 27f.

[14] C.K. Barrett, *The Gospel according to St. John* (2. Aufl.; KEK-Sonderband; Göttingen: Vanderhoeck & Ruprecht, 1978), 15f.; später folgt u.a. J. Blinzler, *Johannes und die Synoptiker* (SBS 5; Stuttgart: Katholisches Bibelwerk, 1965). Blinzler gibt S. 16ff. einen Abriß zur Forschungsgeschichte von H.J. Holtzmann bis in seine Zeit.

[15] A. Dauer, *Die Passionsgeschichte im Johannesevangelium* (SANT 30; München: Koesel, 1972).

literaturwissenschaftlicher Theorien auch auf die Erklärung der Evangelien Einfluß nahmen. Zugleich gerieten einige klassisch gewordene Annahmen der Form- und Traditionsgeschichte in die Kritik. Man konzentriert sich auf das literarische Produkt, so wie es vorliegt, und betont die Flüssigkeit der mündlichen Tradition gegenüber der Fixierbarkeit der Literatur mit der Folge, daß man die mündliche Tradition nur für bedingt aufhellbar hält. Überhaupt wird ein Blick in die Diachronie—vor allem auch zur Suche nach impliziten Quellen—zumindest unwichtig, oder sogar als methodischer Sündenfall verstanden. In solchem Milieu gewann die Frage nach literarischer Benutzung der Synoptiker durch Johannes ganz neues Gewicht. Am nachhaltigsten und extensivsten wollen neuerdings solche Bezüge F. Neirynck und seine Schule[16] wieder begründen. Neben mancher Zustimmung zu dieser Position, die U. Schnelle[17] als "Neubestimmung" und "forschungsgeschichtliche Wende" deklariert, wo sie doch nur eine Rückkehr zum frühkirchlichen Konsens bedeutet, haben unter methodenkritischen Vorzeichen z.B. P. Borgen,[18] W. Reinbold[19] und St. Landis[20] bedeutsame Kritik geübt. Auch I. Dunderberg,[21] der für einige johanneische Stellen literarische Bezüge zu den Synoptikern gelten läßt, hebt sich in der Methode und dem Ergebnis von F. Neirynck deutlich ab.[22]

Im Zusammenhang der literaturgeschichtlichen Theorien ist auch noch auf eine stillschweigende und fragwürdige Konzentration auf den Aspekt der Literaturproduktion allein hingewiesen worden. Es gälte rezeptionsästhetisch, auch mit gleichem Nachdruck den Leser und seine Aneignung der Literatur zu bedenken. Das kann man auf

[16] F. Neirynck hat sich verschiedentlich zu dem Thema geäußert, monographisch: F. Neirynck, *Jean et les Synoptiques* (BETL 49; Leuven: University Press, 1979). Vgl. im übrigen vor allem: F. Van Segbroeck u.a. (hgg.), *The Four Gospels* (3 Bde; FS F. Neirynck; BETL 100; Leuven: University Press, 1992); A. Denaux (hg.), *John and the Synoptics* (BETL 101; Leuven: University Press, 1992).

[17] U. Schnelle, "Johannes und die Synoptiker," in F. Van Segbroeck u.a. (hgg.), *The Four Gospels* (Anm. 16), 3.1799–814, S. 1799.

[18] P. Borgen, "The Independence of the Gospel of John: Some observations," in F. Van Segbroeck u.a. (hgg.), *The Four Gospels* (Anm. 16), 3.1815–34.

[19] Reinbold, *Bericht* (Anm. 13), 27ff.

[20] St. Landis, *Das Verhältnis des Johannesevangeliums zu den Synoptikern* (BZNW 74; Berlin: de Gruyter, 1994).

[21] I. Dunderberg, *Johannes und die Synoptiker* (AASF.DHL 69; Helsinki: Suomalainen Tiedeakatemia, 1994).

[22] Zur Forschungslage vgl. Smith, *John* (Anm. 7); F. Neirynck, "John and the Synoptics," in Denaux (hg.), *John and the Synoptics* (Anm. 16), 3–63.

das Verhältnis von Johannes zu den Synoptikern anwenden. Benutzt der Autor die Synoptiker, aber seine Leser kennen sie nicht? Oder sollen sie geradezu das vierte Evangelium mit Hilfe der Synoptiker lesen? Können sie überhaupt Johannes verstehen, ohne die Synoptiker zu kennen? Die letzte Frage hatte einst schon J. Blinzler[23] gestellt und so beantwortet, daß die johanneische Gemeinde die Synoptiker gekannt haben mußte, um das vierte Evangelium überhaupt voll verstehen zu können. Mit literaturgeschichtlichem Hintergrund versteht neuerdings z.B. H. Thyen[24] die Rezeptionssituation der Gemeinde so, daß sie das vierte Evangelium extensiv im Spiegel der Synoptiker lesen solle. Diesem Konzept ist allerdings auch schon mehrfach widersprochen worden.[25]

So hat es zur Zeit den Anschein, daß wieder alle Möglichkeiten aus der Forschungsgeschichte vertreten werden, einmal die beiden großen Optionen für literarische und traditionsgeschichtliche Abhängigkeit, zum anderen innerhalb dieser beiden Wege eine Fülle von Differenzierungen unter den verschiedensten methodischen Voraussetzungen. Die Vielfalt scheint kaum noch zu überbieten. Lohnt es sich in dieser Situation, die Einzelexegese der (aufs ganze vierte Evangelium gesehen) nicht einmal besonders zahlreichen Stellen, an denen der Entscheid fällt, nochmals zu drehen und zu wenden? Wohl nur sehr bedingt. Nötig erscheint viel eher, die positionellen Vorgaben und die Argumentationswege zu diskutieren, die zum neuen Variantenreichtum der Ergebnisse führen. Dazu wollen die folgenden Ausführungen einen begrenzten Beitrag liefern.

2. *Die externen Bezugstexte des vierten Evangeliums*

Das direkte Selbstzeugnis des Evangeliums in bezug auf seine externe Quellenbenutzung ist eindeutig. Es gibt nur einen Bezugstext an,[26] nämlich die heilige Schrift, die im johanneischen Kreis als *Septuaginta* bekannt war. Sie wird förmlich benannt als "die Schrift" (2:22; 7:38,

[23] Blinzler, *Johannes* (Anm. 14), 52f.

[24] H. Thyen, "Johannes und die Synoptiker," in Denaux (hg.), *John and the Synoptics* (Anm. 16), 81–107.

[25] Zuletzt I. Dunderberg, "Johannine Anomalies and the Synoptics," in J. Nissen – S. Pedersen (hgg.), *New Readings in John* (JSNTSup 182; Sheffield: Sheffield Acad. Press 1999) 108–25, S. 123f.

[26] Dunderberg, *Synoptiker* (Anm. 21), 192.

42 u.ö.) oder "die Schriften" (5,39) und vom "Wort" Jesu unterschieden (2:22). Andere Bezeichnungen sind etwa: "das Gesetz" (1:17; 7:19, 23 usw.) und "das Gesetz und die Propheten" (1:45). Diese Schrift[27] wird—im Unterschied zum 1 Joh, der von der Septuagintabenutzung ganz absieht,—als autoritativer Text mit einführenden formelhaften Wendungen zitiert (1:23; 2:17; 6:31 usw.). Wegen der Eindeutigkeit dieses Tatbestandes liegt hier einer der ganz wenigen Konsense in der johanneischen Forschung vor. Da, soweit man sehen kann, die griechische Sprache für die johanneischen Gemeinden die Alltags- und Gottesdienstsprache war, wird man daneben einer zusätzlichen Benutzung der hebräischen Bibel nicht das Wort reden. Vielmehr ist es empfehlenswert, die Varianten zur Septuaginta bei den johanneischen Bibelzitaten analog dem paulinischen Befund zu erklären, also mit Ungenauigkeiten und auch mit bewußten Gestaltungen zugunsten des eigenen Gedankenganges zu rechnen.[28]

Dieser Befund ist in zwei Richtungen auszuweiten: Der Autor oder die Autoren des Johannesevangeliums haben irgendwelche Evangelien so nicht zitiert, noch pauschal benannt, obwohl in etwa zur gleichen Zeit Lukas ausdrücklich seine Quellen zur Jesusgeschichte jedenfalls summarisch angab (Lk 1:1–4) und zum Beispiel die Didache zeigt, daß man durchaus zur Zeit der Entstehung des Johannesevangeliums schon auf ein Evangelium als einer literarischen Autorität verweisen konnte (Did 8,2; 15,3f.). Mit dem Prolog in Lk 1:1–4 ist in gewisser Weise der Epilog in Joh 21:25 vergleichbar: Jener spricht allgemein von vorhandenen literarischen Darstellungen des Lebens Jesu, dieser in einer floskelhaften Wendung davon, daß man noch mehr Bücher über Jesus schreiben könnte, aber nicht davon, daß solche verwendet wurden. Die Autorität des Evangeliums wird allein auf die Augenzeugenschaft des Lieblingsjüngers gegründet und ist der Anfang einer Abfolge: Lieblingsjünger—Schüler ("Wir"). Vom Lieblingsjünger gilt: Seine Autorität besteht in der (mündlichen) "Martyria",

---

[27] Genauer muß man sagen: wesentliche Teile der Septuaginta, nämlich die Teile, die die Gemeinden als Abschriften besaßen. Zu diesem Problem vgl. den Zugriff auf alttestamentliche Bücher bei Paulus nach der Tabelle bei D.A. Koch, *Die Schrift als Zeuge des Evangeliums* (BHT 69; Tübingen: Mohr, 1986) 33, und etwa Barn, der extensiv das Alte Testament benutzt, aber dabei wohl nur Gen, Dtn, Jes und Ps als Abschriften vor sich hat. Näheres bei K. Wengst, *Die Schriften des Urchristentums*, Band 2: *Didache (Apostellehre), Barnabasbrief, Zweiter Klemensbrief, Schrift an Diognet* (Darmstadt: WBG, 1984) 123 29. Zum 2Clem vgl. A. Lindemann, *Die Apostolischen Väter 1: Die Klemensbriefe* (HNT 17; Tübingen: Mohr, 1992) 193.

[28] Vgl. Koch, *Schrift* (Anm. 27).

die nun "Literatur"[29] wird. Dieser Befund muß zwar Synoptikerbenutzung noch nicht ausschließen, denn man kann das Geschichtsbild, das Joh 21,24 vermitteln will, für ein Konstrukt halten. Aber es ist doch zunächst ein Faktum, daß die Schüler der Abfolge: mündliche Lehre—einmalige literarische Fixierung das Wort reden. In keinem Fall macht Joh 21:24 eine Synoptikerbenutzung zu einer vorrangigen und selbstverständlichen Möglichkeit.

Außerdem ist die Septuagintabenutzung doch wohl geeignet zu zeigen, wie im johanneischen Kreis mit literarischer Autorität umgegangen wurde. Die Freiheit der Benutzung hält sich dabei etwa im Rahmen der paulinischen Verwendung der Schrift. Sie ist aber deutlich weniger frei als bei den synoptischen Beziehungen im vierten Evangelium. Diese größere Freiheit stellt darum ein Problem dar, das detailliert und inhaltlich erklärt und nicht nur pauschal als Behauptung konstatiert sein will. Dies geschieht leider allzuoft. Man darf das Stichwort "freier Umgang" innerhalb der Annahme, Johannes habe die Synoptiker literarisch benutzt, eben nicht dazu mißbrauchen, nur das nicht Erklärbare und Widerständige von seiner Hypothese fernzuhalten. Das Gegenteil ist zu fordern: Gerade die präzise Beschreibung, wie und mit welchen Leitlinien diese Freiheit des Johannes im einzelnen wahrgenommen wird, sollte ein wesentlicher Bestandteil der eigenen Argumentation sein. Der Vergleich mit der Septuagintabenutzung kann dabei eines der Maßstäbe sein, an denen man sich orientiert.

Die nur indirekt nachweisbare *Synoptikerbenutzung*, die also nur in Gestalt einer Hypothese als literarische Abhängigkeit beschrieben werden kann, wird von ihren Befürwortern eigentlich durchweg auf den Kanon konzentriert bedacht. Die Perspektive mit dem vierteiligen Evangelienkanon, an dem sich die Kirchenväter orientierten, ist also stillschweigend übernommen. Doch gibt es zur Zeit der Entstehung des Johannesevangeliums noch keinen Vier-Evangelien-Kanon. Die Verhältnisse zu dieser Zeit sind vielmehr in vielerlei Hinsicht recht kompliziert, zum Teil auch nicht mehr durchschaubar. Man wird *erstens* methodisch zu bedenken haben, daß die Evangelienproduktion in der Frühzeit des Christentums umfangreich war. Das bezeugen die zahlreichen, z.T. nur fragmentarisch oder namentlich bekannten judenchristlichen und gnostischen Evangelien, die später nicht in den

[29] Joh 20:30; 21:24 sind die ältesten Belege dafür, daß ein Evangelium als etwas Geschriebenes, als Buch bezeichnet wird.

Kreis der kanonischen Evangelien aufgenommen wurden. Auch wird es Evangelien gegeben haben, über deren Existenz man nichts mehr sagen kann. Diese Produktionsvielfalt wie die noch erkennbaren einzelnen Bedingungen bei den Produktionsprozessen der zahlreichen Evangelien sollten den Horizont auch der Erklärung des vierten Evangeliums mit abgeben.[30] *Zweitens* mag es wohl so sein, daß das Johannesevangelium das jüngste Werk im Verhältnis zu den Synoptikern ist. Doch alle zeitlichen Fixierungen dieser Art haben eine mehr oder weniger große Unschärfe. Es ist bequem, aber auch ein gutes Stück Abstraktion, etwa von der Reihenfolge Mk-Mt-Lk-Joh auszugehen. Matthäus und Lukas können synchron entstanden sein. Bei Lukas muß man einkalkulieren, daß das dritte Evangelium auch parallel zum Johannesevangelium, ja sogar kurz danach entstanden sein könnte. Dies schließt dann eine direkte Benutzung durch Johannes aus. Außerdem kennt niemand die Schnelligkeit, mit der ein Evangelium von seinem Entstehungsort zu den johanneischen Gemeinden gelangte. Jedenfalls formuliert der, der Johannes literarisch z.B. Lukas benutzen läßt, eine Hypothese zweiten Grades. Er muß nämlich vorab die Abfolge der Entstehung mit Lk-Joh festlegen und dann die Nähe Lk-Joh als literarisch qualifizieren. *Drittens* sieht es nach allem, was noch durch Quellenbelege zu erkunden ist, so aus, daß die Verbreitung der drei Synoptiker zur Zeit der Entstehung des vierten Evangeliums—also für die Zeit von 80–130 n.Chr.—sehr unterschiedlich war. Erst ab der zweiten Hälfte des zweiten Jahrhunderts gibt es unzweideutige Belege, daß alle vier Evangelien in Gemeinden gleichzeitig bekannt und benutzt wurden.[31] Aus der Zeit davor ist jedenfalls eindeutig: Matthäus und Lukas kennen sich gegenseitig nicht, wenn man innerhalb der immer noch gut brauchbaren Zwei-Quellen-Theorie denkt. Dazu paßt, daß z.B. die Didache nur von einem Evangelium spricht, das sie benutzt (Did 8,2). Sie meint damit wohl Matthäus.[32] Auch 1Clem und Ignatius werden nur

---

[30] Wengst, *Schriften* (Anm. 27) 220f., erwägt mit diskutablen Gründen, ob nicht z.B. 2 Clem ein verlorengegangenes synoptikernahes Evangelium benutzt habe und kein synoptisches.

[31] Vgl. K. und B. Aland, *Der Text des Neuen Testaments* (2. Aufl.; Stuttgart: Deutsche Bibelgesellschaft, 1989) 55ff., S. 77; E. Hennecke-W. Schneemelcher (hgg.), *Neutestamentliche Apokryphen* (3. Aufl.; Tübingen: Mohr, 1959) 10–13.

[32] Speziell zur Verbreitung des Matthäusevangeliums vgl. W.-D. Köhler, *Die Rezeption des Matthäusevangeliums in der Zeit vor Irenäus* (WUNT 24; Tübingen: Mohr, 1987).

Matthäus heranziehen. 2 Clem und Polycarp dürften eventuell Matthäus und Lukas verwendet haben, aber kaum Markus, vielleicht auch keinen Synoptiker. Solche Belege sind bekanntlich vermehrbar, wenn sie auch nicht immer wünschenswert eindeutig sind. Auch wird man einkalkulieren, daß Autoren das eine oder andere Evangelium vielleicht kannten, aber in ihren Schriften nicht eigens erwähnten. Zu rechnen ist auch noch damit, daß Gemeinden gar kein synoptisches Evangelium besaßen, andere vielleicht ein nicht-kanonisches. So ist jedenfalls bei einigen Schriften aus der Gruppe der sog. Apostolischen Väter höchst fraglich, ob sie überhaupt eines der synoptischen Evangelien verwendeten.[33] Dazu ist endlich noch überhaupt zu bedenken, daß die meisten urchristlichen Gemeinden "arm" waren, Texte zu vervielfältigen jedoch relativ "teuer" war. Der Wunsch, viele Schriften zu sammeln, stieß also wohl auch oftmals an ökonomische Grenzen. Das führt—auch wenn man den einen oder anderen Fall, der soeben nur thetisch angetippt wurde, anders beurteilen mag—zu dem Ergebnis: Es wäre wohl eher außergewöhnlich, wenn der johanneische Kreis alle drei Synoptiker besessen hätte.[34] Die Möglichkeit, daß er keines dieser Evangelien als Abschrift aufbewahrte, kann nicht ausgeschlossen werden. Als Ergebnis dieses ganzen Abschnittes kann festgehalten werden: Diese dreigestaffelte und nur grob skizzierte Komplexität sollte bei der Auswertung der johanneischen Synoptikernähe immer im Blick sein.

Darum ist auch die manchmal vorteilhafte Diskussion, wer die *Beweislast* zu tragen habe,[35] in diesem Fall kein gangbarer Weg. Es ist schon allgemein kein Zufall, daß solche Diskussion immer dort aufkommt, wo man den anderen die Beweislast aufbürdet, damit man sich selbst einen strategischen Vorteil vorbehält. Darum werden solche "Geschäftsordnungsdebatten" auch meistens als Selbstimmunisierung enttarnt. Daß die literarische Synoptikerbenutzung die vorab selbstverständliche Möglichkeit sei, hätte nur eine einsichtige

[33] Grundlegend immer noch H. Köster, *Synoptische Überlieferung bei den Apostolischen Vätern* (TU 65; Berlin: Akademie Verlag, 1957).

[34] Zu optimistisch schätzt M. Hengel, *Die johanneische Frage* (WUNT 67; Tübingen: Mohr, 1993) 208, die Verbreitung der kanonischen Evangelien ein. In M. Hengel, *Zur urchristlichen Geschichtsschreibung* (Stuttgart: Calwer, 1979), 13, hatte er noch anders geurteilt.

[35] M. Sabbe, "The Arrest of Jesus in Jn 18,1–11", in M. de Jonge (hg.), *L'Évangile de Jean* (BETL 44; Leuven: Leuven University Press, 1977) 203–34. Das Problem ist bei Reinbold, *Bericht* (Anm. 13), 30–32, gut besprochen.

Basis, wenn die voranstehenden Ausführungen nicht gelten würden, und der Vier-Evangelien-Kanon selbstverständlicher und alleiniger Ausgangspunkt der Erörterung sein dürfte. Zwei weitere Gründe kommen hinzu: Die komplexen Verhältnisse der gesamten frühchristlichen Evangelienproduktion lassen nicht nur nicht zu, den Kreis der Quellen vorab festzulegen, sondern lassen auch nur ergebnisoffen diskutieren, ob die Abhängigkeitsverhältnisse literarischer oder traditionsgeschichtlicher Art sind.[36] Auch die Innenverhältnisse im Johannesevangelium sprechen gegen solche Option: Die synoptikernahen Phänomene sind nur eine begrenzte Teilmenge im vierten Evangelium. Die andere respektable Teilmenge will auch auf ihre Herkunft hin bedacht sein. Dies kann nicht ohne traditionsgeschichtliche und/oder literarische Annahmen geschehen. Man kann es drehen und wenden wie man will, wer der literarischen Benutzung der Synoptiker durch den vierten Evangelisten einen Vorrang einräumen will, kann das nur über den Kanonbegriff tun. Er reiht sich dann dem Konsens der Kirchenväter ein, hat aber die historischen Verhältnisse gegen sich.

Eine noch andere Horizontbegrenzung in der Diskussion ist anzusprechen. Diejenigen, die die literarische Benutzung der Synoptiker befürworten, konzentrieren sich meistens, oft ausschließlich auf die synoptikernahen Perikopen und Sätze. Daß hier die Erörterung beginnen kann, ist unbestritten. Aber sie darf hier nicht enden. Solcher Vergleich bezieht sich dann nämlich nur auf die kleinere Schnittmenge der synoptischen und zugleich johanneischen Texte. Sowohl auf synoptischer als auch auf johanneischer Seite sind jedoch die jeweils größeren Textanteile je ganz anderer Art.[37] Eine Verhältnisbestimmung, die dieses *Gesamtphänomen* unbeachtet liegen läßt, bleibt darum immer unzureichend. Ein Kaufmann kann nicht nur seinen Gewinn bilanzieren. Er muß, um seine Firma realistisch einschätzen zu können, eine doppelte Buchführung nach Soll und Haben erstellen. Diese selbstverständliche Regel gilt auch außerhalb des kommerziellen Bereiches.

Da sind zunächst die Beobachtungen zur *Eigenständigkeit* des Johannes! Man kann sich noch gut vorstellen, daß Joh die Taufe Jesu verschwieg—trotz der synoptischen Berichte. Es gibt Erklärungen, warum er den den Synoptikern unbekannten Lieblingsjünger in den Zwölfer-

[36] Vgl. dazu noch einmal Köster, *Überlieferung* (Anm. 33).

[37] Mit vollem Recht mahnte schon Brown, *John* (Anm. 11) 1.XLV an, nicht nur die similarities, sondern auch die dissimilarities zu beachten und zu gewichten.

kreis einband. Das johanneische Weltbild mag verhindert haben, daß im vierten Evangelium kein Exorzismus erzählt ist. Johanneische Theologie kann Erklärung genug sein, daß im vierten Evangelium die Pilatusszene so besonders stark ausgebaut wurde. Auch die Kreuzesworte variieren schon die Synoptiker: Warum sollte nicht auch Johannes hier seine Freiheit genutzt haben? Für die Veränderung der Abfolge Galiläa—Jerusalem (Mk) zu einem mehrfachen Hin und Her zwischen beiden kann man vielleicht auch noch johanneische Theologie als Ursache bemühen. Aber wie will man erklären, daß der vierte Evangelist das synoptische Stichwort "Evangelium" mied? Wieso vermißt man in der Verkündigung des johanneischen Christus bis auf Joh 3:3, 5 das Zentralwort des synoptischen Jesus? Warum sollte der vierte Evangelist hier und da etwas übernehmen, aber die breit und durchgängig bezeugte Gottesreichsverkündigung bis auf die eine Ausnahme in Joh 3 konsequent meiden? Warum fehlen ausnahmlos alle synoptischen Gleichnisse, Parabeln und Allegorien, obwohl es Joh 10 und 15 gibt? Warum fehlen alle synoptischen Gesetzesworte und narrativen Gesetzeskonflikte, obgleich Johannes das Konfliktthema in Joh 5 und 9 bearbeitet? Warum sind die johanneischen Menschensohnaussagen alle so ganz anders als die synoptischen? Warum sollte Johannes bei Kenntnis der Synoptiker ohne Ausnahme die synoptischen alle ausgelassen haben? Warum behandelt er das Liebesgebot so selbständig (Joh 13:34f.; 15:1ff.) und verschmäht es ganz, die synoptischen Variationen zum Thema zu verarbeiten? Warum läßt der vierte Evangelist Mt 23 unbeachtet liegen, wo er doch mit den Pharisäern auch selbst hart ins Gericht geht? Warum erzählt er sieben Wunder und davon nur drei mit Synoptikernähe? Warum gerade dies drei? Warum bleibt Mt 16:17–19 unbenutzt, wo doch in Joh 6:66–71; 21:15ff. eine Sonderstellung des Petrus durchaus im Blick steht? Warum sollte Johannes ohne die Logienquelle zu kennen, just alle Q-Texte ausgelassen haben? Warum hat er Mt 5–7 und Lk 9:51–18:14 achtlos übersehen? Gerade solche Zufälle bei literarisch signifikanten Stücken wie der Logienquelle, der Bergpredigt und der sogenannten großen lukanischen Einschaltung bei der Auswahl kann man sich eigentlich nicht vorstellen. Es bieten sich auch weit und breit keine Gründe an, literarische Kenntnis der Synoptiker vorausgesetzt, diese Phänomene zu erklären. Doch auch für die Phänomene, die durch Themen und Textsorten benannt wurden, gilt insgesamt: Wer für literarische Kenntnis und Benutzung der Synoptiker plädiert, muß diese mit etwas Bibelkunde schnell vermehrbaren Phänomene inhaltlich und konkret erklären können. Eine nur pauschale Deutung mit Verweis auf die Freiheit des Evangelisten ist dabei nicht akzeptabel. Auch der Hinweis, das Kriterium stehe Joh 20:30f.,[38] ist unbrauchbar, weil Joh 20:30f. viel zu summarisch redet. Die gestellten Warum-Fragen weisen auch alle in eine andere Richtung als die einer Synoptikerbenutzung. Ihr Problem erledigt sich gänzlich ohne Ausnahme auf einen Schlag, wenn man die Selbständigkeit des Evangelisten synoptikerunabhängig bestimmt.

Dieser Ansatz erhält eine wichtige Stütze, wenn man die *Widersprüche* zwischen Johannes und den Synoptikern bedenkt. Sie demaskieren vor allem die alles vernebelnde Ergänzungstheorie als das, was sie ist: Eine Erklärungsstrategie, die die Probleme verdunkelt. Also: Kann man sich vorstellen, daß unter anderem folgende Widersprüche in den johanneischen Gemeinden als problemlos galten, wenn die synoptischen Evangelien geachtet und geehrt wurden? Da ist der verschiedene Todestag Jesu, der unausweichlich Konsequenzen für die theologische Auffassung des Todes Jesu und seines letzten Mahles hat. Kalenderfragen sind in der ganzen Antike keine Kleinigkeit, wie man an der essenischen Trennung vom Jerusalemer Tempel und am Osterstreit in der alten Kirchengeschichte ablesen kann (vgl. auch Röm 14:5; Gal 4:10). Nach Joh 6:42 gibt es an Jesu Geburt keine Besonderheit. Dem widersprechen bekanntlich die Kindheitsgeschichten des Matthäus und Lukas. Gerade weil das Johannesevangelium eine "hohe Christologie" vertritt, ist nicht erklärlich, warum—Synoptikerkenntnis vorausgesetzt—die Kindheitsgeschichten der markinischen Seitenreferenten nicht aufgearbeitet wurden, sondern im Gegensatz zu ihnen und unbekümmert geredet wird. Da ist die Angabe in Mk 1:14 parr., die Jesus erst nach der Einkerkerung des Täufers öffentlich auftreten läßt. Doch nach Joh 3:22ff., wirken Jesus und der Täufer in Konkurrenz synchron. Nach Joh 1:21, 25 ist der Täufer nicht Elia, nach Mt 11:14; Lk 1:17; 7:26f. ist er es jedoch ausdrücklich. Nach Mk 1:16–20 erwählt Jesus initiativ vier Jünger aus ihrem Berufsleben heraus. Nach Joh 1:35ff. kommen Jünger selbständig zu Jesus und sind zuvor Täuferschüler. Die unterschiedliche Chronologie bei der Tempelreinigung ist zwischen Johannes und den Synoptikern nicht auszugleichen (Joh 2:14ff.; Mk 11:15–17 parr.). Nach Mt 10:5f. sollen die Jünger Samaria meiden. Nach Joh 4 findet hier sogar Jesu

[38] So U. Schnelle, *Einleitung in das Neue Testament* (2. Aufl.; Göttingen: Vanderhoeck & Ruprecht, 1996) 568f.571.

erste und erfolgreiche Mission statt. Auch die matthäische Gesetzeskontinuität (Mt 5:19–21; 23:1–3) widerspricht den johanneischen Ausführungen (Joh 1:17; 4:21–24; 8:17 usw.). Vom Herrenmahl ist im Johannesevangelium im Gegensatz zu den Synoptikern nicht im Passionszusammenhang gesprochen (Joh 6:51ff.). Die Todesursache Jesu steht nach Joh 11:47ff. in unausgleichbarem Unterschied zu entsprechenden synoptischen Angaben. Diese ausgewählten Fälle wie weitere benennbare Phänomene dieser Art sind wie die voranstehende Liste, bei der es um Auslassungen und nicht erklärbares Übergehen von Textzusammenhängen und Themen ging, wiederum über das ganze vierte Evangelium verteilt und in ihrer Menge signifikant. Wiederum ergibt sich dasselbe Bild: Die Widersprüche zu den Synoptikern werden erst sichtbar, wenn man mit den Synoptikern vergleicht. Das Johannesevangelium steht aber in sämtlichen Fällen in gar keinem expliziten Dialog mit den Synoptikern. Redet es also ganz selbstverständlich eigenständig? Das führt zu der Möglichkeit: Das vierte Evangelium weiß gar nichts von solchen Widersprüchen, weil es keinen Vergleich mit den ihm unbekannten Synoptikern anstellt.

Es ist erstaunlich, daß sich der Vergleich zwischen Johannes und den Synoptikern bisher eigentlich durchweg auf die vier Evangelienschriften allein konzentrierte. Nur noch die Arbeiten am Thomasevangelium haben zum Teil auf Konsequenzen zum Verstehen der Produktionsweisen innerhalb der kanonischen Evangelien aufmerksam gemacht. Es darf jedoch als Mangel der Forschung eingeschätzt werden, daß es für die *frühjüdische Literatur* bisher keine Untersuchung zu solchen Texten gibt, die die Textsorte eines Prätextes reproduzieren und den Inhalt des Prätextes in Anlehnung und Veränderung ein zweites Mal gestalten, um an ihnen abzuklären, welche Rezeptions- und Gestaltungsvorgänge diese in Abhängigkeit erstellten Neufassungen erkennen lassen. Dies könnte sowohl für die Arbeit der Seitenreferenten des Markus wie für eine mögliche Benutzung der Synoptiker durch Johannes literaturgeschichtliche Einblicke und Zuordnungen gestatten, die die Abhängigkeitsphänomene und den Neugestaltungsspielraum jeweils besser einschätzen ließen. Solche reinterpretierenden Neugestaltungen bei Textsortenkontinuität sind im Frühjudentum nicht selten, vielmehr eine spezielle Weise der Literaturproduktion. Zeugen dafür sind unter anderem das chronistische Geschichtswerk, das Jubiläenbuch, die Antiquitates Biblicae und das Genesis-Apokryphon. Es trifft sich gut, daß diese Werke narrative Texte sind, also der

Textsorte Evangelium, wie sie die Synoptiker und Johannes repräsentieren, verwandt sind. Wie schon gesagt, eine Untersuchung der Verhältnisse von solchen nachgestalteten Texten zu ihren Prätexten steht noch aus, doch zeigt eine grobe Durchsicht: Matthäus und Lukas verhalten sich in diesem Großvergleich konform, Johannes fällt aus dem Rahmen. Hat er also vielleicht doch keine synoptischen Prätexte verarbeitet?

Die frühjüdischen Texte, die reinterpretierend Prätexte nachgestalten, setzen sehr wahrscheinlich voraus, daß die Leser die Prätexte (in jedem Fall die Tora) kennen und die neue Interpretationsleistung am bekannten Vortext einschätzen sollen. Insofern geht H. Thyens[39] Ansatz, der die johanneische Gemeinde das vierte Evangelium im Spiegel der Synoptiker lesen läßt, mit der antiken Literaturgeschichte konform. Aber wie ein Text aussah, der wollte, daß sein Prätext mitgelesen wurde, zeigen instruktiv die eben schon genannten Beispiele. Das vierte Evangelium ist von solcher Nähe zu den Synoptikern meilenweit entfernt. Während in diesen Texten die Nähe zur Tora offenkundig ist, bleibt die Nähe, die Thyen aufzeigen möchte, hochgradig subjektiv. Es sind bibelkundliche Einfälle, aber keine begründeten und ausgewiesenen Verbindungen.

Da es heute nicht mehr ganz selbstverständlich ist, gegenüber der klassischen Formgeschichte in modifizierter Weise *mündliche Tradition* als eine Überlieferungsform zur Erklärung der Diachronie anzunehmen, muß zu dieser Möglichkeit zumindest ein knappes Wort gesagt werden, damit die Fixierung allein auf die Möglichkeit literarischer Bezugnahme offener gestaltet wird. Von Paulus[40] bis Papias (Euseb, *h.e.* 3,39) ist eine mündliche Tradition zu Jesu Wirken und Verkündigen bezeugt. Paulus schöpft ausnahmslos aus solcher Tradition und beschreibt sie als mündliche Überlieferung (1 Kor 7:10, 25; 11:23; 15:1f.; 1 Thess 4:15) zum Wirken und zum Geschick Jesu, auf deren Autorität er sich ganz selbstverständlich berufen kann und die auch in den Gemeinden autoritative Geltung besitzt. Papias bevorzugt sie ausdrücklich gegenüber schriftlichen Texten. Auch Matthäus und Lukas bekunden mit ihrem Sondergut, daß sie neben Markus und der Logienquelle mündliche Tradition verarbeiten. Markus unterscheidet zwischen schriftlichem Alten Testament (Mk 12:10, 19, 26),

---

[39] Vgl. oben Thyen, *Synoptiker* (Anm. 24).

[40] Vgl. J. Becker, *Paulus* (2. Aufl.; Tübingen: Mohr, 1992) 119ff.; Borgen, "Independence" (Anm. 16), 1815ff.

einer schriftlichen apokalyptischen Vorlage (Mk 13:14) und mündlichen Gleichnisstoffen (Mk 4:9, 12, 15f., 18, 20, 23f., 33). Die Herrenwortüberlieferung bei den sog. Apostolischen Vätern stammt zu einem guten Teil aus mündlicher Tradition. Auch die Agrapha in der frühen Kirche bezeugen diese mündliche Überlieferung. Wie immer aber die Methodendiskussion zu solcher Mündlichkeit der Tradition geführt werden mag, daß es sie als Jesusüberlieferung gegeben hat, läßt sich schwerlich bestreiten.[41] Wenn das jedoch ein Faktum ist, dann müssen synoptikernahe Phänomene im Johannesevangelium so besprochen werden, daß ausdrücklich begründet wird, ob es besser ist, mit schriftlicher oder traditionsgeschichtlicher Bezugnahme zu rechnen. Jedenfalls buchen F. Neirynck, seine Schüler[42] und ihm nahestehende Autoren solche Nähe viel zu schnell und ausschließlich auf der Seite der literarischen Beziehungen.[43]

Damit ist ein weiteres wesentliches Methodenproblem in der gegenwärtigen Diskussion angesprochen. Sicherlich ist es wichtig, die Nähe zwischen Johannes und den Synoptikern zunächst einmal statistisch festzustellen. Aber solch formales Konstatieren ist auch dann, wenn man ein Dutzend mehr oder weniger lockere Bezüge zu einer Perikope gesammelt hat, noch kein Beweis für irgendeine mögliche These literarischer Abhängigkeit. Aus Quantitäten müssen nämlich erst noch Urteile zur *Qualität der Befunde* gemacht werden. Wer solchen Arbeitsgang ausläßt, muß sich nicht wundern, wenn Vertreter traditionsgeschichtlicher Beziehungen dieses bloße Sammeln als Beweisgang nicht anerkennen. Sie kritisieren die summarische Statistik als solche und im einzelnen in der Regel nur geringfügig und streichen normalerweise aus der aufgestellten Ansammlung von Beziehungen nur diejenigen heraus, die allzu locker oder gar arbiträr sind. Aber sie

[41] Diese Jesustradition bestand nicht nur aus Motiven und Grundaussagen in variabler Sprache, sondern besaß relativ feste Inhalte und Formen. Eines der illustrativen Beispiele dafür bietet gerade das vierte Evangelium: Vgl. Mk 10:15; Mt 18:3; Joh 3:3, 5; Justin, *Apol.* I 61,4.

[42] Vgl. Anm. 16.

[43] Besonders grob argumentiert z.B. Th. Knöppler, *Die theologia crucis des Johannesevangeliums* (WMANT 69; Neukirchen-Vluyn: Neukirchener, 1994). Er sammelt (S. 147–49) alle "Anklänge" aus den johanneischen Abschiedsreden zu synoptischen Aussagen und beschreibt sie dann nur formal statistisch mit vagen Begriffen wie: johanneische Texte "lassen anklingen" oder "erinnern an . . .", gibt sogar zu, daß "von echten Parallelen nicht die Rede sein kann", aber deutet dies alles dann unmittelbar nach seinem Grundsatz, daß Johannes die Synoptiker kenne, sie aber aus dem Gedächtnis verwende (23 Anm. 117).

warten angesichts dieses Befundes auf die entscheidende Argumentation und auf das konkrete Abwägen, welche Möglichkeit der Verhältnisbestimmung wohl angemessener ist.

Diese Diskussion hat mit J. Schniewind und P. Gardner-Smith—von ihnen war oben schon die Rede—begonnen. Bei beiden findet man die ersten *Klassifikationsbemühungen*. Unter den nachfolgenden Beiträgen zum Thema seien die auch schon oben eingeführten Namen von P. Borgen und I. Dunderberg noch genannt. Auch U. Schnelle, der zunächst in seiner Habilitation[44] dieser Qualifikation eigentlich keine Aufmerksamkeit schenkte, hat neuerdings die Notwendigkeit der Qualifizierung erkannt.[45]

Nach Lage der Dinge kann man die Klassifikation leider nicht mit Beziehungen anfangen, die sich durch Selbstevidenz auszeichnen, also mit Zitaten (kenntlich gemachten und freien) oder globalen Verweisen von Johannes auf die Synoptiker. Beginnt man angesichts dieser Fehlanzeige am anderen, also am untersten Ende der Skala, werden im *Wortbereich* besondere Einzelworte, Wortkluster, hapax legomena nur ganz randständige Bedeutung erhalten dürfen, weil sie ebensogut mündlich wie schriftlich zu Verwandtschaften führen können.[46] Satzsyntaktische Phänomene (also die syntaktische Struktur einer Mehrsatzperiode) sind dagegen viel eindeutiger. Da komplexe Perioden eher der Schriftsprache entstammen, sind solche Textstellen qualifizierte Indizien für literarische Wiederaufnahme. Allerdings sind parataktische Satzabfolgen oder Anordnungen von einem Hauptsatz und einem Nebensatz kaum aussagekräftig. So kann man literarisch und mündlich Textgestaltungen vornehmen. Findet man Textabschnitte, bei denen wie im Fall von Mt 3:7–10 = Lk 3:7–9 praktisch nur die Einleitung variiert, im übrigen jedoch Syntax, Wortfolge und Wortwahl gleich sind, kann man sich glücklich schätzen, eine recht große Eindeutigkeit zugunsten literarischen Abhängigkeit vor sich zu haben. Stößt man gleich auf mehrere derartiger Beispiele, ist die Sicherheit des Urteils optimal. Allerdings fehlen solche Beispiele für das Johannesevangelium ganz. Die bloße stoffliche Gleichheit von narrativen Perikopen (Beispiele: Joh 4:46ff. = Mt 8:5ff. par.) besagt jedoch noch nichts. Hier kann erst die Einzelanalyse mit Hilfe der Diskussion zu

[44] U. Schnelle; *Antidoketische Christologie im Johannesevangelium* (FRLANT 144; Göttingen: Vandenhoeck & Ruprecht, 1987).

[45] Schnelle, "Johannes" (Anm. 17), 1800f.

[46] Vgl. dazu auch E.P. Sanders, "Literary Dependence in Colossians", *JBL* 85 (1966) 28–45.

den sonstigen Fällen von Nähe innerhalb der Perikope weiterhelfen. Überhaupt gilt: Lassen sich gehäuft mehrere Beobachtungskategorien für einen Textabschnitt benennen, erhöht dies die Qualität des Urteils.

Die voranstehenden Beispiele blicken isoliert auf Einzelphänomene wie Worte, Sätze und Perikopen. Zu bedenken sind jedoch auch *Kompositionszusammenhänge* und Kontexte. So hat die Abfolge bei Markus: Jüngerberufung—erste Wunder in Kapernaum (Mk 1:16–31) eine Analogie in Joh 1:35–2:12: Auch hier steht nach der Gewinnung der ersten Jünger ein erstes Wunder (mit ausdrücklichem Verweis, daß die soeben berufenen Jünger daraufhin an Jesus glaubten: 2:11). Es ereignet sich allerdings in Kana. Doch die Übersiedlung nach Kapernaum folgt in 2:12 sofort danach. Die verschiedenen Berufungsszenen und die je anderen Wunder schließen es aus, daß Johannes von Markus her diese Komposition übernahm. Aber das Beispiel zeigt, daß es wohl doch ganz allgemein kompositionelle Strukturen gab, deren gegliederte Gestalt Einzeltexte in überschaubare etwas größere Einheiten einband. Ein weiteres Beispiel solcher Art ist die Abfolge in Joh 6 = Mk 6 von Speisungswunder und Seewandel. Dieses Beispiel ist viel diskutiert und muß hier nicht neu besprochen werden.[47] Der Befund läßt im Endeffekt nur zwei Deutungen zu: Da hier der Zufall kaum gewaltet haben kann, liegt entweder Markus-Einfluß vor oder ein vormarkinischer Zusammenhang.

Solche Fälle schrumpfen allerdings—vom Passionsbericht abgesehen—sowohl für die Wortüberlieferung[48] wie für die Erzählungen auf den Fall von Joh 6 zusammen. Die allgemeine Regel lautet also: Die Kontexte und Abfolgen zeigen johanneische Selbständigkeit. Dies ist wohl auch allgemein zugestanden.

Für alle bisher genannten Phänomene gilt nun in jedem Fall noch die besondere Regel, die I. Dunderberg[49] und St. Landis[50] noch einmal vor kurzem unabhängig voneinander energisch ins Methoden-

[47] Vgl. die Diskussionen bei J. Konings, "The Pre-Markan Sequence in Jn VI: A Critical Re-examination," in M. Sabbe (hg.), *L'évangile selon Marc: Tradition et rédaction* (BETL 34; Leuven: Leuven University Press, 1974) 147–77, und bei Dunderberg, *Synoptiker* (Anm. 21), 125–74.

[48] Daß die Wortüberlieferung aus Täufermund in Joh 1:19–34 steht und die synoptischen Analogien eben auch eingangs der Synoptiker zu lesen sind, zeigt zwar einen gleichen Kompositionszusammenhang auf. Er ist aber als solcher nicht auffällig, weil das Täuferthema dies bedingt. Wer die Abhängigkeit des Johannes von Mk diskutieren will, wird andere Beobachtungen benennen.

[49] Dunderberg, *Synoptiker* (Anm. 21), 27f.

[50] Landis, *Verhältnis* (Anm. 20), 41ff.

bewußtsein der Johannesforscher eingeimpft haben: Das entscheidende Kriterium für die Eindeutigkeit des Beweises ist die Forderung, daß johanneische Synoptikerbenutzung dann die stärkste Stütze erhält, wenn die Koinzidenzen sich auf *redaktionelle* Tätigkeiten der Synoptiker beziehen. Allerdings hat auch diese Regel ihre Tücken: Ihre Stärke wird nämlich dadurch begrenzt, daß sie synoptische Analysen voraussetzen, die bestimmen, was zur Redaktion gehört. So schreibt z.B. Dunderberg[51] die Phrase "in dieser Stunde" in Mt 8:13c matthäischer Redaktion zu, also kann für ihn Joh 4:53 als Prätext Matthäus benutzt haben. Anders urteilt St. Landis,[52] der die Angabe für vormatthäisch hält. Weiter bleibt auch immer die Frage, wenn solche redaktionellen Gemeinsamkeiten nur in signifikant kleiner Zahl—bezogen auf den Gesamttext des vierten Evangeliums—vorliegen, ob dann nicht doch eine zufällige Koinzidenz entstand oder es sich um einen Fall von sekundärer Oralität handelt. Doch trotz dieser zwei Einschränkungen bleibt es dabei: Solche redaktionellen Phänomene verdienen höchste Priorität bei der Argumentation.

Ein Sonderfall möglicher Beziehung zu den Synoptikern muß noch Erwähnung finden, wenngleich er im Endeffekt keine Entscheidungshilfe hergibt. Gemeint sind mögliche Fälle, in denen der vierte Evangelist so erzählt, daß er bei den Hörern oder Lesern voraussetzt, sie könnten ganz selbstverständlich seine zufälligen *Erzähllücken* durch Synoptikerkenntnis auffüllen; erst dieser Vorgang mache dann das Verständnis des Textes komplett.[53] Wenn ein solcher Beweis gelänge, besäße er gewiß eine solide argumentative Kraft. Aber er steht immer vor enormen, ja unüberwindlichen Problemen: Einmal muß am johanneischen Text gezeigt werden, daß eine nicht gewollte Informationslücke vorliegt und nicht statt mit einem Erzählfehler mit absichtsvoller Gestaltung zu rechnen ist oder der Erzählfehler nicht anderweitig entstand. Zum anderen muß das nicht erzählte Wissen so definierbar sein, daß es eindeutig nur aus einem literarischen Text der Synoptiker aufgefüllt werden kann, also nicht etwa aus dem allgemeinen Wissen der Gemeinde stammt (oder einem nichtsynoptischen Evangelium). Wird schon die Einschätzung des johanneischen Textes

---

[51] Dunderberg, *Synoptiker* (Anm. 21), 91.

[52] Landis, *Verhältnis* (Anm. 20), 17.

[53] Vgl. dazu etwa F. Büchsel, "Johannes und die Synoptiker", *ZST* 4 (1926/27) 240–65, S. 243–45. Blinzler, *Johannes* (Anm. 14), 52f. Zur Diskussion vgl. Dunderberg, *Synoptiker* (Anm. 21), 113ff.

als lückenhaft immer zwiespältig bleiben, so kann die als notwendig angenommene Synoptikerhilfe überhaupt nie nachgewiesen werden, weil sich Nicht-erzähltes jeder spezifischen Qualifizierung entzieht und damit immer offen bleiben muß, wie das vorausgesetzte Wissen im einzelnen aussah und woher es sich verdanken könnte.

Vom Ansatz her viel verheißungsvoller ist die Diskussion, ob denn nicht die *Textsorte Evangelium* als ganze dazu zwingt, beim vierten Evangelium Synoptikerkenntnis—zumindest das Wissen um die Existenz des Markus—vorauszusetzen. Die Frage lautet: Hat der vierte Evangelist konkrete Kenntnis der Textsorte Evangelium, und gestaltet er im Wissen um diese Textsorte (etwa in Gestalt des Markusevangeliums) sein eigenes Evangelium, oder ist Johannes ein zweiter Markus? Bisher hatte diese Frage ihren systematischen Ort am jeweiligen Abschluß der Diskussion um die synoptikernahen Stellen im vierten Evangelium, also nach der Erörterung der bisher auch in diesem Abschnitt besprochenen Befunde. Sie war gleichsam die alles bündelnde Schlußfrage. Aus dieser Stellung hat sie neuerdings U. Schnelle[54] entfernt und ihr einen eigenständigen Wert zuerkannt, indem er die Strukturelemente im ältesten Evangelium mit denen im vierten Evangelium vergleicht. Er stellt fest, daß erstens Jesus Christus in beiden Fällen als das handelnde Subjekt des Evangeliums auftritt und zweitens die Passion und das Osterzeugnis in beiden Fällen die Fluchtpunkte der Darstellung sind, indem von Anfang an die Verweise auf die Passion (und auf die Auferstehung Jesu Christi) die Leser hin zu den großen Schlußabschnitten beider Evangelien führen. Diese beide Evangelien prägende Makrostruktur kann nicht zufällig gleich sein, sondern spricht für literarische Abhängigkeit—so meint es jedenfalls Schnelle.

Man kann diese Beobachtungsschneise zunächst sogar erweitern: Beide Evangelien behandeln das öffentliche Wirken Jesu, und zwar mit dem Anfang beim Täufer und der Passion (samt Osterzeugnis) als Abschluß. Beide Evangelien wechseln mit erzählerischer Absicht zwischen Erzähltexten und Reden Jesu. Beide strukturieren ihre Großtexte durch Summarien.[55] Beide kennen Erzählerkommentare. Für beide sind Bezüge zum Alten Testament theologisch wichtig. Beide konstituieren die Einheit ihrer Textsorte durch das personelle,[56]

---

[54] U. Schnelle, "Johannes" (Anm. 17), 1801–5.

[55] Bekanntlich kennt die Logienquelle noch keine Summarien. Markus ist in jedem Fall der erste, der sie bei der Gestaltung eines Evangeliums als Stilmittel einsetzt.

[56] Die Hauptfigur steht im perspektivischen Mittelpunkt, die Anhänger sind die

das geographische[57] und zeitliche Inventar.[58] Endlich überschreiten beide in der Art, wie sie Jesu Reden und Wirken schildern, den biographischen Rahmen der Hauptperson und ihrer Lebenszeit. Denn beide lassen in ihre Darstellung Aussagen über Jesu nachösterliche Stellung bei Gott einfließen und geben der nachösterlichen Gemeinde eine geschichtliche und theologische Ortsbestimmung.

Diese auf den ersten Blick frappierende Nähe führt aber nun doch wohl zu einem anderen Ergebnis als dem von Schnelle. Ein Teil solcher Analogien ergibt sich nämlich aufgrund des Gegenstandes der Erzählung von allein: Nicht erst Markus, sondern schon die Logienquelle beginnt mit Johannes dem Täufer. Das heißt: Offenbar war es Allgemeinwissen der frühen Christenheit, Jesu Wirken mit dem Täufer einsetzen zu lassen. Den Passionsbericht wird wohl niemand an anderer Stelle positionieren als am Schluß. Auch daß die Erzählperspektive Jesus Christus ins Zentrum stellt, ist kaum anders zu erwarten und versteht sich von selbst. Weitere Beispiele dieser Art mögen zugunsten einer anderen Beobachtung zurückgestellt werden. Wichtig ist nämlich noch folgender Tatbestand: Diese Übereinstimmungen sind durchweg nur struktureller und funktionaler Art und bekunden keine sonstige Verwandtschaft. So fällt insbesondere auf, daß z.B. die Summarien und Vorankündigungen auf Jesu Geschick in beiden Evangelien je an anderer Stelle kontextuell eingebunden und inhaltlich je ganz anders gestaltet sind: Müßte sich nicht der vierte Evangelist bei Kenntnis des ältesten Evangeliums geradezu höchster asketischer Zurückhaltung befleißigt haben, wenn er zwar von Markus die strukturellen Formen, aber niemals spezifische Sätze übernommen hätte? Diese Frage führt zugleich auf einen letzten wichtigen Gesichtspunkt: Schnelle vergleicht nur Markus und Johannes, unterläßt es aber, die analogen Strukturelemente vor allem in narrativen Texten des Alten Testaments und in der frühjüdischen Literatur aufzusuchen. Ebenso versäumt er es, die religiöse Biographie des Hellenismus in die Untersuchung mit einzubeziehen. Er diskutiert also stillschweigend innerkanonisch und blendet den Blick in die alttestamentliche und frühjüdische Literaturgeschichte und den Helle-

---

Jünger, als Auditorium fungiert das Volk, als Gegner tritt das offizielle Judentum auf, voran die Pharisäer.

[57] Vgl. vor allem den Gegensatz: Galiläa-Jerusalem.

[58] Gemeint ist die ein- oder dreijährige Wirksamkeit Jesu.

nismus aus. Nur dadurch können die strukturellen Koinzidenzen flugs in eine kausale Hypothese umgemünzt werden. Die Doppelfrage, mit welchen strukturellen Mitteln sind die Evangelien gestaltet, und ob diese Beobachtung Licht auf Abhängigkeitsverhältnisse wirft, ist wichtig. Doch wird sie nur angemessen erörtert, wenn sie innerhalb des Großhorizontes der Produktion von analogen Texten aus der Kultur, aus der die Evangelien stammen, besprochen wird. Viele der Strukturelemente erweisen sich dann sehr schnell als allgemeine Mittel der Gestaltung in vergleichbarer Literatur.

Weitgehend zurückgestellt wurde bisher das besondere Problem des *Passionsberichtes*. Die meisten Belege, die von F. Neirynck und M. Sabbe bis U. Schnelle und M. Lang[59] für eine johanneische Abhängigkeit von den Synoptikern aufgezählt wurden, entstammen ihm.[60] Dabei wird in dieser Forschergruppe angenommen, Markus sei der Schöpfer des Passionsberichtes und diesem Erzählzusammenhang sei nie traditionsgeschichtliche Selbständigkeit (vor und nach Markus) eigen gewesen. Diese Position führt dann natürlich mit innerer Konsequenz dazu, sowohl Markus wie auch Johannes als Ganzheiten mit ihren Nähen zueinander zu vergleichen.

Mit diesem Urteil über den Passionsbericht, mit dem ihm eine besondere Traditionsgeschichte abgesprochen wird, wird eine Grundannahme aus den Anfängen formgeschichtlicher Untersuchungen revidiert. Stimmten nämlich schon M. Dibelius und R. Bultmann je auf ihre Weise darin überein, daß Markus am Schluß seines Evangeliums einen alten Erzählzusammenhang aufnahm, und hatten seither viele illustre Exegeten diese besondere Geschichte der Passionserzählung zu erhellen versucht, so lautet das Urteil über diesen Weg nun: Er ist ein Irrweg. Dieses Urteil hat manche Voraussetzungen, u.a. auch literaturtheoretische, die sich hinterfragen lassen. Doch sind sie hier nicht zu diskutieren.

In jedem Fall bleibt die Position der Forschergruppe bis heute umstritten. Das besondere narrative Geflecht des Passionsberichtes[61] und der Umstand, daß nur beim Passionszusammenhang die Akoluthie

---

[59] Vgl. den Forschungsbericht von Lang, *Johannes* (Anm. 5), 21 56. Auf Einzelheiten dieser Darstellung, die für erhebliche Kritik offen ist, gehe ich jetzt nicht ein.

[60] Dies verwundert auch niemanden, der die Diskussion seit Schniewind, *Parallelperikopen* (Anm. 8), überblickt.

[61] Zur Illustration seien beispielhaft diese Punkte genannt: Statt in sich gerundeter kleiner Einheiten, die mehr oder weniger locker redaktionell verbunden sind (so die Typik in Mk 1–13), stößt man im Passionsbericht weitgehend auf aufeinander

der Einzelstücke zwischen Markus und Johannes besonders stimmig ist, ja die Nähe in den Einzelformulierungen zwischen Markus und Johannes besonders signifikant hervorsticht,[62] sprechen dafür, sich intensiv dem Problem zu widmen, wie diese Besonderheiten zu erklären sein können. Sollte der vierte Evangelist wirklich in seinem ersten Hauptteil eine andere Nähe zu Markus aufgebaut haben als im zweiten? Wer Markus zum literarischen Produzenten des Passionsberichtes macht, ist natürlich auf einfache Weise die knifflige Frage los, ob die Diskussion je der Einzelphänomene zu einer literarischen oder traditionsgeschichtlichen Erklärung führt. Er hat sich vorab den Weg freigemacht, nahe Beziehungen allein aufgrund literarischer Rezeption erklären zu können.[63]

Wie immer nun diese benannten Phänomenbeobachtungen (und weitere) einer angemessenen Entstehungshypothese zum Passionsbericht zugeführt werden mögen, methodisch sollte gelten: Man muß nach Lage der Dinge zwei Bilanzen für die Verhältnisbestimmung zwischen Johannes und den Synoptikern aufstellen, eine für den Passionsbericht und eine für das übrige vierte Evangelium. Wer diese Unterscheidung nicht macht, muß sich die Kritik gefallen lassen, sein Ergebnis in einem wesentlichen Punkt vorwegbestimmt zu haben.

Endlich ist nun noch ein Wort zu den *sozialgeschichtlichen Bedingungen* des behandelten Themas angebracht. Man muß mit guten Gründen annehmen, daß die johanneischen Gemeinden in einem übersichtlichen Umfeld lebten, ja wohl wie ein Gemeindeverband eng zusammengehörten. Sie besaßen doch wohl eine numerische Größe, die den Informationsfluß noch gut funktionieren ließ, so daß das gemeinsame Wissen der Gemeinden nahezu deckungsgleich war. Auch zwi-

---

bezogene und aufeinander aufbauende Erzählstücke, deren Reihung nicht ausgetauscht werden kann. Auch bei den Konstituentien jeder Erzählung (Personen, Geographie, Zeit) gibt es ein gut beschreibbares Eigenprofil des Passionsberichtes. Die besondere Beleuchtung der Ereignisse durch ganz bestimmte alttestamentliche Bezüge fällt ebenfalls auf. Sie führt zu einem spezifischen theologischen Gesicht des Passionsberichtes.

[62] Es ist ein Verdienst der Dissertation von Reinbold, *Bericht* (Anm. 13), dies eindrücklich vorgeführt zu haben.

[63] Nur von solcher Vorgabe her verständlich sind z.B. der Aufsatz von Sabbe zu Joh 18:1–11, "Arrest" (Anm. 35), und die Dissertation von Lang, *Johannes* (Anm. 5). Man muß beide Arbeiten nur einmal einer formalen Analyse der Argumentationslogik unterziehen, dann wird offenkundig, wie vorab Verhältnisse geschaffen werden, damit das "Richtige" herauskommt, also jede Einzelstelle nur innerhalb eines bestimmten Wahrnehmungskanals eine Erklärung findet.

schen der Schule oder einem Einzelautor und den Gemeinden wird man die Schnittmenge des Gemeinsamen sehr groß ansetzen. Die Segmentierung einer industriellen und multikulturellen Zivilisation ist jedenfalls weit entfernt von solchen Verhältnissen. Daraus ergibt sich, daß man sehr gute Gründe benötigt, um Quellen, die ein johanneischer Autor benutzt, dem Kenntnisstand der Gemeinden vorzuenthalten. Es ist auch schwer, sich vorzustellen, eine johanneische Quelle benutzt nur Markus, eine andere verarbeitet nur Matthäus, oder die Synoptikernähe sei erst durch eine spätere Redaktion zustande gekommen. Natürlich: Sicher ausschließen lassen sich diese (und ähnliche) Fälle nicht. Aber eine Gesamtauffassung, die der relativ hohen Homogenität der sozialen Situation dieser Gemeinden Rechnung trägt, ist sicher zu bevorzugen. So kann vielleicht der Blick auf die Lebensverhältnisse der johanneischen Gemeinden helfen, dem hohen Differenzierungsgrad der gegenwärtigen Diskussion Grenzen zu ziehen. Es ist sicherlich wichtig, alle Möglichkeiten zu bedenken, aber der Entscheid für eine bestimmte Annahme wird die sozialen Bedingungen, unter der sie existiert haben soll, zu beachten haben.

Diese Ausführungen zu den möglichen externen Bezugstexten des vierten Evangeliums haben hoffentlich alle entscheidenden Probleme angeschnitten,[64] die bei der Aufstellung eines Beweisganges bedacht sein wollen. Dabei ist klar: den Befürwortern einer literarischen Abhängigkeit des Johannes von synoptischen Texten ist mit diesen Ausführungen der Begründungsweg schwerer gemacht, als sie sich ihn selbst gestalten. Prinzipiell ist der vorgeschlagene Weg aber doch wohl der Problemlage angemessen. An dieser Angemessenheit will er beurteilt werden.

---

[64] Absichtlich nicht behandelt wurde die Sonderfrage, ob Johannes, statt die Synoptiker direkt vor sich liegen zu haben, aus dem Gedächtnis zitierte oder sogar nur ganz allgemein von der Existenz eines Evangeliums wußte. Solche Varianten helfen in der Methodendiskussion nicht weiter, weil sie mit der Zufälligkeit der Gedächtnisleistung eine nicht kalkulierbare Unschärfe in Kauf nehmen, bzw. nur ganz allgemein und formal die von Johannes benutzte Textsorte erklären können. Auch die Variante, ob Johannes sich auf ein, zwei oder drei Synoptiker bezog, trägt zur Methodenfrage nichts bei, sondern stellt sich nach der methodengeleiteten Diskussion als Ergebnis ein.

3. *Die internen Bezugstexte des vierten Evangeliums*

Für den kirchenväterlichen Konsens, wie er eingangs beschrieben wurde, erschöpfte sich die Diachronie des vierten Evangeliums wegen der kanonzentrierten Sichtweise wie selbstverständlich auf die Beziehung zu den extern vorhandenen Synoptikern. Erst mit der Literarkritik eines J. Wellhausen wurde der Weg beschritten, die internen Verhältnisse des Johannes auf implizite Bezugstexte hin zu erforschen. Einen forschungsgeschichtlich interessanten und wirksamen Widerspruch dagegen formulierte, wie schon erwähnt, Barrett:[65] Weil Johannes den Markustext sehr frei benutzte, ließe sich, ohne Markus zu kennen, das älteste Evangelium allein aus Johannes heraus nicht rekonstruieren. Darum, sollte Johannes andere nicht extern bekannte Quellen verarbeitet haben, sind sie nicht mehr rekonstruierbar: "All source-criticism of John is guess-work". Und Barrett fügt sogleich hinzu: Wer die Markuskenntnis des Johannes verwirft, steht in noch tieferer Dunkelheit. Aber, so wird man anmerken, mit solcher Verwerfung entfällt auch die Voraussetzung von Barretts eigener Folgerung: Wenn Johannes Markus nicht kennt, kann er das Evangelium auch nicht frei benutzt haben. Also ist die angebliche Freiheit des Johannes kein Grund, interne Quellensuche ganz aufzugeben. Doch diese Kehrseite seines Gedankenganges bedenkt Barrett nicht, weil eine antiliterarkritische Einstellung für ihn auch unabhängig von dem zitierten Gedankengang feststeht. Die Option, den Text so auszulegen, wie er dasteht, gilt nämlich als selbstverständlicher Grundsatz. So wird z.B. zu Joh 1:1–18 zugestanden, daß dem Evangelisten vielleicht in gewissem Umfang externes Material zur Verfügung gestanden haben mag, jedoch habe zu gelten: "The Prologue stands before us as a prose introduction which . . . was specially written . . . to introduce the gospel."[66]

Solcher sektoral begrenzte Zugang zur Textwirklichkeit ist heute mit einigen Modifikationen weit verbreitet. Sofern er begründet wird, sind die typischen Argumentationsgänge zu seinen Gunsten recht gleich. Man kann in manchen Fällen schon so etwas wie ein scholastisches Ritual entdecken: Manche sammeln und wählen nämlich nur noch aus, was in diesem Fall andere schon sagten.[67] Angesichts

[65] Barrett, *Gospel* (Anm. 14), 17.
[66] Barrett, *Gospel* (Anm. 14), 151.
[67] Ein illustratives Beispiel dafür steht bei Hengel, *Frage* (Anm. 34), 226–64.

solcher Gemengelage ist es wohl am sinnvollsten, die typischen Argumente zu sortieren und zu qualifizieren.

Erstaunen erweckt *erstens*, daß man die Frage nach der Diachronie wieder mit der Kanonfrage verknüpfen kann. So sollen Literarkritiker ein unbewältigtes theologisches Problem haben, nämlich die Kanonfrage.[68] Man wird gegenfragen: Sollen wir wirklich noch einmal bei J.S. Semler zu diskutieren anfangen? Die Kanonbildung bestimmt, welche Schriften in Gottesdienst und Lehre der christlichen Kirchen vorrangige Bedeutung haben sollen. Sie bestimmt jedenfalls nicht, wie über die Entstehung der Schriften zu urteilen ist. Die Kanonfrage spielt wohl auch versteckt bei U. Wilckens[69] eine Rolle. Er diagnostiziert bei Literarkritikern eine "interpretatorische Resignation (!) gegenüber dem ungeheuren (!) Anspruch des Textes"[70] und bescheinigt ihnen "Unfähigkeit (!) bzw. Unwilligkeit (!) . . . im theologischen Nach-Denken zusammenzuhalten, was im Text des Joh offensichtlich (!) in eins *gedacht* wird." Das erinnert denn doch an die Typik der antiken Ketzerpolemik:[71] Wer anderer Meinung ist, muß als Subjekt "böse" sein.

Zu vordergründig ist eine *zweite* Gruppe von Argumenten. So wiederholt man vereinfacht die Meinung von Barrett.[72] Doch gesetzt den Fall, Johannes habe Synoptiker benutzt, wieso sind dann andere Quellen ausgeschlossen? Warum übergeht man die berühmten Aporien[73] des vierten Evangeliums und die Menge seiner von den Synoptikern unabhängigen Textpartien bei solchem Argumentationsgang?

---

[68] Vgl. H. Thyen, "Aus der Literatur zum Johannesevangelium", *TRu* 39 (1974) 1–69, S. 39.52; idem, "Johannesevangelium", *TRE* 17, 1988, 200–25, S. 211; F. Frey, *Die johanneische Eschatologie* I (WUNT 96; Tübingen: Mohr, 1997), 296f.

[69] U. Wilckens, *Das Evangelium nach Johannes* (NTD 4; Göttingen: Vandenhoeck & Ruprecht, 1998), 9.

[70] U. Wilckens, "Rez. G. Richter *Studien zum Johannesevangelium*", *TLZ* 106 (1981) 817. Die Ausrufungszeichen stammen von mir.

[71] Vgl. dazu Becker, *Paulus* (Anm. 40), 175. An die Ketzerpolemik in der Antike erinnert in diesem Zusammenhang auch die bewußte Überzeichnung und Ironisierung anderer Positionen. Beispiele: Hengel, *Frage* (Anm. 34), 263; Knöppler, *Theologia crucis* (Anm. 43), 23 Anm. 119; M. Lang, *Johannes* (Anm. 5), 49f.; Frey, *Eschatologie* (Anm. 68), 296f. Sollte nicht Trajans Wort: nec nostri saeculi est, wieder mehr Gewicht bekommen?

[72] Beispiel Hengel, *Frage* (Anm. 34), 253.

[73] E. Schwartz, "Aporien im vierten Evangelium", *Nachrichten von der Königlichen Gesellschaft der Wissenschaften zu Göttingen, Philologisch-historische Klasse*, 1907, 342–72; 1908, 115–48; 149–88; 497–567. Vgl. die Übersicht bei Thyen, "Johannesevangelium (TRE)" (Anm. 68), 203ff.

Eine Variante dieser Auffassung baut U. Schnelle[74] auf: Er geht von dem "positiven Vor-Urteil" aus, das vierte Evangelium sei als schriftstellerisches Werk eines großen Theologen aufzufassen. Darum sei "eine extensive Literarkritik als Quellenkritik" aus "methodischen (!) Gründen" abzulehnen. Dennoch sei der "vielfach behauptete Vorrang der synchronen Textanalyse vor der diachronen ... sehr fragwürdig". Darum müsse eine "begrenzte Literarkritik" nach der Geschichte von Einzelüberlieferungen fragen (Diachronie) und nach ihrer Bearbeitung durch den Evangelisten (Synchronie). Nun ist schon eine Methode, die vorab in ihrer Ertragserzielung eingegrenzt wird und nicht mehr ergebnisoffen arbeiten darf, ein Unding. Doch auch die Analogie zu den Synoptikern läßt diese Position scheitern: Alle Synoptiker sind zweifelsfrei "hervorragende Theologen", die ein kohärentes Werk schufen. Zumindest Matthäus und Lukas verarbeiteten dennoch nicht nur Einzeltraditionen, sondern auch Quellen. An ihnen haben sich—in der Sprache von Schnelle—gerade die "begrenzte" und "extensive Literarkritik" zusammen bewährt.

Nicht unbeliebt ist manchenorts *drittens* auch der Verweis auf die Textgeschichte des vierten Evangeliums: Die Ergebnisse der Literarkritiker hätten an der Textgeschichte keine Spuren hinterlassen, darum seien sie höchst fraglich.[75] Da aber die gesamte neutestamentliche Textgeschichte, wie sie noch erkennbar ist, viel später beginnt als die zur Diskussion stehende Frühzeit, ist solche Argumentation natürlich eine reine Luftbuchung.[76] Umgekehrt ist es eine meist übersehene Tatsache, daß jeder Philologe und Historiker der Antike vor dem ärgerlichen Befund steht, daß in einem erstaunlich großem Maße Texte der Antike verlorengegangen sind. Ein Blick in jedes Lexikon mit antiken Autorennamen bietet dafür eine erschreckend große Fülle an Exempeln. Das Urchristentum bildet innerhalb der antiken Kultur

---

[74] Schnelle, *Christologie* (Anm. 44), 49–51. Ebenso Knöppler, *Theologia crucis* (Anm. 43), 22ff.

[75] So zuletzt wieder Hengel, *Frage* (Anm. 34), 237.263. Vgl. auch Thyen, "Johannesevangelium (TRE)" (Anm. 68), 200.

[76] Frühestens an P^{66} (Anfang des dritten Jahrhunderts; P^{52} und P^{75} sind zu fragmentarisch) ist überprüfbar, daß die Verbreitung des vierten Evangeliums außerhalb der johanneischen Gemeinden in der Gestalt von Joh 1–21 erfolgte. Das sind rund 100 Jahre nach der Entstehung des Evangeliums! Möglich ist: die Verbreitung des Johannesevangeliums außerhalb des johanneischen Kreises erfolgte (ab wann?) nur, nachdem der Endredaktor von Joh 21 den Text abschließend redigierte. Für die Zeit vor dieser Endredaktion kann die Textgeschichte weder etwas Positives noch etwas Negatives beitragen.

dazu keine Ausnahme, wie z.B. die Logienquelle und Stellen wie 1 Kor 5:9; 7:1; 2 Kor 3:1 erhärten. Angesichts dieses Befundes sollte es zugestanden sein, daß die Suche nach nur noch implizit erkennbaren Quellen eine legitime Aufgabe des Exegeten ist.

Viertens und letztens bedenkt man die Literarkritik mit Negativurteilen wie: sie sei ganz allgemein viel zu hypothetisch. Ihre Ergebnisse erschöpften sich in unübersichtlicher Vielfalt. Sie müsse im jetzigen Text ständig Gegensätze konstruieren, die es gar nicht gibt; man dürfe also auch nicht die Maßstäbe neuzeitlicher logischer Gedankenführung an den Text legen. Sie huldige dem Grundsatz vom guten Autor und schlechten Redaktor. Sie ließe sich von historichen Usprungsfragen leiten und instrumentalisiere damit die Textanalyse. Zu dieser ergänzungsoffenen Auswahl ist zu sagen: Literarkritik ist nie fehlerfrei. Das gilt im übrigen für alle anderen Methoden ausnnahmslos in gleicher Weise. Literarkritik hat—wie alle anderen Methoden—auch immer wieder Kritik nötig. Doch was an diesen Negativurteilen unangemessen ist, ist ihre pauschalierende Funktionalisierung zur globalen Ablehnung der Methode. Denn die Kritikpunkte betreffen einzelne Vorgehensweisen. Sie eignen sich darum gut, je am Einzelfall den kritischen Dialog zu führen. Von Korrekturbedingtheit im einzelnen läßt sich aber nicht auf eine Ablehnung einer ganzen Methode schließen. Dann müßte man alle anderen Methoden—weil alle kritischen Nachfragen gegenüber offen sind—ebenfalls ablehnen.

Wie komplex im einzelnen diese Gruppe der abwertenden Urteile ist, soll wenigstens an zwei Beispielen noch aufgedeckt werden: Wer der Literarkritik das Etikett "viel zu hypothetisch" anheftet und die Ergebnisfülle moniert, beobachtet mit Einschränkungen etwas Richtiges: Ohne Hypothetik in möglichst gesteuerter Form und abgewogener Begründung geht es nicht. Auch entstehen auf diesem Feld keine Einheitsergebnisse. Doch bei den beobachteten Phänomenen und den Deutemustern gibt es gerade auch bei der literarkritischen Exegese am Johannesevangelium eine beschreibbare Einheit in der Vielfalt. Denn Textbeobachtungen, Auswertungen des Befundes und das Umsetzen in eine Gesamtanschauung sind in diesem Fall nicht einfach konturenlos vielfältig. Doch davon ganz abgesehen: Alle anderen Methoden, die man in der Exegese benutzen mag, unterliegen ausnahmslos denselben Bedingungen. Dies ist das Schicksal aller Forschung, bei der geistesgeschichtliche Aspekte mit im Spiel sind, weil—auf die Exegese bezogen—die Vagheit in jedem Text, die positionelle Subjektivität jedes Exegeten und die Unvollkommenheit jeder

Methode nichts anderes zulassen.[77] Das andere Beispiel: Die Funktionalisierung der Literarkritik als Weg zum historischen Ursprung hat immerhin die Zwei-Quellen-Theorie hervorgebracht: Sie lebt heute, gelöst von solcher Instrumentalisierung, mit guten Gründen weiter.

Nun gibt es außerdem grundsätzliche Optionen und Deutemuster, die bei der Diskussion um die johanneische Literarkritik entscheidendes Gewicht erhalten haben und so die Wahrnehmung und Deutung der Exegeten mitbestimmen. Drei Begriffspaare, die dabei die Debatte besonders intensiv beherrschen, sollen im folgenden bedacht werden. Es sind dies die Paarungen: Synchronie—Diachronie, Autorpersönlichkeit—(anonyme) Schule und Einheitlichkeit—kohärente Komplexität.

Das erste Paar *Synchronie* und *Diachronie* bezeichnet zwei Brennpunkte, die mit der jüngsten Neuorientierung in der exegetischen Methodenfrage zusammenhängen, also mit strukturellen und literaturwissenschaftlichen Fragestellungen. Dabei haben das Bedenken des strukturellen Geflechtes der Textebene und die Analyse der Dialogsituation vom Autor über den Text zum Leser in der neuesten methodischen Textentwicklung der Exegese einen deutlichen Erkenntnisschub erbracht.[78] Auch wer die sich überschlagenden Einzeltheorien auf diesem Gebiet zum Teil mit gemischten Gefühlen zur Kenntnis nimmt, wird zustimmen, daß die klassisch gewordene Redaktionsgeschichte, wie sie einst praktiziert wurde, zwar eine Pionierleistung darstellte, jedoch durch diese neuere Methodendiskussion eine ganz andere Qualität bekommen hat.

Im Zusammenhang dieser Diskussion ist oft die absolute Vorherr-

---

[77] Um es konkret zu illustrieren: Hengel, *Frage* (Anm. 34), der besonders häufig die Hypothetik der johanneischen Literarkritik hervorhebt, baut selbst ein Gebäude auf, das aus mehrgradiger Hypothetik, manchem Vermutungswissen und einigen Unklarheiten gezimmert ist. Schnelle, *Einleitung* (Anm. 38), 554f., der—wie gezeigt—der "extensiven Literarkritik" entgehen will, führt zu Joh 14:31; 18:1—einem Testfall für johanneische Literarkritik—eine ungemein hypothetische und komplizierte Lösung vor, die das Postulat eines einzigen Autors aller Abschiedsreden untermauern soll. Dazu hat A. Dettwiler, *Die Gegenwart des Erhöhten*, (FRLANT 169; Göttingen: Vandenhoeck & Ruprecht, 1995) 39–41, vorgeführt, daß demgegenüber die literarkritische Lösung einer späteren Redaktion von Joh 15–17 geradezu arm an Hypothetik ist.

[78] Vgl. nur St. Alkier – R. Brucker, *Exegese und Methodendiskussion* (TANZ 23; Tübingen: Francke, 1998); J. Zumstein, "Narrative Analyse und neutestamentliche Exegese in der frankophonen Welt", *VuF* 41 (1996) 5–27; G. Schunack, "Neuere literarturkritische Interpretationsverfahren in der anglo-amerikanischen Exegese", *VuF* 41 (1996) 28–55.

schaft und Autarkie des Ist-Bestandes eines Textgeflechtes behauptet worden.[79] Der Vorrang der Synchronie blockiert dann schon die Frage nach einer möglichen Diachronie ab. So sind Aporien, Spannungen und Brüche im vierten Evangelium für H. Thyen[80] nicht mehr Anlaß, unter anderem auch mit literarkritischer Methode nach diachronen Lösungsversuchen Ausschau zu halten. Vielmehr sind sie nach dem "Prinzip (!) der Textkohärenz" zu interpretieren, also als synchrone auf den Leser bezogene Verstehenshilfen. Die "Flucht (!) in die Literarkritik" (als Frage nach Quellen und Traditionen) und die Frage nach "textexternen Informationen" gilt als Kapitulation vor der eigentlichen Exegese, die die Autarkie des Textes und die Leserorientierung zu bedenken hat.[81]

Solche Exegese mit Hilfe exklusiv gesetzter Prinzipien zugunsten der Synchronie ist glücklicherweise nicht mehr oft anzutreffen. Es mehren sich die Stimmen, die den Vorrang der Synchronie nicht absolut setzen und der Erfragung der internen Diachronie eines Textes ein eigenes Recht zugestehen. Dies kann auch kaum anders sein: Autoren und Leser stehen nicht nur in einer Sprachgemeinschaft, die geschichtlich geworden ist und jeweils durch synchrone Dialoge fortgeschrieben wird. Verstehen zwischen ihnen kann sich auch nur ereignen, wenn sie einen gemeinsamen Fundus von Orientierungs- und Sachwissen ihr eigen nennen, das heißt, wenn sie an einem sich möglichst weit überschneidenden Überzeugungskanon partizipieren. Dies gilt in einem besonders hohen Maße von Gruppen, die in überschaubarer Größe leben und miteinander eine gemeinsame Geschichte durchlebten. Dazu gehört der johanneische Gemeindeverband. Das Überzeugungswissen und die gemeinsame Geschichte sind bei einem Autor und seinem Leser in solchen Fällen präsent als individuelles und kollektives Gedächtnis (vgl. Joh 2,17; 14,26), als weiter gegebene und aktualisierte Überlieferung (Joh 21:24) und als Literatur (im johanneischen Kreis z.B. als Septuaginta). Wie ein Autor aus solchem

---

[79] Vgl. dazu die Beispiele bei J. Becker, "Das Johannesevangelium im Streit der Methoden (1980–1984)", in idem, *Annäherungen* (hrsg. U. Mell; BZNW 76; Berlin: de Gruyter, 1995) 204–81, S. 210ff.

[80] Thyen, "Johannesevangelium (TRE)" (Anm. 68), 216f. Die Ausrufungszeichen stammen von mir.

[81] Neuerdings ist Thyen, "Synoptiker" davon etwas abgerückt, wenn für ihn das vierte Evangelium als Auslegung der textexternen Synoptiker zu lesen ist (Anm. 24). Mit gleichem Textverständnis (freilich mit ganz anderem Ergebnis) arbeitet auch L. Schenke, *Johannes: Kommentar* (Düsseldorf: Patmos, 1998).

Hintergrund heraus sein literarisches Produkt schafft, so eignen sich seine Erstleser dieses an, indem sie es von diesem Hintergrund her verstehen. Die heutige diachrone Betrachtung des Textes macht es sich also mit Recht zur Aufgabe, diesen (meist nur implizit bestimmbaren) Hintergrund zu erfragen. Diese Frage aus prinzipiellen Gründen abzublocken, hieße Autor und Erstleser zu geschichtslosen Monaden zu machen.

Über diese grundsätzlichen hermeneutischen Erwägungen kann man natürlich trefflich dicke Bücher schreiben. Doch mag hier der knappe Aufriß des Horizonts genügen, in dem das geschehen müßte.[82] Wer sich nicht dem Vorwurf aussetzen will, er betreibe Exegese, indem er Texte monothetisch als Fallbeispiele bestimmter neuzeitlicher Theorien behandelt, wird nicht nur die in der Gegenwart geführte Theoriediskussion immer wieder aktualisieren, sondern vor allem auch die antiken Texte aus ihrer Zeit und ihrem damaligen Textverständnis heraus verstehen müssen. Das bedeutet: Es gilt das Textverständnis, die Art der Textproduktion und die Textrezeption der Antike zu erforschen, wenn man antike Texte angemessen auslegen will. In bezug auf dieses Terrain übt man sich in der Regel noch allzuoft in einer Verweigerungshaltung. Dabei ist es sehr die Frage, ob die neuzeitlichen Texttheorien, geboren aus neuzeitlichem Autoren- und Textverständnis, so ohne weiteres und glatt auf die antike Kultur und ihr Autoren- und Textverständnis anwendbar sind. Wer sich dieser Diskussion nicht stellt, muß sich den Vorwurf gefallen lassen, durch methodische Prinzipienentscheide den Wahrnehmungskorridor auf die Textwirklichkeit willkürlich einzugrenzen, statt der Regel Geltung zu verschaffen, daß die Textwirklichkeit zu bestimmen hat, welche methodischen Fragen angemessen und notwendig sind. Methoden stehen im Dienst der Texte. Texte sind nicht nur Fallbeispiele für Methoden. Wer hier dienstbarer Geist des anderen ist, sollte nicht in Vergessenheit geraten.

Um es für das Johannesevangelium für einen Hauptaspekt anzudeuten: Wie will man Literarkritik als solche für methodisch überholt halten, wenn ein großer Teil der bekannten antiken Literatur mehrschichtig ist und oft die Gleichung: ein Autor = ein Text wirk-

[82] Ich habe mich schon früher, nicht nur wie hier, konzentriert auf Autor und Erstleser, dazu geäußert, vgl. Becker, "Streit" (Anm. 79), 217–19; "Aus der Literatur zum Johannesevangelium (1978–1980)", in idem, *Annäherungen*, 139–203, S. 153f.

lichkeitsfremd ist, weil man es unter anderem mit reformulierten, redigierten, korrigierten, ergänzten und kumulativ zusammengestellten Texten zu tun hat, deren Produzenten zwar "schriftgelehrte" Einzelpersonen waren, deren Produkte jedoch keinesfalls als ihr geistiges Eigentum galten? Vielmehr dienten sie einer Überzeugungsgemeinschaft, deren Mitglieder solche Textprodukte als Gesamteigentum der Gemeinschaft betrachteten. Darum konnte diese Gemeinschaft auch in einen Dialog mit solchen Texten treten, in dem einzelne aus ihr den Text fortschrieben, umschrieben oder in andere Textprodukte aufnahmen. Solche Texte wandern auch von einer Gemeinschaft zu einer anderen, wenn beide etwa einer gemeinsamen Religions- oder Kulturgemeinschaft angehören. Solcher Übergang erhöht die Freiheit zur Neuverwendung und Umschreibung.

Solches hier nur skizzierte Literaturverständnis muß nicht erst hypothetisch durch Literarkritik erhoben werden. Es ist also nicht eine Gesamtanschauung, die sich erst nach "umstrittener" Literarkritik an den Textbefunden ergibt. Sie ist durch handschriftliche Überlieferung gegeben.[83] Sie wird auch von antiken Autoren[84] selbst bezeugt. Natürlich erhält sie darüberhinaus kräftige Bestätigung durch Texte, deren Ist-Zustand gar keine andere Wahl lassen, als mit Schichtungen zu rechnen.[85] Leider fehlt bis heute eine umfassende Untersuchung darüber, mit welchen Mitteln im einzelnen die Autoren insgesamt arbeiteten, die am literarischen Prozess solcher Traditionsliteratur beteiligt waren. Dabei wären unter anderem zu beschreiben: Die Erstellung von nacherzählenden Texten, die einen Prätext, der erhalten bleibt, teils paraphrasierend, teils wörtlich aufgreifen und eine neue Gesamtdeutung vertreten (z.B. 1/2 Chr.; *Jub; LibAnt*); die Konstituierung neuer Großtexte durch Einarbeitung von Quellen und Einzeltraditionen (Beispiel: *äthHen*); die laufende Verzahnung einst selbständiger Texte zu einem neuen Text (Beispiel: Matthäus und Lukas); durchgehende inhaltliche Rezensionen, die neue Akzente setzen (vgl. die deuteronomistische Redaktion im Alten Testament und den Weg von 1QM zu den 4QM-Texten); die kumulative Erweiterung

---

[83] Man vergleiche nur beispielhaft die Septuaginta (etwa zu 1 Kön 3–11; Dan; Est) oder die Textüberlieferung zu den *Test* XII; *JosAs* oder die Qumranhandschriften zur Kriegsregel und Sektenschrift oder die Überlieferung zum *EvThom*.

[84] Vgl. etwa die Quellenangaben in 1–2 Reg; bei Josephus oder Jub bis hin zu Lk 1:1–4.

[85] Ich erwähne jetzt nur *äthHen* und *VitAd/ApkMos*.

durch Texte oder Traditionen, die als Relecture zu verstehen sind;[86] die Einfügung von Fremdtexten, die heutige Leser als erratische Blöcke empfinden (vgl. die noachitischen Stücke im *äthHen*) und die Anfügung literarischer Nachträge am Schluß eines Werkes (vgl. Mk 16:9ff.; *äthHen* 70; 71; Joh 21). Diese phänotypische Aufzählung ist sicher so noch unvollkommen. Doch weist sie den Weg, was zu bedenken ist, wenn man diese Sparte antiker Literatur angemessen begreifen will. Sie hat in jedem Fall zur Folge, daß man Synchronie und Diachronie nicht gegeneinander ausspielen darf. Das Verstehen beider Aspekte eines Textes ist vielmehr geboten.

Dieser aufgerissene Horizont hilft nun auch das zweite Paar *Autorpersönlichkeit—(anonyme) Schule* zu erörtern. Insbesondere M. Hengel[87] hat sich dafür mit Vehemenz stark gemacht,[88] daß das vierte Evangelium von "eine(r) beherrschende(n) schöpferische(n) Lehrerpersönlichkeit" stammt, einem "recht selbstbewußten Lehrer", und einer "beherrschenden Persönlichkeit . . . als eines theologischen Lehrers mit einer weitgespannten Dialektik und großen Integrationskraft". Kurzum: nur ein "durch und durch im besten Sinne . . . theologisches 'Original' von faszinierender Geisteskraft" könne das theologisch so gehaltvolle Johannesevangelium geschrieben haben. "Ein Kollektiv einer anonymen Schule" ist "nie wirklich schöpferisch", erst recht nicht das "Kollektiv" Gemeinde. Darum sei die Annahme, das vierte Evangelium sei durch redigierende Schüler erweitert worden, ein "fragwürdiger" und "unkritischer" Konsens, zumal "auch unter Theologen" heute "die Freude an 'kreativen Kollektiven' . . . verflogen ist."

Was hier geschieht, ist deutlich: Die Person des Evangelisten wird mit olympischen Ausmaßen beschrieben und umgekehrt die johanneische Schule (und Gemeinde) zu einem zu fast nichts Selbständigem mehr fähigen Kollektiv degradiert. Dahinter steht die Auffassung: Geschichtsmächtige Persönlichkeiten beherrschen die Massen, bzw. Kollektive. Dieses Geschichtsbild wird instrumentell benutzt, um so die These von der Einheitlichkeit des vierten Evangeliums zu stützen.

---

[86] Vgl. dazu Dettwiler, *Gegenwart* (Anm. 77).

[87] Hengel, *Frage* (Anm. 34), 25, 253, 273, 268, 257, 262, 250f., 274.

[88] Nahe bei Hengel stehen J. Schneider, *Das Evangelium nach Johannes* (THKNT-Sonderband; 1. Aufl. Berlin: Evangelische Verlagsanstalt, 1988) 31; Schnelle, Christologie (Anm. 44), 8; idem, *Das Evangelium nach Johannes* (THKNT 4; Leipzig: Deichert, 1998) 237f.

Doch wie Jesu "Persönlichkeit" nicht mehr geschichtlich greifbar ist, so auch die des vierten Evangelisten nicht.[89] Daß im Urchristentum das Verhältnis von herausragenden Personen zu Schülern und Gemeinden zumindest bei Paulus, seinen Mitarbeitern und Gemeinden ein ganz anderes war, als das eines "selbstbewußten Lehrers" zu einem "Kollektiv", muß nicht abermals ausführlich beschrieben werden.[90] Wegen des Geist- und Gemeindeverständnisses im vierten Evangelium[91] wird man auch für die johanneische Schule und den Gemeindeverband in etwa paulinische Verhältnisse annehmen müssen. Zusätzlich läßt sich zeigen, woher Hengels Deutekategorie stammt: Sie prägt das Geschichtsbild von Herder über Ranke und Burckhardt bis zu Carlyle.[92] Es ist also ein recht neuzeitliches Verständnis, das Hengel in die Zeit des ausgehenden ersten Jahrhunderts zurückprojiziert.

Scheidet diese Deutekategorie also als Mittel zur Einschätzung johanneischer Verhältnisse aus, dann ist der Weg frei, das Verhältnis von Lehrer (Autor), Schule und Gemeinde(n) vorurteilsfreier zu bestimmen. Dazu geben Joh 21:24f. und 1 Joh entscheidende Informationen: Der Verfasser des 1 Joh kann zwar in der Ich-Form sprechen, ordnet sich aber zugleich einer besonderen Gruppe zu, die von der Gemeinde unterschieden ist (1 Joh 1:1–5). Auch Joh 21:24f. wird eine sich äußernde Gruppe und die Gemeinden als Adressaten unterschieden. Dabei weiß diese Gruppe, daß der "Lieblingsjünger" ihre Autorität und die entscheidende Autorität für die Gemeinden ist. Joh 13:16f, 20; 20:21–23 ergänzen: Letztlich geht die Sendung der Jünger, die später die "Wir" aus Joh 21:24f. werden, auf Jesus zurück, der sie zu den Gemeinden sendet. Weiter setzten der 2 und 3 Joh Verhältnisse voraus, nach denen johanneische Gemeinden untereinander durch Boten, Briefe und Gesandtschaften von Wandermissionaren kommunizieren. Dieses Bild läßt sich gewiß noch genauer erfassen, führt aber auch schon so zu folgender Annahme: Der johanneische Gemeindekreis wird von einer Missionars- und Predigerschule betreut. Sie führt ihre Autorität letztlich auf Jesu Sendung zurück, kennt aber auch die herausgehobene Person des Lieblingsjüngers, der offenbar

[89] Von den urchristlichen Gestalten ist allenfalls Paulus (in bestimmten Grenzen) eine Ausnahme.

[90] Verwiesen sei jetzt nur auf Becker, *Paulus* (Anm. 40), 189ff., 254ff.

[91] Vgl. dazu J. Becker, "Das Geist- und Gemeindeverständnis des vierten Evangelisten", *ZNW* 89 (1998) 217–34.

[92] Vgl. G. Theißen – D. Winter, *Die Kriterienfrage in der Jesusforschung* (NTOA 34; Freiburg, Schweiz: Universitätsverlag 1997) 42–63.

als der besondere Gründer der johanneischen Schule galt. Zu ihr wird auch der Presbyter des 2/3 Joh gehören. Auch der vierte Evangelist wird dieser Schule zuzurechnen sein. Presbyter und Evangelist sind literarisch tätig. Dasselbe gilt für die Schulmitglieder aus Joh 21 und den Autor des 1 Joh. Daraus darf man folgern: Wie immer man die literarischen Verhältnisse im Johannesevangelium beurteilen will, der innere Befund der johanneischen Schriften selbst würde einer Annahme, das vierte Evangelium sei das Produkt einer Schule, bestens entsprechen.

Damit kann zur dritten Paarung übergegangen werden: Die Entscheidung zwischen der *Einheitlichkeit* und *kohärenten Komplexität* des vierten Evangeliums zugunsten der ersten Annahme wird vor allem mit der johanneischen Sprache begründet. Sie ist im vierten Evangelium einschließlich der der johanneischen Briefe für E. Ruckstuhl-P. Dschulnigg[93] so einheitlich, daß es praktisch zwingend ist, einen und nicht mehrere Verfasser anzunehmen. Sprachstatistische Argumentationen werden wohl im Zeitalter der Computer eher zu- als abnehmen, damit wohl leider auch die positivistische Überschätzung der Methode als angeblich zwingende Argumentation für Einheitlichkeit oder Schichtenspezifik. Meistens wird schon die angeblich zwingende Objektivität durch Grundregeln der statistischen Mathematik enttarnt.[94] Weiter steht johanneische Sprachstatistik vor dem Problem, wieweit es sich dabei um einen Idiolekt oder einen Soziolekt[95] handelt. Es ist unsinnig, johanneische Spracheigentümlichkeiten ausschließlich pauschal als Idiolekt zu deuten, da jeder Idiolekt weitgehend aus sozial vermittelter Sprache besteht. Wer immer als Einzelperson oder als Schule das vierte Evangelium schrieb, alle wollten von den Erstadressaten verstanden werden. Das erfordert eine große Schnittmenge an gemeinsamer Sprache. Da niemand die Sprache der johanneischen Gemeinden unabhängig von der johanneischen Literatur kennt, bleibt es immer ungeklärt, welche Spracheigentümlichkeiten

[93] E. Ruckstuhl – P. Dschulnigg, *Stilkritik und Verfasserfrage im Johannesevangelium* (NTOA 17; Freiburg, Schweiz: Universitätsverlag, 1991). Vgl. dazu Becker, "Geisterfahrung" (Anm. 2), 430f.

[94] Eine erweiterungsfähige Kostprobe solcher Kritik bietet Sch. Deck, "Wortstatistik—ein immer beliebter werdendes exegetisches Handwerkzeug auf dem (mathematischen) Prüfstand", *BN* 60 (1991) 7–12.

[95] Dazu vergleiche man die deuteronomistische und priesterschriftliche Sprache im Alten Testament.

Soziolekt, welche vielleicht Idiolekt sein können. Da die Idiolekteigentümlichkeiten eigentlich immer geringer sind als der sozial vermittelte Sprachstil, wird man überhaupt gut tun, die johanneische Sprache als Soziolekt zu verstehen. Ein weiteres Problem ist dieses: Die Spracheigentümlichkeiten von Joh und 1–3 Joh sind gar nicht so komplett einheitlich, wie manche gerne annehmen: Es gibt Unterschiede zwischen den Briefen, zwischen dem Evangelium und dem ersten Brief und z.B. zwischen Joh 1–20 und Joh 21. Es fällt auf, daß die narrativen Texte des vierten Evangeliums nur ganz gering von dualistischer Sprache und von der Sprache der Gesandtenchristologie geprägt sind. Diese Beobachtungen sind noch keine sicheren Beweise für verschiedene Autoren, aber solche Phänomene erschüttern in jedem Fall die angeblich nur als Idiolekt zu deutenden Befunde des vierten Evangeliums. Weiter muß gelten: Wer Traditionen und Quellen übernimmt, kann sie unwillkürlich seiner Sprache anpassen. Es gibt Sprachimitationen. Statistisch und formal gleiche Sprache kann Sinnveränderungen enthalten. Sprache ist überhaupt etwas Lebendiges. Diese Eigenschaft kann man nicht in positivistischer Statistik erfassen. Damit sind Sprachstatistiken noch nicht überflüssig, aber im Fall des Johannesevangeliums kann damit nie und nimmer belegt werden, daß das vierte Evangelium (und die drei Briefe) nur einen Autor haben könne(n).

Im übrigen bleiben, auch wenn man das annimmt, noch genügend Probleme, die das vierte Evangelium zu lösen aufgibt. Es sind dabei nicht zuletzt die Aporien des Johannesevangeliums, die dann immer noch einer Erklärung zugeführt werden müssen. Dabei gilt: Kein synoptisches Evangelium, kein Text aus der urchristlichen Briefliteratur hat eine solche Fülle von Auffälligkeiten, nämlich zerbrochene Itinerare, situationslose Stücke, gestörte Zusammenhänge, in sich brüchige Abschnitte, gehäufte Wiederholungen, verschiedene Deutungen einer erzählten Handlung oder einer Grundaussage, Stücke, die ein Thema, das eigentlich abgeschlossen war, fortsetzen und nicht vorbereitet sind, Spannungen im sachlichen Bereich, kenntlich gemachte Korrekturen, reinterpretierende Wiederholungen usw. Dies alles beobachtet man neben sehr gut strukturierten Teilen und Stücken mit herausragender und anspruchsvoller Gedankenführung. Dieses Janusgesicht ist das kompositorische Problem des vierten Evangeliums. Man mag die beispielhaft gezeigten Auffälligkeiten zum Teil als "meditativen Stil" deklarieren oder zu Eigenwilligkeiten des Evangelisten erheben. Erklärt hat man damit nichts. Auch die Deutung des Evangeliums als nicht fertig gewordenes und sukzessive erstelltes Altenwerk eines Autors[96] ist solange eine reine Vermutung, als man dafür aus dem Altertum keine Analogie beibringt und nicht nachweisen kann, daß der Verfasser wirklich alt war und mit relativer Wahrscheinlichkeit tatsächlich immer wieder an seinem Werk gestaltend arbeitete. Gut erklären läßt sich der Kontrast einer exzellenten Komposition einerseits zu den aufgezählten Auffälligkeiten andererseits allerdings mit der Arbeit einer Schule. Dafür sind auch außerjohanneische Analogien vorhanden.

So ist Joh 1–21 nicht einheitlich wie ein neuzeitlicher Roman. Aber der Text besitzt eine kohärente Komplexität, deren Kohärenz in Gestalt der im Groben literarisch strukturierten Form besteht, vor allem aber mit dem inhaltlichen Überzeugungswissen des Evangeliums gegeben ist, das den Rezipienten vertraut war und das sie vor allem beim Lesen abriefen. Weil sie sich dieser Wahrnehmungsschneise bedienten und man im johanneischen Gemeindeverband vielleicht wußte, daß sich der Text der Schule des Kreises verdankte, waren die Aporien kein Rezeptionsproblem. Sie konnten vernachlässigt werden, wie z.B. später auch von M. Luther.[97]

Damit kann als Ergebnis festgehalten werden: Die Suche nach internen Texten macht weiterhin Sinn. Sie ganz abzublocken oder vorab zu begrenzen, ist nicht ratsam.

4. *Zusammenfassung*

Die Ausführungen wollten dafür werben, angesichts der methodischen Diskussion innerhalb der Forschungsgeschichte zum vierten Evangelium die Diskussion über die externen Quellen—also die Frage nach der Verwendung der Synoptiker—nicht vorschnell nur durch die relativ wenigen Parallelitäten positiv zugunsten der Synoptikerbenutzung zu entscheiden, sondern diese Phänomene der Nähe zu

[96] G. Hoffmann, *Das Johannesevangelium als Alterswerk* (Gütersloh: Bertelsmann, 1933); W. Wilkens: *Die Entstehungsgeschichte des vierten Evangeliums* (Zollikon, Schweiz: Evangelischer Verlag, 1958). Diese Annahme wird bis in jüngste Zeit immer wieder einmal aufgeboten.

[97] J. Becker, "Luther als Bibelausleger", in idem (hg.), *Luthers bleibende Bedeutung* (Husum: Husumer Druck- und Verlagsgesellschaft, 1983) 7–21, S. 15f.

qualifizieren und mit den Beobachtungen zur Selbständigkeit des vierten Evangeliums zu bilanzieren. Sie plädierten weiter bei der Frage nach internen Quellen dafür, den Blick in die Diachronie nicht vorschnell abzublocken. Dieses Plädoyer ergibt sich aus dem Ist-Zustand des Johannesevangeliums und aus der Textproduktion in der Antike. An beiden sind neuzeitliche Texttheorien zu überprüfen.

THE BELOVED DISCIPLE IN JOHN: IDEAL FIGURE IN AN EARLY CHRISTIAN CONTROVERSY

Ismo Dunderberg

The enigmatic "disciple whom Jesus loved" is a figure of great importance in the Gospel of John. He is not only one of Jesus' disciples and an eyewitness of him, but also identified with the author of the gospel (John 21:24). Yet he is a very elusive character. He appears only in certain passages in John,[1] usually rather abruptly, and he is completely absent in the synoptic parallels to these passages.[2] The fact that he is left anonymous in John has led to a plethora of possible identifications.[3] Renewed interest in the search for the Beloved Disciple is signalled by the full-scale monographs by Martin Hengel and James Charlesworth. Hengel's suggestion is that the editors of the Fourth Gospel gave the Beloved Disciple a double identity of John the Elder and John the son of Zebedee,[4] while Charlesworth

[1] The Beloved Disciple is mentioned in John 13:21–30; 19:25–27; 20:2–10; 21:7, 20–25. In addition, reference is made to him most likely in John 19:35–36, and probably in John 18:15–16 (see below on p. 257). His identification with one of the two disciples mentioned in John 1:35–37 is less likely; cf. F. Neirynck, "The Anonymous Disciple in John 1", in idem, *Evangelica II: 1982–1991 Collected Essays* (BETL 99; Leuven: Leuven University Press/Peeters, 1991) 617–49; see also R.A. Culpepper, *John, the Son of Zebedee: The Life of a Legend* (Studies on Personalities of the New Testament; Columbia, SC: University of South Carolina Press, 1994) 59; J. Kügler, *Der Jünger, den Jesus liebte: Literarische, theologische und historische Untersuchungen zu einer Schlüsselgestalt johanneischer Theologie und Geschichte; mit einem Exkurs über die Brotrede in Joh 6* (SBB 16; Stuttgart: Katholisches Bibelwerk, 1988) 421–24.

[2] Nevertheless, I am inclined to believe that the Johannine Beloved Disciple passages betray knowledge of the synoptic gospels. For example, John 13:27 seems to presuppose Luke 22:3, which most likely is Luke's editorial addition to Mark 14:10, and John 20:2–10 can be seen as being based upon the short account of Peter's visit to the tomb of Jesus in Luke 24:12 (see below on p. 254).

[3] These identifications have traditionally included John the Elder; John Mark (cf. Acts 12:12); Lazarus (cf. John 11:3, 5); Matthias (cf. Acts 1:15–26); the rich youth (cf. Mark 10:17–22); Paul (cf. Gal 2:20). These suggestions, and others, have been sufficiently discussed in other recent studies; cf. Kügler, *Der Jünger, den Jesus liebte*, 439–48; Culpepper, *John, the Son of Zebedee*, 72–84; J.H. Charlesworth, *The Beloved Disciple: Whose Witness Validates the Gospel of John?* (Valley Forge, Pennsylvania: Trinity Press International, 1995) 127–224.

[4] M. Hengel, *The Johannine Question* (trans. J. Bowden; London/Philadelphia: SCM Press/Trinity Press International, 1989); idem, *Die johanneische Frage: Ein Lösungsversuch* (WUNT 67; Tübingen: Mohr, 1993). Hengel seeks to support his view of two Johns

argues that the Beloved Disciple was Thomas.[5] A major difficulty with these views is, however, that they need to be supported by referring to "a veiled way",[6] or "extremely subtle ways",[7] in which the right solution is pointed by the author (or the editors) of the gospel to "perceptive readers".[8] Already the fact that Hengel and Charlesworth end up with so different theories shows that this "mystifying" argument remains quite inconclusive. In fact, the same argument could be made with equal justification in support of *any* identification of the Beloved Disciple.

It is unlikely, therefore, that these new theories bring the new quest for the Beloved Disciple's identity to an end,[9] nor do they ren-

---

by arguing that the present title of the Fourth Gospel (εὐαγγέλιον κατὰ Ἰωάννην) stems from the editors of this writing (*The Johannine Question*, 74–76; *Die johanneische Frage*, 204–9). This theory, however, is untenable, as Hartwig Thyen and Michael Theobald have shown. Most likely such titles of the gospels became necessary only in the process of their canonization, as these gospels needed to be distinguished from each other. Moreover, Theobald refers to Turner's assessment that even in P66 (Papyrus Bodmer II), on which Hengel largely builds his case, the title "seems to be a later addition." Cf. H. Thyen, "Noch einmal: Johannes 21 und der Jünger, den Jesus liebte", in T. Fornberg & D. Hellholm (eds.), *Texts and Contexts: Biblical Texts in their Textual and Situational Contexts* (FS Lars Hartman; Oslo etc.: Scandinavian University Press 1995) 147–89, on p. 157 n. 29; M. Theobald, "Der Jünger, den Jesus liebte: Beobachtungen zum narrativen Konzept der johanneischen Redaktion", in H. Cancik, H. Lichtenberger and P. Schäfer (eds.), *Geschichte—Tradition—Reflexion: Festschrift für Martin Hengel zum 70. Geburtstag*, vol. 3: *Frühes Christentum* (Tübingen: Mohr, 1996) 219–55, on p. 251. Also Hengel's use of patristic witnesses is open to critique, as Culpepper has pointed out (*John, the Son of Zebedee*, 307): "The linchpin of the argument—the identification of the Elder John (from one single reference in Papias) with the elder of 2 John 1 and 3 John 1—will not bear the weight of the argument that is built on it."

[5] Charlesworth, *The Beloved Disciple*, passim. I have discussed this theory elsewhere; cf. I. Dunderberg, "Thomas and the Beloved Disciple", in R. Uro (ed.), *Thomas at the Crossroads: Essays on the Gospel of Thomas* (Edinburgh: T & T Clark, 1998) 65–88, pp. 73–75. In my view, Charlesworth relies too heavily on what simply seems to be a blank in the Johannine narrative between John 19:35–36 (in which it is told that the Beloved Disciple saw Jesus' pierced side) and John 20:21 (in which Thomas asks to see the wound in Jesus' side); what really matters is that the reader of the gospel already knows about Jesus' wounds and is thus able to understand the Thomas pericope in John. For an insightful discussion about the interpretation of gaps in modern narrative criticism, see now P. Merenlahti, "Poetics for the Gospels: Rethinking Narrative Criticism" (Diss. University of Helsinki, 1999) ch. 5 (pp. 81–97). Among other things, Merenlahti reminds us that narratives often contain blanks, that is, "what is omitted for lack of interest" (ibid. 85, with reference to Sternberg's distinction between more meaningful "gaps" and less meaningful "blanks").

[6] Hengel, *The Johannine Question*, 132 (= *Die johanneische Frage*, 321).

[7] Charlesworth, *The Beloved Disciple*, 21.

[8] Charlesworth, *The Beloved Disciple*, 21.

[9] In two recent Internet publications, it has been suggested that the Beloved

der ill-founded the sweeping doubts expressed in other recent studies as regards this enterprise.[10] What can be discussed with more confidence is the Johannine characterization of the Beloved Disciple. Most scholars agree that he is, in some sense, an ideal figure, but this assessment needs more precision. For although the Beloved Disciple is no doubt portrayed as an ideal witness in John, there are other ideal aspects often associated with him by scholars, such as his perceptiveness, that are not so clearly visible in the Johannine text as is often assumed. In any case, as will be shown below, he is less clearly characterized in terms of his insight than several beloved disciples of Jesus presented in other early Christian writings.

The present article, in fact, goes back to a question Heikki Räisänen posed years ago in a seminar after hearing the very first draft of this paper. That paper was confined to developing an argument to the effect that the Beloved Disciple in John is a fictional character. As is his wont, Räisänen was sharp-eyed in spotting the crucial difficulty in that argument and pointed it out with a seemingly innocent question that went something like this: "Well, if this figure was only fictional, why is he called with the name 'the disciple Jesus

Disciple is Mary Magdalene; cf. E.A. de Boer, "Mary Magdalene and the Disciple Jesus Loved", *Lectio difficilior* 1/2000 (http://www.lectio.unibe.ch); R.K. Jusino, "Mary Magdalene, author of the Fourth Gospel", at http://www.BelovedDisciple.org (for this theory, see below p. 263 n. 75). The hypothesis that the Beloved Disciple was Lazarus has been resuscitated by M.W.G. Stibbe, *John as Storyteller: Narrative Criticism and the Fourth Gospel* (SNTSMS 73; Cambridge: Cambridge University Press, 1992), 77–82; idem, "A Tomb with a View: John 11.1–44 in Narrative-Critical Perspective", *NTS* 40 (1994) 38–54, on p. 48; cf. also M.W. Meyer, "The Youth in Secret Mark and the Beloved Disciple in John", in J.E. Goehring et al. (eds.), *Gospel Origins & Christian Beginnings: In Honor of James M. Robinson* (Sonoma: Polebridge Press, 1990) 94–105, on p. 104. What makes this identification problematic, as Raimo Hakola has recently pointed out, is that "... the chief priests planned to kill Lazarus (12.10–11), whereas the other disciple in 18.15, who is identified with the Beloved Disciple by Stibbe and many others, had access to the court of the chief priest because he was known to him." R. Hakola, "A Character Resurrected: Lazarus in the Fourth Gospel and Afterwards", in D. Rhoads & K. Syreeni (eds.), *Characterization in the Gospels: Reconceiving Narrative Criticism* (JSNTSup 184; Sheffield: Sheffield Academic Press, 1999) 223–63, on p. 247 n. 57.

[10] Cf. K. Quast, *Peter and the Beloved Disciple: Figures for a Community in Crisis* (JSNTSup 32; Sheffield: JSOT Press/Sheffield Academic Press, 1989) 12: "If centuries of intense and wide ranging search for the Beloved Disciple have not satisfied anyone, then perhaps it is time to ask different questions of the text." Kügler, in turn, points out that in all attempts to disclose the Beloved Disciple's identity "the anonymity established by the text is always regarded as something negative that needs to be resolved and destroyed" (*Der Jünger, den Jesus liebte*, 448; cf. also Thyen, "Johannes 21", 156–57).

loved'? Why wasn't he simply identified with some better known disciple?" I no longer recall my hasty response that I gave to this question on that occasion, but now I attempt to provide a two-fold answer to it. First, I argue that the designation "the disciple Jesus loved" is closely associated with his role as the authenticator of the Gospel of John. Second, my tentative suggestion is that this designation is also related to early Christian debates as to who can lay claim to the legacy of Jesus.

1. *Ideal is not Always Paradigmatic*

Although scholars usually consider the Beloved Disciple is an ideal character, it is not always clear what they exactly mean by "ideal" in this context. Already Bacon considered the Beloved Disciple "a purely ideal figure",[11] which meant for him that this character is "no disciple of flesh and blood."[12] "Ideal" in connection of the Beloved Disciple can, thus, mean that this figure is considered a mere fiction. However, most scholars nowadays assume that the Beloved Disciple was a historical figure, probably the founder and leader of the Johannine community, but that he did not belong to the inner circle of Jesus' closest followers, as the Gospel of John maintains. These scholars usually think that the gospel presents a more or less "idealized" picture of him.[13] Yet the term "ideal" can also denote particular features attached to this figure in John, such as his faith (John 20:8). This is usually associated with the view that the Beloved Disciple is presented in John as the disciple *par excellence*, being more perceptive to what Jesus says than the others. Closely related to this view, and often inferred from it, is the assumption that the Beloved

---

[11] B.W. Bacon, *The Fourth Gospel in Research and Debate: A Series of Essays on Problems Concerning the Origin and Value of the Anonymous Writings Attributed to the Apostle John* (London/Leipzig: T. Fisher Unwin, 1910) 320.

[12] Bacon, *The Fourth Gospel*, 317, 319. Bacon was not very consistent on this point, however, for he also affirmed that "(t)he 'disciple whom Jesus loved' is something more than a purely ideal figure. A very real man has sat for the portrait . . .". This model was, in Bacon's opinion, Paul, and it was only the later editor of the fourth gospel who confused the Beloved Disciple with John the son of Zebedee (ibid. 325–26).

[13] Thus, e.g., T. Lorenzen, *Der Lieblingsjünger im Johannesevangelium* (SBS 55; Stuttgart: Katholisches Bibelwerk, 1971) 82, 107–8, R.A. Culpepper, *The Johannine School: An Evaluation of the Johannine-School Hypothesis Based on an Investigation of the Nature of Ancient Schools* (SBLDS 26; Missoula: Scholars Press, 1975) 265, 270.

Disciple is a paradigmatic figure in John, setting the standard of true discipleship to the audience of the gospel.[14]

The different connotations of the term "ideal" are not mutually exclusive. Rather, they often merge into each other in scholarly opinions of the Beloved Disciple. Sometimes this has led to shaky conclusions. For example, the paradigmatic interpretation of the Beloved Disciple's role in John is not self-evident, though it is often taken for granted. Ideal figures can in fact assume different functions in ancient texts. It is only one possibility among others that they are cast as models to be followed by the audience. This is well demonstrated by John Collins's and George Nickelsburg's classification of four different kinds of roles assigned to ideal figures in ancient Jewish writings. Certainly, "a number of the figures lend themselves readily enough as examples to be imitated; they are paradigmatic."[15] Yet this function does not apply to the presentation of ideal figures in Jewish visionary literature. In this body of literature, their usual function is, rather, ". . . to lend weight to and authenticate the content of the revelation."[16] Likewise, Collins and Nickelsburg point out that miracle workers and eschatological figures portrayed in ancient Jewish writings offer no models for behaviour in a strict sense.[17]

In light of this wide variety of the functions ideal figures can assume in ancient writings, the ideal aspects of the Beloved Disciple in John and their functions need to be delineated more carefully than is usually done. This issue has been taken up recently by Richard Bauckham, who voices criticism against the prevalent scholarly opinion that this figure "represents, as model for others, the ideal of discipleship."[18] Instead, Bauckham suggests, ". . . the beloved disciple is portrayed in the Gospel narrative in such a way as to show that he

---

[14] Cf., e.g., Theobald, "Der Jünger, den Jesus liebte", 243.

[15] J.J. Collins & G.W.E. Nickelsburg, "Introduction", in J.J. Collins & G.W.E. Nickelsburg (eds.), *Ideal Figures in Ancient Judaism: Profiles and Paradigms* (SBLSCS 12; Chico, CA: Scholars Press, 1980) 1–12, on p. 7.

[16] Collins-Nickelsburg, "Introduction", 8.

[17] Collins-Nickelsburg, "Introduction", 8: "The miracle working of Hanina ben Dosa . . . would scarcely have admitted of imitation in any case. Tales of miracles are, rather, designed to inspire awe and respect for the miracle worker and lend a supernatural aura to his way of life. The eschatological figures, again, are not models for direct imitation, but they give expression to ideals which influence behavior."

[18] R. Bauckham, "The Beloved Disciple as Ideal Author", *JSNT* 49 (1993) 21–44, on p. 33.

is ideally qualified to be the author of the Gospel."[19] This point merits attention, even though Bauckham employs it to support what seems to be an overly confident view about the historical reliability of the fourth gospel.[20] What Bauckham's rethinking of this issue shows best is that most ideal features attached to the Beloved Disciple in John are closely connected with his role as the one who lends authenticity to this gospel, whereas it is *not* necessary to assume that he is portrayed as ideal in all other possible meanings of the word as well.

The various aspects of the Beloved Disciple's characterization in John will be dealt with below, but before doing that it seems necessary to discuss the rumour at the end of John that the Beloved Disciple would not die (John 21:22–23). Most conclusions about the historical figure of the Beloved Disciple are usually drawn from this passage, but, in my view, scholars have greatly exaggerated its value for this purpose.

2. *The Leader of the Johannine Community?*

In John 21:23, it is said that a rumour was spread among "the brothers" that the Beloved Disciple would not die. This rumour is explained by the narrator as a misconception about what Jesus said (John 21:23). Most scholars not only regard this passage as a sure proof for the historicity of the Beloved Disciple, but also infer from it his leadership in the Johannine community. Two recent assessments suffice to show the importance of this passage in tracing the historical figure of the Beloved Disciple:

> . . . by referring to the death of the Beloved Disciple, John 21 makes clear that he was indeed a historical person. . . . From John 21:20–23

[19] Bauckham, "The Beloved Disciple", 24.

[20] If it is really true that the fourth gospel, as Bauckham maintains, "*correctly* represents the author as a personal disciple of Jesus and eyewitness of some of the events of the Gospel story" ("The Beloved Disciple", 32; my emphasis), the Beloved Disciple, of course, can no longer be an *idealized* figure in John. What poses the greatest difficulty to Bauckham's confidence in the Johannine presentation of the Beloved Disciple, however, is the absence of this figure in the synoptics. Notably, Bauckham does not discuss this problem at all, but is content with simple affirmations of the reliability of the Johannine account, such as: "If the figure of the beloved disciple is due to the redactor, he cannot have been mistaken in supposing that the author had been a personal disciple of Jesus who witnessed significant events in the Gospel story." (Bauckham, "The Beloved Disciple", 32.)

we can gather that the Johannine community was confronted with the unexpected death of the Beloved Disciple and the accompanying threat to their communal faith and identity.[21]

Solutions that interpret the Beloved Disciple solely as a symbolic figure do not satisfactorily explain the concern in John 21:20–23 over the death of the Beloved Disciple. As has often been remarked, symbolic figures do not die. What we have then is a historical figure who has been given an idealized role in the crucial scenes of the farewell discourse, trial, death, and resurrection of Jesus.[22]

In these statements, which could easily be multiplied,[23] it is assumed that (a) the Johannine text refers to the death of the Beloved Disciple, and (b) that this proves that he must have been a historical figure. However, (b) is not a necessary inference from (a); although Kügler considers the Beloved Disciple a fictional figure, he thinks that John 21:20–23 speaks about the death of this figure.[24] It could also be asked whether an account of a person's death really provides us with a sure proof for his or her historicity. It goes—or it at least *should* go—that also *fictional* characters, be they Adam or Sherlock Holmes, can die.

A more serious problem is that the death of the Beloved Disciple is not indicated very clearly in John 21:20–23. Contrary to what most scholars seem to believe, the Johannine text contains no direct references to sweeping despair (vividly described by modern scholars) that would have been occasioned by his death in the Johannine community,[25] or to his advanced age that would have contributed to the rumour that he would no die,[26] not to speak of "the *natural*

[21] Quast, *Peter and the Beloved Disciple*, 150.

[22] Culpepper, *John, the Son of Zebedee*, 70; cf. also idem, *The Johannine School*, 269; *Anatomy of the Fourth Gospel*, 47.

[23] Cf., e.g., R.E. Brown, *The Community of the Beloved Disciple* (New York etc.: Paulist Press 1979) 31; Charlesworth, *The Beloved Disciple*, xiv, xviii, 5, 13, 18, 20, 47, 65 etc.; T.K. Heckel, *Vom Evangelium des Markus zur viergestaltigen Evangelium* (WUNT, 120; Tübingen: Mohr, 1999) 175, 180; Hengel, *Die johanneische Frage*, 213–14; H. Thyen, "Entwicklungen innerhalb der johanneischen Theologie und Kirche im Spiegel von Joh. 21 und der Lieblingsjüngertexte des Evangeliums", in M. de Jonge (ed.), *L'Évangile de Jean: Sources, redaction, theologie* (BETL 44; Leuven: University Press 1977) 259–99, on p. 293; idem, "Johannes 21", 162–64.

[24] Kügler, *Der Jünger, den Jesus liebte*, 481–84.

[25] Cf. Theobald, "Der Jünger, den Jesus liebte", 250: "21,20–23 dient nicht der Aufarbeitung eines vermeintlichen Schocks, den die Gemeinde wegen seines Sterbens erlitten hätte." Even so, also Theobald thinks that the text presupposes the death of the Beloved Disciple (ibid. 249).

[26] The advanced age of the Beloved Disciple is particularly crucial for Hengel's

death of the community's founder and chief authority."[27] These features are merely inferred from the rumour and its correction, but they are far from being inevitable.

In fact, it is not absolutely necessary to assume that it was the death of the Beloved Disciple that led to reflections concerning his immortality in John 21:20–23. Rather, The real issue seems to have been the delayed parusia. The strongly conditioned form of Jesus' promise (ἐὰν θέλω) in John forms a striking contrast to a more affirmative version of his words attested in Mark 9:1: "Truly, I say to you, there are some standing here who will not taste death before they see the kingdom of God come with power." Already the author of Mark reinterpreted this radical saying by linking it with the story of the transfiguration of Jesus (Mark 9:2–9), the result being that, in this gospel, it is this story that already appears as a fulfilment of Jesus' promise.

The Johannine author takes a major step away from Mark by explaining the expectation of physical immortality (ὅτι οὐκ ἀποθνῄσκει, John 21:23) as a *false* interpretation of Jesus' words. This affirmation is especially important in John, given that in this gospel it is often promised to the believers that they are not going to die (John 6:51, 58; 8:51; 11:25–26). It is possible to read John 21:22–23 as a warning against possible misunderstanding of these affirmations:[28] since even the Beloved Disciple is *subject to death* (if Jesus does not want otherwise), the gospel's promises of immortality certainly cannot be understood in terms of avoiding physical death.

In addition, patristic accounts of Menander show that the distinction between immortality and the avoidance of physical death was not self-evident in early Christianity From Justin (*1. Apol.*, 26.4) and Irenaeus (*Haer.*, 1.23.5) can be inferred that Menander promised to his followers physical immortality as a consequence of being baptized into him. Such currents could have made it necessary to separate physical death and immortality as clearly from each other as

---

solution (see, e.g., *The Johannine Question*, 134), but it is often assumed by other scholars too; cf., e.g., S.R. Johnson, "The Identity and Significance of the *Neaniskos* in Mark", *Forum* 8 (1992) 123–39, p. 136; Theobald, "Der Jünger, den Jesus liebte", 250.

[27] Thus T.V. Smith, *Petrine Controversies in Early Christianity: Attitudes towards Peter in Christian Writings of the First Two Centuries* (WUNT 2/15; Tübingen: Mohr, 1985) 150.

[28] Cf. Kügler, *Der Jünger, den Jesus liebte*, 483.

possible. The Gospel of Luke certainly goes in this direction,[29] and it is possible to apply this explanation also to John 21:22–23. It is not necessary to read the Johannine passage as a direct reaction against Menander and his followers, but this group bears witness to a possibility that ideas of immortality similar to theirs were in circulation and needed to be combatted already at the start of the second century CE, as the Gospel of John was written.

This setting offers, in my view, a sufficient rationale for introducing the rumour that the Beloved Disciple would not die; the widely held assumption of his unexpected death is not necessary. Hence, John 21:21–23 does not supply us with a rock-solid evidence for the Beloved Disciple as a historical figure, not to speak of his role as the founder or leader of the Johannine community. The latter theory is difficult also in the light of the Johannine epistles, which never mention the Beloved Disciple. If he were a figure of great importance in the Johannine group, this silence about him in these epistles stemming from the same group would be quite surprising.[30] The evidence for the historical figure of the Beloved Disciple remains, after all, very thin.[31]

3. *Jesus' Closest Disciple*

There are many aspects of the Johannine figure of the Beloved Disciple that cannot be "exemplary" for the audience of the gospel. His position by Jesus' bosom at the last supper, his presence at the cross, and his visit to the empty tomb are unique features that cannot be imitated.[32] Nevertheless, the Beloved Disciple is often portrayed as being superior to other characters in the Johannine narrative. His special affinity to Jesus is emphasized in various ways. He is

[29] It is affirmed in Luke 20:36, in addition to Mark 12:25, that it is those who have their part in the resurrection who "cannot die anymore"; immortality is, thus, understood as a future quality that does not exclude physical death.

[30] Culpepper (*The Johannine School*, 282) tackles with this difficulty, advancing a theory that the silence about the Beloved Disciple in 1 John was due to the *opponents* of this letter who "were claiming his authority." This is, however, a highly circular conclusion, because the only evidence that can be called for in support of it is that the Beloved Disciple is not mentioned in 1 John. To be sure, the author of 1 John identifies himself with eyewitnesses of Jesus (1 John 1:1), but even here there is no specific reference to the Beloved Disciple.

[31] At this point I concur with Kügler, *Der Jünger, den Jesus liebte*, 478–88.

[32] Bauckham, "The Beloved Disciple", 33.

introduced to the readers as "one of his disciples . . . whom Jesus loved" (John 13:23), and this is the only name given to him in the whole narrative (John 19:26; 20:3; 21:7, 20). The name is not necessarily a traditionally fixed expression for a certain figure well-known to early readers of John, because there are two different forms of the name "the disciple Jesus loved" in this gospel,[33] but it no doubt makes the Beloved Disciple a distinguished follower of Jesus, since this or a similar name is never used of any other disciples in John. It will be argued later that also this name is closely related to the main function of this figure in John as the authenticator of this gospel.

The Beloved Disciple's affinity to Jesus is also indicated by a remark that he rested at the last supper "in the bosom of Jesus" (ἐν τῷ κόλπῳ τοῦ Ἰησοῦ, John 13:23). This remark shows that the Beloved Disciple has an honourary position at the last supper.[34] The importance of this aspect is shown by repeating it in John 13:25 and recalling it again at the end of the gospel (John 21:20). In the Johannine last supper scene, the intimate position of the Beloved Disciple makes it possible for him to act as a mediator between the other disciples and Jesus, as they are puzzled because of Jesus' words about the betrayer among them (John 13:23–25). Also this role of the Beloved Disciple is emphatically recalled in John 21:20.

More features that make the Beloved Disciple a distinctive figure are introduced in the Johannine passion narrative (John 18–19). It is not entirely certain whether "the other disciple" mentioned in John 18:15 is the Beloved Disciple.[35] If so,[36] a contrast can be drawn

[33] ὃν ἠγάπα (John 13:23; 19:26; 21:7,20) and ὃν ἐφίλει (John 20:2).

[34] Sjef van Tilborg, *Imaginative Love in John* (Biblical Interpretation Series 2; Leiden/New York/Köln: Brill 1993) 89, points to connotations of "bosom" to "marital sexual relations" and "the protective love for a child in the womb" to warrant his interpretation that the usage of this word, among other things, indicates that the Johannine story lends expression to "the classical idea of the παιδεραστία". What van Tilborg does not mention is that the expression can also denote "(a)t a meal the place of the guest of honour . . . and hence fig. an inward relationship" (R. Meyer, "κόλπος", *TDNT* 3.824–26).

[35] For a thorough survey of this issue, see F. Neirynck, "'The Other Disciple' in Jn 18,15–16", in idem, *Evangelica: Gospel Studies—Études d'Évangile: Collected Essays* (BETL 60; Leuven: Leuven University Press/Peeters, 1982) 335–64, esp. pp. 335–48.

[36] "The other disciple" appears in John 18 together with Peter, as the Beloved Disciple customarily does in John (John 13:23–24; 20:2–10 and 21:1–14, 20–22); the Beloved Disciple is called "the other disciple" in John 20:2; and the identification of the "other disciple" in John 18:15 with the Beloved Disciple would account for the latter's presence at the crucifixion (John 19:25–27, 35–37). Admittedly, the last

between him and Peter, for he is supposed to have escorted Jesus to the courtyard, while Peter was going to deny Jesus (John 18:17–18, 25–27). Yet the Beloved Disciple is not depicted as too daring in this passage, for his admission to the courtyard is not explained in terms of his courage, but as due to his acquaintance with the high priest.

At the crucifixion, the Beloved Disciple is portrayed as the only disciple present and as the one to whom Jesus assigns the care of his mother (John 19:25–27).[37] The Beloved Disciple is thus portrayed as the replacement for Jesus's brothers, for he is supposed to take over a task of her guardian that would have belonged to them.[38] This interpretation is congruent with the totally negative picture drawn of Jesus' brothers elsewhere in John. It was said already in John 7 that they did not believe in him, and, by implication, that they were representatives of the cosmos hostile to Jesus (John 7:5–7).[39] The implicit contradiction between the Beloved Disciple and the brothers of Jesus in John is noteworthy, since it hints, as will be argued below, at a historical setting in which this figure became necessary.

argument can be used only with some caution, for it is peculiar to the Johannine depiction of the Beloved Disciple that he shows up abruptly in different passages. Given his "incidental character" (thus Neirynck, "'The Other Disciple'", 363) in John, the Beloved Disciple *could* be portrayed as being present at the cross also without indicating that he followed Jesus first to the courtyard and then to the cross.

[37] John possibly draws on Luke here. While according to Mark all disciples left Jesus at Gethsemane, it is affirmed in Luke 23:49 that many of his friends (γνωστοί) were present at the crucifixion.

[38] Cf. A. Dauer, "Das Wort des Gekreuzigten an seine Mutter und den 'Jünger den er liebte': Eine traditionsgeschichtliche und theologische Untersuchung zu Joh 19,25–27", *BZ* 11 (1967) 222–239; *BZ* 12 (1968) 80–93, esp. 2.81–82; see also Tilborg, *Imaginative Love*, 94 (also expressing some reservations as to Dauer's arguments), and M. Rese, "Das Selbstzeugnis des Johannesevangeliums über seinen Verfasser", *ETL* 72 (1996) 75–111, on p. 95.

[39] John Painter remarks correctly that "(t)he treatment of the brothers of Jesus must be read against the tendency to exalt the Beloved Disciple"; J. Painter, *Just James: The Brother of Jesus in History and Tradition* (Studies on Personalities of the New Testament; Edinburgh: T & T Clark, 1999) 15. Yet his suggestion that the brothers of Jesus "are portrayed as 'fallible followers' rather than outright unbelievers" (ibid. 17) is not convincing. It is said of no other "fallible followers" of Jesus in John *in expressis verbis* that they did not believe in Jesus, as is done in John 7:5; in fact, the opposite seems to be the case: their faith is affirmed, for instance, in John 12:42. Moreover, it is noteworthy that in John 7:5 the unbelief of the brothers of Jesus is expressed by using exactly the same phrase (οὐκ ἐπίστευον) that appears in connection of a more generalizing statement of the unbelief of the Jews in John 12:38.

The notion that the Beloved Disciple became the guardian of Jesus' mother is not directly related to the claim of his authorship of the gospel. Nevertheless, this scene doubtless adds to his portrayal as the most reliable disciple of Jesus, which is useful also for his depiction as the reliable witness and the author of the gospel. As Heikki Räisänen suggested in his early work, John 19:25–27 "serves as a kind of legitimation of the Beloved Disciple", and "Mary assumes in certain manner the role of the protector of the Johannine tradition."[40]

The Beloved Disciple's portrayal in the Johannine empty tomb stories involves many difficulties of interpretation. John 20:2–10 is based either directly on the short account of Peter's visit in Luke 24:12,[41] or on a tradition similar to it.[42] Either way, the Beloved Disciple is most likely part of the secondary expansion of this earlier account. As to the relationship between him and Peter, it is not necessary to assume a rivalry between Johannine and "pro-Petrine" Christians behind this story;[43] at least, such a rivalry can hardly be inferred from their running race to the empty tomb (John 20:3–4).

Nevertheless, the affirmation of the Beloved Disciple's faith in John 20:8 seems to make him superior to Peter, whose faith is not mentioned in the story. What makes the interpretation of this verse notoriously difficult, however, is that the following narrative aside points out the ignorance of scripture of both disciples (John 20:9). Some scholars suggest that the purpose of this aside is to say that "a lack of insight into scripture of both disciples is . . . replaced through seeing as the basis of the resurrection faith."[44] However, this suggestion seems to involve too strong a contrast between faith and scripture,

---

[40] H. Räisänen, *Die Mutter Jesu im Neuen Testament* (AASF B, 158; Helsinki: The Finnish Academy of Science and Letters, 1969) 179–80.

[41] Thus Neirynck in several articles published in his *Evangelica*, 365–455 (esp. pp. 390–96, 399, 432–40, 452–55); Neirynck's view is adopted by Kügler, *Der Jünger, den Jesus liebte*, 346–49.

[42] E.g., Lorenzen, *Der Lieblingsjünger*, 28–29, 31–32; Quast, *Peter and the Beloved Disciple*, 107.

[43] Cf., e.g., R.A. Brown, *The Gospel According to John* (2 vols.; AB 29–29A; Garden City: Doubleday, 1966/1970) 1004–7; Quast, *Peter and the Beloved Disciple*, 119. For a convenient summary of different interpretations about Peter's and the Beloved Disciple's relationship in terms of a rivalry between early Christian groups, see Smith, *Petrine Controversies*, 146–48.

[44] Kügler, *Der Jünger, den Jesus liebte*, 330. For similar views, see R.G. Maccini, *Her Testimony is True: Women as Witnesses According to John* (JSNTSup 125; Sheffield: Sheffield Academic Press, 1996) 211; Rese, "Selbstzeugnis", 96; Theobald, "Der Jünger, den Jesus liebte", 245–46.

for the correct understanding of scripture is presented elsewhere in John as a positive consequence of the resurrection of Jesus (John 2:22; 12:16). The positive evaluation of scripture is in fact visible also in John 20:9. The divine δεῖ is used in this verse to affirm that scripture shows that the resurrection of Jesus was inevitable, and οὐδέπω ("not yet") anticipates in this verse, like John 2:22 and 12:16, that scripture *will be* understood correctly by the disciples in future.

One possible solution to the difficult juxtaposition of John 20:8 and 20:9 is to assume that John 20:8 does not refer to the resurrection faith of the Beloved Disciple. In its narrative context, the Beloved Disciple's "faith" could be understood only as a verification of Mary's testimony that the tomb is empty (John 20:2).[45] This interpretation would also account for the fact that the narrator mentions no consequences of the Beloved Disciple's faith.[46] What this theory fails to explain, however, is the absolute use of the verb πιστεύειν in John 20:8. This usage suggests that the Beloved Disciple's faith must be understood in a fuller sense (cf. John 19:35; 20:25, 29).[47] Yet it is not clear whether John 20:8 really denotes the full-blown resurrection faith of the Beloved Disciple.[48] If one also tries to take into account what is said in John 20:9, it may seem more likely that "his faith, like Martha's ([John] 11,27.39), did not entail full comprehension."[49]

In addition, faith based upon seeing usually calls forth some reservations in John. Most importantly, in the following Doubting Thomas pericope (John 20:24–29) Thomas' faith based on seeing is contrasted with a blessing of those who believe without seeing. This blessing is not a complete rejection of the eye-witnesses' faith, given

---

[45] To the proponents of this viewlisted in Kügler, *Der Jünger, den Jesus liebte*, 331 n. 2, can now be added Charlesworth, *The Beloved Disciple* (on pp. 79, 83, 94).

[46] Cf. P.S. Minear, "'We don't know where . . .' John 20:2", *Int* 30 (1976) 125–39, on p. 127.

[47] Theobald, "Der Jünger, den Jesus liebte", 235 n. 89; cf. also Kügler, *Der Jünger, den Jesus liebte*, 331; G. Koester, "Hearing, Seeing, and Believing in the Gospel of John", *Bib* 70 (1989) 327–48, on p. 344. The verb is used in a similar manner in John 4:53, and I find it likely that what is believed in must be inferred from the context also here. In light of John 4:48, it seems likely that John 4:53 is a confirmation of the royal officer's faith in miracles, but there are also other interpretations.

[48] Notably, the verb is used absolutely also in John 4:53 without a reference to Jesus' resurrection.

[49] Koester, "Hearing", 344.

the weight measured to their testimony throughout the Gospel of John, starting from ἐθεασάμεθα in John 1:14. However, the blessing adds an important aspect to the eye-witnesses' faith: it is affirmed that the readers of the gospel, though unable to see Jesus, have an equal, if not even a better, opportunity of believing in him as did the figures in the Johannine narrative.

This insight possibly sheds some light on the odd juxtaposition of faith and scripture in John 20:8–9. The figures in the narrative were able to inspect the tomb, but this would not be possible for the readers of the gospel. Hence the affirmation that sufficient proof for the resurrection can be found in scripture—by the readers of the gospel. The point in John 20:9 seems to be similar to that in John 20:29: it is possible to believe without seeing. In this case, there is no stark contrast between the Beloved Disciple's faith based on what he saw and that of the implied readers based upon their knowledge and correct interpretation of scripture. The narrator seems to say in John 20:8–9 simply that both the Beloved Disciple and scripture bear witness to the resurrection of Jesus. If so, the Beloved Disciple's faith could be understood as exemplary to the audience of the gospel. But even here the Beloved Disciple is not clearly cast as a role model to the implied readers; the narrator rather emphasizes scripture as the basis of *their* faith.

In John 21:1–14, the Beloved Disciple is portrayed as the one who recognizes the risen Jesus before the other disciples (John 21:7). Yet it remains unclear whether this feature indicates his better understanding of, or superior faith in, Jesus. No specific attention is paid on these issues by the Johannine narrator.

The claim that the Beloved Disciple wrote the Gospel of John is made at the closure of this writing (21:24–25). This claim is closely related with his portrayal as an eyewitness of Jesus. Reliability of his testimony is emphasized in a similar manner with reference to his role as the eyewitness and as the author (John 19:35; 21:24), and the function assigned to the Beloved Disciple's eyewitness testimony in John 19:35 is identical with the goal of the whole gospel (John 20:30–31): the purpose of both is to evoke faith in the recipients of the gospel.[50]

[50] Cf. B. Bonsack, "Der Presbyter des dritten Briefes und der geliebte Jünger des Evangeliums nach Johannes", *ZNW* 79 (1988) 45–62, on pp. 52–53. This goal is

It has been often suggested that the Johannine portrayal of the Beloved Disciple is closely related to that of the Paraclete,[51] but I find this connection somewhat vague in John.[52] The Beloved Disciple shares only one of the features attributed to the Paraclete: they both bear witness to Jesus.[53] Yet this similarity implies no specific link between the two, since in John 15:27 *all* disciples are told to bear witness of Jesus. There are no other verbal connections between the Beloved Disciple and the Paraclete that would suggest a specific affinity between them.

The Beloved Disciple's portrayal is in fact more closely related in John to that of Jesus than to that of the Paraclete. The name "the disciple whom Jesus loved" is similar to the Johannine affirmation that the Father loves the Son (John 3:35; 5:20; 10:17; 15:19; 17:23–26), and the expression "in the bosom of Jesus" used of the Beloved Disciple recalls the prologue's depiction of Jesus "in the bosom of Father" (John 1:18).[54] Moreover, both the Beloved Disciple and Jesus are presented as eyewitnesses in John: Jesus is the one who has seen the Father (John 5:19–20, 37; 6:46), while the Beloved Disciple has seen Jesus. Jesus bears witness to the Father, as the Beloved Disciple bears witness to Jesus, and the reliability of Jesus' witness is emphasized in a manner similar to that of the Beloved Disciple's testimony (John 3:11, 32; 8:38).

The affinities between the portrayals of Jesus and the Beloved Disciple are strong enough to suggest a deliberate literary device in John. They enable us to posit a Johannine "hierarchy of revelation". This hierarchy is based upon what the Father has taught and shown to the beloved Son; then the Father's teachings have been revealed by the Son to his disciples; and this revelation is reliably documented

---

of course a relatively common feature in John; it is also affirmed with reference to John the Baptist (John 1:7) and Jesus himself (John 11:15, 42; 14:29; 17:21).

[51] E.g., Culpepper, *The Johannine School*, 267–70, and Kügler, *Der Jünger, den Jesus liebte*, 435–38.

[52] Cf. Heckel, *Evangelium*, 82.

[53] In addition to bearing witness to Jesus (John 15:26), the functions ascribed to the Paraclete include glorifying Jesus (16:14), teaching and recalling his words (14:26), and guiding the disciples in truth (14:16; 16:13).

[54] This affinity between Jesus and the Beloved Disciple was noticed already by Origenes (*In Ioa.* 32.20.264), and pointed out virtually by all modern interpreters of John 13:23; cf. Charlesworth, *The Beloved Disciple*, 54; Dauer, "Das Wort des Gekreuzigten", 237; Kügler, *Der Jünger, den Jesus liebte*, 147 (with a thorough list of references to earlier literature); Quast, *Peter and the Beloved Disciple*, 58; Rese, "Selbstzeugnis", 91 etc.

and transmitted to the audience of the gospel by the Beloved Disciple. What is emphasized with this hierarchy of revelation is that there is a chain of transmission extending from Father to the audience of the gospel, and there are no weak links in this chain.

The Beloved Disciple's role in this communication process accounts, in part, for the name used of him in John. Given that there has been the beloved Son who bore witness to his Father in front of his disciples, there *must* be also the Beloved Disciple who reliably passes on the Son's testimony. Hence, the name "the disciple Jesus loved" is, within the Gospel of John, closely related to his function as the one who legitimates this writing. The Beloved Disciple can be left anonymous, because it is not his name but his *status* as the closest disciple of Jesus that is of importance as regards his role as the guarantor of this gospel.[55]

The Beloved Disciple is, however, no unique phenomenon in early Christian literature, and it will be suggested below that there are also extratextual reasons that contributed to introducing him and using the designation "the disciple Jesus loved" of him in John. Before turning to that issue, it is necessary to discuss those cases in which scholars seem to have gone too far in tracing ideal aspects in the Johannine presentation of the Beloved Disciple. In what follows, I try to argue that the popular notion of the Beloved Disciple showing better understanding or secret knowledge of what Jesus says is *not* clearly visible in John; futher, it is precisely here that there is a major difference between the Beloved Disciple in John and the favourite disciples of Jesus presented in other early Christian writings.

4. *The Perceptive Disciple?*

From similarities between John 1:18 and John 13:23 (see above) it has been often inferred that the Beloved Disciple is an *interpreter* of Jesus, in a similar manner as Jesus is portrayed as the one who "interpreted" (ἐξηγήσατο) the Father in John 1:18. If so, the Beloved Disciple could be a figure similar to the Teacher of Righteousness in the Qumran community.[56] In addition, many scholars have con-

[55] In this regard, the Johannine Beloved Disciple is similar to the anonymous Elder of 3 John, as Bonsack has pointed out ("Der Presbyter", 52).

[56] Cf. J. Roloff, "Der johanneische 'Lieblingsjünger' und der Lehrer der Gerechtigkeit", *NTS* 15 (1968/1969) 129–51.

sidered the Beloved Disciple a particularly perceptive character in John, who believes in Jesus sooner, understands him better than the other disciples (cf. John 20:8 and 21:7), and acts as his confidant.[57]

There is, however, little evidence in John for these characterizations of the Beloved Disciple. Jesus is indeed presented as the Father's interpreter in John 1:18, but no similar statement is made of the Beloved Disciple. Rather, his role is restricted to the reliable *transmission* of Jesus' interpretation of the Father.[58]

The view of the Beloved Disciple as Jesus' confidant is usually based on the Johannine last supper scene (John 13:21–30). This passage is often read so as to suggest that Jesus revealed the identity of the betrayer only to the Beloved Disciple, who for some reason withheld this information from the other disciples. In that case, Jesus and he share a secret, whereas the other disciples remain completely ignorant of what is going on (John 13:28). Yet "this text cannot be understood as introducing the Beloved Disciple as 'having a special knowledge of Jesus'."[59] Not only does the text not indicate that only the Beloved Disciple would have heard Jesus' answer.[60] It also does not imply in any other way a secrecy motif either here or later in the narrative.[61] It is *not* affirmed in the text, for instance, that Jesus and the Beloved Disciple conversed with each other in a "quiet manner".[62]

In addition, John 13:21–30 is a typical Johannine story of the disciples' misunderstanding related, as usual, to the issues pertaining to Jesus' death and glorification.[63] Jesus could not have been more

[57] Cf., e.g., Dauer, "Das Wort des Gekreuzigten", 1.237; D.J. Hawkin, "The Function of the Beloved Disciple Motif in the Johannine Redaction", *Laval théologique et philosophique* 33 (1977) 135–50, on p. 150; Tilborg, *Imaginative Love*, 91.

[58] It should be noted that the Gospel of John does not *present* itself as an interpretation of either Father or Jesus—though it, of course, is one.

[59] Thus Quast, *Peter and the Beloved Disciple*, 63, making a reference to Hawkin's interpretation ("The Function of the Beloved Disciple Motif", 143).

[60] Jesus' answer in John 13:26 is not confined to the Beloved Disciple; it is introduced without defining the addressees at all (ἀποκρίνεται Ἰησοῦς).

[61] John 21:20, for example, would have provided a good opportunity to disclose that the exchange between Jesus and the beloved disciple was kept in secret from the others, for the Beloved Disciple's position "in the bosom of Jesus" and his question are recalled in a precise manner in this verse.

[62] Thus Quast, *Peter and the Beloved Disciple*, 64: "Jesus was giving an answer to the Beloved Disciple in the same quiet manner in which the question was asked." It is somewhat surprising that Quast supports this view, for he otherwise rejects the "secrecy theory" in his interpretation of John 13:23–30.

[63] Cf. Culpepper, *Anatomy of the Fourth Gospel*, 163: "The theme that appears most

explicit in identifying the betrayer in the Johannine narrative. First he says that he will dip a morsel and give it to the betrayer; then he dips the morsel and gives it to Judas (John 13:26–27). In spite of these quite open gestures by which Jesus reveals the betrayer's identity, the disciples fail to recognize him and start to ponder other "earthly" explanations for Judas' departure (John 13:29), so the narrator needs to point out that "no one at the table" understood Jesus' words to Judas (John 13:28). The idea of a private exchange between Jesus and the Beloved Disciple is, however, incompatible with this reading of John 13:21–30 as a misunderstanding of the disciples. If only Jesus and the Beloved Disciple knew the betrayer, the other disciples would be denied even the opportunity of recognizing him—which means that there would be no misunderstanding either.

In short, there is no sufficient proof for the notion that it was the narrator's intention in John 13 to show that the Beloved Disciple knew more or was more perceptive than the other disciples.[64] Nothing in the text justifies the contention that "the evangelist is in 13:28 no longer *thinking* of the anonymous disciple in 13:23–25."[65] Rather, in this passage the Beloved Disciple seems to be "as ignorant as the rest of the disciples, he displays no special knowledge of Jesus and after asking the disciples' question, he appears to remain as ignorant as he was before."[66] The Johannine narrator points out elsewhere that Jesus was understood by his disciples only after his resurrection (John 2:22; 12:16);[67] even the Beloved Disciple seems to be no expection to this rule in John.

---

frequently in the misunderstandings is Jesus' death/resurrection/glorification (eight times: 2:19–21; 6:51–53; 7:33–36; 8:21–22; 12:32–34; 13:36–38; 14:4–6; 16:16–19)."

[64] Similarly Quast, *Peter and the Beloved Disciple,* 64; see also Charlesworth, *The Beloved Disciple*, 54.

[65] R. Mahoney, *The Two Disciples at the Tomb: The Background and Message of John 20.1–10* (Theologie und Wirklichkeit 6; Bern: Herbert Lang/Frankfurt am Main: Peter Lang, 1974) 93; for similar views, see, e.g., Lorenzen, *Der Lieblingsjünger*, 17; Theobald, "Der Jünger, den Jesus liebte", 229; Roloff, "Der johanneische 'Lieblingsjünger'", 133 n. 1.

[66] Quast, *Peter and the Beloved Disciple*, 160–61. Although this seems to be precisely opposite to Mahoney's view quoted above, Quast voices agreement with it elsewhere in his study (*Peter and the Beloved Disciple*, 67).

[67] What is striking in John is that the narrator is apparently hesitant to give up misunderstanding stories even after the resurrection of Jesus. Contrary to what might be expected in light of John 2:22 and 12:16, the disciples do not show much more understanding in the Johannine resurrection narratives (John 20–21) than they did in earlier parts of the narrative.

5. *Beloved Disciples of Jesus in Other Early Christian Writings*

The claim made in the Gospel of John that it was written by the closest follower of Jesus is, of course, not unique in early Christian literature. Thomas is a good example of a similar figure. He is portrayed as the author of the *Gospel of Thomas* and as the favourite disciple of Jesus (*Gos. Thom.* 13). In fact, Thomas is in this writing portrayed as the perceptive disciple, the confidant of Jesus who has access to his secret words, and the paradigm of true faith in a much more clearer manner than the Beloved Disciple in John.[68]

What is missing in this portrait of Thomas is the designation "the disciple Jesus loved".[69] Special disciples are often characterized with language implying a relationship of love between them and their teachers not only in other early Christian writings but also in contemporary Jewish and Greco-Roman texts. Josephus, for instance, mentions that Hyrcanos, High Priest during the years 76–67 and 63–40 BCE, was before his clash with the Pharisees "their disciple whom they loved very much" (μαθητὴς δὲ αὐτῶν ἦν καὶ Ὑρκανός, καὶ σφόρδα ὑπ' αὐτῶν ἠγαπᾶτο, *Ant.* 13.289). Language of love was employed to denote an especially close affinity between a teacher and his disciple also in Greek philosophical schools. In our ancient descriptions of them, the teacher could be defined as ἐραστής, "lover", and the disciple as ἐρώμενος, "beloved". In particular, the latter term was used of those who became successors of their teachers in a certain school.[70] However, some Hellenistic philosophers did not consider this an adequate expression for discipleship, because it implied a too affectionate, or erotic, relationship between the teacher and the disciple.[71] In addition, the lack of the specific terms ἐραστής and ἐρώμενος

---

[68] This is a summary of what I have argued more fully in "Thomas and the Beloved Disciple", 75–80.

[69] Nevertheless, in the *Book of Thomas* 138.7–8, Thomas is called by Jesus "my true friend" (*pašbrmmēe*). Hans-Martin Schenke sees here a link to the Johannine designation of "the disciple Jesus loved", but this view is far from being convincing; cf. H.-M. Schenke, "The Function and Background of the Beloved Disciple in the Gospel of John", in C.W. Hedrick – R. Hodgson (eds.), *Nag Hammadi, Gnosticism, and Early Christianity* Peabody, Mass.: Hendrickson 1986) 111–25, and my discussion of this view in "Thomas and the Beloved Disciple", 71.

[70] Tilborg, *Imaginative Love*, 85–87; cf. Diogenes Laertius, 4.19.21–22.29.32 (quoted in Tilborg, *Imaginative Love*, 86).

[71] Cf. Plutarch, *Moralia* 448E: "So again, when young men happen upon their cultivated teachers, they follow them and admire them at first because of their usefulness; but later they come to feel affection for them also, and in place of famil-

in John indicates that the Greek manner of speaking of a love relationship between teachers and their special disciples provides only a remote parallel to the Johannine portrayal of the Beloved Disciple.[72]

Closer parallels to the Johannine Beloved Disciple can be found in other early Christian writings, in which several disciples of Jesus are called either "the disciple Jesus loved" or his "beloved".[73] The language about love is usually associated with disciples who allegedly have some specific knowledge of Jesus' teachings, which makes a secrecy motif an essential part in the characterizations of these figures. This secrecy motif can be either inclusive or exclusive. In the former case, the beloved disciple readily reveals his or her secret knowledge to other figures in the narrative, while in the latter case he or she is reluctant to do so.

To the former group belongs obviously Mary Magdalene as portrayed in the *Gospel of Philip* and the *Gospel of Mary*.[74] In the *Gospel of Philip*, the other disciples raise the question of why Jesus loves Mary more than the rest of them. Her specific affinity to Jesus is also shown in the affirmation that Jesus used to kiss her often (*Gos. Phil.* 63.32–64.9). Similarly, in the *Gospel of Mary* it is said that the Saviour loved Mary more than other disciples and other women. In this writing, the intimate relationship between the Saviour and Mary explains why revelation is given to her by him and transmitted by her to the other disciples (*Gos. Mary* 10.1–6; 18.14–15).

iar companions and pupils (μαθητῶν) they are called lovers (ἐρασταί) and are actually so (trans. Helmbold, LCL)." Such love is, in Plutarch's view, but one sign of human irrationality (*Moralia*, 448D). On the other hand, Plutarch can speak in positive terms of pederasty—as far as it does not involve "flashing with desire" (*Moralia*, 751, referred to by Tilborg, *Imaginative Love*, 80–81). It is impossible to discuss here various aspects of pederasty in Greek society and literature; a concise, but informative survey of this issue is now provided by M. Nissinen, *Homoeroticism in the Biblical World: A Historical Perspective* (Minneapolis: Fortress, 1998) 57–69.

[72] Thus van Tilborg's interpretation of the Johannine portrait of the Beloved Disciple seems far-fetched. Van Tilborg maintains (*Imaginative Love* 247–48) that this portrait should be understood as lending expression to "imaginary homosexual behaviour", which, however, "is not an expression of homosexuality. It is an expression of παιδεραστία, the love for παῖς as the perfect entrance into the knowledge of God's love for his son and consequently of God's love for the cosmos."

[73] Schenke has drawn attention to many of the examples discussed below ("The Function and Background"), albeit only in passing, since he is mostly interested in presenting support for his thesis that Thomas is a historical model for the Beloved Disciple.

[74] On Mary Magdalene in these writings, see A. Marjanen, *The Woman Jesus Loved: Mary Magdalene in the Nag Hammadi Library and Related Documents* (NHMS 49; Leiden: Brill, 1996) 94–121, 147–69.

Mary cannot be identified as the Johannine Beloved Disciple on the basis of these texts,[75] but there are other aspects in her character that call for a comparison. The function of Mary in the *Gospel of Mary* is no doubt similar to that of the Beloved Disciple in John: the language about a love relationship is used to authenticate both writings. The fact that the other disciples raise doubts about Mary's vision in the *Gospel of Mary* (*Gos. Mary* 17.10–19.2) suggests that the teachings included in it were not expected to be accepted without reservations,[76] which makes this kind of authentication necessary. There is, however, another trait that makes Mary different from the Beloved Disciple in John: she is apparently portrayed as the one who knows more than the other disciples because of her private vision of Jesus (*Gos. Mary* 10.10ff.).

A more exclusivistic form of the secrecy motif is present in the portrayal of an anonymous youth called "the one Jesus loved" (ὃν ἠγάπα αὐτόν ὅ Ἰησοῦς) in the *Secret Gospel of Mark* (3.15–16). As is well known, the authenticity of this text is debated, as is its relationship to the canonical gospels.[77] These vexing problems cannot be settled here, but it is in any case noteworthy that in *Secret Mark* the love relationship between Jesus and his beloved one leads to the latter's initiation into "the mystery of the kingdom of God" (τὸ μυστήριον τῆς βασιλεὶας τοῦ θεοῦ). Jesus' teaching to the youth is, as far as can be inferred from the extant fragments of *Secret Mark*, disclosed neither to the other figures in the narrative nor to the audience of the text.[78] Moreover, it is noteworthy that *Secret Mark* depicts

[75] Pace Jusino, "Mary Magdalene". What makes it difficult to identify Mary with the Beloved Disciple is that the latter is referred to as a male figure in John. He is also called "son" by Jesus in John 19:26 (cf. Charlersworth, *The Beloved Disciple*, 5–6). The parallelism between the sentences "behold your son" and "behold your mother" in this verse makes de Boer's suggestion ("Mary Magdalene") that Jesus would speak here of himself as the son untenable. Moreover, Mary Magdalene and the Beloved Disciple are portrayed as distinct persons in John 20:2. De Boer's theory that the expression "the *other* disciple Jesus loved" in this verse "suggests that either Mary Magdalene or Peter could be the disciple Jesus loved, who is mentioned earlier in 19,25–27" seems strained. The more natural way of reading John 20:2 is that Mary went to two disciples of Jesus, of whom the *already known* (note the definite article τόν in John 20:2) Beloved Disciple was the other one.

[76] Cf. Marjanen, *The Woman Jesus Loved*, 113–14, 119–21.

[77] For a short account of the discovery of and subsequent debates about the *Secret Mark*, see M.W. Meyer, "The Youth in the *Secret Gospel of Mark*", *Semeia* 49 (1990) 129–53, esp. 129–30, 134–38; idem, "Beloved Disciple", 94–96.

[78] The exclusivism characteristic of the *Secret Mark* comes to expression also in

a *reciprocal* love relationship between Jesus and the youth; not only does Jesus love the youth, but the youth also loves Jesus. The latter aspect makes the youth different from the Johannine Beloved Disciple, for the Beloved Disciple's love for Jesus is never expressly mentioned in John.

In addition to these texts, there are several writings in which Jesus addresses his disciples as his "beloved". In the *Questions of Bartholomew*, a writing possibly dating from the 3rd century CE, Bartholomew is often called "beloved" by Jesus (*Quest. Barth.* 1:5, 8, 26; 4:67). This text depicts Bartholomew as a recipient of mysteries, but he is also told to "entrust them to all who are faithful and keep them for themselves" (*Quest. Barth.* 4:67, NTA), or, even more widely, to "preach this (secret) word to everyone who wishes it" (*Quest. Barth.* 5:6, NTA). As in John, eternal life is promised in this text too to those who believe in this message guaranteed by the beloved disciple of Jesus (*Quest. Barth.* 5:6).

James is called "my beloved" by Jesus in the (*Second*) *Apocalypse of James* and the *Apocryphon of James.* Again, the address is used as an introduction to Jesus' subsequent revelation:

> My beloved (*pamerit*)! Behold, I shall reveal to you those (things) that neither [the] heavens nor their archons have known. Behold, I shall reveal to you those (things) that he did not know, he who boasted . . . (*2 Apoc. Jas.* 56.16–23, trans. Hedrick)

Like the Beloved Disciple in John, James is connected with authorial fictions in the writings in which he plays the crucial role. He is presented as the author of the *Apocryphon of James*, his vision is related in the first person in the (*First*) *Apocalypse of James* (*1 Apoc. Jas.* 24.11),[79] and the (*Second*) *Apocalypses of James* introduces itself as a discourse of James (*2 Apoc. Jas.* 44.1). He also incorporates several other recurring traits of the favourite disciples of Jesus. Like Mary, he is kissed by Jesus (*2 Apoc. Jas.* 56.14–16), but he also embraces and kisses Jesus (*1 Apoc. Jas. 31.4–5*). Like Mary and Thomas in the texts mentioned above, James is praised for his understanding of Jesus' words (*1 Apoc. Jas.* 29.4–5; 40,9–10). Like Thomas, James is portrayed as

Jesus' outright rejection of the women accompanying the anonymous youth in this document; cf. Meyer, "The Youth", 144.

[79] However, the authorial fiction of *1. Apoc. Jas.* is that this writing has been written down by Addai (*1 Apoc. Jas.* 36.20–24).

Jesus' brother (*1 Apoc. Jas.* 24.14–16; *2 Apoc. Jas.* 50.11–23). Notably, it seems important to add that he is not "materially" similar to Jesus. James is only *called* the brother of Jesus (*1 Apoc. Jas.* 24.14–16),[80] and even though they were nourished with the same milk, Jesus had another father (*2 Apoc. Jas.* 50.11–23).

James is similar to the Johannine Beloved Disciple and Bartholomew in the *Questions of Bartholomew* in that the purpose of Jesus' revelation to him is to evoke faith:

> The Lord said: "James, after these things I shall reveal to you everything, not for your sake alone but for the sake of [the] unbelief of men, so that the [faith] may exist in them. For a multitude will [attain] to faith, [and] they will increase [in . . .] (*1 Apoc. Jas.* 29.19–28, trans. Schoedel)

What is also reminiscent of the figure of the Johannine Beloved Disciple is that Jesus himself too is called "beloved" in the (*Second*) *Apocalypse of James* (49.8). Thus, there is in this text an equivalence similar to that in John drawn between the beloved Son of God and his beloved disciple.[81]

In the *Apocryphon of James*, the term "beloved" is used of both James and Peter. A love relationship is in this text associated with the life-giving function of these two disciples ("You are the beloved; you are they who will be the cause of life in many"; *Ap. Jas.* 10:29–32; trans. Williams) but also with the possibility of becoming equal to Jesus:[82]

> If you do his (i.e., Father's) will, I [say] that he will love you, and make you equal to me, and reckon [you] to have become beloved through his providence by your own choice (*Ap. Jas.* 4.40–5.6, trans. Williams).

---

[80] Cf. similar assessments about James made in Eusebius (*Hist. eccl.* 1.12.5; 2.1.2; cf. Painter, *Just James*, 111), and about Thomas in *Thom. Cont.* 138.10.

[81] The whole section of *2 Apoc. Jas.* 49.8–15 is reminiscent of the christological language of the Fourth Gospel. Nonetheless, it cannot be taken for granted that *2 Apoc. Jas.* made use of the New Testament traditions; cf. below p. 00.

[82] The hope of becoming equal to Jesus is also visible in *Gospel of Thomas* 13 and 108, but it is also more widely attested in early Christian writings. In addition to *Gos. Thom.* 108, Williams cites the following examples: 1 John 3:2; Irenaeus, *Haer.* 1.25.1; Tertullianus, *De Anima* 32; *Gos. Phil.* 61.30–31; 67.21–27; *Pistis Sophia* 96; F.E. Williams, "[Notes to] The Apocryphon of James", in H.W. Attridge (ed.), *Nag Hammadi Codex I* (*The Jung Codex*), vol. 2: *Notes* (NHS 23; Brill: Leiden, 1985) 7–37, on p. 15.

In the *Apocryphon of James*, however, the term "beloved" is not restricted to the two favorite disciples of Jesus. It can be used in a more generic manner for those who will be saved (or belong to the divine realm already) (*Ap. Jas.* 16.8–12). What is explicit also in this writing is the exclusive secrecy motif associated with these two disciples: it is pointed out that James and Peter do not give a full account of their revelation to the other disciples (*Ap. Jas.* 15.34–16.2).[83]

The address "beloved" (*pmerit*) appears also in *Pistis Sophia* 68 and 78 as part of Jesus' praise of James' understanding: "Excellent, James, thou beloved one." This form of Jesus' response is characteristic of *Pistis Sophia*, and it is not confined to James; the same address including the designation "beloved" is also used of other speakers in *Pistis Sophia*: Philip (*PS* 44), John (*PS* 64), Matthew (*PS* 72). Thus *Pistis Sophia* bears witness to a notably inclusive understanding of the term "beloved". It no longer denotes one favourite disciple of Jesus but is associated with all his followers.[84] In keeping with this "egalitarian" tendency, in *Pistis Sophia* "all the disciples who engage themselves in conversation with Jesus seem to understand Jesus' instruction well."[85]

The habit of designating certain disciples or all of them as "beloved" is most likely a tradition that is originally independent from John. The Coptic term *merit* (e.g., *2. Apoc. Jas.* 56.15–16; *PS* 68 etc.) presupposes the Greek word ἀγαπητός rather the verbal phrases used of the Beloved Disciple in John (ὃν ἠγάπα/ἐφίλει). In addition, there seems to be a Jewish background for this tradition. The expression "beloved" occurs in a similar form in LXX and Jewish pseudepigrapha (cf. Tob. 10:13; *T. Levi* 18:13; *T. Benj.* 11:2), and, more importantly, it can be associated in the latter with the revelation of secrets, as is done for instance in the *Apocalypse of Abraham* (which

[83] A notable contrast to this description of James can be found in a quotation attributed to Clement of Alexandria by Eusebius. In this passage, James (together with Peter and John) is depicted as a recipient of "the higher knowledge", but it is also emphasized that "they imparted it to the other apostles" (*Hist. eccl.* 2.1.4; cf. Painter, *Just James*, 111, 115–16).

[84] Cf. also *PS* 138, where the disciples as a group are addressed by Jesus as "my beloved".

[85] Marjanen, *The Woman Jesus Loved*, 175. This can be seen in the fact that the interlocutors are constantly praised by Jesus in *Pistis Sophia* with the words "excellent" (*euge*), "well done" (*kalōs*), and "blessed" (*makarios*) in addition to the word "beloved".

possibly dates from the first or second century CE). In this writing, the apocalyptic revealer addresses Abraham as his beloved:

> I will announce to you guarded things and you will see great things which you have not seen, because you desired to search for me, and I called you my beloved (*Apoc. Abraham* 9:6, trans. Rubinkiewicz-Lunt, OTP).

It may well be that the depictions of beloved disciples of Jesus to whom he grants secret knowledge emerge from this kind of Jewish tradition of the beloved ones of God as recipients of secret things. Above all, the Nag Hammadi tractates associated with James incorporate some early traditions,[86] some of which suggest a Jewish-Christian background.[87] Hence, also the tradition of portraying James as the beloved one of Jesus and his confidant could possibly have been already in air, as the Gospel of John was written.

Conclusion

The comparative material presented above shows that the language about a love relationship is well attested in early Christian presentations of the disciples of Jesus who are act as authenticating figures. In this regard, the Johannine Beloved Disciple is no exceptional character. What makes him different from most other star disciples of Jesus mentioned above is however the absence of an explicit secrecy motif in his characterization. While the others are mostly portrayed

[86] Ron Cameron has demonstrated that the *Apocryphon of James* contains some very early traditions of the sayings of Jesus, and Charles Hedrick argues that, in the (*Second*) *Apocalypse of James*, "(t)he absence of allusions to the later developed gnostic systems, the issues to which the author addresses himself . . ., and the almost total absence of allusions to the New Testament tradition suggest an early date for the origin of the tractate." Cf. R. Cameron, *Sayings Traditions in the Apocryphon of James* (HTS 34; Philadelphia: Fortress Press, 1984); C.W. Hedrick, "The (Second) Apocalypse of James [Introduction]", in D. Parrott (ed.), *Nag Hammadi Codices* V, 2–5 *with Papyrus Berolinensis 8502,* 1 *and* 4 (NHS 11; Leiden: Brill, 1979) 105–9, on p. 108.

[87] The *(First) Apocalypse of James*, though it must be a later work (because of its affinities with Valentinian teaching), still betrays knowledge of James' death before or during the Jewish War (*1 Apoc. Jas. 36,16–19*); cf. A. Böhlig, "Der judenchristliche Hintergrund in gnostischen Schriften der Nag Hammadi", in idem, *Mysterion und Wahrheit: Gesammelte Beiträge zur spätantiken Religionsgeschichte* (AGSJU 6; Leiden: Brill, 1968) 102–11, on p. 110; W. Schoedel, "The (First) Apocalypse of James [Introduction]", in Parrott (ed.), *Nag Hammadi Codices* V, 2–5, 65–67, on p. 66.

as having knowledge and understanding of Jesus' hidden revelations, these traits are far from being clear in John's portrait of the Beloved Disciple. Rather, the Johannine literary fiction is that his testimony provides *common knowledge* that can be guaranteed by the "we" mentioned in John 21:24.[88]

Given that the Beloved Disciple appears to be, among other things, part of the Johannine polemic against the brothers of Jesus, it is noteworthy that Thomas and James are portrayed in the writings discussed above in terms of their brotherhood with Jesus, and James also as his beloved. This raises the question of a possible historical context that made it necessary to introduce the Beloved Disciple in John. Could it be that he was created to form a contrast to either of these figures?

Thomas can hardly be the specific target of the Johannine polemic against the brothers of Jesus—though this theory would concur with an increasingly popular assumption of a real-life controversy between Johannine and Thomasine Christians—[89] for he is nowhere in John associated with Jesus' brothers. James could be a better candidate for this purpose,[90] for his brotherhood with Jesus and leadership of the Jewish-Christian community must have been well-known to early Christians (cf. Gal 1:17–19; 2:6–10; cf. Acts 12:17; 15:13; 21:18).[91] In light of his established status in Jerusalem, the outright condemnation of Jesus' brothers as those who "did not believe in him" in John 7:5 is all the more striking, as is also the fact that it is the disciples who are called the brothers of Jesus after his resurrection (John 20:17–18). It is not only the Beloved Disciple who takes the place of Jesus' brothers in John but also the other disciples are portrayed as substitutes for them.

Yet our evidence is too limited to substantiate a theory that the polemic against the brothers of Jesus in John was directed against those still adhering to James. What we have to hand is the follow-

[88] Most scholars think that "we" in John 21:24 refers to the editors of the fourth gospel or to the Johannine circle in general. Yet in the Johannine story world "we" could also refer to the other disciples of Jesus. They as his eye-witnesses are the ones who really can confirm the accuracy of the Beloved Disciple's account. In addition, already in John 1:14 "we" is used to denote those who have seen Jesus.

[89] This theory is advanced, above all, by G. Riley, *Resurrection Reconsidered: Thomas and John in Controversy* (Minneapolis: Fortress, 1995).

[90] Cf. Rese, "Selbstzeugnis", 95 n. 65.

[91] On James' leadership of the Christian community in Jerusalem, see now Painter, *Just James*, 44, 54–56.

ing: in certain documents James, the brother of Jesus, is called by him "my beloved", while in John there is a polemical slur against the brothers of Jesus and the Beloved Disciple appears as a substitute for them. These observations may suggest some link between James and the Beloved Disciple, but this is far from being certain. For there is no specific polemic against James in John—he is not even mentioned by name; nor are the unbelieving brothers of Jesus as a group linked with those Jews who believe in Jesus but are rejected by him (John 8:31). Thus even if the latter group would represent Jewish Christians, which in itself would be a possibility, they are not directly associated with James.

Accordingly, any conclusions about the historical context of the Beloved Disciple must be put in a more cautious way. What seems evident is that the repudiation of Jesus' brothers and the introduction of the Beloved Disciple are related to each other in John. The fact that no brother of Jesus is mentioned by name in John could indicate that the Beloved Disciple is introduced in John in order to disqualify not a certain "brother" of Jesus, but more generally *all* current attempts to seek authority with claims to the membership of Jesus' family. The increasing popularity of such "dynastic" claims is shown not only by the texts attributed to Thomas and James, but also by the pseudonymous New Testament epistles attributed to James and Jude. All these claims bear witness to early Christian controversies about the legacy of Jesus and to the "dynastic" claims as part of them. My suggestion is that these debates not only gave rise to the invention of the Beloved Disciple, but also account, to some degree, for the designation "the disciple Jesus loved" chosen for him in John.

PART THREE

PAUL IN CONFLICT

NOCH EINMAL "WORKS OF THE LAW": THE DIALOGUE CONTINUES

James D.G. Dunn

Debating with Heikki Räisänen over issues of Pauline interpretation has been one of the most stimulating and enjoyable experiences of my work on Paul. We have both turned our attention elsewhere since then, but the debates and disputes have continued in the meantime and I hope Heikki will find some pleasure in this brief attempt to re-engage in some of our old dialogue.

The overlap of our interests was quite extensive,[1] but hopefully he will forgive me if I return to a question which became a particular concern of mine and which seems at times to have generated more heat than light—what Paul meant by the phrase "works of the law". The ongoing debate has retained a surprising vitality, principally for two reasons, I suppose. One is that what I chanced to describe as "the new perspective on Paul"[2] has now been around long enough for a new generation of scholars to treat it as one of the more "established" options, and thus as calling for fresh scrutiny in its turn—just as my own generation, instructed by Sanders[3] and challenged by Räisänen,[4] found it necessary to subject the established "Lutheran paradigm" to fresh scrutiny. The second is, of course, the publication of the Qumran text 4QMMT, with, at last (!), an example of the very phrase "the works of the law" in a document nearly contemporaneous with Paul, or at least referring to an attitude to the law which was contemporary with Paul and which was evidently summed up by the same phrase, "the works of the law".

---

[1] As indicated already by the overlap in topics as between my *Jesus, Paul and the Law: Studies in Mark and Galatians* (London: SPCK, 1990) and Heikki's *Jesus, Paul and Torah: Collected Essays* (JSNTS 43; Sheffield: JSOT, 1992).

[2] "The New Perspective on Paul", *BJRL* 65 (1983) 95–122, reprinted in *Jesus, Paul and the Law*, 183–206.

[3] E.P. Sanders, *Paul and Palestinian Judaism* (London: SCM, 1977).

[4] In re-reading Heikki's *Paul and the Law* (WUNT 29; Tübingen: Mohr-Siebeck, 1983) I was delighted to note again the extent of our agreement in his chapter on "The antithesis between works of the law and faith in Christ" (162–77), though we began to drift apart thereafter (177–91).

Since my earlier formulations on the subject of "works of the law" in Paul can be included among those which may have generated more heat than light, at least in some circles,[5] it will perhaps not be regarded as too self-indulgent if I begin by explaining how I came to my view of the phrase's reference in Paul. Since I subsequently found the usage of 4QMMT to be supportive of my interpretation of Paul's phrase, it will then be necessary to enter into dialogue with those who have found 4QMMT telling a somewhat different story. It will also be appropriate to reflect a little further on what "works of the law" and the "works" by reference to which final judgment will be rendered have to do with each other in Paul's scheme of things.

I

The observation regarding "works of the law" stemmed from my initial reaction to E.P. Sanders' *Paul and Palestinian Judaism*, as outlined in the 1982 T.W. Manson Memorial Lecture, "The New Perspective on Paul". In that lecture I focused on Gal 2:16, which can certainly be classified as the first extant use of the phrase "works of the law" in Paul's writings and theology.[6] What struck me then was the fact that Paul introduces the phrase in what is most obviously to be understood as Paul's summing up of the lessons he had learned through the disputes which he has just described, the dispute in Jerusalem on whether Titus should be circumcised (Gal 2:1–10), and the dispute at Antioch arising from Peter's refusal to

[5] For earlier attempts to clarify misunderstandings: Additional Note in *Jesus, Paul and the Law*, 206–14; in response to C.E.B. Cranfield, "'The Works of the Law' in the Epistle to the Romans", *JSNT* 43 (1991) 89–101, see my "Yet Once More—'The Works of the Law': A Response", *JSNT* 46 (1992) 99–117; in response to P. Stuhlmacher, *Biblische Theologie des Neuen Testaments*, vol. 1: *Grundlegung von Jesus zu Paulus* (Göttingen: Vandenhoeck & Ruprecht, 1992) 264, see my *The Theology of Paul the Apostle* (Grand Rapids: Eerdmans/Edinburgh: T & T Clark, 1998) 358 n. 97; also "A Response to Peter Stuhlmacher", in F. Avemarie und H. Lichtenberger (eds.), *Auferstelhung-Resurrection* (Tübingen: Mohr Siebech, 2001) 363–8.

[6] The Additional Note in *Jesus, Paul and the Law*, 206–9 already responded to Heikki's response to that lecture, "Galatians 2.16 and Paul's Break with Judaism", *NTS* 31 (1985) 543–53, reprinted *Jesus, Paul and Torah*, 112–26. I still relish his slightly backhanded compliment that "Dunn comes close to describing Paul's position as Paul himself wished it to be understood" (*Jesus, Paul and Torah*, 125). For my more recent exposition see *Theology of Paul*, particularly 354–79, bibliography on 335.

eat with Gentile believers (2:11–14). If others prefer to say that Gal 2:16 represents what Paul had always stood for and what motivated the stands he took at Jerusalem and at Antioch, it makes little difference for the point I am making.[7] For on the present point the outcome is more or less the same: Paul introduced the phrase "works of the law" to express a key element of the principles on which or for which he had fought to safeguard "the truth of the gospel" (2:5, 14) at Jerusalem and Antioch.

I stress the importance of thus setting in context Paul's first reference to "works of the law". It has been a sound principle of hermeneutics since the Renaissance that in order for a text to be properly understood it must first be read in context.[8] But too often still we find that a text like Gal 2:16 is seized upon, rather like a prize artefact in an early (pre-scientific) archaeological enterprise, regardless of its precisely stratified location (historical context), and plundered for the theological insight it brings to the profundities of Pauline theology understood as timeless verities independent of particular historical circumstances. Paul's central theological affirmations may indeed prove to be so ("timeless verities . . ."), in one degree or other. But *the first task is still to read Gal 2:16 in the sequence of thought which gave rise to its formulation.* The opening hermeneutical gambit has to be the recognition that the phrase "works of the law" first emerged in what Paul obviously intended as an expression of "the truth of the gospel" which had come under such threat at Jerusalem and Antioch.

The point, of course, is that the issues in both cases (Jerusalem and Antioch) focused on what religious Jews, at least since the Maccabean resistance, had regarded as fundamental and essential to the practice of their Judaism[9]—viz. circumcision and food laws (I

[7] Though Räisänen and I agree that Paul's theology regarding "works of the law" was decisively shaped by the events at Jerusalem and Antioch.

[8] Thus Schleiermacher, the father of modern hermeneutics: "The meaning of each word of a passage must be determined by the context in which it serves" (*Hermeneutics: The Handwritten Manuscripts by F.D.E. Schleiermacher*, ed. H. Kimmerle [ET Missoula, MT: Scholars, 1977] excerpted by K. Mueller-Vollmer, *The Hermeneutics Reader* [New York: Continuum, 1994] 90).

[9] One of the weaknesses of Räisänen's response to my "New Perspective" article was that he used "Judaism" in a too monolithic, undifferentiated way ("Paul's break with Judaism"). We need not go all the way with those who think it more appropriate to speak in terms of many/several Judaisms (plural) for the period. It is enough to note the tension within the terms "Jew" and "Judaism" as denoting either an ethnic or a religious identity or both. See further my *Theology of Paul*,

need cite no more than 1 Macc 1:60–63). Evidently the traditional Jews within the ranks of the believers in Messiah Jesus[10] insisted that these laws continued to be inviolable for all Jews, and that this fact must govern their relations with such Gentiles as also came to belief in this Jesus.[11] It can hardly be accidental, then, that Paul chooses to introduce just this phrase, "works of the law", in his summing up of what was at stake in these two incidents. The clear implication of Gal 2:16 is that Paul saw the traditionalists as requiring "works of the law" in addition to faith in Jesus Christ.[12] Which is also to say that in formulating the phrase "works of the law" he had in mind particularly circumcision and food laws. That is not to say Paul had only these particular laws in mind; some have so read the wording of my 1983 article,[13] but I hope subsequent clarifications have made the point plain.[14] The point, once again, is that these two laws *in particular* had brought the issue summed up in Gal 2:16 to clarity or at least to focus for Paul. *Whatever else he had in mind when he wrote of "works of the law" in 2:16, Paul certainly had in mind circumcision and food laws.* I would hope that that observation is beyond reasonable dispute.

The question would then be, why these two in particular. Once again, the immediate context indicates the answer, since the above logic works in reverse. Paul had in mind just these two, because it was precisely these two which were being insisted on as essential in addition to faith in Christ. That is, insisted on as rules which must govern relations between believing Jews and believing Gentiles. It is simply impossible in the context of Galatians 2 to avoid the Jew/Gentile issue. The "works of the law" which Paul had particularly in mind were rules which, unless embraced by Gentiles, should prevent full

347–9; S.J.D. Cohen, *The Beginnings of Jewishness: Boundaries, Varieties, Uncertainties* (Berkeley: University of California, 1999) particularly chs. 3–4.

[10] They must be so described despite Paul describing them dismissively as "false brothers" (Gal 2:4) and allusively as "some from James" (2:12); but they were certainly regarded in Jerusalem as disciples of Messiah Jesus (cf. 2:15–16).

[11] It is not necessary to achieve sharper resolution in thus referring to the incident at Antioch. What is clear is that the issues focused on the rights and wrongs of Jews eating with Gentiles, as determined by reference to the various food laws which governed the social relations of the meal table.

[12] It will be noted that I remain unpersuaded by the north American fashion to take πίστις Χριστοῦ as a reference to "the faith of Christ"; see *Theology of Paul*, 379–85, and further below n. 34.

[13] *BJRL* 65 (1983) 107 = *Jesus, Paul and the Law*, 191.

[14] See again n. 5 above.

acceptance of these Gentiles. In other words, it still seems to me impossible to avoid the strong inference here that the works of the law in view were seen as important by the Jewish traditionalists for what I have called their "boundary defining function". They marked out the distinction between the chosen nation and all others (= Gentiles). And by observing these laws, religious Jews maintained the boundary between Israel and the other nations. That is to say, they safeguarded Israel's set-apartness to God, Israel's holy status as God's covenant people.[15]

It is certainly open to exegetes and interpreters to argue out from these basic observations. (1) That "works of the law" must include all and any laws to which obedience is required as a necessary part of the salvation process. (2) That the principle articulated in Gal 2:16 is deeper or broader than simply the issue of relations between Jewish and Gentile believers in Messiah Jesus. I would have no quarrel in either case. Where I want to stand firm, however, is in insisting that the context leading up to Gal 2:16 be given more weight in determining the immediate thrust of 2:16. Moreover, if the reference of 2:16 is deepened or broadened to some more fundamental principle, I also want to insist that the immediate reference to relations between Jewish and Gentile believers be not marginalized or lost to sight.

Let me say a little more on the last point. Some have expressed surprise that I could diminish Paul's hostility to the law to a hostility towards an attitude to the law or an attitude encouraged by the law.[16] I accept that "attitude" is a weak word for what I see to have been at stake. And I see that the term has allowed a too simplistic antithesis between "attitude" and "conduct expressive of that attitude". So let me attempt to make my point more clearly.

My argument is that Paul in or as a result of his conversion reacted particularly against Jewish exclusivism.[17] Not against the fundamental

---

[15] I don't think this point is much in dispute; but the attitude is well illustrated, e.g., by Lev 20:22–26; Num 23:9; and the attitude of Peter and the other Jewish believers which had to be overcome in Acts 10 (see again *Theology of Paul*, 355–56).

[16] Including Räisänen, *Jesus, Paul and Torah*, 122.

[17] To avoid misunderstanding I should make it clear that I am *not* posing the old antithesis of Jewish particularism versus Christian universalism; see my "Was Judaism Particularist or Universalist?", in J. Neusner & A.J. Avery-Peck (eds.), *Judaism in Late Antiquity Part Three, Where we Stand: Issues and Debates in Ancient Judaism Vol. Two* (Leiden: Brill, 1999) 57–73.

belief in Israel's election as such. But against what had become a more and more dominant feature of Jewish belief in the preceding two hundred years—a zeal for the law which treated other Jews as sinners and apostates in effect, and, in extension of the same zeal, regarded Gentiles as "beyond the pale".[18] Paul expresses this in Galatians in describing his conversion as a turning from such zeal to the conviction that he had been called to take the news of God's Son to the Gentiles (1:13–16)—as complete a 180 degree about-turn as one could conceive. My point here is that we should not underestimate the seriousness of the exclusivistic attitude against which Paul now reacted. We have been reminded of just how serious such an attitude can be in the horrors of the Holocaust and more recently in the horrific savagery of the intra-ethnic and inter-ethnic conflicts of former Yugoslavia and Rwanda. It was precisely the same attitude, the same "zeal" which had inspired Paul himself to "seek to destroy the church of God" (Gal 1:13; Phil 3:6). The seriousness of an exclusivist attitude to the law is that it leads inexorably to exclusivist conduct. It is a kind of fundamentalism which can only safeguard the correctness of its belief by persecuting those who disagree or by seeking to eliminate (through conversion or otherwise) those who hold divergent views. That sort of exclusivism can produce a complete spectrum of violence, from the most subtle of social pressure to outright force. It was that sort of 'attitude to the law' which Paul came to abhor.[19]

Again we do not need to clarify here how soon Paul reached these convictions. Nor whether he entered the confrontations at Jerusalem and Antioch with these convictions already clearly drawn, including any formulation involving "works of the law". It should be clear, however, that the crisis for Paul in these confrontations was occa-

---

[18] T.L. Donaldson, *Paul and the Gentiles: Remapping the Apostle's Convictional World* (Minneapolis: Fortress, 1997) argues that prior to his conversion Paul had been interested in attracting proselytes to Judaism (e.g. 78). In my view this gives unjustified weight to a possible interpretation of Gal 5:11 at the expense of the far weightier considerations which flow from the fact of Paul's "zeal" as a persecutor (see e.g. my *Theology of Paul*, 346–54).

[19] V.M. Smiles, *The Gospel and the Law in Galatia: Paul's Response to Jewish-Christian Separatism and the Threat of Galatian Apostasy* (Collegeville, Minn.: Liturgical, 1998) recognizes that "Jewish-Christian separatism" was the problem addressed by Paul, but chides me with confusing the "social function" of the law and its "theological function". Instead he somehow finds Galatians contesting "the law's claims on the entire world" (125–28), which reads into Galatians more than the text can bear.

sioned by the outworking of the same old exclusivism within the ranks of believers in Messiah Jesus: uncircumcised, unobservant Gentile believers should be "excluded, regarded as outsiders" (ἐκκλείω—Gal 4:17). At Jerusalem and Antioch Paul resisted this policy with the same forthrightness as he had enacted it prior to his conversion. And in Gal 2:16 it is that exclusivism which is encapsulated in one degree or other in the phrase "works of the law". To Peter he says, or would like to have said in person, "You must agree that we cannot regard such exclusivist practices as consonant with the gospel; we cannot think that believing Gentiles should either still suffer from such an attitude/practices or should themselves be expected to order their own conduct accordingly".

In short, whatever else Gal 2:16 may mean or may be taken to mean, it certainly was intended to warn against "works of the law" as constituting or erecting barriers to the free extension of God's grace to Gentiles. The phrase did not include any thought evident on the surface of the argument that "works of the law" were necessary to gain initial acceptance by God. What Paul objected to was the thought that the law, as expressed particularly in or epitomised by circumcision and food laws, continued to be a *sine qua non* requirement for believing Jews in governing their acceptance of and relations with believing Gentiles, or in a word, that works of the law were necessary in addition to faith in Christ.

II

One of the most forceful challenges to this view of works of the law (ἔργα νόμου) has been mounted by Michael Bachmann. In a 1993 article he had already argued that "works of the law" refers to the regulations of the law itself.[20] His most weighty arguments are that references to ἔργα elsewhere (as in Jas 2:14–26) are not relevant, since the Pauline phrase is ἔργα <u>νόμου</u> not "works" of a person. On

[20] "Rechtfertigung und Gestezeswerke bei Paulus", *TZ* 49 (1993) 1–33, reprinted in *Antijudaismus im Galaterbrief: Exegetische Studien zu einem polemischen Schreiben und zur Theologie des Apostels Paulus* (NTOA 40; Freiburg: Universitätsverlag, 1999) 1–31: "Paulus meint mit dem Ausdruck 'Werke des Gesetzes' nicht etwas, was auf der durch das Tun gemäss den Regelungen des Gesetzes markierten Ebene liegt, insbesondere nicht: Gebotserfüllungen, sondern er meint mit dem Syntagma 'Werke des Gesetzes' die Regelungen des Gesetzes selber" (14).

the analogy of John 6:28–29 ("the work(s) of God") the fuller phrase should be understood as the works commanded by the law/God, or simply as the commands of the law/God. Moreover, "works of the law" and "law" often stand in parallel in Paul (e.g. Rom 3:21 and 28), implying that by "works of the law" Paul means nothing other than the regulations of the law.

In a subsequent article Bachmann presses the now famous 4QMMT text into service on behalf of the same thesis.[21] Rather like Gal 2:16, the key phrase, *ma'ase hatorah*, is used to sum up the case being made in the body of the letter: "We have also written to you some of the works of the Torah (*miqsat ma'ase hatorah*) which we think are good for you and for your people" (4QMMT C26–27).[22] The allusion back to the beginning of the second/main section of the text is beyond dispute: "these are some of our rulings (*miqsat debarenu*) . . . which are . . . the works (*ma'asim*) . . ." (B1).[23] What clearly are in view are the intervening content of the letter, the "series of halakhic rulings, chiefly relating to temple, priesthood, sacrifices and purity".[24] Bachmann accepts my account on this point, referring particularly to the further summary phrase, "some of our words/rulings (*miqsat debarenu*)", in C30. His point, however, is, once again, that what is in view is not the "*fulfilment* of these regulations . . . but the specific *judgment* of halakhic questions on the part of this 'Qumran people'".[25] The "works" in question are nothing other than the sect's halakhoth.[26]

The argument has obvious weight. Bachmann cites Qimron and Strugnell as noting the singular *ma'aseh* in Ex 18:20 in reference to the law, and in Second Temple Jewish writings the "widespread use

[21] "4QMMT und Galaterbrief, *ma'ase hatorah* und *ERGA NOMOU*", *ZNW* 89 (1998) 91–113; reprinted in *Antijudaismus*, 33–56; in response to my own "4QMMT and Galatians", *NTS* 43 (1997) 147–53.

[22] I follow the verse numbering in E. Qimron & J. Strugnell, *Miqsat Ma'ase Ha-Torah* (*DJD* 10.5; Oxford: Clarendon, 1994), but will refer also to F. García Martínez, *The Dead Sea Scrolls Translated: The Qumran Texts in English* (Leiden: Brill/Grand Rapids: Eerdmans, 1994, 2nd ed., 1996); G. Vermes, *The Complete Dead Sea Scrolls in English* (London: Penguin, 1997).

[23] The various translations fill out the text differently, e.g. García Martínez: "These are some of our regulations [concerning the law of G]od, which are pa[rt of] the works we [are examining and] they [a]ll relate to [. . .] and purity"; Vermes: "These are some of our teachings [ ] which are [the] works which w[e think and a]ll of them concern [ ] and the purity of . . .".

[24] Bachmann here quotes my own summary (Dunn, "4QMMT", 150).

[25] Bachmann, "4QMMT", 43–44.

[26] Bachmann, "4QMMT", 47.

of the plural *ma'asim* as a term designating the laws or commandments".[27] Qimron and Strugnell translate the phrase *ma'ase hatorah* as "the precepts of the Torah", and Vermes as "the observances of the Law". García Martínez initially followed Qimron and Strugnell, but in his second edition changed to "the works of the Torah".[28]

My only concern is that Bachmann is driving a wedge between two meanings of *ma'aseh/ma'asim* which is quite unjustified. He treats what is in effect a spectrum of meaning as two disconnected and separate meanings. But the root meaning of *'asah* is "to do, make". And the only reason why *ma'aseh* can refer to "precept" is because what is in mind is *the conduct and actions thus prescribed*. It would be more accurate to translate *ma'aseh* as "prescribed deed", since it is an extended sense of the basic sense "deed". Vermes' "observance" catches the sense quite well, given that "observance" has more or less the same ambiguity or spectrum of meaning as *ma'aseh*.[29] The point should have been plain from Ex 18:20: "teach them the statutes and instructions (*hatoroth*), and make known to them the way they are to go (*yelekhu*) and the things (*hama'ase*) they are to do (*ya'asun*)" (NRSV). The last phrase clearly has in mind "the deeds prescribed which they are to do". To drive a wedge between "precept/prescription" and "deed (prescribed)", as though the former could be grasped without thought of the latter, puts a distinction between a regulation and its fulfilment which is quite foreign to the thought.[30]

Similarly with 4QMMT. It should surely be self-evident that the writers of 4QMMT were not simply trying to achieve an act of intellectual persuasion, merely to convince the addressees to accept the legitimacy of the halakhic rulings contained in the letter. Here again the term itself, halakhah (from *halakh*, "to walk"), should be given its proper weight: *halakhoth* refers to rulings on how they are to walk (Ex 18:20—*yelekhu*). These "rulings" indicated how the Torah should be *observed in conduct* in the various matters of disputed practice. What the letter writer(s) wanted was to convince the addressees to follow

[27] Bachmann, "4QMMT", 45–46; referring to Qimron & Strugnell, "Miqsat Ma'ase Ha-Torah", 139.

[28] I recounted García Martínez's change of mind in Dunn, "4QMMT", 150.

[29] Similarly J.L. Martyn, *Galatians* (AB 33A; New York: Doubleday, 1997), translates ἔργα νόμου as "observance of the Law" (ad loc.).

[30] See also D. Flusser, "Die Gesetzeswerke in Qumran und bei Paulus", in H. Cancik et al. (eds.), *Geschichte—Tradition—Reflexion: Festschrift für Martin Hengel*, vol. 1: *Judentum* (Tübingen: Mohr-Siebeck, 1996) 395–403.

the sect's halakhoth. So too, the hope held out at the end of the letter is that "at the end of time, you may rejoice in finding that some of our words/practices (*miqsat debarenu*) are true/correct. And it shall be reckoned to you for righteousness in doing what is upright and good before him" (C30–31). Once again it is important to recall that *dabar* has a spectrum of meaning—"word, saying, matter (the thing about which one speaks)". The hope is clearly that those addressed will find that "some of our words/rulings" are true *by doing them*, by following the sect's halakhoth.[31] Assuredly the hope was not that those addressed would be "reckoned righteous" simply by virtue of changing their minds on some disputed points. Only if they did "what is upright and good before him", that is, by *doing* what the sect commended, could they hope for final vindication.

The point is the same with regard to Paul's use of the phrase, "works of the law". How did Paul's opponents understand "justification by works of the law (ἐξ ἔργων νόμου)"? Surely not simply that justification would be granted on the basis of having the law, the regulations of the law understood as a kind of talisman or amulet. As I noted in commenting on Rom 2:13, Paul's observation that "not the hearers of the law are just before God but the doers of the law shall be justified" was one which no scripture-instructed Jew would dispute.[32] At this point, the issue was not *whether* the law should be "done", but *how* it should be done.[33] My objection to Bachmann is not that he is wrong to affirm that "works of the law" in Paul can mean the "regulations of the law". My objection is rather that he denies that the phrase *also* refers to the implementation of these regulations in daily living. No more than at Qumran would the hope disputed in Gal 2:16, or Rom 3:20, 28, be for final vindication on the basis of having been persuaded concerning certain halakhic niceties. The hope was rather that a life lived in accordance with the law (manifesting the works of the law) would be vindicated by God.

Bachmann makes a good deal of the much puzzled-over Gal 3:10.[34]

---

[31] Qimron & Strugnell translate "some our practices" (C30).

[32] *Romans* (WBC 38; Dallas: Word, 1988) 97; see again Flusser, "Gesetzeswerke".

[33] Paul sees faith, the Spirit and love as the key to the "how" (Rom 3:31; 8:4; 13:8–10; Gal 5:14); see further my *Theology of Paul*, ch. 8; see also C. Burchard, "Nicht aus Werken des Gesetzes, sondern aus Glauben an Jesus Christus—seit wann?", in H. Cancik et al. (eds.), *Geschichte—Tradition—Reflexion: Festschrift für Martin Hengel*, vol. 3: *Frühes Christentum* (Tübingen: Mohr-Siebeck, 1996) 405–15.

[34] Bachmann, "4QMMT", 53–55, referring back to the fuller exposition of "Rechtfertigung", 23–26.

The puzzle is how Paul can regard those who are "from works of the law" (ἐξ ἔργων νόμου) as "under a curse". It is the usual interpretation of "works of the law", as referring to *performance* of the law, which causes the problem, since scripture explicitly pronounces the curse on all who *fail* to perform the law (3:10b). In contrast, Bachmann thinks that to understand "works of the law" as referring only to the regulations of the law resolves the puzzle: those who define themselves by reference to such regulations can be said to be under the curse precisely by virtue of their *failure* to fulfil these regulations. I might respond by pointing out that such quite traditional reasoning imports a consideration which is not present in the text: the logic that it is impossible for anyone to fulfil the law (therefore all are under the curse) has to be imported into the text. But that is another issue which I cannot enter into here.[35]

The only point I need to make here is the same point already made above. I agree that ὅσοι ἐξ ἔργων νόμου can be well explicated as "those who define themselves by reference to the ἔργα νόμου". But that must mean that they define themselves in terms of their *obedience* to the law. What sense does it make to envisage Jews who defined themselves by reference to the law of circumcision but who excluded thereby the affirmation that they themselves had, of course, been circumcised? When Paul categorizes Jews as "the circumcision (ἡ περιτομή)"[36] he hardly refers to an intellectual appreciation of the rite's significance as distinguished from the performance of the rite itself. The phrase does indeed denote those who defined themselves by reference to ἔργα νόμου. But it must mean those who defined themselves over against others (Gentiles, and other Jews?) in terms of the halakhoth by which they lived. This is the basis for my own interpretation of Gal 3:10, which understands Paul to mean that the very act and life-style of defining oneself over against others in a condemnatory and dismissive (exclusive) way is itself a failure to live out what the book of the law envisaged (cf. Rom 9:31–32).[37] But here again to pursue that debate would take us too far from our present, necessarily circumscribed task.

In short, Bachmann's attempt to resolve the issue of what Paul

[35] See already my *Galatians* (BNTC; London: A. & C. Black, 1993) 170–74; *Theology of Paul*, 361–62.

[36] Rom 2:26–27; 3:30; 4:9; Gal 2:7–9; Col 3:11.

[37] See again n. 33 above.

meant by "the works of the law" must be judged as misconceived. Not because he has advocated an inadmissable sense for the term. Not at all. But because he has thought it possible to distinguish and separate this sense ("the regulations of the law") from the sense of obeying these regulations ("doing what the law requires"). Paul in turn assuredly did not understand those ἐκ πίστεως as those who cherished a particular opinion about Christ.[38] οἱ ἐκ πίστεως were those who expressed and lived out of faith, as had Abraham before them (Rom 4:16; Gal 3:7–9), and who could therefore be defined in terms of that faith.

III

A different critique has been offered by Tom Wright—basically that the parallel argued between Paul's use of ἔργα νόμου and 4QMMT C27 is disproportionate.[39] (1) "MMT defines one group of Jews over against the rest. The 'works' which Paul opposes, however, define all Jews and proselytes over against the gentile or pagan world". (2) MMT is concerned with "highly tuned postbiblical regulations" regarding animal foetuses, banning the blind and lame from the Temple, the purity or otherwise of streams of liquid, and such like; whereas Paul is concerned with "the biblical marks of Jewish identity (circumcision, sabbath, food laws)". (3) MMT's regulations refer to the Jerusalem Temple and its purity. But neither Paul nor his opponents mention the Temple itself, or the purity codes required for its operation. The two situations are related "only very obliquely".

All of which distinguishing detail is quite correct. But Wright nevertheless misses the fuller and more fundamental parallel involved. That parallel is indicated not only by the phrase "works of the law", but by two of the other points of contact between MMT and Galatians to which I had directed attention.[40] (1) The writers of MMT remind

---

[38] Here I am tempted to point out the parallel between Bachmann's interpretation of ἔργα νόμου and the popular "faith of Christ" interpretation of πίστις Χριστοῦ. In both cases what would be in view was the means to salvation (regulations, Christ's faithfulness), but not its implementation (deeds, faith). In contrast my own view is that in the one case what is in view is not simply the halakhah but its observance seen as necessary, in the other not simply a saving Christ but the means by which that saving act becomes effectual in individual cases.

[39] N.T. Wright, "Paul and Qumran", *Bible Review* 14/5 (1998) 18, 54; Wright's original working title was "4QMMT and Paul: What Sort of 'Works'?".

[40] Dunn. "4QMMT", 147–48, 151–52.

the addressees that "we have separated ourselves from the multitude of the people [and from all their impurity]" (Qimron & Strugnell C7).[41] The letter itself is obviously intended at least in some measure to provide an explanation of why they had thus "separated" themselves. The verb used is precisely equivalent to the verb used by Paul to describe the action of Peter, followed by the other Jewish believers, who "separated himself (ἀφώριζεν ἑαυτόν)" from the Gentile believers in Antioch, having previously eaten with them (Gal 2:12–13). The point is that the attitude behind both "separations" is the same. It is true that the Qumranites "separated" themselves from the rest of Israel, whereas Peter and the other Jewish believers "separated" themselves from the Gentile believers. But in each case the primary concern on the part of the "separatists" was their own purity: they "separated" because they feared the defilement which would be contracted by associating with those who did not maintain the same degree of purity.[42] In short, the motivation and theological rationale were the same in MMT and Antioch: that it was necessary for Torah-true, covenant-loyal Jews to separate themselves from impurity, whether the impurity of apostate Jews or the impurity of Gentiles. That is what Paul objected to.

(2) The parallel extends to the idea of righteousness as dependent on observing such regulations: "This will be 'reckoned to you for righteousness' in doing what is upright and good before him" (C31), with the same echo of Gen 15:6 which was central to Paul's reasoning on the subject (Gal 3:6; Rom 4:3–22). Clearly the letter writer(s) believed that those who followed Qumran's halakhoth would be "reckoned righteous"; that is, they would be "reckoned righteous by reference to their *ma'ase hatorah*", or, in the term used by Paul, they would be "justified ἐξ ἔργων νόμου". In both cases, that is to

[41] Whether Qimron & Strugnell's completion of the lacuna is correct or not, the overall concern of MMT with purity issues is hardly disputable.

[42] The point probably needs to be repeated that the laws of clean and unclean were both essentially purity concerns, and reflected precisely the separation of Israel from the nations (Lev 20:24–26; Acts 10:14–15, 28). Since purity was an issue correlated directly with the Temple (to be pure enough to take part in the Temple ritual) it is worth noting that such purity concerns were evidently a factor determining table fellowship not only within the land of Israel (Pharisees and Jesus as "eating with taxcollectors and sinners") but also beyond (Romans 14). See further my *The Partings of the Ways between Christianity and Judaism* (London: SCM, 1991) 107–13, 130–34; also *Romans*, 818–19, 825–26; and the discussion of purity concerns among the Diaspora in E.P. Sanders, *Jewish Law from Jesus to the Mishnah* (London: SCM, 1990) 258–71.

say, what was seen to be at stake by the separatists was their own righteousness/justification; their own righteousness/justification would somehow be imperilled by association with those who did not so understand and practise the Torah, that is, by the impurity of these others. And, once again, it is precisely that attitude and praxis to which Paul objects.

Wright in fact is very much on target when he indicates that what was at stake in one case was self-definition, and in the other self-identity. For in each case the integrity of their own identity (as Israel, as believers) was understood to be put at risk by association with the non-observant (other Jews, Gentiles). By the same token, the observance of the Torah (halakhoth, food laws) was vital to that self-definition, to maintaining that identity. What has proved so interesting about 4QMMT at this point is that it has used the very same phrase, "the works of the law", in the very same way as does Paul in characterising the attitude of Peter, and with the very same implication that such "works of the law" were deemed by the observant to be necessary bulwarks to sustain and preserve their self-definition, their identity.

I press the point simply to underscore the way in which it strengthens my basic thesis about "works of the law". Despite Wright, the parallel between MMT and Galatians is close and significant. Not because the specific issues/rulings/halakhoth/practices in view were the same. But because the *attitude and concerns* expressed in the phrase "works of the law" were the same. The writers of MMT used the phrase to indicate those halakhoth and practices which were of such importance for them as to necessitate their separation from the rest of the people.[43] Paul used the phrase to describe the Torah-faithful practices which Peter and the other Jewish believers regarded as of such importance as to necessitate their separation from the rest of

[43] The earlier complaint about failure to read a text in context (above n. 8) applies also to MMT's reference to "works of the law". E.g., in disputing my view B. Witherington, *Grace in Galatia: A Commentary on Paul's Letter to the Galatians* (Grand Rapids: Eerdmans, 1998) 176–77, ignores both the obvious inference that "some works of the law", "some of our rulings/practices" (C27, 30) refer back to the rulings laid out in the letter, and that these constituted a dividing line of separation from the rest of the people. T.R. Schreiner, *Romans* (Grand Rapids: Baker, 1998) 173 ignores the context altogether. H.-J. Eckstein, *Verheißung und Gesetz: Eine exegetische Untersuchung zu Galater 2.15–4.7* (WUNT 86; Tübingen: Mohr-Siebeck, 1996) does not even mention 4QMMT!

the believers in Messiah Jesus. Both sets of separatists were making such "works of the law" essential to being reckoned righteous by God. Not, to say it again, because these "works of the law" were thought somehow to achieve an initial acceptability to God, but because such "works of the law" enforced and enacted separation from others of Israel or others of faith.[44] Whereas for Paul, faith alone, faith in Christ, was the sole ground of acceptance by God and for social fellowship with others who shared that faith.

IV

There is one further aspect which deserves some attention. The current debate regarding "works of the law" in Paul has been carried forward without sufficient regard to the fact that the key word, "works (ἔργα)", appears elsewhere in other passages where justification/acquittal is in view. I refer, of course, to the fact that Paul envisages the final judgment as being determined with reference to the "works" of those being judged. God "will render to each according to his works", whether good or evil (Rom 2:6). The "work" of each will be tested by fire (1 Cor 3:13–15). "We must all appear before the judgment seat of Christ, in order that each may receive recompense for what he has done in the body, whether good or evil" (2 Cor 5:10). Bachmann, of course, defuses the issue by making a sharp distinction between such humanly wrought "works" and the "works (= regulations) of the law".[45] And Wright recognizes the importance of the eschatological aspect to the discussion, though he pursues it in his own characteristic way.[46] But the issue cannot be avoided either way. The issue is this: if "works of the law" are indeed the deeds prescribed by the law, then how does Paul relate them to the "works" by reference to which final judgment shall be rendered?

The issue, of course, is all the sharper for those who understand "works of the law" to refer to the whole range of conduct required by the law. For then Paul's various statements on the subject of

[44] See now also M.A. Abegg, "4QMMT C 27, 31 and 'Works Righteousness'", *Dead Sea Discoveries* 6 (1999) 139–47.

[45] Bachmann, "Rechtfertigung" 14–19.

[46] "Towering over these issues is MMT's *biblical eschatology* (something ignored by scholars so far), and the way this relates to its 'works of the law' on the one hand and to Paul's 'works' on the other" (Wright).

"works" seem to fall into complete confusion. He certainly denies that justification/acquittal is "from works (of the law)". But then, on the one hand, he asserts that the law is fulfilled in the command for neighbour love (Gal 5:14), and that believers who "love their neighbour" do in fact fulfil the law (Rom 13:8, 10); are those who "love their neighbour" *not* doing "the work(s) of the law"? Moreover, he affirms that final judgment/acquittal is "in accordance with works"; presumably love of neighbour is the sort of "work(s)" which will survive the fiery test and by reference to which acquittal will be recorded.

Ironically, we encounter here a feature of Paul's theology which seems, to the surprise of some, very similar to the theology of his Jewish contemporaries: that judgment will be according to works. Christian scholarship generally has been so anxious to mark out the difference and distance between Paul and Second Temple Judaism on the issue of justification that we have neglected this point of similarity.[47] But the future emphasis in Paul's teaching on justification must not be neglected. For example, as already noted, the thought of Rom 2:13 is no different from the traditional emphases of Second Temple Judaism: it is "the doers of the law (who) shall be justified". And when in Gal 5:5 Paul talks of "awaiting the hope of righteousness", that can hardly be different from the hope of future acquittal, of being accounted righteous at the final judgment.[48] The logic here cannot be escaped by arguing that reference to the gospel in Rom 2:16 changes the picture of 2:13, or that the "but now" of Rom 3:21 signals a change in the terms of judgment, so that it will no longer be "in terms of works". For we have already noted that Paul paints the same picture of final judgment on work, on actions

---

[47] The charge should not be laid at Sanders' door since he emphasized the importance of "staying in" in his definitions of "covenantal nomism": "the covenant requires as the proper response of man his obedience to its commandments . . ."; "obedience maintains one position in the covenant . . ."; "righteousness in Judaism is a term which implies the maintenance of status among the group of the elect" (*Paul and Palestinian Judaism*, 75, 420, 544).

My own treatment in *Theology of Paul* may have encouraged such an inference, since I treated "justification by faith" solely in terms of the beginning of the process of salvation (ch. 14), and the issue of final justification "according to works" was likely to be lost sight of in ch. 18.

[48] The future tenses of δικαιόω should not be ignored here—Rom 2:13 (note the context, 2:5–13, 15–16); 3:20, 30; God's role as justifier, ὁ δικαιῶν (Rom 3:26; 4:5; 8:33) will be most fully demonstrated in final judgment (3:4–6; 8:33); salvation likewise is not fully achieved until the end (5:9–10; 11:26; 13:11; Phil 1:19; 2:12; 1 Thess 5:8–9).

done in the body, for believers too (1 Cor 3:13–15; 2 Cor 5:10). The extent to which Paul has simply taken over and integrated into his own theology the traditional Jewish understanding of final judgment as "according to works" cannot be escaped and should not be ignored.[49]

The upshot is further confirmation that in denying that justification is ἔξ ἔργων νόμου, Paul cannot have intended to discourage his readers from doing "good works", since he certainly also believed that judgment would have reference to just such "good (deeds/works)" done during life (Rom 2:7, 10; 2 Cor 5:10). What then was being denied in Gal 2:16? The answer seems to have two parts.

1) The first obviously lies in the antithesis between faith and works of the law. Paul asserts that faith alone is necessary. Any attempt to require more than faith is unacceptable to Paul, denies "the truth of the gospel". That, however, as we have now seen, does not mean that believers are not expected to produce any "works". It must simply mean that the works to be tested in the final judgment are works which are themselves the expression of that faith, works, if you like, ἐκ πίστεως,[50] or as Paul himself puts it, "faith working through love" (Gal 5:6). It is the failure of Peter to appreciate that faith remains the single constant, while "works" as the expression of that faith are variable and cannot be narrowly prescribed, which Paul condemns. Alternatively, we might say, Paul insists that the grace which first established the covenant with Israel remains the single determinant of membership of the covenant (Rom 11:6), even though he expects that grace to fructify in the fruit of good character and relationships (Gal 5:22–23).

---

[49] F. Avemarie, *Tora und Leben: Untersuchungen zur Heilsbedeutung der Tora in der frühen rabbinischen Literatur* (WUNT; Tübingen: Mohr/Siebeck, 1996), also "Erwählung und Vergeltung: Zur optionalen Struktur rabbinischen Soteriologie", *NTS* 45 (1999) 108–26, stresses this aspect in describing the "structure of rabbinic soteriology", as a correction or qualification of Sanders' "covenantal nomism". But it is also necessary to note how similar is the "structure of Pauline soteriology" at this point. I have developed the point in "Jesus the Judge: Further Thoughts of Paul's Christology and Soteriology", (forthcoming in FS G. O'Collins, 2000). Cf. P. Stuhlmacher, *Der Brief an die Römer* (NTD 6; Göttingen: Vandenhoeck & Ruprecht, 1989): "Die Paulusbriefe bieten keinen Anlaß, diese Vorstellungswelt als 'vorchristlich' oder 'bloß jüdisch' abzutun. Der Apostel hat sie nicht als Widerspruch zu seiner Rechtfertigungsverkündigung empfunden, vielmehr sein Evangelium in eben diesem Erwartungshorizont entfaltet" (44).

[50] It will readily be recognized that I have in mind the old Protestant tag that "works are the fruit, not the root of faith".

2) The second part of the answer lies in the recognition, once again, that "the works of the law" must be rather more circumscribed than is usually assumed. There are "works of the law" which provide no basis for justification, and "works" by reference to which final judgment shall be reached. Paul cannot have the same "works" in view in both cases. What is so wrong about "the works of the law" of Gal 2:16? Evidently that they have proved antithetical to the openness of faith, to the claim that a Gentile's faith alone is sufficient ground for full acceptance, not least at the meal table, by believing Jews. Once again, then, we are driven by the logic of Paul's wider thought to the conclusion that by "works of the law" Paul had in mind that obedience to the precepts of the law which was deemed still necessary for believing Jews, particularly at the point where it meant treating believing Gentiles as outside the community of salvation.

If he has persevered thus far I can well imagine Heikki giving a wry smile at this point (if not well before). There are surely more important issues for biblical scholarship and theology than to pursue such finer exegetical points at such length. My only defence is that the issue "not from works of the law" was evidently important for Paul. And since Paul has been such a creative force in Christian theology, it is well worth while persevering in an attempt to ensure that nuances which were important for Paul when he first drew the phrase into his theology are not lost to sight. But such a defence simply invites a widening of our dialogue beyond what is appropriate here. Next time perhaps. *Ad multos annos*, Heikki.

PAUL AND BARNABAS: THE ANATOMY AND CHRONOLOGY OF A PARTING OF THE WAYS

Alexander J.M. Wedderburn

Both the Letter of Paul to the Galatians (2:11–14) and the Book of Acts (15:36–41) refer to a disagreement between Paul and Barnabas. In the former, although Barnabas is not the main protagonist, he is mentioned as siding with Peter and the other Jewish Christians in the church in Antioch-on-the-Orontes who are persuaded by "those from James" to withdraw from table-fellowship with the Gentile Christians in that church. He is, however, singled out from amongst all the other Jewish Christians there and mentioned by name; this may simply be because Paul has already mentioned him as also present as a delegate of the Antioch church at the meeting described in Gal 2:1–10. It would, however, have an added point if the Galatian churches to whom Paul writes are in fact those in the southern part of the Roman province of Galatia, which, according to Acts 13 and 14, Barnabas and Paul founded on the so-called first missionary journey.

This identification of the churches addressed has long enjoyed considerable support in English-speaking scholarship; until recently this theory has found little favour in the German-speaking world, which has preferred the so-called "North Galatian"-theory, but now certain voices have called this dominant consensus in question.[1] The strength of the case of these scholars lies, above all, in the difficulty of postulating a plausible route for the travels of the apostle which would take him from the southern part of the province northwards into that area which is postulated as an alternative, the heart-land of the territory of the ethnic Galatians around Ancyra.

[1] See Martin Hengel, "Der vorchristliche Paulus", in idem and Ulrich Heckel (eds.), *Paulus und das antike Judentum* (WUNT 58; Tübingen: Mohr-Siebeck, 1991) 177–293, here 201, and Hengel and Anna Maria Schwemer, *Paul between Damascus and Antioch: The Unknown Years* (London: SCM/Louisville: Westminster John Knox, 1997; German: WUNT 108; Tübingen: Mohr-Siebeck, 1998) 261, 302 (German 395, 453); Rainer Riesner, *Die Frühzeit des Apostels Paulus: Studien zur Chronologie, Missionsstrategie und Theologie* (WUNT 71; Tübingen: Mohr-Siebeck, 1994) esp. pp. 254–59; Cilliers Breytenbach, *Paul und Barnabas in der Provinz Galatien* (AGJU 38; Leiden etc.: Brill, 1996) esp. pp. 99–126, 172–73.

Breytenbach, for instance, regards a route via Pessinus and Germa as the only possibility within northern Galatia, but points out that only in the case of Ancyra is there evidence of pre-Constantinian Christianity in this area; further Acts 16:6–8 and 18:23, usually seen as evidence of Paul's work in northern Galatia, say nothing of missionary work there (147). Although one may not want to exclude the possibility of emissaries as responsible for the troubles in the Galatian churches (not only Jewish patterns of self-propagation are relevant here, but also Christian ones), Breytenbach, who sees Galatian Jewish Christians who remained loyal to the synagogues of the region as responsible for the troubles, is correct in supposing that such a situation, whoever provoked it, is more plausible in the area further to the south, where a far more considerable Jewish presence is attested. Yet one need not assume that it is also necessary to prove the existence of people of Celtic descent in the southern region in order to justify Paul's addressing them as Γαλάται (Gal 3:1). That there were also Celts in the the south may be assumed, but that the churches founded in this region contained only converts of Celtic extraction is most unlikely. In an area containing such a mixed population Riesner's question (255) is a legitimate one: "How could the apostle have addressed Lycaonians, Phrygians, Pisidians, those who spoke Greek and Roman colonists collectively if not by reference to the province to which they jointly belonged?"

Whether the account in Galatians 2 requires that we assume that Barnabas and Paul were still working together at the time of this dispute is an issue to which we must return; it would, of course, make Barnabas' taking sides against Paul a yet more grievous betrayal, but is that necessarily meant here? Paul's disagreement with Barnabas in this account is, at any rate, a most serious matter: effectively it threatened to split both the Antioch church and the Gentile mission in two: if "those from James" had their way, Gentile Christians, in Antioch and by implication elsewhere, would henceforth have to choose between two alternatives: either they must accept the demands which the Jewish Christians laid upon them which would enable them to have table-fellowship with the Jewish Christians without endangering the latter's status as Jews, or they would exist as a separate community, unable to enjoy full fellowship, including presumably eucharistic fellowship, with their Jewish Christian sisters and brothers. The latter alternative in turn raised the question of the status of the Gentile Christians: the people of God was either one and undivided and both groups could not then belong to it, or it was divided. And Paul never recounts that his arguments won the day; does that then mean that he failed to persuade his fellow Jewish Christians? In all probability it does, for to be able to tell of a victory here would have helped his cause with the Galatian churches immensely.[2]

At first sight the dispute of which Acts 15 tells seems trivial by comparison. It is already, however, foreshadowed in 13:13, where the author mentions that a certain John left Barnabas and Paul when they reached Perga in Pamphylia, and returned to Jerusalem. (In 12:12 and 25 he has already told us that this John was also named Mark; this is necessary, because two Johns have already been mentioned in this work, the Baptist and the son of Zebedee.) In ch. 15, when Paul proposes that they should revisit the churches founded in the journey described in the previous two chapters, Barnabas wishes to take John Mark with them.[3] Paul, however, demurs, holding him to be unsuitable because of his action during the previous journey. There is a sharp and bitter dispute (a παροξυσμός) and Barnabas and Paul split up, Barnabas going with John Mark to his

[2] So Ernst Haenchen, *Die Apostelgeschichte* (KEK 3; Göttingen: Vandenhoeck & Ruprecht, 7/16th ed. 1977) 459.

[3] Acts does not explain how he came to be available in Antioch, since in 13:13 he had returned to Jerusalem (cf. Haenchen, *Apg*, 456); there is a similar problem with regard to Silas if the same person is meant who had come down to Antioch from Jerusalem with Judas Barsabbas (15:22, 27, 32): seemingly he had returned to Jerusalem in 15:33 (this problem Gerd Lüdemann, *Das frühe Christentum nach den Traditionen der Apostelgeschichte: Ein Kommentar* [Göttingen: Vandenhoeck & Ruprecht, 1987] 175, following Alfons Weiser, *Die Apostelgeschichte* [2 vols.; ÖTK 5; Gütersloh: Mohn/Würzburg: Echter, 1981] 1.153, solves by postulating that v. 40 is traditional, the earlier reff. to Silas in this ch. redactional).

Nor does Acts mention that John Mark was related to Barnabas (Col 4:10). Quite what the relationship was is uncertain: "(first) cousin" is the only meaning of ἀνεψιός recognized by LSJ, but BA also give "Neffe". (Eduard Schweizer, *Der Brief an die Kolosser* [EKKNT; Zürich etc: Benziger/Neukirchen-Vluyn: Neukirchener Verlag, 1976] gives "Neffe" in his translation, "Vetter" in the comm.!) The Lat. *nepos* is, however, related and can mean "nephew" as well as "grandson". Whether Luke withholds the information lest Barnabas seem guilty of nepotism (Theodor Zahn, *Die Apostelgeschichte des Lucas* [KNT 5; 2 vols.; Leipzig: Deichert/Scholl, 3rd–4th ed. 1927] 556) is questionable.

Are we to infer from Philemon 24 that Paul and John Mark were later reconciled? Or from 1 Cor 9:6 that Paul and Barnabas patched things up? (Richard Bauckham, "Barnabas in Galatians", *JSNT* 2 [1979] 61–70, makes things even more complicated by completely identifying Gal 2:1–10 with the famine-relief visit to Jerusalem of Acts 11 and 12 and setting Gal 2:11–14 immediately after this: as a result relations between these two apostles have to patched up again by the time of Acts 15:1ff., only to break down yet again in 15:36–41.) Luke T. Johnson, for instance, argues on the basis of Col 4:10 and 1 Cor 9:6 that the rift between Paul and Barnabas (and his cousin) was not a permanent one: *The Acts of the Apostles*

home-territory of Cyprus (4:36), which had already been their initial destination on their previous journey (13:4–12), and Paul taking Silas with him as he sets out through Syria and Cilicia towards Derbe and Lystra.[4] The quarrel may have been a sharp one, but what is at issue seems to be far more a clash of personalities rather than the fundamental issues affecting the very nature of the Christian church which were at stake in the dispute at Antioch. How are these two quarrels related to one another?

I

To this question a great variety of answers have been proposed by exegetes and no consensus has emerged in recent years:

1. Luke knew of the account in Galatians 2, but the serious doctrinal disagreement reflected in that account did not accord with his picture of a harmonious early Christianity, united on the basis of the teaching of the apostles; instead he substituted the less damaging picture of a clash of personalities. The two quarrels are therefore in the last analysis one and the same. But this explanation has found less favour in modern scholarship.[5] And yet if the meeting described in Acts 15:1–29 is identified more or less with that of Gal 2:1–10 then there is a natural tendency to identify their respective

(Sacra Pagina 5; Collegeville: Liturgical, 1992) 283. That 1 Cor 9:6 is evidence of such a reconciliation is denied by Hengel and Schwemer (*Paul*, 210, German 321): in the later Galatians (2:13) Paul's resentment still surfaces in the text. In Col it is Barnabas' relative Mark who is with Paul and in 1 Cor it is enough that the Corinthians know of Barnabas (just as they know of Peter, to whom some of them are in Paul's eyes over-attached: 1:12). Johnson is, at any rate, not prepared to go as far as postulating a complete reconciliation: these passages give "no hint of a particularly close working relationship between Paul and Barnabas, or an estrangement". Haenchen questions, however, whether this is the same Mark (and Marcus was indeed a common name): *Apg*, 456 n. 2 (cf. Hans Conzelmann, *Die Apostelgeschichte* [HNT 7; Tübingen: Mohr, 2nd ed. 1972] 96). If he were the same, it would seem unlikelier that he had been involved in opposition to Paul's law-free mission as Pesch suggests (see below).

[4] In other words travelling overland by way of the pass through the Taurus Mountains known as the Cilician Gates.

It is to be noted that in this way the two parties, at least initially, revisit two parts of the areas covered by the journey of Acts 13–14; the difference between the two parties is, of course, that Paul and Silas, having revisited their part of the area of the previous journey, launch out on a far more ambitious journey.

[5] Haenchen, *Apg*, 459: so Franz Overbeck in the 4th ed. of Wilhelm M.L. de Wette, *Kurze Erklärung der Apostelgeschichte* (Leipzig: Hirsel, 1870) 216; Alfred Loisy,

sequels as well. Yet that becomes less cogent as soon as one is prepared to argue that (a) the contents of Acts 15:1–29 reflect two different meetings, at one of which Paul was present, but not at the other, and (b) that the meeting at which Paul was present did not take place at this point chronologically, but rather earlier.

2. Luke did not know of the quarrel recorded in Galatians 2, but found an account of a personal quarrel in his sources, an account which was, however, in fact an alternative version of the Galatians quarrel. So Conzelmann, for instance, holds that Gal 2:11–14 lies behind Acts 15:39, but Luke did not know of that account. It is the traditions which he used which have transmuted a doctrinal quarrel into a personal one.[6] Jervell, too, maintains that Luke did not know of the quarrel recorded in Galatians 2 and probably did not know either that Barnabas had taken sides against Paul on that occasion, and most likely believed that the quarrel between the two missionaries took this form.[7]

3. Luke simply inferred from the change in Paul's travelling companions, reflected in the sources at his disposal, that something must have happened to occasion this change. The quarrel in Acts is then largely Luke's own composition in order to explain this situation. Although Haenchen favours this solution,[8] it has rightly been objected that other less discreditable explanations could have been found if

Les Actes des Apôtres (Paris: Nourry, 1920) 607–18. This position is most clearly represented in the newer commentaries by Weiser (*Apg*, 394–95; cf. 397): this episode is yet another example of Luke's tendency to tone down basic theological conflicts in earliest Christianity; Luke knew of the Antioch quarrel as the real reason for Paul's break with Barnabas, but chose to tell the story otherwise. Josef Zmijewski also seems to incline in this direction, although he asks whether John Mark was named in the traditions at Luke's disposal as responsible for the breach in Antioch and hesitates to say whether or not Luke was responsible for this different tradition (cf. position 2 below) (*Die Apostelgeschichte* [RNT; Regensburg: Pustet, 1994] 581–82).

[6] Conzelmann, *Apg*, 96.

[7] Jacob Jervell, *Die Apostelgeschichte* (KEK 3; Göttingen: Vandenhoeck & Ruprecht, 17th ed. 1998) 410. Cf. here Walter Schmithals, *Die Apostelgeschichte des Lukas* (ZBK 3.2; Zürich: TVZ, 1982) 144–45: the conflict is the same as in Gal 2:11–14; yet Schmithals finds it difficult to decide whether Luke himself has defused this account or whether he did not know of Gal 2:11–14 (cf. also Bernd Kollmann, *Joseph Barnabas: Leben und Wirkungsgeschichte* [SBS 175; Stuttgart: Kath. Bibelwerk, 1998] 56). Gerhard Schneider, too, regards the connection between a quarrel and John Mark as traditional, but sees 15:37–40 as "recalling" the Antioch conflict of Galatians 2 (*Die Apostelgeschichte* [2 vols.; HTK 5; Freiburg, etc.: Herder, 1980] 2.195).

[8] Haenchen, *Apg*, 460.

Luke had had a fully free hand; for a bitter quarrel is scarcely in keeping with that unanimity which he repeatedly depicts in the life of the early church (Acts 1:14; 2:46; 4:24; 5:12, etc.).[9] Therefore others rightly argue that this is a cogent argument for treating this episode as basically coming from Luke's sources.[10]

4. There was one quarrel between Paul and Barnabas, but it had two sides to it, a doctrinal and a personal, and Paul depicted the one, Acts the other. So Roloff views the quarrel over John Mark as only one part of a theological controversy, but regards it as uncertain whether Luke was deliberately playing the theological issues down or was genuinely unaware of this dimension of the problem; he regards the latter as more likely.[11] Here one should also mention the hypothesis of Pesch, who regards it as conceivable that behind John Mark's desertion of Barnabas and Paul in Pamphylia lies a mistrust of the law-free gospel that this pair was preaching;[12] John Mark had accordingly played his part in provoking the quarrel in Antioch described in Galatians 2, in that it was his (critical) report on the situation in Antioch to the Jerusalem church that provoked James' sending of emissaries.[13] In his commentary, however, Pesch rather complicates the situation by his argument that the incident in Acts is rightly placed, since 15:5–12a and 13–33 describe the solution of the Antioch quarrel by means of the Apostolic Decree.[14] But

---

[9] Cf. Charles K. Barrett, *A Critical and Exegetical Commentary on the Acts of the Apostles* 2 (ICC; Edinburgh: Clark, 1998) 756–57: "There is no reason to think that the story about Mark is totally untrue, for there is no reason why it should have been invented. Luke could have remained silent about the trouble described in Galatians 2, simply saying that, after a period of shared ministry (v. 36), Barnabas accompanied by Mark decided to go to Cyprus, and Paul, accompanied by Silas, to go to Syria and Cilicia."

[10] So, e.g., Schmithals, *Apg*, 143.

[11] Jürgen Roloff, *Die Apostelgeschichte* (NTD 5; Göttingen: Vandenhoeck & Ruprecht, 1981) 236–37.

[12] Cf. also Roloff, *Apg*, 236. Contrast, e.g., Frederick F. Bruce, *New Testament History* (1969; Garden City NY: Doubleday, 1972) 273: John Mark's turning back was due merely to his having had enough of the rigours of missionary journeyings.

[13] Rudolf Pesch, *Die Apostelgeschichte* (2 vols.; EKKNT 5; Zürich etc.: Benziger/ Neukirchen-Vluyn: Neukirchener Verlag, 1986) 2.93; Barrett, who remains largely agnostic about the question of the relation of the two quarrels, grants that Pesch may be right here: *Acts*, 756.

[14] Pesch, *Apg*, 2.91; cf. also the shorter account in his "Das Jerusalemer Abkommen und die Lösung des Antiochenischen Konflikts: Ein Versuch über Gal 2, Apg 10,1–11, 18, Apg 11,27–30; 12,5 und Apg 15,1–41", in P.G. Müller, W. Stenger

if 15:36–41 is the quarrel or part of it, then should it not *precede* the solution described in the earlier part of the chapter? In other words, it would be more appropriate if the Decree had played a part in provoking the quarrel of Gal 2:11–14, as some have indeed suggested.[15] On the whole, however, the Decree is more plausibly interpreted as a response to the sort of problems which surfaced in Antioch rather than their cause, even if it was neither so widely recognized nor so widely applied as the Acts account might suggest; its distribution was perhaps as limited as the address of the letter in Acts 15:23 in fact implies and its purpose may above all have been to eliminate various aspects of the "pollutions of idols" (cf. 15:20).[16]

5. There were two different quarrels.[17] Naturally the one may have had a bearing on the other: so Marshall asks tentatively whether the memory of the dispute of Gal 2:11–14 still lingered on and made Paul uncertain of Barnabas' attitude in the tricky situation in the Galatian churches.[18] And on the face of it there indeed seems to be little in common between the two incidents apart from their location in Antioch and the involvement of both Paul and Barnabas, as the following section will substantiate.

II

The two quarrels may seem to occur at precisely the same point in the narratives of Acts and Galatians, that is in each case immediately or almost immediately (Acts 15:36, "after some days"), or in

(eds.), *Kontinuität und Einheit* (FS F. Mußner; Freiburg etc.: Herder, 1981) 105–22, esp. p. 120.

[15] Cf., e.g., David R. Catchpole, "Paul, James and the Apostolic Decree", *NTS* 23 (1976/7) 428–44. But Andreas Wechsler (*Geschichtsbild und Apostelstreit: Eine forschungsgeschichtliche und exegetische Studie über den antiochenischen Zwischenfall (Gal 2,11–14)* [BZNW 62; Berlin/New York: de Gruyter, 1991] 171–78) rightly points to an illustrious predecessor in the person of Albrecht Ritschl in the 2nd ed. of his *Die Entstehung der altkatholischen Kirche: Eine kirchen- und dogmengeschichtliche Monographie* (Bonn: Marcus, 1850, 2nd ed. 1857) 145.

[16] Cf. further my "The 'Apostolic Decree': Tradition and Redaction", *NovT* 35 (1993) 362–89.

[17] So Frederick F. Bruce, *The Acts of the Apostles* (London: Tyndale, 1951, 2nd ed. 1952) 306; Hengel and Schwemer, *Paul*, 216 (German 330).

[18] I. Howard Marshall, *Acts* (TNTC; Leicester: IVP, 1980) 257; that presupposes that Gal 2:11–14 occurred *before* Acts 15:36–41 and that the situation in the Galatian churches was already "tricky"; both assumptions are questionable.

the case of Galatians some time after,[19] meetings in Jerusalem which apparently handled such similar themes that it is difficult to deny the connection between the two accounts.[20] And yet it is clear that the content of the two accounts is very different:

1. Different persons are involved: Barnabas may be present on both occasions, but in Galatians he is only caught up in a quarrel which is primarily between Paul on the one hand and Peter together with the delegates of James on the other. In Acts, on the other hand, there is no hint that Peter was present then in Antioch and Paul's quarrel is directly with Barnabas. There is no hint that Peter was there, let alone the emissaries from James.

2. Even more serious is the difference in the content of the quarrels and the issues at stake on each occasion: despite the attempts to read the issues of the one into the background of the other, these explanations undeniably read something into the text which appears nowhere on its surface. The Acts account describes a quarrel which involves John Mark's suitability for the coming journey, and the possibility that his unsuitability (in Paul's eyes) lies in his opposition to the missionary policy of Paul and Barnabas is not the only one; other, less theologically significant aspects of their missionary journeys could have put him off. If this reason for his desertion lay behind the quarrel, then it would seem that Barnabas was won over and now shared his misgivings; that would mean that, had Barnabas and John Mark taken part in the following journey, they would have required the preaching of the gospel to be on different terms to those

[19] Assuming that Gal 2:1–10 and 11–14 are mentioned in their correct chronological sequence. That they are may be defended by the argument that only after the question of the legitimacy of the gospel offered to Gentiles by the Antioch church had been settled could the question of the relationship between Gentile and Jewish Christians arise: if Gentiles needed instead to become Jews at the same time as becoming Christians, then Jewish Christians' table-fellowship with them would be no problem. But see Gerd Lüdemann, *Paulus, der Heidenapostel*, vol. 1: *Studien zur Chronologie* (FRLANT 123; Göttingen: Vandenhoeck & Ruprecht, 1980) esp. pp. 101–5.

[20] And yet the issue which is common to both accounts, i.e. whether Gentile Christians need to be circumcised and keep the Jewish law, which is clearly the issue in Galatians and exemplified in the person of Titus (Gal 2:3), is the apparent trigger for the meeting in Acts (15:1, 5, 10), but then is lost from sight. Perhaps it is implicit that the Apostolic Decree (15:20, 29) solves the question by saying that only its 4 prohibitions are required of Gentile Christians, but it is no more than implicit (and the whole matter of the recognition of the validity of the mission of the Antioch church and of Paul is also unmentioned).

which Barnabas and Paul had hitherto preached. And in turn that would presumably have necessitated a correction of their previous message as they revisited the churches founded during the journey of Acts 13 and 14 (15:36). To presuppose all that involves reading a great deal between the lines of Acts 15:36–41.

In Gal 2:11–14 nothing is said about John Mark or about the terms of the Christian message which is to be preached by evangelists, although such a dimension to the dispute would be more directly relevant to the situation in the Galatian churches than the question of table-fellowship in the Antioch church. It is a matter of the relations between Jewish Christians and Gentile Christians at Antioch and whether the former can continue to eat with the latter without endangering their Jewish status and also, to put it mildly, the tolerability of their conduct in the eyes of non-Christian Jews. Pressure is put on the Jewish Christians and they yield to the demands of the emissaries from James, with the exception of Paul; nothing is said about anything being demanded of Gentile Christians and to that extent the terms of the agreement reached in 2:1–10 are presumably not violated—at least in the eyes of the other Jewish Christians, although Paul saw it very differently. And the implications of the course taken by the Jewish Christians for the Gentile Christians in Antioch show that much was indeed at stake, as I have already mentioned: either the latter must fulfil whatever conditions the Jewish Christians stipulate or there are two separate Antioch churches that are no longer in communion with one another.

Barnabas, however, sides with the other Jewish Christians and against Paul. Here we have to ask how he may have reconciled this behaviour with the Christian gospel which he has until very recently been preaching along with Paul, according to the usual reconstructions of the course of events. Was this indeed a very sudden volte-face? Did it only strike him for the first time that the missionary policy which he had been pursuing until now was objectionable in the eyes of his fellow Jewish Christians? (That is hardly intelligible if John Mark had in fact parted from him and from Paul for that very reason in Pamphylia.) Or is his conduct more easily intelligible if he had already quite some time before parted company with Paul and had distanced himself from Paul's missionary policy? In other words important questions of the relative chronology of these various events arise at this point and we must turn to this aspect of the problem in the next section.

In short the elements in common between the two accounts of the quarrels are very limited: both incidents involved Paul and Barnabas and both are placed after an account of a meeting in Jerusalem; these two meetings have much, but, as already indicated, by no means all in common. Efforts to merge these two quarrels into one have only a limited success and raise as many questions as they solve. Yet it must be stressed that, even if one regards the quarrels as separate ones, that by no means solves the (perhaps insoluble) question whether or not Luke knew that there was another quarrel. In other words this answer to the question of the relation of the two accounts still leaves it open that Luke knew of the other quarrel, but suppressed it as far too damaging for the picture of the early church which he wanted to paint. For having just shown Paul, James and Peter in splendid harmony over the way in which to deal with the troublemakers who had disturbed the Antioch church, he could hardly have relished a story, had he known it, which showed Paul's work being in essence rejected and undermined by the other two leading apostles and by his former travelling-companion.

III

If one accepts that there were two separate quarrels then that poses a chronological question, as I have already indicated, and that a twofold one: which quarrel came first? And how and when did they occur within the sequence of events during Paul's missionary travels?

When scholars offer an opinion as to the first question, which is rather infrequent, then, perhaps rather surprisingly, their preference is to set the quarrel of Galatians 2 before that of Acts 15.[21] That answer is perhaps intelligible if the second quarrel followed hard on the heels of the first, so that it was more or less a continuation of that one, but it is still surprising. Can one really imagine Paul proposing further missionary work with a partner who has just stabbed him in the back in this way?[22] And if Acts is wrong in attributing the

---

[21] Bruce, *Acts*, 306; Haenchen, *Apg*, 458 (mentioned as a possibility by Marshall, *Acts*, 257).

[22] The seriousness of Barnabas' conduct in Paul's eyes is hardly to be played down in the way in which it is in Bruce's commentary: "Barnabas played only a minor and temporary part, for which he is almost excused by Paul" (*Acts*, 306; but cf. Barrett, *Acts*, 756). Paul concentrates on Peter's role, but that is quite probably

proposal to Paul, is it likelier that Barnabas would suggest such a thing? And the unacceptability of the proposal, whoever made it, surely rested on more serious and fundamental considerations than the suitability of a travelling-companion.

However, if one takes seriously the likelihood that Paul's arguments did not carry the day and that, as a consequence, the Antioch church was either split into two camps or accepted the basis of a life together and of table-fellowship on the terms demanded by the emissaries from James, then the question is whether any further work in or with the Antioch church was possible for Paul, as well as whether he could still work with Barnabas.[23] Yet the quarrel of Acts 15 is set in Antioch. Is that incorrect, or does it not rather suggest that the chronological relation of the two quarrels is in fact the other way round, that of Acts 15 *before* that of Galatians 2?

For it seems to be an at least unspoken assumption of many accounts that at the time of Gal 2:11–14 Paul and Barnabas were still working together, whether in the Antioch church or in missionary activities at the behest of the Antioch church. The separate mention of Barnabas may, however, be otherwise explained, as I have already indicated at the start: he was an important person, perhaps particularly important for the Galatian churches,[24] and he had worked together with Paul so that his attitude at this juncture would be a particularly bitter blow. So what sort of picture emerges if we question this assumption and posit instead a different sequence: quarrel over John Mark—parting of the two missionaries and separate missions—quarrel over table-fellowship in the Antioch church?[25]

Matters of Pauline chronology are regrettably complex, but nevertheless form the backbone of any reconstruction of the history of

because Peter (and the Jerusalem church under James) featured more prominently in the arguments of the intruders in the Galatian churches than Barnabas ever did.

[23] As Haenchen rightly notes: *Apg*, 459.

[24] Is then Paul's implicit message to the Galatian churches at this point something like the following?—If even my fellow-missionary Barnabas backed down at this stage you can see how I alone have defended your interests and have stuck up for your rights as fully-fledged members of God's people. (For Bauckham, "Barnabas", Barnabas' part in founding the Galatian churches makes his desertion of Paul all the more embarrassing and damaging to Paul's arguments in the letter.)

[25] A corollary of this is, of course, that the letter to the Galatians cannot be dated very early, even if one thinks that its addressees were the churches founded in Acts 13–14.

the earliest church in general.[26] I propose to tackle the aspects which affect this question in three steps:

1. The setting of the quarrel of Acts 15:36–41 within Paul's journeys.
2. The setting of the quarrel of Gal 2:11–14 within Paul's journeys.
3. The setting of the meeting of Gal 2:1–10 and Acts 15:1–29 (in part) within Paul's journeys.

In this way I hope that the sequence of events and the relationship of the two quarrels to one another will become clearer and more intelligible.

1. *The setting of the quarrel of Acts 15:36–41 within Paul's journeys*

There is a wide measure of agreement that the author of Acts found in his sources an account of a journey of Paul with Barnabas through Cyprus and southern Asia Minor (as in Acts 13 and 14) and another in which Paul and a new travelling companion, Silas, set out through the area previously visited in southern Asia Minor on a journey which was to take them through Macedonia to Achaea (as in Acts 15:41–18:22). Unless the quarrel over John Mark has been invented just to explain the change of travelling companions, its logical setting would indeed be between these two journeys. But that raises one further question: during the journey of Acts 13 and 14 Barnabas and Paul are emissaries of the Antioch church (13:1–3). Did Paul's relation to the Antioch church change as a result of the quarrel with Barnabas? Acts' answer is a clear "No": Paul and Silas' journey is undertaken with the blessing of the Antioch church (15:40) and on completion of the journey Paul returns to Antioch in 18:22. Now that could simply be the result of Luke's tendentious efforts to depict a harmonious church in which the legitimacy of Paul's work was as widely as possible endorsed and supported. But it need not be and Paul's return to Antioch in 18:22 is mentioned very briefly, with no hint that a significant point is being made here. It is, therefore, possible that the Antioch church was indeed still behind Paul's work during his travels in Acts 15:41–18:22 and that their solution to the strife between the two missionaries was to endorse two separate mis-

[26] I offered an attempt at a chronology of Paul's ministry in "Some Recent Pauline Chronologies", *ExpTim* 92 (1981) 103–8; the present article contains some modifications of the scheme that I offered there.

sions (although Acts neglects to mention a separate endorsement of Barnabas' mission with John Mark; but Barnabas now, from this moment on, becomes an irrelevance from the point of view of the story of Acts).

2. *The setting of the quarrel of Gal 2:11–14 within Paul's journeys*

The dispute of Gal 2:11–14 is a far more serious one that affects the very basis of Paul's missionary work, the sort of gospel that he could preach, and the sort of churches which he could establish. It is hard to see how, after this quarrel, Paul could continue to work with the Antioch church, or at least with the Jewish Christian portion of it, or how this church could continue to endorse and commission him. For it is from this point on that it first becomes clear that there is another, official version of Christianity as opposed to Paul's version; hitherto Paul and his Jewish Christian colleagues have contrived to patch up their differences, whatever the tensions, but now that was no longer possible and the Antioch church has decided to back the line taken by the Jerusalem church and in opposition to Paul.

Yet according to Acts Paul continued to remain in contact with the Antioch church after his travels in 15:41–18:22 and it is only thereafter that this account is silent about any further contact between him and that church. Yet that silence is surely rather significant when the journey involved is Paul's last journey to Jerusalem, a journey on which, as we learn from his letters rather than from Acts, Paul was bringing with him the money collected from amongst his churches for the Jerusalem church. On this occasion he sails directly from Patara, past Cyprus, to Tyre (21:3). Now it may of course simply be that that was the route of the ship which happened to be available, and a more direct one at that, but the omission of Antioch may still be significant. (For a start it sets a question-mark against the view that the collection which Paul has now raised is a fulfilment of the agreement mentioned in Gal 2:10, to remember the poor of the Jerusalem church. That agreement was an agreement of the Antioch church with that of Jerusalem, even if Paul's oscillation between 1st person singular and 1st person plural throughout this passage rather obscures this fact. It seems, however, that the Antioch church has absolutely nothing to do with this project in the form in which Paul has now brought it to completion. Unnecessary detours may have been highly undesirable and have increased the risk of mishaps, such as either shipwreck or robbery; the route from Patara to Tyre via Antioch would have kept nearer the coast—and potential robbers?—but would, on the other hand, have offered more chance of a safe anchorage in the event of sudden storms.)

Yet the question must be raised: does the Acts account not then suggest that Paul's relations with the Antioch church remained intact until the end of the journey of 15:41–18:22 and that the breach occurred thereafter?[27] Now some experts in Pauline chronology have argued that this was the point of time at which the meeting of Gal 2:1–10 in fact took place,[28] and if the quarrel at Antioch was its sequel[29] then of course it in turn cannot be placed earlier. But is so late a date for the Jerusalem meeting likely?

3. *The setting of the meeting of Gal 2:1–10 and Acts 15:1–29 (in part) within Paul's journeys*

In the attempt to place the meeting of Gal 2:1–10 chronologically the information in Gal 1:21 that Paul was at this stage in the regions of Syria and Cilicia is highly significant, particularly if a major concern of Paul's in this argument is to show his independence and distance from the Jerusalem church. Does that mean, then, that during the period up to the meeting he was never further removed from Jerusalem than the provinces of Syria and Cilicia?[30] It is true that this has been denied, either because of a reluctance to admit the possibility of so long a period in Paul's life (2:1) about whose content we know so little, or because scholars are concerned to bring together chronologically the agreement of Gal 2:10 and the actual process of the gathering of the collection. Yet the latter argument is greatly weakened if the collection that is actually gathered in Paul's

---

[27] Breytenbach's question (*Paulus*, 173) whether it is significant that Paul is now accompanied, no longer by Silas from Antioch, but by Timothy and Titus from the southern Galatian region, is a suggestive one.

[28] So, e.g., John Knox, *Chapters in a Life of Paul* (New York: Abingdon-Cokesbury, 1950/London: Black, 1954) esp. 68; John C. Hurd, Art. "Chronology, Pauline", in *IDBSuppl.* (1979) 166–67; Robert Jewett, *Dating Paul's Life* (London: SCM, 1979 [= *A Chronology of Paul's Life* (1979)]) 5 *et passim* (see also the older exegetes as well as the chronologies of Hubaut and Légasse cited by Riesner, *Frühzeit*, 6, 25).

[29] Which Lüdemann denies (see above n. 19).

[30] Cf. Alfred Suhl, *Paulus und seine Briefe: Ein Beitrag zur paulinischen Chronologie* (SNT 11; Gütersloh: Mohn, 1975).

churches is not in fact the fulfilment of an agreement which was instead the concern of the Antioch church. That, of course, leaves open the question whether the latter may not have suggested the idea of the former to Paul. And the first argument based on the emptiness of these 14 years begs a great many questions about the nature of Paul's activities in the years after his conversion and about the nature and completeness of our sources of information. The argument based on Gal 1:21 would then be that Paul mentions Syria and Cilicia, but not Cyprus, Pamphylia or Lycaonia or any parts of the Roman province of Galatia, let alone Macedonia or Achaea, because the double province of Syria and Cilicia is the furthest away from Jerusalem that he has been during this period. And had he in fact been in the area of the Galatian churches at this time then, so far from arguing that he simply passes that over in silence as something the Galatians already know, is it not far likelier that he would explicitly appeal to this known fact to reinforce his argument?[31]

This argument has two corollaries:

1) the agreement reached in Gal 2:1–10 can then be seen as the basis upon which the Antioch church undertakes further missionary expansion and despatches Barnabas and Paul as recounted in Acts 13:1–3. That is in itself thoroughly plausible: the state of affairs in the Antioch church and the instructions that the Christians there have been giving to Gentile Christians have been challenged by Jewish Christians (Gal 2:4; Acts 15:1–2) and the meeting that is held subsequently endorses the validity of the Antioch church's mission to the Gentiles and its responsibility for this side of the mission of the whole church. Reassured by this and commissioned to take on a wider area of responsibility the Antioch church now decides to send out missionaries, and Barnabas and Paul set out, first for Cyprus which is Barnabas' home, and then for the nearby regions in southern Asia Minor lying to the west of Cilicia.

2) The point of time at which the meeting then took place coincides in the account of Acts with another Jerusalem visit, the visit mentioned in Acts 11:27–30 (12:25). In that case Gal 2:1–10 would correspond chronologically to this visit, even if the matters discussed

[31] And even Riesner, who wants to place the journey of Acts 13–14 before the council meeting, grants that to mention South Galatia would have helped make the apostle's point in Gal 1–2, namely his independence and separation from Jerusalem (*Frühzeit*, 254).

correspond rather to the issues raised in Acts 15:1–5 (if not to the subsequent discussions in that chapter). This chronology may be significant: in the first place we may then be best to translate the present subjunctive μνημονεύωμεν in Gal 2:10 as "continue to remember", if the Antioch church had already helped the poor in Jerusalem. But, secondly, we also need to ask whether the gift that had been brought in Acts 11:29 did not already have something of the same significance which Paul was later to give to his collection, namely as a financial inducement to persuade the Jerusalem church to recognize their partnership with the Antioch church. Was Agabus then not the only visitor from Jerusalem in those days (and Acts does speak of "prophets", 11:27) and was his warning of impending, perhaps already threatening famine not the only message brought from that church? Are we to date the activities of those mentioned in 15:1 also to this period and to see the relief that was sent as also a means of persuading the Jerusalem church to curb these unwelcome efforts of their emissaries? If that was their purpose then it succeeded very well—for a time. The authorities of the Jerusalem church endorsed the mission of the Antioch church and the Christian message which it proclaimed.

But only for a time. Partnership with a church of this nature would become more and more dangerous for the Jerusalem Christians at a time of rising nationalist feelings and pressure in Judaea[32] and the matter would be aggravated if the leading apostle, Peter, who had been recognized as responsible for evangelizing Jews, was found to be compromised by participating in the life and table-fellowship of the Antioch church. But the agreement may have worked for a time and we have to leave some time anyway for a change of opinion and second thoughts about the matter in the Jerusalem church. And if we separate Barnabas' split with Paul from the Antioch quarrel of Galatians 2 then the lapse of some time in this case may help to explain Barnabas' conduct on the latter occasion. For his readiness not only to desert Paul, but also in effect repudiate his own previous work as a missionary is the more easily intelligible if he had in fact for some time been pursuing his own course, perhaps one that increasingly differed from that of Paul on the question of the demands to be made of Gentile converts.

---

[32] Cf. Robert Jewett, "The Agitators and the Galatian Congregation", *NTS* 17 (1970/71) 198–212.

These various considerations suggest a sequence of events like the following:

1. Meeting in Jerusalem
2. Missionary travels in southern Asia Minor (Acts 13 and 14)
3. Quarrel of Acts 15:36–41
4. Paul's missionary travels of Acts 15:41–18:22
5. Antioch quarrel of Gal 2:11–14
6. Paul's missionary work independent of the Antioch church

This account then assumes that Paul returned from Achaea in 18:22 to be confronted with the situation which he describes in Gal 2:11–14.[33] That some considerable time had indeed by now passed since the Jerusalem agreement seems to me on the whole most probable. For one has to ask oneself how the Jerusalem church, which had seemingly endorsed the status quo in the Antioch church, should now appear to call what had been agreed into question. Second thoughts are always a possibility, but that they should arise is the more easily explicable if enough time had elapsed for a new situation, above all a new balance of power, to arise in the Jerusalem church—a new situation, for instance, in which Peter was no longer present (for he was now in Antioch) and the reins were in the hands of James the Righteous; if the situation had already begun to resemble that which Acts depicts on the occasion of Paul's last visit to Jerusalem, with its (probably exaggerated) reference to "many thousands" of Jewish Christians zealous for the Law (21:20), then it is intelligible that the Jerusalem church, even if it was not prepared simply to repudiate the earlier agreement, nevertheless wished to limit the damage and the danger to itself which stemmed from the outworking of the agreement. And the very least that it had to do was to ensure that Jewish Christians remained true Jews in the eyes of their fellow Jews, to show that they were, in short, not promoting apostasy from Judaism. But such a sea change is unlikely to have occurred overnight and is far more readily intelligible the longer the span of time between the agreement and the quarrel is.

Such a reconstruction has, of course, further implications, for instance for the dating of the letter to the Galatians and for the

[33] Hengel and Schwemer also express themselves in favour of dating the Antioch quarrel after the so-called second missionary journey (*Paul*, 159, 215 [German 247–48, 329]).

course of the organization of the collection. According to these proposals Galatians cannot be a particularly early letter of Paul's, for it self-evidently presupposes that the Antioch quarrel has already taken place.[34] In that case, however, it is the more surprising that no mention is made of the Galatians' participation in the collection or of the instructions given to them (as mentioned in 1 Cor 16:1). That difficulty one could solve by supposing either that the gathering of the collection had already taken place, which few would suppose,[35] or that it had not yet been set in motion. If Galatians is to be dated relatively early then this latter explanation poses no problems; if one sets it as late as is suggested here then rather more precision is required, for not too much time can elapse before Paul is in Ephesus and refers to his instructions to the Galatians in 1 Cor 16:1. That is still possible if one supposes the following sequence:

- Antioch quarrel of Gal 2:11–14.
- News reaches Paul of the intruders in the Galatian churches. (Does this sequence suggest that they may have been very directly part of the same movement as the emissaries whom James sent to the Antioch church? That is very possible, whether or not James himself was so directly responsible for sending them as well. This would still hold good if they took their cue from his intervention in the Antioch church.)
- The writing of Galatians.[36]
- Paul decides upon the collection as a means of bringing pressure upon the Jerusalem church to recognize his churches and his mission and thus to repair the severely damaged unity of the church.
- Paul travels through the southern Galatian provinces (Acts 18:23) and issues instructions about the collection,[37] before proceeding

[34] At least this seems to me self-evident, but Riesner, *Frühzeit*, e.g. 286, seems to regard it as possible that Galatians was written before the Council and he regards the quarrel in Antioch as a sequel to this (249); yet were this letter really so early, it is hard to see how Riesner could consistently confine himself to 1Thess in the account of the early theology of Paul with which this work concludes.

[35] Yet cf. now François Vouga, *An die Galater* (HNT 10; Tübingen: Mohr-Siebeck, 1998) 3–5: he sees the letter as the last of Paul's main letters and his principal piece of evidence is the fact that Paul does not commend the collection to them, because it is already past.

[36] Breytenbach, *Paulus*, 173, regards a dating of the letter immediately after the quarrel in Antioch as possible.

[37] The word which Acts 18:23 uses, ἐπιστηρίζων, would hardly be the most appropriate term in view of the tone of Paul's letter unless his reception in those

into the province of Asia. If the Apostolic Decree is to be seen as a response to the problems raised by the quarrel in Antioch, then its promulgation is presumably also to be dated to this period, perhaps as a regulation for the Antioch church and its immediate sphere of influence.

Such a sequence is, I believe, a credible one.[38] And these reflections on Pauline chronology, never the easiest of topics, have the value of forcing us to think concretely about the sequence of events which led eventually to Paul's finding himself bearing ultimately the sole responsibility for what he considered to be the only legitimate Gentile mission. In fact it was probably only now, after the quarrel at Antioch, and the rejection of his arguments by Peter and the other Jewish Christians there, that Paul came to see himself as *the* apostle to the Gentiles.[39] And that has, in turn, important implications for our understanding of what Paul understood immediately after his experience on the way to Damascus. Although Gal 1:16 may give the impression that Paul from this moment on understood himself to be at least *an* apostle to the Gentiles, even if not *the* apostle to them, it is likelier that Paul wrote thus with the advantage of the insights gained up to the point of time when Galatians was written. And by that time Peter, Barnabas and the Jewish Christians at Antioch, indeed perhaps the whole Antioch church, had failed, had not kept the truth of the gospel intact for others like the Galatian churches (cf. Gal 2:5), and Paul saw himself as the only apostle who had remained true to this vital insight and who offered this God-given gospel unsullied and without compromise or dilution to the Gentiles.

But chronology has not been the main purpose of this article, nor

churches, and therefore probably the impact of the letter too, were surprisingly positive; and yet the list of Acts 20:4, if it is, unacknowledged by the author, a list of the delegates accompanying Paul from the churches which had contributed to the collection, could indeed suggest, through the naming of Timothy, that the churches from this part of the Galatian province felt themselves able to back Paul in this venture.

[38] Up to this point I have concentrated on reconstructing a relative chronology; I incline to an absolute chronology along approximately the following lines: 45 or 46, council; 46/7, journey to southern Galatia; early 48, quarrel with Barnabas and Paul's departure on his journey to Macedonia and Achaea; 51/2, quarrel in Antioch and start of the last period of travels and the organizing of the collection.

[39] As opposed, that is, to *an* apostle whose task was to win Gentiles but also Jews as well, or *an* apostle who was jointly responsible with others (Barnabas/the Antioch church) for the Gentile mission.

even biography, either of Paul or of Barnabas. But these should be seen rather as a means by which one can better understand those concatenations of events and the actions of those who were involved in them. Paul's quarrel with Barnabas in Acts 15 may seem thoroughly trivial, but if the alienation involved in it prepared the way for Barnabas' later desertion of Paul at a most critical point in the latter's life and in the whole history of the earliest church, then it is in retrospect by no means so insignificant as it might at first seem. The reconstruction of the details of these developments means that the rise of new, theologically profound insights can be "rooted" in a concrete history. In much the same way Heikki Räisänen could most plausibly show that Paul's attitude to the Law could in large measure be traced back to, and thus "rooted" in, the concrete situation of a Paul who had once persecuted Stephen and his group for their attitude towards the Gentiles and, as a consequence, also towards the Law which should have regulated their relations with non-Jews: the former persecutor found himself all of a sudden on the same side as the persecuted and presumably sharing their convictions and their way of life.[40] I write this, therefore, in the hope that my Finnish colleague may recognize in this essay something that breathes the same spirit as his own trail-blazing studies and in its own small way follows in his tracks.

---

[40] Cf. Heikki Räisänen, *Paul and the Law* (WUNT 29; Tübingen: Mohr-Siebeck, 1983, 2nd ed. 1987) 251–63; what I have written above should also be seen as more directly endorsing his observation that "the Antiochian episode reveals . . . a great deal of how Paul's 'final' theology of the law took shape" (259).

RÖM 9–11—EINE AUSEINANDERSETZUNG DES PAULUS MIT ISRAEL UND MIT SICH SELBST: VERSUCH EINER PSYCHOLOGISCHEN AUSLEGUNG

Gerd Theißen

Paulus war kein systematischer Theologe. Sein Denken ist voll von Widersprüchen. Man wird ihm gerechter, wenn man sie nicht weginterpretiert, sondern historisch und psychologisch interpretiert. Das hat H. Räisänen in vielen Beiträgen gezeigt. Paulus ist in seiner Theologie damit beschäftigt, neue Erfahrung mit alten Traditionen zu legitimieren. Wer neuen Wein in alte Schläuche füllt, muss riskieren, dass die Schläuche reißen oder der neue Wein in ihnen verborgen bleibt.[1] Er läuft Gefahr, an der Unvereinbarkeit des Alten und Neuen zu scheitern. Die folgenden Ausführungen wollen zeigen: Bei Paulus scheitern Gedanken an den Widersprüchen seines Lebens. Seine widersprüchlichen Aussagen über Israel in Röm 9–11 sind Ausdruck seiner Ambivalenz sich selbst gegenüber: Er hat durch seine Wende vom Christenverfolger zum Christenmissionar einen tiefen Bruch erfahren. Und sie sind zugleich Ausdruck seiner Ambivalenz gegenüber Israel: Er schwankt vor seiner Jerusalemreise zwischen Todesfurcht und Heilserwartung. Paulus setzt sich mit sich selbst und mit Israel auseinander. Beides ist unlösbar miteinander verbunden. Röm 9–11, ein vermeintlich spekulativer Teil des Römerbriefs,[2] ist einer seiner persönlichsten Texte, der mit hoher Ich-Beteiligung[3] geschrieben ist.

---

[1] H. Räisänen hat das besonders an Röm 9–11 gezeigt: "Paulus will in Römer 9–11 gleichzeitig zwei unterschiedliche Soteriologien vertreten: Einmal die christozentrische Anschauung, die alles auf Gottes neues Handeln setzt; das andere Mal die klassische Bundestheologie, die auf Gottes erbarmendem Handeln an den Vätern basiert und Gottes bleibende Treue gegen das Volk Israel, die Nachkommen der Väter, betont. Einmal muß man sich bekehren, um in eine neue Gemeinschaft durch einen neuen Initiationsritus eingegliedert zu werden; das andere Mal soll man als Jude der Gemeinschaft treu bleiben, in die man geboren wurde. Das erstere ist die normale Sicht des Paulus. Wo er sich, wie in Röm 11, auf das letztere einläßt, muß er eine neuartige Ekklesiologie gleichsam ad hoc entwerfen." H. Räisänen, "Römer 9–11: Analyse eines geistigen Ringens", *ANRW* II 25.4 (Berlin/New York: de Gruyter 1987) 2891–939, dort S. 2933f.

[2] R. Bultmann, *Theologie des Neuen Testaments* (8. Aufl.: Tübingen: Mohr 1980) 484: Das in Röm 11,25ff. dargestellte heilsgeschichtliche Geheimnis entspringe der "spekulierenden Phantasie".

[3] Ich-Beteiligung oder Ego-Involvement meint das Engagement, das eine Person

1. *Ich-Beteiligung: Die persönlichen Einleitungen in Röm 9–11*

Drei Mal leitet Paulus einen Gedankengang mit einer ganz persönlichen Bemerkung ein. Das "Ich", das dabei spricht, ist ein "Ich" im "biographischen" Sinn—anders als in Röm 7,7ff., wo es sich m.E. um ein typisches Ich handelt, das biographisch gefärbt, aber nicht autobiographisch gemeint ist. In Röm 9,1ff. ist es umgekehrt: Dies Ich ist zweifellos ein individuelles Ich, es spricht mit großem persönlichem Engagement, aber hinter ihm werden "Typen" aus dem Alten Testament sichtbar. Was Paulus von sich aussagt, ist nach Mustern und Vorbildern gestaltet, die er bewusst oder unbewusst aus seiner Tradition aufgegriffen hat.

a) *Paulus als geborener Israelit und die Privilegien Israels (Röm 9,1–5)*

In Röm 9,1ff. äußert er den irrealen Gebetswunsch, anstelle Israels den Fluch Gottes zu tragen: "Ich selber wünschte, verflucht (ἀνάθεμα) und von Christus getrennt zu sein für meine Brüder, die meine Stammverwandten sind nach dem Fleisch . . .". Paulus denkt als Modell vielleicht an Mose, der sein Leben als stellvertretende Sühne für den Abfall seines Volkes anbot (Ex 32,32), oder an Christus, der den Fluch (κατάρα) für alle (ὑπὲρ ἡμῶν) trug (Gal 3,13), den niemand mit 'Ανάθεμα 'Ιησοῦς verfluchen kann, der vom Geist getrieben ist (1 Kor 12,3). In jedem Falle äußert Paulus einen irrealen Wunsch. Sofern Paulus an Mose denkt, hat er eine unerfüllte Bitte vor Augen; denn Gott lehnte es ab, dass Mose für den Abfall Israels mit seinem Leben sühnt. Sofern er an Christus denkt, kann er nur eine unerfüllbare Bitte meinen; denn er kann unmöglich die Rolle des Erlösers übernehmen. Sein unerfüllbarer Wunsch beleuchtet indirekt, welch dunklen Schatten er über seinem Volk liegen sieht: Es steht unter einem Fluch, weil es "getrennt von Christus" ist. Paulus will diesen Fluch stellvertretend für (ὑπέρ) seine Brüder tragen. Dadurch wird seine dunkle Aussage erträglich. Aber es besteht kein Zweifel: Paulus selbst steht auf Seiten Christi. Er ist von seinem Volk getrennt, so wie dies Volk in seiner überwiegenden Mehrheit von Christus getrennt ist.

Dieser Schatten wird noch dunkler, wenn Paulus die Privilegien Israels mit seiner Unheilssituation kontrastiert. Er zählt sie in

bei einer Sache entwickelt. Der Begriff geht auf M. Sherif – H. Cantril, *The psychology of ego-involvement* (New York: Wiley 1947), zurück.

zwei korrespondierenden Reihen auf. Paulus will für seine Brüder eintreten:

	τῶν συγγενῶν μου		κατὰ σάρκα,		οἵτινές εἰσιν Ἰσραηλῖται	
ὧν	ἡ υἱοθεσία	καὶ	ἡ δόξα	καὶ	αἱ διαθῆκαι	καὶ
	ἡ νομοθεσία	καὶ	ἡ λατρφεία	καὶ	αἱ ἐπαγγελίαι,	
ὧν	οἱ πατέρες	καὶ				
ἐξ ὧν	ὁ Χριστὸς	τὸ	κατὰ σάρκα			

Die Verleihung von Sohnschaft und Gesetz entsprechen einander. Der Gleichklang von -θεσία unterstreicht das. Die Erscheinung der Herrlichkeit geschieht im Gottesdienst, beides wird durch die Endung auf -α lose verbunden. Die Bundesschlüsse sind Verheißungen: Der Bund mit Noah zielt auf die Wiederkehr von Sommer und Winter, der Bundesschluss mit Abraham auf Nachkommenschaft und Land, der Bund am Sinai verheißt Fluch und Segen, der Bund mit David den Messias. Umrahmt wird diese Aufzählung durch den Hinweis auf die Verwandten des Paulus κατὰ σάρκα und den Messias τὸ κατὰ σάρκα. Die Betonung der physischen Herkunft zeigt: Diese Privilegien verbinden Paulus und alle Israeliten aufgrund leiblicher Abstammung von denselben "Vätern". Was Paulus hier aufzählt, entspricht seinem Stolz als geborener Israelit—lange vor der Begegnung mit dem Christentum. Alle Aussagen über die Privilegien Israels sind daher auch Aussagen über Paulus selbst: Es sind seine Vorrechte.[4]

Das Bild von Israel ist in dieser Einleitung von tiefer Ambivalenz geprägt: Israel steht einerseits unter einem Fluch, andererseits unter dem Segen seiner Vorrechte. Dem korrespondiert ein Selbstbild des Paulus, das von tiefer Zerrissenheit geprägt ist: Auf der einen Seite erfüllt "große Traurigkeit und Schmerzen ohne Unterlass" sein Herz (9,2), auf der anderen preist er wegen Israels Privilegien den, "der da ist Gott über alles, gelobt sei er in Ewigkeit. Amen" (9,5).

Diesem Präludium, in dem Paulus und Israel "zerrissen" erscheinen, entspricht der Inhalt von Röm 9: Eine Spaltung geht durch Israel. Israel gehört sowohl zu den auserwählten "Gefäßen" als auch zu den "Gefäßen des Zorns" (9,22). Es wird repräsentiert von Jakob,

[4] Dieser Stolz des vorchristlichen Paulus bricht manchmal noch bei dem christlichen Missionar durch, etwa wenn er betont: "Wir sind von Geburt Juden und nicht Sünder aus den Heiden" (Gal 2,15), oder wenn er im Blick auf seine vorchristliche Zeit seine Vorzüge lobt (Phil 3,4–6).

den Gott liebt, und von Esau, den Gott hasst (9,13). Es erscheint in der Gestalt des Mose, dessen sich Gott erbarmt, und des Pharao, den Gott verhärtet (9,14ff.). Diese Spaltung in Israel basiert auf Erwählung durch Gott vor jedem menschlichen Handeln. Das entspricht in etwa der Einleitung. So wie Paulus von Geburt an die Privilegien Israels teilt, so ist Jakob von Geburt an geliebt und Esau gehasst. Nur dass die Erwählung nicht durch Geburt, sondern durch Gnadenwahl Gottes vor der Geburt geschah.[5] Durch sie gab es schon immer zwei Gruppen in Israel. Nicht alle Israeliten waren wirkliche Israeliten kraft Erwählung. Aber in der Gegenwart hat sich etwas verändert: Heiden wurden hinzuberufen. Sie gehören zum Volk Israel. Das bisherige Israel geriet in eine Katastrophe. Nur ein kleiner Rest wurde gerettet: die Judenchristen. Ohne diesen geretteten Rest wäre es Israel wie Sodom und Gomorra gegangen (9,29 = Jes 1,9). Erst von 9,30ff ab wird dies finstere Bild korrigiert: Israel hat sich aufrichtig um die Gerechtigkeit des Gesetzes bemüht, auch wenn es nicht zum Ziel gekommen ist.[6]

b) *Paulus als ungläubiger Eiferer und der Eifer Israels in Röm 10,1f.*

In 10,1f tritt an die Stelle eines irrealen Gebetswunsches (von 9,3) ein "reales" Gebet: "Brüder, meines Herzens Wunsch ist, und ich

[5] Wir finden in Röm 9,6ff. eine Steigerung der Unabhängigkeit des Heils und Unheils vom Menschen. Nacheinander wird es zurückgeführt auf Vorhersage, Vorherbestimmung und Schöpfung. Es ist (1.) abhängig von einer vorhergehenden innergeschichtlichen Verheißung (einem λόγος)—wie die Verheißung der Geburt Isaaks an Abraham und Sara (9,9), (2.) von einer vorgeburtlichen Prädestination von Menschen (von einer πρόθεσις)—wie bei Esau und Jakob (9,10–13), womit nicht gesagt ist, dass diese Prädestination vorgeschichtlich geschah; sie ist (3.) abhängig von der Formung des Menschen durch seinen Schöpfer im Töpfergleichnis (von einem ποιεῖν). Damit könnte an die creatio continua gedacht sein, die sich bei der Entstehung jedes Menschen fortsetzt. Auch die Kontrastierung von Mose und Pharao in Röm 9,14ff. könnte im Übrigen so verstanden werden: Gott erbarmt sich des Mose in grundlosem Erbarmen—genau zu der Zeit, in der er ihm begegnet (Ex 33,19 = Röm 9,15); und er verhärtet den Pharao genau zu der Zeit, als Mose ihm gegenübertritt (Ex 9,16 = Röm 9,17).

[6] Wichtig ist: Erst in der Gegenwart verschieben sich die Verhältnisse zwischen dem Verheißungs-Israel und dem Abstammungs-Israel dramatisch: Erst jetzt gehört nur noch ein kleiner Rest zu dem Israel, dem die Verheißung gilt. Denn erst jetzt antwortet Israel überwiegend mit Unglauben auf die Botschaft von Christus. Paulus könnte sich theoretisch durchaus vorstellen, dass in der vorhergehenden Geschichte eine sehr viel größere Menge zum Verheißungs-Israel gehörte. Zu Elias Zeiten waren es freilich auch nach ihm nur 7000 (Röm 11,4). Und Paulus weiß: Schon Jesaja klagte über den Unglauben, auf den seine Botschaft traf (10,17).

flehe auch zu Gott für sie, dass sie gerettet werden. Denn ich bezeuge ihnen, dass sie Eifer für Gott (ζῆλος θεοῦ) haben, aber ohne Einsicht (οὐ κατ᾽ ἐπίγνωσιν)." In diesem Gebet tritt Paulus als Entlastungszeuge für Israel ein:[7] Die Israeliten mögen auf dem falschen Wege sein und am "Stein des Anstoßes" durch Unglauben zu Fall gekommen sein (9,33), aber sie haben Eifer für Gott, wenn auch "blinden" Eifer ohne Einsicht.

Das Entlastungszeugnis des Paulus bezieht sich auf den vorhergehenden Abschnitt. Hier hat er das Verhalten Israels geschildert, für das er um Verständnis wirbt. Er unterschied in 9,30ff. zwei Wege zum Ziel des Gesetzes. Der erfolglose ist der Weg der "Werke", der erfolgreiche der des Glaubens. Heiden sind ans Ziel gelangt, weil sie Gerechtigkeit aus Glauben (ἐκ πίστεως) empfingen, ohne danach gesucht zu haben (9,30.32). Israel hat dagegen die vom Gesetz verheißene Gerechtigkeit (den νόμον δικαιοσύνης) nicht erreicht (9,31), weil es irrtümlich meinte, Werke könnten Gerechtigkeit schaffen (9,32). Abzulehnen sind nicht die Werke an sich, sondern die Meinung, man könne durch sie (ὡς ἐξ ἔργων) zum Ziel gelangen.[8] Neben diese subjektive Ursache tritt ein objektiver Grund für die Erfolglosigkeit Israels: Gott hat in Zion einen Stein des Anstoßes gesetzt, an dem Israel angestoßen ist (9,33 = Jes 28,16 + 8,14). Dieser Fels des Anstoßes (πέτρα σκανδάλου) ist Christus, der Gekreuzigte, der für Juden ein Ärgernis (σκάνδαλον) ist und eine Torheit für Griechen (1 Kor 1,18ff.).

Beide, der subjektive und der objektive Grund für das Versagen Israels, werden in der Fürsprache des Paulus 10,2ff erneut aufgegriffen und intensiviert—als würden durch die Begegnung Israels mit Christus schon vorher vorhandene Fehlhaltungen gesteigert: Die durch ὡς ἐξ ἔργων angedeutete subjektive Fehlhaltung kehrt als fehlende Einsicht wieder (vgl. οὐ κατ᾽ ἐπίγνωσιν und ἀγνοοῦντες γάρ in 10,2f.). Die "Werkgerechtigkeit" wird dabei gesteigert zum "Eifer für Gott" (ζῆλος θεοῦ), mit dem Israel seine "eigene Gerechtigkeit" aufrichten will (Röm 10,2). Der objektive Grund, Christus, wird aus einem Stein

[7] Im Hintergrund dürfte als Modell wieder Mose stehen. Dafür spricht, dass von Mose in 10,5ff. direkt die Rede ist.

[8] Das ὡς weist auf eine subjektive Meinung: "mit der Behauptung, dass", "unter dem Vorgeben, dass" bzw. "im Gedanken, dass" (Vgl. *BDR* § 425.3).

[9] In dem langen Streit um die Übersetzung von τέλος νόμου als "Ziel" oder "Ende" spricht m.E. ein kleines Plus für die Bedeutung "Endpunkt" (was sich von "Ziel" wenig unterscheidet)—mit einer gewissen Zweideutigkeit, da dieser Endpunkt

des Anstoßes und Ärgernisses zum "Endpunkt des Gesetzes" (10,4).[9] Die Übersetzung mit "Endpunkt" lässt eine gewisse Doppeldeutigkeit zu. Denn Christus ist ein Endpunkt des Gesetzes (τέλος νόμου) für "jeden Glaubenden", also sowohl für Juden wie für Heiden.[10] Er konnte aber auf keinen Fall für beide Gruppen in derselben Weise τέλος νόμου sein. Für Heiden konnte Christus nicht das "Ende" des Gesetzes sein. Denn Heiden hatten nie unter dem Mosegesetz gestanden und nicht nach ihm gesucht. Sie gelangen erst durch Christus zum Gesetz, das im Liebesgebot erfüllt ist (Gal 5,14; Röm 13,8–10). Juden aber erreichen mit Christus, was sie im Gesetz erreichen wollten. Paulus hatte erst soeben davon gesprochen, dass Israel den νόμον δικαιοσύνης angestrebt, aber nicht erreicht hatte: "Sie (d.h. Juden) gelangten nicht zum Gesetz" (9,31). Das Gesetz ist für Juden also Endpunkt ihres Laufes (= Ziel), aber mit Erreichen dieses Ziels ist das Strebens nach ihm mit Hilfe von Werken zu Ende. Entscheidet man sich für die Übersetzung mit "Endpunkt (= Ziel)", so kann man für Juden und Heiden eine ähnliche Bedeutung von τέλος annehmen. Paulus nutzt dabei eine gewisse Doppeldeutigkeit des Begriffs τέλος bewusst aus.

---

für Judenchristen nicht dasselbe bedeuten kann wie für Heidenchristen. Die wichtigsten Argumente für "Endpunkt" sind:

1. Syntagmatisch greift die Verbindung τέλος νόμου εἰς δικαιοσύνην die Verbindung νόμος δικαιοσύνης (von Röm 9,31) auf. In Übereinstimmung mit 9,30ff. könnte Paulus allenfalls von einem τέλος τῶν ἔργων νόμου (= Ende der Werke des Gesetzes) sprechen, nicht aber von einem "Ende des Gesetzes". Das Gesetz soll nach 9,31 ja gerade als Ziel erreicht werden.
2. Metaphorisch begegnet seit 9,30ff. das Bild vom Lauf, das schon in Röm 9,16 vorlag und in 11,11 noch einmal aufgegriffen wird. Zu ihm gehört, dass der Lauf ein "Ziel" hat, bei dem er endet, aber auch, dass ein "Stolperstein" als Hindernis vor dem Ziel auftauchen kann. Die Inkongruenz im Bild—Christus ist sowohl der Stolperstein auf dem Weg als auch das Ziel selbst—ist m.E. in paulinischen Bildern denkbar.
3. Im folgenden Schriftzitat aus Dtn 30,12 tritt Christus an die Stelle des Gesetzes, sofern die Worte des Mose: "Das Wort ist dir nahe in deinem Munde und in deinem Herzen" (Röm 11,8) vom Gesetz auf die Botschaft von Christus übertragen werden.
4. Die Aussage "Endpunkt" des Gesetzes (im Sinne eines Ziels) würde gut zu den positiven Gesetzesaussagen im Römerbrief passen (3,31; 7,12.14; 8,4 und 13,8.10), zumal in den nächstliegenden Textpassagen vorher und nachher (8,2–7; 13,8–10) positiv von einer Erfüllung des Gesetzes die Rede ist: vom πληρωθῆναι des Gesetzes durch den Geist (8,4; 13,8) und vom πλήρωμα νόμου (13,10).

[10] Vgl. die Wendung "einem jeden Glaubenden, dem Juden zuerst und dann dem Griechen" in der Themenangabe des Römerbriefs 1,16, die hier deutlich anklingt, so dass man beide Gruppen, Juden und Heiden, hier ergänzen muss—von denen ja seit 9,30ff. explizit geredet wurde. Ein "τέλος des Gesetzes" aber muss für diese beiden Gruppen etwas Verschiedenes bedeuten.

Der mit Paulus vertraute Leser kann in Röm 9,30–10,4 leicht einen persönlichen Hintergrund erkennen: Paulus selbst war einst ὡς ἐξ ἔργων unterwegs zum Ziel der Gesetzesgerechtigkeit gewesen. Paulus selbst hatte Anstoß genommen am "Stein des Anstoßes und am Fels des Ärgernisses". Er selbst war ein "Eiferer" für die väterlichen Überlieferungen (Gal 1,14) gewesen, der die Kirche κατὰ ζῆλος verfolgt hatte (Phil 3,6), um dann aufgrund der überwältigenden "Erkenntnis" (γνῶσις) Jesu Christi dies als Fehlweg zu erkennen. Paulus selbst hatte Christus als τέλος νόμου erfahren. Die Schilderung Israels in 9,30–10,4 ist eine Parallele zur Schilderung der Bekehrung des Paulus in Phil 3,6ff.: Die Pointe ist hier wie dort, dass falscher (aktiver) "Eifer", der sich im Streben nach "eigener Gerechtigkeit" äußerte, durch eine (passiv) von Gott empfangene Gerechtigkeit überwunden wird—hier wie dort durch die Erkenntnis Jesu Christi und den Glauben an ihn. Wegen dieser Parallelität zwischen seiner Biographie und dem kollektiven Verhalten Israels,[11] kann Paulus als glaubwürdiger Entlastungszeuge auftreten. Sein Zeugnis besteht in seiner ganzen Existenz.

Während Paulus in 9,1ff auf seine Zeit vor der Begegnung mit der christlichen Botschaft zurückgreift, hat Paulus in 9,30ff. die Folgen dieser Begegnung für ihn (und Israel) vor Augen. Erst in Konfrontation mit dem Fels des Ärgernisses wurde aus der Meinung, man könne "wie aus Werken" das Ziel der Gerechtigkeit erlangen, ein falscher "Eifer", der andere Menschen unter Druck setzt, um ihnen die eigene Heilsvorstellung aufzunötigen. Erst durch Konfrontation mit Christus wurde aus der Gerechtigkeit des Gesetzes eine "eigene Gerechtigkeit", die sich jener "Gerechtigkeit Gottes" widersetzt, die in Christus das Heil geschaffen hat. Zwischen 9,1ff. und 10,1ff. liegt somit eine "chronologische" Verschiebung beim Rückgriff auf das Leben des Paulus: In 9,1ff. identifiziert er sich mit Israel aufgrund von Geburt und Herkunft. In 10,1ff. (bzw. ab 9,30ff.) identifiziert er sich mit seinen Stammverwandten aufgrund ihres Unglaubens: Juden und Paulus sind dadurch verbunden, dass sie alle Anstoß und Ärgernis genommen und in falschem "Eifer" gehandelt haben.[12]

---

[11] U. Wilckens, *Der Brief an die Römer* (3 Bde; EKK 6; Neukirchen: Neukirchener 1978–82) 2.221, betont die Parallelität zwischen Röm 10,3 und Phil 3,9, hebt aber mit Recht einen Unterschied hervor: Phil 3 schildert eine subjektive Bekehrung aus menschlicher Perspektive, Röm 10 dagegen den objektiven Wandel einer "Heilsordnung".

[12] Was Paulus hier über das Judentum insgesamt sagt, ist natürlich eine Aussage über "sein" Judentum. Das Ideal des Eifers war im Judentum zwar weit verbreitet,

Auch in Röm 10 entspricht diesem Präludium der folgende Gedankengang: Paulus zeigt in seiner persönlichen Einleitung, wie Israel und Paulus auf die Botschaft reagieren, und er spricht im ganzen Kapitel 10 von dieser Botschaft. Sie ist in die ganze Welt ergangen, fand aber nicht überall Glauben. Sie wurde nicht verstanden. Wenn Israel ohne Einsicht (ἐπίγνωσις) in die Irre ging (10,2), so tat Gott doch alles, um diese Einsicht zu ermöglichen—vergeblich. Paulus resigniert: "Ich frage aber: Hat Israel nicht verstanden (οὐκ ἔγνω)? Als erster spricht Mose: 'Ich will euch eifersüchtig machen (παραζηλώσω) auf ein Nichtvolk, und über ein unverständiges Volk will ich euch zornig machen'" (10,19 = Dtn 32,21). Παραζηλοῦν greift hier auf ζῆλος in 10,2 zurück. Schon dort hatte Paulus seinen "Eifer" als aggressives Vorgehen gegen andere im Blick. Dieses Eifern setzt sich im Widerstand von Juden gegen Heidenchristen fort. Und wieder steht am Ende die Andeutung einer positiven Wende: Israel hat zwar die Botschaft abgelehnt, aber Gott streckt trotzdem seine Hände nach einem ungehorsamen und widerspenstigen Volk aus (10,21 = Jes 65,2). In dieser Anklage wird indirekt eine Hoffnung formuliert: Gott lässt sich durch die Ablehnung Israels nicht beirren, sich ihm weiterhin zuzuwenden.

c) *Paulus als erwählter Israelit und die bleibende Erwählung Israels (Röm 11,1ff.)*

Während sich Paulus in 9,1ff. und 10,1f. in Wünschen und Gebeten Israel näherte, besteht die persönliche Einleitung in 11,1f. in apodiktischen Feststellungen: Er, Paulus, ist ein Israelit. Und weil er nicht verstoßen ist, kann auch Israel nicht verstoßen sein! Jetzt identifiziert sich Paulus direkt mit Israel, und zwar als einer, der sich seines Heils gewiss ist. Und wieder wählt er—diesmal explizit—ein Modell, Elia, in dessen Licht er die Aussagen über seine Person formuliert. Zwischen Elia und Paulus gibt es drei Vergleichspunkte:[13]

---

aber es beherrschte nicht alle. Philo und Josephus vertreten es nicht. Was Paulus hier über das Judentum sagt, ist eine unzutreffende Generalisierung, aber keine völlige Verzerrung: Für einen Teil des Judentums ist es zutreffend, dass Juden "in der Meinung, durch Werke zum Ziel zu gelangen", das Gesetz praktizierten.

[13] W. Schmithals, *Der Römerbrief: Ein Kommentar* (Gütersloh: Mohn 1988) 388: "Ob neben den Typos 'Rest' in V.2b–5 auch eine Typologie Elia-Paulus tritt, wie viele Ausleger vermuten, erscheint unsicher. Zwar wird Paulus wie Elia von den eigenen Volksgenossen verfolgt, und er kämpft wie dieser auf scheinbar verlorenem Posten, aber Paulus führt solche Analogien nicht aus, und da Paulus selbst kein Judenmissionar

1) Elia ist in Todesgefahr. Er klagt in 1 Kg 19,10: "Deine Altäre haben sie zerstört und deine Propheten getötet mit dem Schwert." Paulus stellt die beiden Klagen um, so dass er mit der für seine Situation entscheidenden Klage einsetzt: "Deine Propheten haben sie getötet". Die Umstandsbestimmung "mit dem Schwert" lässt er weg, vielleicht weil eine Prophetentötung eher eine Steinigung war (vgl. Lk 13,34).[14] An zweiter Stelle nennt er die Zerstörung der Altäre (womit die Zerstörung christlicher Gemeinden und ihres Gottesdienstes gemeint sein könnte).[15] Auf jeden Fall denkt er an seine eigene Situation. Denn er fordert in Röm 15,30 die römische Gemeinde auf, für ihn zu beten, "damit ich errettet werde von den Ungläubigen in Judäa".[16] Paulus erlebt sich genauso bedroht wie Elia.
2) Elia ist allein übriggeblieben. Weil Paulus von vornherein Elia im Blick hat, beruft er sich nur auf seine eigene Person, um die These von der Verstoßung Israels zurückzuweisen (und nicht auf alle Judenchristen). Denn Elia glaubte, "allein" übriggeblieben zu sein: ὑπελείφθην μόνος schreibt Paulus in Röm 11,3 = 1 Kg 19,10

war, während Gott dem Elia 7000 Bekenner aus Israel zur Seite stellte, dürfte dem Apostel diese persönliche Typologie kaum vorschweben." Aber Paulus vergleicht sich mit Elia nicht in seiner Eigenschaft als Judenmissionar, sondern als Judenchrist. Den 7000 Bekennern des Elia entspricht der "Rest" aus Judenchristen (11,5), dem Eintreten des Elia gegen Israel das Zeugnis des Paulus für Israel (10,1f.), dem "Gottesspruch" an Elia das "Mysterion" des Paulus (11,25), der Verfolgung des Elia das "Eifersüchtigmachen", das in 10,19 noch eine negative Tönung hat: Es ist ein Aufreizen zum Zorn (παραζηλώσω und παροργιῶ stehen in Röm 10,19 = Dtn 32,21 LXX parallel).—Erwägenswert ist die Annahme, dass Elia schon für den vorchristlichen Eiferer Paulus ein Vorbild war (so K. Haacker, *Der Brief des Paulus an die Römer* [THK 6; Leipzig: Ev. Verlagsanstalt 1999] 222 Anm. 23). Relevant ist auf jeden Fall, dass Paulus in Röm 11,3 den Anfang der Klage Elias aus 3 Rg 19,10 nicht übernimmt: Ζηλῶν ἐζήλωκα τῷ κυρίῳ παντοκράτορι κτλ. Paulus versteht sich nicht mehr als ein Eiferer im Sinne des Elia. Nicht alle potentiellen Züge einer Eliatypologie werden ausgewertet. Der Abfall der Israeliten zu Baal hat im Verhalten der ungläubigen Juden keine direkte Parallele, es sei denn man führt ihre Verblendung auf den "Gott dieser Welt" zurück (vgl. 2 Kor 4,4). Baal wäre dann als Satan verstanden.

[14] Die Tötung christlicher Propheten ist in früher Zeit denkbar, wie das Schicksal des Stephanus zeigt.

[15] Vgl. das πορθεῖν, mit dem Paulus seine Verfolgungstätigkeit beschreibt (Gal 1,13) und mit der sie auch von den betroffenen Gemeinden beschrieben wird (Gal 1,23). Auch die Apg gebraucht dies starke Wort "zerstören" (Apg 9,21).

[16] Er benutzt in Röm 11,26 σώζεσθαι und in Röm 15,30 das Verb ῥύεσθαι. Das macht keinen Unterschied, wie der Übergang von σώζεσθαι (in der Formulierung des Paulus) zu ῥύεσθαι im alttestamentlichen Zitat von Jes 59,20 in Röm 11,26 zeigt. Vgl. auch Röm 7,24 mit 8,24.

(in der LXX 3 Rg 19,10 steht sogar ἐγώ μονώτατος). Wenn Paulus sich typologisch auf Elia beziehen will, muss er als Einzelner zum Gegenbeleg gegen die pauschale Verwerfungsthese werden![17] Wir werden sehen, dass es noch weitere Gründe für diese Zuspitzung der Argumentation auf Paulus allein gibt.

3) Elia empfängt aufgrund seines Gebetes eine Offenbarung: Wie Elia hat Paulus zu Gott gefleht und geklagt (vgl. 10,1f)—und wie Elia ist er durch eine Offenbarung getröstet worden. Elia empfing den Gottesspruch (χρηματισμός) über 7000 treue Gläubige. "Ich habe mir übriggelassen siebentausend Mann, die ihre Knie nicht gebeugt haben vor dem Baal" (11,4). Paulus wurde ein "Geheimnis" (μυστήριον) von der Rettung ganz Israels offenbart (11,25ff). Auch hier ist die persönliche Einleitung von Röm 11 ein Präludium für das ganze Kapitel.

Während in den bisherigen Kapiteln das biographische Ich des Paulus nach den persönlichen Einleitungen verschwindet, begegnet es in Röm 11 noch einmal. Paulus spricht in 11,13 als Heidenmissionar: "Euch Heiden aber sage ich: Weil ich Apostel der Heiden bin, preise ich mein Amt, ob ich vielleicht meine Stammverwandten zum Nacheifern reizen und einige von ihnen retten könnte".

Zusammenfassend sei festgestellt: Die persönlichen Einleitungen in Röm 9–11 folgen einer gewissen biographischen Ordnung: Wir hören nacheinander etwas von dem geborenen (9,1ff.) und dem ungläubigen "Saulus" (10,1ff.), dann von dem erwählten (11,1ff.) und missionierenden "Paulus" (11,13). Sein Verhältnis zu Israel stellt er verschieden dar: Er beginnt damit, dass er sich mit dem unter einem Fluch stehenden Israel solidarisiert (9,1ff.), und endet damit, dass er sich als Apostel um die Erlösung Israels müht (11,13ff.). Israel erscheint dabei einerseits als "Objekt" seines Wünschens und Bemühens, so dass zwischen Paulus und Israel deutlich unterschieden wird (9,3; 10,1f; 11,13). Andererseits erscheint Paulus als Teil Israels, da er ja selbst Israelit ist (11,1, vgl. 9,3), so dass alle seine Aussagen über Israel auch Aussagen über ihn selbst sind. Sie können entweder "selb-

[17] Wären die *vielen* Judenchristen neben ihm nicht ein besseres Argument gegen falsche Generalisierungen über das jüdische Volk als er, der nur *ein* Jude ist? Paulus hatte schon in 9,27ff. von den Judenchristen als Rest gesprochen, und dieser Rest war schon dort ein Argument für die Erfullung der Zusage Gottes an Israel. Die 7000 Getreuen des Elia sollen vielleicht für alle Judenchristen in der Gegenwart stehen.

streferenziell" verstanden werden, d.h. bezogen auf Paulus selbst, oder "fremdreferenziell", d.h. bezogen auf das Israel, mit dem sich Paulus auseinandersetzen muss. Das gilt nicht nur für die persönlichen Einleitungen. Paulus spricht ja auch sonst in Röm 9–11 von Israel. Meine These ist, dass viele dieser Aussagen fremd- oder selbstreferenziell verstanden werden können: Sie bringen etwas über die Einstellung des Paulus zu Israel und über ihn selbst (als einen Israeliten) zum Ausdruck. Wir gehen im Folgenden noch einmal Röm 9–11 durch, um die Aussagen über Israel zunächst fremdreferenziell als Aussagen des Paulus über sein Verhältnis zu Israel zu lesen.

2. *Paulus im Gegenüber zu Israel: Die Ambivalenz des Paulus gegenüber Israel und der Jerusalemreise*

Paulus spricht von Israel in den drei Kapiteln sehr verschieden: In Röm 9 entwickelt er ein düsteres Bild von der Spaltung Israels in Erwählte und Nicht-Erwählte, das im Katastrophenbild vom übriggebliebenen "Rest" ausläuft. Grund dieser Spaltung ist allein die irrationale Entscheidung *Gottes*. In Röm 10 wird Israel als Adressat der Misssionspredigt angesprochen und seine "eifersüchtige und zornige" Ablehnung der christlichen Botschaft als unverständlicher Ungehorsam angeklagt. Grund für die Ablehnung ist der Unglaube der *Menschen*. Röm 11 wendet die Aussagen der vorherigen Kapitel ins Positive. In 11,1ff. wird der Rest-Gedanke aus Röm 9 neu bewertet: Aus dem Überrest einer Katastrophe wird die Vorhut der Rettung von ganz Israel.[18] Ausgangspunkt ist, dass wenigstens *ein* Israelit gerettet ist: Paulus selbst. In Röm 11,11ff. wird der Eifersuchtsgedanke aus Röm 10 neu interpretiert. Aus der aggressiven Ablehnung wird eine nachahmende Konkurrenz von Juden und Christen auf dem Weg zum gleichen Ziel. Jetzt sind es schon "*einige*", die gerettet werden. In Röm 11,25ff. entfaltet Paulus schließlich sein "Mysterion" von Israels Rettung: Jetzt werden *alle* gerettet. Im folgenden sei der Gedanke entfaltet, dass die Aussagen über Israel immer Aussagen über das Verhältnis des Paulus zu Israel sind—und zwar in einer Situation, in der er sich dazu motivieren muss, nach Jerusalem zu reisen, während er Todesangst vor seinen dortigen Gegnern hat.

[18] Zur Neubewertung des Restgedankens vgl. O. Hofius, "Das Evangelium und Israel: Erwägungen zu Römer 9–11", *ZTK* 83 (1986) 297–324, dort S. 304ff.

a) *Röm 9: Die Spaltung Israels und die Ambivalenz des Paulus gegenüber Israel*

In Röm 9,6ff. stellt Paulus eine tiefgreifende Spaltung in Israel heraus: Die Verheißungen an Israel sind gültig—aber sie galten von Anfang an nicht allen leiblichen Nachkommen Abrahams, sondern nur den "Kindern der Verheißung" wie Isaak, dessen Geburt durch eine Verheißung angekündigt wurde, oder Mose, dem Gott seine Barmherzigkeit offenbarte. Bei dieser "Spaltung" Israels fällt auf, dass Ismael,[19] Esau und Pharao Israel repräsentieren, obwohl sie eigentlich für fremde Völker wie Araber, Edomiter und Ägypter stehen. Paulus redet von seinem eigenen Volk, als sei es ein fremdes Volk.[20] Diese Spaltung Israels hat sich in der Gegenwart dramatisch zugespitzt: Fremde Völker, Heiden, wurden hinzuberufen, Nicht-Völker wurden zum Volk Gottes (9,24ff.). Vom alten Gottesvolk blieb nur ein "Rest" (9,27ff.). Das ist ein direkter Widerspruch zu Röm 11,25ff., wonach "ganz Israel" gerettet wird. Und doch legt Paulus schon in Röm 9 die Grundlage für diesen überraschenden Wechsel von der Verlorenheit Israels zur Rettung Israels, oder genauer: von der Rettung eines Restes zur Rettung von ganz Israel.

1. Die Unterscheidung zwischen Erwählten und Nicht-Erwählten gilt als völlig irrational. Es gibt keinen Grund für sie. Und dennoch wird ein Grund für die an sich grundlose Entscheidung Gottes indirekt erkennbar. Der erwählte und berufene Teil Israels war immer der schwächere: Isaak wurde von überalterten Eltern geboren, Jakob war der Jüngere, Mose vertrat gegenüber dem Pharao die versklavten Israeliten. Mit dieser Vorzugswahl der Schwächeren aber ist eine Verheißung verbunden: Sobald (das ungläubige) Israel in die Rolle des Geringeren und Schwächeren eintritt, könnte es eine erneute Chance haben. Eben dies behauptet Paulus in 11,11ff.: Das ungläubige Israel ist gegenüber den Heidenchristen ins Hintertreffen geraten.
2. Die Prädestination bestimmt über Heil und Unheil des Menschen unabhängig von seinem Glauben. In 9,12 wird zwar Rechtfertigungs-

[19] Isaak wird im Text nicht explizit genannt, ist aber vorausgesetzt (vgl. Gal 4,21ff.).

[20] Schon im Galaterbrief identifizierte er Hagar mit dem ungläubigen Israel, Sara aber mit den Christen—einschließlich der Heidenchristen.

terminologie benutzt, um das zum Ausdruck zu bringen: Erwählung geschieht "nicht aus Verdienst der Werke, sondern durch die Gnade des Berufenden". Aber anders als in der Rechtfertigungslehre des Paulus sonst ist der Glaube nicht entscheidend. Gottes Entscheidung trifft Menschen schon vor der Geburt, ehe sie Gutes und Böses getan haben. Wenn Erwählung unabhängig vom Glauben ist—dann ist sie auch unabhängig vom Unglauben.[21] Wenn Gott konsequent souverän gedacht wird, kann er sich auch gegen den Unglauben und die Feindschaft von Menschen durchsetzen. In 11,25ff. hat dann Paulus tatsächlich eine Rettung Israels im Blick, die unabhängig vom Unglauben Israels ist.

3. Die Endgültigkeit der Einteilung in Erwählte und Nicht-Erwählte ist nicht so sicher, wie oft suggeriert wird. Esau ist gehasst, Jakob geliebt—und das grundlos vor ihrer Geburt (9,13). Aber aus von Gott nichtgeliebten Menschen können geliebte Menschen werden. Daher zitiert Paulus Hos 2,25: "Ich will nennen . . . meine Geliebte, die nicht meine Geliebte war." (Röm 9,25). Ist es ganz ausgeschlossen, dass auch Esau, der Nicht-Geliebte, zum "Geliebten" wird? Wenn das ungläubige Israel in die Rolle heidnischer Völker tritt, in die Rolle Ismaels, Esaus, des Pharao—sollten ihm dann nicht alle Verheißungen gelten, die für die "Heiden" gelten? Auch die Verheißung, dass die Heiden aus Ungeliebten zu Geliebten werden? In Röm 11 lässt Paulus in der Tat die Verheißungen für ganz Israel wieder aufleben, weil Israel de facto in die Rolle von Heiden getreten ist (vgl. 11,30–32).

Man kann zwar nicht sagen, dass Paulus seine überraschende Wende in seiner Einstellung zu Israel in Röm 9 logisch vorbereitet hätte. Im Gegenteil, von der Argumentation her läuft alles auf ein düsteres Ende zu. Aber auch in dieser düsteren Darstellung Israels ist so viel Ambivalenz enthalten, dass die Wende zum Heil "psychologisch" gut vorbereitet erscheint: Noch die kritischsten Aussagen über das nichterwählte Israel enthalten versteckt viel Positives, so dass die später durchbrechende Zuwendung zu Israel nicht ganz überraschend kommt—zumal, wenn man Röm 9 im Lichte der persönlichen Einleitung liest.

---

[21] H. Räisänen, "Römer 9–11", 2934, sieht hier mit Recht einen "dritten soteriologischen Ansatz neben dem erbarmenden Handeln an den Vätern . . . und dem eschatologischen Handeln in Christus: das Handeln aus lauter Allmacht durch völlig freie Verfügungen."

Dies düstere Bild von Israel aber ist von der persönlichen Situation des Paulus gefärbt. Wenn Israel in die Rolle der Feinde Israels eintritt—in die Rolle Ismaels, Esaus und des Pharao, so könnte das damit zusammenhängen, dass Paulus seine Reise nach Jerusalem so erlebt, als betrete er "Feindesland". Besonders erstaunlich ist die Darstellung des Pharao. Er ist der klassische Feind Israels. Paulus tritt ihm gegenüber in die Rolle des Mose, der sein Volk herausführen will. Er hat die Botschaft gehört: "Ich erbarme mich dessen, dessen ich mich erbarme" (Röm 9,15 = Ex 33,19). Und alle seine Gegner müssen letztlich wie Pharao dazu dienen, gegen ihren eigenen Willen die "Macht" Gottes zu zeigen und Gottes Namen auf der ganzen Erde bekannt zu machen. So wie Paulus ja auch Jerusalem nur als Zwischenstation für seine weltweite Mission betrachtet, um die Botschaft in der ganzen Welt bekannt zu machen. Natürlich darf man solche Aussagen nicht "eins für eins" auf die Situation des Paulus übertragen. Sie haben ihr durch Traditionen vorgegebenes Eigengewicht. Aber in einem Punkt sind sie eindeutig: Paulus macht sich mit ihnen Mut für seine Reise.

Ein Blick zurück auf die persönliche Einleitung und ihren Kontext lässt die Situation des Paulus noch deutlicher hervortreten. Paulus hatte das 8. Kapitel des Römerbriefs mit einem Lobpreis auf die Liebe Gottes abgeschlossen, der einen Peristasen- und einen Mächtekatalog umfasst: eine Aufzählung von Leiderfahrungen auf Erden (8,35f.) und von mythischen Mächten im Himmel (8,38f.). Schon hier waren dunkle Töne laut geworden: Christen werden wie Schlachtschafe getötet. Dennoch können Tod und Leben sie nicht von Gott trennen. Muss Paulus nicht schon hier die Todesgefahr vor Augen haben, der er sich durch seine Jerusalemreise aussetzt? Wenn er unmittelbar danach den Israelteil mit dem (irrealen) Wunsch beginnt, er möge stellvertretend für Israel verflucht sein—muss man darin nicht den Gedanken eines Menschen sehen, der bald eines der Schlachtschafe sein könnte und der wünschte, seinem möglichen Tod doch noch einen Sinn für Israel geben zu können? Aber motiviert sich Paulus nur durch Unterdrückung von Angst und Furcht für seine Reise? Muss er nicht auch positive Erwartungen haben? Vielleicht treten sie in Röm 10 deutlicher hervor!

b) *Röm 10: Das Evangelium als Motivation für die Zuwendung zu Israel*

Paulus setzt in Röm 10 noch einmal mit einer intensiven Zuwendung zum ungläubigen Israel ein. Aber auch hier finden wir eine tiefe Ambivalenz gegenüber Israel. Sie erscheint jetzt nicht mehr als Kontrast zwischen erwähltem und nicht-erwähltem Israel wie in Röm 9, sondern als Kontrast zwischen Gesetzes- und Glaubensgerechtigkeit. Er wird oft so gedeutet, als würde Moses auf der einen Seite, die Glaubensgerechtigkeit auf der anderen Seite stehen und beide sich verschiedener Medien bedienen: "Mose *schreibt* mit Bezug auf die Gerechtigkeit aus dem Gesetz: 'Der Mensch, der das tut, wird dadurch leben'" (10,5 = Lev 18,5). Die Glaubensgerechtigkeit *spricht* vom Aufstieg in den Himmel und Abstieg in die Hölle: von dem, was kein Mensch tun kann (10,6f. = Dtn 30,12).[22]

Aber meinen "Schreiben" und "Sprechen" wirklich den tötenden Buchstaben (des Gesetzes) und die viva vox (des Evangeliums)? Wohl kaum! Denn Paulus kann im selben Kapitel das Deuteronomium mit der Formel zitieren: "Mose spricht (λέγει)" (10,19 = Dtn 32,21). Mose wird also nicht auf die "Schrift" festgelegt. Paulus verbindet ferner Schreiben und Sprechen in der Zitationsformel: "Denn es spricht (λέγει) die Schrift (ἡ γραφή)" (Röm 10,11). Beides gehört in antiker Lesepraxis zusammen: Schriften wurden vorgelesen und "gesprochen".

Wenn man genau hinschaut, ist der Gegensatz nicht: "Mose und die Glaubensgerechtigkeit", sondern "Gesetzesgerechtigkeit und Glaubensgerechtigkeit". Erstere bezeugt Mose in Dtn 30,12,[23] letztere in Lev 18,5. Nichts weist darauf, Paulus habe die Worte der Glaubensgerechtigkeit nicht dem Mose zugeschrieben. Paulus bringt eine gute Botschaft mit den Worten des Mose: Sie ist für alle zugänglich, erfordert nichts Unmögliches, keinen Aufstieg zum Himmel und keinen Abstieg zur Hölle. Vielmehr ist seine Botschaft "nahe in deinem Munde und in deinem Herzen" (Röm 10,8 = Dtn 30,14)! Wenn selbst Mose diese Botschaft—das Wort, "das wir predigen" (10,8)—bezeugt, sollte sie dann nicht doch eine Chance in Israel haben? Ist Paulus mit dieser Botschaft wirklich unwillkommen in

[22] Der Mensch kann nur glauben, dass Gott eben das an Christus getan hat, was ein Mensch unmöglich tun kann.

[23] Mose ist auch der Schreiber von Dtn 30,12, schrieb er doch nach Dtn 31,9 das Gesetz auf, um es immer wieder vorlesen zu lassen.

Israel? Gilt nicht auch hier Jes 52,7: "Wie lieblich sind die Füße der Freudenboten, die Gutes verkündigen" (Röm 10,15). Paulus setzt hier den Singular (den Freudenboten aus Jes 52,7) in den Plural. Er hat viele christliche Missionare vor Augen, nicht nur sich selbst. Aber auch er darf sich auf seinem schwierigen Weg nach Jerusalem als "Freudenbote" verstehen!

Gerade weil Mose die allen leicht zugängliche Glaubensgerechtigkeit bezeugt und (Deutero-)Jesaja ihren positiven Charakter betont, wird der Unglauben Israels erst recht rätselhaft. Nicht alle wurden dem Evangelium gehorsam.[24] Paulus tröstet sich mit dem Gedanken, dass schon Jesaja mit seiner Botschaft keinen Glauben fand (10,16). Dem stehen andere Erfolge gegenüber: Die Verkündigung ist (durch Paulus selbst) in alle Lande gegangen (Röm 10,18 = Ps 18,5 LXX). Gott wurde unter denen offenbar, die ihn nicht suchten—und das rief in Israel aggressive Eifersucht und Zorn gegen die Heidenchristen hervor. Es besteht m.E. kein Zweifel: Paulus spricht hier von seiner Heidenmission und führt den Widerstand Israels gegen die Botschaft auf sie zurück.

c) *Die Rettung Israels und die Rettung des Paulus in Röm 11*

Wenn Paulus gedanklich um die Rettung von ganz Israel ringt, so ringt er um die Chancen für seine Rettung. Je größer seine Gewissheit wird, dass Gott mit Israel noch viel Positives vorhat—umso größer darf seine Zuversicht sein, dass auch er in Israel Positives erfahren wird.

Zunächst macht Paulus sich mit dem Beispiel des Elia Mut (11,2ff.). Auch wenn er isoliert in Israel (und unter seinen judenchristlichen Glaubensbrüdern) steht, so hat er viel mehr Verbündete, als er weiß. Die Verstockung der großen Mehrheit der Juden interpretiert er in eine vorübergehende Betäubung um. Paulus verändert entsprechend ein Zitat aus Dtn 29,3 LXX. Er las dort: "Und nicht gab ihnen der Herr, der Gott, ein Herz zu verstehen und Augen zu sehen und Ohren zu hören bis auf diesen Tag." Im Kontext ist vorausgesetzt: Heute gab Gott ihnen endlich Herz und Sinne, um seine Gebote

[24] "Nicht alle" ist eine Litotes, wenn man nur an Israel denkt. Es könnte sich aber auf alle Hörer des Evangeliums beziehen, auf Juden und Heiden (vgl. Röm 10,12), zumal auch in 10,18 die weltweite Mission vor Augen steht. Erst 10,19 und 21 wenden sich eindeutig nur an Israel!

zu verstehen. Paulus betont noch entschiedener den vorübergehenden Charakter dieses Unverständnisses, indem er das Herz, ein konstantes Organ, gegen einen vorübergehenden Zustand, den Geist der Betäubung (aus Jes 29,10), eintauscht: "Gott gab ihnen einen Geist der Betäubung..."

In 11,11ff. wendet er den Eifersuchtsgedanken ins Positive. Die Kritik an der Heidenmission schafft zwar viel Ärger—aber sie könnte auch zu einer Eifersucht werden, die zur Nachahmung reizt. Und dadurch könnte sie doch noch zur Rettung einiger Juden führen.

Mehr noch als abstrakte Gedanken können Bilder Gewissheit verbreiten. In Röm 9,19ff. hatte Paulus das Töpferbild beschworen, um die Souveränität Gottes zu demonstrieren, die einen Gefäße für den Gebrauch, die anderen zum Wegwerfen zu bereiten. Kein Gefäß kann seinen Schöpfer zur Rechenschaft ziehen. Dies Töpferbild wird in Röm 11 durch das Ölbaumgleichnis abgelöst.[25] Wichtig ist hier der Unterschied zum Töpfergleichnis: Gegenüber dem Ton tritt Gott als souveräner Schöpfer auf, gegenüber dem Ölbaum als Gärtner. Der Töpfer formt nach Belieben den Ton, der Gärtner pflegt seinen Ölbaum. Ein einmal weggeworfenes Töpfergut bleibt unbrauchbar. Nicht so ein abgebrochener Zweig. Er hält (innerhalb des von Paulus entfalteten Bildes) weiterhin seine natürliche Eignung für den Ölbaum und kann gegebenenfalls wieder eingepfropft werden.[26] Das aber heißt: Auch die im Unglauben in der Gegenwart vom Ölbaum getrennten Glieder bewahren ihre natürliche Zugehörigkeit zum Ölbaum. Israel hat einen character indelebilis. Im Laufe des Bildes wächst seine Gewissheit. Noch in 11,23 betont er: Gott *kann* die abgebrochenen Glieder wieder einsetzen. Schon im nächsten Satz geht er weiter: Sie *werden* wieder eingesetzt werden. Das kann zwar ein logisches Futur sein. Im Lichte des folgenden Kontextes wirkt es aber wie eine konkrete Ankündigung!

Diese konkrete Ankündigung finden wir im "Mysterium" in Röm 11,25ff.: Ganz Israel wird nach dem Eingehen der Heiden gerettet

---

[25] Im Grunde ist es ein Doppelgleichnis vom Teig und Ölbaum (Röm 11,16). Das Teigbildnis hat ein Proprium: Der Teig ist eine homogene Masse. Er ist als ganzer heilig, wenn die Erstlingsgabe geheiligt ist. Die Wurzel und die Zweige des Ölbaums sind dagegen verschiedenartig. Aber sie passen trotz ihrer Verschiedenartigkeit auch in der Trennung gut zueinander.

[26] Zum Ölbaumgleichnis einschließlich des realen Hintergrunds des Wiedereinpfropfens vgl. P. v. Gemünden, *Vegetationsmetaphorik im Neuen Testament und seiner Umwelt: Eine Bildfelduntersuchung* (NTOA 18; Freiburg, Schweiz: Universitätsverlag/ Göttingen: Vandenhoeck 1993) 275–94.

werden. Zunächst belegt Paulus durch ein alttestamentliches Mischzitat diese Gewissheit. Danach bringt er in eigener Formulierung eine Anwendung des "Mysteriums" wie des AT-Zitats, sachlich in Kategorien der Rechtfertigungstheologie, sprachlich mit Worten von Ungehorsam und Erbarmen. In ihr wird die Feindseligkeit der ungläubigen Israeliten zu einer Durchgangsphase. Sie dient dazu, alle im Ungehorsam zusammenzuschließen, damit sich Gott aller erbarmen kann. Schon immer war sie keine unbegrenzte Feindschaft. Denn die Israeliten waren immer zugleich "Feinde um des Evangeliums", aber "Geliebte Gottes" um der Väter willen (11,28).

Meine Deutung mag zunächst trivial klingen: Wenn Paulus wegen seiner vielen Feinde in Judäa Angst um sein Leben hat, dann schwindet die Angst, wenn deren Feindschaft nicht das letzte Wort bleibt. Wenn ganz Israel gerettet wird, hat auch Paulus eine Chance "vor den Ungehorsamen in Judäa" gerettet zu werden (Röm 15,31). Aber es geht nicht nur um solche Angstüberwindung. Wenn der Erlöser kommt, wird er nicht nur Angst, sondern Schuld überwinden. Und auch das können wir auf die Einstellung des Paulus zu Israel beziehen: Der zur Parusie kommende Christus, der Israel trotz seiner Feindschaft vergibt—das ist die religiöse Imagination eines Menschen, der nach Jerusalem reist und den Tod von denen befürchtet, denen am Ende vergeben wird! Das dürfen wir so verstehen: Auch Paulus wird am Ende denen verzeihen können, die sich seiner Heidenmission in den Weg gestellt haben und von denen er Schlimmes befürchtet.

Wir fassen unsere Überlegungen zu einer fremdreferenziellen Deutung von Israelaussagen zusammen. Die Aussagen über Israel sind durch die Ambivalenz des Paulus gegenüber Israel bestimmt: In Röm 9 stellt er die Spaltung Israels dar. Vor dem nicht-erwählten Teil hat er Furcht. Er stellt sie daher als die Feinde Israels dar. Der erwählte Rest aber ist verschwindend klein. In Röm 10 setzt er gegen diese Furcht eine positive Gegenmotivation: Seine Botschaft ist für die Juden eine willkommene Freudenbotschaft. Wenn sie abgelehnt wird, so hindert das Gott nicht daran, sich trotzdem Israel zuzuwenden. Eben das vollzieht Paulus nach: Wenn er nach Jerusalem reist, so ist seine Reise das Ausstrecken der Hand Gottes nach seinem Volk. Diese Botschaft ist nicht zum Misserfolg verurteilt. In Röm 11 zeigt Paulus: Die Verstockung der Israeliten ist nur eine vorübergehende Betäubung. So wie Elia sich schließlich trotz aller Gefahren durchsetzte, so wird es auch Paulus mit seiner Botschaft tun.

3. *Paulus als Teil Israels: Selbstreferenzielle Deutung der Israelaussagen*

Jede Reise in ein Land, in dem man eine wichtige Zeit gelebt hat,[27] ist eine Reise in die Vergangenheit und eine Begegnung mit sich selbst. Das gilt auch für Paulus. Er wird durch seine bevorstehende Reise nach Jerusalem mit seiner Vergangenheit als Jude konfrontiert. In Röm 11,1f. schließt er nach folgender Logik von sich auf Israel. Was für ihn gilt, kann für Israel nicht verneint werden. Gott hat sein Volk nicht verstoßen: "Denn auch ich bin ein Israelit, vom Samen Abrahams, aus dem Stamm Benjamin." Darf man die hier zutage tretende Identifizierung mit Israel schon in 9,6ff. voraussetzen, wenn er dort vom "Samen Abrahams" spricht? Theoretisch gilt zwar: Alle Aussagen über Israel schließen logisch Aussagen über Paulus ein—und sind psychologisch durch sein Leben gefärbt. Aber gilt es auch konkret? Noch einmal gehen wir Röm 9–11 darauf hin durch.

a) *Die Spaltung Israels—eine Spaltung auch im Leben des Paulus?*

In der Einleitung von Röm 9 äußert Paulus den irrealen Wunsch, an die Stelle des unerlösten Israels zu treten. Bleibt dieser Wunsch in Röm 9,6ff so "irreal" wie am Anfang? Oder bringt die Spaltung Israels in Erwählte und Nicht-Erwählte eine Spaltung im Leben des Paulus zum Ausdruck? Und muss man deshalb nicht alle Aussagen über Israel auch als Aussagen über Paulus lesen?

Paulus ist zweifellos "Same Abrahams". Er zählt sich zu den "Kindern der Verheißung" und nicht zu Ismael, dem Sohn ohne Verheißung. Man fragt sich natürlich: War er nicht einmal Ismael? In Gal 4,29 sagt er über Ismael und Isaak: Der, der nach dem Fleisch gezeugt war, verfolgte den, der nach dem Geist gezeugt war. Gehörte nicht Paulus selbst zu den Verfolgern? Verkörpert Ismael nicht etwas in seinem Leben? Aber in Röm 9,6ff. erwähnt Paulus

---

[27] Es ist umstritten, ob Paulus in Jerusalem selbst erzogen worden ist, wie die Apostelgeschichte behauptet, oder in der Diaspora. Zuletzt hat M. Hengel, "Der vorchristliche Paulus", in M. Hengel und U. Heckel, *Paulus und das antike Judentum* (WUNT 58; Tübingen: Mohr 1991) 177–294, dort S. 212ff., mit guten Argumenten für Jerusalem plädiert. Aber auch wenn Paulus erst später dorthin gekommen wäre, wäre er hier Petrus begegnet und hätte hier das Apostelkonzil erlebt—entscheidende Punkte in seinem vergangenen Leben. Er begegnet in jedem Falle seiner eigenen Vergangenheit.

ihn nicht einmal. Bewusst identifiziert sich Paulus nur mit Isaak.[28]

Auch beim zweiten Beispiel ist die Zuordnung eindeutig: Rebekka hat zwei Söhne, Typen des ungläubigen und gläubigen Israels. Den einen hat Gott geliebt, den andern gehasst. Musste Paulus nicht in Esau seine vorchristliche Zeit sehen? War nicht auch er, der Verfolger, "von Gott gehasst"? Und war er nicht als Christ von Gott geliebt? War er nacheinander Esau und Jakob? Wohl kaum! Denn Paulus führt die Unterscheidung der beiden Brüder auf eine vorgeburtliche Prädestination Gottes zurück. Bewusst zieht er eine scharfe Grenze zwischen Esau und Jakob, wie sie schärfer nicht sein könnte. Eine bewusste Identifikation liegt wieder nur mit Jakob vor.

Beim dritten Beispielpaar streift Paulus seine Biographie noch mehr. Wenn Gott zu Pharao sagt: "Eben dazu habe ich dich erweckt, damit ich an dir meine Macht (δύναμις) erweise (ἐνδείξωμαι) und damit mein Name (ὄνομα) auf der ganzen Erde verkündigt werde." (Ex 9,16 = Röm 9,17), so passt alles auf Paulus: Auch an ihm hatte Gott seine Macht erwiesen (vgl. δύναμις in 2 Kor 12,9). Auch durch ihn wurde sein Name verbreitet—dort, wo Christus noch nicht genannt worden war (ὠνομάσθη) (Röm 15,20). Auch ihn hatte Gott "verhärtet", als er die Christen unterdrückte wie Pharao einst Israel! Aber auf ihn passt auch, was Gott Mose sagt: "Wem ich gnädig bin, dem bin ich gnädig, und wessen ich mich erbarme, dessen erbarme ich mich." (Ex 33,19 = Röm 9,14). Denn auch Paulus ist ἠλεημένος ὑπὸ κυρίου (1 Kor 7,25).[29] Eine Identifikation des Paulus mit Pharao läge nahe. Bewusst aber wird sie nicht vollzogen, sondern eher abgewehrt!

Man darf schließlich fragen: Musste Paulus nicht schließlich an sich denken, wenn er die Gegenüberstellung der Gefäße des Zorns und des Erbarmens in einem Anakoluth abbricht: "Da aber Gott seinen Zorn erzeigen (ἐνδείξασθαι) und seine Macht (τὸ δυνατόν)[30] kundtun wollte, hat er mit großer Geduld ertragen die Gefäße des Zorns, die zum Verderben gefertigt wurden . . ." (9,22f.). Schweigt er über das Ende der Gefäße des Zorns, weil er damit sein eigenes Verderben aussagen würde? Beschränkt er sich deshalb auf die "positive" Aussage, dass Gott diese Gefäße ertragen hat? War er nicht

[28] Auch in Gal 4,29 rechnet sich Paulus, wie Gal 5,11 zeigt, eher zu den Verfolgten, als dass er sich mit seiner ehemaligen Verfolgertätigkeit identifiziert.

[29] Wenn er seine Berufung χάρις nennt, meint er sachlich dasselbe (vgl. Röm 1,5; 12,3; 15,15; 1 Kor 3,10; 15,10).

[30] Mit den Stichworten ἐνδείξασθαι und τὸ δυνατόν greift Paulus in 9,22 auf Röm 9,17 = Ex 9,16 zurück.

selbst so ein "Gefäß des Zorns"? Aber wieder muss man betonen: Es findet sich kein bewusster Hinweis auf die nahe liegende Identifikation des Paulus mit den Gefäßen des Zorns. Im Gegenteil: Wir finden eine schroffe Abgrenzung. Innerhalb der Logik des Töpfergleichnisses gibt es keinen Übergang von den Gefäßen des Zorns zu den Gefäßen des Erbarmens![31]

Erst am Ende des Kapitels (in 9,30–10,4), als er aus der Perspektive des erwählenden und verwerfenden Gottes zur Perspektive der handelnden und glaubenden Menschen übergeht, schildert Paulus den Weg Israels so, dass an der impliziten Identifikation des Paulus mit dem ungläubigen Israel kein Zweifel bestehen kann: Paulus hatte genauso wie Israel das Ziel der Gesetzesgerechtigkeit verfolgt—mit Hilfe seiner Werke. Er hatte Anstoß genommen an Christus—genauso wie Israel. Er hatte auf diesem Wege das "Gesetz nicht erreicht"—wie Israel. Er war ein Eiferer geworden—wie Israel. Er hatte seine eigene Gerechtigkeit zu bewahren versucht—eben das, was er Israel vorwirft. Während die Identifikation des Paulus mit dem ungläubigen Israel im ganzen Kapitel so "irreal" bleibt wie die in der persönlichen Einleitung beteuerte Solidarität mit Israel, wird sie am Ende des Kapitels real. Wie soll man diese Verbindung von nahe liegender Identifikation und schroffer Abgrenzung deuten?

Paulus kennt in Röm 9,6–29 nur den Dualismus zweier Gruppen—und trennt sie durch den souveränen Willen Gottes, der die einen erwählt und die anderen verhärtet. Paulus steht auf der Seite der Erwählten als Christ, mit seiner vorchristlichen Existenz dagegen auf der Seite der Verworfenen. Was in der persönlichen Einleitung als irreale Möglichkeit erscheint, dass Paulus wie seine ungläubigen Stammesgenossen verflucht und von Christus getrennt sei,—das erscheint ständig als Möglichkeit, die dann doch nicht realisiert wird! Das legt

[31] Oder deutet Paulus diese Identifikation in 9,24f an? Hier sagt er über die Gefäße des Erbarmens: "Als solche hat er uns auch berufen nicht allein aus Juden sondern auch aus Heiden, wie er denn auch durch Hosea spricht: 'Ich will das mein Volk nennen, das nicht mein Volk war, und meine Geliebte, die nicht meine Geliebte war.'" (Hos 2,25 = Röm 9,25). Meist bezieht man das Hoseazitat nur auf die Heiden. Nur sie wären dann das Nicht-Volk, das zum Volk Gottes wurde. Theoretisch aber könnte man es *auch* auf die Juden beziehen, dann wären Juden eingeschlossen, die Paulus zuvor mit Ismael, Esau und Mose wie heidnische Völker (wie Araber, Edomiter und Ägypter) angesprochen hatte. Der unerwählte Teil Israels war ihm ein fremdes Volk geworden! Auch dieser Teil Israels würde wieder aus einem Nicht-Volk zu einem Volk! Aber auch das ist noch kein sicherer Hinweis auf eine selbstreferenzielle Beziehung der Aussagen über Israel auf Paulus selbst!

den Gedanken nahe, im schroffen Erwählungsdualismus von Röm 9 eine Abwehr des Gedankens zu sehen, dass Paulus nicht nur auf der Seite des erwählten Israels steht—sondern auch auf der anderen Seite. Dieser Gedanke war zu bedrohlich, als dass Paulus ihn zulassen konnte. Er verdrängt ihn unter Aufbietung massiver theologischer Überzeugungen und geht dabei über alle seine bisherigen Aussagen über Israel hinaus: Israel ist nicht nur verblendet. Es liegt nicht nur in Reaktion auf das Evangelium eine Decke auf seinem Herzen (wie in 2 Kor 3,14f.). Es verhindert nicht nur eine satanische Macht seine Einsicht (2 Kor 4,4). Vielmehr hat der Schöpfer selbst von Anfang an endgültig die einen in Israel zum Heil, die andern zum Unheil bestimmt![32] Tiefer kann die Kluft zwischen dem erwählten und dem nicht-erwählten Israel nicht aufgerissen werden. Sie ist unüberbrückbar! Aber Paulus kommt in Röm 11 zu ganz anderen Ergebnissen. Wie ist das möglich?

b) *Das ablehnende Israel—und die Ablehnung des Evangeliums durch den vorchristlichen Paulus in Röm 10*

Es liegt nahe, den Schlüssel für die Wende vom Erwählungsdualismus in Röm 9 zum Heilsuniversalismus in 11 im 10. Kapitel des Römerbriefs zu suchen (oder genauer in 9,30–10,21). Hier werden die zwei entscheidenden neuen Größen eingeführt: Christus auf Seiten des objektiven Heils, der Glauben auf Seiten des menschlichen Subjekts. Beide beziehen sich aufeinander—als Glauben an Christus. Beide durchbrechen die Grenzen zwischen Erwählten und Nicht-Erwählten, zwischen Juden und Heiden.

Aus der Christologie begegnen in Röm 9,30–10,21 die beiden Grunddaten Kreuz und Auferstehung, das Kreuz in Form des Jesajazitats vom Stein des Anstoßes (9,33), die Auferstehung durch Zitat der urchristlichen Bekenntnisformel, dass "Gott ihn von den Toten auferweckt hat" (10,9).[33]

---

[32] H. Räisänen, "Römer 9–11", 2929, betont mit Recht: Die "Vorstellung einer, wie es scheint, endgültigen Verstockung, die Gott allein wegen seiner souveränen Macht heraufgeführt hat, ist . . . einmalig bei Paulus". Ebenso aber "übertrifft die positive Sicht von Israels *character indelebilis* und die Vorstellung von Israel als dem bleibenden Raum des Heils (der 'Ölbaum') bei weitem alles, was Paulus sonst positiv über Israel sagt." Sowohl im Negativen wie im Positiven kommt er in Röm 9 und 11 zu neuen Spitzenaussagen.

[33] Auffällig ist, dass wir in Röm 9–10 zwar einen Bezug auf Kreuz und Auferstehung finden, aber keinen Rückgriff auf die soteriologische Deutung des Todes für die

Das Kreuz ist als Stein des Anstoßes und Felsen des Ärgernisses τέλος νόμου für *jeden* Glaubenden (παντὶ τῷ πιστεύοντι)—und das heißt: für Juden *und* Heiden, wie aus der parallelen Formulierung in der Themenangabe des Römerbriefs hervorgeht: Das Evangelium ist "eine Kraft Gottes zur Rettung für *jeden* Glaubenden (παντὶ τῷ πιστεύοντι), Juden zuerst und Griechen" (1,16). Die Gerechtigkeit Gottes, der sich die ungläubigen Juden widersetzen, ist also von vornherein eine Gerechtigkeit "für alle Glaubenden. Denn es ist hier kein Unterschied" (3,22). Beim (impliziten) Leser des Römerbriefs wird das als Zentralaussage des Briefes schon vorausgesetzt. Er muss daher Röm 10, 1ff. so verstehen: Die eigene Gerechtigkeit Israels (10,3) steht nicht nur in Kontrast zu Gottes Gerechtigkeit, sondern auch zu den anderen Völkern, den "Sündern aus den Heiden" (Gal 2,15). Sie betont den Unterschied zu ihnen, während die Glaubensgerechtigkeit die Grenzen der Völker transzendiert.

Dasselbe gilt von der Auferstehung. Aufgrund der Auferstehung wird Jesus zum KYRIOS über alle. "Jeder, der an ihn glaubt, wird nicht zuschanden werden. Denn es ist hier kein Unterschied zwischen Juden und Griechen: er ist über alle derselbe KYRIOS" (10,11f.). Der Glaube an den Auferstandenen transzendiert die Grenzen zwischen den Völkern. Nach Röm 9,6f. aber sind das die Grenzen auch zwischen Erwählten und Nicht-Erwählten. Sogar das nicht-erwählte Israel trat dort in die Rolle des fremden Volkes, dargestellt als Ismael, Esau und Pharao.

Man könnte noch weiter gehen. In Röm 10,6–8 wird das Gesetz in Dtn 30,12–14 durch Christus ersetzt. Er ist so nahe, wie es das Gesetz ist. Christus muss nicht erst vom Himmel herab, aber auch nicht aus der Unterwelt heraufgeholt werden. Gott bringt ihn vom Himmel,[34] Gott hat ihn aus dem Totenreich auferweckt. Er ist nahe im Bekenntnis des Mundes und im Glauben des Herzens. Paulus hat gegenüber Dtn 30,12–14 alle Hinweise auf das Tun des Gesetzes gestrichen und verändert auch die Topologie des Geschehens: In Dtn 30,13 wird gesagt: Man muss das Gesetz nicht jenseits des

Sünden der Menschen. Die Sündenvergebung (gegenüber Israel) wird in Röm 11,26f. mit der Parusie verbunden, nicht mit dem Kreuz.

[34] Offen ist hier, ob Paulus eher an die Inkarnation denkt. Dafür spricht die Reihenfolge: Abstieg vom Himmel, Heraufholen aus der Unterwelt. Oder ob er an die Parusie vom Himmel denkt. Man könnte auch erwägen, ob er zeitgenössische Offenbarungsschriften im Auge hat, die durch Reisen in die Himmelswelt und die Unterwelt geheime Offenbarungen vermitteln (wie z.B. der Äthiopische Henoch).

"Meeres" holen.[35] Bei Paulus aber wird daraus die "Unterwelt" (ἄβυσσον). Himmel und Hölle werden kontrastiert. Und beide werden durchlässig. Das Christusgeschehen durchbricht die Grenze von Himmel und Hölle. Wenn aber der "Dualismus" von Himmel und Hölle durch Christus aufgehoben wird, wird dann nicht auch der Dualismus von "Gefäßen des Erbarmens" und "Gefäßen des Zorns" (Röm 9,22) überwunden?

Der Erwählungsdualismus in Röm 9 ist ein Dualismus remoto Christo. Der irreversible Dualismus von Erwählten und Nicht-Erwählten gilt nur unter der Voraussetzung, dass Christus nicht gekommen wäre. Mit seinem Kommen wird diese Grenze durchbrochen. Das, was Nicht-Volk war, wird nun zum Volk (Hos 2,25 = Röm 9,25). Himmel und Hölle werden durchlässig. Juden und Griechen (= Heiden) werden im Glauben an ihn als KYRIOS vereint.

Paulus identifiziert sich mit dieser Botschaft: Sie ist das Wort, "das *wir* predigen" (10,8). Eigentlich würde man jetzt den großen Durchbruch erwarten: Diese Botschaft ist allen zugänglich (10,6ff.), ist Freudenbotschaft und müsste willkommen und ersehnt sein (10,15). Aber durch die Reaktion auf diese Botschaft werden die Probleme noch einmal verschärft—nicht durch Gottes Erwählen und Verwerfen, sondern durch menschlichen Gehorsam und Ungehorsam: Nicht alle akzeptieren diese Botschaft, Israel lehnt sie mehrheitlich ab. Erst am Ende (ab V.19ff) spricht Paulus wieder explizit Israel an. Und wieder erkennt man in den Aussagen über das ungehorsame Israel Aussagen über Paulus selbst. Gott hat Israel "wütend" gemacht auf ein Nicht-Volk und gegen ein unverständiges Volk erzürnt (10,19 = Dtn 12,21). Trotzdem hat er seine Hände ausgestreckt nach einem ungehorsamen und widerspenstigen Volk (10,21 = Jes 65 65,2). All das passt

[35] Vgl. Dtn 30,13: "Es (= das Gebot) ist auch nicht jenseits des Meeres, dass du sagen müsstest: Wer will für uns über das Meer fahren und es uns holen, dass wir's hören und tun?" Dieselbe Topologie kehrt in Bar 3,30f wieder, wo Dtn 30,11–14 auf die Weisheit bezogen wird: "Wer ist übers Meer gefahren und hat sie gefunden und für kostbares Gold hergebracht? Es gibt niemand, der den Weg weiß, wo man die Weisheit findet, noch über den Pfad zu ihr nachdenkt." Der Gedanke der leichten Zugänglichkeit des Gesetzes ist hier umgeschlagen in das resignative Motiv der unauffindbaren Weisheit. Dieser Pessimismus ist nur möglich, weil Baruch (wie Paulus) alle Hinweise auf das Tun des Gebotes streicht. Optimistisch wird dagegen Dtn 30,11–14 bei Philo (*Praem* 80–82) ausgelegt: Das Gute ist nahe dem Mund, dem Herzen und den Händen. Das wird gedeutet auf Rede, Gedanken und Handlungen. Das Gute kann getan werden. Auch hier wird die Topologie von Dtn 30 beibehalten: Das Gute muss nicht jenseits des Meeres gesucht werden. Die Abwandlung des Meeres zur Unterwelt ist ein spezifisch paulinischer Zug.

zum Leben des vorchristlichen Paulus: Paulus war erzürnt über die Christen—und dennoch hat sich Gott ihm zugewandt. Dass sich auch Paulus hier mit betroffen weiß, geht rückwirkend aus 11,1ff. hervor.

c) *Paulus der Berufene als Modell für die Rettung Israels in Röm 11*

Wenn Paulus am Anfang von Kap. 11 emphatisch ausruft: Ich bin ein Israelit!, dann sagt er nach dem vorhergehenden Kontext: Auch ich war einer von jenem Volk, denen Gott trotz seines Ungehorsams und seiner Widerspenstigkeit seine Hände entgegen gestreckt hat. Jetzt verstehen wir, warum Paulus als Gegenbeleg zur These einer generellen Verwerfung Israels nicht auf die große Schar der Judenchristen verweist, sondern nur auf sich. Paulus war in der Tat einzigartig: Unter den Judenchristen hatte nur er sich vom Verfolger zum Missionar bekehrt. An seiner Person konnte er zeigen, dass Juden, die als ungehorsames und widerspenstiges Volk (10,21) die Botschaft abgelehnt hatten, nicht endgültig verstoßen sind. Eben darauf will er in Röm 11 hinaus.

Warum braucht er dazu die Elia-Typologie? Sie passt zunächst, wie wir oben gesehen haben, zu einem Einzelkämpfer gegen eine überwältigende Mehrheit. Die Berührung mit Elia ist aber noch enger: Elia ist ein Beispiel für "Eifer". Paulus signalisiert mit seiner Hilfe: Israel ist *trotz* (nicht *wegen*) seines "Eifers" angenommen! Denn mochte sich Paulus auch früher als ein Eiferer nach dem Modell des Elia und des Pinehas verstanden haben,[36] so tut er es jetzt nicht mehr. Sein ζῆλος gehört für ihn zu den Dingen, die er einst als Vorzug, jetzt aber als Schaden betrachtet (Phil 3,4ff.). Deswegen lässt er in der Klage des Elia in 3 Rg 19,10 LXX das Motiv des Eifers aus (ζηλῶν ἐζήλωκα κτλ.). Wir erhalten dann eine sinnvolle Reihenfolge in den persönlichen Einleitungen des Paulus in Kap. 10 und 11: In Röm 10,1f tritt Paulus (wie Mose) *für* das eifernde Israel ein und in 11,1ff. (wie Elia) *gegen* Israel—als ehemaliger Eiferer, der seinen Eifer jetzt konstruktiv einsetzt, um Israel zu gewinnen. Noch wichtiger aber ist das dritte Motiv, das konkretisiert, wie sich Paulus um Israel müht: durch Gebet. Gott antwortet auf das Gebet durch Offenbarung.

---

[36] Zum Eifer des Elia und des Pinehas als zeitgenössisches Leitbild im Judentum vgl. M. Hengel, *Die Zeloten: Untersuchungen zur jüdischen Freiheitsbewegung in der Zeit von Herodes I. bis 70 n. Chr.* (2. Aufl.; AGAJU 1; Leiden/Köln: Brill 1976) 154ff.

Das Gebet des Paulus in Röm 10,1f. wird implizit durch Dtn 30,11–14 beantwortet: Gott hat alles getan, um alle zu retten—und diese Rettung ist nahe und für alle zugänglich.[37] Das Gebet des Elia in Röm 11,3 wird sogar explizit durch einen Gottesspruch beantwortet: Gott hat einen Rest von 7000 Getreuen übriggelassen (1 Kg 19,18 = Röm 11,4). Dem χρηματισμός in 11,4 entspricht das μυστήριον in 11,25.[38] So wie Elia offenbart wurde, dass weit mehr als er allein Gott treu geblieben sind, so erhält Paulus die Offenbarung: Nicht nur ein Rest, sondern ganz Israel wird gerettet werden.

Trotzdem grenzt Paulus im folgenden Abschnitt die Erwählten im Volk noch einmal schroff von den "Übrigen" ab (Röm 11,7ff.). Die anderen sind verstockt. Das wird mit zwei Zitaten belegt, die durch das Stichwort "Nicht-Sehen" verbunden sind (vgl. τοῦ μὴ βλέπειν in Dtn 29,3 und Ps 68,23f. LXX). Aber Paulus verwandelt hier durch Einschub des Geistes der Betäubung (aus Jes 29,10) in das erste Zitat die Verstockung in eine vorübergehende Betäubung. Damit wird der Weg frei, Hoffnung für die Verstockten zu haben. Im Hintergrund dürfte seine persönliche Erfahrung stehen, dass ihm seine Blindheit und Verstockung vor Damaskus genommen wurde. Auch sie war nur eine vorübergehende Betäubung seines Geistes. Im zweiten Zitat wird Paulus aber noch einmal in vehementer Weise aggressiv: Während die Abgrenzung der beiden Gruppen in Israel bisher nur durch das Handeln Gottes geschah, bringt Paulus jetzt im Zitat (also nicht in Eigenformulierung) die Aufforderung Davids: "Ihren Rücken beuge allezeit!" (Ps 68,24 LXX = Röm 11,10b).[39] Soll das eine Aufforderung

[37] Im Hintergrund steht wohl eine Mosetypologie: Die Fürbitte des Mose in Ex 32, 30ff. wird in Ex 32,33f. durch Offenbarung Gottes beantwortet.

[38] U.B. Müller, *Prophetie und Predigt im Neuen Testament* (SNT 10; Gütersloh: Mohn 1975) 177f., vertritt die ansprechende These, dass das Mysterion in Röm 11,25f sachlich die Antwort Gottes auf das Gebet des Paulus in 10,1 darstellt, durch welche die ältere Prophetie von 1 Thess 2,14f. aufgehoben wurde. Diese Deutung ist unabhängig davon, ob Paulus diese neue Offenbarung vor oder während der Niederschrift von Röm 11 empfangen hatte (für eine Offenbarung während der Niederschrift von Röm 11 spricht sich aus: B. Noack, "Current and Backwater in the Epistle to the Romans", *ST* 19 [1965] 155–66, dort 165f). Auch in Röm 1,18ff. spricht Paulus manchmal so, als hätte er noch nicht die "Offenbarung" der Gerechtigkeit Gottes, wie er sie in Röm 3,21ff. schildert, vor Augen—und trotzdem besteht kein Zweifel, dass er die Gewissheit dieser Offenbarung schon vor der Niederschrift des Römerbriefs besaß. Er spricht in Röm 2,1ff. remoto Christo vom Gesetz nach den Werken, so wie er in Röm 9 remoto Christo von einer dualistischen Erwählung spricht.

[39] Auch wenn das ein AT-Zitat ist, so hätte Paulus doch diesen Satz nicht mehr aus Ps 68,24 LXX übernehmen müssen. Der Kontext erfordert nicht die Wiedergabe dieses Satzes.

sein, dass David, der Messias oder andere Völker das ungläubige Israel beherrschen und unterdrücken sollen? Ich wage folgende Deutung: Paulus hat soeben die Verstockungsaussage "aufgeweicht". Verstockung ist nur vorübergehende Verblendung. Wenn aber nicht mehr das souveräne göttliche Handeln zwischen Erwählten und Nicht-Erwählten die Grenze zieht (wie es in Röm 9 geschah), dann muss es der Mensch selbst tun. Paulus führt hier den unfreien Status der Juden auf ihre Ablehnung des Messias zurück, der für Israel Freiheit bringen sollte. Ähnlich argumentierte er Gal 4,21ff.: Israel ist unfrei, weil es nicht Kind der Sara ist—nämlich nicht den Glauben an Christus annahm, der wahre Abrahamskindschaft verleiht. Gleichzeitig aber fordert er sich selbst zur Unterdrückung und Verdrängung dessen auf, was auch in ihm blind und verstockt war. Noch einmal bricht sein Distanzierungswille gegenüber seiner eigenen Vorzeit durch.

Dieser aggressive Gedanke wird aber sofort zurückgewiesen: Israel ist zwar gestrauchelt, aber nicht gefallen (Röm 10,11). Das Heil ging zu den Heiden. Aber diese reizen nun Israel zur Nachahmung. Es kommt zu einer Konkurrenz von ungläubigen Juden und gläubigen Heiden auf dem Weg zum gleichen Ziel. Der Dualismus der Erwählten und Nicht-Erwählten wird überwunden. Beide sind nicht nur einander entgegengesetzt, sondern streben zum gleichen Ziel. Dabei erinnert die Schilderung des Wegs Israels als Verlust (ἥττημα) und Reichtum (πλοῦτος) an das Wortfeld, in dem Paulus auch seine Bekehrung geschildert hat, als Gewinn (κέρδη) und Schaden (ζημία) (Phil 3,7). An die Stelle der Verdrängung tritt die Konkurrenz. Aus dem aggressiven παραζηλοῦν (von Röm 10,19) wird das imitative παραζηλοῦν von 11,11. Aus dem verfehlten Eifer (dem ζῆλος) in 10,2 wird ein konstruktiver Wetteifer in 11,11ff. An die Stelle der Verwerfung Israels tritt seine Annahme (11,15). Selbstreferenziell auf Paulus bezogen, heißt das: Was Paulus bisher—auch in sich selbst—"verworfen" hat, kann er wieder annehmen und—auch in sich selbst—akzeptieren.

Wir hatten gesehen: In Röm 10 wird die Wende vom Erwählungsdualismus von Röm 9 zum Heilsuniversalismus von Röm 11 durch zwei Motive vorbereitet: durch den allen zugänglichen Glauben und durch die Christologie. Beide Motive begegnen noch einmal in Röm 11.

Das Ölbaumgleichnis entfaltet das Glaubensmotiv. Wie so oft bereiten Bilder und nicht abstrakte Gedanken die entscheidende Wende vor. Zwar sind Zweige entfernt worden. Aber sie haben aufgrund ihrer natürlichen Zugehörigkeit zum Ölbaum eine bleibende Verbundenheit mit ihm—auch in ihrer Trennung von ihm. Das, was einmal abgetrennt war, muss nicht entfernt und vernichtet werden (vgl. dagegen Joh 15, 6), im Gegenteil: Es soll durch den Gärtner gepflegt werden, und der kann es wieder einsetzen. Ohne Bild gesprochen geht es hier um die ungläubigen Juden im Unterschied zum erwählten Israel aus Juden- und Heidenchristen. In selbstreferenzieller Rückwendung auf Paulus aber ist damit zugleich gesagt: Die abgetrennten Zweige, die wieder eingepfropft werden sollen, sind ein Symbol für die Wiederaneignung dessen, was er in sich verdrängt, unterdrückt und "abgeschnitten" hat. Damit ist gegenüber dem Töpfergleichnis in Röm 9,19ff. ein entscheidender Wandel eingetreten. Der Töpfer kennt nur zwei Arten von Gefäßen. Sind sie gebrannt, so ist es nicht mehr möglich, sie umzuformen. Sie sind für immer Gefäße des Erbarmens oder des Zorns, sind endgültig zum Gebrauch oder zur Vernichtung bestimmt! Das Ölbaumgleichnis aber kennt diese Alternative nicht mehr. Es löst den Dualismus von Erwählten und Nicht-Erwählten auf. Alle, die einmal "abgeschnitten" wurden, können zurückkehren!

Das Mysterion in 11,25ff. entfaltet daraufhin die objektive Seite dieses Heilsuniversalismus und geht noch einen Schritt über alles Bisherige hinaus: Gott *kann* nicht nur alle ungläubigen Israeliten wieder zum Glauben bringen, er *wird* es auch tun! Paulus stellt sich diese Erlösung Israels in zwei Akten vor. Der erste Akt ist das "Eingehen der Vollzahl der Heiden"—also die Völkerwallfahrt, durch die alle Völker zum Zion strömen, um dort in die Gottesherrschaft einzugehen. Die Feststellung: "Und so (καὶ οὕτως) wird ganz Israel gerettet" (in 11,26a) bezieht sich auf diese Völkerwallfahrt zurück. Dann folgt ein begründendes Schriftzitat: "Wie (καθὼς γέγραπται) geschrieben steht: Aus Zion wird der Erlöser kommen . . .". Auch dies Schriftzitat bezieht sich auf die Erlösung Israels, so dass es eine theoretische Frage ist, ob Israel durch das Eingehen der Heiden oder durch den zur Parusie kommenden Christus gerettet wird. Beide Akte gehören zur Rettung Israels. In die Darstellung beider Akte könnte Erfahrung des Paulus eingehen.

Der erste eschatologische Akt, das Eingehen aller Heiden, wird die Abgrenzung Israels von den Heiden ad absurdum führen. Der Widerstand Israels gegen die Heidenmission war ja für Paulus die eigentliche Verblendung und "Sünde" Israels (vgl. 1 Thess 2,14–16). Sie wäre definitiv überholt, wenn die Vollzahl der Heiden zum Heil gekommen ist. Dahinter könnte eine persönliche Erfahrung stecken, auch wenn es nicht ganz sicher ist: Wir dürfen vermuten, dass Paulus in seiner vorchristlichen Zeit durch die Offenheit der Christen für die Heiden gegen das Christentum aufgebracht worden ist—etwa durch den Traum von der Völkerwallfahrt, dem baldigen Einzug von Heiden in die Gottesherrschaft (Mt 8,10f.) oder deren baldige Zulassung zum Tempelgottesdienst (Mk 11,17). Das könnte ihn einmal als Provokation "zum Glauben gereizt"—und damit zur Konfrontation mit dem Erhöhten geführt haben, die für ihn unmittelbar eine Berufung zum Heidenmissionar war (Gal 1,15ff.). In Analogie dazu stellt er sich wahrscheinlich die Rettung ganz Israels vor. Die Verblendung Israels gegenüber Gottes Zuwendung zu den Heiden wird aufgehoben, wenn Israel sieht, dass auch die Heiden zum Heil eingehen.

Dasselbe gilt für den zweiten eschatologischen Akt: So wie Paulus als ungläubiger Israelit durch eine Erscheinung vom Himmel bekehrt wurde, so wird auch ganz Israel durch den zur Parusie kommenden Christus gerettet werden.[40] Ganz Israel hat eine zweite Chance bei der Parusie—dann wenn der Stein des Anstoßes und der Fels des Ärgernisses sichtbar überwunden ist. Die Herrlichkeit des Erhöhten wird keine Zweifel daran lassen, wer der Messias ist. Als Parusieort stellt sich Paulus Jerusalem vor. Der Erlöser kommt nicht "wegen Zions" (wie es Jes 59,20 in der LXX heißt), sondern "aus Zion". Von Jerusalem kommend,[41] wird er das weltweit zerstreute Israel ("ganz Israel") einsammeln—und ihm seinen bisherigen Unglauben und seine Feindseligkeit vergeben,—so wie er einst Paulus seine Verfolgung und Feindschaft vergeben hat. Ist das ein "Sonderweg" Israels zur Erlösung? Es ist gewiss kein Weg an Christus vorbei, auch kein Weg ohne Glauben, wohl aber ein Weg an der "Kirche" vorbei: Juden werden gerettet werden, ohne dass sie durch die Verkündigung der Kirche für den Glauben gewonnen oder in die christliche Kirche aufgenommen wurden. Ihr Glauben wird insofern ein anderer

[40] So O. Hofius, "Das Evangelium und Israel: Erwägungen zu Römer 9–11", *ZTK* 83 (1986) 297–324, S. 320: "Israel kommt auf die gleiche Weise zum Glauben wie Paulus selbst! . . . Paulus sieht und weiß sich als den Prototyp des dem Evangelium gegenüber verschlossenen *und* des von dem erwählenden Gott nicht preisgegebenen Israel!"

[41] Man muss hier also nicht unbedingt an das himmlische Jerusalem denken. Dass der zur Parusie kommende Christus vom Himmel kommt, ist ohnehin selbstverständlich.

sein als der der meisten Christen: Denn er braucht den Anstoß des Kreuzes nicht mehr überwinden. Er ist bei der Parusie ja schon lange überwunden! Aber dieser Glaube ist im Kern nicht wesentlich unterschieden vom Glauben des Paulus, der ja auch durch eine unmittelbare Begegnung mit dem Erhöhten zum Glauben gekommen war.[42]

Wir hatten gesehen: Schon in Kap. 10 hatten Glauben und Christologie die schroffe Aufteilung in Erwählte und Nichterwählte, in Juden und Heiden, Himmel und Hölle, überwunden. Diese frohe Botschaft hatte bei Juden wenig Anklang gefunden. Sie grollten weiterhin den Heiden, lehnten den weltweit sich verbreitenden Glauben ab. In Röm 11 wird daher noch einmal ein Wunder erwartet:

Das Ölbaumgleichnis sagt: Gott kann Glauben bei denen schaffen, die wie die ungläubigen Juden trotz Unglaubens einen character indelebilis bewahrt haben. Er kann auch abgebrochene Zweige wieder einsetzen. Wir hatten das auch auf Paulus persönlich bezogen: Das, was in ihm "abgeschnitten" und "verdrängt" war—sein Judentum als Eiferer und Feind des Christentums, kann er im Glauben wieder aneignen. Wie verformt dies eifernde Judentum in ihm auch war, es gehört zum "Teig", der durch und durch heilig ist. Er darf sich zu ihm bekennen.

Das "Mysterion" sagt darüber hinaus: Wenn alle Völker zum Heil "eingehen" werden, dann wird Christus zur Parusie kommen, um denen zu vergeben, die sich gegen die Öffnung des Heils für die Heiden gesträubt haben. Und auch das können wir auf Paulus beziehen: Auch ihm ist seine Feindschaft gegen die Christen verziehen worden. Er macht in seinen Schriften kein großes Aufsehen davon. Man hat ihm in dieser Hinsicht ein "robustes Gewissen" zugeschrieben.[43] Dies robuste Gewissen wäre das Ergebnis eines Verdrängungsaktes, den er im Vorgriff auf die Vergebung der Sünden Israels am Ende der Zeiten aufhebt. Oder sollte sich Paulus ausgerechnet selbst aus der Masse der Ungehorsamen ausschließen?

Am Ende seiner Gedanken hat Paulus nichts in den vielen Wider-

[42] Ist die Rettung von ganz Israel innergeschichtlich als unwahrscheinlicher Erfolg der Mission zu verstehen? Wohl kaum. Schon in Röm 11,15 hatte Paulus betont, dass die endzeitliche "Annahme" Israels durch Gott "Totenauferstehung" sei (und nicht nur "wie" eine Totenauferstehung). Das weist auf ein Wunder jenseits der Geschichte.

[43] K. Stendahl, "The Apostle Paul and the Introspective Conscience of the West", *HTR* 56 (1963) 199–215.

sprüchen aufgelöst, die Röm 9–11 logisch charakterisieren. Aber er hat Zuversicht gewonnen, dass sich der Widerspruch seines Lebens lösen wird, und Mut, um nach Jerusalem zu reisen—trotz aller Feindschaft, die ihn dort erwartet. Er ist eins mit sich. Und das heißt auch: Er ist eins mit seiner jüdischen Herkunft und versöhnt mit seinen jüdischen Feinden. Was er in 11,15 schreibt: "Denn wenn ihre Verwerfung die Versöhnung der Welt ist, was wird ihre Annahme anderes sein als Leben aus den Toten!", können wir als Aussage auch über ihn hören: Wenn die Verwerfung des Judentums durch Paulus Versöhnung für alle Menschen brachte, was wird dessen Wiederannahme anders sein als neues Leben aus dem Tode! Und daher kann er Gott loben und preisen—für seine unerforschlichen Wege mit Israel, mit der Menschheit und auch mit ihm (Röm 11,33–36).

THE QUESTION OF SALARY IN THE CONFLICT BETWEEN PAUL AND THE "SUPER APOSTLES" IN CORINTH

Lars Aejmelaeus

1. *The living and contextual way of Paul's argumentation*

When as a young pastor in the beginning of 1970's I came back from the provinces to Helsinki to write my dissertation, the situation in the Department of Biblical Studies was changed. My old teacher, Aimo T. Nikolainen, had become a bishop and a young promising scholar, Heikki Räisänen, was responsible for New Testament Exegetics. It was not difficult to observe that new fresh winds were blowing. Heikki had already written about the Gospels and was now beginning to work with Paul and the law questions. His studies were later published in the important books *Paul and the Law* and *The Torah and Christ.*[1]

In these books Räisänen concentrates on the Romans and Galatians, whereas I was and have also later been mostly interested in the Corinthian correspondence. Nevertheless, I received important stimulus also for the Corinthian problems from the new professor. The ideas which Räisänen emphasized were useful for my aims. One of the key ideas which made Räisänen's investigation about the law so successful was the viewpoint he took concerning the *consistency* of Paul's thoughts: You did not need to think that Paul always had only one and the same conception about a matter:

> Paul was indeed an original thinker, and his letters are full of seminal insights and thought-provoking suggestions. He is, however, first and foremost a missionary, a man of practical religion who develops a line of thought to make a practical point, to influence the conduct of his readers; in the next moment he is quite capable of putting

[1] H. Räisänen, *Paul and the Law* (WUNT 29; Tübingen: J.C.B. Mohr [Paul Siebeck], 1983); idem, *The Torah and Christ: Essays in German and English on the Problem of the Law in Early Christianity* (PFES 45; Helsinki: The Finnish Exegetical Society, 1986).

> forward a statement which logically contradicts the previous one when trying to make a different point or, rather, struggling with a different problem.[2]

This was the way Paul was able to handle the, for him, so difficult question about the Jewish Law. The different situations in Romans and Galatians demanded different answers to the questions. Inside Paul's mind there were different models of how to solve the problems. He had experienced great things. He was convinced that Jesus Christ was the right answer on all the questions of salvation and of living a good life before God. There were, nevertheless, many valuable things in his old Jewish religion which he could not simply throw away although they did not easily suit his new religious conviction. Because he was no strict systematic thinker, more a religious man, he had no great difficulties living with contradictions. The changes of viewpoints and of definitions of words belong to this connection.

All this can be seen in the chapters in which Paul is writing about the Jewish law. Therefore, a scholar must not explain all the difficulties in the Pauline letters away so that nothing but total harmony is left. He/she is not allowed to make artificial compromises between different Pauline thoughts. Räisänen emphasized that we must be able to live with this inconsequence in the Pauline writings. Only so we can reach an interpretation which does justice to Paul and understand what he really meant.

Once in the autumn of 1974, Heikki was asked to visit a working group led by Professor Henrik Zilliacus from the Department of Greek Literature. I gave a paper about the new approach of Hans Dieter Betz to 2 Cor 10–13.[3] A young scholar who was interested in the interpretation of Paul's rhetorical argumentation could benefit by hearing how Räisänen emphasized that by reading the old texts you must always, besides the writer, also keep *the readers* in mind. Paul, as all other authors, surely wanted to be understood. It means that he would hardly write such thoughts which only he himself would be able to understand correctly and in the right light. Ergo the verses 2 Cor 12:1–10 should not be interpreted as a parody. Otherwise there would have been clear signs in the text which would have helped the readers to understand the text as such.

---

[2] Räisänen, *Law*, 267.

[3] H.D. Betz, *Der Apostel Paulus und die sokratische Tradition: Eine exegetische Untersuchung zu seiner "Apologie" 2 Korinther 10–13* (Tübingen: J.C.B. Mohr [Paul Siebeck], 1972).

With these instructions in mind, I began my own wrestling with the texts of Paul. I was able—that was in any case the subjective feeling I had—to see light in the contradictory and paradoxical pericopes of 2 Cor 10–13. Here also Paul need not be understood as consistent. He could change his point of view not only when he was writing about the law, but also when he was arguing with his enemies about the right Christian way of living and about the right characteristics of an apostle. The problems Paul had were not limited only to the Jewish Law. He also had heavy arguments with people who had a different vision of the way in which the divine strength was visible in an apostle.

In studying 2 Cor 10–13 ("Letter of Tears"), it is very important to try to understand what the situation actually was.[4] Many questions need answers: What people were the opponents? What was their theology and way of life? On what points were they criticizing Paul? These questions could also be formulated as follows: In which respects were they superior to Paul as apostles of Christ?[5] To achieve a correct understanding of the chapters, the scholar must also try to understand the reactions of the congregation. How deeply had it already accepted the teachings of the new apostles and rejected the teachings of Paul? Everything is more complicated because we are not dealing here with an exact report of the facts, what really happened. Several things point to the direction that Paul, while writing his letter, saw the situation in much darker colours than it really was. The "Letter of Reconciliation" (2 Cor 1–9), and especially the chapters 2 and 7 in it, which were written later than the chapters 10–13, can easily be understood as indicating that Paul himself admits having been too severe and having exaggerated the depth of the "downfall" of the Corinthians in his Letter of Tears. For the correct interpretation of the Letter of Tears one must first try to understand which details are written only from the subjective viewpoint

[4] The chapters 2 Cor 10–13 were written before the chapters 2 Cor 1–9 ("Letter of Reconciliation") and constitute the "Letter of Tears", about which Paul speaks in 2 Cor 2:4. My arguments for the solution in L. Aejmelaeus, *Streit und Versöhnung: Das Problem der Zusammensetzung des 2. Korintherbriefes* (PFES 46; Helsinki: The Finnish Exegetical Society, 1987). Cf. also my answer to the newer discussion in *Schwachheit als Waffe: Die Argumentation des Paulus im Tränenbrief (2 Kor 10–13)* (PFES 78; Helsinki/Göttingen: The Finnish Exegetical Society/Vandenhoeck & Ruprecht, 2000) 19–26.

[5] It is not possible to give a clear picture of Paul's opponents in this article. My opinion about their character is to be read in Aejmelaeus, *Schwachheit*, 26–35.

of Paul. Only this actually matters. It was naturally this subjective analysis of his as well as his subjective strong feelings for the Corinthians and against the super apostles which gave rise to his argumentation.

It is also of great importance for the right interpretation of the Letter of Tears to consider whom Paul is addressing in the various parts of the letter, whether he is addressing the members of the congregation or the "super apostles". It is especially important to recognize which rhetorical style Paul is using in the various parts of the letter. Nowhere else, not even in Galatians, is Paul so ironic, even sarcastic, as in the Letter of Tears. The nature of irony is such that one must be well acquainted with the person who is writing as well as with the exact situation he is writing about in order to be able to recognize the ironic nature of the text for certain. Unfortunately, we have no other real witness to the character of Paul and to the Corinthian conflict apart from Paul's own text. Therefore it is no wonder that the scholarly opinion about Paul's intentions in distinct parts of 2 Cor 10–13 is all but unanimous.

2. *The question of Paul's salary as a problem*

In this article I want to examine only one example of the rhetorical problems of the Pauline argumentation, but one of the most sinuous ones. The way Paul wrote about it was so convoluted that most scholars, according to my sincere opinion, have come to wrong solutions. It is the tenacious problem about the salary that Paul had not received from the Corinthian congregation. The culmination point of Paul's dealing with this problem can be seen in 2 Cor 11:7–12. He writes about the theme also in 2 Cor 12:13–18. In both places Paul is expressing himself in such a way that it has been very difficult for later readers to understand his point. Paul was able to write in a sinuous way here because the Corinthians knew the facts, i.e. their own situation. Therefore they clearly knew where Paul was only joking and where he was serious.

2 Cor 11:7–12 and 2 Cor 12:13–18 are part of the Letter of Tears. This means that Paul was in a very special situation when he took the theme of his apostolic salary under discussion. He was in the middle of struggling for his apostolate against criticism which had been directed against him in the Corinthian congregation. The struggle was still acute while Paul was writing. The new preachers

from outside who have snatched away the members of the congregation and who lie behind the criticism were still in Corinth. Nobody was yet able to see what the outcome of the struggle would be. In this situation, Paul uses every means he thinks could be useful to enable him to win the battle for the souls of the members of the congregation.

Just before beginning the salary theme, Paul claims in 2 Cor 11:5 that he in no way at all is inferior to the "super apostles" (οἱ ὑπερλίαν ἀπόστολοι)—as he calls the intruders. In 11:6 he then also rebuts an accusation which concerns the way he is proclaiming God's word. He has no problems with this matter, too, although he is "unskilled in speech" (ἰδιώτης τῷ λόγῳ).

When the table has been cleared concerning the question of how Paul preaches—and here he seems to have, at least at the moment, no bigger problems—Paul begins in 11:7 to handle another subject in which he does seem to have dangerous deficiencies. Concerning this subject, too, he wants to show that he is not inferior to his opponents. In 11:5–6 Paul wanted to emphasize that in Corinth he had preached the full and genuine gospel although not with rhetorical splendour. In this matter nobody can blame him. But would somebody be able to blame him for having done it without taking a salary from the congregation? This is the problem which Paul begins to handle in 11:7–12.

With this problem, Paul comes back to a theme which he had already written about in 1 Cor 9. He scrutinized there the right of a servant of the gospel to accept a salary from the congregation, but also his refusal to take support from the congregation. The question now has a new aspect in a situation where the "super apostles" differ from Paul's practice in their attitude towards the salary regulations. It is important for Paul to scrutinize the question anew. This can easily be recognized from the amount of text Paul writes in the Letter of Tears about the salary problem. Taken together, verses 11:7–12 and 12:13–18 make up about 14 per cent of the total verses of the whole letter.

Why is it so important to write about this problem? It was surely not the main problem between Paul and his opponents in the battle for the souls of the congregation. The main issues were theological, christological and pneumatological problems, as one can see from the charges against Paul (cf. 2 Cor 10:1,3,7,10; 11:6,23; 12:1,12;

13:3).[6] In any case many scholars think that the Corinthians were continuing to criticize Paul on this matter after the writing of this account in 1 Cor 9 and especially after the coming of the new apostles. The scholars often explain the issue according the following scheme: The way the opponents used their right to support proved for Corinthians that they were genuine apostles of Christ while Paul's attitude proved that there was something wrong in his apostolate. Paul must have been uncertain about his apostolate because of his refusal of support.[7]

Josef Zmijewski, who is a typical representative of this pattern, thinks that the criticism against Paul can be read rather directly in 11:7. Paul was criticized because he had humbled himself by preaching the gospel for nothing. The use of the privilege of an apostle was at the same time the testimony of the genuine apostolate. Zmijewski continues:

> Offenbar gehört nach Ansicht der Gegner die Unterstützung durch die Gemeinde zu den 'Zeichen des Apostels' (vgl. 12,12). Daß Paulus auf seine Unterstützung verzichtet, ist in ihren Augen nicht nur ein Zeichen von Lieblosigkeit (vgl. 11,11) und bezeichnender Hinterlist (vgl.

[6] This means that P. Marshall, *Enmity in Corinth: Social Conventions in Paul's Relations with the Corinthians* (WUNT 2/23; Tübingen: J.C.B. Mohr [Paul Siebeck], 1987) 261, is exaggerating when he considers "Paul's refusal of aid in Corinth and the resultant charge of inconstancy in his relations with others" as "one major reason for distrust".

[7] For example, the following scholars interpret the case according to this pattern: A. Plummer, *A Critical and Exegetical Commentary on the Second Epistle of St Paul to the Corinthians* (3rd ed.; ICC; Edinburgh: T & T Clark, 1948) 307; H. Lietzmann, *An die Korinther I/II* (5th ed.; HNT 9; Tübingen: J.C.B. Mohr [Paul Siebeck], 1969) 147; R.H. Strachan, *The Second Epistle of Paul to the Corinthians* (4th ed.; MNTC; London, 1946) 22; D. Georgi, *Die Gegner des Paulus im 2. Korintherbrief: Studien zur religiösen Propaganda in der Spätantike* (WMANT 1; Neukirchen: Neukirchener Verlag, 1964) 239 n. 1; G. Dautzenberg, "Der Verzicht auf das apostolische Unterhaltsrecht: Eine exegetische Untersuchung zu 1 Kor 9", *Bib* 50 (1969) 213 n. 2; Betz, *Tradition*, 100; W. Pratscher, "Der Verzicht des Paulus auf finanziellen Unterhalt durch seine Gemeinden: ein Aspekt seiner Missionsweise", *NTS* 25 (1979) 294–95; G. Theissen, *Studien zur Soziologie des Urchristentums* (WUNT 19, Tübingen: J.C.B. Mohr [Paul Siebeck], 1979) 215–19; V.P. Furnish, *II Corinthians* (AB; Garden City, New York: Doubleday, 1984) 506–9; C. Wolff, *Der zweite Brief an die Korinther* (THKNT 8; Berlin: Evang. Verl.-Anst., 1989) 220; E. Lohse, "Das kirchliche Amt des Apostels und das apostolische Amt der Kirche", in idem (ed.), *Verteidigung und Begründung des apostolischen Amtes (2 Kor 10–13)* (Benedictina, Monographische Reihe, Biblisch-Ökumenische Abteilung 11; Rom 1992) 132, 137; U. Heckel, *Kraft in Schwachheit: Untersuchungen zu 2 Kor 10–13* (WUNT 56. Tübingen: J.C.B. Mohr [Paul Siebeck], 1993) 16, 25–26.

> 12,16), sondern darüber hinaus ein Zugeständnis seiner grundsätzlichen 'Unterlegenheit' gegenüber den anderen Aposteln.[8]

In the light of 1 Cor 9, the representatives of such an interpretation must think that the Corinthians have either totally forgotten what Paul had written earlier or they have not understood or accepted what Paul wrote. Paul had already asked in 1 Cor 9:1 whether he was an apostle despite his refusal to take the salary and had already answered the question positively. The answer was long and thorough. Has the Pauline argumentation in 1 Cor 9 been fruitless, so that he must handle the same matter once again, or has he other grounds for doing so? Is the interpretation that here Paul is defending himself against critics and suspicions the best solution, or is the bringing up of the question about salary under scrutiny here better understood in another way?

The way Paul argues is puzzling. One could think that in 2 Cor 11:7–12 he is even contradictory. For a better understanding of his thoughts, we must first see what he writes about the question in other places (1 Cor 9; 2 Cor 12:13–18). It is also important to concentrate on the common rules and habits in the Jewish and general Hellenistic environments concerning the ways a religious or philosophical teacher or preacher earned his living among the people with whom he or she was interacting. In recent decades, there have been new attempts to interpret the Pauline difficulties concerning his support with the help of patterns which were usual—or at least existed—in the Hellenistic culture of that time.

3. *The assumed contemptibility towards working at a craft*

Paul's working with own hands during his missionary travels became a problem for him and other Christians. Otherwise, he would not have written so much about it in many places, especially in 1 Cor 9. Why was it a problem? The Pauline texts are not, for many reasons, very clear here. In any case, the scholars cannot find consensus in their answers to the question. Often they try to explain the Pauline

[8] J. Zmijewski, *Der Stil der paulinischen "Narrenrede": Analyse der Sprachgestaltung in 2 Kor 11,1–12,10 als Beitrag zur Methodik von Stiluntersuchungen neutestamentlicher Texte* (BBB 52; Köln-Bonn: Peter Hanstein, 1978) 127. Compare also F. Lang, *Die Briefe an die Korinther* (NTD 7; Göttingen: Vandenhoeck & Ruprecht, 1986) 338, 352.

utterances in a way which is not satisfying, and which is often even contradictory in itself. It is easy to go astray here if one does not pay sufficient attention to the rhetorical character of the text. All is not always what it seems to be.

Besides the rhetoric, it is important to know something about the real life conditions of the time in question. When we try to understand the texts of Paul correctly we must have a good general picture about the conditions of the situation, in which Paul is an itinerant preacher in the antique world, a religious teacher among Hellenistic city people. Under what circumstances concerning support did a missionary create suspicion or indignation in the distant past? How was he generally allowed to earn his bread, if he was not so rich that he could teach at his own expense?

Paul mainly paid his own expenses by working with his hands as an artisan during the time he travelled as a missionary. The attitude towards such a solution in Hellenistic culture was ambiguous. The upper class despised craftsmen, as Ronald F. Hock writes: "To those of wealth and power, the appearance (σχῆμα) of the artisan was that befitting a slave (δουλοπρεπής)." Hock, like many other scholars, thinks that we have *here* the explanation for the Pauline apology in 1 Cor 9. Hock goes on writing: "It is no wonder . . . that Paul thought it necessary to defend his practice of supporting himself by his work at trade (1 Cor 9:1–27) and that the dominant theme of his defence was whether he was free or slavish (vv. 1, 19)." Hock further thinks that it was especially before the eyes of the rich members of the Corinthian congregation that Paul was defending himself. They despised him because of his working at a trade. "To Corinthians who, relative to Paul, appeared to be rich, wise, powerful, and respected (cf. 4:8,10), their lowly apostle had seemed to have enslaved himself with his plying a trade (cf. 9:19)."[9] Also Victor Paul Furnish similarly describes the grounds for criticism of Paul in Corinth: "Among the philosophers and itinerant teachers of Paul's day, continuing to work at a craft was regarded as the least acceptable way of providing for life's necessities. This accords with the generally low estimate of craftsmen in the ancient world."[10]

[9] R.F. Hock, *The Social Context of Paul's Ministry: Tentmaking and Apostleship* (Philadelphia: Fortress, 1980) 60.

[10] Furnish, *II Corinthians*, 506–7. Furnish refers here to Lucian, *The Dream* 13, and

It can well be that in the eyes of the upper class an artisan was despised and that the way Hock describes this attitude is right: "Stigmatized as slavish, uneducated, and often useless, artisans, to judge from scattered references, were frequently reviled or abused, often victimized, seldom if ever invited to dinner, never accorded status, and even excluded from one Stoic utopia."[11] We must, however, keep in mind that this is only the opinion of the upper class. It comes out in so many testimonies from antiquity only because it was mostly the upper class which was able to express their opinion on this matter in a way which reaches us today. The number of members of the upper class was decreasing, however. The great majority of the people belonged to other classes. They were peasants, labourers of various kinds, artisans, storekeepers, and slaves. Their attitude towards genuine craftsmanship cannot have been as negative as that of the upper class.

Ramsay MacMullen stresses in his book *Roman Social Relations 50 B.C. to A.D. 284* the small upper class population during the time with which we are dealing and the misinterpretation of the real social conditions if we are satisfied only with the testimony of a minimal group of men who belonged to the upper class and who mostly lived on the Italian peninsula. He writes:

> Modern historians speak . . . of 'the contempt the ancient felt for any servile activity . . .; all paid work was held in contempt.' Had it really been so, Trimalchio would never have commissioned for his own house a wall-painting that showed him being bought and sold as a slave, nor would an auctioneer, a shopkeeper, a weaver, a fuller, or any member of the "despised" occupations have advertised on his tombstone for all to see, down through eternity, exactly what work he did and where in the city he did it. Only the More Honorable despised him, too many miles above his head to matter.[12]

Paul could hardly have been despised by the Corinthians just because he worked as an artisan. Among the members of the Corinthian congregation, there were unlikely to have been people who belonged to the small upper class of the really rich people in the Roman Empire. Paul describes the social structure of the congregation as

---

to the examples in R. MacMullen, *Roman Social Relations 50 B.C. to A.D. 284* (New Haven-London: Yale University Press, 1974) 114–15.

[11] Hock, *Social Context*, 35–36.

[12] MacMullen, *Roman Social Relations*, 88–120 (the citation on p. 120).

follows: "Look at your own calling as Christians; there are among you not many who are wise by human standards, not many who are powerful, not many who are nobly born" (1 Cor 1:26). What follows in the Pauline description strengthens the impression that the general picture of the congregation is more proletarian than noble (1 Cor 1:27–28). Even the sparse number of the "nobly born" seems not to belong to the highest class of the Empire, which had hardly any representatives among the population of the town. Consequently, Paul had no need to be ashamed of working as an artisan because the members of the congregation would have despised work itself. That was what they themselves were doing. The problems which Paul had because of his working for his living must have arisen from other reasons.

4. *The theory of patron and client relationship*

If the solution for the Pauline difficulties in the support question does not lie in the direct contemptibility for work as such, it is, according to a popular scholarly opinion, possible that the attitudes and habits of the antique upper class paid a role here in another way. Many modern scholars have fixed their attention on a special institution, namely the relationship between a patron and his client. For example, Victor Paul Furnish wants to explain the problem with the help of the conditions which belonged to this institution. He writes:

> In the ancient world, giving and receiving, placing someone under and being oneself placed under financial obligation were extremely important components of the social structure . . . The wealthy expressed and enhanced their power by becoming patrons of the needy . . . To be the recipient of a benefaction was to be placed immediately under an obligation of gratitude to the benefactor, and the gratitude of the beneficiary in turn placed the benefactor under further obligation. Therefore, to accept a gift was to become a client of and dependent upon the more privileged person . . . To refuse a benefaction was an act of social enmity." Thus, Paul's refusal to accept financial support from the Corinthians "was a renunciation of their status as a patron congregation" (cf. 2 Cor 12:13) and therefore a repudiation of their friendship (cf. 11:11), as well as a regrettable act of self-humiliation.[13]

[13] Furnish, *II Corinthians*, 507–8. Furnish follows here Marshall's interpretation. Marshall, *Enmity*, builds a total analysis of the Corinthian dispute on the ground of

Although the patron-client-model is popular in interpreting the Pauline support difficulties in Corinth, it is still not convincing. We have already mentioned that in Corinth there were hardly any persons who would have been so rich that they could have acted like the Roman patrons. If there were some from this class, they did not yet belong to the congregation. The wealthy people of the congregation had houses where the congregation could come together, and they surely could also support the work of the missionaries and help the poor members, but all this is still far away from the manner of living of the really rich patrons in Italy.[14]

The term "upper class" in these connections is quite variable, and the scholars define it in their own way. Theissen points out that there were some rich people in the congregation, but it is clear in the light of his account that they did not belong to the real "jet set" of the Empire. If, against all probabilities, there had been some person who would have liked to play a patron in his relationship with Paul, he would soon have seen how impossible it would have been. The cases which Furnish uses as parallels concern private persons with their private clients. In his missionary work, Paul always established relationships with whole communities, as when he addresses the whole community in his letters and when he teaches and rebukes his fellow Christians (the Letter to Philemon is an exception which can easily be explained). There are no real hints at any individual

---

the described relationship between patron and recipient. His extensive book has many good sporadic points but the overall pattern is not convincing. This can well be seen in the very details when the writer tries to analyze the concrete text in the light of this overall hypothesis. C. Forbes, "Comparison, Self-Praise and Irony: Paul's Boasting and the Conventions of Hellenistic Rhetoric", *NTS* 32 (1986) 1–30, also interprets Paul's relationship to the Corinthians in the same way (on pp. 14, 24). This basic interpretation seems to be accepted also, for example, by J.A. Crafton, *The Agency of the Apostle: A Dramatistic Analysis of Paul's Responses to Conflict in 2 Corinthians* (JSNTSup 51; Sheffield: JSOT Press, 1991) 55–56; J.K. Chow, *Patronage and Power: A Study of Social Networks in Corinth* (JSNTSup 75; Sheffield: JSOT Press, 1992) 109–10, 173–74; A. Eriksson, *Traditions as Rhetorical Proof: Pauline Argumentation in 1 Corinthians* (CB New Testament Series 29; Stockholm: Almqvist & Wiksell, 1998) 146.

[14] About the sociological structure in Corinth, see Theissen, *Soziologie*, 231–71. Compare also N.A. Dahl (assisted by P. Donahue), *Studies in Paul: Theology for the Early Christian Mission* (Minneapolis, Minnesota, 1977) 27–28; W.A. Meeks, *The First Urban Christians: The Social World of the Apostle Paul* (New Haven/London: Yale University Press 1983) 51–73; H.D. Betz, "The Problem of Rhetoric and Theology according to the Apostle Paul", in A. Vanhoye (ed.), *L'apôtre Paul: Personnalité, style et conception du ministére* (BETL 73; Leuven: University Press, 1986) 16–48, esp. p. 24 n. 48.

"patrons" in the letters. Because of this fact, Furnish does not talk about private patrons, but about "patron congregations".[15] Such a collective institution has no real parallel in Greek and Roman culture.[16]

The only "private patron" of Paul was Jesus Christ, and all must have very soon understood this, so that it is not probable that somebody would have wanted to begin to play this role in the life of Paul—not to mention that he would have been injured if Paul refused to accept him as his patron. Paul had the self-esteem of an apostle of Christ, and it was impossible for him to become the court chaplain of some congregation which he himself had founded, or the private preacher of some rich household. This must have been clear to the Corinthians from the very beginning.

5. *The normal attitude towards a working preacher*

How did the people in antiquity usually think about the combination of craftmanship and spiritual or intellectual work? From what we have said above, it is clear what the upper class thought about the issue, but it is not important for our purposes. We ask what the attitude of the ordinary people was to the question. Even if they did not have as many opportunities to concentrate on deeper intellectual learning, they still had their own religious interests. In this area, special persons took care of these things on their behalf, and they were owed gratitude. How was this gratitude shown in situations similar to that of Paul?

First, there is quite a lot of material about the issue in the Jewish sources. Although much of it belongs to the time after the catastrophe of A.D. 70, it is possible to draw some conclusions from the Jewish standpoints on the time before this.

---

[15] Furnish, *II Corinthians*, 507–8. So also J.L. Sumney, *Identifying Paul's Opponents: The Question of Method in 2 Corinthians* (JSNTSup 40; Sheffield: JSOT Press, 1990) 165.

[16] Critical views against the patronage solution of Marshall and Furnish are to be found also in H. Probst, *Paulus und der Brief: Die Rhetorik des antiken Briefes als Form der paulinischen Korintherkorrespondenz (1 Kor 8–10)* (WUNT 2/45; Tübingen: J.C.B. Mohr [Paul Siebeck], 1991) 179–80; T. Haraguchi, "Das Unterhaltsrecht des frühchristlichen Verkündigers: Eine Untersuchung zur Bezeichnung ἐργάτης im Neuen Testament", *ZNW* 84 (1993) 178–95, T. Schmeller, *Hierarchie und Egalität: Eine sozialgeschichtliche Untersuchung paulinischer Gemeinden und griechisch-römischer Vereine* (SBS 162; Stuttgart: Verlag Katholisches Bibelwerk, 1995). See further Aejmelaeus, *Schwachheit*, 137–40.

In Jewish writings we can also surely see glimpses of the negative upper-class attitude towards handiwork (cf. Sir. 38). What Sirach writes here can, however, be considered atypical of the usual Jewish attitude.[17] Usually the attitude was more positive. There is a famous rabbinic maxim (*bQidd* 30b): "Who doesn't teach his son a craft, makes him a robber." This really seems to reflect the way the Jewish people and their teachers in the synagogue thought about the matter.

Ronald F. Hock thinks that the positive attitude towards working with one's own hands together with the spiritual activity and the corresponding practice in the life-style of a rabbi first developed *after* the catastrophe.[18] Although the difficult circumstances after the Jewish War naturally strengthened such an attitude, it can hardly be true that the ideals and real circumstances in the synagogue life would earlier have been build on other grounds. Even before the catastrophe, ordinary Jewish people and their religious teachers were not rich. We are not speaking now about the high priests of Jerusalem, but about the rabbis of many Jewish communities throughout Palestine and the Hellenistic world. Paul's relationship to his congregations can better be compared with the synagogue leaders to their communities than to the aristocratic high priests' living conditions.

In the rabbinic literature there are also voices which plead for the rights and ideals of a religious teacher to concentrate only on spiritual things and to live at the cost of others, but the mainstream Jewish thinking went in another direction. Göran Agrell describes this as follows: "The study of the Torah and worldly labour are . . . both seen as positive, of aid to each other and to a morally proper life."[19] This has, with all probability, been the case during the time of Paul as well. He was not the person who invented this attitude towards craft within the Jewish culture. That a teacher, a preacher

[17] W. Bienert, *Die Arbeit nach der Lehre der Bibel: Ein Beitrag zur evangelischen Sozialethik* (2nd ed.; Stuttgart: Ev. Verlagswerk, 1956) 142–50; G. Agrell, *Work, Toil and Sustenance: An Examination of the View of Work in the New Testament, Taking into Consideration Views Found in Old Testament, Intertestamental, and Early Rabbinic Writings* (Stockholm: Verbum, 1976) 38.

[18] R.F. Hock, "Paul's Tentmaking and the Problem of His Social Class", *JBL* 97 (1978) 557; idem, *Social Context*, 66.

[19] Agrell, *Work*, 47–67 (the citation on page 50). Cf. also F. Hauck, *Die Stellung des Urchristentums zu Arbeit und Geld* (BFCT 2/3; Gütersloh: Gütersloher Verlagshaus Gerd Mohn, 1921) 11–16; Paul Billerbeck, *Kommentar zum Neuen Testament aus Talmud und Midrasch*, vol. 2: *Das Evangelium nach Markus, Lukas und Johannes und die Apostelgeschichte* (München: C.H. Beck, 1924) 745–46.

or even a missionary works with his own hands besides doing religious work was, seen from the Jewish point of view, not unusual, wrong or shameful—rather, the contrary.[20]

Hock gives a good picture about the varying ways the philosophers in antiquity got their support. He concludes his presentation as follows: "Four options were debated: charging fees, entering a household as its resident intellectual, begging, and working . . . Philosophers clearly preferred charging fees or entering a household. Begging appealed only to homeless and shameless Cynics. Working was the least popular option."[21] Had Paul been a philosopher—and in the eyes of the people of antiquity the difference was not great—he would have belonged in the last group. From his Jewish point of view, it was natural to Paul to choose the fourth alternative. Even if the itinerant non-Jewish teachers and philosophers themselves did not gladly choose this uncomfortable alternative, it was nevertheless no ground for despising them or their message. There were, however, Christian missionaries who had made another choice, and this was the reason why Paul writes so much about the theme. It was an inner-Christian discussion where the rules had not yet been settled.

6. *The support of a preacher in the Christian context*

If craftmanship in itself was not a problem in Corinth, could the explanation for the difficulties Paul seemed to have arise from the fact that *his* primary calling was not craft but preaching the gospel? Must the problem be explained through the conviction some had that a man of God was not allowed to do anything else but what belonged to the area of spirituality? This is indeed the way many modern scholars try to solve the Pauline difficulties in the matter. They want to explain the difficulties by interpreting the matter as a special problem within Christianity itself. They maintain that the

[20] Betz, *Tradition*, 115, has seen the situation correctly, when he writes: "Wenn Paulus sich also freimütig dazu bekennt, daß er in der Vergangenheit tatsächlich auf finanziellen Unterhalt durch die Gemeinde in Korinth verzichtet hat, befindet er sich in Übereinstimmung mit sehr alten und ehrwürdigen Haltungen, die im Judentum auf die Propheten und im Griechentum auf die sokratische Tradition zurückgehen."

[21] Hock, *Social Context*, 52–59.

early Christians demanded that the missionaries refuse to work with their hands. They had to live on support from others.

One influential representative of this interpretation, Gerd Theissen, thinks that Paul had to give a reckoning in 1 Cor 9 of his way of living because it differed from the rules of the itinerant charismatics of the early Christian movement. This was serious because Paul was breaking the clear commands of Jesus himself. Theissen writes:

> In the synoptic commissioning speeches Christian missionaries are put under obligation to a demonstrable ascetism. They may not make the slightest provision for life but must trust God's grace as simply and completely as do the birds of the air and the lilies of the field. Foresight is distrust in the face of God's grace. The missionary stands under the demand for charismatic poverty.

By breaking these rules, Paul gave evidence in the judgment of many fellow Christians that he was not at all a genuine apostle of Jesus Christ. Theissen describes the criticism against Paul as follows: "The charge could be leveled at him that he has deliberately evaded the requirement of charismatic poverty, and that his work as a craftsman displays a lack of trust in the grace of God, who will also supply the material needs of his missionaries." In his apology in 1 Cor 9, therefore, Paul tries to change a command of Christ that the missionaries should live by the gospel (1 Cor 9:14) to a mere privilege.[22]

In such an interpretation, the role of the synoptic rules (Matt. 10:5ff., Mark 6:8–11; Luke 10:4–11) in the missionary work of early Christianity is surely overemphasized. The logic of the Pauline text in 1 Cor 9 does not speak for it, either. In 1 Cor 9 Paul is not defending his behaviour, but on the contrary is struggling for his and every apostle's principal right to refuse to work and to live on the support of the congregation, as if somebody had tried to deny it.[23] The point

---

[22] G. Theissen, *The Social Setting of Pauline Christianity: Essays on Corinth* (edited and translated by J.H. Schütz; Philadelphia: Fortress, 1982) 28, 42–44. In the same way also: Schmeller, *Hierarchie*, 59; H.-G. Sundermann, *Der schwache Apostel und die Kraft der Rede: Eine rhetorische Analyse von 2 Kor 10–13* (Europäische Hochschulschriften 23/575; Frankfurt am Main: Peter Lang, 1996) 225. Also B. Holmberg, *Paul and Power: The Structure of Authority in the Primitive Church as Reflected in the Pauline Epistles* (ConB New Testament Series 11; Lund: CWK Gleerup, 1978) 90, writes: "The Palestinian missionaries who have visited Corinth (perhaps Cephas was among them) may have asked critical questions when they heard that Paul had not followed this clear command of the Lord, but had worked for his own living. And this is why Paul re-interprets this duty to live without making plans, totally dependent on others, to a privilege that he has not availed himself of."

[23] W.L. Willis, *Idol Meat in Corinth: The Pauline Argument in 1 Corinthians 8 and 10*

of the Pauline rhetoric is here obvious: Only after Paul has made this principal right very clear, are the Corinthians able to admire the greatness of his abstinence. In the macro context (1 Cor 8–10), Paul wants to emphasize the importance of the voluntary refusal of a Christian of his rights when a weak fellow Christian is in need.[24] Paul here offers himself as a good example of this voluntary refusal.

Paul formulates his thought in 1 Cor 9:14 in a way which has given incitement to the contrary interpretation: "In the same way too the Lord has ordained (διέταξεν) for those who preach the Gospel, that they should live by the Gospel." If the verse is separated from the context, one could indeed think that it is a holy order of the Lord that must be followed so that a preacher is not allowed to earn his livelihood by working with his own hands. In the context of the whole chapter 1 Cor 9 this interpretation is, however, highly improbable. The expression "the Lord has ordained" implies here more a charge to the members of the congregation than to the preachers: They have to take care of the needs of the preachers, if they need help.

The verb διατάσσειν here must not be emphasized too strongly. Although Paul has actually the congregation in view he does not mean that the congregation had broken some important order either. Nobody is criticized here. The Greek verb as such is often not very harsh when Paul uses it.[25] If Paul had thought that a strict order of

(SBLDS 68; Chico, California: Scholar Press, 1985) 35: "The claims or illustrations in 9.4–14 can hardly be a defense of Paul's right to support, as if he were called into question by some in Corinth. Their brevity suggests that they are only illustrations, not arguments . . . So the function of vv. 4–14 is not to establish Paul's right to support, but to remind the readers that his authority (ἐξουσία) in this regard is secure." M.M. Mitchell, *Paul and the Rhetoric of Reconciliation: An Exegetical Investigation of the Language and Composition of 1 Corinthians* (HUT 28; Tübingen: J.C.B. Mohr [Paul Siebeck], 1991) 244, also hits the target when she writes: "All attempts to analyze 1 Cor 9 as a true defense against actual charges have failed." See also S.J. Hafemann, *Suffering and the Spirit: An Exegetical Study of II Cor 2:14–3:3 within the Context of the Corinthian Correspondence* (WUNT 2/19. Tübingen: J.C.B. Mohr [Paul Siebeck], 1986) 127–32; Jürgen Becker, *Paulus: Der Apostel der Völker* (Tübingen: J.C.B. Mohr [Paul Siebeck], 1989) 205–6; Wolfgang Schrage, *Der erste Brief an die Korinther* (3 vols.; EKKNT 7; Solothurn/Düsseldorf/Neukirchen-Vluyn: Benziger Verlag, Neukirchener Verlag, 1995) 2. 278–79, 310. Cf. Marshall, *Enmity*, 222, who represents the opposite view.

[24] Cf. how Bienert, *Arbeit*, 304, and Agrell, *Work*, 109–10, also criticize an interpretation like that of Theissen and Holmberg.

[25] See, for example, 1 Cor 16:1, where Paul uses it when he speaks about the collect regulations.

the Lord really existed concerning a preacher's duties in this matter, he would not have used the verb here in so easy and nonchalant a way. Also the whole formulation of the verse would surely have been different.

The length and zeal with which Paul actually explains his principal rights as apostle, however, reveal that there was some obscurity concerning the matter in the congregations, although it was not of the kind mentioned above. We can understand the matter when we take into account that there were no well-established rules regulating the way a missionary should earn his living. The habits of the apostles and other wandering Christian preachers and teachers were changing. The actual ability of individual missionaries to get their own livelihood from their own work was different. Theissen himself states in this context that Paul represented a type of missionary different from the charismatic preachers: a "community organizer" missionary. This means that also from his point of view the Corinthians must have been aware of different models, among which no one could easily claim the status of being the only right model. Theissen describes the different preconditions of the preachers well:

> It is immediately evident that fishermen and farmers turned itinerant preachers had to give up their work if they were to missionize in rural environs. They could not pack up and carry along their fields and lakes as one might one's tools. Peter the fisherman is forced by necessity to accept the "privilege of support"; Paul the craftsman can afford to renounce it.[26]

I suppose that all participants did realize and accept this without bigger problems.

Although it was relatively easy for Paul to begin to work for his living, this way of life as such was very hard. Paul describes it himself in 1 Thess 2:9: "And you remember, brothers, our hard labour and toil (τὸν κόπον ἡμῶν καὶ τὸν μόχθον); it was while we worked day and night so as not to be a charge on any of you, that we preached

[26] Theissen, *Social Setting*, 37–38. Cf. how M. Hengel, "Die Arbeit im frühen Christentum", *TBei* 17 (1986) 196–97, describes the actual way of Paul's working as follows: "Vermutlich verarbeitete er Leder zu Zelten (und andere Lederwaren), möglicherweise belieferte er zuweilen selbst die römische Armee, da das Heer der größte Abnehmer von Lederzelten war. Für sein Handwerk benötigte er offenbar nur einfaches Handwerksgerät, so daß er sich in den verschiedenen Städten relativ leicht Arbeit verschaffen konnte." More by Hock, *Social Context*, 20–21; Billerbeck, *Kommentar*, 2.746–47; Bienert, *Arbeit*, 300–4.

to you the gospel of God." Hock describes Paul's work as follows: "Making tents meant rising before dawn, toiling until sunset with leather, knives, and awls, and accepting the various social stigmas and humilations that were part of the artisan's lot, not to mention the poverty—being cold, hungry, and poorly clothed."[27]

It is no wonder that the working life of Paul, in particular, played a major role in his catalogues of hardships (cf., for example, 1 Cor 4:12; 2 Cor 11:27). The work is here in the role of a proof of Paul's voluntarily sacrificing himself in the interests of the Gospel. It is a thing he is proud of. Paul is therefore surely not including the work "as a significant shame element in his peristasis", as Marshall claims.[28]

Paul's status as apostle was of a special character (cf. 1 Cor 15:8–9) and therefore vulnerable. There were also people who did not want to accept his apostolate (cf. 1 Cor 9:2: "If I am not an apostle to others, yet at least to you I am"). Therefore the theme of apostolate easily entered discussions even where it would not have been necessary. It is enough to think that somebody in Corinth had only wondered why Paul's way of living was different from the way of living of the "the prince of apostles", Peter. Paul was indeed sensible in his relationship to Peter and the other "Pillars of Jerusalem". When we consider the First Letter to the Corinthians as a whole, it becomes very clear that the writer does not have the smallest doubts about his full authority as an apostle of Christ among the Corinthians. His status has not been seriously criticized by anyone in Corinth—not because of his refusing support or for other reasons.

When we are studying the problems of the Pauline salary in Corinth, we must not pass over the testimony of 1 Thess 2:5–12 as a whole and see how the fact that Paul was working with his own hands for his living conditions was, in fact, a positive thing in his relationship to the members of the congregation. Concerning the missionary work, in the Jewish context there was not only the rule that the preacher has a right to salary from the congregation, but along with it there was also the rule that God's word must be preached free of charge (δωρεὰν ἐλάβετε, δωρεὰν δότε, Matt 10:8).[29] Through his labouring Paul made it quite clear that he did not belong to the large and notorious group of wandering philosophers

[27] Hock, *Social Context*, 37.
[28] Contra Marshall, *Enmity*, 212.
[29] Agrell, *Work*, 63; Pratscher, "Verzicht", 291.

or prophets of new religions whose main purpose was to get for themselves a carefree living at the cost of others. The work gave evidence that Paul was a genuine and serious envoy of the truth. Paul is therefore proud, not apologetic, when he refers to his way of life.[30] It cannot be assumed that the attitude of the Corinthians was totally different from that of the Thessalonians in this matter. In the eyes of the Corinthians, the fact that Paul worked with his own hands must have also had its strong positive aspects while the problem of wandering religious cheats existed in Corinth, too.

Especially at the beginning of the proclaiming of the gospel in a new town, it was important for Paul not to take support from his listeners. When the congregation had been established and there were no doubts about Paul's motives, the possibilities were at hand to make other arrangements. In the Pauline texts, we can read that he had received support from the established congregations for his needs in other congregations (2 Cor 11:8–9; Phil 2:25–30, 4:10–18). From the Pauline material one could come to the conclusion that Paul did not take support from the congregation in which he was actually teaching, but it was possible for him to take support from outside.[31] It can also be that it was only the Macedonian congregations with which his relationship was so cordial that this was possible. From the text in 1 Cor 9, it becomes clear that the Corinthians had never supported their apostle, neither when he was in the town nor when he was outside.

At the beginning the rules concerning the salary in early Christianity seem to have been more a purely practical rather than a theological question.[32] It was important that the gospel spread as rapidly and smoothly as possible and that the preachers try to diminish all kinds of obstacles in their missionary work. The conditions in Palestine were different from those in Greece and Asia Minor. In Palestine the distances between the small villages were short and the net of

[30] More by E. von Dobschütz, *Die Thessalonicher-Briefe* (Nachdruck der Ausgabe von 1909, herausgegeben von Ferdinand Hahn; Göttingen: Vandenhoeck & Ruprecht, 1974) 2–6, 82–107; Hauck, *Stellung*, 105; E. Best, *A Commentary on the First and Second Epistles to the Thessalonians* (Black's New Testament Commentaries, London: Adam & Charles Black, 1972) 99; Theissen, *Soziologie*, 211–13; Lang, *Korinther*, 338; Wolff, *Der zweite Brief*, 222.

[31] Pratscher, "Verzicht", 290.

[32] Theissen, *Social Setting*, 54, sees the question in another way: "The theological question of an apostle's legitimacy is indissolubly linked with the material question of the apostle's subsistence."

sympathizers was thick. The rules in Luke 10:4–11 par. could be followed there whereas everything was different in the regions where Paul was travelling. It would have been madness to prescribe or even to suggest to Paul that he follow the same rules.

Theissen also emphasizes the differences between the conditions of "the itinerant charismatics in Palestine" and those of the "missionaries to the Gentiles" and describes them well. Nevertheless, he builds his total interpretation of the conflict between Paul and the "super apostles" on the hypothesis that the new apostles had taken the Palestinian rules for missionary work with them to Corinth and criticized Paul in the light of them: Paul should preach the gospel following a life style which was possible only in the rural land of Palestine and among the Jewish people! Theissen wants to point out that in the Hellinistic world outside Palestine there also was an analogous movement: the Cynic wandering teachers. Theissen describes the Cynics and the link between them and the Christian preachers as follows:

> Here too we find an elevated ethos of independence from earthly necessities based on an unqualified trust in God's will. The early Christian itinerant charismatic movement originating in Palestine could link up in the Greek world with the ethos of the Cynic itinerant preacher.[33]

Theissen can well be correct when he links the "super apostles" with the Cynics' way of living, but this conclusion brings these apostles hardly nearer to the early Jesus movement and to its rules in Palestine. The Jesus movement cannot be seen as a subordinate branch of the Cynic movement of that time, although there were some points of contact between the attitudes both had towards living conditions. The way of living of the "super apostles" can best be explained with the help of the general attitude of the wandering philosophers of that time. This was one model of how an important message could be spread, but it was not the only permissible and sanctified way. The "super apostles" also acted in a way different from what the synoptic rules ordained. The synoptic rules, for example, said nothing about the recommendation letters which seem to have played an important role in the travelling activity of the "super apostles" (2 Cor 3:1–3; 12:11–12). The rules for wandering preachers in Did 11:4–6 reflect similar living conditions as the ones in Synoptic Gospels.

[33] Theissen, *Social Setting*, 47.

When we, in addition, take these rules into consideration, it becomes more obvious how different the situation was in Syria-Palestine compared with that in Greece. The preachers in Palestine were in a continuous movement from village to village, but the "super apostles" had come to stay in Corinth.[34]

7. *The Corinthian congregation as a special case*

It was quite in accordance with his usual habit that Paul did not take support from the Corinthian congregation when he was there for the first time. But it seems exceptional that he proclaims in an extreme strong way that he "would rather die" than take support from them in the future either (1 Cor 9:15). Why does he proclaim his decision so strongly here? Why was his relationship to the Corinthian congregation so strict and so different?

The overall rule which regulated Paul's acting in the matter of salary was that he wanted "to put no obstacle in the way of the gospel of Christ" (1 Cor 9:12). Göran Agrell explicates the contents of this obstacle as follows:

> The most crucial hindrance to the reception of the gospel would have been that people might have thought that Paul and Barnabas preached in order to receive support or pay, like the γόητες ('imposters') of their time . . . Furthermore, those who would be forced to provide their support—especially the poor—might be deterred from receiving the gospel and entering the church. A further possibility is that Paul was in danger of becoming dependent on those who supported him, and could not then offer reproof without the suspicion being raised that he had been bought. Finally, the gathering of the collection for Jerusalem might be misinterpreted if Paul did not provide for himself.[35]

It is, however, not likely that Paul had *all* these points in view, but probably only the two first motives were important for him.[36]

---

[34] About the interpretation of Did 11:4–6 see K. Niederwimmer, *Die Didache* (KAV 1; Göttingen: Vandenhoeck & Ruprecht, 1989) 215–17.

[35] Agrell, *Work*, 110–11.

[36] Cf. also Lietzmann, *Korinther*, 42; G. Sass, *Apostelamt und Kirche: Eine theologisch-exegetische Untersuchung des paulinischen Apostelbegriffs* (Forschungen zur Geschichte und Lehre des Protentantismus 9/2; München, 1939) 61–62; H.-D. Wendland, *Die Briefe an die Korinther* (13th ed.; NTD 7; Göttingen: Vandenhoeck & Ruprecht, 1972) 73; H.D. Betz, *Lukian von Samosata und das Neue Testament: Religionsgeschichtliche und paränetische Parallelen* (TU 76; Berlin, 1961) 114; Dautzenberg, "Verzicht", 219.

Only when Paul could be sure that the condition "not to put an obstacle" was fulfilled in some congregation could he take support from it, or as Bengt Holmberg describes the rule: "Only when (and if) the relation between the apostle and the church has developed into a full, trusting κοινωνία does Paul accept any money from the church."[37] When Paul writes 1 Cor 9, he is thinking—surely not without some amount of vehemence—that his relationship to this congregation would never become such that he would be able to take support from it. The Corinthian congregation seems to be an exception.[38]

Why is the congregation an exception? To rephrase the question: Why is Paul writing about the congregation as if it would stay as an exception forever? Why does Paul seem to be so inflamed in his feelings when writing about this theme? We cannot suppose that we could find the only right and sure answer, but one possible answer could be as follows: The way the matter was brought into the discussion in the congregation before the writing of 1 Cor had insulted Paul's feelings. The Corinthians had compared Paul's way of living with the way of living of other apostles (1 Cor 9:4–6), and they had asked some questions about the reasons for the difference. The questions seem to have insulted Paul deeply—not because he feared for his apostolate in the eyes of the Corinthians, but because the Corinthians seem to mistake his motives completely. Paul thought he had done something praiseworthy in the eyes of others. The Corinthians seemed, however, for Paul's great disappointment to consider something which ought to have been ground for his boasting as a proof of his weakness. It was especially the *comparison* with Peter and the others from this wrong point of view that seems to have been insulting for Paul.

In 1 Cor 9 Paul had two reasons to use his refusal as an example. The first and—according the logical line of thought—most important reason was that it was a very good example for the right application of Christian freedom. Secondly, by choosing this example Paul was able to make clear an annoying misunderstanding: The

[37] Holmberg, *Power*, 94.

[38] Betz, *Tradition*, 105, 117, informatively describes Paul's relationship to the Corinthians and concludes: "Es hat den Anschein, als sei Paulus aus irgendeinem Grunde der Meinung gewesen, daß er in Korinth das Evangelium nur dann ungehindert verkündigen könne, wenn er auf dortige Unterstützung verzichte." He can, however, give no explanations for the reasons for Paul's decision. Cf. also Marshall, *Enmity*, 237, 240.

refusal of support was in fact his own voluntary choice and nobody was allowed to diminish its value.[39] Although the second reason came into the Pauline writing only secondarily, it soon captured the main role when Paul continued to develop his thoughts. In 1 Cor 9:15 Paul seems to lose all moderation when he wanted to stop the Corinthians from drawing wrong conclusions. That explains why he wrote his unhappy words that he "would rather die than" (ever take money from the congregation). The expression is hyperbole and does not present Paul's real thoughts about his future relationships to the Corinthians.

After the Corinthians had received the letter and had read the Pauline exposition about his motives in the question of support and his assurance that he would never even in the future take support from the Corinthians, it was their turn to be insulted. Paul's unfortunate formulations could then have produced the allegations he alludes to in 2 Cor: He did not love and trust them as much as other congregations because he refused to take support from them, although he took it from other congregations.

This is also the way Bengt Holmberg, for example, explains the development of the relationships between Paul and the Corinthian congregation. He writes:

> Unfortunately Paul's reluctance to ask for or accept financial support from this church led into a growing distrust, which eventually broke into open conflict . . . The church could not lightly accept the fact that their apostle received money from Macedonia while staying there and explaining to them that it was on principle impossible for him to accept support from Corinth, as he was a slave of the gospel. Once the facts are clear, it is difficult for the Corinthians not to draw the conclusion that they are less respected and less loved by the apostle than are other churches (2 Cor 11:11; 12:13,15).[40]

[39] Cf. D.L. Dungan, *The Sayings of Jesus in the Churches of Paul: The Use of the Synoptic Tradition in the Regulation of Early Church Life* (Oxford, 1971), 6: "There seems to be a certain defensiveness about Paul's argument in Chapter 9. As we can see from v. 5, Paul and his associates are being compared with Peter, the brothers of the Lord and other apostles, and some Corinthians must have been confused as to why Paul's group had not accepted their financial support as they had . . . Paul takes this opportunity to kill two birds with one stone. He argues, concerning meat sacrified to idols, why that legitimate right ought not to be observed when it would be injurious to the weaker brethren, and, at the same time, he takes as an illustration his own practice of not observing a certain legitimate authority of an apostle, when to do so would be injurious to the Church."

[40] Holmberg, *Power*, 95.

When Holmberg continues developing his interpretation, he is no longer convincing. He thinks that the accusation of lack of love brought with it further critique against Paul in Corinth. It brought the members of the congregation

> . . . to an even less favourable interpretation of his reluctance to accept Corinthian money: perhaps Paul had not given them their full share of spiritual gifts either (2 Cor 12:13a), or maybe this is tacit acknowledgment of the fact that he is inferior to other apostles who do not hesitate one moment to accept support (2 Cor 11:5ff.,20; 12:11ff.).[41]

Holmberg also unites the Corinthians' suspicions concerning the collection of money for the poor of Jerusalem with Paul's refusal of support. The appeal for the collection could, in their minds, be "Paul's indirect, clandestine way of claiming acknowledgment as an apostle." It might even be "a sly trick to acquire money through an intermediary (2 Cor 12:16ff.)".[42]

This is, indeed, not the most convincing interpretation of the verses in question. It is important to observe that in these verses we have already moved into the Letter of Tears with its special situation and special ironic rhetoric where one needs to be cautious in interpreting what Paul really means. Paul's alleged lack of love (2 Cor 11:11) was surely an embarrassment in the relationship between Paul and the Corinthians after he had sent the first presentation of the matter (1 Cor 9). The theme got new weight when, after the receiving of 1 Cor, new apostles came to Corinth who did not refuse salary from the congregation. Paul's behaviour now came into a new light. Did Paul's status in the eyes of the Corinthians become worse or better in this situation? The scholars usually answer in the former way, as Holmberg did also. Peter Marshall especially emphasizes that the new apostles had explicitly used Paul's refusal as a weapon against him in Corinth.[43] Victor Paul Furnish even suggests that perhaps first Paul's rivals "encouraged the Corinthians to think that Paul's remaining financially independent of them shows that he does not love them."[44] Yet, the Pauline statements about the matter can hardly be explained in this way when we concentrate on the actual text and style of the Letter of Tears.

---

[41] Ibid.
[42] Ibid.
[43] Marshall, *Enmity*, 177.
[44] Furnish, *II Corinthians*, 506.

8. *Paul's ironic humbling of himself (2 Cor 11:7; 12:13)*

What Paul wanted to explain in 1 Cor 9 had surely become clear in the minds of the Corinthians. There is, in fact, no real hint in the abundant material about the matter in 2 Cor that somebody had seen in Paul's independence a testimony about his weakness as an apostle although many scholars want to interpret the text in this way.

The fact that the Corinthians did not criticize the genuineness of Paul's apostolate from this point of view is obvious when we take into consideration what Paul writes in 2 Cor 11:11. After having said that he is—nota bene!—*boasting* about not to have been burdensome to the Corinthians and about keeping himself in the future from being burdensome to them (2 Cor 11:9–10), he continues with the question "Why?" He answers with a new question on behalf of the Corinthians, insinuating what he thinks they have wrongly concluded: "Because I do not love you?" Note that he does not write "Because I am not an apostle?" The theme of lack of love was the only difficulty concerning the refusal of salary which remained between Paul and the congregation after the sending of 1 Cor. This is the only real charge Paul defends himself against.[45]

In 2 Cor 11:11 Paul is serious, as the expression "God knows" shows. Some verses earlier, in 2 Cor 11:7, Paul wrote: "Or did I commit a sin in humbling myself that you might be exalted, by preaching the Gospel of God to you for nothing?" Is he also here raising serious questions and is he really anxious that he has done wrong in the past when he preached in Corinth without taking money from the members of the congregation? This is the way in which, for example, Ronald F. Hock interprets the situation. He thinks that the charge of the opponents played an important role here and connects the accusation of lack of love to the subject matter of 2 Cor 11:7:

> We may find the explanation by recalling the debates over the appropriate means of support for philosophers and other intellectuals. We recall that one justification for entering a household . . . was the bond

[45] Here I agree with Zmijewski, *Stil*, 142: "Der Apostel greift offensichtlich auf einen konkreten Vorwurf zurück, der ihm . . . seitens der korinthischen Gemeinde . . . gemacht wurde. Der Vorwurf mag gelautet haben: 'Du liebst uns nicht . . ., weil du gerade von uns keine Unterstützung annimmst.'" Theissen, *Social Setting*, 48, again thinks that Paul was not able to persuade the Corinthians with the help of 1 Cor 9.

> of friendship between philosopher and patron, with friendship being the reason for having all things in common. Perhaps the opponents, basing their having received support from the Corinthians (11:20; cf. 2:17) on friendship, had argued that Paul's refusal to be supported reflected a lack of friendship, or love, on his part toward them.[46]

As I already have pointed out, the solution with the model patron and his house chaplain can nevertheless hardly be a sound way of interpretation here.

In interpreting 2 Cor 11:7, we must think that Paul is speaking here in an extremely ironical way. The answer to the question of the verse is self-evident: That Paul had given the Corinthians the Gospel with all its blessings was clearly no sin. Similarly self-evident was the blamelessness of the other part of his behaviour. He had not taken money for doing these things, but had worked hard for his own living. Such an attitude to his apostolate could indeed not be considered as sin, and nobody had really suggested it. This is also the interpretation of 2 Cor 11:7 which most scholars have chosen. All of them have yet not understood that 2 Cor 12:13 must also be interpreted in a similar way. There is no serious or other accusation against Paul when he formulates his thoughts as follows: "In what respect were you put lower than the other churches, except that I myself did not make myself a burden to you? Forgive me this injury." Paul does not defend himself here against any charges of not having given all his spiritual knowledge to the Corinthians—or whatever the accusations could be. He is just playing a bitter rhetorical game with self-evident facts and so stressing the very strong sides of his altruistic behaviour.[47]

We cannot understand the contents of the Letter of Tears right if we do not correctly understand the style which Paul uses in the letter. 2 Cor 10–13 is full of irony of a special kind, but not all material in these chapters is ironic. Paul changes his style and can often be very serious, too. On the superficial level, taken only as representative of one style, the text seems contradictory. The interpreter has to be able to separate the ironic statements from the normal speech.

The irony Paul uses is in many places rather simple; he writes the opposite of what he really has in mind. That Paul often gives

[46] Hock, *Social Context*, 62–63.

[47] For the interpretation of 2 Cor 12:13–18, see Aejmelaeus, *Schwachheit*, 164–70.

no clear hint about the fact that he is speaking the opposite of what he really thinks is part of his ironic style. Paul usually does not say, "Look, here I say what I don't really mean." The places where he says that he speaks "like a fool" point more to forbidden subjects than to travesty (2 Cor 11:1,16–19,21; 12:11), although this way of speaking, as such, indicates that the text as a whole may also include other traps for the reader. But where these are located is not pointed out clearly. The only sure hints we find are the places in which the exaggeration is already so heavy that the sayings cannot possibly be taken seriously, as in 2 Cor 11:16–21a, or in the cases where some clearly ironical terms like "super apostles" (2 Cor 11:5; 12:11) indicate an ironic approach. Most frequently the readers must realize the irony without any clear hints, and the first readers of 2 Cor 10–13 also certainly understood well when Paul was only playing a bitter game with them. They knew very well the real situation and what they themselves and the "super apostles" had claimed concerning Paul, his behaviour and his value as an apostle. When they heard that Paul was defending himself against charges which were never suggested by them, they automatically realized that the text was ironic. The later readers no longer have the same keys to automatically understanding the text correctly. This is also our situation today. All scholars agree that there is much irony in the chapters, but opinions are divided in the details when we try to define the character of isolated verses.[48]

I think that there is a great deal of irony in the way Paul defends himself about his refusal of salary. He is only pretending that he defends himself while in reality he is, in fact, attacking his opponents.[49] The Letter of Tears is a fighting letter in which Paul's aim is by every possible means to win back the congregation which is drifting farther away from him through the influence of the "super apostles". Bitter irony is one of his weapons. With its help, he thinks he is better able to point out his advantages compared with his opponents.

Irony is also a good weapon concerning the religious inhibitions which Paul has against directly boasting about himself. Speaking in a contrary way, the Pauline overall rule "If anyone is to boast, let

[48] Theissen, *Soziologie*, 217–20, is able to uphold his interpretation about the nature of the conflict in Corinth only because he takes the material which, in my opinion, must be understood as ironic in 2 Cor 10–13 as non-ironic.

[49] Cf. the opposite interpretation of the situation by Marshall, *Enmity*, 225.

him boast in the Lord" (2 Cor 10:17) has not been broken. While Paul is seemingly defending himself in 2 Cor 11:7, he is in fact emphasizing one point where he has a much stronger position than the new apostles: He has not been living on the support of the congregation, but the "super apostles" have. In 2 Cor 11:8 Paul changes his style. Now he is no longer saying the opposite from reality but exaggerating very heavily his behaviour: He claims that he "robbed other churches" by taking payment from them in order that he "might be able to serve" the Corinthians.

9. *The aspirations of the adversaries to be like Paul (2 Cor 11:12)*

After 2 Cor 11:8 Paul by and by abandons the irony. In 2 Cor 11:12 he is already fully serious when he writes the difficult sentence: Ὃ δὲ ποιῶ, καὶ ποιήσω, ἵνα ἐκκόψω τὴν ἀφορμὴν τῶν θελόντων ἀφορμήν, ἵνα ἐν ᾧ καυχῶνται εὑρεθῶσιν καθὼς καὶ ἡμεῖς. In translating the verse, the key word is ἀφορμή. The Liddell-Scott Lexicon gives to it the meanings "starting-point, esp. in war", "base of operations".[50] These meanings in their metaphorical sense suit well to this verse. Knowing this, we can accept the following translation (after C.K. Barrett):[51] "But what I am doing, that I will also continue to do, in order to cut off opportunity from those who would like to have an opportunity to become, in their boasting, just what we are." Paul's practice of preaching and working which recently seemed to be a sin is suddenly something so valuable that he does not want to abandon it. It is something which even the "super apostles" envy. The contents of the verse make a contradictory impression compared with the earlier verses because Paul has left the irony for a moment and speaks openly about how things really are from his point of view. His financial independence is something unique, and he will

[50] H.G. Liddell – R. Scott, *A Greek-English Lexicon* (ed. H.S. Jones and R. McKenzie; 9th ed.; Oxford: Clarendon Press, 1968) s.v. Cf. Zmijewski, *Stil*, 151: "Auch das Substantiv ἡ ἀφορμή stellt einen recht plastischen Ausdruck dar und ist zudem noch mehrdeutig: Es bedeutet nicht nur 'Anlaß' bzw. 'Gelegenheit', sondern meint auch den 'Ausgangs- u. Stützpunkt einer Expedition'. Genau dies dürfte Paulus hier betonen wollen: Die Gegner suchen gleichsam einen strategischen 'Stützpunkt', von dem aus sie den Apostel bekämpfen können, um auf diese Weise für sich selbst Kapital zu schlagen."

[51] C.K. Barrett, *A Commentary on the Second Epistle to the Corinthians* (Black's New Testament Commentaries; London: Adam & Charles Black, 1973) 270–71.

not change it. He is not willing to descend to the same level as the new apostles. They would be only too happy if he would do so.

It is only natural that the complicated verse and the situation behind it has had many different interpretations among scholars. Many of them have choosen a more or less different way from that presented above. One of these is Theissen, whose interpretation is present in the following quotation, in which he describes the conflict between Paul and the new charismatic apostles:

> Itinerant charismatics arriving in Corinth made a claim on support from the community. The members reacted at first by pointing to Paul: our apostle Paul never raised any such claims. In response, the itinerant charismatics could point to the words of Jesus as a justification for their position. As regards Paul, that left but two choices. Either they must convert him to their style of life or deny him his claim to apostolicity. Possibly they tried the first; at any rate Paul protests: "And what I do (namely, forgoing my right to subsistence) I will continue to do, in order to undermine the claim of those who would like to claim that in their boasted mission they work on the same terms as we do" (2 Cor 11:12).[52]

When the new apostles came to Corinth, the members of the congregation had already read Paul's answer in 1 Cor 9 so that the issue of the salary of a preacher and the different ways the preachers actually lived was no longer new to them. They did not need to ask anything when the new apostles wanted to be supported by them. It has also become clear that "the words of Jesus" played no crucial role in this discussion. In addition Paul is hardly speaking here about any clear "claims" of the new apostles, but more about the secret hopes which he concludes they must have in their evil minds.[53]

---

[52] Theissen, *Social Setting*, 53. Also Pratscher, "Verzicht", 295–96, interprets in the same manner and describes the activity of the new apostles as follows: "Immerhin ist ein doppelbödiges Spiel der Gegner erkennbar: einerseits benutzen sie den Verzicht des Paulus als Argument gegen ihn, andererseits sehen sie in demselben Verzicht etwas, das er ihnen voraus hat und das er durch die von ihnen gewünschte Annahme von Unterstützung einbüßen soll."

[53] Betz, *Tradition*, 102, interprets the vers as follows: "Mit seinem Hinweis, daß er (sc. Paul) von den Korinthern finanziell nicht unterstützt worden ist noch unterstützt werden will, kann er gegenüber den Gegnern einen Vorteil für sich buchen. Das erkennen offenbar die Gegner stillschweigend damit an, daß sie durch die Korinther versucht haben, Paulus zur Annahme von Geld und also zur Aufgabe seiner vorteilhaften Position zu bewegen. Dieser ist freilich zu klug, um in die Falle hineinzulaufen. Er macht den Unterschied zwischen seinem und dem Verhalten der Gegner möglichst augenfällig, damit diese nicht in die Lage versetzt werden

It is difficult to believe that the new apostles really had tried to get Paul to take money from the congregation. Besides the unlikelihood of such an attempt as such it is also difficult to imagine the concrete situation and the real life circumstances in which Paul could have encountered such attempts by the new apostles.

The new men had first come to Corinth after Paul had left the town and been away a long time. During his second short, sad visit in Corinth he met the new apostles. Was it during this visit they did try "to convert him to their style of life"? This is unlikely because Paul's *short* visit to Corinth gave no real opportunity for such attempts by the "super apostles". There were two preconditions for the new arrangement of the economic relationship between the congregation and Paul that were not fulfilled. 1) To convert to the style of life of the intruders was not a simple matter of accepting once some amount of cash from the congregation. It would have been presupposed that Paul really *stayed* there a longer time and *lived* there as their teacher. 2) An agreement on economic arrangements would also have required that Paul's relationship to the Corinthians had been unproblematic. People discuss such things in an atmosphere of trust and peace, not when they are quarrelling with each other. It is therefore difficult to believe that the "super apostles" had made a real and concrete attempt during Paul's short visit in the town for the purpose of getting him to take money from the congregation. There surely were other subject matters which were much more important such as the real charges against Paul, the charges of the weakness of Paul's preaching and of his person, and the accusations that he was not spiritual enough when compared with the intruders (2 Cor 10:1,10; 11:5–6; 13:3).

The interpretation that the opponents really did try to make Paul accept money from the Corinthians in order that he would descend to their level, that he would become like them, is in fact too complicated to be true. The presuppositions which must be assumed in order to accept this solution are not from real life. The whole thought about the wishes of the new apostles cannot be more than Paul's speculation, his conclusion on how they must see the issue. Paul is

können zu sagen, mit ihnen verhielte es sich genauso wie mit Paulus." I agree with this interpretation in other aspects, but not in the notion that the opponents really would have tried to make the Corinthians to give Paul money in order that Paul by accepting salary from the congregation would become like them.

speaking only about "wishes" (τῶν θελόντων)—and that must mean secret wishes, the existence of which Paul only supposes—not about real statements.

The "super apostles" had taken support from the congregation and in doing so they had done nothing wrong; the Christian missionaries were allowed to do so. Paul does not claim that taking support would be wrong as such. Peter, Apollos and others, whom Paul does not want to attack, did so, too. Concerning the "super apostles", Paul only wants to point out that they have exaggerated this privilege in Corinth. That is what Paul wants to point out in the very ironical verses 2 Cor 11:16–21a. He asserts that the new apostles have robbed the congregation and that the Corinthians have enjoyed it: "If anyone enslaves you, if anyone eats you out of house and home, if anyone strikes you on the face, you put up with him." He begs to be forgiven that he himself has been too weak to give them the same pleasure.

Although Paul is in 2 Cor 11:16–21a surely exaggerating the actual behaviour of the new apostles, the benefits of his own modest life style become so very clear. Comparing his own refusal of support with the exaggerated picture of the greediness of the new apostles, Paul wants to designate them religious cheats. This suspicion was never far away in connection with travelling teachers of that time especially in connection with money.[54]

Paul emphasizes that the new apostles would like to be like him in their relationship towards the congregation but they will never reach this state. Paul is and stays in a unique relationship with his congregation. The congregation has only one father, and Paul has this status.[55] With the help of this picture, Paul is also able to explain the charges of his lack of love to his own advantage. Paul does this very skilfully in 2 Cor 12:13–15. In an ironic way, he begs forgiveness that he "did not make himself a burden" to the Corinthians as

---

[54] Cf. Betz, *Tradition*, 115: "Paulus versetzt den Gegnern zwei Schläge. Einmal ist sein Verzicht auf finanzielle Zuwendungen ein für damalige Ansicht eindeutiger Beweis dafür, daß man ihn nicht als Goet einstufen kann. Leute, die das dennoch tun, machen sich selbst verdächtig. Paulus scheut sich nicht, den Spieß herumzudrehen: seine Gegner sind es, die sich mit ihrer Bereitschaft, Geld anzunehmen, als Goeten ausweisen."

[55] Marshall, *Enmity*, 247–51, gives a good analysis of the pattern of parent and child relationship in antiquity and used by Paul.

he had done with other congregations (2 Cor 12:13).[56] When the members of the congregation up till now had suspected that the explanation for this fact was that Paul did not love and did not respect them as much as other congregations, Paul gives them now another explanation: His attitude is, on the contrary, a sign of the deepest love relationship there is, namely, the relationship between a father and his children. "Children ought not to save up for their parents, but parents for their children" (2 Cor 12:14). His refusal of support was rightly understood not as lovelessness towards the Corinthians, but as deepest love. "If I love you more abundantly, am I loved the less?" (2 Cor 12:15). Because of his refusal, the Corinthians should only love him more and not think ill of him. The "super apostles" had indeed reason to envy him and his unique place in the Corinthian congregation.

10. *Conclusion*

Those parts of the Letter of Tears in which Paul is apologizing for *not* having taken support from the congregation are severely misunderstood if one does not regard much of this material as ironic. In fact, Paul was not accused of not having taken salary from the congregation. This conclusion can be build on the following four points:

1) The text itself is contradictory if it is taken at its face value, on one stylistic level only, as if Paul is continuously serious about what he is saying. If one interprets the Pauline expressions so that he only pretends to apologize and defend himself against accusations of *not* having taken money from the congregation, everything becomes very clear.

2) The interpretation that Paul—or anybody—could have proved himself a genuine apostle by only accepting money from the congregation is already from the common sense viewpoint all too simple. If Paul had only said to the Corinthians: "Give me money", they would have been satisfied, had believed in his apostleship and most of Paul's troubles would have been swept away. This way of proving one's apostleship would have been too easy to be plausible.

[56] The ironic character of 2 Cor 12:13–15 is well emphasized by Betz, *Tradition*, 116–17.

3) There was nothing in the Hellenistic tradition—neither in the Jewish religion, in the pagan religiosity nor in the conditions of life in the social environment of Paul—which would have forced Paul to take a salary from the congregation if he wanted to be taken seriously as an apostle; things were rather the other way around.

4) When one examines the different accusations against Paul, it becomes very clear that all the other accusations belong to another area, namely to spiritual weakness in speaking and appearance and lack of ecstatic experiences. The accusations concerning money belong to a category which makes a strange impression in this connection. This also hints at the solution that this issue does not stem from the Pauline opponents but is an ironic counterattack of Paul himself whereby he wishes to demonstrate his special relationship to the congregation.

What was the real situation behind the Pauline salary utterances, if he is not defending himself against some clear accusations? It seems to be clear that the support of Paul in Corinth had from the very beginning little to do with the problem of his apostolate. The different practices among the apostles and other Christian preachers had brought about some disturbance in the minds of the members of the Corinthian congregation, and Paul deals with these problems when he writes about the Christian freedom in 1 Cor 9. He did it nevertheless in such an indiscreet way that the Corinthians were insulted because they could draw the conclusion that he did not love and respect them as much as other congregations.

The whole matter was still not a serious obstacle between Paul and his congregation. Serious problems first arose after new Christian teachers, who stood for a different conception of the Christian faith and how ministers of Christ must conduct themselves, came to Corinth. The new teachers criticized Paul on the grounds of the spiritual characteristics of an apostle, and they also succeeded in undermining Paul's authority in the eyes of the congregation.

In this situation, Paul defends himself with all available means, mostly attacking heavily the "super apostles" and emphasizing his own worth and achievements. He does this often in an ironic way, speaking the opposite of what he really has in mind. The readers of the letter understood Paul's points without difficulty because they knew very well the real facts. What Paul says about support is to be seen in this light. He only seemingly defends himself in this matter because his refusal of salary is an advantage for him when compared with the behaviour of the new apostles, who lived at the expense of the congregation. In this new situation, Paul was able to skilfully change the reproof of lovelessness to the reverse. That he himself was not taking support from the congregation was clear proof of his unique status. He was the only apostolic father of the Corinthians. Therefore, his action was according to the action of a father towards his children. His refusal was proof of the deepest love. The intruders behaved differently and could only envy Paul and his special relationship to the congregation. This is, in any case, how Paul himself wanted to explain the situation.

PHILIPPIANS: PHANTOM OPPONENTS AND THE REAL SOURCE OF CONFLICT

MORNA D. HOOKER

1. *Introduction: The Nature of the Opposition*

Who were Paul's "opponents" in Philippi? This much-debated question[1] should perhaps give way to the more fundamental question: *were* there any opponents within the Philippian community? That there were opponents *to* the Christian community in Philippi is plain, for they are clearly referred to in 1:28. Since very little is said about them, except that they are heading for destruction and are causing the Philippians suffering, and since there is no hint that they are preaching the "wrong" gospel, this group must almost certainly have consisted of outsiders,[2] who were opposed to the gospel and were persecuting the Christians in Philippi, much as Paul himself had suffered at their hands.[3] What, then, is the evidence for opposition to Paul's gospel *within* the Christian community? In 3:2 Paul issues a peremptory warning against "the dogs", who were clearly Judaizers of some kind, but the warning serves mainly to introduce a discussion of his own renunciation of Jewish privilege, which reflects Christ's own self-emptying. There is no evidence of any significant Jewish presence in Philippi, and no hint that these people were already at work in that city; the warning here seems to be a general one—be careful if you come across such people!—rather than referring to a specific, known danger. In 3:18–19 Paul refers to those who "live as enemies of the cross of Christ", but, remarkably, says that he has

[1] For a recent summary of some of the main suggestions, see Peter O'Brien, *The Epistle to the Philippians* (New International Greek Testament Commentary; Grand Rapids, Mich: Eerdmans, 1991) 26–35. For later discussion, see Günter Klein, "Antipaulinismus in Philippi: Eine Problemskizze", in D.-A. Koch et al. (eds.), *Jesu Rede von Gott und ihre Nachgeschichte im frühen Christentum: Beiträge zur Verkündigung Jesu und zum Kerygma der Kirche* (FS Willi Marxsen; Gütersloh: Gerd Mohn, 1989) 297–313; Christoph Kähler, "Konflikt, Kompromiss und Bekenntnis: Paulus und seine Gegner im Philipperbrief", *KD* 40 (1994) 47–64.

[2] In Philippi, the opposition was almost certainly pagan.

[3] Phil 1:30; Acts 16:19–24.

often told the Philippians about them—suggesting, again, that this was a danger that had not yet invaded the community.[4] Finally, we have in 4:2–3 Paul's plea to Euodia and Syntyche "to be of the same mind in the Lord". Here we are clearly dealing, not with false teaching or opposition to Paul (since both have wrestled side by side with Paul "in the gospel", together with others who are all Paul's co-workers), but rather with some personal dispute. It is not surprising, then, that some recent commentators have concluded that the notion that the Philippian community had been invaded by opponents to Paul's gospel is the product of scholars' faulty "mirror-reading" of the text.[5] There is, indeed, *no* evidence that there were *any* "false teachers" in the Philippian community.

Our concern in this paper, however, centres on a somewhat different problem, which arises from personal rivalry rather than doctrinal opposition, and involves not the Philippians, but Paul himself. In 1:12–26, Paul explains his own situation to the Philippians, declaring that his imprisonment has in fact helped to advance the gospel, both because news of the reason for his imprisonment has spread but also because many members of the Christian community in the city where he is imprisoned[6] have been inspired by his courage and confidence in the Lord to preach the gospel.[7] Some of them, however, do so for the wrong reasons—out of strife and rivalry, and because of their own selfish ambition. Strangely, Paul does not directly condemn these people, but concludes that, whatever their motives, Christ is nevertheless being proclaimed, and that this is all that matters.

Although commentators have sometimes identified these people as "Judaizers", it is difficult to see how this could be the case. How

[4] It would seem that this is a different group from the "dogs" in 3:2. For a brief summary of the issues, see M.D. Hooker, "Philippians" in L.E. Keck et al. (eds.), *New Interpreter's Bible* (Nashville, Tenn.: Abingdon, 2000) 11.534b–535a.

[5] Gordon D. Fee, *Paul's Letter to the Philippians* (New International Commentary on the New Testament; Grand Rapids, Mich.: Eerdmans, 1995) 7–10; Markus Bockmuehl, *The Epistle to the Philippians* (Black's New Testament Commentaries; London: A. & C. Black, 1997) 18–19.

[6] Rome, Caesarea and Ephesus have all been suggested as the place of Paul's imprisonment, but Rome is by far the most likely, and the difficulties with this solution have been exaggerated. See the major commentaries for summaries of the arguments. In this essay we shall assume that the letter was written from Rome.

[7] Paul in fact expresses this more modestly: it is others who have been made confident in the Lord by his bonds. Here we see the same paradoxical sharing of strength and consolation "in Christ" by those who are weak or afflicted, that we find in passages such as 2 Cor 12:8–9; 1:3–7.

could he describe Judaizers as "proclaiming Christ", when in Gal 1:6–7 he refers to their teaching as "another gospel", and indeed quickly denies that it is a gospel at all? Suggestions that he has "mellowed" in his opposition to the Judaizers since writing Galatians founder when we turn to Phil 3:2.[8] Moreover, there is no criticism here of the content of this group's preaching. Paul clearly recognizes these people as fellow-Christians: they are included among those whom he describes as "brothers in the Lord" (1:14), and they are said to "speak the word" (1:14), to "preach Christ" (1:15) and to "proclaim Christ" (1:17). Though he thinks they are doing the right thing for the wrong motive, they can hardly be described as "opponents". He refuses to regard them as rivals, even though he obviously believes that they see *themselves* as his rivals. The problem (as in 4:2–3) concerns personal conflicts rather than doctrinal disputes.

Yet this distinction between "doctrine" and personal rivalry immediately raises a further problem. Were not the gospel and personal attitudes inextricably linked? Did not the message of Christ's own self-emptying, death and exaltation imply the necessity for Christians to be conformed to the same pattern in their everyday lives? Certainly this seems to be Paul's basic argument throughout Phil 1:27–3:21! Did he not argue that the image of Christ must be stamped on the Christian?[9] Is it not perfectly clear that conformity to that image excludes such things as φθόνος, ἔρις and ἐριθεία?[10] Did Paul not consider personal rivalry and bickering to be a danger to the Church?[11] Is it not essential that those who preach the gospel must preach Christ, not themselves,[12] and that this must be demonstrated in the preachers' own lives?[13] Describing his call in Gal 1:16, Paul speaks

[8] I have argued elsewhere for the unity of Philippians, on the basis that chapter 3 reflects and continues the argument of chapter 2. See M.D. Hooker, "Philippians 2:6–11" in E. Earle Ellis & Erich Grässer (eds.), *Jesus und Paulus* (FS Werner Georg Kümmel; Göttingen: Vandenhoeck & Ruprecht, 1975) 151–64; reprinted in M.D. Hooker, *From Adam to Christ* (Cambridge: CUP 1990) 88–100.

[9] Rom 6:1–11; 2 Cor 3:18.

[10] All three terms are included in the list of "the works of the flesh" in Gal 5:19–21. Cf. also 2 Cor 12:20, where we find ἔρις and ἐριθεία in the list of what Paul regards as possible dangers to the community.

[11] Cf. 1 Cor 1–3, where those who encourage such attitudes are said to be in danger of destroying the temple of the Holy Spirit, 1 Cor 3:16–17.

[12] 2 Cor 4:5. Cf. 1 Cor 3:5–9.

[13] See, e.g., 2 Cor 4:5: "ourselves as your slaves, for Jesus' sake". Cf. 1 Cor 9:19–23: I have discussed this passage elsewhere; see M.D. Hooker, "A Partner in the Gospel: Paul's Understanding of His Ministry", in Eugene H. Lovering and

of God choosing ἀποκαλύψαι τὸν Υἱὸν αὐτοῦ ἐν ἐμοί, and if we take that ἐν seriously, then Paul is placing the emphasis on Christ being revealed through what he, Paul, becomes—i.e. his manner of life—rather than through what he proclaims. This is hardly surprising, since he goes on to declare: "It is no longer I who live, but it is Christ who lives in me" (Gal 2:20). This is why he dares to urge his converts to imitate his example.[14]

In accusing these people of preaching Christ because of envy and strife (v. 15), and as the result of selfish ambition (v. 17), it would seem that Paul is making the kind of criticism that was brought against himself in Corinth (2 Cor 4:5). We might expect him to say that their selfish ambition emptied the cross of its power, as he does in 1 Cor 1:17, when attacking the rivalry that was endemic in Corinth. In Paul's view, concern for one's self contradicts the underlying principle of the gospel, which must be reflected in concern for others. Yet here he insists that in spite of their mixed motives these preachers *are* "proclaiming Christ".

Paul's unhappiness regarding the motives of his fellow-Christians in Rome surfaces again in Phil 2:20–21, when he complains that of those whom he might send to Philippi he can trust only Timothy to have the interests of the Philippians at heart, since the rest are all concerned about their own interests. The people whom Paul has in mind here are presumably a smaller group than those he refers to in 1:15, 17, and do not necessarily overlap with them, but their general attitude is similar: they are concerned with their own welfare, rather than that of others. It seems that Paul is determined that his envoy to Philippi should be the ideal role-model.

Finally, we notice that there are hints that Paul believes that the same infection may be creeping into the Philippian congregation. The clearest indication of this comes in 4:2–3, where he refers to a disagreement between two leading members of the Christian community. We are not told the cause of the disagreement, and Paul does not accuse Euodia and Syntyche of rivalry and ambition, but the fact that he urges them to be of the same mind in the Lord suggests that he believes that each of them is more concerned about having her own way than with the truth of the gospel. It sounds

Jerry L. Sumney (eds.), *Theology and Ethics in Paul and His Interpreters* (FS Victor Paul Furnish; Nashville, Tenn.: Abingdon, 1996) 83–100.

[14] 1 Cor 4:16; Phil 3:17.

very much as though Paul suspects that the strife and rivalry which he has encountered in Rome may be present in Philippi. If so, then the way in which he spells out the gospel in terms of Christ's self-emptying and stresses its implications for Christian living is clearly relevant to the Philippian community.[15] This perhaps explains why he is so anxious to send the right envoy to Philippi, someone who will provide the right example to the community. Yet Paul speaks warmly of these two women as having struggled alongside him in the work of the gospel; and having urged them to "agree in the Lord", and requested his "loyal companion" to assist them, he drops the matter: the danger appears to be minimal, and certainly does not affect Paul's overwhelming joy regarding the Philippians' genuine faith and their "partnership in the gospel".[16] The characteristic note of the epistle is joy, and he refers to the Philippian Christians as his "joy and crown"[17] Whatever the dispute between the two women, it appears not to have been a major problem.[18]

We need, then, to examine further two related issues:

First, why does Paul refuse to regard the group referred to in 1:15, 17 as opponents, and insist that these people *are* preaching Christ, in spite of attitudes which might be thought to negate the gospel?

Second, what were the problems and concerns that led Paul to write the letter to the Philippians? Did it perhaps arise out of and reflect his own situation and problems as much as those of the Philippians?

2. *Paul's "Rivals" in Philippians 1:15–17*

Paul's reference to those who are preaching Christ as a result of his imprisonment is set out in chiastic form, drawing a clear contrast between honest and false motives:

[15] Phil 1:27–2:18.
[16] Phil 1:5–11; 4:15–20.
[17] Phil 4:1.
[18] The recent study by Davorin Peterlin, *Paul's Letter to the Philippians in the Light of Disunity in the Church* (NovTSup 79; Leiden/New York/Köln: Brill, 1995) greatly exaggerates the problems by excessive "mirror-reading".

τινὲς μὲν καὶ διὰ φθόνον καὶ ἔριν,
τινὲς δὲ καὶ δι' εὐδοκίαν
τὸν Χριστὸν κηρύσσουσιν·

οἱ μὲν ἐξ ἀγάπης,
εἰδότες ὅτι εἰς ἀπολογίαν τοῦ εὐαγγελίου κεῖμαι,
οἱ δὲ ἐξ ἐριθείας
τὸν Χριστὸν καταγγέλλουσιν,
οὐχ ἁγνῶς, οἰόμενοι θλῖψιν ἐγείρειν τοῖς δεσμοῖς μου.

Τί γάρ; πλὴν ὅτι παντὶ τρόπῳ,
εἴτε προφάσει
εἴτε ἀληθείᾳ,
Χριστὸν καταγγέλλεται
καὶ ἐν τούτῳ χαίρω.

On the one hand we have φθόνος, ἔρις and ἐριθεία. In Rom 1:29, φθόνος and ἔρις are both said to characterize fallen humanity, while in the following chapter (2:8), those who are doomed to wrath are those who live ἐξ ἐριθείας and who disobey the truth (ἀλήθεια). But this does not mean that these attitudes are no longer found in the Christian community! In 13:12–13, the Romans are urged to lay aside the works of darkness, which include ἔρις (here linked with ζῆλος). In 1 Cor 1:11 we learn that there are ἔριδες in Corinth and in 1 Cor 3:3, ἔρις and ζῆλος are seen as a sign that the Corinthians are not πνευματικός but σαρκικός. In 2 Cor 12:20 Paul expresses his fear that he will not find the community to be what he would like them to be; the catalogue of what he fears he *will* find includes both ἔρις and ἐριθεία. Gal 5:20–21 refers to all three terms in a list of the works of the flesh which are opposed to the Spirit, but the warning against them indicates that there is a real danger that the Galatians may succumb to them. Finally, we note that the Philippians themselves are urged to do nothing from ἐριθεία in 2:3.

It is worth noting that φθόνος and ἔρις appear together in secular Greek as attitudes which were considered to endanger the common good. Thus Dio Chrysostom (writing a little later than Paul) condemns them as opposing concord in the community, and regards them as inappropriate behaviour for the manly and high minded.[19] In an earlier discourse,[20] he contrasts those who are motivated by

[19] *Or.* 77/78.37–39.
[20] *Or.* 38.8–9.

concern for the good of others and those who are seeking personal glory. This is remarkably similar to Paul's antipathy to these attitudes. Yet Paul's concern goes beyond this, for he regards these things as belonging to the sphere of the flesh, not the Spirit, and it is clear in 1 Corinthians 1 that he sees them as endangering the unity of the body of Christ.

In opposition to φθόνος and ἔρις, Paul sets εὐδοκία, whose meaning is far from straightforward. Whose good will is in mind? The word's normal meaning in the LXX and New Testament is "God's will or purpose",[21] though in Rom 10:1 Paul uses it of his own resolve.[22] But this is hardly what we understood by "goodwill", which is the meaning normally given to the term here. The word is used again in Phil 2:13, and though some commentators interpret it there also as meaning "goodwill", it is more naturally understood as referring to God's good pleasure or purpose: it is God who is at work in the Christian community in Philippi, bringing about the fulfilment of his will. Some have argued, therefore, that the word has the same meaning in 1:15:[23] if this is correct, what Paul is contrasting to φθόνος and ἔρις is not simply goodwill towards himself, but a willingness to be used by God for the sake of his purposes.

However we interpret this word, the issue focuses on attitudes towards Paul in the next contrast, which is between ἀγαπή and ἐριθεία. There is little need to explore the appropriateness of ἀγαπή in this context, for it sums up, as does no other term, the quality which should characterize life in the Spirit. In 1 Corinthians 13 it is the supreme gift which holds the body together—in contrast to the ἔριδες of 1:11 that are in danger of tearing it apart. Love is the very opposite of selfish ambition.

In Phil 1:16–17 the contrast between ἀγαπή and ἐριθεία is filled out and made specific by two defining clauses. On the one hand, those motivated by love know that Paul has been put in prison for the defence of the gospel. On the other, those motivated by selfish ambition are not sincere but imagine that they can increase his sufferings. It looks, then, as though the particular problem being described here has something to do with the way in which Paul's

[21] In the Pauline literature, see Eph 1:5, 9.
[22] Cf. also 2 Thess 1:11, where the meaning is ambiguous.
[23] Bockmuehl, *Philippians*, in loc.

fellow-Christians view his imprisonment. If the first group know that Paul has been imprisoned for the defence of the gospel, this is presumably something that the members of the second group have failed to grasp.

What exactly is Paul claiming here? The word κεῖμαι in v. 16 suggests that he thinks of himself as being "placed" in prison or "appointed" to be there. The purpose of this is conveyed by the word ἀπολογία, a term which was linked in v. 7 with βεβαιώσις, confirmation, and it is already clear from vv. 12–14 that his defence of the gospel has helped to spread it; his expectation of a positive outcome from this "defence" (whatever the verdict at the trial!) will be affirmed in v. 20.

This very positive attitude towards Paul's imprisonment—that it has, in effect, been part of God's εὐδοκία—is set in contrast to a very negative view, held by the other group. Paul obviously believes that the members of this group see themselves as his rivals; if, as he says, they imagine that he will be hurt to learn of their successful preaching, then they must see *him* as a failure. Do they perhaps think that he is in danger of bringing the Christian community into disrepute, and thus *damaging* the cause? Do they think that Paul has come into unnecessary conflict with the political authorities? Do they therefore consider him an embarrassment, and rejoice that he is out of the way? Do they perhaps even believe that his imprisonment is a sign of divine punishment?

What we have in Phil 1:15, 17 is, of course, Paul's own assessment of this group's motives, and we cannot be sure that he has understood them correctly! He accuses these people of supposing (wrongly!) that they are adding to his affliction, but perhaps it is he who is wrong in his supposition that this is their motive. Certainly he seems to believe that they have misunderstood the significance of his imprisonment. He insists, therefore, that he has been set in prison in order to defend the gospel, and that his very imprisonment has served to forward it. His "eager expectation and hope" are that he will not be put to shame and that, whatever happens to him, Christ will be exalted through him, whether by his life or his death (v. 20). Like the Corinthians, the members of this group have perhaps failed to understand the implications of the gospel, and so cannot see his sufferings as part of the paradox of the cross. Whether or not Paul is correct in thinking that they wish to cause him pain, we can be sure that their understanding of the apostolic role would have been very different from the one he sums up in 1 Cor 4:8–21.[24] Paul may well be right, then, in thinking that they are to some extent motivated by ἐριθεία. Were they perhaps boasting, in effect, that if Paul had converted thousands, they would convert ten thousands?[25]

Since vv. 16–17 focus on Paul, it is probable that we should understand the envy and strife of v. 15 as being directed chiefly towards him, in which case we may suppose that the εὐδοκία in that verse also concerns him. But this does not necessarily mean that we should understand the term as meaning simply "human goodwill", for this second group's attitude towards Paul will presumably be grounded in the divine purpose. Moreover, as we have seen, these people (like Paul himself) understand Paul's chains to be themselves part of the divine purpose. They are certainly not preaching Christ because they wish to be nice to Paul! Rather, their response to Paul's imprisonment is to carry on his work of proclaiming the gospel. Human goodwill, then, seems an inadequate understanding of the term: their preaching, like his imprisonment, has its part in God's plan.

The contrast between the two groups is summed up in 1:18: Christ is being proclaimed, we are told, whether as the result of pretext (πρόφασις) or of truth (ἀληθεία). Paul uses the term πρόφασις in 1 Thess 2:5, where he denies that his mission to the Thessalonians had been motivated ἐν προφάσει πλεοναξίας. In a similar—but much more passionate—context in 2 Corinthians 4, he insists that he has preached the word of God in an open declaration of the truth. We see, then, that these words are terms that Paul has used in defending his *own* ministry: he himself has been accused of πρόφασις, and he has claimed that, on the contrary, he is motivated by ἀλήθεια.

Remarkably, however, Paul affirms that *both* groups are proclaiming Christ; those whom he criticizes are not preaching "another Jesus"[26] or "a different gospel",[27] but are preaching the right gospel for the wrong reasons. If we are puzzled by his failure to condemn them, then it is perhaps partly explained by the fact that the second group's failing appears to be primarily animosity towards Paul himself. At

[24] There is no need to imagine, as do some (e.g. Robert Jewett, "Conflicting movements in the early church as reflected in Philippians", *NovT* 12 [1970] 362–90), that "divine-men" missionaries are the cause of the problem.

[25] 1 Sam 18:7.

[26] As in 2 Cor 11:4.

[27] 2 Cor 11:4; Gal 1:6.

the heart of the disagreement seems to be their unwillingness to recognize that his imprisonment is furthering the gospel. But just as the Corinthians, though "infants in Christ", are nevertheless *in Christ*,[28] so these preachers are in Christ and are "preaching Christ". Their misunderstanding does not invalidate their gospel.

We need to remember also that Paul was under no illusions about the continuing existence of inappropriate attitudes and behaviour within the Christian community, as his continual warnings against them make clear. His constant appeal to his converts is: "You are in Christ: live as those who are in Christ *should* live!" His scathing comments to the Corinthians in 1 Cor 4:8–13 are addressed to those whom in v. 14 he terms his "beloved children". Paul himself, as he will remind the Philippians in 3:12, does not consider himself to be perfect. 2 Corinthians 10–13 demonstrate that he was painfully aware of the dangers of boasting in his achievements as an apostle—a danger which besets all preachers and to which many succumb. Though the message of the cross *should* be reflected in the life of the preacher, as in the lives of all Christians, the reflection in this life is only partial, and the process of transformation incomplete.[29] It would seem, however, that the power of the gospel is sufficient to negate human failure. If the message of the cross is being effectively proclaimed, though from the wrong motives, we find that even here, the "weakness of God", displayed in the cross, is stronger than the "human strength" of those who proclaim it.

We turn now to our second question, and ask how this matter relates to the rest of the letter. Are the issues that concern Paul in prison reflected in the teaching directed towards the Philippians?

3. *Paul's* Apologia

The letter to the Philippians is unusual among Paul's epistles in that much of the section that follows immediately after the thanksgiving in 1:3–11 is devoted to telling the readers about his own situation. It would seem that the Philippians are concerned about him[30] and are eager to know how he fares, but Paul introduces the subject of

---

[28] 1 Cor 3:1.
[29] 2 Cor 3:18.
[30] Phil 2:25–30.

his imprisonment in a triumphant way: "I want you to know that what has happened to me has actually helped to advance the gospel." He is clearly anxious that the Philippians should have no doubts about why he is in prison: it is for the defence of the gospel (v. 16). He does not wish to risk any misunderstanding of the kind that he has encountered in Rome. He seems anxious, too, to set his own view of the coming trial down on paper. Whatever happens, he is confident that he will not be put to shame, but that through their prayers and the help of the Spirit of Jesus Christ he will be vindicated before God and enabled to speak boldly, so that Christ will be "magnified" through him. For Paul, the whole process—imprisonment, trial, verdict and possible punishment—serves to spread the gospel. The Philippians need to be reassured that what is happening to him will further God's plan, but Paul perhaps has another reason for explaining how he views his situation: Phil 1:12–26 is not only a defence against those who misunderstand his plight (vv. 15, 17) and a reassurance to the Philippians that the outcome will serve the gospel (vv. 12–20), but a "final testimony" (in case of an unfavourable verdict at the trial) explaining the underlying principle of his ministry: "to me, to live is Christ and to die is gain" (v. 21).

One tends to assume that from 1:27 onwards, when Paul turns his attention back to the Philippians, we have a letter whose primary concern is to encourage the Philippians to "live in a manner that is worthy of the gospel". Yet there are frequent references to his own situation and ministry, suggesting that the manner of life he is anxious to foster in his converts is inextricably linked with this explanation of his own manner of life and ministry. This is hardly surprising, for the Philippians are "his joy and his crown" (4:1) and his partners in the gospel (1:5). The pattern which he urges on them (of conformity to Christ's own attitudes) is the one that has governed his own ministry. His appeal to them is to join in "imitating" him (3:17), just as he has clearly "imitated" Christ (3:7–11).[31] There are others among them who live according to the model—τύπος—which they have in Paul. Side by side with his encouragement to the Philippians to follow this way of life (1:27–2:18) he shows how he

[31] The command Συνμιμηταί μου γένεσθε should perhaps be understood to mean "Be imitators *with* me"—i.e. *of* Christ. For the literature on this point, see Hooker, "Πίστις Χριστοῦ", *NTS* 35 (1989) 332–33; reprinted in Hooker, *Adam*, 176–77. But however we translate the phrase, the twin ideas that Paul and Christ are to be seen as "models" of Christian living are both present.

has followed it himself (3:4–16). His argument seems to be: "the principle that to live is Christ and to die is gain has governed my life; may it govern yours also".

The teaching in 1:27–2:18 is clearly related to matters which affect Paul in prison, and may be prompted as much by his own experience as by what is going on in Philippi. What echoes of his own situation, then, are to be found there?

We note first that Paul begins his teaching by urging the Philippians to stand firm against opposition from outside. They must not be intimidated by their opponents, for what is taking place is "from God" (v. 28), who has "granted" them the privilege, not simply of believing in Christ but of suffering for his sake—an idea which is emphasized by being expressed twice (ὑπὲρ Χριστοῦ . . . ὑπὲρ αὐτοῦ, v. 29), echoing the phrase used elsewhere when speaking of Christ's suffering and death "for us". The Philippians are thus "having the same struggle" that they had once seen Paul engaged in (while he was among them) and now hear him to be having (in Rome). Just as Paul believes that God is at work in his own circumstances, and that he has been "placed" in prison for the defence of the gospel (v. 16), so he believes that the opportunity to suffer for Christ has been "granted" to the Philippians. He is confident that the outcome of his own sufferings will be σωτηρία (v. 19), and assures the Philippians that their own firmness in the face of opposition is proof of *their* σωτηρία (v. 28).

If Paul, in prison, is finding himself lacking in support from many of his fellow-Christians, it is hardly surprising if he urges the Philippians to "stand firm in one Spirit,[32] striving side by side as one person for the faith of the gospel" (v. 27). Nor is it surprising if he continues, in Philippians 2, by appealing to the "encouragement found in Christ", the "consolation of love", and the "fellowship of the Spirit", and urging the Philippians to complete *his* joy by "thinking the same thing, having the same love, being of one accord and thinking the one thing" (vv. 1–2). As in 1:15–18, we have a contrast between two attitudes: the one they should pursue has been set out in 2:1–2, where one of the key terms used in 1:16, ἀγαπή, has been picked up; now, in v. 3, where Paul sets out what they should avoid, we

[32] It is likely that πνεῦμα here, as in 2:1, refers to the Holy Spirit. For discussion of the point see the commentaries.

find the second, ἐριθεία: "do nothing from selfish ambition or conceit". Paul is anxious that the Philippians should get it right, and be motivated by ἀγαπή, not ἐριθεία: so far, however, the only cause of his anxiety for which we have evidence is his experience in Rome.

After repeating the contrast in v. 4, Paul sets out the basis of his appeal: the *reason* why they should be governed by love, not by selfish ambition, is that this is what the gospel itself is about. In 2:6–11 we see how Christ himself was governed by concern for others, not himself. The function of the so-called "hymn" is both kerygmatic *and* ethical. The gospel demands that Christians have "the same mind" that is seen in Christ and that belongs to them *in* Christ: to live in any other way is a denial of the gospel itself. Therefore the Philippians—who have "always obeyed" Paul—must "continue to work out" their own σωτηρία, for God is at work in them (vv. 12–13). The goal is expressed in the phrase ὑπὲρ τῆς εὐδοκίας: all is "for the sake of his will". The purpose of God—which in 1:15 motivated one of the groups of Christians in Rome—is worked out also in the Philippians, as they respond to the gospel and allow it to govern their lives.

Another—implied—contrast lies behind 2:14–15, where the Philippians are urged to do everything "without complaining or arguing". Perhaps Paul again has the ἔρις of 1:15 in mind; certainly he is thinking of the people of Israel, for the phrase is a clear echo of Deut 32:5. But the Philippians are not, like them, the "crooked and perverse generation"; on the contrary, they shine among them like lights. So Paul returns to the thought of the opposition that confronts the Philippians, and urges them to "hold fast[33] the word of life". Then he will be able to boast on the day of Christ that he has not run in vain or toiled in vain.[34] In other words, the Philippians will provide the proof of the authenticity of his work. Once again, Paul may have those who criticize him in mind, and in v. 17 he appears to return to the matter that is uppermost in his mind—the possible verdict of death that looms over him. To be sure, his reference to being poured out as a libation does not necessarily relate specifically to his death, since it can be understood of his whole

[33] It is possible to understand the verb ἐπέχω here as meaning "to hold out/proffer". So, e.g., Fee, *Philippians*, in loc. The idea of Paul's "boasting" in them, however, suggests that he has in mind their steadfastness.

[34] The second phrase echoes Isa 49:4.

ministry, but the two are closely linked, since it is the manner of that ministry that is leading him into the danger of death—just as it was Christ's self-emptying and manner of living that led to *his* death. Again, the Philippians' "offering" could be understood to refer to the gift the Philippians have sent him—except that the offering is defined as being τῆς πίστεως. Moreover, there is a logical link (already established in v. 16) between Paul's death and the Philippians' steadfastness, and it is therefore more likely that Paul is seeing his death as a libation that accompanies the Philippians' "sacrifice" and "offering", which consist of lives lived in accordance with the faith of the Gospel. Once again, Paul links his own situation with that of the Philippians, who are maintaining the faith.

We have noted already that in the passage immediately following this section of teaching, Paul refers again to the motives of his fellow-Christians in Rome (2:21). Here the contrast is between Timothy, who will genuinely care for the Philippians' well-being, and the rest, who "seek their own interests, not those of Christ Jesus". Timothy's value is already known to the Philippians, since he has served (δουλεύω) with Paul in the cause of the gospel (v. 22). Paul described himself and Timothy as δοῦλοι Χριστοῦ Ἰησοῦ in 1:1,[35] and though the appellation is an honorific one,[36] it nevertheless echoes the language of 2:5–11. Paul and Timothy are the δοῦλοι of the one who is now κύριος, and proud to be so: but Christ was made κύριος because he was content to become a δοῦλος, and the manner of their service will therefore be modelled on his. Timothy will, in turn, be a model to the Philippians, whom Paul has urged to be concerned for one another's interests, not their own (μὴ τὰ ἑαυτῶν, 2:4)—unlike those referred to in 2:21, who seek τὰ ἑαυτῶν. Paul hopes to send Timothy soon (vv. 19, 23), but he is still "confident in the Lord" that he himself will be able to come soon (v. 24). Paul's confidence surprises us, but it echoes what he said in 1:25, where his conviction that he was needed by his churches persuaded him that, in spite of his personal desire to be "with Christ", he would "remain" with them. Nevertheless, this has to be seen in the context of his awareness that the outcome of the trial is far from certain (1:20–23). His own convictions about

[35] The use of δοῦλος in a prescript is rare: see only Rom 1:1.
[36] Cf. the descriptions of Moses and David as "my servant" in, e.g., Num 12:7; Ps 89:20 (LXX 88:21).

what would be good for the churches are challenged throughout the epistle by the reality of his situation, and lead him to seize the opportunity to write what is in effect a "farewell letter".

Paul then turns from Timothy to Epaphroditus, whose return to Philippi has probably triggered the writing of the letter (2:25–30). Epaphroditus has been the Philippians' messenger and a minister to Paul in his need in captivity: he has endeavoured to minister to Paul on the Philippians' behalf, and has risked his life in the process. The whole passage resonates with concern for others: the Philippians for Paul and for Epaphroditus, Epaphroditus for Paul and for the Philippians, Paul for Epaphroditus and for the Philippians. Though the language is not this time picked up, the theme is again that of 2:4, since each is concerned for the interests of others.

But why, when Paul turns back to teaching, does he issue the stern warning against Judaizers in 3:2–3? There is no reason to believe that these people are already troubling the Philippians, and it may simply be that Paul is warning them against all possible dangers—understandable, if he thinks it possible that he won't have the opportunity to visit them, or even to write to them, again. The interesting fact from our viewpoint, however, is that the warning immediately triggers Paul's account of what he has done in response to the gospel—in effect, "emptying" himself of his Jewish privileges[37] and regarding them as worthless for the sake of knowing Christ, gaining Christ, and being found in him. For Paul, as for Christ, this process lasts even to death. Once again, Paul's mind has turned to what he may soon have to face; he wants to know "the power of Christ's resurrection", which is experienced through the "sharing of his sufferings" and by "being conformed to his death" (3:10). For Paul, response to the gospel means becoming like Christ and sharing his attitudes: this is what has led to his imprisonment, and to the prospect of becoming like him in death, trusting that "to die is gain" (1:21). The process of conformity to Christ is not yet complete, and the prize is not yet won (3:12–14). Paul again links the Philippians with himself with the words Τοῦτο φρονῶμεν, echoing the command of 2:6 and showing that he and they are taking part in a common endeavour. And if any of them thinks differently, then God will reveal this to them (v. 15)! This brief reference to possible

[37] The verb, ἥγημαι and ἥγουμαι (x 2), echoes ἡγήσατο in 2:6.

dissent is dropped as soon as it is introduced, and does not suggest that Paul suspects any serious disagreement. If anyone *does* think differently, then he is confident that he or she will be corrected.

For Paul the end is in sight, and the prize will soon be gained (v. 14). It is because he himself has given up everything for the sake of Christ and longs to share his resurrection by being conformed to his death that he dares to urge the Philippians to "observe those who live according to the example that you have in us" (v. 17). They are to join in imitating him (or perhaps to be joint imitators *with* him),[38] but the ultimate model is, of course, Christ himself. Once again, Paul contrasts two ways of life: over against the example (τύπος) that the Philippians have in Christ, stand those who "live as enemies of the cross" (v. 18). Why does Paul mention these "negative models"? Clearly they have caused him much pain and distress, since he has "often" told the Philippians about them—which suggests that they are not present in Philippi. There is nothing to indicate that these people are the "dogs" of 3:2;[39] it is possible that they do not even claim to be Christians, though both Paul's distress at their life-style and the reference to "the cross of Christ" suggest that they do. The accusation that "their god is their belly" and that "their minds are set on earthly things" (v. 19) makes it probable that they were living a licentious, antinomian life, believing that the gospel brings freedom from all constraint. The context suggests that the shame in which these people glory may well be sexual licence,[40] but whatever it is, it is the antithesis of true glory. Presumably Paul's words are intended as a warning against their way of life: they do not have to be physically present in Philippi for their philosophy to represent a danger. Their manner of life is precisely the opposite of the one that Paul has been advocating, for it is based on self-indulgence, and their minds are set on earthly things instead of heavenly. The way of life that Paul has been commending (πολιτεύεσθε, 1:27) is now seen to relate to a heavenly "commonwealth" (πολίτευμα, 3:20),[41] from which Christians expect a saviour—the Lord Jesus Christ, whose

[38] See above, n. 31.

[39] See above, n. 4.

[40] See the commentaries for discussion of the various suggestions.

[41] The use of the term in this context suggests that Paul is not primarily concerned with civic responsibility in 1:27, *pace* Bruce Winter, *Seek the Welfare of the City: Christians as Benefactors and Citizens* (Grand Rapids, Mich: Eerdmans/Carlisle: Paternoster, 1994) 81–104.

exaltation was described in 2:9–11. The one who in 2:7–8 was said to have been found in fashion (σχῆμα) as a man and who humbled himself (ἐταπείνωσεν ἑαυτὸν) will now transform (μετασχηματίσει) the body of our humiliation (τὸ σῶμα τῆς ταπεινώσεως ἡμῶν); he who took the form of a slave (μορφὴ δούλου) will conform (σύμμορφον) that body to his body of glory (δόξα, in contrast to the false δόξα of v. 19), by the power that enables him to make all things subject to himself (echoing 2:9–11).

Paul's eye is clearly still on the heavenly prize. But the imagery has reverted from running a race to "standing firm". He urges the Philippians to stand firm "thus"—i.e., in accordance with his teaching from 1:27 onwards. They are his joy and crown (4:1, cf. 2:16)—the symbol of victory that will be given him at the end of the race.

In 4:2–3 we finally come to a clear indication of some sort of trouble in the Philippian church. But after all that he has said, Paul apparently feels that there is little more that *needs* to be said, beyond urging them to "think the same thing in the Lord" (4:2, echoing 2:2). He simply asks other members of the congregation to help the two women to agree, and so offer the kind of mutual support that we expect among those who share the mind of Christ.

After a few general admonitions (4:4–8) and encouragement to continue to follow Paul's teaching and example (v. 9), Paul turns again to his own situation in prison, and to the help that the Philippians have given him there (4:10–19); this help is "a fragrant offering, an acceptable sacrifice, well pleasing to God" (v. 18), since these gifts, like the earlier ones they made for his work (vv. 15–16), are a "sharing in the gospel" (1:5), modelled on Christ's self-giving.

4. *Conclusion*

The letter to the Philippians is not simply a pastoral letter to one of Paul's congregations. Pastoral concern is certainly part of its purpose, for in spite of Paul's expressions of confidence that he will be spared, it would seem that he is anxious to set out his understanding of the manner of life that is appropriate to Christians. In that sense, it is part of his final testimony. But it is also testimony to the underlying policy of his mission which, like his understanding of the Christian life, is modelled on the gospel story itself. If the gospel is about Christ's self-emptying and exaltation, then the Christian must be prepared to abandon concern for self, to share his sufferings and death, and so share his glory. The paradox of the cross, seen in Christian humility and final glory, is reflected in Paul's ministry: in particular, it is seen in his imprisonment—which has served to spread the gospel—and will continue to be seen in whatever happens to him, whether through his life of his death, since for him "to live is Christ, and to die is gain". In so far as others are blind to this principle, and regard his imprisonment as a sign of failure, Paul's letter is a defence of his understanding of his apostolic mission.

The real source of conflict, then, is found in Rome (if that is where Paul is imprisoned), not in Philippi, and centres on Paul himself.[42] The epistle's explanation is to be found in Paul's own situation, quite as much as that of the congregation to whom he writes. In this respect, Philippians is perhaps analogous to Romans, which many have argued is addressed to Paul's own concerns rather than those of the Romans. If so, however, it is for a very different reason: not because he was writing to a church he did not know, and whom he wishes to inform of his position, but because he is writing to a church he knows intimately. The epistle is a presentation of his gospel and of his pastoral theology. Writing to those who were his "joy and crown", Paul ensured that his understanding of *how the gospel should be lived* was preserved. The Philippians were surely encouraged and inspired by his letter to them, not rebuked.

The irony is that once his pastoral warnings about those who might lead his converts astray became detached from their original

---

[42] It is worth noting that in 1 Clement, the deaths of Peter and Paul are attributed to ζῆλος and φθόνος (5:2), and that of Paul to ζῆλος and ἔρις (5:5)—a combination used by Paul himself in Rom 13:13 and 1 Cor 3:3. There are other interesting echoes of Philippians, such as the use of πολιτεία etc. in 2:8 and 3:4, the reference to Paul showing the way to a crown (βραβείον, 5:5. cf. Phil 3:14), the reference to Clement and the Corinthians being engaged in the same strife (ὁ αὐτὸς . . . ἀγών, 7:1, cf. Phil 1:30) as those who preceded them, the appeal to be imitators of the prophets (μιμηταί γενώμεθα, 17:1), and the frequent references in the early chapters to humility (2:1; 3:1; 16:1; 19:1). The source of the jealousy, envy and strife experienced by Peter and Paul is not specified, but the theme is introduced because it is relevant to Clement's purpose. His letter is addressed to the church in Corinth, where there are strifes and factions (ἔρεις καὶ θυμοὶ, 46:5), and Clement links these present controversies with the divisions which existed there in Paul's day. The parallel Clement draws between the problems that assailed the Corinthian Church and those that confronted Paul himself in Rome supports our suggestion that for Paul, also, the opposition he encountered from Christians in Rome would have had obvious links with the strife within the Corinthian community.

situation, they helped to contribute to later conflict: in particular, his comments about "Judaizers" in 3:2–3 became a source of anti-Jewish sentiment.

If this essay "swims against the tide", and finds less conflict in the Philippian situation than Professor Räisänen himself would perhaps argue for, it is hoped that this will nevertheless make it an appropriate offering for a scholar who has never been afraid to rebel against commonly-accepted views.

JAMES AND THE PAULINE LEGACY: POWER PLAY IN CORINTH?

Kari Syreeni

Few documents within early Christian literature have proved so resistant to being placed in terms of their tradition-history as the letter of James. The first line of demarcation is whether the main body of the letter is basically of Christian origin or not. While modern commentators unanimously reject the hypothesis of an underlying Jewish writing, a wide range of opinion still remains.[1] The second main division is between defenders of an early Palestinian origin—whereby James the Just would count as the writer or at least the transmitter of the supposedly Jesuanic traditions preserved in the letter[2]—and those who would rather view the document in a wider Hellenistic or Diaspora Jewish setting. If the former option can be excluded, as I think it can, the question is whether anything more precise can be said about the ideological, social and geographical provenance of the letter.

---

[1] The interpolation hypotheses are discussed at some length by Dean B. Deppe in his doctoral thesis, *The Sayings of Jesus in the Epistle of James* (Chelsea, Mi.: Bookcrafters, 1989) 21–24. For a general history of research, see the contributions in *ANRW* 25.5. (1988) by Peter H. Davies ("The Epistle of James in Modern Discussion", pp. 3621–45) and Ernst Baasland ("Literarische Form, Thematik und geschichtliche Einordnung des Jakobusbriefes", pp. 3646–84).

[2] A strong defense of the authenticity of Jas is Gerhard Kittel, "Der geschichtliche Ort des Jakobusbriefes", *ZNW* 41 (1942) 71–105. Among more recent similar assessments, the most solid exposition is Franz Mussner's commentary originating in 1963 (Herder 13/1; 5th ed. 1987). A pre-70 Palestinian setting is also advocated by Ralph Martin, "The Life-Setting of the Epistle of James in the Light of Jewish History" in G.A. Tuttle (ed.), *Biblical and Near Eastern Studies* (Grand Rapids: Eerdmans, 1978) 97–103. Peter H. Davids is somewhat obscure in his *ANRW* article (above, n. 1) but more explicit in opting for the authenticity of the main bulk of material in his commentaries. He reckons with a later but pre-70 redaction of the letter, obviously to make the authenticity hypothesis more immune to criticism without substantially sacrificing the conservative outlook: "The editor improved the Greek, but acted conservatively so as not to obscure James' voice" (*James*, NIBC 15; Peabody: Hendrickson, 1983/1989, p. 7). For a more critical encounter with Jas suggesting a Palestinian or Syrian location, see Benedict T. Viviano, "The Perfect Law of Freedom: James 1:25 and the Law", in K.J. Illman et al. (ed.), *A Bouquet of Wisdom: Essays in Honour of Karl-Gustav Sandelin* (Åbo: Åbo Akademi, 2000) 217–30.

For a number of exegetes since Dibelius, there is no getting beyond the broad picture of Jas as an exponent of late first-century or early second-century Hellenistic Jewish Christianity. Some attempts have been made to give detail to the picture.[3] It may seem less than encouraging to observe that the suggested locations stretch from Alexandria through Palestine (Ceasarea or Tiberias) and Syria (preferably Antioch) over to Asia Minor, Greece and Rome.[4] The various geographical options, however, are mostly derivative of the overall tradition-historical question of how to relate Jas to Pauline Christianity.[5] The more closely Jas is seen to reflect the situation of post-Pauline communities and to address their specific problems, the more plausible a location in Asia Minor, Greece or Rome will appear. By contrast, the more independent from Pauline issues Jas appears, and the closer it is drawn to, say, Matthew's Gospel and the Didache, the more probably is its place of origin to be sought in Syria or Palestine.[6]

In either case it must be borne in mind that the tradition-historical placement is a much wider issue than the actual place of writing;

---

[3] One of the most unconvincing hypotheses is that Luke is the final editor of Jas; thus John Painter, *Just James: The Brother of Jesus in History and Tradition* (Minneapolis: Fortress, 1999) 245–46. Instead, Luke probably knew Jas and used it in Acts 15 (James's speech and letter), Luke 6 (woes) and Luke 4:25 (eighteen months).

[4] Franz Schnider, *Der Jakobusbrief* (RNT; Regensburg: Friedrich Pustet, 1987) 16–19 is original in suggesting Alexandria. The arguments are rather general and weak: 1) polemic against a misconceived Paul; a Hellenistic Jewish Christian theology; 2) literary proximity to the Testaments of the Twelve Patriarchs and 3) Philo of Alexandria, and 4) references to seafaring and travelling merchants. While arguments 2 and 3 mainly reproduce Dibelius's general view of the paraenetic genre, the fourth argument is not exclusive to Alexandria; for instance, Corinth would qualify just as well.

[5] Cf. Wiard Popkes, *Adressaten, Situation und Form des Jakobusbriefes* (SBS 125/126; Stuttgart: Katholisches Bibelwerk, 1986). He opts for a post-Pauline setting for Jas: "Als entscheidend für die Gesamteinschätzung hat sich ferner die Relation zu Paulus bzw. zum Paulinismus herausgestellt; die Waagschale neigt sich zu einer nach-paulinischen Situation. Daraus folgt, dass man die Adressaten am ehesten im Bereich der hellenistischen Missionskirche zu suchen hat, während das Gewicht der judenchristlichen Tradition zurückgeht." (p. 41). I concur with Popkes's view of the addressees; but there is no reason to deny the importance of other than Pauline traditions in Jas.

[6] Jas's knowledge of Matthew's Gospel is argued by M.H. Shepherd in a classic essay, "The Epistle of James and the Gospel of Matthew", *JBL* 75 (1956) 40–51. See, however, the detailed discussion in Deppe, *Sayings*, 151–66. ("It is unnecessary to assume contact with one or more of the Synoptic gospels", p. 166.) Matthias Konradt, *Christliche Existenz nach dem Jakobusbrief: Eine Studie zu seiner soteriologischen und ethischen Konzeption* (Göttingen: Vandenhoeck & Ruprecht, 1998), concludes that Jas belongs in a tradition-historical "triangle" together with Matthew and 1 Peter (which Konradt locates in Antioch).

firstly, because the author and the addressees may be geographically remote, and secondly, because the writer may be familiar with other traditions besides those he has in common with the recipients of the letter. Nonetheless, in determining the provenance of Jas one crucial task is to assess its relationship with Paul's letters and theology. Paul's earliest *Wirkungsgeschichte* is presumably found in the communities to which his letters were addressed and where these were continuously read, discussed and reflected upon. As will appear soon, I contend that Jas is deeply engaged in debates concerning the Pauline legacy. This by no means implies that the author was a Pauline theologian. While taking up and developing many central Pauline concepts and topics he advances a profiled and carefully argued alternative to Paul's theology and its practical consequences, as these were understood *post Paulum locutum.*

This thesis, if shown to be feasible, concurs with some of the broad lines of Bo Reicke's 1964 Anchor Bible commentary, where Jas was interpreted against the background of the politically turbulent years towards the end of Domitian's reign. Reicke did not decide on the precise location of the writing of Jas, but apparently he was thinking of Rome or a major city in Greece or Asia Minor.[7] Sophie Laws, in her unpublished 1968 Oxford dissertation and her 1980 commentary, was more specific in suggesting Rome.[8] She was followed by Dean B. Deppe, whose 1989 Amsterdam dissertation is oddly in two minds about the authenticity of Jas but nevertheless gives some fresh arguments for the Roman hypothesis.[9] The strength of this

[7] Bo Reicke, *The Epistles of James, Peter and Jude* (AB 19; Garden City: Doubleday, 2nd ed. 1964) 5–6.

[8] Sophie Laws, *A Commentary on the Epistle of James* (Black's NT Commentaries; London: Black, 1980) 26: "That the epistle of James had its origin in some part of the Roman community is a plausible, if not provable, hypothesis." The Roman hypothesis as such is an old one. It was already discussed by Dibelius who, however, in his 1921 commentary (KEK 15; Göttingen: Vandenhoeck & Ruprecht) deemed it just a possibility. "So the attempt to fix the place of the composition of Jas must be abandoned," was his conclusion (quoted from the Hermeneia series translation, reworked by H. Greeven, Philadelphia: Fortress, 1976, p. 47). Viviano ("The Perfect Law of Freedom", 219) thus greatly exaggerates Dibelius's "bold strokes" (Dibelius also dated Jas between 80–130, not "in the first half of the second century").

[9] Deppe (*The Sayings of Jesus*) discusses the possibility of a Roman provenance seriously and finds evidence for a date in the 80's (pp. 211–18). Yet he would not definitely abandon the hypothesis of an early Palestinian setting and authorship by James of Jerusalem. Then, however, "we must admit that the traditional picture of

hypothesis is that Jas shows important literary connections with 1 Peter, 1 Clement and the Shepherd of Hermas, all of which seem to have been written in Rome (although the location of 1 Peter is less certain). In addition, as will be argued below, the author of Jas is familiar with Paul's letter to the Romans, together with his Corinthian correspondence and possibly Galatians. While I doubt that Rome is the place of origin, I suggest we need not go too far east of the capital city to find a plausible context for the situation addressed in Jas.

Before discussing James's reception of and response to (post-)Pauline theology and praxis, three concise remarks by Heikki Räisänen in his *Paul and the Law* deserve attention. First, Räisänen rightly points out that the dispute with Paul in Jas shows that even central issues in Paul's letters were "difficult to understand" (2 Pet 3:16), and that indeed misunderstandings were inevitable.[10] Since my focus is on the letter of James, I am more concerned with this particular (mis)reading of Paul than to do justice to Paul or his sympathetic readers. Secondly, Räisänen remarks that the common view of Jas as merely 'paraenesis' and 'ethos' without any consistent theology needs to be revised[11]—a prophecy fulfilled in recent scholarship on James. While concentrating on James's reception of Paul, I also try to depict the central agenda of the letter. As Ulrich Luck rightly notes, the theology of Jas is not primarily *antipaulinisch*, but *jakobäisch*—it represents another kind of theology with a thought structure of its own.[12] At the same time, however, I will try to show how some decisive elements of James's religious ideology owe to a critical appraisal of Paul's theology.

Thirdly, Räisänen follows Dibelius in contending that there is no dispute over the Jewish law nor any trace of the Jewish-Gentile problem in Jas.[13] This conclusion, too, I surmise, is now in need of some revision. My thesis is that Jas does take a position against Paul or Paulines in both these matters, yet in an intricate way, in part using

an ascetic, legalistic James who spoke primarily Aramaic and emphasized the ceremonial dimensions of the law does not fit the givens of this epistle. Therefore, we must either adjust our image of James, the brother of Jesus, or assign the epistle to an unknown James in the provenance of Rome." (p. 218)

[10] Heikki Räisänen, *Paul and the Law* (WUNT 29; Tübingen: Mohr, 1983) 197.

[11] Räisänen, *Paul and the Law*, 210 n. 34.

[12] Ulrich Luck, "Die Theologie des Jakobusbriefes", *ZTK* 81 (1984) 1–30, esp. p. 23.

[13] Räisänen, *Paul and the Law*, 210.

Paul against Paulines. This peculiar relation to the Pauline legacy may explain why, for instance, Michael Goulder in his breathtaking retelling of the Tübingen tale of two missions found no place for the letter of James.[14]

James vs. Paul on faith and works

Any discussion of the literary and theological relationship between Jas and Paul is likely to begin with the lengthy treatise on faith and works in Jas 2:14–26. This need not be the case. For one thing, the conflict starts right in the first verse of Jas, where the humble yet proud self-designation Ἰάκωβος θεοῦ καὶ κυρίου Ἰησοῦ Χριστοῦ δοῦλος echoes the opening of Romans (Παῦλος δοῦλος Χριστοῦ Ἰησοῦ). Together with the programmatic address to ταῖς δώδεκα φυλαῖς ταῖς ἐν τῇ διασπορᾷ this self-presentation prepares for a contest between the two servants of Christ, the one—James, Jacob—being not only the respected Jerusalem pillar and Paul's antagonist (Gal 2) but also the legitimate "patriarch" of God's people worldwide.[15] Secondly, too much of Jas's basic theological concerns should not be extracted from a polemical passage where Pauline terminology and argumentation sets the agenda, so much so as the polemic in Jas may have been partly triggered by a social conflict.

But surely the *locus classicus* Jas 2:14–26 is a good point of departure in other respects. Not only does it heavily draw on Paul, it goes very decidedly into a debate with well-known Pauline statements. The reluctance of many scholars to see a literary dependence here is stunning.[16] Perhaps it is thought that an author misconceiving the

---

[14] M. Goulder, *A Tale of Two Missions* (London: SCM, 1994).

[15] In this very limited sense the idea of Jacob the patriarch as the text-internal sender seems plausible. Due to the modest and allusive references to James the brother of Jesus in Jas—besides the possible reference to his death in 5:6, only the mention of 'the poor' and the anti-Pauline posture rely on this fiction—the author was able to include aspects of the OT patriarch's role in the image of the implied sender. As the leader of the Jerusalem church, James could metaphorically take on the patriarch's role as the head of all Israel (i.e., the church), cf. 1 Clem 31:4 ("to him was given the sceptre of the twelve tribes of Israel"). The "patriarchal" connotation coheres with the *covenantal diaspora letter* genre that highlights some aspects of Jas; see Karl-Wilhelm Niebuhr, "Der Jakobusbrief im Licht frühjüdischer Diasporabriefe", *NTS* 44 (1998) 420–43, and Donald J. Verseput, "Wisdom, 4Q185, and the Epistle of James", *JBL* 117 (1998) 691–797, esp. pp. 702–5.

[16] Fortunately there are some exceptions, especially during the recent years, such

slogans of latter-day Paulinists would be theologically more palatable than an actual critical reader of Paul.[17]

No doubt, James's polemic has a more contemporary address besides Paul. It is also true that Jas is fighting here a "Paul become a formula".[18] Yet the formula was coined by Paul himself in Gal 2:16 and repeated in Rom 3:28. Both times, Paul uses the generalizing ἄνθρωπος, the passive δικαιοῦται/δικαιοῦσθαι and the antithetical structure (*not* works *but* faith/faith *without* works of law) to make his point. All three distinctive features together recur in the treatise of James, but nowhere else in the New Testament or in the early Christian literature. Thus Jas 2:24 puts forward the precise antithesis of Paul's formula: "man is justified" "by works" and "not by faith" alone.[19] Moreover, in both Pauline contexts the statement

as J.T. Sanders, *Ethics in the New Testament: Change and Development* (Philadelphia: Fortress, 1975) 115–28; Gerd Lüdemann, *Paulus, der Heidenapostel*, vol. 2: *Antipaulinismus im frühen Christentum* (Göttingen: Vandenhoeck & Ruprecht, 1983) 194–205; Migaku Sato, "Wozu würde der Jakobusbrief geschrieben?", *AJBI* 17 (1991) 55–76, esp. 67–68; Hans Hübner, *Biblische Theologie des Neuen Testaments*, vol. 2: *Die Theologie des Paulus und ihre neutestamentliche Wirkungsgeschichte* (Göttingen: Vandenhoeck & Ruprecht, 1993) 384; Manabu Tsuji, *Glaube zwischen Vollkommenheit und Verweltlichung: Eine Untersuchung zur literarischen Gestalt und zur inhaltlichen Kohärenz des Jakobusbriefes* (WUNT 2/93; Tübingen 1997) 189–98.

[17] This attitude often goes together with the arbitrary argument, or rather presupposition, that had the author of Jas read Paul's letters, he would necessarily have understood Paul's theological concepts and intentions "rightly", i.e., in the way Paul meant. Against this reasoning, see Tsuji's (*Glaube*, 188) sound judgment: "Dass Jakobus von den Begriffen Glaube und Werke nicht im paulinischen Sinne redet, ist zwar eine an sich richtige Beobachtung, bedeutet aber nicht, dass er keine Kritik an Paulus beabsichtigt. Denn man kann nicht . . . voraussetzen, dass der Verfasser des Jak die paulinischen Aussagen genauso verstanden hat, wie sie von Paulus intendiert waren. Daher soll es eigentlich nicht um einen Vergleich zwischen dem von Paulus intendierten Sinne und der Interpretation des Jakobus gehen, sondern um einen Vergleich zwischen der schriftlich vorliegenden Rechtfertigungslehre und Jakobus als deren Leser."

[18] Räisänen, *Paul and the Law*, 196 n. 176, referring to G. Eichholz.

[19] The added 'alone' is, of course, absent from Paul's formulation. Luck remarks that this *particula exclusiva* is "pikanterweise" a creation of Jas ("Theologie", 2). It is not, however, a misunderstanding but only renders poignantly and concisely what Paul is saying in both places with so many more words, cf. Gal 2:16: ἵνα δικαιωθῶμεν ἐκ πίστεως Χριστοῦ καὶ οὐκ ἐξ ἔργων νόμου, ὅτι ἐξ ἔργων νόμου οὐ δικαιωθήσεται πᾶσα σάρξ. The only inaccuracy in Jas's rendering of Paul's diction is the use of 'works' instead of 'works of the law', and it is a matter of quite sophisticated exegesis whether this shortening involves a crucial misunderstanding of Paul or not. James Dunn (*The Theology of Paul the Apostle* [Grand Rapids/Cambridge: Eerdmans, 1998]), while finding the formulation of James quite appropriate to describe Paul's stance (pp. 371–79: a chapter entitled "By faith alone"), insists that in Paul's thought the 'works' contrasted with faith are especially those works prescribed by the Jewish

is introduced with a paradosis-like expression (λογιζόμεθα, εἰδότες) which gives it an air of doctrinal declaration: "for it is our contention" (Rom 3:28), "for we know" (Gal 2:16). In the place of this introduction, Jas 2:24 has the argumentative ὁρᾶτε: "so there you see". Paul's contention is proved wrong, the opposite case is shown. In Romans, Paul too had provided an argument for his contention: a lengthy exegesis of Gen 15:6 (Rom 4:1–12). Jas is sure to select this very proof text of Paul's (Jas 2:23).[20] By taking an example of Abraham's work of faith (Jas 2:21), he shows that Paul's interpretation of Gen 15:6 was inconclusive.[21]

At places even the style of the treatise in Jas 2:14–26 seems reminiscent of Paul's diatribic discussion in the opening chapters of Romans.[22] In the introductory verse to the discussion on faith and works in Jas, there is also finely tuned irony,[23] as the rhetorical argument according to usefulness, typical of Paul not least in his Corinthian letters, is adopted in defining the issue: "What does it *profit* (τί τὸ ὄφελος),[24] my brethren,[25] if a man says he has faith but has not

torah which protected Israel's privileged status as God's people (pp. 354–66). Cf. Räisänen, *Paul and the Law*, 171: "Thus works of the law are something that *separates* the Jew from the Gentile, and *not* (against Bultmann) something characteristic of man in general." It may be significant and even intentional (thus Tsuji, *Glaube*, 194–98) that the author of Jas avoids the specific Pauline connotation as he simply speaks of 'works'.

[20] Rom 4, Gal 3, and Jas 2 are the only instances in all early Christian literature that we know where the topic of Abraham's justification occurs, together with the quotation of Gen 15:6. See Wiard Popkes, "James and Scripture: An Exercise in Intertextuality", *NTS* 45 (1999) 213–29, esp. 222.

[21] I am not suggesting that Jas's arguments make more sense than Paul's. Both may have their respective strengths and moot points. However, the Pauline bias among scholars sometimes takes extreme forms, as when E.M. Sidebottom (*James, Jude, 2 Peter* [NCBC; Grand Rapids: Eerdmans, 1967/1982]) contends that "it is hard to see how anyone who was directly acqainted with Paul's teaching could offer so incompetent a critique of it" (p. 16).

[22] Consider, e.g., the casual use of σύ in Jas 2:18–20. In Rom 1–4, the provocative σύ style is used most pregnantly in 2:17–24, where a hypothetical Jew—one who is proud of the law and thinks he is an able teacher to the Gentiles—is being addressed. The vocative ὦ ἄνθρωπε κενέ in Jas 2:20 has a partial parallel in Rom 2:1,3 (ὦ ἄνθρωπε). This is but one example of Jas's sensitive stylistic response to Paul. (The sensitivity of Jas is, as will be seen, remarkable in issues that touch upon the fundamentals of Jewish—or Jewish Christian—*honour*. This is confirmed by another reaction against Rom 2:24 in Jas 2:7.)

[23] A touch of irony seems also present in Jas 2:19 (καλῶς ποιεῖς etc.), where Paul's argument from the monotheistic credo is confronted.

[24] The exact phrase τί τὸ ὄφελος is found in 1 Cor 15:32 and Jas 2:14.16, but not elsewhere in the New Testament.

[25] "(My) brethren" is, besides being typical of the diaspora letter style and early

works?" (2:14; cf. also v. 16). Another peculiar feature in the treatise Jas 2:14–26 is its reference to the monotheistic credo εἷς ἐστιν ὁ θεός (v. 19). The credo seems at first out of place in this treatise, but then again, this was Paul's concluding argument in Rom 3:30 in favour of righteousness without works.

Moreover, in Jas 1 all the vital themes of the letter are introduced. In 1:22, the main point of 2:14–26 is anticipated by elaborating on Romans 2:13 (note the antithesis between "doers of the word/law" vs. "hearers").[26] If all this is not evidence that Jas is referring to Paul's diction, I cannot see what might be. But what precisely does Jas wish to prove against Paul and his advocates, and what might have occasioned such a heavy attack on the Pauline formula?

A look at Jas 2:14–26 in its larger context may give us some clues. The warning against partiality is a vital issue in the whole of chapter 2. It is connected with the theme of faith already in 2:1: 'Αδελφοί μου, μὴ ἐν προσωπολημψίαις ἔχετε τὴν πίστιν τοῦ κυρίου ἡμων etc.[27] After the prime example of partiality in vv. 2–7, the author reminds his readers of the danger of προσωπολημψία again in v. 9. The first practical example of "faith without works" in vv. 15–16 resembles vv. 2–7 in showing that impartiality in practice implies, somewhat paradoxically, a *partiality* towards the poor and the needy (cf. v. 5: οὐχ ὁ θεὸς ἐξελέξατο τοὺς πτωχοὺς τῷ κόσμῳ etc.). Thus, it seems suggested that the works that keep faith alive (v. 26) and show one's (im)partial neighbourly love (vv. 8–9) are especially such works that benefit the poor. Partiality in the community (2:1–7), neglect of neighbourly love (2.8–13) and the absence of works (2:14–26) all imply that some community members are ill-treated or neglected. This is

---

Christian paraenesis in general, a Pauline favourite expression. In Jas, the expression is used very pointedly in the openings of new major sections so as to structure the letter. For a similar Pauline usage, see Jonas Holmstrand, *Markers and meaning in Paul: An analysis of 1 Thessalonians, Philippians and Galatians* (CBNTS 28; Stockholm: Almqvist & Wiksell, 1997) 239 (Greek index) *et passim.*

[26] The substantive ποιητής is found elsewhere in the new Testament only in Jas 4:11 and in Acts 17:28 (a 'poet'); ἀκροατής is used nowhere else in the New Testament.

[27] Partiality (προσωωποληµψία) is an issue in Rom 2:11, too, but there Paul speaks of God, not humans. While there are no *prima facie* thematic connections or further verbal agreements between Rom 2:11 and Jas 2:1, it is not excluded that Jas was indirectly influenced by Paul's diction. Jas 2.9, which takes up the theme of partiality anew, echoes Rom 2:12, and in Jas 1:22 an allusion is found to Rom 2:13.

the author's concern already in 1:27 (ἐπισκέπτεσθαι ὀρφανοὺς καὶ χήρας ἐν τῇ θλίψει αὐτῶν).

Consequently, the caring of the needy in 2:15–16 is not "an arbitrary example"[28] but illustrates a major point in the whole chapter. In this connection the theme of hospitality deserves special attention. The hypothetical τις ἐξ ὑμῶν in v. 16 not only fails to help the brother or sister in need, but more specifically refuses to receive them in his house, saying, "Go in peace". This is where Rahab the harlot acted differently; she received those who needed protection.[29] The scriptural arguments in vv. 21–25 indirectly make an even stronger point, implying the danger of losing one's life: Isaac was being offered upon the altar, the messengers' lives were at stake. Similarly in 2:15–16, a brother or a sister who is facing cold and hunger is not provided with τὰ ἐπιτήδεια τοῦ σώματος. In 2:11, the readers are warned not to *kill*. This is often felt to be a huge exaggeration, but the accusation of killing recurs in 4:2 and 5:6 and therefore seems suggestive of a rather inflected situation.

Another point of interest is the possible reference to proselytes.[30] Both Abraham and Rahab were often seen as paradigmatic proselytes. This aspect of Abraham figures in Rom 4 in that Paul emphasises his faith that preceded circumcision; by virtue of this faith Abraham become the "forefather" (Rom 4:1) of both Jews and Gentiles—"our" father, as James (2:21) reminds. Rahab might have been suggested to the author of Jas as a female representative of a righteous non-Jew. If this aspect of meaning is intentional—which seems not too far-fetched in view of the reference to the missionary implications of the credo in Jas 2:19 and the possibility that the rich man in 2:2–3 represents a Gentile benefactor of the community—then the author of Jas has taken up the vital point of Rom 2–3. Paul was intent on showing that faith in Christ is the sole ground for justification. The law, with all the 'works' it summoned, was an unhappy though perhaps necessary intervention. As Rom 7 so vividly

---

[28] So Sanders, *Ethics*, 125.

[29] It is often suggested that the mention of Abraham may remind the reader of his celebrated hospitality as well. For the image of Abraham, see, e.g., Klaus Berger, "Abraham II: Im Frühjudentum und Neuen Testament", *TRE* 1.372–82. But admittedly Abraham's endurance in trials seems here the most naturally evoked idea (so Berger, p. 374).

[30] See Tsuji, *Glaube*, 195.

describes, the law was only there to produce temptation, sin and death, and to be replaced by faith in Christ. Against this, Jas urges that the law and the proper works still need to be done. Obviously, such a reminder would make best sense if the addressees include Gentile converts claiming that the Torah is not for them.

If the two aspects are taken together, the argument in Jas 2 would seem to be that Gentile members and newcomers to the community, including rich benefactors, should fulfil the law by showing righteous works, especially such works of neighbourly love and hospitality that further the dignity (2:5–7), well-being and safety of others in the community. If such a strong reminder of impartiality[31] was needed, in particular concerning the security of life, then we do well to consider the possibility of a serious social conflict behind Jas. If the Pauline slogan of a faith *without* works was repeated in a situation where not all community members received the care and protection they needed, the irritation reflected in the letter is not difficult to understand.[32]

That some practical, rather than theological, motivation has contributed to the polemic tone in Jas 2:14–26 would also explain why the author uses concepts that are less fitted to, and even counteract his own theological concerns. In order to challenge the Pauline maxim the author adopts Paul's language. Had not Paul contrasted faith and works, it would hardly have occurred to the author of Jas to do that so vehemently; for obviously the whole thrust of the letter is that these two *cannot* be separated from each other. In a conflict situation, the opposing parties are often driven to extreme formulations. In Galatians Paul speaks of a *faith active in love* (πίστις δι' ἀγάπης ἐνεργουμένη, Gal 5:6), which however is overshadowed by his polemical statement about 'faith without works of law' in the same letter. The former formulation is not so far from what Jas might have said; but

[31] Here we see what in the Pauline speech of *God's impartiality* towards Gentiles and Jews in Rom 2:11 troubled the author of Jas. His response was that then also the Christians should show impartiality, and that towards Gentile and Jewish members alike. In this way, the author's choice of terms may indirectly owe to his reading of Rom 2:11. We see a similar move in Jas 1:20, where Paul's "God talk" is applied anthropologically.

[32] I do not suggest that some Paulines used the slogan as an *argument* or *excuse* for their policy. However, that need not have prevented the author of Jas from associating the Pauline concept of faith without works with the notion of *moral laxity*. Laws (*James*, 131) thinks that the opponents represented "quietism".

as the writer takes issue with the latter statement, he seems led to another extreme. To be sure, he is careful enough (and surprisingly Pauline) to add the crucial word μόνον in 2:24, so that faith is not abandoned for the sake of proper works. But the unwanted dichotomy between faith and works remains, and the author does what he can to indicate that these two cannot really be separated, or else both will suffer. Faith without works would be like a body without the life-giving spirit (2:26),[33] that is dead (νεκρά, 2:26), or ineffective, unproductive, and powerless (ἀργή).[34]

Any dualism of faith and works is thus basically foreign to the author. What appears to suggest such a dichotomy is caused by his attempt to challenge a Pauline formulation by means of its opposite. This does not mean that Paul's language of faith and works only affected the author's way of expressing his theological stance. The Pauline theological concepts seem to have contributed to James's understanding of faith and works on a deeper level too. To match

[33] The bold imagery in Jas 2:26, something of an *oxymoron* ('body' for *faith* and 'spirit' for *works*), easily meets the suspicious reader's eyes, as exemplified by Christoph Burchard, "Gemeinde der strohernen Epistel: Mutmassungen über Jakobus", in Dieter Lührmann & Georg Strecker (eds.), *Kirche* (FS Günther Bornkamm; Tübingen: Mohr, 1980) 315–328. Burchard first claims that Jas separates faith from works (p. 326) and then comments on Jas 2:24, which he thinks corroborates his interpretation: "Aber ein 'toter Leib' verwirklicht sich nicht im Geist" ("Gemeinde", 326 n. 75). The same argument is found in Burchard's exegesis of Jas 2:14–26 in *ZNW* 71 (1980) 27–35, where he speaks of v. 26 as a ceterum censeo (p. 45) but precisely therefore especially indicative of Jas's concerns (p. 31). In fact, the metaphor of a dead body only shows that to the extent Jas *does* imagine a faith without works, it is no real faith. In Jas 2:1 'faith' is a comprehensive term for describing the proper Christian way of life: 'your faith in our Lord Jesus Christ of glory' should naturally *include* impartiality, which in turn is an integral part of fulfilling 'the sovereign law' (2:8–9). No doubt Paul and Jas had different conceptions of faith, but exegetes should try to understand both of them on their own terms. If there was a misinterpreted Paul, there is certainly a misunderstood James, too.

[34] ἀργή is suggestive of something barren, unproductive, thus useless and, with a slightly different nuance, of something imperfect, not completed. Both aspects of meaning are also present when Jas speaks of a "dead" (νεκρά) faith in 2:26. It is obviously the aspect of imperfection that bothers the critics of Jas; it would seem that works *add* to faith. The notion of cooperation or synergism (ἡ πίστις συνήργει τοῖς ἔργοις) is another disturbing feature to many Protestant interpreters. However, a reflection on Gal 5:6 might result in precisely the argument advanced by Jas: if faith does *not* work (ἐνεργουμένη) so as to produce works of love, then obviously it is unproductive (ἀργή). But the author of Jas need not have thought of Gal 5:6 in formulating 2:26. In Rom 7 Paul argued that the law, destructively working as 'the law of sin' in one's *body*, is the source of *death*. Jas claims that precisely the opposite is the case: the law, or the works, is what gives life to the body. Besides, did not Paul admit that the law in itself is πνευματικός (Rom 7:14)?

the Pauline emphasis on faith, Jas elaborates on the idea of 'work'. While Paul's theology of faith led to a pejorative speech of many 'works'—suggesting that these are something derivative and at worst harmful appendices to the one 'faith'—Jas 1:4 strikingly articulates the idea of perfection as ἔργον τέλειον. This peculiar expression, with the singular form 'work' indicating the final goal of Christian existence, highlights the theology of James better than does the more polemical, anti-Pauline juxtaposition of faith and work*s*. To appreciate better the differing concepts, we should compare Gal 5:6 (faith working through love) with Jas 1:4 (a complete work), rather than take sides in the directly polemical discussion between Rom 3 and Jas 2. Of course, not all differences will vanish in that comparison, nor can we distill Jas's authentic, pure theology apart from its anti-Pauline posture. As will be argued in the next section on James's anthropology, even Jas 1:2–4 is a critical response to Paul; but there we find the author concisely articulating a more comprehensive stance where the concept of 'work' carries rich theological implications.

In the case of *justification* language too, the heavy polemical tone in Jas 2:14–26 obscures rather than reveals the author's deeper dependence on, and critical reworking of, Pauline theology. Some scholars see a difference between Paul's argument in Rom 4 and Gal 3 on the one hand and Jas 2:14–26 on the other hand to the effect that Paul is speaking of God's righteousness—the righteousness belonging to, shown and given by God—whereas Jas speaks of man's righteousness before God. The justification language makes the chasm look even worse than the disagreement between "faith *without* works" and "faith *and* works" alone would necessitate.

However, the difference between two concepts of righteousness does not lie at the heart of the dispute. Jas is not simply saying that righteousness is a matter of one's (faith completed with) works. In the terse formulation, ὀργὴ γὰρ ἀνδρὸς δικαιοσύνην θεοῦ οὐκ ἐργάζεται (Jas 1:20), righteousness rather appears to be God's property. A reader familiar with Romans will here feel a strange intertextual twist. Paul spoke of the wrath of *God* (ὀργὴ θεοῦ, Rom 1:18) as the background for the manifestation of God's salvific righteousness in Christ. In reorganizing the Pauline terms of God's wrath and righteousness, Jas effectively turns upside down the whole train of thought in the opening chapters of Romans. Wrath belongs to imperfect humans, while God is invariably good and righteous. God does not first direct his wrath against a humankind that fails to fulfil the law, in order then to manifest his righteousness apart from the law through faith in Christ. According to Jas, God does not change: "With him there is no variation, no play of passing shadows" (1:17). God's ways remain the same. It is man who must change to match God's unchangeable righteousness by receiving the perfect gift from above (πᾶσα δόσις ἀγαθὴ καὶ πᾶν δώρημα τέλειον ἄνωθεν ἐστιν καταβαῖνον ἀπὸ τοῦ πατρὸς τῶν φώτων, 1:17). So the righteousness of man before God is a gift from God who is righteous. While Paul and Jas have differing conceptions of God, there is no necessary disagreement when it comes to the righteousness of God as the ultimate source for justification.

In Jas 2:13, we see another articulation of the theology of work. Here the abstract ἔλεος functionally parallels the ἔργον τέλειον in expressing the human appropriation of God's merciful righteousness.[35] It is not simply a human property, let alone a merit before God, but indicates rather a middle term between God and humans: mercy as the perfect work. In a similar, yet so different fashion Paul posited faith as the means of appropriating God's free gift. Thus Jas 2:13 is something of a response to Paul's "exclusion of boasting" (Rom 3:27): it is quite in place for those who fulfil the royal law and show mercy to boast at the judgment, not for their good works but for God's perfect ἔλεος shown in their perfect ἔργον.

In the final analysis, the issue of "justification" is a Pauline rather than a genuinely Jacobean concern. The deeper disagreement concerns the role of the law in the Christian way of life. The route to this discussion goes through anthropology, more precisely through the question of the origin, nature, and goal of *Christian* existence.[36]

[35] The word ἔλεος might be understood as an abstract equivalent to 'those who show mercy'. Cf. 2 Pet 3:13 ('righteousness' for 'the righteous'). Then the notion of boasting would be less surprising, for it is humans who may (or may not) boast. As in Paul, who (besides boasting where he shouldn't) boasted of the power of Christ that was "outside" yet "in" himself, so in Jas the ἔλεος that rightfully 'boasts against' the standards of judgment comes from God but dwells in the Christian.

[36] For both Paul and Jas, anthropology is primarily a matter of explicating the *Christian* condition rather than a general theory of the *human* existence. Konradt (*Christliche Existenz*, 268 and *passim*) therefore occasionally speaks of Jas's "christianology" instead of anthropology.

James vs. Paul on perfection, baptism, and the law of liberty

While Rudolf Bultmann in his *New Testament Theology* obviously overemphasized the role of anthropology in Paul's thought,[37] it remains true that Paul in this respect was an exceptionally creative thinker within early Christianity. And here too, the author of Jas read Paul critically, developing a profiled alternative to Paul's view of the (human and) Christian condition.

This discussion is already introduced in Jas 1:2–4, which can be compared with Paul's dictum in Rom 5:1–5.[38] The chain structures in both sequences lead to remarkably opposite conclusions. In Paul, justification by faith (δικαιωθέντες οὖν, 5:1) grants the believers peace with God and gives a hope of God's glory (v. 2). This hope, or as Paul somewhat carelessly puts it, the affliction itself produces endurance (ἡ θλῖψις ὑπομονὴν κατεργάζεται, v. 3), which then brings proof that the believers stand the test and leads to an unfailing hope (ἡ δοκιμὴ ἐλπιδα, v. 4) because God's love has been poured into the believers though the Spirit (v. 5).

In spite of its rhetorical appeal, Paul's argument seems circular. It starts with faith, justification and hope, and ends up with hope. Should there not be some progress? Moreover, if afflictions cause endurance, it would appear that sufferings and temptations are God's educational means for the benefit of the believers. Jas 1:2–4 discards the Pauline notions of a stagnant faith and God as the originator of afflictions. Yet there is, as in Paul, the notion of rejoicing amidst trials in the awareness that faith, provided that it is genuine and unwavering faith (τὸ δοκίμιον ὑμῶν τῆς πίστεως), will produce endurance. Such a tested faith should lead to the perfect work and the perfect human being. The conclusion indicates that these two aspects of perfection are inseparable: ἡ δὲ ὑπομονὴ ἔργον τέλειον ἐχέτω, ἵνα ἦτε τέλειοι καὶ ὁλόκληροι ἐν μηδενὶ λειπόμενοι (1:4).

Thus an anti-Pauline anthropological programme is launched in the opening paraenesis of Jas. Surely Paul, too, spoke of Christians

[37] See H. Räisänen, *Beyond New Testament Theology: A Story and a Programme*, (London-Philadelphia: SCM/Trinity, 1990) 37–42. Räisänen aptly describes Bultmann's project as "a system which has anthropology as its core" (p. 40; this description is not included in the new edition of the book).

[38] Cf. Konradt, *Christliche Existenz*, 101–9. Konradt takes great pains to explain the similarity between Rom 5:3–4 and Jas 1:2–3 without assuming Jas's knowledge of Paul's letter.

as τέλειοι (1 Cor 2:6) in describing the secret wisdom he was proclaiming to the Corinthians (λαλοῦμεν θεοῦ σοφίαν ἐν μυστηρίῳ, τὴν ἀποκεκρυμμένην, v. 7). While Paul's perfection language has a strong intellectual flavour,[39] the author of Jas, for all his emphasis on the wisdom coming from above, is much more down to earth.[40] Perfection in Jas is no secret knowledge of God, but God's *law* and salvific *word* leading to proper *deeds* and the perfect *work*.

Other peculiar features in Paul's conception of perfection are its eschatological orientation, and its problematic relation to the law and the human condition. According to 1 Cor 13:10, perfection is yet "to come" (ὅταν δὲ ἔλθῃ τὸ τέλειον). Together with the intellectual overtones, this futurist aspect elevates perfection from the moral sphere to a more speculative realm. The coming perfection will include a perfect, immediate knowledge of God and a fulfilment of the love between God and humans in a face-to-face relationship (1 Cor 13:12). It also implies the resurrectional transformation of the believers, described by Paul in 1 Cor 15. There, Paul vividly describes the sudden change (πάντες δὲ ἀλλαγησόμεθα, ἐν ἀτόμῳ, ἐν ῥιπῇ ὀφθαλμοῦ, vv. 51–52), but making clear that it is a future event (ἐν τῇ ἐσχάτῃ σάλπιγγι, v. 52). Notably, the transformation will free the Christians not only from sin and death, but from the law as well; for "the sting of death is sin, and sin gains its power from the law" (v. 56).

There is, to be sure, a subtle dialectic between the present and the future aspects in Paul's theology, so that Christians are *already* freed from law, sin and death (and yet not quite so). Some such dialectic is not foreign to Jas either. But whereas imperfection for Jas is to be removed through a prayer for wisdom (1:5–8), Paul's theology of hope curiously seems a message of human *weakness*. In Rom 8:26, Paul's hope is in the Spirit's assistance in the midst of our weakness, for we do not even know how to *pray*! Jas's understanding of prayer in 1:5–8 stands in a sharp contrast with Paul's praise of hopeful weakness.

---

[39] Besides 1 Cor 2:6, consider Rom 12:2, 1 Cor 13:10, 14:10, Phil 3:15. In all cases perfection has to do with one's perception, understanding, evaluation, or the like, rather than deeds. Jas stands here closer to Matthew (cf. Matt 5:48, 19:21).

[40] The role of wisdom in Jas is not so prominent as is sometimes suggested. Rightly Konradt, *Christliche Existenz*, 249–65; Donald J. Verseput, "Wisdom, 4Q185, and the Epistle of James", 705–7. Yet there is some truth in the notion that Jas is

In Paul, human weakness is coupled with the power of law and evil desire. In Rom 7:7–11, attempting to eschew the devastating conclusions concerning the law that his previous statements in that letter suggest, Paul explains that there is nothing wrong with the law in itself. Paul's reasoning is notoriously obscure, but his readers will learn that there is a close connection between law, evil desire, sin and death. Apart from the peculiar role of the law, Paul seems to suggest that evil desire lies at the root of the trouble. Lust leads to sin; and sin to death.[41] Interestingly, this is in essence what Jas 1:14–15 says: ἕκαστος δὲ πειράζεται ὑπὸ τῆς ἰδίας ἐπιθυμίας ἐξελκόμενος καὶ δελεαζόμενος· εἶτα ἡ ἐπιθυμία συλλαβοῦσα τίκτει ἁμαρτίαν, ἡ δὲ ἁμαρτία ἀποτελεσθεῖσα ἀποκύει θάνατον.

So far James is fairly Pauline, using Paul's chain structure to describe the destructive effects of evil desire. However, the main point in Jas is directed against Paul's insinuation that God (by giving the law) is the initiator of lust and sin. Jas points out that the individual human being is responsible for leaving room for evil desires. In introducing this teaching, the author explicitly says that God cannot be blamed for the desire (1:13), and in what follows he again warns his readers not to be misled in this matter (μὴ πλανᾶσθε, ἀδελφοί μου ἀγαπητοί), for God is the giver of all good things and perfect gifts (1:16).

What must have seemed especially annoying in the eyes of the author when reading (or hearing) Rom 7 is the dilemma of the "I" who is torn into two pieces in a tremendous struggle between God's will and the power of sin.[42] Jas contends that Christians ought not, and need not be torn apart like that. A Christian should be perfect and whole, not double-minded (δίψυχος, 1:8). The term δίψυχος is first known to us in Jas and indeed has been suggested as the author's

critical of "cosmic-speculative wisdom" and urges a more modest and practical ("Solomonic") approach; thus Walther Bindemann, "Weisheit versus Weisheit: Der Jakobusbrief als innerkirchlicher Diskurs", *ZNW* 86 (1995) 189–217. Jas's criticism need not be primarily against Paul; even Paul had difficulties in meeting the wisdom teaching in Corinth.

[41] The last move is described repeatedly by Paul in the same letter, cf. Rom 5:12, 6:23.

[42] See also Gal 5:17. Both Rom 7 (cf. Rom 7:23 and Jas 4:1) and Gal 5:12–17 (cf. especially Gal 5:14 and Jas 4:12) may have contributed to some formulations in Jas 4:1–12, where the Jacobean wholeness paraenesis is directed against internal strifes within the community.

own coinage or also a 'local term' used in Rome.[43] Whatever its origin, the term in Jas 1:8 (recurring in the plural in 4:8) in effect describes the "I" of Rom 7 as many of Paul's early readers, rightly or wrongly, must have understood it: a weak Christian who wants to do God's will but has not the strength. How could that be a proper description of the Christian condition? Besides, was not Paul himself precisely such a weak Christian? It is Paul who here says "I".[44] Is not his exclamation 7:24 ταλαίπωρος ἐγὼ ἄνθρωπος proof that he got it all wrong? That might just be how the author of Jas felt when describing the ἀνὴρ δίψυχος, the unstable (and therefore sinning, 4:8) Christian in 1:5–8. The message of Jas 4:9 to such δίψυχοι is uncompromising: ταλαιπωρήσατε καὶ πενθήσατε καὶ κλαύσατε![45]

Not only does Paul admit that Christians are weak; in his Corinthian letters he keeps saying he is *proud* of his weakness (1 Cor 1:31, 2:3, 2 Cor 11:30, 12:5; 12:9). Naturally Paul is not speaking of a sinful weakness; but a critical reader would nonetheless find Paul's pride out of place. Jas 3:13–14 emphasises that the rightful boasting comes from one's actual deeds (τὰ ἔργα αὐτοῦ), shown wisely in humility (ἐν πραΰτητι σοφίας); everything else is wrong and *against the truth* (μὴ κατακαυχᾶσθε καὶ ψεύδεσθε κατὰ τῆς ἀληθείας).

---

[43] A Roman provenance for the term is suggested by Sophie Laws, *James*, 61. See also her earlier article, Sophie Marshall, "DIPSYKHOS: A local term?", *StEv* 6 (TU 112; Berlin 1973) 351. Stanley Porter, "Is '*dipsuchos*' (James 1,8; 4:8) a 'Christian' Word?", *Bib* 71 (1990) 469–98 thinks that the term was coined by Jas. Konradt, *Christliche Existenz*, 271 n. 15, however contends that a Jacobean coinage is to be excluded "mit an Sicherheit grenzender Wahrscheinlichkeit". Konradt assumes a Jewish origin for the word, stressing its occurence in Did 4:4 and Barn 19:5 and the fact that 1 Clem 23:3–4 and 2 Clem 11:2–4 have it in a quotation from an unknown source. I concur with Konradt that the word was hardly coined by the author of Jas, but would not exclude an origin in (Hellenistic) Jewish Christian circles around him, either at the place of writing of Jas or elsewhere where the author had travelled.

[44] See Brian Dodd, *Paul's Paradigmatic "I": Personal Example as Literary Strategy* (JSNTS 177; Sheffield: Sheffield Academic, 1999) 221–34. I find Dodd's interpretation plausible in its main lines: "The Romans 7 'I' is used as a stylized theological portrayal in which Paul draws together diatribal and biblical elements . . . and probably combines them with personal experience or reflection (esp. 7:14–25) . . . Paul is not excluded from 'I', but neither is he writing straightforwardly about himself." Whether or not the author of Jas sensed the full complexity of Paul's rhetorical and theological 'I', he would not have been altogether wrong in including Paul himself in the 'I' of Rom 7. Apart from that, he certainly recognized the more general theological (anthropological) implications of Paul's first-person description.

[45] In the New Testament, almost all occurrences of ταλαιπωρια, ταλαίπωρος and ταλαιπωρέω are found in Rom and Jas; the only other occurrence is ταλαίπωρος in Rev 3:17.

One wonders whether Paul would have passed this test. In his Corinthian correspondence he hardly showed meekness, boasting not only of his powerful weakness, but also of his Jewish descent and secret visions (2 Cor 11:22–23, 12:1–4), and often stressing that his boasting is *truthful* (2 Cor 7:14, 11:10, 12:6; consider also the very phrase κατὰ τῆς ἀληθείας, 2 Cor 13:8). It was also Paul who emphasised that his 'yes' is really 'yes' and 'no' is 'no' (2 Cor 1:17), a phrase captured *verbatim* in Jas 5:12.[46] Elsewhere (3:14) Jas strongly warns that one should not lie against the truth. It seems possible that the peculiar boasting language in Jas was inspired by Paul's letters, and partly used as a corrective of his dubious self-appraisal.[47]

One source for the complexity of Paul's dialectic is his understanding of *baptism*. Here we have a common ground that unites Paul and Jas much more deeply than is often realised,[48] but it is also a watershed where—because of their opposite conceptions of the role of the law in relation to baptism—Paul and Jas drift apart most fundamentally. Paul explicates his baptismal theology particularly in Rom 6. His basic view of baptism as the beginning of the

[46] The prohibition of swearing in Jas 5:12 comes from another tradition (cf. Matt 5:33–37), but significantly Jas's wording parallels 2 Cor 1:17 exactly where James, according to many interpreters, is supposed to be more authentic than Matthew, i.e., in being closer to an authentic saying of Jesus. Jas may not be consciously drawing on Paul here, but it is worth noting that the expression in Paul is extremely suggestive with christological overtones. Paul's emphatic language may have affected his later readers.

[47] Another contribution to Jas's sensitivity to Paul's boast language is probably the connection Paul made between (the Jews') boasting and the law (Rom 2:17, 3:27 etc.). In terms of word statistics, the boasting language is very typical of Paul; out of 59 occurrences of καυχάομαι, καύχησις and καύχημα in the New Testament, 54 appear in Paul's seven authentic letters (I read καύχησωμαι in 1 Cor 13:3) and 3 in Jas (1:9; 4:16 *bis*), while elsewhere only occurring in Eph 2:9 and Hebr 3:6. The majority of the occurrences in Paul are found in his Corinthian letters. The compound verb κατακαυχάομαι occurs twice in Rom 11:18 (of Gentile Christians who should not boast against Jews), twice in Jas (2:13; 3:14) and nowhere else in the New Testament.

[48] Scholars often miss this basic affinity between Pauline/post-Pauline and James's theology by taking Paul's baptismal theology as a pan-Christian phenomenon. However, while there was a wide agreement that baptism was the practical beginning of the Christian life, and while important elements of Paul's baptismal theology come from his tradition, by no means all strands of early Christianity ascribed to baptism the theological importance that we find in Paul. For our discussion, it is instructive to note how differently Matthew—for many interpreters the writer closest to Jas—conceived of the significance of baptism; see Petri Luomanen, *Entering the Kingdom of Heaven: A Study on the Structure of Matthew's View of Salvation* (WUNT 2/101; Tübingen: Mohr, 1998) 216.

Christian life, another "birth" after one's natural birth, no doubt reflects a wide tradition. Even the further metaphor of "dying away" from the former life is inherent in the immersion rite itself.

Paul's further step, to juxtapose dying and rebirth at the baptism to the death and resurrection of Jesus, may be his own contribution, with its suggestive expression and participation-theological depth: "We were buried therefore with him by baptism into death, so that as Christ was raised from the dead by the glory of the Father, we too might walk in newness of life" (Rom 6:4). Still more original is Paul's next move, as he changes the flow of the metaphor and has *Christ* die away from his former life: "For we know that Christ being raised from the dead will never die again; death no longer has dominion over him. The death he died he did to sin, once for all, but the life he lives he lives to God" (vv. 9–10). The shift is impressive but dangerous: did Christ live in sin before dying to it (cf. Rom 8:3)? But Paul immediately shifts again, focusing on *the Christian's* once-for-all death and new life. The dangerous move only motivates the participation aspect in v. 11: "So you also must consider yourself dead to sin and alive to God *in Christ Jesus*." But another crux comes from the connection between sin and law. This final move is made in v. 14: "For sin will have no dominion over you, since you are not under law but under grace."

Baptism, then, for Paul is the site of freedom from the law. This freedom is a prominent theme in Romans and Galatians, being perhaps most suggestively articulated in Gal 5:1 (τῇ ἐλευθερίᾳ ἡμᾶς Χριστὸς ἠλευθέρωσεν); or one may think of other principled, definition-like formulations such as 2 Cor 3:17 (οὗ δὲ τὸ πνεῦμα κυρίου, ἐλευθερία). But Paul's metaphors then transform the freedom language into what appears to be its precise opposite. The Christians' freedom from law, sin, and death is namely nothing but a new "slavery" for God (e.g., Rom 6:22 ἐλευθερωθέντες ἀπὸ τῆς ἁμαρτίας δουλωθέντες δὲ τῷ θεῷ) and righteousness (Rom 6:18). The "slaves" now live under another law, that of Christ (Gal 6:2 τὸν νόμον τοῦ Χριστοῦ; cf. 1 Cor 9:21 ἔννομος Χριστοῦ), of faith (Rom 3:27 διὰ νόμου πίστεως), or of the Spirit of life (Rom 8:2 ὁ νόμος τοῦ πνεύματος τῆς ζωῆς). In effect, Paul only says that the Christians have been freed from their previous master; but they are still "slaves" and under a "law".[49]

[49] Regrettably, the subtleties in Paul's thought (what precisely is the relation

It does not really help that Paul exclaims his freedom before the Corinthians (1 Cor 9:1 οὐκ εἰμὶ ἐλεύθερος)—only to admit that he has become a slave again (1 Cor 9:19 πᾶσιν ἐμαυτὸν ἐδούλωσα).[50]

So Paul spoke of a freedom from the law at baptism. But why should we be freed from God's law which is good, just, holy, spiritual (Rom 7) and meant precisely to give us *life* (v. 10)? And why a new enslavement—were not Christians supposed to be *free*? Paul's confusing language may carry deep insights; but I suggest that this is how the author of Jas read his Paul in advancing a simple yet ingenious theological counter-position. Paul had made two completely unnecessary moves by first removing the law and then postulating a new slavery. As Jas saw it, there was never anything wrong with God's law.[51] On the contrary, it has precisely the life-giving and liberating power that Paul had been looking for in his baptismal theology. In Jas 1:18, the baptismal turning-point is referred to as God's salvific action (βουληθεὶς ἀπεκύησεν ἡμᾶς) through the word of truth (λόγῳ ἀληθείας).[52]

between the torah and the new "law"?) cannot be discussed here. Hans Hübner may have a point in suggesting a change of the role of the law from Gal to Rom, and that the constant between them is the teaching of justification (see briefly his article on νόμος in *EDNT* 2, 476). However, even in Rom the role of the law is ambivalent, and there is another constant too between Rom and Gal, namely the concept of participation. In fact the (dualistic) participatory thread in Paul's theology is a cause of some trouble. It implies that a human or a Christian is never free but "belongs" to one of two opposite sides. Paul advances a suggestive existential version of the dualistic participation scheme (cf. Gal 2:20, Rom 7:25), but the scheme nevertheless forces a sharp distinction between two realms, ages or "masters". How the law is abolished, transformed or remains the same in passing from one realm to another, or from one master to another, is the question.

[50] Once again, Paul says he is weak—now because of his slavery for the gospel (v. 22).

[51] By now, it is obvious how Jas's heavy criticism of Paul's conception of God and theology of weakness relates to the discussion of the law. In Rom 7, Paul's decisive argument against the law was human weakness. For Jas, that is to *beg the question*. The law is *not* weakened by the weakness of the flesh; God does *not* need to replace the law with something else. Instead, the law—God's life-giving word—is the *means* of freeing the Christians from the weakness of the flesh.

[52] Here Jas, like Paul elsewhere, credits the baptized with a special status among the whole creation (εἰς τὸ εἶναι ἡμᾶς ἀπαρχήν τινα τῶν αὐτοῦ κτισμάτων). The substantive ἀπαρχή appears in Rom 8:23; 11:16; 16:5; 1 Cor 15:20; 16:15; Jas 1:18; Rev 14:4; 2 Thess 2:13 (?). In Jas (and Rev) it seems to be a cultic metaphor (the flawless "first fruits" given to God) without necessarily implying the temporal, expansive notions typical of Paul's usage (e.g., 1 Cor 16:15: the household of Stephanas were the *first* Christians of Achaia). However, the difference should not be exaggerated. In Rom 11:16 ("if the dough offered as first fruit is holy, so is the whole lump") Paul could unite cultic and missionary aspects.

In referring to "the word of truth", Jas 1:18 shows tradition-historical proximity to post-Pauline developments[53] but is still in dialogue with Paul in juxtaposing "the word" and the law. This dialogue is evident in 1:23, where the expression ποιηταὶ λόγου renders the ποιηταὶ νόμου of Rom 2:13. With some systematisation, it can be inferred that in Jas νόμος is the ethical or imperative aspect of the life-giving λόγος that was "planted in your hearts" and that "can bring you salvation" (1:21).[54] Especially in post-Pauline traditions, the power of God's word is emphasised.[55] As Jas combines "word" and "law", this dynamic view of God's word is transferred to the law. Paul's κήρυγμα should furnish those who believe with "Christ, the power of God and the wisdom of God" (1 Cor 1:24). In Jas, God's power and wisdom is the law.

However, Jas points out that the planted word has power and salvific effect only when the former life is "put away" and the word is properly "received" in meekness (Jas 1:21). Receiving is more than just hearing the word (and being baptized); the word must be "done" as well. Jas reminds his readers of this teaching of Paul's (Rom 2:13), and goes on to explicate the intimate relation between receiving and doing. The law is by no means abolished at baptism; it is there that it *begins* to exert its powerful and salvific effect. Therefore Christians should continually live "in front of" the law, and with the planted word "in" them, to attain to perfection.

In Jas 1:23–25, this perseverance is described as staying in front of a *mirror*.[56] The passage is to be compared with 1 Cor 13:12, the

[53] The post-Pauline concept of "the word (of God)" is remarkably oscillating, and thus very convenient in stressing salvation-historical unity. 1 Pet 1:23–25, a close parallel to Jas 1:18 (and 1:11), is an illustrative example: the "word" is the imperishable word of God, once praised by prophets (v. 24), then proclaimed to the Christian community (v. 25b), and now operating as the seed which gives new birth within the individual Christian. It is obviously this kind of combination that Jas presupposes, rather than the narrower doctrinal "word of the truth" of 2 Tim 2:15.

[54] See Konradt, *Christliche Existenz*, 67–74.

[55] Typically Heb 4:12.

[56] The imagery of Jas 1:23–25 is admittedly open to various interpretations; see, e.g., Timothy B. Cargal, *Restoring the diaspora: Discursive structure and purpose in the Epistle of James*, (SBL DS 144; Atlanta: Scholars, 1993) 100–5; Konradt, *Christliche Existenz*, 171–76. I think it plausible to understand the mirror imagery as governing the whole passage, since the author has decidedly worked out a contrast between the forgetful man in front of the mirror (vv. 23–24) and the persevering looker (v. 25). The slight inconsistency in the presentation may be due to a reworking of existing materials. It is vital to the logic of the passage that the first parable takes a plain

scant verbal agreement (only ἔσοπτρον in common) and the strikingly different use of the mirror metaphor notwithstanding. In Paul, the presence of the mirror is contrasted with the coming fulfilment when the unclear and fragmentary image is replaced with an immediate seeing—a far cry from the notion of Jas that the Christians should *stay* (παραμείνας) in front of the mirror of the word/law. For Paul, the Christian knowledge is defective (ἐκ μέρους), a theme launched already in the preceding verses: we know defectively now, and this imperfection will pass away (καταργήσεται, 1 Cor 13:8.19), indeed must be rejected (cf. κατήργηκα, v. 10). Another relevant Pauline passage 2 Cor 3:17–18 seems to suggest that the eschatological perfection comes from seeing of the glory of the Lord. In the same chapter, Paul admits that the law of Moses already was glorious (διὰ δόξης), but stresses that it is perishing (τὸ καταργούμενον, v. 11).

For Jas, Paul's vision was at best partially true. The law is not powerless nor defective. As the *perfect* law, it has precisely the transformative power Paul described in speaking of the glory of the Lord. Therefore there is no reason to leave the mirror of the word in a hope of receiving something better. As the mirror lets one see one's natural human face, that is, the shape given in one's natural birth (τὸ πρόσωπον τῆς γενέσεως αὐτοῦ, v. 23), so does the mirror of "the perfect law of liberty" reveal one's perfect shape of being (v. 25). There is no greater secret wisdom, no better cause for boasting, than the *perfect* law of *liberty*.[57] The Christian goal of perfection is nothing more, and nothing less, than the perfect *work* that this law produces.

What the role of faith and of Christ would be in such a theology remains highly conjectural, but the reference to "the faith of our Lord Jesus Christ of glory" (Jas 2:1) may give a clue. The appended τῆς δόξης seems here unmotivated and is grammatically awkward, but it is then all the more noteworthy that the author of

everyday situation (a "natural" face is seen: no-one is expected to stay at the mirror), while the second parable makes an advanced theological point (one's perfect image is seen: then one should stay in front of the mirror).

[57] The deep roots of Jas's discussion of the law in Pauline theology suggest that the attributes 'perfect' and 'of liberty' be understood against this background. It is noteworthy, however, that the term 'the law of liberty' is "familiar to Jew and Greek alike" (Laws, *James*, 87), likewise the notion of a 'perfect' law. Here, as often elsewhere, Jas stands on a common ground and underlines such aspects of the Christian, Jewish and Hellenistic philosophical tradition that all his readers might concur with.

Jas did append the genetive attribute to describe Jesus. In 1 Cor 2:8 Paul used a similar expression (τὸν κύριον τῆς δόξης). Paul never again used this phrasing in his extant letters, but his casual coinage would easily occur to his readers when coming to 2 Cor 3, where the different grades of Moses's and Christ's δόξα are compared.

Whether Jas already presupposes a christological application of the mirror metaphor—with Christ as the perfect work/man whose image one sees in the mirror as the ultimate "face" of one's existence—cannot be known. In 1 Clem we find a reflection upon 1 Cor 13 where the mirror metaphor is developed further and combined with the idea of seeing the shape of Christ in the mirror (ἐνοπτριζόμεθα τὴν ἄμωμον καὶ ὑπερτάτην ὄψιν αὐτοῦ, v. 2).[58] In the Johannine letters, the Pauline path of tradition is followed along the eschatological line of "hope" (a future transformation of God's children, 1 Joh 3:1–3), but there is no mirror imagery. In the Jewish Christian, slightly gnosticizing *Odes of Solomon* (13:1–4) the Lord is indeed the mirror through which the Christian sees his ideal self as the image of the Lord, and the fulfilment is in being with the Lord (thus in front of the mirror) "at all times".[59] A similar imagery is found in the *Acts of John* with a somewhat clearer gnostic slant.[60]

In view of these parallels, a christological application of the mirror metaphor may be somewhat later than Jas. The concise formulation in Jas 1:23–25 need not imply a well-defined system of thought.

[58] Also 1 Clem 49–50 draws heavily on 1 Cor 13. The image of "the bondage of the love of God" (49:2; cf. "love unites us with God", 49:5) is another attempt at explicating the Christian ideal of perfection (τελειότης, 50:1).

[59] "Behold, the Lord is our mirror. Open (your) eyes and see them in Him. And learn the manner of your face, Then declare praises to His Spirit. And wipe the paint from your face, And love His holiness and put it on. Then you will be unblemished att all times with him. Hallelujah." (Trans. J.H. Charlesworth, *The Odes of Solomon*, Oxford: Clarendon, 1973, 64.) The additional ideas are here subordinate to the mirror metaphor: the "putting on" of the Lord's holiness (an idea coming from the common baptismal paraenesis) and the wiping of "paint" (?) from one's face. The latter imagery, if thus read, is a variant of a gnostic theme, understood here in a negative sense (as the removable dirt of one's natural face).

[60] In the Hymn of Christ in the *Acts of John* (96:25), Christ says: "I am a mirror to you who know me." (K. Schäferdiek, engl. transl. G.C. Stead, in W. Schneemelcher (ed.), *New Testament Apocrypha* (2 vols.; Philadelphia: Fortress, 1969, 230). The idea of *portrait* in the same document approximates the mirror image. In the chapter on the portrait of John (*Acts of John* 26–29), Jesus is said to be the one "who paints us all (from life) for himself, who knows the shapes and forms and figures and dispositions and types of your souls". The "colours" to be painted with include faith in God, knowledge, reverence, kindness, etc.

Jas 2:1 *may* indicate that Christ is given the "glory" that Paul attributed to the law *and* Christ, but in any case the author of Jas must have modified the Pauline view that the Torah is outdated. He could either admit that a superior, perfect understanding of the law has come with Christ,[61] or then simply assimilate law and Christ as equal bearers of God's glory.

A similar problem arises in Jas 2:8–11, if we try to pinpoint the precise content and the theological implications of the law. Does "the whole law" (v. 10) include circumcision and all food and purity laws, or is it the new Christian law as expounded by Jesus, that is, neighbourly love and the ethics of the kingdom? The first alternative would imply, from a Gentile Christian viewpoint, that Jas represents a wholesale Judaizing attack on Paul.[62] But nothing in Jas suggests that, and the emphasis laid on baptismal "birth" hardly complies with a programme of circumcision.[63] The second alternative, to the extent it implies the concept of a "new" law as distinct from an "old" and abolished one, would jeopardize the whole of Jas's argument against the Pauline understanding of law. So either a tacit assimilation between the torah and its Christian (epitomised) version or a more nuanced "teleological" and Christ-oriented fulfilment theology is the most plausible option here too.[64]

In either case, Jas quite willingly refers to Paul's teaching on the Christian law. Both in Gal 5:14 and Rom 13:8–9 Paul speaks of the

[61] The argument in 2 Cor 3 could well be used to that effect; the conclusion that the greater δόξα of Christ completely disqualifies the lesser δόξα of the Mosaic law is a typical Pauline *non sequitur*. If the two possible interpretations of τέλος in Rom 10:4 (I find it very difficult to choose between 'goal' and 'end' there) are applied to 2 Cor 3, 'goal' might well be the Jacobean reading: with Christ the perfect, liberating law has come.

[62] Viviano, "The Perfect Law of Freedom" (note 3), assumes that Jas quite naturally includes circumcision in the "whole" law.

[63] Konradt, *Christliche Existenz*, 318, rightly refers to the concept of covenantal nomism (E.P. Sanders) and sees Jas as a representative of its Christianized version; the basic difference is that election pertains to the individual through conversion (through baptism). Konradt also points out that this modification of covenantal nomism by no means contradicts the profound Jewish elements in the symbolic world of Jas.

[64] Whether or not there is refined teleology behind Jas's concept of the law, its assimilating force is undeniable. The perfect law of liberty is also the implanted "word", which in itself already combines (OT) Scripture and the Christian message; and probably the author would have welcomed other equations, too, including the Hellenistic idea of a divine principle. The assimilating and Christianized nature of Jas 2:8 is rightly emphasised by Heikki Räisänen, "Freiheit vom Gesetz im Urchristentum", *StTh* 46 (1992) 55–67, on pp. 62–63.

love commandment as the fulfilment of the *whole* law. Jas 2:8–9 gladly agrees,[65] but while Paul in Rom 13:8–9 emphasises that not committing adultery, not killing etc. are all fulfilled in this one command, Jas points out the *negative* conclusion that no one committing adultery or killing fulfils the law. Obviously the author is recalling the Romans passage rather than Gal. This is confirmed by the fact that Jas here combines the love commandment with two other themes present in Romans 2, namely partiality (Rom 2:12) and transgression of individual commandments (Rom 2:25). The tenor of his argument would be, "if you really wish to fulfil the love command as Paul taught you, then *do* the law and *stop* showing partiality and despising the poor in the community".

Here again we get a glimpse of the infected social situation that motivates James's paraenesis. Can more be detected?

James vs. Paul on the rich and the poor, teaching authority, and community order

Jas's concern for the poor and polemic against the rich surfaces in several passages, whose implied social setting is however not easily determined. The obscurity about the situation may indicate the author's indebtedness to traditional material. It is not always possible to tell the general paraenetic intention from the author's interpretation. A specific address may not be intended everywhere. But the situation itself may be complex too, and may be further confused by the author's generalizing and associative procedures; people drawn into the nearness of some group are indiscriminatively counted as belonging to it ("guilt by association"). Finally, the terms have symbolic overtones and therefore need not always refer to people who outwardly meet the description.

The symbolism of the poor and the rich was already entertained by Paul. He knew that 'the poor ones' was an honourific name for the Jerusalem community (Gal 2:10, Rom 15:26). In 2 Corinthians, he described himself as poor but bringing wealth to many (6:10), and drew a bold parallel between himself and Christ who, being rich, assumed poverty for the sake of the community (2 Cor 8:9).

[65] Here, as in 2:19, the slightly ironic "you do well" signals Jas's relative agreement with Paul(ines).

Whether or not Paul's use of the poverty language affected Jas directly is impossible to say, but the pseudegraphic fiction of Jas indicates that the author was no less conscious of its specific Jewish Christian slant. The odds are then that, to the extent the rich and the poor refer to groupings among the addressees, the schism has to do with (Pauline) Gentile and Jewish Christian members, with the author taking sides with the latter group.

We have already seen that this overall hypothesis makes sense of Jas 2. Two things there help to detail the picture. First, the possible allusions to (Gentile) newcomers who are welcomed without too scrupulous demands concerning the law; second, the image of the rich man attending the synagogue, implying that the community is trying to acquire prominent (Greek or Roman) patrons or benefactors.[66] Both features would signal an alliance between the Gentile Christians and the surrounding pagan society, which would seem a threat to the Jewish minority of the community.

This alliance would to some extent explain why the rich in Jas oscillate between insiders and outsiders. In 1:9–11 the rich would seem to be within the community, as they receive admonition together with the lowly brother. The wealthy man in 2:2–4 attends the synagogue, while the rich ones in 2:6–7 might also be hostile outsiders. In 4:9–10 an address within the community would seem plausible. There the rich ones are not explicitly mentioned, but the tone of the passage is much the same as in 5:1–6, where the rich are addressed—but now apparently outside the community.

The accusation of neglecting the poor and the concern for orphans and widows (1:27) might be compared with Acts 6:1–6, according to which a conflict arose between Hebrews and Hellenists in the early Jerusalem church, as the Hellenists' widows and orphans were neglected. This led to the election of seven deacons. How accurate Luke's account is in this particular case need not worry us here, but if this was a typical issue in a schism between a community's majority and minority, then it is not hard to imagine that Jas is writing to a community facing a similar problem—only that those in majority are Gentile Christians. In light of Jas 2:1–4, the final sentence in Jas 1:27 about "keeping oneself unstained from the world" seems to include political ascetism in relation to those in power. One is

[66] Reicke, *James*, 27.

also reminded of Paul's warning against going to civil courts (1 Cor 6:1–8).[67]

Yet the prophetic section Jas 5:1–6, with its astounding conclusion "you have killed the righteous one", is hard be explain within a purely inner-Christian debate. As Ernst Baasland has pointed out, there is some emphasis in Jas on the "Cainite" sins committed against the Christians.[68] The question is then whether Jas has Jewish opposition in mind. This possibility seems at first to complicate the situation too much. However, there may be a link between the anti-Gentile ethos and the possible experience of Jewish enmity. The bitterness of Jas would be understandable if a considerable part of the community, in trying to make friends with pagan authorities, left the Jewish Christians at the mercy of their compatriots. This would not mean, however, that Jas is addressing the Jews, but only that pressure from the Jewish synagogue was one element of the complicated situation.

Acts provides interesting material for comparison in this issue, too. Luke reports that Crispus, one of the few who were baptized by Paul (1 Cor 1:14), was the former ruler of the synagogue in Corinth (Acts 18:8). If so, he was apparently a man of means. However, as Wayne Meeks remarks, the reports of the Pauline converts in Acts must be treated with caution. In addition to the time span from Paul to Luke (half a century or so), we must remember that Luke "evidently was interested in portraying the Christian sect as one that obtained favor from well-placed, substantial citizens".[69] Furthermore, Luke "is also capable of inventing typical occasions to make his

---

[67] See Gerd Theissen, *The Social Setting of Pauline Christianity: Essays on Corinth* (Philadelphia: Fortress, 1982) 97. The object of the suit in 1 Cor 6:1–8 are βιωτικά, i.e., affairs of property or income. However, Paul's warning also has a political aspect: the community should not associate with those who have earthly power. Rom 13:1–7 seems to reflect a more positive attitude to civil authorities, but the issue there is different from 1 Cor 6; cf. B.W. Winter, "Civil Litigation in Secular Corinth and the Church: The Forensic Background to 1 Corinthians 6:1–8", *NTS* 37 (1991) 559–72.

[68] Baasland, "Literarische Form", 3677. To be sure, his interpretation is not compelling, especially since he considers the whole of Jas 3:13–5:6 in this connection. Moreover, in 1 Clem 4 "Cainite" behaviour is discussed explicitly—with reference to Cain and Abel—in the context of an inner-community conflict which, however, does not exclude the aspect of Jewish/Gentile Christian controversy.

[69] Wayne Meeks, *The First Urban Christians: The Social World of the Apostle Paul* (New Haven and London: Yale University, 1983) 61.

points".[70] Regrettably, Meeks, with the majority of interpreters, is not cautious enough about this particular occasion. In fact, Luke's story in Acts 18 is beset with difficulties that force the question of the value and nature of his sources.[71]

If the author of Acts is less reliable about past incidents, he is in all likelihood better informed of the more recent and contemporary situation in Corinth and elsewhere in the Roman empire. In this regard, it is interesting how he describes the Corinthian incident in Acts 18:12–17. The Jews made an attack upon Paul and brought him before the tribunal, but the Roman proconsul refused to interfere, considering it "a matter of questions about words and names and your own law". As the Jews then seized Sosthenes and beat him in front of the tribunal, "Gallio paid no attention to this". If that was the usual attitude in Luke's time and shortly before, the Christian community could not count on Roman legal protection against Jewish pressures as far as the community was thought to be a Jewish sect. It is likely that the pressure was harder on Jewish Christians and Gentile sympathisers who still had contacts with the synagogue. In such a situation, Gentile members of the Christian community might well be tempted to cut off unnecessary ties with Jewish authorities and turn a deaf ear to Jewish Christians who were thus left at the

[70] Meeks, *The First Urban Christians*, 62.

[71] In Acts 18:17, the ruler of the synagogue in Corinth is suddenly named Sosthenes. If that is more than a lapse, then Luke obviously wants his readers to conclude that Crispus was forced to leave his post after the conversion. But why was his successor immediately mistreated (by his fellow Jews)? Did he, too, have too much sympathy for Christians (and then became one)? In that case, the Corinthian Jews were incredibly unfortunate, to say the least. The obvious explanation is that Luke utilises 1 Cor, where both Sosthenes (1:1) and Crispus (1:14) were mentioned as converted Jews. So Luke employed their names in his Corinthian report, spectacularly made Crispus a synagogue leader and was even tempted to use Sosthenes as a similar paradigm. But *two converted synagogue leaders in one town* may be too good to pass as true. Luke, a writer with unmistakable taste, was careful not to push his luck. The Sosthenes account was therefore kept enigmatic; let the reader (of 1 Cor) understand! (Alternatively, Luke was just inadvertent and wrote "Sosthenes" for "Crispus".) 1 Cor also mentions Apollos, of whom Luke narrates some vivid details which neatly fit in with Paul's scanty hints. It is astonishing how uncritically commentators rely on Luke and his alleged independent "sources". In one of the best modern commentaries to Acts, Jacob Jervell (*Die Apostelgeschichte*; KEK; Göttingen: Vandenhoeck & Ruprecht, 1998; p. 464) notes here: "Historisch stehen wir auf festem Boden." He then enumerates over a dozen proof texts from *Paul*! Yet he is more critical than the average commentator in questioning the last Corinthian incident: "Hat Lukas den Synagogenversteher Sosthenes eingeführt? Wenn ja: wozu?" However, he finds no answer.

mercy of the synagogue. To protect themselves, the Pauline Gentile communities would welcome influential pagan benefactors and allies without being too scrupulous about their religious convictions.[72]

In Romans and 1–2 Corinthians, Paul discussed a division between "the strong" and "the weak". This terminology is more typical of Paul than "the rich" and "the poor", and of special interest in pointing to the Jewish/Gentile Christian problem in the communities. It is no wonder that Jas avoids this favourite Pauline terminology. The author had every reason to discard the suggestion that Jewish Christians, with their possible Gentile Christians allies, were "weak" Christians unlike the "strong" Paulines.

Food laws were important to the "weak" in Paul's communities, and may have been observed by the author of Jas, too. But what has that to do with weakness? For those of Jewish descent, avoiding impure food could appear the most natural thing to do, not only because they knew the Scriptures but also because of habitual dislike of pagan customs, an attitude shared by many Gentile sympathisers of the Jewish religion. At the same time there were weightier matters in the Jewish inheritance: devotion to one God, awareness of standing in a long tradition of law, wisdom and prophecy, high morality, the ethos of neighbourly love. For people of such contention, it must have been traumatic to be blamed—by a continuous reading of Romans and the Corinthian letters—for *weakness* and *lack of knowledge*! We have seen that the annoyance of Jas is very deep and passionate on both issues.

My conclusion then is that the Jewish/Gentile Christian tension is a major issue in Jas, even if it is only taken up indirectly, through the theological and practical *consequences* it had in community life. Nothing was more alien to the author than the self-satisfied deutero-Pauline assertion, based on Gal 3:28, that the newness of life in Christ has removed any distinction between Greek and Jew (Col 3:11).[73] But

---

[72] There need be no contradiction between a low profile policy towards the synagogue and the strategy of presenting the Christian devotion as a form of Judaism to benefit from its status as a *religio licita*. The latter strategy was oriented towards Roman authorities and could in practice be supported by a policy of non-intervention in synagogal affairs. Jas also employs a double strategy which is conceivable in such a situation: the author reminds the addressees of *both* the law (in order to urge neighbourly love, i.e., solidarity and assistence) *and* the faith in Christ (pleading to the central Pauline conviction; consider in particular Jas 2:1).

[73] Much uncritical Paulinism appears in the commentaries at this point. Only

the social background of the conflict in Jas is much more complex than the ethnic distinction. The alliance with powerful members of the larger society brings us to the issue of *patronage*, and here additional factors in the schism come to light.

Paul's Corinthian correspondence gives a vivid picture of a church where some relatively powerful patrons had no scruples in exercising their rights at the cost of the weaker people in the community. Paul's stance in this schism has been a matter of dispute. Gerd Theissen in his seminal essays on the social setting of Pauline Christianity[74] saw that Paul took a middle position with his *love-patriarchalism*. Paul accepted patronage in principle and took social differences for granted, but tried to ameliorate them through an obligation of mutual respect and love. In his 1992 study on the social networks in Corinth, John K. Chow[75] depicts Paul as a more radical critic of patronage.[76] Chow's interpretation highlights Paul's efforts to side with the socially weak in the community. What Chow does not stress enough is the fact that Paul, while being the founding father of the community, was a missionary worker who periodically visited the city (and wrote letters while being absent). Thus Paul confronted the Corinthian patronage as an outsider, and no matter how subversive of the prevailing social order his theological ideal was, it is doubtful that he could bring a lasting change. Besides, his own personal claim for authority was based on an even more pronounced patriarchal ideology than the societal system of patronage.[77] Theissen's interpretation probably

from a limited viewpoint can one conclude, e.g., that "the obliteration in Christ of the old religious distinction between Jew and Gentile . . . was one of the most remarkable achievements of the gospel within a few decades" (F.F. Bruce, *The Epistle to the Colossians, to Philemon and to the Ephesians*, NICNT; Grand Rapids: Eerdmans 1984, 149).

[74] Theissen, *The Social Setting*.

[75] John K. Chow, *Patronage and Power: A Study of Social Networks in Corinth*, JSNTS 75 (Sheffield: Sheffield Academic, 1992).

[76] See also John S. Kloppenborg, "Status und Wohltätigkeit bei Paulus und Jakobus", in *Von Jesus zum Christus* (BZNW 93; Berlin-New York: de Gruyter, 1998) 127–54. Kloppenborg's interesting and richly documented comparison between Paul (mainly his Corinthian letters) and Jas comes to the conclusion that both authors were critical of patronage, even though only Jas ventures a "Frontalangriff auf die Patronage" (p. 153).

[77] Cf. Elisabeth Schüssler Fiorenza, "Rhetorical Situation and Historical Reconstruction in 1 Corinthians", *NTS* 33 (1987) 386–403, p. 397: "In 1 Corinthians Paul introduces the vertical line of patriarchal subordination not only into the social relationships of the *ekklesia*, but into its symbolic universe as well by arrogating the

catches the overall development better. In practice, Paul represented a theologically motivated patriarchalism, which we then meet in a more developed form in the deutero-Pauline letters.

The author of Jas seems to share Paul's position outside the secure power of patronage, but his response is clearly more radical than Paul's. His siding with the poor amounts to a pronounced hostility towards the rich. The "impartiality" he advocates in Jas 2 seems to go beyond the claim for equal rights and is in fact a programme for the supremacy of the poor. This "rule of the poor" is of course an ideological programme hard to turn into practical reality among the addressees, but in 2:5 the author nevertheless discloses his subversive ideal: οὐχ ὁ θεὸς ἐξελέξατο τοὺς πτωχοὺς τῷ κόσμῳ πλουσίους ἐν πίστει καὶ κληρονόμους τῆς βασιλείας ἧς ἐπηγγείλατο τοῖς ἀγαπῶσιν αὐτόν;

The language is here amazingly Pauline, as if the author were alluding to what Paul had taught the Corinthians (1 Cor 1:27–29 and 2:9).[78] The expression τοὺς πτωχοὺς τῷ κόσμῳ is peculiar to Jas, however. It qualifies 'the poor' in relation to 'the world' and should obviously be understood in the light of the anti-cosmic ethos of Jas 1:27 (ἄσπιλον ἑαυτὸν τηρεῖν ἀπὸ τοῦ κόσμου) and 4:4 (ἡ φιλία τοῦ κόσμου ἔχθρα τοῦ θεοῦ ἐστιν). In a 1999 SBL paper entitled, "Who are the 'Poor to the World' in James?",[79] Stephen J. Patterson suggests that the honourific title specifically refers to impoverished, itinerant preachers and charismatic leaders, who in Matthew (19:21) and the Didache (6:2) are called τέλειοι. The schism in Jas would be one between wandering radical prophets and new local leaders and patrons.

authority of God, the 'father', to himself. He does so in order to claim for his interpretation of divine power the authority of the singular father and founder of the community. He thereby seeks to change the understanding of persuasive-consensual authority based on pneumatic competence accessible to all into that of compulsory authority based on the symbolization of ultimate patriarchal power." I basically agree, but Kloppenborg ("Status und Wohltätigkeit", 145) is right to note that Fiorenza's "persuasive-consensual authority" is in this historical setting "probably anachronistic and ethnocentric".

[78] Cf. also Rom 8:28 (τοῖς ἀγαπῶσιν τὸν θεόν), 1 Cor 6:9–10 (θεοῦ βασιλείαν οὐ κληρονομήσουσιν) and the occurrences of κληρονόμοι in Rom and Gal. For Jas 2:6, cf. 1 Cor 11:22 and 1 Cor 6:2,4. However, in what follows the critical tone goes *beyond* Paul (Jas 2:6: a direct attack on the rich) and then indirectly *against* Paul's diction (Jas 2:7; cf. Rom 2:24).

[79] The main thesis is found in *AAR/SBL Abstracts* 1999, 351–52. I thank the author for sending me the manuscript of the paper.

This is an important insight, and I have argued elsewhere[80] that in Matthew's community the group that made claims for perfection—by observing the whole law (Matt 5:19–20) and leaving everything for Christ's sake (19:27)—was called 'the little ones'. The group seems rather heterogeneous, constisting of itinerant prophets, wise men and teachers (10:40–42), ascetics (19:12) and healers, and also charismatic local leaders who, evoking the special authority given by Jesus to Peter (16:16–18) and the core community (18:15–18), wished to decide on disciplinary matters. What was common to them was a Jewish Christian heritage from the early Jesus movement, and the ability to arouse sentiments of originality and charismatic vigour. These were modest and humble people, outside power in the larger community, but no-one should question their authority. The most fatal thing was to *despise* them (18:10).

No doubt Jas 2:5–6 fits the overall picture of the charismatic elite. The poor ones belong to another, subversive order of power and honour. In the Kingdoms's perspective they are the truly rich, so one should show them *respect* (v. 6). An identification of the Jacobean "poor people" with a specific group known from other early Christian sources is not possible, however. The Matthaean term "the little ones" is not found in Jas, and the "poor ones" of Jas are not called τέλειοι. The term τέλειος ἀνήρ (Jas 3:2) indicates the letter's general anthropological ideal and has close parallels in Pauline and particularly in deutero-Pauline letters (Col 1:28, Eph 4:13).

That Jas testifies to a battle between older charismatic leadership and an emerging local leadership with patronage has much to speak for it, but we should remember that the battle was not just a Syrian phenomenon. Paul's struggles in Corinth were already symptomatic of the emerging problem. As for Jas, we may observe that Jas pays little attention to ecclesiastical hierarchy. The formulaic address, "(my beloved) brethren", underscores the fraternal nature of the ideal community. Jas 1:27 does not reckon with a special ministry to take care of orphans and widows, but makes it an obligation for all believers. It is also typical of Jas that the passage dealing with internal battles only commends submission to God (4:7). In 1 Pet 5:8 a similar admo-

[80] K. Syreeni, "Peter as Character and Symbol in the Gospel of Matthew", in David Rhoads & Kari Syreeni (eds.), *Characterization in the Gospels: Reconceiving Narrative Criticism* (JSNTS 184; Sheffield: Sheffield Academic, 1999) 106–52; especially pp. 141, 143, 151.

nition, after advice to presbyters and youngsters, interprets submission to God as obedience to ecclesiastical authorities.

The same reserve is seen when Jas does mention groups exercising power in the community. In 3:1 the addressees are warned: "Let not many of you become teachers, my brethren, for you know that we who teach shall be judged with greater strictness." Here the author reveals himself to be a 'teacher'. A tacit claim for teaching authority runs through the letter from the modest greeting (1:1) to the concluding words (5:5:19–20) which, as Timothy Cargal rightly observes, insinuate that the addresser himself is one who wants "to bring back a sinner from the error of his way".[81] Considering this implicit self-claim, the warning that "not many of you become teachers" may well be more than a paraenetic commonplace.[82] It sounds rather like a suggestion that no other teachers besides the author himself are needed, or at least that teachers with another message should not stand up. The concession, "for we all make many mistakes" (3:2), then only apparently includes the author. Once this sharp tone is heard, it is possible to discern an ecclesiological accent in 3:2b–3. Against the background of Paul's teaching on the community as σῶμα Χριστοῦ (1 Cor 12:27 etc.), Jas insinuates that only the perfect man is able to guide the whole community.[83] After the discussion in 2:14–26, the address of Jas's warning should be obvious enough.[84]

---

[81] Cargal, *Restoring the Diaspora,* passim, finds in the enveloping verses Jas 1:1 and 5:19–20 an expression of the separation between James and his implied readers. Cargal over-emphasizes the connection between the diaspora metaphor and the idea of wandering away from the truth, but I agree that the conclusion of the letter includes a reference to the implied author's humble (1:1) efforts to corrects his readers. This strategy, which runs through the whole epistle, is not sufficiently explained by, e.g., Baaslands's hypothesis of a mainly Jewish Christian community as the implied reader and the Jews as secondary "intended" readers ("Literarische Form", 3676).

[82] Thus Dibelius-Greeven, *James*, 184. Interestingly, Rom 13:2 and Jas 3:2 have in common the phrase κρίμα λήψεσται. In Paul, it refers to those who resist authorities. In Mk 12.40 a similar utterance is directed against false teachers.

[83] According to Reicke (*James*, 37), the "body" is here, as often in Paul, a symbol for the church. That is a bit too much to say, for obviously the primary, literary reference is one's own body. The ecclesiological sense is only a metaphoric overtone. Jas combines individual and collective aspects even later as he parallels "the fightings among you" with "the passions that are at war in your members" (4:1).

[84] Laws (*James*, 140) thinks "it is artificial to suggest that the warning against becoming teachers is related to James's attack on the purveyors of the Pauline slogan", but in the next breath she admits "(t)his initial specific warning stands itself

The presbyters (elders) of the church are mentioned in Jas 5:14, but their role is very subordinate. No suggestion is made that they should exert disciplinary authority. They are called by the sick person to pray over him and anoint him with oil "in the name of the Lord". It is not by their authority that the sick will be saved, but by "the prayer of faith" and, in the last instance, by "the Lord". This description makes the elders vulnerable to criticism. If the sick is not cured, it must be the elders' fault; they did not pray in faith. Consequently, the healing becomes a test for revealing unworthy presbyters. The elders are not said to have the authority of binding or loosing sins; Jas only says the anointed sick "will be forgiven" if he has sinned. In the added teaching on forgiveness and prayer, the elders disappear. The believers are urged to confess their sins to one another and to pray for one another. The power lies in the prayer of "a righteous man" (5:16), such as the Old Testamant prophet Elijah, "a man of like nature with ourselves" (5:17).

In de-emphasising institutional authority in favour of fraternality, Jas resembles Matthew's Gospel, where issues of church discipline (binding and loosing) are interpreted by the evangelist non-hierarchically as foregiveness of one's brother (Matt 18:21–35); teaching authority is restricted to Christ alone (23:8). But there are differences, too. While Matthew's fraternalistic and Christ-centred programme is a compromise to promote unity and the evangelist distances himself from charismatic elitism, Jas is a voice of protest and advocates the ideological supremacy of the poor, the wise, the prophets and healers.

This does not mean that Jas had a firmer hold on ecclesiastical power than Matthew; quite the opposite. Jas is critical of the church establishment occupied by a Pauline front, but he does not offer a practical alternative. He could only play down the role of the community leaders, suggesting that there were unworthy teachers and elders, and invoking the authority of the renowned Jewish Christian leader. It is perhaps the strongest evidence for the author's lack of power that he had to resort to a pseudepigraphic fiction and ascribe his programme to a figure of the past. The authority of James the Just is an ideological, symbolic one. It is a reminder of the Jewish

in some isolation from the passage as a whole". The natural conclusion would be that 3:1–2 is a kind of bridge from 2:14–26 to 3:3ff. (rightly Dibelius & Greeven, *James*, 184).

origins of the Christian faith, a reminder which must have been especially forceful in a community boasting of its Pauline inheritance.

The author of Jas is the spokesman for a minority, a mighty minority[85] though, and one which is aware of its dignity. Hence the vehemence of the effort at theological justification. A kind of historical irony is occasioned by the fact Paul ranked himself among the poor in relation to the Corinthian church. "Already you are filled! Already you have become rich! . . . We are weak, but you are strong. You are held in honour, but we in disrepute. To the present hour we hunger and thirst . . ." (1 Cor 4:8–13). One or two generations later, the author of Jas feels much the same way—again in a Corinthian setting?

Conclusion: A Corinthian conflict?

In the course of the analysis, the hypothesis gradually emerged that the provenance of Jas can be traced more precisely than to a general Hellenistic milieu. The author is deeply versed in Paul's letters to the Romans and the Corinthians. Several observations suggest that Corinth, rather than Rome, should be considered as somehow involved in the writing of Jas. A Roman colony,[86] Corinth is the likely place where both Romans and the Corinthian letters were known and regularly read.[87] The reference to sea (1:6), ships (3:4) and travelling

---

[85] The suggestive term comes from Jacob Jervell, "The Mighty Minority", *StTh* 34 (1980) 13–38.

[86] The attempt by W. Willis, 'Corinthus ne deletus est?', *BZ NF* 35 (1991) 233–41, to shake the scholarly consensus on the Roman nature of first-century Corinth fails to carry conviction; see D.W.J. Gill, 'Corinth: a Roman Colony in Achaea', *BZ NF* 37 (1993) 259–264. The close cultural and administrative contacts between Corinth and the capital city obviously help explain the Roman church's interest in Corinthian affairs (1 Clem).

[87] The two likely places for the earliest collection of Paul's letters are Corinth and Ephesus. See Walter Schmithals, *Paulus und Gnostiker: Untersuchungen zu den kleinen Paulusbriefen* (Theologische Forschung 35; Hamburg-Bergstedt: Evangelische Verlag, 1965) 175–201; Hans-Martin Schenke, 'Das Weiterwirken des Paulus und die Pflege seines Erbes durch die Paulus-Schule', *NTS* 21 (1975) 505–18. The local collections probably showed some variation. It may be significant that while Jas only alludes to Rom and 1–2 Cor, and possibly knew Gal, the deutero-Pauline Colossians and Ephesians seem to exploit a larger corpus of Pauline epistles. In a recent doctoral dissertation, made under the guidance of Heikki Räisänen, entitled, *The Making of Colossians: A Study on the Formation and Purpose of a Deutero-Pauline Letter* (University of Helsinki, 2000), Outi Leppä argues that Colossians makes use of all the seven undisputed Pauline letters. She also argues that Col represents the debate between two different types of early Christianity: Paul's heritage of Christian liberty and an

merchants (5:13–17) are certainly intelligible in a Corinthian setting. More important, Corinth was the site of notorious conflicts in the Christian church, in Paul's day as well as later when 1 Clem was sent there as an intervention by the Roman congregation.

Some basic ideological and social elements in the Corinthian schism seem to have lasted from Paul to Jas and 1 Clem, with these elements being more peculiar to Corinth than Rome or other important centres of early Christianity. First of all, Corinth—unlike Antioch or Galatia—seems unaffected by an extreme Judaizing mission.[88] In Paul's Corinthian correspondence, circumcision was not a major issue; the tone of the passing discussion in 1 Cor 7:18–19 is serene. Jewish particulars were not included in James's agenda, nor does 1 Clem charge the rebels with outstanding doctrinal deviances. Yet some form of Jewish Christianity and its relation to Paul and his adherents was vitally involved in the theological debate. It is beyond the scope of the present study to discuss the parties Paul takes issue with in 1 Cor 1–4 or to review the variety of opinions concerning Paul's opponents in Corinth.[89] What is clear, however, is that Paul connected himself very intimately with the Corinthian community. He was their founding father (1 Cor 15), and they were the seal of his apostleship (1 Cor 9:2). Yet many denied his leadership and would rather follow other celebrities including Peter and, as might be conjectured, the brothers of Jesus (1 Cor 9:5).

---

apocalyptic visionary group that observed stricter regulations, with the book of Revelation orginating among the latter group. Jas has some interesting linguistic resemblances with Rev, and shares with it a keen end-expectation and an anti-Pauline attitude, but obviously it represents another kind of Jewish Christianity. Also, the kind of Pauline heritage we see in Jas differs remarkably from Col and Eph and shows rather more affinity with 1 Pet.

[88] The difference between the Galatian and the Corinthian conflicts may not be due to the missionaries alone. The Galatian Gentile Christians may have been eager to adopt Jewish customs; and the Corinthian Christians who received the missionaries may have been Jewish Christians, so that the problem of circumcision never appeared.

[89] The main scholarly positions are lucidly presented by Niels Hyldahl, "The Corinthian Parties and the Corinthian Crisis", *StTh* 45 (1991) 19–32. To briefly state my general understanding of the Corinthian conflict where Paul was involved, I basically concur with Hyldahl (p. 28) that Paul's opponents were neither Judaizers nor gnostics (in the proper sense) but represented Hellenistic Jewish wisdom traditions. I disagree with Hyldahl as he reduces Paul's opposition to an Apollos-movement. For Paul's possible opponents in 2 Cor 3 especially, see Sini Hulmi, *Paulus und Mose: Argumentation und Polemik in 2 Kor 3* (PFES 77; Helsinki/Gottingen: Finnish Exegetical Society/Vandenhoeck & Ruprecht, 1999) 4–35; she opts for a Petrine opposition.

It is fair to assume that even after Paul the question of his authority remained an important line of demarcation. Inevitably Paul became a symbol of pride for Gentile Christians, both as a proclaimer of faith without works of the law and as the founder of the community, while others continued to have mixed feelings about Paul. As his letters were read and his cathwords repeated, elements of his thought world were digested even by those who would rather have followed other teachers. But was there any teacher authoritative enough to stand against Paul? Living persons seldom match a past saint. 1 Clem 5 refers to Peter together with Paul as the "greatest and most righteous pillars" of the church and the noblest examples for Corinthians to follow.[90] The two apostles in 1 Clem 5 are not representatives of rival parties, but symbolise the Roman hegemony; Peter was already becoming the founder of the Roman church and a guarantor of Pauline traditions, as is probably reflected in 1 Peter. In Corinth by that time Peter was no convenient symbol for an anti-Pauline movement.[91] Instead, James the Lord's brother had all the qualifications. He was independent of Rome, a blameless Jew, a worthy competitor to Paul and a spokesman for the poor. There need not have been a James party at Corinth in Paul's time or afterwards. The cautious fiction in Jas does not necessarily suggest more than a symbolic figure, but it gave a voice to the minority concerns of the Pauline church.[92]

Secondly, we have seen that Jas shares with 1–2 Cor several theological and social interests. Socially, Paul's Corinthian letters and

---

[90] See Raymond E. Brown's discussion of 1 Clem 5:2–7 in R.E. Brown & J.P. Meier, *Antioch and Rome: New Testament Cradles of Catholic Christianity* (London: Geoffrey Chapman, 1983) 123. Also Ignatius, *Rom.* 4:3, mentions Peter and Paul, in this order, as apostles in the Roman church.

[91] If 1 Peter is considered to be earlier than and known by Jas, that would be quite obvious. I am somewhat hesitant about the order of these two letters. Despite many verbal connections and some similarity in the overall arrangement, there is no substantial "communication" between them: Jas is not an answer to 1 Peter, or vice versa. In any case, the probability is that by the time of Jas the figure of Peter was already associated with Rome and pro-Pauline policy.

[92] However, we need not exclude all concreteness from the figure of James. Hegesippus knew a story about two "nephews of Judas and called according to the flesh brothers of the Lord" being brought before Domitian as alleged messianic pretenders (Eusebius, *Hist. eccl.* 4.18–20). According to Hegesippus, the relations of Judas, when released, guided the churches, "since they were witnesses and relatives of the Lord". If the story has any historical ground, it is thinkable that minority groups at Corinth and elsewhere put some hope in the "family" of Jesus.

Jas deal with problems caused by the sharp contrast between the rich and the poor. This is no surprise, for Corinth was known for its pronounced social stratification.[93] In Paul's time, problems arose when the community was gathered to eat the Lord's supper (1 Cor 11:17–34).[94] Going to civil courts was another demonstration of favouritism and social inequality.[95] Paul's reference to "the strong" and "the weak" shows that the social conflict also had to do with the relations between Gentile and Jewish members. In Jas, the situation seems to have grown worse, so that the Jewish Christians together with Gentile sympathizers, who would not cut off all ties with the Jewish synagogue, were left outside the shelter of patronage.

If Jas is viewed as a reaction to such developments, it is easier to appreciate the writer's vigour in inviting the community to stand firm and united in defence of the honourable name of Christ and the royal law of liberty, common to Jewish and Gentile believers alike. The purpose of Jas was, to be sure, not only to ask the Gentile church for help and solidarity, but beyond that to claim implicitly ideological supremacy for the genuine Jewish legacy. From a wider perspective, the letter of James testifies to the great variety of Jewish Christianity.[96] Jas belongs to one strand of the many-faceted Hellenistic Jewish Christianity, being explicit in some of its anti-Pauline emphases and in its claim for social equality and ideological supremacy in a church that seemed to have wandered from the truth. At the same time, it lacks several of the distinctive features often associated with Jewish Christianity, incorporates the palatable parts of the Pauline legacy, and, from its own premises, still strives for the unity of the church.

The bitter tone of the letter indicates that the unity was severely threatened. Perhaps the author had already left the community, or had been forced to do so. If he was an itinerant preacher, he might

---

[93] Theissen, *Social Setting*, 69–119.

[94] Theissen, *Social Setting*, 145–74.

[95] Chow, *Patronage and Power*, 123–41. Chow gives reason to assume that the case of the "immoral man" in 1 Cor 5 concerned the stepmother's dowry and is another illustration of the policy of the rich patrons.

[96] Cf. Jack T. Sanders, *Schismatics, Sectarians, Dissidents, Deviants: The First One Hundred Years of Jewish-Christian Relations* (London: SCM, 1993) 222–24. Sanders points out that the definition of Jewish Christianity as a Christianity that adheres to a strict observance of the ritual laws is very narrow, and that Jas's opposition to Paul's theology is "entirely an opposition from the Jewish side" (p. 223) even though Jas does not comply to that definition of Jewish Christianity.

well have visited other Pauline outposts in Italy, Greece or Asia Minor, and found similar developments. The non-Pauline traditions in Jas, which I have left outside the scope of the present discussion but certainly do not deny, may reflect the author's previous or subsequent contacts with Christian communities east of the Pauline main missionary field. Be that as it may, the overall impression is that Jas, while best understandable against the background of a situation like that in Corinth, also takes a wider angle, and possibly views the conflict from an outside perspective.[97] Hence the address to the whole dispersion and a sender whose fictional location—whether it is also historical cannot be known—is Jerusalem or Antioch rather than Rome or Corinth. In practice such a diaspora letter could not be sent to every community throughout the Roman empire. If Corinth was the main target of the letter, that will of course not exclude a more general address to Pauline churches.

With the lack of external evidence, the Corinthian hypothesis must remain a scholarly guess. What we do know is that a serious conflict took place in Corinth in the 90s, and that 1 Clem was written to solve it. There is some probability that Jas was known to the author of 1 Clem.[98] Unfortunately, the letter is remarkably silent about the actual reasons for the conflict.[99] There is no direct reference to Gentile

[97] Here the situation reflected in Revelation is a good point of comparison. The Jewish Christian writer is familiar with communities in Asia Minor, many of which are dominated by Pauline Christianity. Compelled to move elsewhere, he now looks back and gives his verdict on the life and faith in the communities (Rev 2–3).

[98] See Donald A. Hagner, *The Use of the Old and New Testaments in Clement of Rome* (NovTSup 34; Leiden: E.J. Brill, 1973) 248–56. Hagner remarks that while a number of the parallels between 1 Clem and Jas can be explained on the basis of a fund of common terminology, the use of paraenetic tradition, common knowledge of apocryphal writings no longer extant, some striking parallels yet remain unaccounted for. He therefore concludes "the probability (although not very considerable) of literary dependence" (p. 256).

[99] For various hypotheses, see Horacio E. Lona, *Der erste Clemensbrief* (KAV 2; Göttingen: Vandenhoeck & Ruprecht, 1998) 78–81. Lona holds that the most plausible overall backgound for the conflict was a tension between charismatic and institutional forces within the community. Chrys Caragounis, "From Obscurity to Prominence: The Development of the Roman Church between Romans and 1 Clement", in Karl P. Donfried & Peter Richardson (eds.), *Judaism and Christianity in First-Century Rome* (Grand Rapids/Cambridge: Eerdmans, 1998), 278–79 assumes that "the trouble in Corinth was the desire for a renewal, perhaps, of a charismatic (Pauline) type of church government, which led to the deposition of the old presbyters, who represented a static authority". This may be half true; but I am doubtful that the "charismatic" rebels were Paulines.

and Jewish Christian factions, but the assurance that the recipients are well versed in the scriptures (1 Clem 53:1) and the wealth of Old Testament paraenetic examples may indicate that the author is especially keen to win the Jewish Christians' sympathies.[100] From the Roman point of view, the issue was mainly a disciplinary one: the removed presbyters should be restored to the ministry and the rebels should either repent and submit themselves to the presbyters, or else leave the community. Only a few theological issues are explicitly raised. The defence of resurrection belief in 1 Clem 23–27 is interesting, but whether or not it reflects an ongoing Corinthian discussion about bodily resurrection is hard to say.[101] Another possible hint of the underlying dispute is the unexpected defence of the Pauline doctrine of justification by faith (1 Clem 32:3–4).[102] Of special interest in this connection is the reference to Jacob, who "departed from his country in meekness because of his brother" (31:4; cf. chapters 55–56).[103] No other names are mentioned in 1 Clem besides Cephas

[100] An explanation for the absence of explicit Jewish/Gentile problems in 1 Clem may be that they played a minor role in the Roman church. Probably already in Paul's time the majority of the Roman church were of Gentile origin but had lived as sympathisers on the margins of the synagogue before they became Christians; thus Peter Lampe, "The Roman Christians of Romans 16", in K.P. Donfried (ed.), *The Romans Debate* (2nd rev. ed.; Peabody, Ma: Hendrickson, 1991) 216–42; p. 225. The author of 1 Clem seems to have a similar background; cf. Lona, *Der erste Clemensbrief*, 73–74.

[101] It is adventurous to infer that the Corinthian rebels were Gnostics who denied bodily resurrection, as suggested by Walter Bauer, *Orthodoxy and Heresy in Earliest Christianity* (based on the 2nd German ed.; Philadelphia: Fortress, 1971) 101 and (more cautiously) by Philipp Vielhauer, *Geschichte der urchristlichen Literatur* (Berlin-New York: Walter de Gruyter, 1975) 535. The topic may have occurred to the author because of 1 Cor 15. If there is a more urgent background for Clement's discussion, and if signs of the position attacked should be sought in Jas, one might ask to what extent Jas's stress on the Christian's *birth* (at baptism) by the life-giving and salvific word (the law) renders Paul's resurrection talk obsolete. But such a 'birthing' theology would not necessarily imply a pneumatic resurrection faith, nor is it presentic to the exclusion of the parousia (cf. Jas 5:7).

[102] The context of this passage (after the reference to Jacob) is noteworthy, as is the sudden and ample dealing with "faith and works". It might be conjectured that Clement was aware of the existence of a recent document ascribed to James/Jacob where the problem was raised. For the theology of the passage, see Heikki Räisänen, "Werkgerechtigkeit—eine 'Frühkatholische' Lehre?", in idem, *The Torah and Christ: Essays in German and English on the Problem of the Law in Early Christianity* (PFES 45; Helsinki: Finnish Exegetical Society, 1986) 307–33, esp. pp. 317–324. Räisänen shows that 1 Clem defends the Pauline concept of righteousness without works, even though πίστις in 1 Clem means something else than in Paul.

[103] The verb ἐκχωρεῖν is used for both Jacob (31:4) and the Corinthian rebels who should leave the city (54:2; cf. also 55:1). Lona, *Der erste Clemensbrief*, 342, con-

and Apollos, who were invoked in Paul's day but apparently not during the present conflict (47:4–5). While the social background of the dissension also remains unclear, many admonitions address a situation similar to that of Jas: "Let the strong care for the weak and let the weak reverence the strong. Let the rich man bestow help on the poor and let the poor give thanks to God, that he gave him one to supply his needs; let the wise manifest his wisdom not in words but in good deeds . . ." (38:2).

However balanced Clement tried to sound in the Corinthian ears, it was the Pauline establishment that had his support. "Take up the epistle of the blessed Paul the Apostle" he exhorted (47:1). But if my admittedly very tentative hypothesis should be correct, there would also have been another epistle to be taken up in settling the Corinthian conflict.[104]

cludes: "Es ist möglich, dass die Gestalt Jakobs als Beispiel für Demüt aufgrund des Verlassens des Landes nicht zuletzt in Hinblick auf die Gruppe in der korinthischen Gemeinde dargestellt wurde . . ."

[104] As it happened, not only Paul's letters but also the "long and wonderful" 1 Clem survived in Corinth as authoritative reading in public assembly (Eusebius, *Hist. eccl.* 3.16). Dionysius, Bishop of Corinth about 170, witnesses to the further development of the Corinthian community as a Roman ally and a defender of the right doctrine (Eusebius, *Hist. eccl.* 3.19–20).

PART FOUR

THE PROBLEM OF DIVERSITY IN OTHER EARLY CHRISTIAN LITERATURE

DISSIDENTS AND DEFECTORS: THE LIMITS OF PLURALISM

Stephen G. Wilson

What first caught my eye and caused me to reflect on the theme of this paper was a statement by Eusebius:

> Why are they not ashamed of so calumniating Victor when they know quite well that Victor excommunicated Theodotus the cobbler, the founder and father of this god-denying apostasy (ἀποστασίας) when he first denied that Christ was a real man? For if Victor was so minded towards them as their blasphemy teaches, how could he have thrown out Theodotus who invented this heresy (αἱρέσεως)? (Eus. *H.E.* 5.28.6)

For some time I have been interested in the phenomenon of defection from religious or quasi-religious groups in antiquity.[1] Eusebius' use of "apostasy" and "heresy" as apparent synonyms provokes a number of questions. Was Eusebius typical or does he represent the end of a process that was once more complex and discriminating? Had the terms always been used in this way or had they, and the social reality they allude to, once been considered distinct? If the latter, what was the distinction and to whom did it apply? As classic instances of social labeling, did they evolve and operate in the same way? Can we find parallels in Jewish or pagan groups to the things we can observe in the Christian tradition? What follows is less the pursuit of a particular thesis and more a series of reflections on these and related questions.

What underlies the questions is a simple enough observation. In principle, heretics and apostates (or, to use less theologically loaded terms, dissidents and defectors) could describe two quite different

---

[1] Stephen G. Wilson, "The Apostate Minority", in D. Hellholm, H. Moxnes, T.K. Seim (eds.), *Mighty Minorities? Minorities in Early Christianity—Positions and Strategies: Essays in Honour of Jacob Jervell* (Oslo: Scandinavian University Press, 1995) 201–11; idem, "ΟΙ ΠΟΤΕ ΙΟΥΔΑΙΟΙ: Epigraphic Evidence for Jewish Defectors", in Stephen G. Wilson and Michel Desjardins (eds.), *Text and Artifact in the Religions of Mediterranean Antiquity: Essays in Honour of Peter Richardson* (Waterloo: Wilfrid Laurier University Press, 2000) 354–71; idem, "Defectors and Rivals", forthcoming in L. Vaage (ed.), *Religious Rivalries in the Ancient World* (Waterloo: Wilfrid Laurier University Press, 2001).

groups. First, those who despite deviant belief or behaviour were still considered to be part of a community (dissidents); and second, those who because of deviant belief or behaviour were considered to be no longer part of community (defectors). Such a distinction is not unrelated to one of themes of this volume, for it invites us to consider what the limits of Christian pluralism were. Was there a time when dissidents were treated differently from defectors, when Christian pluralism was capable of including the one even if not the other?

At the outset a number of preliminary observations need to be made. First, a now familiar point: terms like "heretic" and "apostate" are rarely self-designations; rather, they are almost always (in the ancient world, at least) labels applied to an individual or group by someone else. Those so labeled, of course, may not see themselves in the same light at all. This is vividly illustrated by another passage from Eusebius, where he quotes from Dionysius of Alexandria's letter to Rome:

> For those who came over from the heresies (αἱρέσεων), although they had abandoned (ἀποστάντας) the church—or rather, had not abandoned it, but while still reputed members, were charged with frequenting some false teacher—he [Heraclas] drove from the church . . . (*H.E.* 7.7.4)

Those whom the bishop thought to have apostatized in fact remained active in the community and did not see themselves as apostates at all—at least not until the bishop forced the issue. Thus there is an important truth in the observation that heresy and apostasy are terms that do not transparently describe an objective reality; rather, they are social labels applied by others (usually, but not always, those in authority) to those with whom they disagreed.[2] The perspective of the labeler, it is argued, is thus all-important and changes from one writer to another, one time to another and one set of circumstances to another.

---

[2] By far the best discussion of these issues is by J.G. Barclay, "Deviance and Apostasy: Some Applications of Deviance Theory to First-century Judaism and Christianity", in P.E. Esler (ed.), *Modelling Early Christianity: Social Scientific Studies of the New Testament in its Context* (London/New York: Routledge, 1995) 114–27; idem, "Paul among Diaspora Jews: Anomaly or Apostate?", *JSNT* 60 (1995) 89–120; idem, "Who was considered an apostate in the Jewish Diaspora?", in G.N. Stanton and G.G. Strousma (eds.), *Tolerance and Intolerance in Early Judaism and Christianity* (Cambridge, Cambridge University Press) 80–98.

Second, while it is clearly important to consider the range and application of the more obvious linguistic terms (αἵρεσις, ἀποστασία) we need also to distinguish between linguistic usage and social reality. We cannot assume, in particular, that terms that have become familiar through long use in a religious tradition were the only ones used to describe the phenomena we wish to look at. If we restrict ourselves to linguistic surveys we will miss a significant portion of the evidence for dissidence and defection that appears in our sources.

Third, as a sort of extension of the second point and a qualification of the first, we do not necessarily have to be bound by the distinctions—or lack of them—in ancient sources, nor by the perspective of those who provide them. If, for example, some of them do not encourage too sharp a dividing line between heretics and apostates this needs to be noted, but we should not necessarily be bound by it. It still seems to me useful to make a distinction between dissidents who remained within the bounds of a community and defectors who went beyond them, however we label them; though, of course, a person could start as a dissident and end up as a defector. And, while we need to be sensitive to the social dynamics of the process of labeling, not everything is just a matter of perspective. When, in Antioch during the Jewish War, a Jew named Antiochus defected, denounced his father and his fellow Jews and accused them of setting the city centre on fire, and when—to prove the sincerity of his own conversion and his detestation of Jewish customs—he sacrificed in the Greek fashion and forced as many as he was able to abandon their customs and follow his lead (Jos. *War* 7.46–52), this seems unambiguously to be a case of apostasy. And when Pliny speaks of Christians in Bithynia who claimed that they had defected from the movement three, five or even twenty-five years before (*Ep.* 10.96–97) there is no reason to doubt his word, nor that of Lucian when he records the defection of the infamous Peregrinus from Christianity prior to his adoption of a form of Cynicism (Lucian *Pereg.* 333–41). Admittedly these examples are about as clear-cut as they come, but they do illustrate the point that, to bring some clarity to our own discussion, we may need to impose our own judgement as to who belongs in what category, indeed, as to what the categories are to be!

This points, finally, to a related problem, that of boundaries. What defines the difference between a dissident and a defector, or the moment when an individual passes from one category to the other? It is not easy to say. It has been argued, for example, that it is difficult to define the taxonomic indicators the possession of one or more of which signified inclusion in a Jewish or Christian community in the ancient world.[3] It is, by the same token, equally difficult to know which ones have to be absent for an individual to be excluded. The boundaries of Jewish, Christian and pagan communities would of course have been different, often mutually exclusive, but within each group the boundaries could also be defined differently in different places and at different times. This complicates matters, but not, I think, impossibly.

While recognizing that linguistic usage is only one indicator of the phenomena we are looking at, it is nevertheless interesting to look briefly at our two main terms. Outside Judaeo-Christian sources the primary meaning of αἵρεσις was "choice", and its connotation was either neutral or positive, but never pejorative. It came to refer to a conviction, point of view, or doctrine and then by extension to different medical and philosophical schools that were often called αἱρέσεις. More positively it referred to a coherent, articulated doctrine that showed the intellectual talent of its adherents (Sext. Emp. *Pyr.* 1.16).[4] Competing intellectuals or schools of thought often considered their opponents wrong, but they did not convey this by a pejorative use of αἵρεσις. The neutral sense is also found in early Christian and Jewish sources (Acts 5:17, 15:5, 26:5; Jos. *Ant.* 13.5.9; 18.1.2; *War* 2.3.14; Philo *Plant.* 151; *Vit.Cont.* 29) and in some later Christian writers (Justin *Dial.* 17.7, 108.2; *Acts Phil.* 15; Clem. *Strom.* 7.15.89; 7.92.3; Origen *C.Cels.* 3.12–13).

What is striking, and as yet without clear explanation, is the shift from a positive or neutral sense to a negative or pejorative one, the more puzzling because both senses can be implied in the same writer. In addition to the neutral uses mentioned above, Acts may contain

[3] J.Z. Smith, "Fences and Neighbours: Some Contours of Early Judaism", in idem, *Imagining Religion: From Babylon to Jonestown* (Chicago: Chicago University Press, 1982) 1–18.

[4] See M. Desjardins, "Bauer and Beyond: On Recent Scholarly Discussions of Αἵρεσις in the Early Christian Era", *SecCent* 8 (1991) 65–82. See also H. Schlier, "αἵρεσις", *TDNT* 1.180–81; N. Brox, "Häresie", *RAC* 13.248–97; M. Simon, "From Greek *Hairesis* to Christian Heresy", in W.R. Schoedel and R.L. Wilken (eds.), *Early Christian Literature and the Classical Tradition* (Paris: Beauchesne, 1979) 101–116; H. von Staden, "*Hairesis* and heresy: The Case of the *hairesis iatrikai*", in B. Meyer and E.P. Sanders (eds.), *Jewish and Christian Self-Definition*, vol. 3: *Self-Definition in the Greco-Roman World* (Philadelphia: Fortress, 1982) 76–100; A. le Boulluec, *La notion d'hérésie dans la littérature grecque (IIe–IIIe siècles)* (Paris: Études Augustiniennes, 1985).

pejorative uses, when Jews call Christianity a αἵρεσις (Acts 24:5,14; 28:22), and Justin certainly does (*Apol.* 26:8, *Dial.* 35.3, 51.2 etc.).[5] A transitional sense, on the way from neutral to negative, is implied by 1 Cor 11:18f. (in connection with σχίσματα), Gal 5:20, and 2 Pet 2:1, but it is the context or the accompanying adjectives that convey this. Ign. *Trall.* 6:1, in contrast, seems to be an absolute and negative use (and Ign. *Eph.* 6:2?). By the early to mid second century, therefore, αἵρεσις is established as a technical term for "heresy"—false teaching or practice, by individuals or groups whose errors can be traced on one level to Satan and on another level to founding figures (like Simon Magus) or to contamination by paganism. This transition can be demonstrated much more readily than its cause. The use of αἵρεσις, to refer to a doctrine or opinion of a sub-group of Christians is natural enough, but the shift to a largely negative or pejorative sense is not—a problem to which we shall return.

The root meanings of ἀποστασία/ἀποστατέω (from ἀφίστημι) are to "rebel/revolt" or "desert/defect." Mostly the context is political or military, so that in Herodotus and Thucydides ἀπόστασις often describes a rebellion against a ruler or one-time ally, and it is Josephus' preferred term for referring to the Jewish War.[6] An ἀποστάτης is thus typically a rebel or deserter, though it can also refer to a fugitive slave or a runaway dog.[7] The shift towards the sense we are interested in, defection or desertion without necessarily implying military conflict, can be found in the LXX and Josephus.[8] It is worth noting, however, that most of the interesting examples of defection found in Josephus are described not as "apostatizing" but in more

[5] There is some doubt in each case. All the uses in Acts could be neutral and all those in Justin could be negative. It depends on the weight given to the context or the accompanying adjectives, which may convey the negative sense rather than the term αἵρεσις itself? See note 25.

[6] Herod. 3.128; 5.113; 7.4; Thuc. 1.75; 3.13 (4x); 5.81; 8.5 (4x); also Polyb. 5.57.4; Plut. *Cimon* 10 for the verbal form. Josephus uses it in this sense over 60 times (*War* 1.93, 2.39, 73; *Ant.* 18.4,118; *Life* 39, 124–5 etc.). In the LXX see 1 Es 2:27; Neh 2:16; 6:6; 1 Macc 11:14; 13:16; 2 Macc 5:11.

[7] Plut. *Rom.* 9; 2.281.

[8] *Ant.* 4.129–30; 8.191–92; 16.337; 17.227; *War* 2.634; *Life* 125, 158. An interesting example is *War* 2.467, where the Jews of Scythopolis side with their pagan townsmen against marauding Jews (thus "apostatizing" against their fellow Jews). Fighting ensues, but is not a rebellion in the broader sense. Cf Philo *Virt.* 182. In the LXX see Josh 22:22; Ps 118 (119) 118; 2 Chron 29:19; 33:19; Jer 2:19; Is 30:1; 1 Macc 2:15; 2 Macc 5:8.

general terms, such as "leaving" or "abandoning" Jewish traditions. Here καταλείπω is a favourite verb, but it has this sense only in context and is otherwise too variously used to have a technical sense.[9] Christian uses of ἀποστασία/ἀποστατέω, by contrast, often carry the sense of defection or desertion, to the point where we can consider this the normal meaning in that tradition.[10]

Latin terms convey much the same flavour as the Greek. The most common terms, *defectio/defector* and *desisco*, are used mainly in military or political contexts for groups or individuals who abandon previous alliances or commitments.[11] Pliny uses *desisse/desisto* to describe the Christian deserters in Bithynia, and Cyprian later has a lot to say about those who lapsed (*lapsare*) under the pressure of persecution.[12] Other terms that might have been used—traitors (*traditores*) or renegades (*renegares*)—seem not to occur with any frequency.

Thus the terms "apostasy" and "heresy" have this in common: in early Christian usage they take on a largely negative sense. In the case of heresy there is no obvious parallel in Jewish or pagan usage. In the case of apostasy, while there are precedents in Hellenistic Jewish traditions (including the LXX), it is Christians who turn it into a frequent, almost technical term. On the face of it this suggests that we are dealing with Christian innovation, but before reaching that conclusion we need to look at other possible analogies in the ancient world. The immediate issue is linguistic, but broader parallels to the way Christians conceived of and dealt with dissidence and defection are just as interesting.

Before we look for analogies, however, we need to return to Eusebius and his predecessors. The opening quotations from Eusebius are not eccentric. Elsewhere he writes of Tatian, who abandons (ἀποστάς) the church after Justin's death and establishes his own doctrine, described as a heresy (*H.E.* 4.29.3; similarly Iren. *Haer.* 1.28.1), and of Novatian, whose excommunication as the "leader of the

[9] *Ant.* 8.190–91; 8.270; 12.240; 12.269; 12.364; 12.384; 18.141; 20.75.

[10] Acts 21:21; 2 Thess 2:3; 1 Tim 4:1; Heb 3:12; Herm. *Vis.* 1.4.2; 2.3.2; 3.7.2; *Sim.* 8.6.4; 8.8.2,5; 8.9.1–3; 8.10.3; 9.19.1; Eus. *H.E.* 3.27.4 (Paul's apostasy from Judaism), 5.28.6; 7.24.6; Arianus *Decr.* 27; Greg. Nyssa *Eun.* 2; Diod. Sic. *Bib.Hist.* 21.14.1,4.

[11] *Desisco*: Cic. *Sest.* 101; *Sul.* 35; Livy 1.27.4; 9.45.6; Tac. *Hist.* 1.8; 2.77; Caes. *Civ.* 1.60.5. *Defectio/defector*: Cic. *Pis.* 84; *Phil.* 13.39; Caes. *Gall.* 3.10.2; Tac. *Ann.* 4.24; 11.8; 12.50; 16.7; *Hist.* 3.12; Suet. *Tib.* 16.1; *Nero* 43.2.

[12] Pliny *Ep.* 96; Cyprian *De Lapsis*.

heresy" is later described as his "defection (ἀποστασίας) and schism" (*H.E.* 6.43.3; 6.45.1). Eusebius appears to reflect a trend that started well before him. Tertullian, for example, described heretics as apostates (*Praescr.* 4.5; 41.6) and Valentinus as both (*Valent.* 1). Irenaeus sees the followers of Tatian as 'heretics and apostates from the truth, patrons of the serpent and of death' and the gnostics, who for him epitomize heretical belief, as apostates like the serpent in whose footsteps they follow (*Haer.* 3.23.8; 4.1.4).

Earlier, however, things were less clear-cut. The author of 1 Timothy, it is true, describes the false teachers he opposes as those who "renounce/abandon (ἀποστήσονται) the faith," thus apparently equating dissident teaching with defection from the community, rather like later Christian writers (1 Tim 4:1, cf. 1:20). But others, while not always using the specific terms heresy and apostasy, do suggest that the two phenomena were distinguished. The author of Hebrews, for example, alludes to Christians who had reneged on their Christian commitment. They had already tasted the benefits of membership in the Christian community: knowledge of the truth, heavenly gifts, experience of the Spirit and the goodness of God's word. Yet now they had fallen away (παραπεσόντας) and had—to use the unusually strong language of the author—spurned or re-crucified the Son of God and made a mockery of his death. Repentance for such renegades is out of the question and their punishment will be severe, even more severe than the punishment for those who breach the Mosaic law (6:4–8; 10:26–31). What led to the defections is not clear, but the allusion to past experiences of persecution, public harassment, confiscation and imprisonment may be the best clue (10:32–34), suggesting the action of Roman officials. At the same time the author mentions deviant practices to be avoided (13:9–10), and spends much of his time trying to correct his reader's defective christology and unduly positive view of Jewish traditions.[13] That is, the author distinguishes between and reacts differently to deviants who, in their eyes and his, remain within the community (and to whom he appeals), and those who defect and for whom there is no way back.

A somewhat similar situation appears in *Hermas* (*Sim.* 9.19), who contrasts "apostates and blasphemers (ἀποστάτοι καὶ βλάσφημοι) against

[13] See Stephen G. Wilson, *Related Strangers: Jews and Christians 70–170 CE* (Minneapolis: Fortress, 1995) 110–27, for a fuller discussion.

the Lord, and betrayers (προδόται) of God's servants," for whom there is no repentance, with "hypocrites and teachers of evil" for whom repentance is still possible. Asked why, the author says the latter have not blasphemed and betrayed. Here blaspheming and betraying seem to be the very definition of apostasy and, in view of other allusions in the book, almost certainly refer to those who cursed Christ and betrayed fellow Christians when arraigned by Roman authorities (cf. *Sim.* 8.6.4; 9.21.3; 9.26.3–6; 9.28.4). Of the "hypocrites and teachers of evil" it is said that "because of a desire for gain they acted hypocritically, and each one taught to suit the desires of sinful men"—that is, from the author's point of view, they pandered to humanity's baser instincts (cf. *Sim.* 8.6.5). Both groups, interestingly, are labeled "believers" (οἱ πιστεύσαντες), but this seems to be merely a convenient way of identifying them and says nothing profound about their status. Thus the false teachers are dissidents within the community, what we might think of as heretics (the term is not used), whereas the apostates had clearly severed their ties through public denial and betrayal.

A rather different example appears in Justin's discussion of various Christian groups in *Dial.* 47, where the context is not State harassment but church-synagogue interaction. Those of whom Justin approves—others, he admits, disagree with him—are Jewish Christians who do not isolate themselves or impose their views on others, and Gentile judaizers who have taken up Jewish ways yet held to their confession of Christ. Those he condemns are Jewish Christians who try to impose their ways on others and Gentiles who switch allegiance by joining the Jewish community and disavowing their Christian faith. The first two groups—wrongheaded as they are—are given grudging approval, but the second two groups are not. The first two deviate within acceptable limits, the other two go beyond them. Some are unequivocal defectors.

The examples from Hebrews and *Hermas* suggest that some early Christians distinguished between dissidence and defection, reserving the latter for public renunciation of their allegiance to the community, a situation reminiscent of Pliny's account of events in Bithynia in *Ep.* 10.96–97.[14] Justin did likewise, but in the context of Jewish-Christian rivalry.

---

[14] R. Freudenberger, *Das Verhalten der römischen Behörden gegen die Christen im 2*

One place to look for analogies to these Christian developments is in the early rabbinic material roughly contemporaneous with it. That the two traditions were broadly similar—in their notions of tradition and succession in which heresy is a corruption that disturbs the consensus of the faithful—was argued some while ago by Shaye Cohen.[15] He rather too easily elides the concepts of heresy and apostasy, but his general point stands. Further interesting parallels appear when we look more closely at the rabbinic material. To describe heretics the rabbis coined a term, *minim*, whose root meaning remains obscure, but whose every use is pejorative. In early rabbinic sources the *minim* are accused of numerous things: healing by sorcery (*t.Hul.* 2.22–23), conducting worship in unapproved ways (*m.Meg.* 4.8–9), illegal slaughtering of meat (*m.Hul.* 2.9; *t.Hul.* 1.1), reading suspect books (*t.Sab.* 13[14].5), denying the world to come (*m.Ber.* 9.5), and asserting the existence of two powers in heaven (*m.Meg.* 4.9). *Minim* thus appears to be a fluid concept that could be associated with a number of specific actions or beliefs. The early rabbis are consistent, however, in two things: they pass negative judgement on, and urge avoidance of, the *minim.*[16] Here, as in later traditions, the *minim* are likened to the godless nations (*b.Hul.* 41b)—indeed they are sometimes seen to be worse than them (*t.Sab.* 13.5; *b.Sab.* 116a; *t.Hul.* 1.1; *b.Git.* 45b)—and their ultimate destination is Gehenna (*t.Sanh.* 13.4–5).

The two most common rabbinic terms for apostates (neither is in the Mishnah) are *mumar* ("converted") and *meshummad* ("destroyed") and they appear to be interchangeable. One of the earlier definitions of apostates is found in *t.Hor.* 1.5:

Jahrhundert dargestellt am Brief des Plinius an Trajan und das Reskripten Trajans und Hadrians (München: C.H. Beck, 1969) 147.

[15] S.J.D. Cohen, "A Virgin Defiled: Some Rabbinic and Christian Views on the Origins of Heresy", *USQR* 36 (1980) 1–11.

[16] See M. Goodman, "The Function of the Minim in Early Rabbinic Judaism", in P. Schäfer (ed.), *Geschichte—Tradition—Reflexion: Festschrift für Martin Hengel zum 70. Geburtstag*, vol. 1: *Judentum* (Tübingen: Mohr/Siebeck, 1996) 501–10; R. Kalman, "Christians and Heretics in Rabbinic Literature of Late Antiquity", *HTR* 87 (1994) 155–69; N. Janowitz, "Rabbis and their Opponents: The Construction of the 'Min' in Rabbinic Anecdotes", *JECS* 6 (1998) 449–62. Goodman notes that the paucity and vagueness of early sources on the *minim* may be because the rabbis chose to deal with them by ignoring them. The most detailed summary of rabbinic material on both heresy and apostasy is in S. Stern, *Jewish Identity in Early Rabbinic Writings* (Leiden: Brill, 1994) 105–12.

> He who eats carrion and non-kosher meat . . . . . who drinks forbidden (libation) wine, who desecrates the sabbath, and who is de-circumcised. R. Yose b. Yehuda says, even one who wears a garment of wool and linen. R. Shimeon b. El'azer adds, even he who commits a transgression for which there is no natural desire.[17]

There is sometimes a hint of a distinction between "limited apostates," who do one of the above, and "comprehensive apostates" who worshiped *avoda zara* or were "apostates from the whole Torah," but it is not consistently made (*b.Hul.* 4b–5a; *b.Eruv.* 69a–b). Like the *minim*, apostates are considered to be worse than non-Jews, and are condemned to eternal punishment in Gehenna (*m.Shek.* 1.5; *t.Sanh.* 13.4–5).[18] They are frequently mentioned together, including in the infamous *birkat ha-minim* which, like other rabbinic texts, condemns heretics, apostates and informers alike.[19]

Schiffman has suggested the following distinction: heretics diverge from the established religion in their beliefs, apostates in their actions. But rabbinic traditions—where, as we have seen, the *minim* are condemned as much for deviant actions as for false belief—does not support him.[20] It may be that "in some respects the *minim* are no more than a variety of apostates,"[21] but only in some respects. Certainly, heretics and apostates are equally roundly condemned and assigned the same ultimate fate. Apostates appear to be distinguished, however, by their more flagrant deviation from Jewish traditions (see *t.Hor.* 1.5 above), most commonly worship of *avoda zara*, and they are usually condemned for breaches of halakha and not matters of belief.[22] Indeed, for the rabbis one of the problems with the *minim*

---

[17] This list echoes the misdeeds which according to the book of *Jubilees* cause individuals to be rooted out and expelled from Israel: not keeping the sabbath (2:27–33); eating forbidden foods (6:12); effacing circumcision (15:34); intermarriage (30:7, 10).

[18] This summary on *mumar* and *meshummad* is taken from Stern, *Identity*, 106–7, including the translation of *t.Hor.* 1.5. See also L.H. Schiffman, *Who Was A Jew? Rabbinic and Halakhic Perspectives on the Jewish-Christian Schism* (New York: KTAV, 1985) 41–49. In Amoraic sources a distinction is made between apostates out of convenience (following forbidden desires) and apostates out of conviction (spite) (*b.AZ* 26b; *b.Hor.* 11a). *Mumar* may have been substituted for *meshummad* in the printed texts by censors—some of whom were converted Jews—who did not like the nuances of *meshummad*. So S. Zeitlin, "Mumar and Meshumad", *JQR* 54 (1963–64) 84–86.

[19] See the texts collected in William Horbury, "The Benediction of the MINIM and Early Jewish-Christian Controversy", *JTS* 33(1982) 19–61, here 43–44.

[20] Schiffman, *Jew*, 41.

[21] Stern, *Identity*, 111

[22] Although *t.Hul.* 1.1 implies that some of the *minim* were suspected of worship-

was precisely that they didn't stand out but looked in many respects just like other Jews. And there is a further crucial difference: apostates in general were judged to have abandoned the covenant community, while heretics, however troublesome, remained within it.[23] It has been argued that apostates technically retain their identity as part of Israel, at least in this life, but this is often only implicit and is generally underplayed. By contrast, their affinity with the non-Jewish world (who are sometimes seen as less culpable) and their ultimate fate in Gehenna are clearly and emphatically asserted.[24]

Rabbinic and Christian traditions are in some ways similar: they both develop the concepts of heresy and apostasy and describe them with separate terms (in either Greek or Hebrew); and, apart from the non-pejorative (and mostly early) use of αἵρεσις in Christian sources, they both come to understand the terms and the phenomena they refer to in a negative way. In rabbinic sources, however, the distinction between heretics and apostates is more consistently preserved, even if they are equally condemned. Heretics and apostates are two different species, not two ways of talking about the same species. In rabbinic sources, too, there is no evidence of a more lenient attitude towards dissidents than to defectors, such as we find in a few early Christian sources. In interesting ways the traditions run parallel, but they are not identical. Is it likely that they interacted with and influenced each other? Not much encourages such

---

ing *avoda zara* (Stern, *Identity*, 110), this is an exception. The notorious rabbinic defector, Elisha ben Avuyah, is said to have read the books of the *minim*, but is normally referred to by his pejorative nickname, Aher (the other), rather than as an "apostate." A prominent rabbi, whose pupil R. Meier never lost faith in him, Elisha came to epitomize defection that was beyond repentance. The more prominent traditions suggest he erred in belief (about two powers in heaven) and actions (desecrating the sabbath on the day of atonement to dramatize his abandonment of Jewish practise, and discouraging younger Jews from studying the Torah—*y.Hag.* 2.1,77b; *t.Hag.* 2:3; *b.Hag.* 14b–15b). He was said to have been profoundly disillusioned by the slaughter of faithful Jews during the Bar Cochba rebellion.

[23] Stern, *Identity*, 109, defines (rabbinic) apostates as in almost all respects the reverse of proselytes, except that proselytes lose their previous identity and apostates theoretically retain theirs (in this life). See next note.

[24] On apostates and heretics as "Jews" see Schiffman, *Jew*, 48–49; Stern, *Identity*, 107–9. The evidence is slight, scattered and obscure. Nowhere is it as clear as the virtually opposite claim "that the overt apostate is like a non-Jew in all respects" (*y.Eruv.* 6.2, quoted by Stern). To call someone an apostate "Jew" (as in *Israel mumar*) says something about where they are from, but does not necessarily define where, in terms of Jewish identity, they now are. The analogy could be with *Hermas*, discussed above, who calls apostates "believers", but only as a convenient means of telling us who he is talking about.

a view. The use of different languages would have been one barrier, and there is little to suggest that Christians were in general well informed about developments within rabbinic Judaism. The rabbinic movement was itself somewhat insular, and it was not for several centuries that the rabbinic leaders were able to exert widespread control over Jewish communities. There may have been parallel developments in diaspora Judaism, but this we do not know.[25] Perhaps the similarities arise simply because they are similar sorts of tradition.[26] We cannot rule out cross-fertilization, but not much points in this direction.

Where else might we look for analogies? In one of the more extensive discussions of pagan evidence, Norbert Brox concludes that any attempt to find Graeco-Roman parallels to the Christian concept of heresy founders on two obstacles: that disputes and disagreements roughly analogous to those in the churches (e.g. in the philosophical schools) do not affect the semantic field of αἵρεσις in pagan sources; and that the influence of such disputes on Christian concepts of deviation can only be surmised, since there is no instance where we can, as it were, observe it actually occurring.[27] He also notes that the absence of normative beliefs and confessional orthodoxy in the schools, as well as the introduction of the concept of revelation as the source of divine truth in the churches, placed them in radically different worlds. His linguistic point seems correct.[28] However, the contrast in concepts of orthodoxy and revelation is overdrawn and somewhat abstract, and at any rate applies only to the later Christian period when such ideas took hold. Moreover, his focus on linguistic usage tends to override other kinds of pertinent evidence.

In contrast, Shaye Cohen has suggested that the historiographical outlook of the philosophical schools—the pristine teachings of the

[25] Desjardins, "Bauer", 76–77, suggests that the use by Jews of αἵρεσις to refer to Christians (Acts 24:5, 28:22; Justin. *Dial.* 17.1; 108.2) may reflect early Jewish usage. But not all of these are necessarily negative and they may at any rate only witness to Christian usage placed on Jewish lips.

[26] Cohen, "Virgin", 6. He notes that both are book religions, in which doctrines of tradition and succession are inevitable; and that both espouse a form of monotheism, which encourages notions of unity, oneness and exclusivity.

[27] Brox, "Häresie", 248–59.

[28] A check (through *TLG*) of the use of αἵρεσις in a large range of classical writers turned up no parallels to the negative Christian usage.

founder, their transmission through a chain of tradition, the splits and rivalries—may well have influenced both the Jewish (rabbinic) and Christian ideas of heresy.[29] More recently, H. Cancik has argued that the true analogy for what he calls Luke's "institutional history" are the philosophical schools, with their disputes over unity, inheritance and contintuity.[30] There are many instances of disagreement and lively polemic both between and within the Hellenistic schools. A famous schism occurred within the Platonic Academy under Antiochus of Ascalon (died 68 BCE), who introduced a reform which created a "new" academy, but one which they preferred to call the "Old Academy" because they claimed to be harking back to the original teachings of Platonism.[31] Others, like Menedemus, founded new schools but within the same tradition. Equally interesting are those who move from one school or system of thought to another, like Aristo of Alexandria and Cratippus of Pergamum, both of who were said to have "defected from the Academy" (ἀποστατήσαντες τῆς Ἀκαδημείας) when Aristus, Antiochus' brother, took over the reins.[32] This striking use of ἀποστατήσαντες reminds us of Dionysus of Heraclea ('the renegade'), who abandoned (ἀποστάς) Zeno the Stoic and became a hedonist (Diog. Laert. 7.166–67), and of Chrysippus who separated himself (ἀπέστη) from Cleanthes (Diog. Laert. 7.179). A few that

[29] Cohen, "Virgin", 6–8.

[30] H. Cancik, "The History of Culture, Religion, and Institutions in Ancient Historiography: Philological Observations Concerning Luke's History", *JBL* 116 (1997) 673–95. The point of contrast for Cancik is Graeco-Roman religion where he finds no such analogy. He focuses on Acts but, quite apart from the observation that Acts is in many ways the precursor of later concepts of Christian orthodoxy, much of the evidence he collects can be applied more generally to the issue we are looking at. Cancik provides a rich array of examples that can be used to flesh out Cohen's proposal. Loveday Alexander's perceptive comments on the parallels between Christian groups and philosophical and medical schools do not deal directly with the issue that concerns us: "Paul and the Hellenistic Schools: The Evidence of Galen", in T. Engberg-Pedersen (ed.), *Paul in his Hellenistic Context* (Philadelphia: Augsburg Fortress/Edinburgh: T & T Clark, 1994) 60–83. Medical schools are an important point of comparison too, but there is less information about their rifts—see H. von Staden, "Hairesis", 76–110.

[31] J. Barnes, "Antiochus of Ascalon", in M. Griffin and J. Barnes (eds.), *Philosophica Togata: Essays on Philosophy and Roman Society* (Oxford: Clarendon, 1989) 51–96, is the fullest study of Antiochus known to me. One of the earliest, and certainly the most famous, of philosophical schisms came when Aristotle abandoned Plato.

[32] The evidence for Menedemus is in col. 6 and the quotation is in col. 35 of the *Index Academicorum* (not available to me), as found in Cancik, "History", 691. Cancik discusses several other examples of inter- and intra- school competition (686–95).

we know about not only seceded but become savage critics of the system they left behind. The once dedicated Epicurean, Timocrates, abandoned the school, became an implacable opponent, started an influential and often scurrilous tradition of anti-Epicurean polemic, and was vigorously opposed by Epicurus and others of his school (Diog. Laert. 10.6–8). There is no record of him joining another school.

A number of things are worth noting. First, we have evidence of internal divisions within a school, transfer of allegiance from one school to another, and perhaps (in the case of Timocrates) abandonment of philosophy altogether.[33] Associated with this are bitter exchanges, counter-attacks by those who have been abandoned, and endless squabbles over inheritance of the true tradition. Second, while not exactly a technical term, ἀποστατέω is fairly regularly used to describe defection from one school to another or even from philosophy altogether. Thus, although the negative use of αἵρεσις is not found, the negative use of ἀποστατέω is. And although there is no linguistic distinction between dissidents and defectors, both sorts of behaviour can be found in the records. Thus the analogy with the philosophical schools works well, at least for some of the features we are interested in. It is a commonly observed that "philosophy" is the nearest thing in the ancient world to our term "religion", and we know that Christian (like Jewish) apologists often presented themselves as a sort of philosophy.[34] In the second century CE the analogy came natu-

---

[33] Lucian, interestingly, speaks of abandoning (ἀποστάντας) philosophy and living an ordinary life because of the difficulty of making a choice (αἵρεσις) between the various systems of thought (*Herm.* 67.7)—but this is not the use of αἵρεσις we are looking for.

[34] Of course, other cults and associations might provide better analogies for other aspects of early Christianity. Moreover, some philosophical schools would have provided a better analogy than others. The Epicureans, for example, in addition to sharing an emphasis on tradition and transmission, were more communally and religiously minded than other schools. They lived together in well-ordered communities that resembled miniature states. The "religious" element included commemorative festivals, common meals, honouring the founder (the "sole saviour" Epicurus) and the extensive use of statues of their masters. The broad similarity between Epicureans and Christians was observed as early as the second century (Lucian *Alex.*). On the religious element in Epicureanism see C.E. Glad, *Paul and Philodemus: Adaptability in Epicurean and Early Christian Psychagogy* (Leiden: Brill, 1995) 8–9; B. Frischer, *The Sculpted Word: Epicureanism and Philosophical Recruitment in Ancient Greece* (Berkeley/Los Angeles/London: University of California Press, 1982) 52–70; D. Clay, "The Cults of Epicurus", in idem, *Paradosis and Survival: Three Chapters in the History of Epicurean Philosophy* (Ann Arbor: University of Michigan Press, 1998) 75–102.

rally to Galen, who likens Judaism and Christianity to the medical and philosophical schools of his day. It is not implausible to think that on a social level, and perhaps on a linguistic level too, the philosophical schools may well have influenced the way that early Christians conceived of and responded to dissidence and defection.

The sort of middleman through whom such ideas may have been transmitted is Justin. Le Boulluec has already suggested that Justin was the key figure in constructing the Christian notion of heresy, since it is in his writings that the negative use of αἵρεσις occurs fairly consistently for the first time to describe dissidents. He also wrote what was, as far as we know, the first comprehensive anti-heretical tract (*Apol.* 26.8)—no longer extant, but referred to by Justin and used by Irenaeus. Even his brief comments in the extant works reveal an urge to classify, and give a pedigree for, heretical groups—which, interestingly, he likens to the various philosophical schools (*Apol.* 1.26; *Dial.* 35). Of the philosophical schools, so he tells us in his autobiographical sketch in *Dialogue 1–8*, he had first-hand experience, and their modus operandi probably influenced the Christian school he subsequently set up in Rome. Moreover, the *Dialogue* shows that he was aware of currents in the Jewish thought of his day at precisely the time when the Jewish concepts of heresy and apostasy were being developed so that, insofar as this is a place to look for influence, Justin is more likely than most to have been exposed to it. None of this can be proven, but it is not an implausible surmise.

Now we can return to some of out initial questions. There is evidence that the later tendency to fuse heresy and apostasy was less common in the first century or so of the Christian movement. What happened in the process of fusion was that heresy was, so to speak, upgraded to the level of apostasy, and dissidents were increasingly seen as defectors. Precise analogies to these developments cannot be found, but the philosophical schools provide, on the face of it, the more interesting ones. There is no secure parallel, Jewish or pagan, to the pejorative use of "heresy," suggesting that it may have been a linguistic innovation.[35] On the other hand there is both Jewish and pagan evidence for the negative use of "apostasy." In the early period no one Christian author uses both terms to refer to Christian

[35] See note 24 above.

dissidents and defectors; rather, they have use one or the other.[36] Yet the two phenomena are clearly found and, sometimes in the same source, distinguished.

As it relates to the theme of Christian pluralism, what we have discovered comes as no great surprise. In the first and early second centuries churches were capacious enough to contain dissidents within them, to recognize that they belonged even though their practices and beliefs were (from the viewpoint of the writer) questionable, if not unacceptable. Of course, the dissident minority in some communities might well have been those who by later standards were the "orthodox", as Bauer has taught us. Apostates were those who unequivocally and publicly defected. As time went by, however, the two were conflated and the fate of the defector became the fate of the dissident. Those (primarily Marcionites and gnostics) who defied the growing sense of Christian orthodoxy were no longer seen as wayward brethren, but as demonically-inspired renegades. Why? A more confident sense of identity? The need to find a unifying core amidst an increasingly chaotic diversity? A response to views more radical and challenging than anything that had been met before? These and other causes can be surmised. Whatever the causes and whatever the gain, Christian pluralism was the loser.

[36] Acts does have both, but ἀποστασία in Acts 21:21 refers to Paul as a defector from Judaism. Justin uses ἀποστατέω, but with reference to Satan, the angels, or Israel as rebels against God (e.g. *Dial.* 76.3; 79.1, 3; 103.5). Our enquiry might have been simpler if this had not been the case. If, for example Justin had used ἀποστατέω in the way it is used in connection with the philosophical schools that would have greatly strengthened the argument made above.

"WHO WILL BE OUR LEADER?" AUTHORITY AND AUTONOMY IN THE *GOSPEL OF THOMAS*

Risto Uro

A feature that has often invited comments in Thomasine scholarship is the juxtaposition of sayings on James' leadership in *Gos. Thom.* 12 and on Thomas' "wordless confession" in *Gos. Thom.* 13:

> The disciples said to Jesus, "We know that you are going to leave us. Who will be our leader?" [2]Jesus said to them, "No matter where you are, you are to go to James the Just, for whose sake heaven and earth came into being." (*Gos. Thom.* 12)
>
> Jesus said to his disciples, "Compare me to something and tell what I am like." [2]Simon Peter said to him, "You are like a righteous messenger." [3]Matthew said to him, "You are like a wise philosopher." [4]Thomas said to him, "Master, my mouth is utterly unable to say what you are like." [5]Jesus said, "I am not your master. Because you have drunk, you have become intoxicated from the bubbling spring that I have tended."
>
> [6]And he took him, and withdrew, and told him three things. [7]When Thomas came back to his friends, they asked him, "What did Jesus say to you?" [8]Thomas said to them: "If I tell you one of the things he spoke to me, you will pick up rocks and stone me, and fire will come from the rocks and devour you." (*Gos. Thom.* 13)[1]

The appearance of the two figures is indeed striking. James and Thomas are elevated in two sayings which follow each other, but the question of how exactly the authority of these figures should be related does not receive any explanation and is left for the reader to decide. According to one influential interpretation, Thomas' special position in saying 13 serves as something of a corrective to the claim about James' leadership in the previous saying.[2] This, however, opens

---

[1] Transl. modified from R.J. Miller (ed.), *The Complete Gospels: Annotated Scholars Version* (Revised and expanded edition; San Francisco: Harper, 1994), which is the basic English translation of the *Gospel of Thomas* used in this article.

[2] H. Koester has argued in several publications that in *Gos. Thom.* 13 James' authority is "surpassed" or "superseded" by that of Thomas; see "GNOMAI

up a number of further questions. Why is James' authority retained in the first place, if Thomas' position as the recipient of the special revelation and the guarantor of the gospel tradition (cf. prologue) supersedes that of James?[3] Is *Gos. Thom.* 12 a fossilized remnant of an earlier phase of the tradition, which still appealed to the authority of James?[4] Or is the cluster of sayings 12 and 13 an example of a subtle irony used by the author of the gospel to undermine the "ecclesiastical" authority represented by James?[5] Or should James' and Thomas' positions be regarded as parallel or supplementary rather than competing ones?[6]

1. *Apostles as Symbols*

A common presupposition behind many interpretations of *Gos. Thom.* 12–13 is that they take the figures of James and Thomas in the text as representatives of specific groups or traditions in early Christianity.[7]

DIAPHORAI: The Origin and and Nature of Diversification in the History of Early Christianity", in J.M. Robinson and H. Koester, *Trajectories through Early Christianity* (Philadelphia: Fortress, 1971) 114–57, esp. p. 136; idem, "Introduction" [to the *Gospel According to Thomas*], in B. Layton (ed.), *Nag Hammadi Codex II,2–7 together with XIII,2*, Brit. Lib. Or. 4926(1), and P.Oxy. 1, 654, 655* (2 vols.; NHS 20–21; Leiden: Brill, 1989) 1.37–49, esp. p. 40. In another instance, however, Koester may formulate somewhat differently that the contrast between James and Thomas seeks to strengthen the tradition of Thomas against the authority of James, "without denying the latter's claim to leadership in ecclesiastical matters"; see H. Koester, *Introduction to the New Testament*, vol. 2: *History and Literature of Early Christianity* (Philadelphia/Berlin: Fortress/de Gruyter, 1982) 152–52. See also A. Marjanen, *The Woman Jesus Loved: Mary Magdalene in the Nag Hammadi Library and Related Documents* (NHMS 40; Leiden: Brill, 1996) 40–42; idem, "Is *Thomas* a Gnostic Gospel?" in R. Uro (ed.), *Thomas at the Crossroads: Essays on the Gospel of Thomas* (SNTW; Edinburgh: T & T Clark, 1998) 107–39, on p. 119.

[3] S.J. Patterson *The Gospel of Thomas and Jesus* (Foundations and Facets: Reference Series; Sonoma: Polebridge Press, 1993) 116 n. 13.

[4] G. Quispel attributed *Gos. Thom.* 12 to a "Jewish-Christian" source, while saying 13 would derive from an "encratite" source; *Makarius, das Thomasevangelium und das Lied von der Perle* (NovTSup 15; Leiden: Brill, 1967) 97–98. Patterson has suggested that sayings 12 and 13 represent subsequent layers in the compositional history of the gospel. See *Gospel of Thomas*, 118–20. Patterson's stratification has been followed by J.D. Crossan, *The Historical Jesus: The Life of a Mediterrenean Jewish Peasant* (San Francisco: Harper, 1991) 427–28; idem, *The Birth of Christianity: Discovering What Happened in the Years Immediately after the Execution of Jesus* (San Francisco: Harper, 1998) 247–56.

[5] R. Valantasis, *The Gospel of Thomas* (New Testament Readings; London: Routledge, 1997) 73.

[6] Patterson, *Gospel of Thomas*, 116 n. 13.

[7] These alternatives are not of course exclusive since group-identity must have been heavily depended on the idea of a common tradition.

Whatever is known of James and Thomas as historical persons, they later became symbols which some early Christian groups could appeal to as the ideal leaders of the heroic beginnings and guarantors of the truth of their traditions. Although many authors used the concept of apostles (e.g. Ephesians; Ignatius; *1 Clement*) or the idea of the "twelve apostles" (Luke) generally, it has been observed that certain local communities or like-minded groups claimed a link with a particular apostolic figure ("Johannine Christianity" probably being the clearest example).[8] Moreover, scholars have not infrequently seen controversies between groups which venerated the heritage of *different* apostles and figures of authority in critical stories or remarks of one apostle in some text which is interpreted as an attempt to restrict or decrease the influence of the corresponding group.[9] Such controversies may be traced back to the conflicts between the actual historical persons (for example, between the historical Paul and Peter or James), but for later Christian generations the apostolic figures became in any case weapons in both strengthening one's own claim and opposing that of others.

There is no doubt that, for early Christians, figures like James and Thomas were powerful symbols that played an important role in the legitimation of the traditions of various early Christian groups. Both names can be associated with a particular geographical area; James with Jerusalem and "Judas Thomas" with eastern Syria.[10] In the prologue of the gospel, Thomas is described as a "figure of authentication,"[11] who wrote down the "secret words" of the "living

[8] Koester, *Introduction*, 2.6–8.

[9] This approach is, of course, as old as the so-called "Tübingen school" established by Ferdinand Christian Baur. He interpreted first two Christian centuries in light of a bitter conflict between the followers of Peter and Paul. A more recent example is T.V. Smith, *Petrine Controversies in Early Christianity: Attitudes towards Peter in Christian Writings of the First Two Centuries* (WUNT 2/15; Tübingen: Mohr [Siebeck], 1985), which looks for "anti-Peter" and "pro-Peter" traditions in the early Christian writings. Smith does not, however, trace a single Petrine group as Baur did, but rather a number of different groups stemming from widely divergent backgrounds (ibid., 211).

[10] For the East Syrian origin of the name "Judas Thomas", see A.F.J. Klijn, "John XIV 22 and the Name Judas Thomas", in *Studies in John Presented to Prof. J.N. Sevenster on the Occasion of His Seventieth Birthday* (NovTSup 23; Leiden: Brill, 1970) 88–96; Koester, "GNOMAI DIAPHORAI", 127–28; J.J. Gunther, "The Meaning and Origin of the Name 'Judas Thomas'", *Muséon* 93 (1980) 113–48; H.J.W. Drijvers, "Facts and Problems in Early Syriac-Speaking Christianity", *SecCent* 2 (1982) 157–75, esp. pp. 158–59; For recent studies on James, see below note 23.

[11] See especially I. Dunderberg, "*Thomas* and the Beloved Disciple", in Uro (ed.), *Thomas at the Crossroads*, 65–88.

Jesus" and who thus has a special position among the disciples as a recipient of Jesus' teaching. In some other early Christian writings James has a similar role as Thomas in the *Gospel of Thomas*.[12] The high status of James in logion 12 may be contrasted with the silence or suppression of James in many early Christian writings (see below). This seems to give at least some indirect evidence for the claim that controversies continued to be projected onto the apostolic figures during subsequent Christian generations.

However, reading early Christian history through the images of apostles is not without problems. We do know that *different* groups and authors—both geographically and theologically—could appeal to the authority of the *same* apostle. Paul came to be venerated both in "Gnostic"[13] and "ecclesiastical" circles (cf. Pastorals). Peter was honored as a foundational figure in the congregations of Rome and Antioch.[14] Moreover, using stories of the apostolic figures as keys to the conflicts between early Christian groups can be very tricky. A good example is the presentation of Peter in the Gospel of Matthew. It is difficult to decide whether Matthew is promoting Peter's authority as one who has been given the power of the keys (Matt 16:19), or undermining his authority as "a man of little faith" (14:31) who utters Satanic words (16:33) and finally denies his master (26:69–75). In his characterization of Peter Matthew is surely doing more than simply giving a transparent presentation of a contemporary "Petrine group."[15] We should be cautious not to make textual characters into a kinds of mirror images[16] which directly reflect their historical counterparts, whether one thinks of factual historical persons or groups that later identified themselves as the true cultivators of their her-

---

[12] Cf. the *Apocryphon of James*, which reports of the "secret books" revealed to James and Peter (or to James alone) and written down by James.

[13] For the second-century Gnostic interpretation of Paul, see E. Pagels, *The Gnostic Paul: Gnostic Exegesis of the Pauline Letters* (Philadelphia: Fortress, 1975).

[14] Rome revered the memory of both Paul and Peter, whereas Peter became a foundational figure also in Antioch. For the references, see W. Bauer, *Orthodoxy and Heresy in Earliest Christianity* (transl. R. Kraft and G. Krodel; Philadelphia: Fortress, 1971) 111–18.

[15] K. Syreeni's recent narrative-critical analysis of Peter in Matthew from the perspective of the "three-world model" demonstrates well the multidimensional nature of Peter's character; "Peter as Character and Symbol in the Gospel of Matthew", in D. Rhoads and K. Syreeni (eds.), *Characterization in the Gospels: Reconceiving Narrative Criticism* (JSNTSup 184; Sheffield: Sheffield Academic Press, 1999) 106–52. According to Syreeni, Matthew's Peter is "highly ambivalent ecclesiastical symbol" (p. 132).

[16] I owe this metaphor to Syreeni, "Peter as Character and Symbol", 109.

itage. Instead, I think, we should take seriously the *symbolic* nature of these images and realize that their use may be motivated by several concerns, some of which may deal with the narrative logic, others with ideological or "church-political"realities.[17] This may, as seems to be the case in *Gos. Thom.* 12–13, result in a rather complicated network of meanings, which is not easily deciphered into a clear historical interpretation.

One explicit concern in *Gos. Thom.* 12 is the issue of leadership. The disciples ask, who will hold the leading position among them after Jesus' departure, to which Jesus plainly answers that the position belongs to James the Just. The dialogue in *Gos. Thom.* 13 begins as a discussion about the right Christological confession, but the saying deals with the issue of leadership as well. Thomas' answer, "Master, my mouth is utterly unable to say what you are like," is qualified by Jesus with words "I am not your master."[18] On the basis of this saying, some scholars have suggested that the *Gospel of Thomas* champions a "masterless" ideal of discipleship and opposes hierarchic understanding of community-life.[19] This suggestion leads us to intriguing questions. How is *Thomas'* "masterless" ideal related to the development of leadership roles in other early Christian groups? Is *Thomas* against any kind of ecclesiastical authority? How should one interpret James' leadership from this perspective? The *Gospel of Thomas* gives only a few and partially contradictory hints of how organizational roles are envisioned in the gospel. We may, however, shed some more light by comparing *Thomas'* scarce statements with more extensive discussions on leadership in other early Christian documents. In this paper my primary point of comparison is the Gospel of Matthew. I have several reasons for such a choice. Matthew is among those early Christian documents which foster highly egalitarian model of community-life similar to that in *Thomas* (no one should be called "rabbi" or "master;" Matt 23:8–11). At the same time, Matthew highlights the ecclesiastical authority of Peter the Rock in Matt 16:18–19, which provides an analogy to the authority of

[17] Cf. Syreeni's distinction between character (textual phenomenon), person (historical and social reality) and symbol (ideological dimension); "Peter as Character and Symbol", 116–20.

[18] The Coptic word *sah*, a derivative from verb *shai* ("write"), can be translated either as "master" or "teacher."

[19] Marjanen, *The Woman Jesus Loved*, 40–42; idem, "Is *Thomas* a Gnostic Gospel?" 120; Valantasis, *Gospel of Thomas*, 73.

James the Just in *Gos. Thom.* 12.[20] Finally, the whole pericope of Matt 16:13–23 has its closest parallel in *Gos. Thom.* 13, which makes it difficult to escape the question of the relationship between the Matthean and Thomasine traditions.[21]

2. *James' leadership*

The disciples' question in *Gos. Thom.* 12 (lit. "Who will be great over us?") bears some resemblance to the synoptic stories in which the disciples discuss the issue of who is the "greatest" among them (cf. Mark 9:33–37 parr; cf. also Mark 10:35–45 parr.). In these stories Jesus does not however designate any of the disciples as having a special position, but rather gives a general lesson on humble leadership by referring to slaves and children (Mark 9:35–36; 10:43–45 parr.). It is hardly possible that *Gos. Thom.* 12 would have been modeled on the pattern of these synoptic stories.[22] Most likely the saying represents a tradition which belongs to the same category as Jesus' words on Peter's leadership and commission (Matt 16:17–18; cf. also John 21:15–19). One may also refer to the language Paul uses when relating his special calling as an apostle of the gentiles in Gal 1:11–2:10. In the canonical gospels, James is mentioned only in passing in a few instances among Jesus' siblings (Mark 6:3; Matt 13:55). Although in Acts he is depicted as the leader of the Jerusalem church, his role is largely eclipsed by that of Peter and Paul. Recent scholarship on James has become increasingly aware that James

---

[20] M. Hengel, "Jacobus der Herrenbruder—der erste 'Papst?'", in E. Grässer and O. Merk (eds.), *Glaube und Eschatologie* (FS W.G. Kümmel; Tübingen: Mohr [Siebeck] 1985) 79.

[21] A comparison between *Thomas* and Matthew has been made seldom. Koester, *Ancient Christian Gospels: Their History and Development* (London: SCM; Trinity Press International, 1990), typically compares *Thomas* with Matthew only in connection with parables (pp. 103–7). *Thomas'* relation to Q, Mark and John receive major attention.

[22] R.M. Grant and D.N. Freedman argue that the saying is based on John 14:5 as well as on Mark 9:34; 10:43 and the parallels; *The Secret Sayings of Jesus* (London: Collins, 1960) 124–25. Yet the parallelism between the Johannine passage and the disciples' question in *Gos. Thom.* 12:1 is remote. As to the synoptic parallels, even W. Schrage, who generally strongly argues for *Thomas'* dependence on the canonical gospels, concludes that the question must be left open in this case, *Das Verhältnis des Thomas-Evangeliums zur synoptischen Tradition und den koptischen Evangelienübersetzungen: Zugleich ein Beitrag zur gnostischen Synoptikerdeutung* (BZNW 29; Berlin: Töpelmann, 1964) 51.

played much more prominent role in the earliest decades of the Jesus movement than one is able to conclude on the basis of the New Testament.[23] The letters of Paul and Acts, to be sure, contain some important clues to support the suggestion of James' leading position in the Christian movement from the very beginning (Gal 1:17–19; 2:1–14; 1 Cor 15:7; Acts 1:14; 12:17; 15; 21:17–26). Non-canonical sources and Josephus confirm this conclusion and suggest that during the first and second centuries James was venerated among many groups as the most prominent authority of the Christian origins next to Jesus.[24] Some of the sources, most notably the *Gospel of Hebrews*,[25] describe James as being appointed to his position and legitimated by Jesus himself, just like Peter in the canonical texts. With its explicit statement about the position of James as a successor of Jesus, *Gos. Thom.* 12 can be seen as being part of such traditions.

There are further indications that *Gos. Thom.* 12 derives from a group that took James' "primacy" seriously. The saying uses the epithet "Just" or "Righteous" (δίκαιος), which does not appear in the New Testament but is instead found in many of the sources that seem to preserve traces of James' priority.[26] It has sometimes been argued that the epithet was given to him because of his martyrdom,[27] but it is possible that the name was already used during

[23] See e.g. Hengel, "Jacobus der Herrenbruder", 71–104; W. Pratscher, *Der Herrenbruder Jacobus und die Jacobustradition* (FRLANT 139; Göttingen: Vandenhoeck & Ruprecht, 1987); R.B. Ward, "James of Jerusalem in the First Two Centuries", in *ANRW* II 26.1 (1992) 779–812; the articles published in B. Chilton and C.A. Evans (eds.), *James the Just and Christian Origins* (NovTSup 98; Leiden: Brill, 1999); and especially J. Painter, *Just James: The Brother of Jesus in History and Tradition* (Edinburgh: T & T Clark, 1999).

[24] J.D. Crossan makes this point succinctly: "If you read a non-Christian source such as Josephus . . . you would know only two individuals in earliest Christianity: one is Jesus himself and the other is his brother James." *Birth of Christianity*, 463.

[25] The *Gospel of Hebrews* reported of James' participation in the last supper and Jesus' appearance to him after the resurrection; see Jerome, *Vir. ill.* 2 (= *Gos. Hebr.* # 7). Also some traditions preserved by Eusebius seem to presuppose the direct appointment of James by Jesus and James' leading position in Jerusalem right after the resurrection; see the quotation from the *Outlines* Book VIII of Clement of Alexandria in *Hist. eccl.* 2.1 and 7.19.1 (but compare with the quotation from Book VII of Clement's work and *Hist. eccl.* 2.23.1); for an analysis, see Painter, *Just James*, 105–58, esp. p. 114.

[26] *Gos. Hebr.* # 7; *1 Apoc. Jas.* 32,2–3; *2 Apoc. Jas.* 44:14; 59:22; 60:12; 61:14; Eusebius, *Hist. eccl.* 2.23.7.

[27] E.g. Ward, "James of Jerusalem", 801, with references to Wis 2:17f; Matt 23:29,35; Jas 5:6 and Isa 3:10 (Hegesippus quoted the last one in his description of James' death; see Eusebius, *Hist. eccl.* 2.23.15); see also Painter, *Just James*, 157.

James' lifetime because of his exemplary and pious life-style.[28] The peculiar characterization of James as the one "for whose sake heaven and earth came into being" is often noted as a typical Jewish expression, which is used of such exemplary righteous persons as Abraham, Moses, David, Hanina ben Dosa or the Messiah.[29] These features strongly support the view that *Gos. Thom.* 12 goes ultimately back to the circles who venerated James as the most important leader of the Christian movement after Jesus.[30] It is natural to think that these circles were in some way connected with, or rooted in, the Jewish-Christian community in Jerusalem.

There are, on the other hand, signs that in the present context the meaning of the saying is modified with several intratextual references. There is a catchword connection with the statement in the previous saying that "this heaven (*teipe*) will pass away, and the one above it will pass away" (11:1). The statement may be seen as relativizing James' authority as something which is temporary and will pass away. A variant of this saying is found in *Gos. Thom.* 111 ("The heavens and the earth will be rolled up in your presence"), which is glossed with an editor's comment: "Does not Jesus say, 'Those who have found themselves, of them the world is not worthy.'" The latter part of this comment repeats the phrase which is found also in *Gos. Thom.* 56 and 80, two closely parallel sayings on the world as a "body" or "corpse." These sayings characterize the world and the human body as something external to person's true domain.[31] A careful reader of Jesus' sayings in the gospel is thus able to gather that James' leadership, praised in saying 12, belongs ultimately to the sphere of the temporary and the external. Those who understand

[28] Hengel, "Jakobus der Herrenbruder", 80. This does not mean, however, that Hegesippus' description of James (*Hist. eccl.* 2.23) as a nazarite and extreme ascetic with priestly motifs is historically accurate.

[29] Scholars usually refer to L. Ginzberg, *The Legends of the Jews* (vol. 5; Philadelphia: The Jewish Publication Society of America, 1925); J.-É. Menard states that the expression makes *Gos. Thom.* 12 "juif d'apparance, mais antijuif dans son interprétation", since it elevates James to the same position as Torah, Abraham, Moses, and the Messiah; *L'évangile selon Thomas* (NHS 5; Leiden: E.J. Brill, 1975) 97. This misses the point, however.

[30] Similar language is used of James in the *Second Apocalypse of James* 55,24–25 ("You are whom the heavens bless") and 56, 2–5 ("For your sake they will be told [these things], and will come to rest. For your sake they will reign [and will] become kings . . ."). Trans. C. W. Hedrick in J.M. Robinson (ed.), *The Nag Hammadi Library in English* (3rd ed.; San Francisco: Harper & Row, 1988).

[31] Cf. also *Gos. Thom.* 21.

and "have found themselves" are superior to the world ("the world is not worthy of them")[32] and are therefore also superior to their leaders, while the latter are seen as part of the transient structures of this world. Moreover, it should be noted that already at the beginning of the gospel *Thomas'* audience had been encouraged to take a critical attitude toward religious leaders who naively teach that the kingdom is in heaven or in the underworld (*Gos. Thom.* 3). It is somewhat unclear whether the saying refers to the teachers or leaders who were recognized as such by *Thomas'* audience,[33] but in light of what is said about their teaching it seems obvious enough that they were *Christian* leaders.

Another trait of saying 12 which is modified by its context within the collection as a whole is the localization of James' authority. It is possible that originally the somewhat surprising exhortation "wherever you are, you are to go to James" could be explained by the fact that in the tradition James' leadership was firmly placed in the "mother church" of Jerusalem.[34] However, in the Thomasine perspective such localization of authority may be contrasted with the rejection of any attempt to localize the kingdom or Jesus' presence (e.g. *Gos. Thom.* 3; 24; 77:2; 91; 97; 113). When the disciples ask Jesus to show "the place" where he is, Jesus turns their attention to the "light within a person of light" (24).[35] James, in contrast, does have a place where he is, and the disciples are asked to go to him. This creates a tension between the basic thrust of logion 12 and some central theological emphases of *Thomas* found elsewhere in the gospel. These considerations lead us to a closer examination of *Gos. Thom.* 13, which is commonly seen as functioning as a redefinition or modification of James' leadership in the preceding saying.

---

[32] Cf. also Hebr 11:38. The expression is also found in rabbinic literature (e.g. *Mek.* 5a; *Sanh.* 11:1).

[33] The Coptic version uses the expression *netsōk hēt tēytn*, which is best translated as "those who lead you", the verb *sōk hēt* being an equivalent of the Greek ἡγέομαι; see W.E. Crum, *A Coptic Dictionary* (Oxford: Clarendon, 1939) 327. The Greek form (οἱ ἕλκοντες; "those who attract" or "draw you on") may also be understood as referring to outside leaders; see R. Uro, "Neither Here Nor There: Luke 17:20–21 and Related Sayings in Thomas, Mark, and Q", *Occasional Papers* 20 (Claremont: Claremont Graduate School), 15 n. 38, 18 (cf. the synoptic parallels in Mark 13:21–23; Matt 24:23–26; Luke 17: 20–23).

[34] Cf. Patterson (*Gospel of Thomas*, 151), who sees here an indication that Thomas Christians are dispersed and itinerant.

[35] The "the place of life" in *Gos. Thom.* 4, though seemingly local, is in essence a "non-place", a primordial place beyond time and space (cf. also 50:1).

3. *Thomas and Peter*

The form of *Gos. Thom.* 13 is closely related to the synoptic accounts of Peter's confession in Mark 8:27–33 and parallels (cf. also John 6:66–71). Each of the synoptic versions has Jesus asking the disciples about opinions of him with a number of different characterizations of Jesus' identity given, culminating in the final confession of one of the disciples and Jesus' response. Except from Luke, in each gospel a private discussion follows the scene of the confession, although in Mark (8:32) and Matthew (16:22) it is Peter who takes Jesus aside to rebuke him, whereas in *Thomas* Jesus tells Thomas "three things" or "words" (*nšomt nšaje*) in privacy (13:6–8). Only in Matthew and *Thomas* does Jesus' response contain a reference to the divine source of the confession (cf. the blessing in Matt 16:17 and Thomas' intoxication in *Gos. Thom.* 13:5), which is affirmed with the unique role that Jesus assigns to the disciple who has given the appropriate answer. Mark has only the command to keep Jesus' identity in secret (cf. also Matt 16:20; Luke 9:21). The closeness between the Matthean and Thomasine versions is reinforced by the fact that the previous saying on James' leadership (*Gos. Thom.* 12) can be seen, as argued above, as an analogy to the "investiture" of Peter in Matt 16:17–19.

In spite of these affinities between Matt 16:13–20 and *Gos. Thom.* 13, it is not probable that *Thomas* is *directly* dependent on the Gospel of Matthew (or Matthew on *Thomas*, for that matter).[36] The similarities between the Matthean and Thomasine accounts lie more in the general structure of the account than in details that would indicate literary reworking. To be sure, one could argue that this structure has resulted from Matthew's redactional composition, because he added the blessing and the appointment of Peter to Mark's story, where they are absent. In that case one could consider the possibility of "secondary orality," that is, the influence of Matthew's literary redaction on the oral tradition drawn upon by *Thomas*.[37] On

[36] Pace Smith, *Petrine Controversies*, 115, who argues that logion 13 is "a Gnostic version of the *Matthean* Caesarea Philippi event" (Smith's italics). Cf. B. Gärtner, who held that *Gos. Thom.* 13 is "evidently an edited and expanded form of Mark 8:29"; *Ett nytt evangelium? Thomasevangeliets hemliga Jesusord* (Stockholm: Diakonistyrelsens bokförlag, 1960) 114. See also R. McL. Wilson, *Studies in the Gospel of Thomas* (London: A.R. Mowbray, 1960) 112.

[37] Uro, "'Secondary Orality' in the Gospel of Thomas? Logion 14 as a Test

the other hand, it is not at all clear that the abrupt silencing command in Mark 8:30 was the only way in which the story was told in the tradition until Matthew's pen reformulated it. Most scholars are unwilling to regard all of Matt 16:17–19 as Matthew's creation, but then again attempts to place these verses in some other pre-Matthean setting, for example in a post-resurrection appearance story[38] or in the context of the Last Supper (cf. Luke 22:31–34),[39] can be contested.[40] While many scholars have sought to trace a separate pre-Matthean tradition[41] or individual sayings behind Matt 16:17–19,[42] some have argued that there is no better setting for Matt 16:17–19 in the gospel history than the confession at Ceasaraea Philippi.[43] The former view

Case", *Foundations & Facets Forum* 9:3–4 (1993) 305–29, reprinted with the title "*Thomas* and the Oral Gospel Tradition" in Uro (ed.), *Thomas at the Crossroads*, 8–32. Cf. also E.W. Saunders, "A Trio of Thomas Logia", *BR* 8 (1963) 43–59, esp. p. 59.

[38] E.g. R. Bultmann, *The History of the Synoptic Tradition* (2nd ed.; English trans. by J. Marsh; Oxford: Blackwell, 1968) 259. Some scholars limit the post-resurrection tradition to verses 16:18–19, while 16:17 is taken basically as Matthew's composition or creation; see A. Vögtle, "Zum Problem der Herkunft von 'Mt 16,17–19'", in P. Hoffmann (ed.), *Orientierung an Jesus: Zur Theologie der Synoptiker* (FS Josef Schmid; Freiburg: Herder, 1973) 372–93; R.E. Brown, K.P. Donfried and J. Reumann (eds.), *Peter in the New Testament: A Collaborative Assessment by Protestant and Roman Catholic Scholars* (Minneapolis: Augsburg, 1973) 86–91.

[39] E.g. O. Cullmann, *Petrus: Jünger, Apostel, Märtyrer* (Munich: Siebenstern Taschenbuch, 1967) 205–7.

[40] Cullmann's suggestion has not gained much following; see e.g. Brown et al. (eds.), *Peter in the New Testament*, 85. Much more common is the claim that Matt 16:17–19 (or part of it) was originally a post-resurrection tradition. Bultmann (*History of Synoptic Tradition*, 259) referred to "a clear parallel" in the post-resurrection episode John 21:15–19 (cf. also 20:22–23) and argued that this tradition derived ultimately from the first appearance of the risen Christ to Peter (cf. 1 Cor 15:5). Yet the parallelism with John 20:15–19 is not as "clear" as Bultmann suggests; for criticism, see B.P. Robinson, "Peter and His Successors: Tradition and Redaction in Matthew 16.17–19", *JSNT* 21 (1984) 85–104, esp. pp. 87–88; W.D. Davies and D.C. Allison, *The Gospel According to Saint Matthew*, vol. 2: *Commentary on Matthew VIII–XVIII* (ICC; Edinburgh: T & T Clark, 1991) 608–9. Moreover, in whatever context Peter's confession was originally told, the confession, the blessing and the investiture make a good story. The suggestion that a lost account of the first appearance to Peter was later replaced with stories like Matt 16:13–20 and John 21:15–19 is strained.

[41] E.g. G. Künzel, *Studien zum Gemeindeverständnis des Matthäus-Evangeliums* (Calwer Theologische Monographien 10; Stuttgart: Calwer, 1978) 180–93.

[42] E.g. Robinson, "Peter and His Successors", 85–104; U. Luz, *Das Evangelium nach Matthäus* 2 (EKKNT 1:2. Zürich: Benziger Verlag; Neukirchen-Vluyn: Neukirchener Verlag, 1990) 453–59.

[43] Davies and Allison, *The Gospel According to Saint Matthew*, 602–47, esp. pp. 606–7. They also argue that "many of the arguments against a dominical origin are not as persuasive as often thought, and there are weighty points to be made on the other side" (p. 615). See also the arguments for the authenticity of Matt 16:17–19 in B.F. Meyer, *The Aims of Jesus* (London: SCM, 1979) 185–97. In my opinion,

leaves us with an isolated tradition or sayings (e.g. the "rock saying" v. 18; cf. John 1:42; Eph 2:20; Rev 21:14 and "binding and loosing" v. 19bc; cf. Matt 18:18 and John 20:23), but it must be admitted that the latter argument has some force. It is natural to think that the appointment of Peter as the foundational "rock" in v. 18 was preceded by some kind of positive initiative on Peter's part. The "confession" is the best context we can imagine. To be sure, this argument can be used to support the view that all of Matt 16:17–19 is more or less Matthew's creation. Yet one cannot exclude the possibility that Matthew used an existing story in which not only an abrupt command to silence but also an affirmation and Peter's appointment followed the confession. Perhaps the most weighty point in support of the latter conclusion is Matthew's ambivalent attitude toward Peter's ecclesiastical authority. Would Matthew have created the sayings on Peter's investiture just to be able to formulate an ironic contrast between Peter as a "rock" and as a "stumbling block" (Matt 16:23)?[44]

Should one then regard *Gos. Thom.* 13 as a polemical response to the tradition behind (or born of) Matt 16:13–20, elevating Thomas' authority and undermining that of Peter?[45] In *Thomas* it is Peter who, together with Matthew, gives an inadequate answer, whereas in the synoptic accounts the inadequate answers are presented as popular opinions and not as opinions of particular disciples. *Thomas'* formulation can thus be seen as accentuating Peter's (and Matthew's) inadequacy.[46] It has been furthermore noticed that in *Gos. Thom.* 114

however, a much more natural setting for the origin of the tradition is a later time, when the issues of legitimation and leadership had become acute.

[44] Cf. Mark 8:33, in which the "stumbling block" is lacking. Some scholars have emphasized the irony in Matthew's presentation; see e.g. A. Stock, "Is Matthew's Presentation of Peter Ironic?" *BTB* 17 (1987) 64–69. The ambivalence of Matthew has made the pericope an easy target of an deconstructionist analysis; W.W. Bubar, "Killing Two Birds with One Stone: The Utter De(con)struction of Matthew and His Church", *BibInt* 3:2 (1995) 144–57.

[45] Smith (*Petrine Controversies*, 116) sees an "anti-Peter stance" in sayings 12 and 13. Note also that scholars have often interpreted Matt 16:17–19 as being polemical; e.g. T.W. Manson, *The Sayings of Jesus* (London: SCM, 1957 [originally published 1937]) 203–4 (against Paul) and W.D. Davies, *The Setting of the Sermon of the Mount* (Cambridge: Cambridge University Press, 1964) 338–39 (against James).

[46] It has sometimes been suggested that Matthew and Peter stand as representative figures for the apostolic tradition contained in the gospels of Matthew and Mark, the latter gospel being guaranteed by the authority of Peter; see A.F. Walls, "The References to Apostles in the Gospel of Thomas", *NTS* 7 (1960–61) 266–70, esp. p. 267; Smith, *Petrine Controversies*, 115.

Peter similarly gives an opinion that Jesus corrects. On the other hand, one should not overemphasize *Peter's* lack of understanding in the *Gospel of Thomas*. The incomprehension of the disciples is a well-known theme in the gospel tradition, the most striking example being the Gospel of Mark,[47] but this theme is in no way restricted to Mark. For example, just before Peter's confession, Matthew can depict the disciples as complete fools who are not able to understand a simple figure of speech, i.e. the "leaven" of Phrarisees and Sadducees (Matt 16:5–12; cf. Mark 8:14–21). *Thomas* elaborates the traditional theme of incomprehension in several sayings, in which the disciples' (or the audience's) failure has an important rhetorical function in contrasting the human situation to Jesus' divine revelation.[48] Thus, if *Thomas* were to be described as "anti-Petrine" it should also be characterized as showing antipathy toward the (male)[49] disciples in general (except for Thomas, of course). More consistently than in Mark, which is the most striking example of the synoptics in this respect, the disciples in *Thomas* never explicitly say that they understand Jesus' teaching.[50] *Thomas'* description of Peter must therefore be put into a broader context than that of specifically anti-Petrine polemics. Peter is a rank-and-file disciple just like Matthew, but there is no strong case for the view that *Gos. Thom.* 13 should be read as a deliberate attack against Peter's leadership or against a group that venerated Peter's authority.[51] A far more probable explanation is that the saying uses the motif of the disciples' incomprehension as a foil to elevate one

[47] H. Räisänen, *The "Messianic Secret" in Mark's Gospel* (SNTW; Edinburgh: T & T Clark, 1990) 195–222.

[48] Typically e.g. *Gos. Thom.* 43; see also *Gos. Thom.* 22; 24; 51; 52; 53; 91; 92; 99; 104; 113; 114.

[49] It seems that the female disciples are not depicted as ones who completely lack understanding; see Marjanen, "Women Disciples in the *Gospel of Thomas*", in Uro (ed.), *Thomas at the Crossroads*, 89–106, esp. p. 92.

[50] The incomprehension of the disciples as one of the main themes of *Thomas* was pointed out by P. Sellew in a paper read at Thomas Christianity Consultation of the SBL 1993 Annual Meeting in Washington, DC, "The Construction of Jesus in the Gospel of Thomas." Can the Thomasine Jesus, then, be seen as speaking over the head of the disciples to the elect and solitary? Cf. sayings 19 and 21, which seem to make a distinction between the audience and the "true disciples."

[51] Cf. K. Berger, "Unfehlbare Offenbarung: Petrus in der gnostischen und apokalyptischen Offenbarungsliteratur", in P.-G. Müller and W. Strenger (eds.), *Kontinuität und Einheit* (FS F. Müssner; Freiburg: Herder, 1981) 261–326. Berger points out that the role of Peter in *Gos. Thom.* 13 is not merely connected with Peter's person. "Was nach der Mehrzahl der Texte von Petrus gilt, kann in anderen Texten auch von Johannes, Jacobus, Thomas oder anderen gesagt werden" (p. 282).

particular disciple, that is Thomas, as a recipient of special revelation. The inability of the other disciples to deal with such deeper enlightenment becomes evident at the end of the saying, where it is said that, had the other disciples been told one of the things revealed to Thomas, they would "pick up stones and throw them" at Thomas.[52]

Even though it may be difficult to describe the precise relationship between *Gos. Thom.* 13 and its synoptic parallels in terms of tradition history, some differences and similarities can be observed in the gospels' use of the secrecy motif. In Mark 8:27–30, Peter utters the messianic confession as the *spokesman* of the disciples: Jesus addresses and responds to all of them. There is no indication of Peter's having reached understanding or received a revelation beyond those of the other disciples. In Matthew's version, Peter clearly occupies a unique position, even though in the context of the whole gospel his confession or the power given to him are not as unique as one would expect on the basis of the episode in Matt 16:13–20 (cf. 14:33; 18:18).[53] Compared with other gospels, *Thomas* is most consistent in its emphasis on the incomprehension of the other disciples and in its description of Thomas' unique position as the recipient of a special revelation. In *Thomas* only one chosen disciple fully understands that Jesus' identity is unutterable. Yet one cannot avoid the impression that there is an interesting similarity between the Markan secrecy motif and the *Gospel of Thomas*: both gospels emphasize the esoteric nature of Jesus' teaching (cf. the *mysterion* of the kingdom in Mark

---

[52] Many speculations about the "three secret words" told to Thomas by Jesus have been presented. There is no way of knowing whether there ever was a fixed tradition about the content of these words, but the reader of the gospel could hardly have missed the connection between the "secret words" written down by Thomas (prologue) and the "three words" uttered to Thomas in *Gos. Thom.* 13:6. For the issue and further references, see Dunderberg, "*Thomas* and the Beloved Disciple", 72–73.

[53] It is a much-debated question whether Peter in Matt 16:13–20 is exalted to a place above the other disciples or whether he continues to act as the spokesman of other disciples. However one interprets Matthew's overall view of Peter, it seems obvious that in this particular passage Peter is clearly singled out from the other disciples and given a unique position. For the issue, see e.g. E. Schweizer, *Matthäus und seine Gemeinde* (SBS 28; Stuttgart: KBW, 1974) 138–70; an English translation of this chapter is in G. Stanton (ed.), *The Interpretation of Matthew* (IRT 3; Philadelphia: Fortress, 1983) 129–55; Brown et al. (eds.), *Peter in the New Testament*, 87; J.D. Kingsbury, "The Figure of Peter in Matthew's Gospel as Theological Problem", *JBL* 98 (1979) 67–83; M.L. Wilkins, *The Concept of Disciple in Matthew's Gospel* (NovTSup 59; Leiden: Brill, 1988); J.A. Overman, *Matthew's Gospel and Formative Judaism: The Social World of The Matthean Community* (Minneapolis: Fortress, 1990) 136–40.

4:11 and, for example, in *Gos. Thom.* 62) and, at the same time, both gospels suggest that even the closest circle of Jesus' followers did not comprehend much or any of his teaching.[54]

In *Thomas* there is not, of course, any "Messianic Secret" in the proper sense, since Jesus' identity is not understood in terms of messiahship or of any other Christological title. As a matter of fact, *Gos. Thom.* 13 can be seen as opposing such Christological categorizations as Peter's confession in the synoptic accounts represents. It should be noticed, however, that the inadequate characterizations of Jesus ("a righteous messenger"; cf. *Gos. Thom.* 88; "wise philosopher") are not polemically formulated against messianic interpretations or any other synoptic type of Christologies, but rather change the culturally particular and historical figures (John the Baptist, Elijah, Jeremiah) into more general categorizations. In this respect, *Gos. Thom.* 13 may be described as a cultural translation[55] of a story like the one in Matt 16:13–20, with Thomas taking the role of the perceptive disciple and providing a model for an alternative interpretation of Jesus' teaching. In the Thomasine perspective, Jesus' identity cannot be confined to the particular since he is "the light above them all" (*Gos. Thom.* 77:1), a manifestation of the universal oneness, in which no particular can exist (cf. *Gos. Thom.* 61; 77:2).

4. *Thomas and James*

Even though *Gos. Thom.* 13 was probably not formulated specifically against *Peter's* authority, one cannot avoid the impression that in the present context the model of Thomas seems in some way to modify *James'* leadership in the previous saying. As noted above, there is a striking contrast between the "masterless" ideal connected with Thomas in *Gos. Thom.* 13:5 and James' leadership position that is entrusted to him by Jesus in *Gos. Thom.* 12. Scholars have often

[54] Would it be possible to see the social situations of Mark and *Thomas* having anything in common, as they both combine the esoteric mystery and incomprehension? It is interesting that scholars have often sensed an *inner-Christian conflict* behind Mark's messianic secret; see for example, Räisänen (*The 'Messianic Secret'*, 242–58), who suggests that Mark was engaged in a debate with "Q-type" Christians. Some features in *Thomas* seem to likewise reflect an inner-Christian conflict (see below).

[55] Cf. Walls, "The References to Apostles", 267. Walls speaks of "transmutation", which may be too strong an expression.

referred to saying 108 as an indication that the model of Thomas in saying 13 is paradigmatic[56] and that the "masterless" ideal can be achieved by anyone who drinks from the mouth of Jesus and becomes one with him. Becoming one and the same person with Jesus logically means that there can no longer exist any master-disciple relationship. The idea has no full New Testament equivalent, even though an "ideological parallel" has sometimes been seen in John 15:15, in which Jesus no longer calls his disciples "servants" but "friends."[57] This intimacy does not, however, blur the hierarchy between Jesus and his followers in the same radical manner as is the case in *Gos. Thom.* 108 (cf. e.g. John 15:1–6).[58] In the Thomasine saying the relationship is expressed in strongly symmetrical terms; not only does the one who drinks from the mouth of Jesus become like Jesus (*ntahe*) but Jesus himself becomes him (*anok hō tinašōpe entof pe*). In view of *Gos. Thom.* 2, this state could be described as the most advanced level of seeking, when, after having found, disturbed, and marveled, one finally rules over all (cf. also *Gos. Thom.* 19). The hierarchical model of James' leadership does not seem to apply to those who have reached this level of spiritual perfection. Is this then a sign of religious elitism? Do the disciples in logion 12 represent those Christians who are less-advanced in their seeking and therefore in need of ecclesiastical authority symbolized by James? In the same vein, the motif of the incomprehension of the disciples (cf. above) could be understood as directed against Christians whose perception is defective. On the other hand, nowhere in the gospel is there evidence for the view that *Thomas* makes a clear-cut distinction between two levels of spiritual maturity (let alone the "Valentinian" distinction between three classes of the human race; i.e. the "fleshly," "pneumatic" and "psychical").[59] Time after time the reader is encouraged to constant

[56] E.g. Patterson, *Gospel of Thomas*, 206; Marjanen, *The Woman Jesus Loved*, 42–43. Dunderberg, "*Thomas* and the Beloved Disciple", 77–78.

[57] R.E. Brown, "The Gospel of Thomas and St John's Gospel", *NTS* 9 (1962–63) 155–77, esp. p. 162. Cf. also Q 6:40.

[58] This holds true also for the other NT passages in which Jesus identifies himself with his disciples; cf. Matt 10:40–42; 25:31–46; 1 Cor 8:12; Acts 9:4–5; 22:8; 26:15.

[59] Irenaeus, *Adv. haer.* 1.7.5. For a recent discussion on determinism and the three-class division of the human race among the Gnostics, see M.A. Williams, *Rethinking "Gnosticism": An Argument for Dismantling a Dubious Category* (Princeton: Princeton University Press, 1996) 189–212. Williams demonstrates convincingly how the caricature presented by Irenaeus does not match the picture inferred from the sources that were produced by Gnostics themselves.

vigilance, seeking and finding. The language is provisional and contingent, and there is no reason to think that *Thomas* suggests fixed stages in the spiritual growth or any kind of "class system."[60] For most of the gospel a dualistic model between insiders ("the elect") and the outsiders prevails, characteristic of the most other early Christian writings.[61]

Thus it seems that the best explanation for the appearance of James and Thomas in *Gos. Thom.* 12–13 is not the suggestion that *Thomas* divides the believers into two distinct and irreconcilable categories, between those in need of the ecclesiastical authority and those who "rule over all" and are under no authority. *Thomas* lays much emphasis on the idea of spiritual growth, which necessarily presupposes some sort of religious elitism, but this elitism does not mean that the gospel elaborates a theory of fixed stages or levels symbolized by the figures of James and Thomas. Other reasons must be sought for the juxtaposition of the two logia. A clue may be found in the fact that in the Syrian tradition "Judas Thomas" was believed to be the twin brother of Jesus, and Thomas may thus be understood as a counterpart to James, the brother to Jesus. The origin of this tradition and the name itself is obscure and a full discussion of the problem is beyond the scope of this article.[62] The *Gospel of Thomas* does not spell out the belief that Judas Thomas is the twin brother of Jesus and does not give an explanation for Judas' nickname "Twin" (Aram. *t*ᵉ*'oma*; Gr. δίδυμος).[63] The belief has

[60] Note also that contrary to the common interpretation the "eschatological reservation" has not disappeared in *Thomas;* R. Uro, "Asceticism and Anti-familial Language in the *Gospel of Thomas*", in H. Moxnes (ed.), *Constructing Early Christian Families: Family as Social Reality and Metaphor* (London: Routledge, 1997) 216–34, esp. pp. 223–24.

[61] This seems to be the case in the Valentinian writings as well. See M.R. Desjardins, *Sin in Valentianism* (SBLDS 108; Atlanta: Scholars Press, 1990).

[62] For literature concerning the origin of "Judas Thomas", see note 10 above.

[63] Scholars have often imagined a real disciple of Jesus whose name was Judas and who was at some point nicknamed "the Twin." Gunther ("Meaning and Origin", 124) offers three possibilities why the proper name Judas was dropped in the gospel tradition: 1) "If his proper name were 'Jesus (Joshua),' this would have been suppressed, as was 'Jesus (Barabbas)' in most mss. of Mt 27:16 (cf. Col. 4:11)." 2) "Thomas was the one who resembled him in appearance, as the Acts of Thomas relates." 3) "[H]is name was dropped because there were two others among the twelve so named." A. De Conick surmises that the "name 'Judas' fell out of favor because it was so closely linked to the man who betrayed Jesus." "'Blessed are Those Who Have Not Seen' (Jn 20:29): Johannine Dramatization of an Early Christian Discourse", in J.D. Turner and A. McGuire (eds.), *The Nag Hammadi Library*

however often been presupposed by the Thomasine scholars on the basis of the explicit references that are made in the *Book of Thomas* (138,1–21) and especially in the *Acts of Thomas*.[64] It is, therefore, possible to argue that the twin motif is later than the *Gospel of Thomas*, and sayings such as 13 and 108 contributed to the emergence of the tradition.[65] Yet, it is also possible that the *combination* of sayings 12 and 13 reveals knowledge of the twin symbolism. According to such an interpretation, *Gos. Thom.* 12–13 puts two brothers of Jesus side by side, James the Just and (Judas) the Twin, since the name of the latter was in some circles understood to mean that he was a twin brother of Jesus.[66] To develop this hypothesis further, one could argue that the *Gospel of Thomas* gives a glimpse of how this peculiar tradition on "Judas Thomas" came into being. It has been assumed that the occurrence of James in logion 12 is a strong indication that the Thomasine trajectory emerged from and then confronted the Jewish Christianity which looked to the authority of James.[67] If, as

After Fifty Years: Proceedings of the 1995 Society of Biblical Literature Commemoration (NHMS 44; Leiden: Brill, 1997) 381–98, on p. 389; see also J. Dart, "Jesus and His Brothers", in R.J. Hoffmann and G.A. Larue (eds.), *Jesus in History and Myth* (New York: Prometheus Books, 1986) 181–90, esp. p. 188. The evidence for reconstructing the historical "Judas/Thomas" is extremely meager, however.

[64] *Acts Thom.* 11–12; 31; 34; 39; 45; 47–49; 57; 147–53. In *Acts* the twinship to Jesus was conceived to be of spiritual rather than physical nature; P.-H. Poirier, "The Writings Ascribed to Thomas and the Thomas Tradition", in Turner and McGuire (eds.), *The Nag Hammadi Library After Fifty Years*, 295–307, esp. p. 302.

[65] Dunderberg, "*Thomas* and the Beloved Disciple", 78. Cf. also Poirier, "The Writings Ascribed to Thomas", 205–307, esp. p. 302. Poirier argues that the *Acts of Thomas* developed a full-fledged twin symbolism, which is based on but not found in the *Gospel of Thomas*.

[66] Koester and others have suggested that the figure "*Judas* Thomas" was early identified with Judas/Jude, brother of James and Jesus (Mark 6:3; Jude 1); "GNOMAI DIAPHORAI", 134; see also Dart, "Jesus and his Brothers", 188. There is, however, no direct evidence for this identification. The apostle called Ἰούδας Ἰακώβου in Luke 6:16 and Acts 1:13 hardly refers to "Judas, the brother of James (and Jesus)" and in any case "Judas (Thomas)" is not identified in *Acts Thom.* 1 with this apostle. For a criticism of Koester's hypothesis, see I. Dunderberg, "John and Thomas in Conflict?" in Turner and McGuire (eds.), *The Nag Hammadi Library After Fifty Years*, 361–80, esp. pp. 372–73. It seems that the "Judas Thomas" tradition did not emphasize the physical brotherhood as much as the spiritual one. Cf. also *Thom. Cont.* 138:8–13: "Now since it *has been said* that you are my twin and true companion, examine yourself and learn who you are, in what way you exist, and how you will come to be. Since you are be called my brother, it is not fitting that you be ignorant of yourself" (trans. by J.D. Turner in B. Layton [ed.], *Nag Hammadi Codex II,2 7*, 2:181; my italics).

[67] Saying 12 is usually taken as a strong argument for the view that at least part of the Thomasine sayings derive from a Jewish-Christian tradition or trajectory; see e.g. Gärtner, *Ett nytt evangelium?* 47; Quispel, *Makarius*, 19. De Conick argues that

the evidence above suggests, there was a branch of early Christianity that appealed to Jesus' family,[68] and the roots of *Thomas* are in that kind of Christianity, the emergence of the religious symbolism exploiting kinship language, such as the idea of Thomas' being the spiritual twin of the Lord, is easy to explain.[69] It may also be relevant to note at this point that *Thomas* seems to be familiar with the idea of a heavenly double (cf. *Gos. Thom.* 84), which is readily associated with the twin symbolism.[70]

It is worth noting that there are traditions in which James' kinship to Jesus is similarly used to demonstrate the unique relationship between Jesus and the apostle (James). The so-called *First Apocalypse of James* opens with the Lord's words to James, whose brotherhood to Jesus is understood in spiritual rather than in fleshly terms.

> See now the completion of my redemption. I have given you a sign of these things, James, my brother. For not without reason have I called you my brother, although your are not my brother materially. And I am not ignorant concerning you; so that when I give you a sign—know and hear. Nothing existed except Him-who is. He is unnameable and ineffable. I myself also am from He-who is, just as I have been [given a] number of names—two from Him-who-is. (*1 Apoc. Jas.* 24,11–24).[71]

"[l]ogion 12 indicates that the Thomasites were tied closely to the law-abiding 'Hebrews' of the primitive Jerusalem organization of which James was the leader." *Seek to See Him: Ascent and Vision Mysticism in the Gospel of Thomas* (VCSup 33; Leiden: Brill, 1996) 129. For an argument that *Thomas* is engaged in a conflict with Jewish-Christian groups, see Uro, "'Washing the Outside of the Cup': *Gos. Thom.* 89 and Synoptic Parallels", in J. Ma. Asgeirsson, K. De Troyer and M.W. Meyer (eds.), *From Quest to Q: Festschrift James M. Robinson* (BETL 146; Leuven: Peeters/Leuven University Press, 2000) 303–22, esp. pp. 319–20.

[68] There is no need to push the argument to the claim that there existed an early Christian "kaliphat", a dynastic form of successive leaders, which legitimated their position by their belonging to the family of the Lord. Arguments against this view were presented by H. von Campenhausen, "Die Nachfolge des Jakobus: Zur Frage eines urchristlichen 'Kalifats'", *ZKG* 63 (1950–51) 133–44. It seems, nonetheless, clear enough that members of the Lord's family were influential in Jerusalem and in Jewish-Christian circles after Jesus' death, probably also after James' death (cf. the traditions on Simeon, who was said to be Jesus' cousin and the second bishop of Jerusalem; see Eusebius, *Hist. eccl.* 3.32.1–6; 4.5.1–4; 4.22.4; for an analysis, see Painter, *Just James*, 105–58). It should be noticed that von Campenhausen did not have the Nag Hammadi traditions on James at his use.

[69] Note also that the idea of spiritual family is strongly emphasized in *Thomas*; cf. Uro, "Asceticism and Anti-familial Language", 216–34.

[70] E.g. B. Layton, *The Gnostic Scriptures* (Garden City: Doubleday, 1987) 359–60. For the motif of the heavenly double in early Christian and Jewish traditions, see De Conick, *Seek to See Him*, 148–72.

[71] Trans. by W.R. Schoedel in J.M. Robinson (ed.), *The Nag Hammadi Library*.

A little later in the apocalypse, James is told that he will finally reach Him-who-is in a mysterious union: "You will no longer be James; rather you are the One-who-is" (27,8–10). The identification here is similar to that expressed in *Gos. Thom.* 108, even though the latter does not refer to Thomas alone; James is a prototype of the Christian who ascends to the heavenly realm (cf. *1 Apoc. Jas.* 28,20–27).[72] These parallels, to be sure, do not *prove* that the juxtaposition of James and Thomas in *Gos. Thom.* 12–13 was motivated by their belonging to Lord's family, but in any case these traditions demonstrate that the notion of the ideal brother of Jesus who resembles him or becomes one with him in the divine mystery was used for both James and Thomas in early Christianity. In this respect, it is also interesting that the Johannine "Beloved Disciple," who functionally resembles Thomas and James,[73] is also connected with Jesus' family by his guardianship of Jesus' mother (John 19:25–27). By this "adoption" the Beloved Disciple replaces the other brothers and in effect becomes a brother of Jesus.[74]

The hypothesis suggested above is at best conjectural. However, given the popularity of the traditions in which various "hereditary" claims were made, it is not implausible that the redactor responsible for the combination of sayings 12–13, and probably for the prologue as well, joined traditions about James and Thomas. The reason for this link was the redactor's belief that Thomas was the twin brother of Jesus and had thus more intimate knowledge of Jesus' identity than any other human being, including James the Just. Even though this hypothesis may shed some light to the origin of the mysterious figure of "Judas the Twin," it does not yet provide a fully satisfactory answer to the question of how James' leadership and the

[72] A striking parallel of applying the "twin" motif to James can be found in the pseudepigraphic *Letter of Ignatius to John*, in which James is said to resemble Christ "in life and manner of conversation, as if he were his twin brother from the same womb; whom they say, he is like seeing Jesus himself in respect to the all *lineamenta* of his body." Gunther refers to this text ("Meaning and Origin", 146; transl. from J.R. Harris, *The Twelve Apostles* [Cambridge: W. Heffer, 1927] 57–58) without noting, however, that this pseudepigraphic letter is usually dated very late, deriving perhaps from 12th century. See Funk – Bihlmeyer, *Die Apostolischen Väter* (3rd ed; SAQ II 1:1; Tübingen: Mohr [Siebeck], 1970) xxxiii.

[73] Dunderberg, "*Thomas* and the Beloved Disciple."

[74] See especially Dunderberg's article in this volume; note also H.-M. Schenke, "The Function and Background of the Beloved Disciple", in C.W. Hedrick and R. Hodgson (eds.), *Nag Hammadi, Gnosticism, and Early Christianity* (Peabody: Hendrickson, 1986) 111–25, esp. p. 119.

model of Thomas should be compared in *Gos. Thom.* 12–13. To be able to provide an answer, we have to locate these sayings in the wider context of organizational debates in early Christian communities which transmitted Jesus' teachings.

5. *Thomas and Matthew on Leadership*

Matthew has often been described as the most "ecclesiastical" of the New Testament gospels, since the gospel alone uses the term ἐκκλησία (Matt 16:18; 18:17), and it often deals issues of Matthew's contemporary community very transparently, the most conspicuous example being the "church order" of Matt 18.[75] Yet by no means is it obvious how Matthew sees the various leadership roles and how far the institutional structures had been developed in his community.[76] The much-discussed question of Matthew's "church" is closely intertwined with other issues of Matthean scholarship, such as Matthew's view of discipleship, his relation to the contemporary Jewish leaders

[75] Post-World War II studies on Matthew's church until 1980 are summarized by G. Stanton, "The Origin and Purpose of Matthew's Gospel: Matthean Scholarship from 1945 to 1980", *ANRW* II 25:3 (1985) 1890–951, esp. pp. 1925–29. For more recent studies relevant to the issue, see L.L. White, "Grid and Group in Matthew's Community: The Righteousness/Honor Code in the Sermon on the Mount", *Semeia* 35 (1986) 61–90; E. Krentz, "Community and Character: Matthew's Vision of the Church", *SBLSP* 26 (1987) 565–73; Overman, *Matthew's Gospel*; D.L. Balch (ed.), *Social History of the Matthean Community: Cross-disciplinary Approaches* (Minneapolis: Fortress, 1991); I. Maisch, "Christsein und Gemeinschaft (Mt 18)", in L. Oberlinner and P. Fiedler (eds.), *Salz der Erde—Licht der Welt: Exegetische Studien zum Matthäusevangelium* (FS A. Vögtle; Stuttgart: Katholisches Bibelwerk, 1991) 239–66; Stanton, "Communities of Matthew", *Int* 46 (1992) 379–91; W. Carter, *Households and Discipleship: A Study of Matthew 19–20* (JSNTSup 103; Sheffield: Sheffield Academic Press, 1994); A.J. Saldarini, *Matthew's Christian-Jewish Community* (Chicago: University of Chicago Press, 1994); P. Luomanen, *Entering the Kingdom of Heaven* (WUNT 2/101; Tübingen: Mohr Siebeck, 1998).

[76] For discussion on leadership roles in Matthew, see e.g. H. von Campenhausen, *Ecclesiastical Authority and Spiritual Power in the Church of the First Three Centuries* (Trans. J.A. Baker; London: Adam & Charles Black, 1969) 124–48; Künzel, *Studien*, 167–79; B.T. Viviano, "Social World and Community Leadership: The Case of Matthew 23.1–12, 34", *JSNT* 39 (1990) 3–21; Overman, *Matthew's Gospel*, 113–24; D.L. Bartlett, *Ministry in the New Testament* (OBT; Minneapolis: Fortress, 1993) 58–88; Saldarini, *Matthew's Christian-Jewish Community*, 102–7; D.C. Duling, "The Matthean Brotherhood and Marginal Scribal Leadership", in P.E. Esler (ed.), *Modelling Early Christianity: Social-scientific Studies of the New Testament and Its Context* (London: Routledge, 1995) 159–82; Stanton, "Ministry in Matthean Christianity", in D.A. Campbell (ed.), *Call to Serve: Essays on Ministry in Honour of Bishop Penny Jamieson* (Sheffield: Sheffield Academic Press, 1996) 142–60.

and formative Judaism.[77] Obviously all these cannot be discussed in detail in this paper. There are, however, a number of features in Matthew's "ecclesiastical" concern that are relevant to our discussion on *Thomas'* view of leadership.

Matthew's ideal is an egalitarian community, in which "all are brothers" or "children" (Matt 23:8–12; 18:1–6; 19:13–15).[78] Honorary titles, such as "father," "rabbi" and "instructor," are specifically condemned (23:8–10). It is also worth noticing that the disciplinary regulations concerning the erring brother in 18:15–20 mention no council of elders or other leaders.[79] In 18:17–18 the power of "binding and loosing" is entrusted to all members of the *ekklēsia*. This ideal egalitarianism notwithstanding, Matthew does show some signs of institutionalization and emergence of various leadership roles.[80] There are, for example, several positive allusions and references to "prophets," "scribes," and "sages" (e.g. 10:40–42; 13:52; 23:34), and it is obvious that the ideal brotherhood of the Matthean ethos does not warrant the conclusion that the Matthean community lacked any kind of established leadership structures. Given the careful attention that the gospel gives to scriptural and legal interpretation, it seems obvi-

[77] For the latter issues, see P. Luomanen' article in this volume.

[78] For Matthew's use of "children" as a metaphor of discipleship, see Carter, *Households and Discipleship*, 90–114. Cf. also the much-discussed expressions "little ones" (Matt 10:42; 18:10,14) and "one of the least of these" (25:40, 45); see S.W. Gray, *"The Least of My Brothers": Matthew 25:31–46: A History of Interpretation* (Atlanta: Scholars Press, 1989). It would be interesting to extend the comparison between Matthew and *Thomas* to the metaphor of children as well, since both gospels seem to give much emphasis to the child-like being of the disciples.

[79] It may be wise not to use this silence as a positive argument for the view that the system of elders did not exist in Matthew's environment; cf. von Campenhausen, *Ecclesiastic Authority*, 128; Davies and Allison, *The Gospel According to Saint Matthew*, 786. Cf. Schweizer ("Matthew's Church", 140) who argues that the Matthean community "seems to know neither elders nor bishops nor deacons."

[80] Overman, *Matthew's Gospel*, 113–24; see also Bartlett, *Ministry*, 76–82; Duling, "The Matthean Brotherhood", 159–82. Some have also laid stress on the charismatic and prophetic authority in Matthew's church. Schweizer, for example, believes that one can trace a trajectory from the Matthean community of "little ones" to an anti-hierarchic "ascetic Judeo-Christian group", which produced the *Apocalypse of Peter* (NHC VII, 3); idem, "Matthew's Church", 129–55, cf. also Stanton, "5 Ezra and Matthean Christianity", in idem, *A Gospel for a New People: Studies in Matthew* (Edinburgh: T & T Clark, 1992 [orig. published 1977]) 256–77. White ("Grid and Group") suggests that Matt 18 "reflects a pattern of organization that places minimal reliance on formally distinguished roles" (p. 75), but also admits that it would be "theologically naive" to "conclude that the community's self-definition fundamentally agrees with its actual composition, character, and circumstances" (p. 85).

ous that teachers were important figures in the Matthean group.[81] Matthew's strong emphasis on humility and his denial of honorary titles may be taken as indirect evidence for the view that the gospel resists some expressions of an emerging hierarchy in his community or environment. Many scholars have seen in the denial of the "synagogue titles" in Matt 23:8–11 a sign that some Christian leaders inside or outside Matthew's group were in fact using these titles[82] or at least showing off in the manner that aroused Matthew's criticism.[83] One could also argue that Matthew's ambivalent presentation of Peter as a figure who is *both* the "rock," on which the church is built, *and* the "stumbling block" (16:13–23) similarly reflects Matthew's reserved attitude toward emerging Christian leadership and legitimation of power in his environment. By democraticizing Peter's authority (cf. 18:18) and holding only to "archaizing" and undifferentiated types of leadership roles ("prophets," "scribes" or "sages"),[84] Matthew tries to maintain the ideal of a small house-church assembly,[85] in which every member has a special charisma and all the important decisions, such as the excommunication of a sinning member (18:15–20; cf. 1 Cor 5; 6:1–11), are made collectively. Perhaps this "conservative" attitude of Matthew explains why he grants the supreme religious and judicial power to the non-Christian Jewish leaders (Matt 23:2–3; 5:21–26) rather than to some specific authority or body of authorities in his own group.

The Gospel of Thomas shares Matthew's egalitarianism in that it problematizes Christian leadership and the master-pupil relationship

[81] Saldarini, *Matthew's Christian-Jewish Community*, 105.

[82] Schweizer, "Matthew's Church", 139; D.E. Garland, *The Intention of Matthew 23* (NovTSup 52; Leiden: Brill) 57–63; Duling, "The Matthean Brotherhood", 166.

[83] Viviano, "Social World", 16.

[84] Viviano ("Social World", 14) characterizes Matthew's list of "offices" as being "conservative or archaizing."

[85] Cf. Stanton (*A Gospel for New People*, 50–51), who estimates that "it would have been difficult to many more than 50 or so people to crowd into even quite a substantial house;" see also idem, "Communities of Matthew", 388, and Luomanen, *Entering the Kingdom of Heaven*, 272. Stanton concludes from this that Matthew must have written to a larger audience than to one small house-church. Such a social location would indeed explain some of Matthew's peculiarities, for example his teaching concerning itinerant teachers (false and good) and contradictions with respect to Jewish heritage. Matthew's "imprecision" with respect to his audience could be explained by the fact that the assemblies Matthew is writing for are diverse. This kind of situation also creates a need for more centralized leadership (cf. Luomanen, ibid.), a development which Matthew can be seen as resisting.

(*Gos. Thom.* 3 and 12–13; cf. also 88). Matthew's utopia seems to be based on such biblical promises as Isa 54:13 and Jer 31:33, according to which at the end of the days the children of God will be taught directly without any human intermediary.[86] *Thomas'* vision is more radical and fundamental, since it plays down the role of Jesus himself as the supreme teacher. Jesus words to Thomas "I am not your master" are almost antithetical to Matthew's "you have one instructor, Christ" (Matt 23:10). Whereas Matthew emphasizes equality under the overarching symbol of Jesus as the final and absolute interpreter of God's law, in *Thomas* the anti-authoritarian model is extended to the symbolic presentation of the equality between the ideal disciple, Thomas, and Jesus himself. Regardless of all of his emphasis on brotherhood and service, Matthew's symbolic world is ultimately a hierarchical one: the heavenly Father and the Son of Man rule at the top, next in order come the twelve disciples (Matt 19:28).[87] The hierarchy is not destroyed, but strongly conditioned by the warning that, as far as human beings are concerned, "many who are first will be last, and the last first" (19:30). The symbolic world of *Thomas* is based on the idea that there is no essential difference between humanity and Divinity, thus there is no heavenly court and hierarchy.[88] Every person is part of God and will eventually return to God, at least if trained to realize his or her divine nature. In this respect, *Thomas* represents a totally different conceptual world compared with Matthew and derives its basic ideological tenor from the ideology widely accepted in the Hellenistic world. In a sense, the Thomasine Jesus resembles the ideal Stoic teacher, who encourages his audience to become one's own pupil and teacher.[89]

[86] J.D.M. Derrett, "Mt 28,8–10 a Midrash on Is 54,13 and Jer 31,33–34", *Bib* 62 (1981) 372–86; Krentz, "Community and Character", 566.

[87] This ethos can aptly be compared to what Gerd Theissen has called "love-patriarchalism" encountered in Pauline and especially in the deutero-Pauline and Pastoral Epistles. "This love-patriarchalism takes social differences for granted but ameliorates them through an obligation of respect and love, an obligation imposed upon those who are socially stronger;" Theissen, "Social Stratification in the Corinthian Community", in idem, *The Social Setting of Pauline Christianity: Essays on Corinth* (edited and translated by J.H. Schütz; Philadelphia: Fortress, 1982) 69–119, on p. 107.

[88] *Gos. Thom.* 15 may be understood as criticizing cultic adoration of anyone "born of a woman" (cf. Gal 4:4; Q 7:28; *Gos. Thom.* 46) rather than as fostering hierarchic symbolism. See Valantasis, *Gospel of Thomas*, 81–82.

[89] Cf. Epictetus, who summons his students to abandon other people's opinions: "Will you not, then, let other men alone, and become your own pupil and your

It is however obvious that a radical symbolic egalitarianism does not automatically generate actions that would aim at removing all social distinctions and patriarchal structures. Most Stoics, for example, did not understood their radically antihierarchical theory as a direct recipe for social and political action.[90] It would be an oversimplification to draw the conclusion that the Matthean church was considerably more patriarchal than the Thomasine circles or that *Thomas* envisioned a fundamentally more egalitarian model of Christian community than Matthew. In spite of their ideological differences, both gospels are suspicious about the Christian leadership structures that were developing in their environments under the auspices of the symbols of Peter and James. Both understand Jesus' role ultimately as that of a teacher, and it is therefore highly probable that the activity of teaching was of vital importance in both communities. It is possible though that the role that the female disciples Mary Magdalene and Salome occasionally have in *Thomas* (*Gos. Thom.* 21; 61; 114) signals a difference between the social worlds of these two gospels.[91] One could argue that women were encouraged to have more active role in the Thomasine community than in the Matthean church, which may be seen as a community of *brothers* rather than that of siblings. The role that the women disciples have in *Thomas* may reflect the same Hellenistic universalism as described above,

own teacher" (*Diatr.* 4.6.11; Transl. by W.A. Oldfather, LCL 131). See also M.C. Nussbaum, *The Therapy of Desire: Theory and Practice in Hellenistic Ethics* (Princeton: Princeton University Press) 345.

[90] T. Engberg-Pedersen, "Stoicism in Philippians", in idem (ed.), *Paul in His Hellenistic Context* (Minneapolis: Fortress, 1995) 256–90, esp. p. 267. This does not mean that the egalitarian and universalist ideal was simply an empty theory without any practical consequences. Epictetus' teaching on slave-master relationship illustrates well the Stoic attitude (I owe this example to N. Huttunen's paper on "Epictetus, Law and Paul", read at the "Centre of Excellence" seminar in Helsinki, August 28, 2000). A gentle reaction to disobedient behavior of a slave at dinner is a thing that is "acceptable to the gods", since one has to remember that slaves are "kinsmen, brothers by nature, that they are the offspring of Zeus" (*Diatr.* 1.13.4; transl. by W.A. Oldfather in *Epictetus* [vol. 1; LCL 131; Cambridge: Harvard University Press, 1995; orig. 1925]). Epictetus does not challenge the institution of slavery nor patriarchal rule in general, but teaches his students to look beyond "these wretched laws of ours" to "the laws of gods" (I 13.5) and to act gently and without angry. This comes close to what Theissen means by "love-patriarchalism" (see above note 82). As a matter of fact it was a widespread ethical ideal in the Hellenistic world; cf. the ideology of "benevolent patriarchalism" described in D.B. Martin, *The Corinthian Body* (New Haven: Yale University Press, 1995) 39–47.

[91] Marjanen, "Women Disciples."

which could sometimes create surprisingly "modern" expressions. According to Musonius Rufus, for example, everyone who possesses the five senses, including women, should study philosophy.[92] On the other hand, one should not fail to notice that Matthew's gospel does not ignore the role of the female followers of Jesus either (cf. e.g. 27:55–56). They may not be named among Jesus' "disciples" (cf. *Gos. Thom.* 61:4),[93] but it would be against the evidence to argue that Matthew aims at diminishing the communal and prophetic activity of women.[94]

There is at least one saying in which differences between the Matthean and Thomasine community ideal are clearly visible. The first part of the Greek form of *Gos. Thom.* 30 (*P.Oxy.* 1:23–27) is virtually an antithesis of Matt 18:20 (the Coptic version, I think, is corrupt).[95] The Greek version combines this saying with the words found in the Coptic version at 77:2 (*P.Oxy.* 1:27–30). My translation is based on Attridge's reconstruction of the Greek text:[96]

> [Jesus said], Where there are [three], they are without God, and where there is [one] alone, I say that I am with [him]. Lift up the stone, and you will find me there. Split the piece of wood, and I am there. (*Gos. Thom.* 30 + 77:2.)

Compare this to the Matthean form of the saying:

> Where two or three are gathered in my name, I am there among them. (Matt 18:20.)

[92] See his treatise on "That Women Too Should Study Philosophy"; transl. and ed. by C.E. Lutz in *YCS* 10 (1957) 39–43.

[93] A.C. Wire, "Gender Roles in a Scribal Community", in Balch (ed.), *Social History*, 87–121, esp. p. 103; T. Mattila, "Naming the Nameless: Gender and Discipleship in Matthew's Passion Narrative", in Rhoads and Syreeni (eds.), *Characterization in the Gospels*, 153–79, esp. p. 159.

[94] M.R. D'Angelo, "(Re)presentations of Women in the Gospel of Matthew and Luke-Acts", in R.S. Kraemer and M.R. D'Angelo (eds.), *Women & Christian Origins* (Oxford: Oxford University Press, 1999) 171–95, esp. pp. 172–80; Mattila, "Naming the Nameless", 153–79.

[95] "Jesus said, 'Where there are three gods, they are gods. Where there are two or one, I am with him.'" Transl. by T.O. Lambdin in B. Layton (ed.) *Nag Hammadi Codex II, 2–7* (vol. 1).

[96] H.W. Attridge, "The Original Text of Gos. Thom., Saying 30", *BASB* 16:3 (1979) 153–57; idem, "The Greek Fragments" [of the *Gospel According to Thomas*], in B. Layton (ed.) *Nag Hammadi Codex II, 2–7*, 119, 127. The translation above differs slightly from Attridge's translation.

If the reconstruction above is correct, *Thomas* does not encourage seeking Jesus' presence in the community of believers, and as a result Matthew's tradition is turned upside down. It is not the community of brothers, minimally consisting of two or three disciples of Jesus, to which the individual Christian's life is anchored, but rather the "aloneness" of a single person, which may be directly linked to the universal cosmos ("lift the stone etc."). In *Thomas* there is no corporate "body of Christ" which would signify the unity and harmony of the Christian community. The self-sufficiency emphasized in *Thomas* is in this respect more "individualistic" than Matthew's ecclesiastical theology (or that of the Pauline letters). This self-sufficiency should not be confused with an individualism that is based on the idea that becoming a unique and distinctive individual is regarded as inherently valuable.[97] *Thomas* does not emphasize uniqueness, but rather "sameness" of the true self with divinity and the realm of light.

In light of saying 30 it thus seems obvious that *Thomas* envisions looser and less group-oriented communal interaction than Matthew.[98] Another question is whether this means that the gospel is advocating radical isolation or itinerancy. *Gos. Thom.* 30 has often been connected with the sayings which praise the *monachoi*, the "solitary ones" (*Gos. Thom.* 16; 39; 75).[99] I have discussed these sayings elsewhere and argued against using this term as evidence for *Thomas'* deriving from a strictly encratite sect that regarded celibacy and ascetic wandering as entrance requirements.[100] I have also warned against reading too much "wandering" into Thomasine sayings,[101] since in fact they say very little about itinerancy or about a Cynic-like lifestyle. Regardless of how we interpret the sayings on "solitary" and *Thomas'* anti-familial ethos, the reconstructed Greek form of saying 30 need

[97] Cf. the helpful considerations on the idea of "being yourself" in Hellenistic ethics by C. Gill, "Panaetius on the Virtue of Being Yourself", in A. Bulloch, E.S. Gruen, A.A. Long, and A. Stewart (eds.), *Images and Ideologies: Self-definition in the Hellenistic World* (Berkeley: University of California Press, 1993) 330–53, esp. pp. 351–52. For the wide range of meanings that "individualism" has carried in western thought, see S. Lukes, *Individualism* (Key Concepts in the Social Sciences; Oxford: Basil Blackwell, 1973).

[98] Similarly Patterson, *Gospel of Thomas*, 151 (although emphasizing that the Thomasine Christianity was "a loosely structured movement of wanderers"); Valantasis, *Gospel of Thomas*, 69 ("a loosely formed community").

[99] E.g. Patterson, *Gospel of Thomas*, 152–52.

[100] Uro, "Is *Thomas* an Encratite Gospel?" 156–62.

[101] Uro, "Asceticism and Anti-familial Language", 218–19.

not be taken as pointing to some sort of "anchoritic" solitariness. *Thomas* may isolate its readers from tightly organized assemblies, but the internal logic of the gospel seems to presuppose some sort of loosely structured school in which the sayings of Jesus were read and meditated. Moreover, one may raise the question whether the emphasis on "aloneness" in saying 30 should be set against *Thomas'* confrontation with a clearly defined Christian church which celebrated Jesus' presence in its cult meetings and deemed the Thomasine Christians more or less outsiders. If this assumption is on the right track, then we have one more important difference between the Thomasine and the Matthean critiques of leadership. Whereas Matthew still largely defines the ideal communal structure against non-Christian formative Judaism, *Thomas* is engaged in criticism of Christian leadership and hierarchical formation *within* Christian communities. However, given Matthew's reserved attitude toward the hierarchical structures that were emerging inside and outside his community, one may also see both gospels as resisting the church hierarchy developing at the turn of the second century. Ironically it was Matthew who left in Peter's "investiture" one of the strongest weapons for the legitimation of a monarchical episcopate. *Thomas'* radical model of teaching authority could hardly have been accepted by those who championed the monarchical episcopate in Christian communities from the early second century onwards.[102]

[102] The criticism of monarchical episcopate and church offices continued among the second and third-century Gnostic groups; see E. Pagels, "'The Demiurge and His Archons'—A Gnostic View of the Bishop and Presbyters?" *HTR* 69 (1976) 301–24; K. Koschorke, *Die Polemik der Gnostiker gegen das kirchliche Christentum* (NHS 12; Leiden: Brill, 1978), esp. pp. 67–71. At the end of the second century, however, "school" and the "monarchical episcopate" still constituted two distinct institutions in Alexandria represented by Clement and bishop Demetrius. D.J. Kyrtatas stresses the social integration and the economic basis of the latter institution: The school "tended to become, in a manner of speaking, secular. It divided Christianity into sects using intellectual criteria; it had no hierarchy in the strict sense and was in need of no special funds: a member became teacher because of his learning. . . . The monarchical episcopate, by contrast, can be termed more religious. It struggled to integrate all local communities into one church, it had a rigid hierarchy which depended on fixed salaries and organized charity—hence the prime importance of finance; its members were promoted to successive grades through internal mechanisms inaccessible to outsiders." *The Social Structure of the Early Christian Communities* (London: Verso, 1987) 141–42.

6. *Conclusion*

The comparison between the Matthean and Thomasine views on leadership shows that, in spite of the different ideological frameworks, both gospels share an antihierarchical stance which may be set against the background of emerging church offices at their times. This can especially be seen in the ways in which both gospels deal with the major figures of ecclesiastical power, Peter and James. Yet a fundamental difference exists between their criticisms of church hierarchy. Whereas Matthew ultimately accepts the power of the keys, although strongly conditioning it with demands of humility, *Thomas* adds to James' leadership a different kind of model, one based on self-sufficiency and independence. Thomas exemplifies this model and through the prologue of the gospel becomes the guarantor of the tradition which promulgates this understanding of discipleship. Matthew's view became *the* Christian pattern, whereas Thomas' model was pushed to the margin of Christian life and culture until its resurgence in post-modern religiosity.

THE SUFFERING OF ONE WHO IS A STRANGER TO SUFFERING: THE CRUCIFIXION OF JESUS IN THE LETTER OF PETER TO PHILIP

Antti Marjanen

1. *Introduction*

One of the stereotypes which tended to characterize the pre-Nag Hammadi views of the so-called Christian Gnosticism was that the crucifixion of Jesus played a minimal role in the formation of its thinking.[1] If the crucifixion was mentioned in some Christian Gnostic sources, it was assumed that the reference had to be conceived in terms of a docetic understanding.[2] According to this conception, Christ did not undergo bodily suffering because he was man only in appearance or because it was not the Savior himself who suffered and died on the cross but another person, a substitute, whose body the Savior had used in order to fool the worldly powers.[3]

The first docetic model has its prototypes in the descriptions of the docetic opponents in the First and Second Epistle of John and in the Letters of Ignatius and the second in Irenaeus' account of

[1] A desire not to be satisfied with stereotypical (and therefore often false or misleading) views is an essential part of the research ethos of Heikki Räisänen, my teacher and my friend. As I present him my warmest congratulations I hope that this short article can to a small degree demonstrate that the years I have heard him speaking about fair play in the field of research has not been in vain.

[2] A typical representative of this view is F. Loofs, *Leitfaden zum Studium der Dogmengeschichte: 1. und 2. Teil: Alte Kirche, Mittelalter und Katholizismus bis zur Gegenwart* (6. durchgesehene Auflage hrsg. von K. Aland; Tübingen: Max Niemeyer, 1959) 80–81.

[3] Some scholars insist that it is only the first alternative which properly describes docetism. However, M. Slusser, "Docetism: A Historical Definition", *SecCent* 1 (1981) 163–71, has convincingly shown that docetism, as it was used and understood by the second-century church fathers, included both alternatives. Slusser concludes his discussion on the historical definition of docetism: ". . . the malice of those who taught a 'seeming' Christ lay in their denial that the heavenly Savior was ever really involved in the material and human realities of this creation as we experience them. This denial was no less complete in the case of doctrines which separated the heavenly Christ from the earthly Jesus than it was in the case of doctrines which held that Jesus was a phantom."

Basilides' interpretation of the crucifixion. The opponents of the Johannine Epistles deny that "Jesus Christ has come in the flesh" (1 John 4:2; 2 John 7), and Ignatius accuses some unbelievers of falsely insisting that Christ "only seemed to suffer" (*Smyrn.* 2:1; *Trall.* 10). In these references to a docetic understanding of Jesus, many scholars have seen indications of a kind of (proto-)Gnostic current in Syria and Asia Minor.[4] This current is taken as a predecessor of later similar docetic teachers and movements which Irenaeus and others refer to.[5] Basilides' view of Jesus is the classic example of the laughing Savior who avoids all suffering and watches by the cross how his replacement, Simon of Cyrene, is crucified in his stead (1.24.4).[6] In his report Irenaeus states that Basilides emphasized two things: first, the Savior did not suffer; second, the crucifixion did not have a positive function. In fact, according to Irenaeus, Basilides maintained that all those who denied the crucified Jesus were freed from the worldly rulers and had a saving acquaintance with the first principle.

2. *Docetism and the Nag Hammadi Library*

The stereotypical understanding of the Christian "Gnostic" interpretation of the crucifixion, as advanced in the two models introduced above, was shaken by the discovery of the Nag Hammadi

[4] A classic example is R. Bultmann, *Theology of the New Testament* (2 vols.; translated by Kendrick Grobel; London: SCM) 1.169. For those who argue for a (proto-) Gnostic tendency among the opponents of the author of the First and Second Epistle of John, see also W. Schmithals, *Das Neue Testament und Gnosis* (ErFor 208; Darmstadt: Wissenschaftliche Buchgesellschaft, 1984) 104–10; for an anti-Gnostic stand of Ignatius, see K. Rudolph, *Die Gnosis: Wesen und Geschichte einer spätantiken Religion* (Göttingen: Vandenhoeck & Ruprecht, 1978) 322; cf. also H. Koester, *Introduction to the New Testament*, vol. 2: *History and Literature of Early Christianity* (Philadelphia: Fortress, 1980) 286.

[5] E.g. Irenaeus, *Adv. haer.* 1.24.1–2 (Satorninos); Irenaeus, *Adv. haer.* 3.18.5–6; Hippolytus, *Ref.* 8.1–4; Eusebius, *Hist. eccl.* 6.12.6; Epiphanius, *Panarion* 26.10.5 (Gnostics or Borborites); 40.8.2 (Archontics).

[6] An interesting variant is the view Irenaeus attributes to Ptolemy or to Ptolemy's disciples (*Adv. haer.* 1.6.1; 1.7.2). According to that view, it was not the heavenly, anointed Christ who underwent the crucifixion and suffering but an animate son of the Demiurge (cf. also *Gos. Phil.* 68.26–29). The heavenly, spiritual Christ departed from the animate Christ when he was brought before Pilate. The animate Christ, the son of the Demiurge, suffered but even he only appeared to be a man but was not really. This is due to the fact that in Ptolemy's system the animate Christ (as well as an animate human being) is capable of salvation if he is not spoiled by material essence.

Library. One of the surprises it provided was that it contains so many texts which refer to the death and crucifixion of Jesus.[7] To be sure, at least one of the writings, namely the *Teachings of Silvanus*,[8] is not "Gnostic" according to any definition of the term, and some of the tractates, such as the *Second Treatise of the Great Seth* and the *Apocalypse of Peter*, come pretty close to the stereotypical picture of the Christian "Gnostic" view of the crucifixion deduced from Irenaeus' report of Basilides' teaching.[9] Nonetheless, there are also writings in the Nag Hammadi Library which can be regarded as Valentinian (e.g., the *Gospel of Truth* and the *Interpretation of Knowledge*) or other Christian "Gnostic" texts (the *Concept of Our Great Power*) which contain interpretations of the crucifixion clearly deviating from or at least modifying the stereotypical idea of docetism.[10]

This article will concentrate on a further example of a "Gnostic" Nag Hammadi writing which contains references to Jesus' suffering and crucifixion but which does not lend itself very well to a docetic interpretation. The text is the *Letter of Peter to Philip*, the second tractate of the eighth codex of the Nag Hammadi Library.[11]

3. *Introducing the Letter of Peter to Philip*

The tractate begins with a letter of Peter addressing Philip and asking him to join the other disciples in order that they might plan how to proclaim the gospel (132.12–133.8). Philip consents to the invitation, and all the apostles go together to the Mount of Olives

[7] For the evidence, see M. Franzmann, *Jesus in the Nag Hammadi Writings* (Edinburgh: T & T Clark, 1996) 135–56.

[8] *Teach. Silv.* 107.9–17.

[9] Cf. *Treat. Seth* 56.4–20; *Apoc. Pet.* 81.28–83.4; G. Riley ("NHC VII,2: Second Treatise of the Great Seth", in B.A. Pearson [ed.], *Nag Hammadi Codex VII* [Nag Hammadi and Manichaean Studies 30; Leiden: E.J. Brill, 1996] 137–38) is probably right when he insists that neither of the writings are Basilidean in the sense that they maintain that Simon of Cyrene was the one who died in the place of Jesus. Yet, both of the writings emphasize that a substitute for Christ undergoes the suffering whereas the Savior himself is laughing at the foolishness of those who tried, but failed, to seize him.

[10] Cf. *Gos. Truth* 20.10–21.2; *Interp. Know.* 5.30–35; *Great Pow.* 41.9–42.8.

[11] The critical edition of the text by M.W. Meyer ("NHC VIII,2: Letter of Peter to Philip: Introduction and Commentary") has appeared in J.H. Sieber (ed.), *Nag Hammadi Codex VIII* (NHS 31; Leiden: E.J. Brill, 1991) 227–51; cf. also H.-G. Bethge, *Der Brief des Petrus an Philippus: Ein neutestamentliches Apokryphon aus dem Fund von Nag Hammadi (NHC VIII,2)* (TU 141; Berlin: Akademie Verlag, 1997).

where they have a visionary experience during which they converse with the Risen Jesus (133.8–138.7). After the revelatory dialogue, the apostles return to Jerusalem and on the way they discuss the fearful possibility that they also have to undergo sufferings in the way Jesus did. During the conversation, Jesus reappears and consoles the apostles (138.7–139.4). In Jerusalem they go to the temple, heal people and instruct them in the matters of salvation. After that Peter is filled with the Spirit and gives a sermon (139.4–140.1). The situation recalls the Pentecost scene of the Book of Acts.[12] After Peter's sermon, the apostles are again filled with the Spirit, perform cures and depart in order to preach the message of the Lord Jesus (140.1–13). After the preaching tour they meet again. Jesus appears and assures them of his perpetual presence. The text ends with a reference to a new journey of the apostles (140.13–27).

This brief summary of the *Letter of Peter to Philip* shows that the author of the text is quite familiar with several New Testament writings, including the gospels of Matthew and Luke as well as the Book of Acts.[13] In the first part of the tractate, which contains a dialogue between the Risen Jesus and the apostles, it becomes clear that the author also knows a version of a cosmological myth resembling that of the *Apocryphon of John* although it is lacking the most characteristic features of the Sethian system.[14] All this suggests that the document is to be considered "Gnostic"[15] and has to be dated to the end

[12] This was pointed out by K. Koschorke, "Eine gnostische Pfingstpredigt: Zur Auseinandersetzung zwischen gnostischen und kirchlichen Christentum am Beispiel der 'Epistula Petri ad Philippum' (NHC VIII,2)", *ZTK* 74 (1977) 323–43.

[13] Koschorke, "Eine gnostische Pfingstpredigt", 326–27; C.M. Tuckett, *Nag Hammadi and the Gospel Tradition: Synoptic Tradition in the Nag Hammadi Library* (Studies of the New Testament and Its World; Edinburgh: T & T. Clark, 1986) 112–17. K. Koschorke, "Eine gnostische Paraphrase des johanneischen Prologs: Zur Interpretation von 'Epistula Petri ad Philippum' (NHC VIII,2) 136,16–137,4", *VC* 33 (1979) 383–92, has also argued that the *Letter of Peter to Philip* contains a paraphrase of the Johannine prologue. This has been questioned by M.W. Meyer, *The Letter of Peter to Philip* (SBLDS 53; Chico, California: Scholars Press, 1981) 132–33; Bethge, *Der Brief des Petrus*, 95–96.

[14] For the Sethian Gnosticism, see H.-M. Schenke, "The Phenomenon and Significance of Gnostic Sethianism", in B. Layton (ed.), *The Rediscovery of Gnosticism: Proceedings of the International Conference on Gnosticism at Yale, New Haven, Connecticut, March 28–31, 1978*, vol. 2: *Sethian Gnosticism* (Studies in the History of Religions [Supplements to *Numen*] 41; Leiden: E.J. Brill, 1981) 588–616.

[15] So also J. Hartenstein, "Gedanken zur Koharenz und Absicht des 'Brief des Petrus an Philippus' (NHC VIII,2)", in S. Emmel et al. (ed.), *Ägypten und Nubien in spätantiker und christlicher Zeit: Akten des 6. Internationalen Koptologenkongresses, Münster, 20.–*

of the second century or to the beginning of the third.[16] The likely provenance of the *Letter of Peter to Philip* has to be sought in an environment where the Jesus material of the New Testament is interpreted in a "Gnostic" fashion even to the extent that it can be conflated with a more or less classical type of "Gnostic" cosmological myth.

I shall deal with the topic of Jesus' suffering and crucifixion in the *Letter of Peter to Philip* in three parts: 1) the earthly body of the Lord Jesus; 2) the nature of Jesus' suffering and crucifixion; and 3) the significance of Jesus' suffering and crucifixion.

4. *The Earthly Body of the Lord Jesus*

There are several references to the earthly bodily existence of Jesus in the *Letter of Peter to Philip*. The first one appears at the beginning of the dialogue section which describes how the apostles gathered together and went upon the Mount of Olives, to the place where they used to go when "the blessed Christ was in the body (= *efhn sōma*)" (133.17).[17] The same expression is later repeated twice (138.3;[18] 139.11). How is one to interpret this phrase? There are certainly writings and passages in which "going into the body/being in the body" presupposes a docetic understanding. A good example is *Treat. Seth* 51.21–24.[19] In that text the docetic understanding of Christ's appearance in the world is underlined by the fact that Christ himself, while taking hold of his bodily dwelling, casts out the earlier occupant. It is worth noting that later in the tractate it is not only Christ but also his own ones who are considered to have come into their bodies in a docetic fashion (59.19–22).

On the other hand, the phrase "to be in the body" need not be conceived in a docetic sense in early Christian texts. There are several instances in which "being in the body" is simply tantamount to

26. Juli 1996, vol. 2: *Schrifttum, Sprache und Gedankenwelt* (Sprachen und Kulturen des Christlichen Orients; Wiesbaden: Reichert Verlag, 1999) 475–76.

[16] So also Meyer, "Letter of Peter", 231.

[17] The translations of the *Letter of Peter to Philip* derive from Meyer, "Letter of Peter", unless otherwise stated.

[18] The Coptic equivalent of the expression "in the body" here contains a definite article *hm psōma*, but it does not seem to affect its meaning.

[19] For the rendering of the text, see G. Riley, "Second Treatise", 129–99.

the description of earthly existence.[20] The clearest example is Hebr. 13:3, in which the author exhorts his readers to show compassion to those who have been badly treated in this world ὡς καὶ αὐτοὶ ὄντες ἐν σώματι "because they (the readers themselves) too are in the body," i.e., "because they too are subject to the conditions of earthly existence."[21] In the face of this, one can conclude that the phrase "when Jesus was in the body" itself does not necessarily imply a docetic understanding of Jesus' bodily existence.

Nevertheless, in one instance there is an additional comment in the context of this phrase in the *Letter of Peter to Philip* which has persuaded scholars to suggest docetic interpretations of Jesus' earthly existence. In the passage 136.16–22, Jesus instructs his disciples as follows: "I am the one who was sent into the body because of the seed which had fallen away. I came into their (i.e., the powers') mortal mold. But they did not recognize me. They were thinking that I am a mortal man." Since the mortal mold in this text obviously serves as a disguise which hides Jesus' real character, the text has been taken as an indication of a docetic view of Jesus in the *Letter of Peter to Philip*.[22] I believe that this interpretation is possible but not inevitable.

What I want to suggest is that the act of "coming into a mortal mold" of the Lord need not mean any more than the phrase "coming into the body," i.e., "becoming subject to the predicament of earthly existence." This is shown by the fact that in 137.9 the expression *hnrōme eumoout* "mortal beings" is a general way to describe all human beings. Thus, in a text, such as the *Letter of Peter to Philip*, in which a mortal person is a common description of a human being who is living in the earthly realm (137.6–9), the phrase *aiei ehrai epeuplasma etmoout* "I came down into their mortal mold" does not necessitate an especially docetic understanding of Jesus' being.

To be sure, the word *plasma* obviously stands for a body molded by the powers (136.11–13). However, this does not mean that the Savior is pictured as a phantom who was man only in appearance and who occupied someone else's body as his earthly dwelling. There

---

[20] Cf. Meyer, *The Letter of Peter*, 100.

[21] Paul uses at least twice a similar phrase to express the same thing (2 Cor 5:6,10; 12.2), cf. also Gal 2:20; Phil 1:22 although in both instances he is using ἐν σαρκί instead of ἐν σώματι.

[22] Koschorke, "Eine gnostische Paraphrase", 389.

is no indication of this in the text. On the contrary, the passage 136.16–20 refers to a sort of incarnation. The only extraordinary trait in the description is the fact that the body the Savior receives is a creation of the archontic powers. In this way, the passage stresses that the Savior had to live under the same severe limitations which mark all the human life on the earth. If this is true, Jesus did not betray the authorities of the *authadēs*, the Arrogant One, by being some other than he was but *by being precisely what they were thinking he was, a mortal human being in his body.*

5. *The Nature of Jesus' Suffering and Crucifixion*

My suggestion concerning the non-docetic character of Jesus' earthly existence in the *Letter of Peter to Philip* must, of course, be tested in light of what the text says about the suffering and crucifixion of Jesus. There are two passages which deal with the topic. The first one occurs in connection with the return of the disciples from the Mount of Olives to Jerusalem (138.13–139.4), and the second is part of the so-called little Pentecost sermon of Peter in the temple of Jerusalem (139.15–20).

For this discussion, it is important to note that it is clearly asserted in both of these passages that Jesus really suffered. In the first text this is stated by an anonymous apostle who opens the discussion on the way from the Mount of Olives by saying: "If he, our Lord, suffered, then how much must we suffer?" (138.15–16). The non-docetic character of Jesus' suffering is also confirmed by Peter in his reply to this question and later, more strongly, in his Pentecost sermon in which he cites a confessional formula which declares that "Jesus came down and was crucified. And he bore a crown of thorns. And he put on a purple garment. And he was crucified on a tree and he was buried in a tomb" (139.15–20). When Peter later speaks about the suffering of the apostles caused by the transgression of the mother (139.22–25),[23] he states that because of this Jesus had to

[23] The mother is most likely to be identified with Sophia; so also Koschorke, "Eine gnostische Pfingstpredigt", 330; C. Scholten, *Martyrium und Sophiamythos im Gnostizismus nach den Texten von Nag Hammadi* (JAC Ergänzungsband 14; Münster: Aschendorffsche Verlagsbuchhandlung, 1987) 269. Bethge, *Der Brief des Petrus*, 136–37, has argued that "the transgression of the mother" refers to that of Eve, because the word *parabasis* usually designates the Fall in Gen. 3 (cf. also Rom. 5:14). In the

undergo the same fate as his apostles. The similarity of his experience with that of his apostles is underlined by the phrase *afeire nhōb nim kata oueine hrai nhētn* (139.24–25). As Meyer has pointed out, *kata oueine hrai nhētn* does not emphasize the unreal or apparent character of Jesus' activity ("he did everything in appearance among us")[24] but it stresses the strong resemblance between the experiences of Jesus and his disciples ("he did everything like us").[25] Its Greek equivalent can be found in an expression κατὰ τὸ ὁμοίωμα εἰς/ἐν ("just as"; cf. Ignatius, *Trall.* 9:2).[26]

All of these references clearly testify to the reality of Jesus' suffering, including his crucifixion. In these statements there can be seen no insinuation that the talk about Jesus' suffering should be understood in terms of any kind of docetism. In view of this, it is quite astonishing that Peter, after his confessional formula, after having referred to Jesus' mockery, crucifixion and burial, makes a comment: "Jesus is a stranger to this suffering" (139.21–22). The comment is so startling that it has caused many scholars to favor a docetic interpretation of Jesus in their analyses of the *Letter of Peter to Philip*. In his first introduction to the text, Hans-Gebhard Bethge, for example, maintains that "the Savior only suffered as far as his body, the substance of the archons, was concerned, whereas he himself, as the one coming from the upper realm, had nothing to do with suffering."[27] Marvin Meyer, who does not otherwise see docetic traits in the *Letter of Peter to Philip*, is also ready to admit that at this point a docetic

face of *Ep. Pet. Phil.* 135.8–14, which surely refers to the imprudence of Sophia, it is nevertheless difficult to escape the impression that both texts speak about the same incident. In addition, *parabasis* does not only refer to the Fall in the Nag Hammadi texts. In *Orig. World* 107.25 the term is used of the arrogant behavior of the Demiurge which undeniably has a resemblance with the activity of Sophia.

[24] F. Siegert, *Nag-Hammadi-Register: Wörterbuch zur Erfassung der Begriffe in den koptisch-gnostischen Schriften von Nag-Hammadi* (WUNT 26; Tübingen: J.C.B. Mohr [Paul Siebeck], 1982) 22, translates *kata oueine* "scheinbar" and adds in the brackets "(Doketismus)".

[25] Meyer, *The Letter of Peter*, 155; cf. also Bethge, *Der Brief des Petrus*, 138.

[26] Meyer, *The Letter of Peter*, 155.

[27] H.-G. Bethge, "Der sogenannte 'Brief des Petrus an Philippus': Die zweite 'Schrift' aus Nag-Hammadi-Codex VIII, eingeleitet und übersetzt vom Berliner Arbeitskreis für koptisch-gnostische Schriften", *TLZ* 103 (1978) 164. A similar docetic understanding of Christ's appearance and suffering in the *Letter of Peter to Philip* has also been advocated by J.-É. Ménard, *La Lettre de Pierre à Philippe* (Bibliothèque copte de Nag Hammadi, Section "Textes" 1; Quebec: Les presses de l'Université Laval, 1977) 9. In his later works, Bethge has modified his position; see Bethge, *Der Brief des Petrus*, 65–66, 117–18, 136.

glimmer is shining through. This observation leads him to conclude that there is a Christological tension in the *Letter of Peter to Philip*. For the author, "Jesus is both invulnerable and vulnerable, both immortal and dying . . . his body is both a mortal disguise and a body of death."[28]

It cannot be excluded that Bethge's and Meyer's interpretations of the nature of Jesus' suffering made on the basis of this one phrase "Jesus is a stranger to this suffering" are on the right track. Nonetheless, I cannot help wondering why the other evidence points to another direction and emphasizes the reality of Jesus' suffering. Therefore, I have tried to look for other plausible explanations for the phrase "Jesus is a stranger to this suffering." There seem to be two viable options.

First, the phrase may reflect a general outlook on life which dominated in the early centuries of the common era. Most clearly, this came into expression in Stoicism which represented a sort of philosophic *koine* in the period, as James Francis has put it.[29] According to this view, humans are supposed to pass through suffering being untouched by the experience[30] or, to use the expression coined by the author of the *Letter of Peter to Philip*, being "a stranger to it." Epictetus, for example, indeed admits that suffering, pain and death are impediments of human life but with the right attitude they do not have to affect one's real self (*Handbook* 9). Taking into account a contemporary philosophical trend such as this, there is no need to insist on a docetic interpretation of the phrase "Jesus is a stranger to this suffering." The phrase does not have to deny the reality of the suffering but it emphasizes that even though Jesus underwent suffering, it did not upset and disturb him. To be sure, the *Letter of Peter to Philip* cannot be considered a writing with a large amount of Stoic influence but this does not mean that the author could not have picked up a common idea of a self that can be exempt from the experience of suffering and death. Another way to look at the phrase "being a stranger to suffering" is to see it as an indication that the suffering Jesus underwent was not due to his own actions

[28] Meyer, *The Letter of Peter*, 156.

[29] J. Francis, *Subversive Virtue: Asceticism and Authority in the Second-Century Pagan World* (University Park: Pennsylvania State University Press, 1995) 1.

[30] See J. Perkins, *The Suffering Self: Pain and Narrative Representation in the Early Christian Era* (London: Routledge) 77–103.

but the suffering had a substitutionary character. This is actually explicitly stated in *Ep. Pet. Phil.* 138.18, when Peter replies to the question of an anonymous apostle. Peter states: "Jesus suffered on our behalf..." The substitutionary nature of Jesus' suffering is obliquely confirmed also by the passage 139.21–23 itself. After it has been stated that "Jesus is a stranger to this suffering," it is further related that the apostles "have suffered through the transgression of the mother" and therefore Jesus also had to suffer (139.24–25). The fact that the apostles, as a consequence of the mother's action,[31] were obliged to come to the world of oblivion (134.18–135.2) thus compelled Jesus to come and to suffer in order to rescue "the seed which had fallen away" (136.16–18).

A similar understanding of Jesus' suffering is reflected in two other Nag Hammadi writings, the *Interpretation of Knowledge* and the *Tripartite Tractate*.[32] The former text contains a credal statement in which it is asserted that Jesus was crucified and died, but not his own death, for he did not deserve to die (5.30–32). The same idea is developed in *Tri. Trac.* 115.3–11. The author of the *Tripartite Tractate* states that the Savior not only did "take upon <himself> the death of those whom he thought to save, but he also accepted their smallness to which they had descended when they were <born> in body and soul."[33] Both of these texts, as well as the *Letter of Peter to Philip*, seem to imply that the suffering of Jesus was real but it happened on behalf of others.[34] There is another interesting resemblance between the *Tripartite Tractate* and the *Letter of Peter to Philip*. Both writings depict the worldly existence as smallness (*Tri. Trac.* 115.6; *Ep. Pet. Phil.* 138.20).[35] In the *Tripartite Tractate* it is even clearly asserted that the Savior himself accepts this smallness, and on the whole, the treatment of his incarnation is undeniably non-docetic.[36] Although the

---

[31] This refers to the imprudence of Sophia; see note 24 above.

[32] The similarity among the three writings at this point has been pointed out by U.-K. Plisch, *Die Auslegung der Erkenntnis (Nag-Hammadi-Codex XI,1)* (TU 142; Berlin: Akademie Verlag, 1996) 94–96; cf. also Franzmann, *Jesus in the Nag Hammadi Writings*, 146.

[33] The translation is taken from H.W. Attridge – E.H. Pagels, "The Tripartite Tractate", in H.W. Attridge, *Nag Hammadi Codex I (The Jung Codex)*, vol. 1: *Introductions, Texts, Translations, Indices* (NHS 22; Leiden: E.J. Brill, 1985) 301.

[34] Plisch, *Die Auslegung der Erkenntnis*, 96; so also Bethge in his latest study of the *Letter of Peter to Philip* (*Der Brief des Petrus*, 136).

[35] *Tri. Trac.* 115.6: *tmntšēm*; *Ep. Pet. Phil.* 138.20: *tmntkoui*; cf. also *Gos. Phil.* 57.28–58.10, in which smallness seems to stand for wordly limitations.

[36] So also Attridge – Pagels, "The Tripartite Tractate", 186.

Letter of Peter to Philip does not say explicitly that the Savior became small, the same effect is produced by maintaining that the Savior did everything like the apostles (139.24–25).

In view of the previous observations, one can conclude that the phrase "Jesus is a stranger to this suffering" does not call for a docetic interpretation. Both alternative interpretations presented above offer a more plausible solution to the understanding of the expression. They do not even exclude each other, although in the context of the *Letter of Peter to Philip* the latter alternative, according to which Jesus was a stranger to suffering because he suffered on behalf of others, may alone give a sufficient explanation for the phrase. In any case, both interpretations fit well together with a non-docetic understanding of Jesus' earthly existence and suffering which otherwise seems to dominate in the *Letter of Peter to Philip*.

6. *The Significance of Jesus' Suffering*

One final question remains to be asked. What is actually the significance of Jesus' suffering in the *Letter of Peter to Philip*? This question is important because it may help us to perceive why a non-docetic Christological alternative may have been developed in a Christian "Gnostic" setting.

If we ask the text why Jesus had to suffer, it does not give an explicit answer. In *Ep. Pet. Phil.* 138.18 Peter indeed says: "He suffered on our behalf." But it does not specify the reason. Yet if the suffering does not only refer to Jesus' actual death on the cross but to his entire earthly life, as it seems likely, Jesus' mission has to do with the deliverance of the seed fallen away (136.16–18). In other words, he is the mediator of the saving knowledge. But this is not the whole story.

Jesus' suffering has also an exemplary function. Since he has suffered, the apostles and evidently also their followers cannot expect any other fate. In a way Jesus' suffering makes the suffering of his followers easier however.[37] In addition, Jesus emphasizes that without

[37] Second- and third-century martyr acts form an interesting parallel. It is worth noting how they describe the suffering of martyrs. A Christian martyr may be completely bruised but still entirely unaffected by torture since there is no pain where Christ's glory is manifested. In a way, a martyr is also a stranger to the suffering she or he experiences. In the *Passion of Perpetua and Felicitas* (for the text, see P. Habermehl, *Perpetua und der Ägypter oder Bilder des bösen im frühen afrikanischen Christentum: Ein Versuch zur Passio Sanctarum Perpetuae et Felicitatis* [TU 140; Berlin: Akademie Verlag, 1990]

suffering they will not reach their goal.[38] In the face of this, it is very likely that the *Letter of Peter to Philip* has been written in a situation in which the author and the readers have been persecuted. The inevitability with which Jesus speaks about the future suffering of his disciples does not leave very much room for any other alternative. Whether a persecution can generally contribute to the development of a non- or less docetic understanding of Christology, it is difficult to say, but at least with regard to the *Letter of Peter to Philip* this seems to be the case. It is only the Savior who did everything on behalf of his disciples, even suffered on behalf of them, who can say: "Behold, I am with you forever" (140.22–23).

5–29) there is a description of a young woman martyr called Felicitas who is pregnant and has severe pains in the prison while waiting to be tortured and killed in an arena. When a guard wonders how she is going to endure the actual pain of the final torture, Felicitas replies: "What I now suffer I suffer on my own. In the arena there will be another in me who is going to suffer for me, because I also will suffer for him" (15.2).

[38] Although the beginning of page 139 is badly damaged, it is very likely that the passage 138.27–139.4 contains an encouragement not to avoid suffering, because the one who endures it will be rewarded; cf. Bethge, *Der Brief des Petrus*, 121–22.

PART FIVE

HERMENEUTICAL ISSUES

DIALOG UND DIALEKTIK: ZUM WISSENSCHAFTSTHEORETISCHEN GESPRÄCH MIT HEIKKI RÄISÄNEN

Hans Hübner

Der Einladung, einen Beitrag zur Festschrift für Heikki Räisänen zu schreiben, folge ich gern. Sie bietet in besonderer Weise die Möglichkeit, mit dem finnischen Kollegen das mit ihm schon seit Jahrzehnten geführte wissenschaftliche Gespräch fortzusetzen und zu intensivieren. Es war—ich denke, ich kann es sicherlich so umschreiben—ein bisher im Geiste der Freundschaft geführter Dialog sowohl über Inhalte, in denen wir übereinstimmten, als auch über Fragen, zum Teil sogar Grundsatzfragen, in denen unsere Auffassungen und Überzeugungen recht weit auseinander liegen.

Nun ist ein *Dialog* etwas, was in seinem Gelingen oder Mißlingen nicht allein von denen abhängt, die ihn führen. Natürlich spielt die gegenseitige *bona voluntas* beider Partner eine sehr große Rolle. Denn man darf ja wohl voraussetzen, daß derjenige, der sich im Dialog befindet, die Absicht hat, den anderen zu verstehen und von ihm verstanden zu werden. Aber es darf nie übersehen werden, daß sich dieser gute Wille auf beiden Seiten in einem Bedingungsgefüge befindet, das nicht allein vom Wollen und Planen der Dialogpartner bestimmt ist. Diese gehen nämlich von bestimmten *Vorverständnissen* aus, von denen sie in der Regel annehmen, daß sie sie durchschauten. Die Wurzeln unserer Vorverständnisse sind uns aber zum großen Teil—kann man vielleicht sogar sagen: zum größten Teil?—nicht recht transparent. Wir denken in Denkbahnen, deren Grenzen wir uns sicherlich immer wieder bewußt zu machen versucht haben. Ein wenig vom kritischen Geist Immanuel Kants wollen wir uns doch alle, die wir ernsthaft zu argumentieren bemüht sind, zu eigen machen, nämlich mittels unserer Vernunft die Grenzen unserer Vernunft zu erkennen. Aber wer wirklich mit realistischer wissenschaftlicher Einstellung ans eigene Denken herangeht, auch und gerade ans eigene kritische Denken sich selbst gegenüber, weiß um die Gefahr der Illusion und Selbsttäuschung, der weiß um die Gefahr der leider nicht ganz durchschauten und durchschaubaren Grundüberzeugungen, die oft Resultat unterschiedlicher Komponenten unserer Sozialisationen sind, Resultat unserer immer noch bestehenden Gefangenschaft in nur teilweise erkannten Emotionen—einmal ganz zu schweigen von den Kräften des Unterbewußten, wozu ich mich in diesen Zeilen schon allein aus Kompetenzmangel nicht äußere. Es geht mir keineswegs darum, die hier nur kurz skizzierte hermeneutische Situation in ihrer Gefährdung zu dramatisieren und den aus unterschiedlichen Denkweisen geschehenen und geschehenden Dialog mit Kassandra-Rufen als weithin gescheitert zu erklären. Aber das *caveat* sollte doch wohl ausgesprochen werden. Denn Heikki Räisänen und ich werden wohl kaum ein halbes Jahr nach Erscheinen dieses meines Beitrags zu seiner Festschrift feststellen, daß wir uns plötzlich in allen fundamentalen Fragen über das Wesen der neutestamentlichen Exegese geeinigt haben. Wäre das der Fall, dann hätte zumindest einer von uns beiden nicht jahrzehntelang mit Sorgfalt und wissenschaftlicher Akribie an seiner Grundkonzeption gearbeitet. Beide sind wir in jahrzehntelangen Bemühungen zu einer exegetischen Gesamtsicht gelangt, haben uns bemüht, sie wissenschaftstheoretisch zu fundieren, haben sie in Selbstkritik bedacht und in der Kritik entgegengesetzter Positionen mit Argumenten verteidigt. Aber das eine ist vielleicht doch durch diese Zeilen möglich, nämlich daß wir den jeweils anderen ein wenig mehr noch als bisher verstehen. So sei das, was ich hier schreibe, nicht nur ein Gruß an den Jubilar, sondern auch der Versuch, das gegenseitige Verstehen erneut zu fördern.

Vom Dialog war soeben die Rede—doch jetzt zum zweiten Begriff der Überschrift, der *Dialektik*. Kein Geringerer als Hans-Georg Gadamer, einer der bedeutendsten Philosophen auf dem Gebiet der philosophischen Hermeneutik,—sein wichtigstes Werk *Wahrheit und Methode*[1] ist zur Genüge bekannt—hat die Affinität von Dialog und Dialektik herausgearbeitet, u.a. in seinem 1983 publizierten Aufsatz "Texte und Interpretationen".[2] Darin faßt er Dialektik zunächst von der hermeneutischen Rückbesinnung auf die vom Deutschen Idealismus entwickelte und vollendete spekulative Methode; er denkt sie aber dann

[1] H.-G. Gadamer, *Hermeneutik I: Wahrheit und Methode: Grundzüge einer philosophischen Hermeneutik* (Gesammelte Werke, Band 1; Tübingen: Mohr, 2., durchgesehene Auflage 1990).

[2] Jetzt in: H.-G. Gadamer, "Texte und Interpretationen", in ders., *Hermeneutik II: Wahrheit und Methode, Ergänzungen. Register* (Gesammelte Werke, Band 2; Tübingen: Mohr, 1993), 330–60.

weiter als Korrektiv gegenüber dem Methodenideal der neuzeitlichen Dialektik, die sich im Idealismus des Absoluten vollendete, indem er ihre hermeneutische Struktur nicht mehr so sehr an der Erfahrung ihrer Verarbeitung in der Wissenschaft aufsuchte, sondern an der Erfahrung der Kunst und der Geschichte selber: "Für das Kunstwerk, wie sehr auch immer es als eine geschichtliche Gegebenheit und damit als möglicher Gegenstand wissenschaftlicher Erforschung erscheinen mag, gilt, daß es selber uns etwas sagt—und das so, daß seine Aussage niemals abschließend im Begriff ausgeschöpft werden kann."[3] Ich möchte jedoch in den nun folgenden Überlegungen den Begriff "Dialektik" ein klein wenig modifizieren, doch im Prinzipiellen an dem festhalten, was Gadamer hermeneutisch vertritt. In welcher Weise ich diese Modifikation vornehme, wird sich aus dem Gesamtduktus der Darlegungen ergeben.

Es ist sicherlich kein uninteressanter Sachverhalt, sicherlich auch ein bezeichnender Sachverhalt, daß Heikki Räisänen und ich oft, wenn auch nicht immer, in der Analyse von Texten übereinstimmen, aber fast immer in prinzipieller Hinsicht, wenn es um Fragen theologischer Interpretationen geht, in unserer Auffassung differieren. Das ist zwar ein wenig holzschnittartig gesagt. Aber als ungefähre Ortsangabe unseres Verhältnisses in exegetischen Problemen mag die Aussage für diesen Aufsatz hinreichen, zumal durch die weiteren Ausführungen das Holzschnittartige noch ein wenig präzisiert wird. Für die Unterschiedlichkeit unserer Auffassungen nur zwei Beispiele: Ich habe 1985 die erste Auflage seines Buches "Paul and the Law"[4] rezensiert.[5] Daß es dabei auch um die unter uns kontrovers gesehene Frage nach einer Entwicklung der paulinischen Theologie gegangen ist, versteht sich von selbst, ist aber für die hier zur Debatte stehende Frage kaum von größerem Belang. Relevant für unsere Diskussionslage ist aber jetzt vor allem, daß ich bei Heikki Räisänen eine Aufsplitterung der Aussagen des Paulus meinte feststellen zu müssen und in der Konsequenz eine eigentliche *Theologie* des Paulus vermißte. Und so habe ich dann geschrieben: "Als Theologe, der ja der Exeget sein soll, fragt man sich freilich nach der Lektüre von Räisänens Paulusbuch ein wenig besorgt: '*Quo vadis, theologia?*'" Des

---

[3] Gadamer, *Hermeneutik II*, 332.
[4] H. Räisänen, *Paul and the Law* (WUNT 29; Tübingen: Mohr, 1983).
[5] *TLZ* 110 (1985), 894–96.

weiteren habe ich damals moniert, daß er den Protestantismus im Banne der widersprüchlichen "Rationalisierung" des Paulus sehe; der Protestantismus, so Räisänen, solle lieber zur "*Intuition*" des Apostels zurückkehren. Denn durch seine Intuition habe Paulus wichtige Einsichten in die Freiheit des Christen gewonnen."[6] Räisänen seinerseits hat Anstoß daran genommen, daß ich, nachdem ich den 1. Band meiner "Biblischen Theologie des Neuen Testaments" einem (damals) noch Lebenden und den 2. Band *in memoriam* einem verstorbenen Kollegen und Freund gewidmet hatte, den 3. Band dann mit *Deo uno et trino* überschrieb. Eine solche Widmung empfand er anscheinend für ein wissenschaftliches Werk als unpassend. Dies liegt ganz auf seiner Linie, im Gefolge William Wredes statt biblische oder neutestamentliche Theologie urchristliche Religionsgeschichte zu betreiben. Ist doch in seinen Augen die Aufgabe des Exegeten eine historische, wie er es programmatisch in seiner Schrift "Beyond New Testament Theology"[7] fordert. Doch finden sich in ihr auch interessante Aspekte von hermeneutischer Relevanz.

Das Problem ist, was unter "historisch" zu verstehen ist. Im Deutschen unterscheiden wir zwischen "*historisch*" und "*geschichtlich*", wobei dem Historischen je nach Autor mehr oder weniger der positivistische Aspekt eignet, während dem Geschichtlichen, auch hier wieder von Autor zu Autor verschieden, der existentiale Aspekt anhängt. Ins Englische oder auch in eine andere moderne Sprachen ist diese Unterscheidung von "historisch"/"Historie" und "geschichtlich"/"Geschichte" nur schwer zu übersetzen, wie mir leidvoll aus der Übersetzung eigener Publikationen zur Genüge bekannt ist. Aber, so ist nun grundsätzlicher zu fragen, ist es überhaupt berechtigt, auf das, was im Deutschen das "Historische" oder gar das "rein Historische" besagen soll, den positivistischen Akzent so stark zu setzen? Ist "Historie" wirklich nur das bloße Ensemble von empirisch gewonnenen Fakten, allenthalben noch die Summe ihrer Kausalverbindungen? Bekommt man damit überhaupt die *Geschichte* im Vollsinn dessen, was mit diesem Wort gemeint ist, *in all ihrer Lebendigkeit* und *ihren individuellen Ausprägungen* in den Griff, oder verbleibt es bei einer Betonung

[6] *TLZ* 110, 896.

[7] H. Räisänen, *Beyond New Testament Theology* (London: SCM Press; Philadelphia: Trinity Press International, 1990; 2. Aufl. 2000). Ich setze in den folgenden Ausführungen die in diesem Buch vertretene Grundthese voraus, ohne jedoch zumeist im einzelnen auf sie einzugehen.

des Faktischen nicht bei bloßen und blassen Abstraktionen? Ist es nicht der Gewinn der Entwicklung der hermeneutischen Wissenschaft—wie immer man auch in Einzelfragen zu ihr steht—, daß sie uns gelehrt hat, daß *nur das Leben das Leben versteht*? Auch wenn man hier und dort in der Geschichtsschreibung und Geschichtsbetrachtung eine Überbetonung eines vielleicht tatsächlich überspitzten Individualismus zurückschrauben will oder gar muß—*daß* das Leben eines Individuums unter der dringenden Mahnung des *individuum ineffabile* steht (auch für ein "Kollektiv"[8] gilt Analoges!), kann meines Erachtens derjenige nicht bestreiten, der sich wissenschaftlich oder auf andere ernsthafte Art ausführlich mit der Geschichte beschäftigt. Wo immer wir mit sogenannten "Fakten" konfrontiert sind, begegnen uns diese immer schon als interpretierte Fakten. *In vita nostra facta semper interpretata et interpretanda sunt.* An diesem Axiom kommt kein Historiker vorbei, es sei denn, er wolle lediglich eine museale Sammlung empirisch gewonnener Geschichtsdaten präsentieren. Um nicht falsch verstanden zu werden: Eine solche wirklichkeitsferne Grundeinstellung werfe ich auf keinen Fall dem Jubilar, dem diese Festschrift gewidmet ist, vor. Seine Sicht der Religionsgeschichte ist von solch primitiver Sehweise weit entfernt. Allerdings bin ich davon überzeugt, daß das genannte Axiom Weiterungen impliziert, die—ich will es vorsichtig formulieren—meiner Sicht von Theologie, auch und gerade von kirchlich verantwortlicher Theologie, recht günstig sind.

Kommen wir auf den Begriff "Dialektik" zurück! Ich möchte mit diesem Begriff zum Ausdruck bringen, daß wir vor einer *doppelten Aufgabe* stehen, einer dialektischen Aufgabe nämlich. Wollen wir in der geschichtlichen Vergangenheit ein Ereignis, eine Person, ein Volk, eine Religion, einen geschichtlichen Zusammenhang, ein Überzeugung oder was auch sonst in der Vergangenheit geschichtlichen Charakter hatte, verstehen, so müssen wir *auf der einen Seite* das Faktische zur Kenntnis nehmen, also Zeiten und Orte, Personen, Gemeinschaften und Gesellschaften in ihrem faktischen Gegebensein konstatieren; wir müssen aber zugleich *auf der anderen Seite*, eben weil wir als Historiker, die wir ja geschichtliche Wesen sind, Geschichtliches verstehen wollen, unsere eigene geschichtliche Existenz mit einbringen; wir müssen gerade als Historiker ein Stück Selbstverstehen realisieren. Als

[8] "Kollektiv" natürlich nicht im ideologischen Sinn einer kollektivistischen Weltanschauung verstanden! Der Autor dieser Zeilen hält nichts von solchen Weltanschauungen, die er unseligen Angedenkens im eigenen Vaterland erleben mußte.

Verstehende unserer Gegenwart verstehen wir, wie in der Vergangenheit Verstehende sich selbst verstanden haben, auch wenn sie es nicht eigens unter dem Gesichtspunkt des Selbstverstehens taten. Denn dieses sich selbst Verstehen gehört notwendig zu unserem Dasein hinzu. Dasein ist immer verstehendes und sich selbst verstehendes Dasein, mag solches Verstehen reflektiert geschehen oder nicht. So steht also immer Faktisches und notwendig Geschichtliches in unlösbarer Verbindung, wenn wir wirklich eine geschichtliche Vergangenheit verstehen wollen.

Am Rande bemerkt: Was ich soeben ausgeführt habe, läßt sich unleugbar bestens in die Fundamentalontologie von Martin Heideggers *Sein und Zeit*[9] einfügen. Aber der geschilderte "Sach"-Verhalt[10] ist auch unabhängig von Heideggers Philosophie evident. In meinen Augen ist allerdings seine Analyse des menschlichen Daseins, zu dem wesenhaft das Verstehen und Selbst-Verstehen als Existenzial hinzugehören, eine seiner wichtigen Erkenntnisse, die es uns erleichtert, über unser Verstehen, auch unser alltägliches Verstehen, nachzudenken. Und das heißt auch, daß diese Erkenntnis uns in besonderer Weise befähigt, uns als menschliche Existenz zu verstehen.

Das also ist eine zentrale Voraussetzung, die ich in jeder Exegese, jeder Auslegung eines biblischen Textes mache: *Feststellung von Fakten*—freilich eine idealtypische Aussage, weil es Fakten als solche, von jeglicher Interpretation isolierte oder auch nur isolierbare Fakten nicht gibt, nicht geben kann; *bruta facta* sind eine Fiktion—und *Interpretation von Fakten* (beziehungsweise von dem, was sich irgendwie dem Begriff "Fakten" nähert, ohne es jedoch in strengen Sinne des Wortes sein zu können) stehen *in einer dialektischen Einheit.* Fakten sind immer auf Interpretation aus, da es keine "reinen" Fakten gibt; und Interpretation ist immer faktenbezogen, Interpretation ist immer nur Interpretation von Interpretiertem. Anders formuliert: Interpretation ist immer *intentionale Interpretation*; es gibt keine Interpretation außer der von Interpretiertem. Die gegenseitige Angewiesenheit von Faktum und Interpretation macht ein Wesenselement des geschichtlichen Denkens aus. Und mag vielleicht das zuletzt Gesagte gewissermaßen als Tautologie vorkommen—es ist keine Tautologie, es kann keine Tautologie sein, was sofort einleuchten sollte, wenn man sich in der

[9] M. Heidegger, *Sein und Zeit* (14. Aufl.; Tübingen: Niemeyer, 1977).

[10] "Sache" bewußt in Anführungszeichen, weil der Begriff "Sache" in "Sachverhalt" das Ausgesagte verdinglicht, der Mensch aber kein Ding, keine Sache ist.

Geschichte der Philosophie die Geschichte des Begriffs "Intentionalität" vergegenwärtigt.[11]

Wir sind mit diesen Überlegungen noch nicht beim theologischen Problem als solchem angekommen, wohl aber bei der auch für die Theologie bedeutsamen Frage nach dem, was *Geschichtsschreibung* vermag und soll. Ausgesprochen habe ich mich in den soeben vorgetragenen Überlegungen gegen ein bestimmtes Verständnis von *Historismus*—bekanntlich ist "Historismus" ein äußerst vieldeutiger und daher wenig präziser Begriff—, nämlich gegen jene Spielart des Positivismus, die als *"historischer Positivismus"* zu verstehen ist. G. Scholz umschreibt ihn als "zur Stoffhuberei ausgewucherte Tatsachenforschung und -aufreihung, die alles Vergangene thematisieren kann, ohne nach Sinn und Beziehung zur Gegenwart zu fragen, die alles und jedes genetisch herleitet und so auch den Standpunkt des erkennenden Subjektes historisch relativiert, kurz: Historismus als Indiz für den Auseinanderfall von Subjektivität und Objektivität".[12] Die genialste Auseinandersetzung mit dieser Art von Historismus und Positivismus ist immer noch *Friedrich Nietzsches* Streitschrift "Vom Nutzen und Nachtheil der Historie für das Leben", seine zweite "Unzeitgemäße Betrachtung".[13] Es ist erfreulich, daß Scholz in seinem *HWP*-Artikel im Zusammenhang mit dem historischen Positivismus auf diese Schrift Nietzsches verweist. Während ich diese Zeilen schreibe (im Jahre 2000), begehen wir das Nietzsche-Jahr (hundert Jahre nach seinem Tod). Als zugespitzte These erlaube ich mir zu sagen: Die *Affinität der Denkstrukturen* Nietzsches, innerhalb derer er die Geschichte reflektierte, und die Denkstrukturen, deren sich der Theologe für die Interpretation des Neuen Testaments bedient, relativierte erheblich den Gegensatz von Nietzsches aggressivem Atheismus und dem christlichen Gottesglauben; vielleicht kann man sagen, daß er ihn sogar in den Schatten stellt.[14] Das bedeutet, daß sich Nietzsche und die

---

[11] Ich kann hier schon allein aus Platzgründen nicht auf diese Frage eingehen; vielleicht genügt es, wenn ich auf U. Claesges, "Intentionalität", *HWP* 4 (Darmstadt: Wissenschaftliche Buchgesellschaft, 1976), 475, verweise.

[12] G. Scholz, "Historismus", *HWP* 3 (Darmstadt: Wissenschaftliche Buchgesellschaft, 1974) 1141–47, S. 1142.

[13] F. Nietzsche, *Unzeitgemässe Betrachtungen. Zweites Stück: Vom Nutzen und Nachtheil der Historie für das Leben* in ders., *Sämtliche Werke: Kritische Studienausgabe* (15 Bde; herausgegeben von G. Colli und M. Montinari; Berlin: de Gruyter 1999), 1.243–334.

[14] Im Rahmen des Nietzsche-Jahres halte ich in diesem Semester (SS 2000) an der Göttinger Universität eine Vorlesung für Hörer aller Fakultäten "Friedrich

Interpreten des Neuen Testaments im Grundverständnis der *Hermeneutik* recht nahe sind. Natürlich soll und darf auf keinen Fall mit dieser Feststellung der absolute Gegensatz zwischen Nietzsche und dem Neuen Testament in der Gottesfrage verharmlost werden. Eine andere Frage, der wir hier nicht nachgehen können, ist es allerdings, ob nicht in den Motiven Nietzsches für seinen so radikalen Atheismus Implikationen verborgen sein könnten, deren Wurzeln, ohne daß es ihm bewußt gewesen wäre, in theologischen Denkstrukturen virulent sind.

Bleiben wir noch einen Augenblick bei Friedrich Nietzsche! Den Nutzen der Historie sieht er darin, daß er—ich sage es einmal zum Teil in eigenen Worten—vom Historiker die *Perspektivität* fordert, nämlich die Auswahl von dem aus dem Gesamtgeschehen in der Vergangenheit, was im Dienst des *Lebens* stand. Ist doch in der Überschrift der zweiten "Unzeitgemäßen Betrachtung" die Rede vom *Nutzen* der Historie für das Leben. Historie hat also die Vergangenheit auf das in ihr gewesene Leben um des Lebens in der Gegenwart willen zu befragen. Um es auf eine Kurzformel zu bringen: *Damaliges Leben um des heutigen Lebens willen!* Einige Aussagen in Nietzsches Schrift über die Historie sollen diesen Gesichtspunkt ein wenig konkretisieren. Die wenigen im folgenden genannten Stellen können mühelos vervielfacht werden. Zu bedenken ist in diesem Zusammenhang, daß sich Nietzsche aber nicht nur als Philosoph verstand, sondern auch als Pädagoge, der sich für das von ihm vertretene Bildungsziel tatkräftig engagierte. Dies tat er auch in der von uns hier herangezogenen Schrift. So erklärte er, daß die *historische Bildung* nur "im Gefolge einer mächtigen neuen Lebensströmung . . . etwas Heilsames und Zukunft-Verheissendes" sei.[15] Geschichte werde nur von starken Persönlichkeiten ertragen, die schwachen lösche sie vollends aus.[16] Er hebt auf die Erfahrung des Historikers ab, wenn dieser wirklich Historiker im echten Sinne sei: "Geschichte schreibt der *Erfahrene* und Ueberlegene. Wer nicht Einiges grösser und höher erlebt hat als Alle, wird auch nichts Grosses und Hohes aus der Vergangenheit zu deuten wissen."[17] So könne die Kultur nur aus dem Leben hervorwachsen und

---

Nietzsche und das Neue Testament", in der ich gerade auf die *Zweite Unzeitgemäße Betrachtung* sehr ausführlich eingehe. Inzwischen ist erschienen: H. Hübner, *Nietzsche und das Neue Testament* (Tübingen: Mohr Siebeck, 2000).

[15] Nietzsche, *Vom Nutzen*, 257; alle Nietzsche-Zitate bringe ich in der Orthographie der neuen kritischen Ausgabe von Colli und Montinari.

[16] Nietzsche, *Vom Nutzen*, 283.

[17] Nietzsche, *Vom Nutzen*, 294.

herausblühen. Erkenntnistheoretische Programmatik findet sich in folgendem Satz: "Das Erkennen setzt das Leben voraus."[18] Es geht ihm also nicht um "das leere 'Sein'", sondern um "das volle und grüne 'Leben'"; also nicht mit Decartes *cogito ergo sum*, sondern *vivo ergo cogito*! Und er bringt dann das Wortspiel, daß er, wenn er in Begriffen denke, kein *animal*, sondern nur ein *cogital* sei.[19]

Damit ist aber der letztlich entscheidende Punkt genannt: Wenn es der Historie um Leben geht, also um die lebendige Vergangenheit, die dem Leben in der Gegenwart zu weiterer Lebendigkeit verhelfen soll, dann sind es gerade nicht die Begriffe, die die historische Wissenschaft schaffen soll. Begriffe sind bei Nietzsche der Gegensatz zum Leben. Sie sind der Versuch, eine nicht realisierbare "Objektivität" zu schaffen. "Historische 'Objektivität'" ist für ihn das Ideal einer "fürchterlichen Species von Historikern", die er als "naive Historiker", als "enge Köpfe" charakterisiert.[20] Sie verstehen vom Leben rein gar nichts! Aber diese "Species von Historikern" bestimmt nach Nietzsches Einschätzung das historische Denken seiner Gegenwart, so daß er in der ersten Person Plural sprechen kann: "wir sind ohne Bildung, noch mehr, wir sind zum Leben, zum richtigen und einfachen Sehen und Hören, zum glücklichen Ergreifen des Nächsten und Natürlichen verdorben und haben bis jetzt noch nicht einmal das Fundament einer Kultur, weil wir selbst davon nicht überzeugt sind, ein wahrhaftiges Leben in uns zu haben."[21] Genau in diesem Zusammenhang spricht er, und zwar zur Begründung des soeben Zitierten, davon, daß wir "mit *Begriffen* wie mit *Drachenzähnen* übersäet (sind), *Begriffs-Drachen* erzeugend, dazu an der Krankheit der Worte leidend und ohne Vertrauen zu jeder Empfindung, die noch nicht mit Worten abgestempelt ist"; und begründet er seine elende Existenz als *cogital* damit, daß er sich "als eine solche *unlebendige* und doch unheimlich regsame *Begriffs- und Wort-Fabrik*" denunziert.[22] Es ist also das Wort, als Begriff verstanden, das er als lebenszerstörend zeichnet; freilich nicht das Wort schlechthin, sondern das Wort, insofern es vom Leben abschnitten ist, das kastrierte Wort, das das Leben von sich abstoßende Wort. In anderem Zusammenhang spricht er vom (bloßen)

---

[18] Nietzsche, *Vom Nutzen*, 331.
[19] Nietzsche, *Vom Nutzen*, 329.
[20] Nietzsche, *Vom Nutzen*, 285ff.; das Thema der historischen "Objektivität" bringt er im 6. Kapitel der Schrift; Zitate des letzten Satzes S. 285.289.
[21] Nietzsche, *Vom Nutzen*, 328f.
[22] Nietzsche, *Vom Nutzen*, 329; Kursiven durch mich.

"Erkenntnisphänomen", zu dem ein "historisches Phänomen" aufgelöst worden sei,[23] also jener Vorgang,—so können wir interpretieren—in dem das *Sein* der Vergangenheit zum rein ideellen *Denkobjekt* reduziert und somit das ursprüngliche historische Phänomen aller lebendigen Wirklichkeit entnommen, also kein historisches Phänomen mehr ist. Bloßes Erkennen ist für Nietzsche danach lediglich ein rein begriffliches und folglich wirklichkeitsloses Phantom, etwas ohne jegliche Realität, ohne jegliches Leben. Begriff *contra* Leben, Leben *contra* Begriff! Das ist sein Kampfruf.

Vielleicht denkt der eine oder andere Leser, ich hätte über meiner Argumentation mit Friedrich Nietzsche Heikki Räisänen schon längst vergessen. Genau das ist nicht der Fall! Die ganzen Ausführungen über Nietzsches zweite "Unzeitgemäße Betrachtung" geschehen ganz im Blick auf den finnischen Jubilar. Es mag an jener Rezension deutlich werden, die ich damals über sein Buch "Paul and the Law" geschrieben und zu Beginn dieses Festschrift-Beitrags genannt habe. Ich möchte versuchen, an eben jener Stelle weiterzudenken, an der ich damals meinen Einspruch gegen Heikki Räisänens Paulus-Interpretation geäußert habe, nämlich daß der Apostel nicht der große Denker, "the prince of thinkers", "the theologian par excellence" gewesen sei, als der er in der Regel hingestellt wird, sondern ein Mann der gedanklichen Widersprüche, von dem wir als evangelische Christen aber lernen könnten, was "*Intuition*" ist. Ich möchte versuchen, an genau dieser Stelle noch einmal den Dialog mit dem finnischen Exegeten aufzunehmen, und zwar in der gerade von ihm behaupteten *Dialektik* von *Paulus als dem Denker* und *Paulus als dem Mann der Intuition.* Ich gestehe allerdings sofort zu Beginn dieses Teils meiner Ausführungen, daß ich immer noch der Meinung bin, daß Räisänen Paulus in seiner denkerischen Kraft unterschätzt. Dennoch möchte ich den Versuch unternehmen, durch einen differenzierteren Blick auf Paulus mit dem Bau der theologische Brücke zu Heikki Räisänen über die Distanz Göttingen—Helsinki zu beginnen, ohne hoffen zu dürfen, hiermit diesen Brückenbau zu vollenden. Um im Bild zu bleiben: Ohne das andere Ufer völlig zu erreichen. Aber vielleicht könnte zumindest die Distanz zwischen den beiden Universitätsstädten in Deutschland und Finnland, was ihn und mich betrifft, etwas kleiner werden.

---

[23] Nietzsche, *Vom Nutzen*, 257.

Um von Paulus als Denker zu sprechen, müßte man sich zunächst einmal einigen, was man überhaupt unter "*Denken*" versteht. Meinen wir ein Denken in Syllogismen? Meinen wir in diesem Sinne ein *ratiocinari*? Meinen wir ein begriffliches, in unserem Falle: ein theologisch begriffliches Denken? Sicherlich sind bei Paulus immer wieder Ansätze zur Begrifflichkeit konstatierbar. Sicherlich gibt es bei ihm ein Denken in größerem konzeptionellen Zusammenhang. Dafür ist der Römerbrief ein beredtes Beispiel. Aber man wird Paulus als Denker nicht gerecht, wenn wir in ihm einen virtuosen Begriffsakrobaten sehen wollen. Begrifflichkeit ist zwar bei ihm vorhanden, aber sein theologisches Denken ist bei ihm kein von Begriffen exakt konstruierter System. Selbst der Römerbrief ist kein Lehrbuch der Systematischen Theologie, § xy, Rechtfertigungslehre.

Derjenige Philosoph, der sich im 20. Jahrhundert in besonderer Weise um das Denken bemüht hat und dabei dem begrifflichen und logischen Denken ein anderes Denken entgegengesetzt hat, ist der so umstrittene Martin Heidegger. Es ist bekannt, daß er die formale Logik nicht ins Zentrum der Philosophie hineingelassen hat. Sein Verdienst ist es meines Erachtens—ich weiß, daß andere in diesem Punkte anders urteilen—, daß er dem begrifflichen, also auf Definitionen zielenden Denken ein Denken *aus* dem Sein (oder: Seyn) entgegenstellte. Es kann hier und jetzt nicht unsere Aufgabe sein, dieses Denken aus dem Sein zu reflektieren oder gar ihm gegenüber Zustimmung oder Ablehnung zu äußern. Das ist schon allein deshalb in hiesigen Zusammenhang nicht möglich, weil dann die ontologische Frage in ihren Prinzipialität zu bedenken wäre, auch im Blick auf das Sein Gottes, das schon allein im interkonfessionellen Sinn zu Belastungen geführt hat und auch noch führt. Man denke nur an das heiß diskutierte Problem der *analogia entis*. Aber man kann sehr ernsthaft fragen, ob Heideggers Alternative zum begrifflichen Denken nicht einen Anstoß geben könnte, auch *innerhalb des Bereichs des theologischen Denkens zu einem alternativen Denken gegenüber einer rein begrifflichen theologischen Argumentation* zu gelangen. Ich habe dazu, unter anderem auch 1997 vor der Martin-Heidegger-Gesellschaft, Stellung genommen, kann aber auf diesen anfänglichen Denk-Versuch hier nicht näher eingehen, will aber wohl um der "Sache" willen kurz auf ihn verweisen.[24] Meine Anregung war, nach der Möglichkeit eines Denkens

[24] H. Hübner, "'Vom Ereignis' und vom Ereignis Gott. Ein theologischer Beitrag zu den "Beiträgen zur Philosophie", in P.-L. Coriando (Hg.), *"Herkunft aber bleibt*

aus der Offenbarung des sich offenbarenden Gottes zu fragen: Gibt es eine, wie auch immer zu denkende, Entsprechung zwischen dem *cogitare ex* . . . bei Heidegger und in der christlichen Theologie? Ich möchte nur kurz zur Erläuterung sagen, daß ich ein theologisches *cogitare ex revelatione* nicht offenbarungspositivistisch verstehe. Eine Verständigung mit Heikki Räisänen auf offenbarungspositivistischer Basis wäre wohl auch undenkbar.

Doch nun zu diesem selbst. Räisänen gesteht zu: "Paul was indeed an original and imaginative thinker, and his letters are full of seminal and thought-provoking suggestions."[25] Möglicherweise kommt er mit diesem Urteil, das ich in dieser Formulierung unterschreiben könnte, dem nahe, wie ich das theologische Denken des Apostels fasse. Verstehe ich Heikki Räisänens Paulus-Verständnis richtig, wenn ich es, von ihm als originales und ideenreiches Denken charakterisiert, bestimmt oder zumindest mitbestimmt sehe von dem, was er kurz danach ausführt, nämlich daß Paulus auf dem Wege der *Intuition* oder, was er anscheinend als damit identisch begreift, aufgrund seines Glaubens an Christus (er fügt hinzu: "if you like") zu wichtigen Einsichten beispielsweise hinsichtlich der christlichen Freiheit gekommen sei?[26] Ich möchte dieses Urteil so verstehen, daß der den ganzen Menschen mit all seinen Fähigkeiten des Daseins erfassende Glaube in innigste Verbundenheit mit dem Denken gekommen ist. Anders gesagt: Was die gesamte Existenz des Menschen ausmacht, erfaßt zusammen mit seinem Denkvermögen den Glauben (*fides quae creditur*) und verbindet sich so zum Glauben (*fides qua creditur*). Daß sich dabei in meiner Vorstellung auch das einfindet, was man seit Rudolf Bultmann "existentiale Interpretation" nennt, brauche ich wohl nicht zu begründen.

Heikki Räisänen bezieht sich an dieser Stelle seiner Darlegungen auch auf Adolf Deissmanns Paulus-Buch, in dem dieser die *intuitiv-*

---

stets Zukunft": Martin Heidegger und die Gottesfrage (Martin-Heidegger-Gesellschaft Schriftenreihe 5; Frankfurt a.M.: Klostermann, 1998), 135–58; ders., "Martin Heideggers Götter und der christliche Gott. Theologische Besinnung über Heideggers "Besinnung" (Band 66)", *Heidegger Studien* 15 (Berlin: Duncker & Humblot, 1999) 127–151.

[25] Räisänen, *Paul and the Law*, 267.

[26] Räisänen, *Paul and the Law*, 26; s. dazu auch Räisänen, *Beyond New Testament Theology*, 106: "A history of early Christian thought as I see it ought to make abundantly clear the connections of the thoughts und ideas with the experiences of individuals and groups. The development of thought is to be analysed precisely in the light of the interaction between experiences and interpretations."

kontemplative Begabung des Apostels herausstellt.[27] Kontemplation versteht Deissmann als “Reaktion auf eine Begegnung mit Gott”. Er schildert diesen Zustand in nahezu poetischer Diktion: “die inneren Saiten vibrieren unter den Fingern Gottes; die erschütterte Seele reagiert auf die Offenbarung, in den schweren Wehen schaffenden Gestaltens oder im verzückten Jauchzen des Psalmisten.”[28] Und so charakterisiert er Kontemplation als “bald ein Sichversenken des Gläubigen, ein Hinabtauchen in die geoffenbarten ‘Tiefen Gottes’, bald ein Ringen mit praktischen Problemen, die nicht als theologisch-wissenschaftlich interessant, sondern als religiös quälend empfunden werden”.[29] Und so kann Deissmann auch sagen: “Eine neue Stellung zu Gott hat Paulus gefunden, *nicht* eine neue *Lehre* von Gott.”[30] Er spricht vom Gotteserlebnis des Paulus, das dem Gotteserlebnis Jesu nahe verwandt sei. Der Unterschied sei, daß Jesus mit seinem Gotteserlebnis auf sich selbst stehe, Paulus aber nicht; er bedürfe der Vermittlung.[31] Die Christologie des Paulus sei nicht der Weg zu Christus, sondern der Reflex Christi. So sei auch eine bloß intellektuelle Christologie wertlos. “Was man paulinische Christologie nennt, ist nichts vorwiegend Intellektuelles, erscheint vielmehr vom mystischen Christuserlebnis und vom Christuskult aufs stärkste inspiriert, ist Kontemplation.”[32] Nun ist es beim heutigen Forschungsstand kaum noch angebracht, von der Mystik des Paulus zu sprechen; lassen wir aber einmal diesen etwas überholten Begriff beiseite, so läßt sich Deissmanns Urteil *insofern* halten, als es als Umschreibung einer Theologie interpretiert wird, die nicht mit theologischen Begriffen konstruiert ist, aber auch nicht bestreitet, daß Paulus ein tiefer Denker ist. Es ist schon richtig, seine Christologie nicht als eine *bloß* intellektuelle zu beschreiben. So verstanden, kann ich Räisänens Bezug auf Deissmann im Prinzip zustimmen.

Daß er für die Theologie des Paulus die *Intuition* statt begriffliches Denken als charakteristisch sieht, läßt erneut die Assoziation Friedrich Nietzsche aufkommen. Denn dieser hat in seiner nachgelassenen

[27] Räisenen, *Paul and the Law*, 268, Anm. 19.

[28] A. Deissmann, *Paulus: Eine kultur- und religionsgeschichtliche Skizze* (2. völlig neubearbeitete und vermehrte Auflage; Tübingen: Mohr, 1925) 85.

[29] Deissmann, *Paulus*, 85.

[30] Deissmann, *Paulus*, 145; Kursive durch mich.

[31] Deissmann, *Paulus*, 145.

[32] Deissmann, *Paulus*, 147.

Schrift *Ueber Wahrheit und Lüge im aussermoralischen Sinne*[33] in sehr polemischer Weise die Antithese "Begriff—Intuition" vorgestellt. Zwar ist der Gesamtzusammenhang dieser Ausführungen ein anderer als der bei Räisänen bedachte. Trotzdem lohnt ein Vergleich. Nietzsche wertet den Intellekt des Menschen erheblich ab; er sei lediglich ein Mittel zur Erhaltung des Individuums und entfalte dafür seine Hauptkräfte in der Verstellung. Es kommt auch zur Abwertung des Wortes. Der Intellekt bilde nämlich Worte zu Begriffen, indem er für zahllose, mehr oder weniger ähnliche, niemals aber gleiche Fälle ein und denselben Begriff entstehen lasse; so gebe uns der Begriff das Übersehen des Individuellen und Wirklichen.[34] Er antwortet dann auf die Frage, was die *Wahrheit* sei: "Ein bewegliches Heer von Metaphern, Metonymien, Anthropomorphismen kurz eine Summe von menschlichen Relationen, die, poetisch und rhetorisch gesteigert, übertragen, geschmückt wurden, und die nach langem Gebrauche einem Volk fest, canonisch und verbindlich dünken: *die Wahrheiten sind Illusionen*, von denen man vergessen hat, dass sie welche sind, Metaphern, die abgenutzt und sinnlich kraftlos geworden sind, Münzen, die ihr Bild verloren haben und nun als Metall, nicht mehr als Münzen in Betracht kommen."[35] Was Nietzsche hier vor allem tadelt, ist, daß *ein Bild in einen Begriff aufgelöst* wird.[36] Zunächst wird man als Wahrheitsmoment dieser Annahme anerkennen, daß das Bild die Grundlage für die Metapher ist. Wo aber vom Bild die Rede ist, da ist auch das Thema der *Kunst* berührt. Wo sich jedoch der Mensch unter die Herrschaft der immerhin von ihm gebildeten Begriffe begibt, da ergibt er sich dem Irrtum, er habe die Dinge unmittelbar als *Objekt* vor sich: "Er vergisst also die originalen Anschauungsmetaphern als Metaphern und nimmt sie als die Dinge selbst."[37] Damit sind wir auf das Problem der *Subjekt-Objekt-Spaltung* gestoßen, das bekanntlich seit Heidegger und Bultmann in der Diskussion über die Auslegung der biblischen Schriften zum dominierenden Thema geworden ist. Indem sich das Subjekt das Objekt *gegenüber*-stellt, nimmt es sich selbst aus dem Verstehen des "Objekts" heraus; es vergißt, daß es selbst

[33] F. Nietzsche, *Ueber Wahrheit und Lüge im aussermoralischen Sinne* in ders., *Sämtliche Werke* 1.873–90.
[34] Nietzsche, *Wahrheit und Lüge*, 879f.
[35] Nietzsche, *Wahrheit und Lüge*, 880f.; Kursive durch mich.
[36] Nietzsche, *Wahrheit und Lüge*, 881.
[37] Nietzsche, *Wahrheit und Lüge*, 883.

im Prozeß des Verstehens notwendig zum verstandenen "Objekt" hinzugehört. In gewisser Weise hat also Nietzsche schon die von Heidegger im Bereich der Philosophie und von Bultmann im Bereich der Theologie bekämpfte Subjekt-Objekt-Spaltung, deren Wurzeln beide vor allem bei Descartes gesehen haben, vorweggenommen.

Nietzsche sieht am Bau der Begriffe also zuerst die Sprache arbeiten, in späteren Zeiten dann die Wissenschaft. Diese "arbeitet . . . unaufhaltsam an jenem grossen Columbarium der Begriffe, der Begräbnisstätte der Anschauung, baut immer neue und höhere Stockwerke . . . und ist vor allem bemüht, jenes in's Ungeheure aufgethürmte Fachwerk zu füllen und die ganze empirische Welt d.h. die anthropomorphische Welt hineinzuordnen."[38] Das ist nämlich Nietzsches Grundvorwurf an die mit Begriffen arbeitende Wissenschaft, daß sie sich in Verkennung der grundsätzlichen und unvermeidbaren anthropomorphen Grenzen der Begriffsbildung ihrem eigenen, nicht durchschauten Anthropomorphismus unterwirft. An dieser Stelle erkennt der Mensch sein Klein-Sein nicht; er erkennt nicht, daß nur er auf diese Weise seine Begriffe bildet, nur so bilden kann. Er baut sich seinen "complizirten Begriffsdom" und ringt nach einem Verstehen der Welt, die er als ein bloß menschenartiges Ding voll und ganz begreifen will.[39] Es gibt aber auch ganz andere Wege der Erfassung der Wirklichkeit: "Könnten wir uns aber mit der Mücke verständigen, so würden wir vernehmen, dass auch sie mit diesem Pathos[40] durch die Luft schwimmt und in sich das fliegende Centrum dieser Welt fühlt."[41]

So unterscheidet Nietzsche zwischen dem *von Begriffenen und Abstraktionen geleiteten Menschen* und dem *von Intuitionen geleiteten Menschen.*[42] Der intuitive Mensch erntet durch seine Intuitionen, inmitten in einer Kultur stehend, "eine fortwährend einströmende Erhellung, Aufheiterung, Erlösung".[43] Doch auch er wird allerdings von Nietzsche mit einigen negativen Zügen gezeichnet. Aber er vermag als der der Kunst Nahe, als der das Bild noch *als* Bild Erkennende die Wirklichkeit angemessener zu erfahren; er ist der Wirklichkeit näher als der unter der Diktatur der von ihm selbst konstruierten Begriffe Stehende.

[38] Nietzsche, *Wahrheit und Lüge*, 886.
[39] Nietzsche, *Wahrheit und Lüge*, 882f.
[40] Verglichen mit dem pathetischen Hochmut, mit dem der Mensch auf sein erkennen schaut.
[41] Nietzsche, *Wahrheit und Lüge*, 875.
[42] Nietzsche, *Wahrheit und Lüge*, 888.
[43] Nietzsche, *Wahrheit und Lüge*, 889.

Wir können freilich die Gedanken dieser kleinen Studie Nietzsches jetzt nicht einfach auf die Überlegungen Räisänens übertragen. Aber ihr Grundgedanke enthält doch ein gehöriges Quantum an Wahrheit. Den absoluten Pessimismus im Blick auf Begrifflichkeit können wir sicherlich nicht teilen. Er ist maßlos übertrieben. Aber daß Begriffe anthropomorph sind, hat ja nicht Nietzsche zum ersten Mal gesagt. Und daß wir sie stets auf ihr anthropomorphe Bedingtheit untersuchen müssen, bedarf keiner Begründung. Derjenige Realismus, der in den Begriffen das getreue Abbild des von ihnen Intendierten sieht, ist primitiv. Aber das ist ja die uns im *theologischen* Zusammenhang bewegende Frage, wie *wir* die im Kommen Jesu Christi in unsere Welt hereingebrochene *Welt Gottes* verstehen können, ohne Gott in anthropomorpher Begrifflichkeit zu vermenschlichen, also selbst ohne Opfer unseres notwendig verstellenden Anthropomorphismus zu werden und ohne Gottes Sein durch anthropomorphe Begriffe zu entstellen. Daß wir Gott und die Wirklichkeit seines Gnadenhandelns nicht in Begriffe einzwängen dürfen—Gott ist ja nicht de-*fin*-ierbar, ist kein begrenzbares, in feste Grenzen einschließbares Wesen!—, läßt ja nur einen Erkenntnisweg zu, der auf keinen Fall ein Weg mit Begriffen ist. Es ist aber dann zu fragen, ob mit dem, was Nietzsche in *seinem* Kontext und was Räisänen im theologisch-exegetischen Kontext mit *Intuition* beschreiben, ein *fundamentaltheologischer Zugang zum Verstehen des* sich eben nicht mit Begriffen begreifbaren *Handelns Gottes* ermöglicht ist. Wie können wir die Theologie dessen, dem Räisänen den Titel "prince of thinkers" verweigert, den ich ihm aber doch geben möchte—freilich mit der Präzisierung: Fürst der theologischen Denker, die Gottes Sein und Handeln nicht mit notwendig anthropomorphen Begriffen definieren wollen (man sehe mir bitte diese so umständliche Sprache nach!)—, ohne in Grenzen zwingende Begriffe in unser geschichtlich bedingtes und begrenztes Verstehen übersetzen? Ist die Intuition eine theologische Rettungsmöglichkeit? Kann der Dialog mit Räisänen dadurch ein Stück weiter geführt werden, daß wir uns, wie auch immer, auf den Weg eines *intuitiven Verstehens* begeben? Versuchen wir also in einem letzten Schritt unserer heutigen Bemühungen den Dialog mit ihm zu intensivieren und das noch klarer herauszustellen, was in der Überschrift mit "Dialektik" zum Ausdruck gebracht worden ist.

Kommen wir auf die Überschrift unseres Aufsatzes zurück: *Dialog* und *Dialektik.* Gedacht ist jetzt, um Grundbegriffe unseres jahrzehntelangen Gesprächs zu nennen, an die Dialektik von *Religionsgeschichte* und *Theologie*. Religionsgeschichte war und ist das Anliegen meines finnischen Gesprächspartners, Theologie war und ist mein Anliegen. Beides ist notwendig und unverzichtbar. Die Auslegung des Alten Testaments ist ohne gründlichste religionsgeschichtliche Forschung nicht möglich. Schon allein die im Alten Testament dargestellte und reflektierte Geschichte ist ein Geschichte der Jahwäh-Religion und anderer vor allem vorderasiatischen Religionen, die zum Teil in die Jahwäh-Religion integriert wurden. Und auch das Neue Testament steht mitten in der damaligen Religionsgeschichte Vorderasiens und Europas. Was die Theologie betrifft, so bleibe ich hier einmal nur auf meinem Fachgebiet, dem Neuen Testament, und frage: *Wie können religionsgeschichtliche Aussagen des Neuen Testaments*, die sich ja in der Regel gar nicht als solche ausgeben, *mit den theologischen Intentionen des Neuen Testaments vermittelt werden?*[44]

Das Neue Testament enthält weithin *theologische Aussagen*, die von seinen Autoren *als* theologische Aussagen intendiert sind. Es sind Aussagen, die Gott und sein Handeln vorstellen, die diese Aussagen auch in kerygmatischer Intention bringen, sie also bei ihren Lesern zum Verstehen bringen wollen. *Theologische Aussagen wollen aber theologisch verstanden werden.* Die exegetische Aufgabe besteht dann darin, damalige theologische Aussagen so zur Sprache zu bringen, daß sie im heutigen Verstehenshorizont theologisch verstanden werden können. Die theologische Interpretation neutestamentlicher Aussagen gehört also aufgrund des Charakters der neutestamentlichen Schriften unverzichtbar zum Kern der neutestamentlichen Exegese. Und wenn wir sie nun als Aussagen nehmen, die gerade nicht als begriffliche Aussagen verstanden werden wollen, weil sie sonst ihres Gehaltes verlustig gingen, so wäre ein theologisches Verstehen als ein Begreifen theologischer Begriffe *kontraintentional* zur Intention dieser Aussagen. Ich hoffe, daß ich Heikki Räisänen, der, wie oben gezeigt, in genau diesem Zusammenhang von Intuition und Glauben spricht, in der Hinsicht richtig verstanden habe, daß er das Verstehen theologischer Aussagen des Neuen Testaments mit solcher Intuition und mit Glauben zusammenbringen will.

---

[44] Auf die Frage nach dem Verhältnis von der Theologie des Neuen Testaments zu den Theologien im Neuen Testament gehe ich hier nicht ein. Ich habe mich dazu, wie ich hoffe, ausführlich genug geäußert in: H. Hübner, *Biblische Theologie des Neuen Testaments* (3 Bde; Göttingen: Vandenhoeck & Ruprecht, 1990–1995).

Nehmen wir—es ist sozusagen die Probe aufs Exempel!—das Wort "*Gott*". Daß zwar im Laufe der christlichen Theologiegeschichte immer wieder das Erfassen dieses Wortes als begriffliche Aufgabe gesehen wurde, ist ein Faktum, das der Theologe heute nicht ignorieren kann und darf. Daß damit auch griechisches Erbe wirksam ist, bedarf keiner Begründung. Schaut man auf die Entwicklung der antiken griechischen Philosophie, so zeigt sich dort ein ständiges den Gottesgedanken weitertreibende Bemühen, und zwar sowohl in begrifflicher als auch in einer bewußt Begriffe vermeidenden Weise. So hat sich z.B. Xenophanes (ca. 570–475 v. Chr.)[45] sehr energisch gegen alle anthropomorphe Begrifflichkeit und alles anthropomorphe Vorstellen Gottes sehr energisch gewandt (s. nur Diels/Kranz 21 B 15!). Andererseits haben z.B. Aristoteles und die Stoa viel in die begriffliche Erfassung Gottes investiert. Nehmen wir nun die neutestamentlichen Gottesaussagen—ich wähle die des Paulus aus—, so will dieser in seinen Briefen die, die lesen, wie er Gott theologisch zur Sprache gebracht hat, dazu bewegen, *Gott als die sie bestimmende Wirklichkeit* zu verstehen. In seinen Augen hat keiner Gott in seinem begnadenden Handeln verstanden, der dieses in Begriffe bringt, die auch unabhängig vom Glauben begriffen werden könnten. Das Evangelium vom befreienden Handeln Gottes hat für ihn nur verstanden, wer zugleich sich selbst als von diesem Gott befreit versteht. Gottes "Existenz" ist also in der paulinischen Aussage mitgedacht und mitausgesagt. Nach Paulus hat keiner verstanden, was er von Gott verkündet, wenn er nicht zugleich an Gott als den für ihn Existierenden glaubt. Im Verstehen des paulinischen Gottesgedankens ist also bereits das Erfassen des rettenden Daseins Gottes mitgesetzt. Paulus würde daher eine Antwort auf seine Verkündigung wie "Ich verstehe, daß Gott nach deiner Verkündigung der rettende Gott ist; ich glaube das aber nicht" antworten: "Du hast nicht verstanden, was ich verkündige. Denn du hast Gott nur als etwas rein Ideelles aufgefaßt, nicht aber das Entscheidende, nämlich sein Dasein, das im zu verstehenden Gottesgedanken mitgesetzt ist." In mittelalterlicher scholastischer Terminologie: Gottes *essentia* impliziert seine *existentia*; wer den Gedanken seiner *essentia* wirklich verstanden hat, hat zugleich

---

[45] Zu Xenophanes im Blick auf die alttestamentliche Entwicklung des Gottesgedankens s. Hübner, *Biblische Theologie* 1.248f.

seine *existentia* als gegeben verstanden.[46] Freilich—dieser Gedanke des Paulus, sei er in der soeben formulirten Terminologie ausgesprochen oder nicht—kann nur als Glaubenssatz ausgesprochen werden. Für den, der an den Gott glaubt, der in Jesus Christus soteriologisch gehandelt hat, ist es ein überzeugender Satz. Wer ihn außerhalb des Glaubens vernimmt, für den bleibt er mit Notwendigkeit ein inhaltsleerer Satz. Nur innerhalb des christlichen Glaubens ist also die Rede vom theologischen Verstehen der theologischen Botschaft des Neuen Testaments keine inhaltsleere Rede. Außerhalb des christlichen Glaubens ist es eine religionsgeschichtliche Aussage, die auf gleicher Ebene liegt wie beispielsweise die Aussage eines Christen über das Nirvana. Denn nach buddhistischer Überzeugung wäre eine solche christliche Aussage eine Aussage ohne Substanz und ohne wirkliches und eigentliches Verstehen. Für den Christen ist aber—und damit sind wir wieder beim Ausgangspunkt unserer Überlegungen angelangt—die religionsgeschichtliche Betrachtung des Neuen Testaments eine Betrachtung, die theologische Aussagen impliziert. Die *Dialektik* von unverzichtbarer *Religionsgeschichte* und unverzichtbarer *Theologie* ist also eine sinnvolle Dialektik, sofern sie innerhalb der hier versuchten Argumentation ausgesprochen ist. Die Frage an Heikki Räisänen ist dann, ob diese meine Überlegungen einen Schritt im gemeinsamen Bemühen um das, was das Neue Testament sagt, weitergführt haben.

[46] Das Wahrheitsmoment des ontologischen Gottesbeweises *Anselms von Canterbury*, das auch unanhängig davon besteht, ob man diesen Gottesbeweis gelten läßt oder nicht.

GRANDMA, RÄISÄNEN, AND THE GLOBAL VILLAGE: A FEMINIST APPROACH TO ETHICAL CRITICISM

Hanna Stenström

I

In a recent lecture in Uppsala entitled, "On the Way to Moral Criticism", Heikki Räisänen gave a number of historical and contemporary examples of moral or ethical criticism in biblical studies, as well as a programme with ten theses for the makeup of such criticism.[1] Shortly before, I had defended my doctoral thesis on the Book of Revelation, where I also discussed ethical and political accountability, laying a feminist perspective on both the biblical text and its scholarly interpretations.[2] When I was given the opportunity to give a faculty lecture in Uppsala on March 27, 2000, in the same room where Räisänen had spoken, it seemed appropriate to address his programme for moral criticism. I found that many of my own concerns had been taken up by him, but also that there were more things that should be said, especially from a feminist point of view.

While being a response to Prof. Räisänen, my lecture was actually dedicated to the memory of my grandmother, Märta Dorotea Forsberg, born Sedvall, who died on March 27, 1977. Grandma Märta gave birth to fourteen children; the God of her youth's free-church environment was believed to punish all who would try to prevent the inception and completion of a new life. In the end, she was no longer able to believe in such a god, but she never lost her confidence that Jesus would come and take her with him. By narrating incidents from my own grandmother's life, I wanted to write her into the history of all those women who experienced the double role of the God of Christian scriptures as "enemy and friend, tormentor

[1] The lecture was given in Swedish (original title "På väg mot en etisk bibelkritik") and published in SEÅ 65 (2000) 227–42.

[2] Hanna Stenström, *The Book of Revelation: A Vision of the Ultimate Liberation or the Ultimate Backlash? A Study in 20th Century Interpretation of Rev. 14:1–5, with special emphasis on feminist exegesis* (University of Uppsala, 1999).

and saviour".[3] She was one of those who, living in and being shaped by an oppressive tradition and patriarchal culture, nevertheless became subjects. As subjects, these women were capable of expressing both a joy of life and a protest against the life circumstances they were allotted. Theirs was both a belief in God and an awareness of the wrongs of the image of God in the traditional piety around them.

So my lecture on the ethical responsibility of biblical scholars was given "in memory of her". Now, reworking that lecture with Heikki Räisänen's 60th birthday in mind, I hope to contribute a warm (but not uncritical) greeting to him which continues the discussion on topics that are crucial to both of us—and not us alone.

The following section II is a reworked form of the main section of my lecture, including some material that space did not allow to present at that time. In a new section III, I enclose some reflections on the book *Reading the Bible in the Global Village: Helsinki*.[4] This book continues the same discussion as Heikki Räisänen's and my lectures sought to further, but there the feminist stance is voiced by Elisabeth Schüssler Fiorenza.

II

When speaking of ethical issues in biblical scholarship, we may distinguish three closely related but not identical fields. First, there is the question of the exegete's "professional ethics". The second field is "moral criticism" of the Bible, that is, ethically motivated criticism of biblical texts and their interpretations. The third field of discussion comprises "biblical ethics", i.e., the formulations of ethics and morality found in the biblical documents.

---

[3] The quotation is from Mary Ann Tolbert, "Defining the Problem: The Bible and Feminist hermeneutics", *Semeia* 28 (1983) 113–26, on p. 126. Cf. also Alice Suskin Ostriker, *Feminist Revision and the Bible* (The Bucknell Lectures in Literary Theory; Oxford: Blackwell, 1993) 86: "If the Bible is a flaming sword forbidding our entrance to the garden, it is also a burning bush urging us toward freedom. It is what we wrestle with all night and from which we may, if we demand it, wrest a blessing."

[4] Heikki Räisänen, Elisabeth Schüssler Fiorenza, R.S. Sugirtharajah, Krister Stendahl and James Barr, *Reading the Bible in the Global Village: Helsinki* (Atlanta: SBL, 2000). This book originates from the SBL International Meeting 1999 in Helsinki and includes Heikki Räisänen's introductory lecture "Biblical Critics in the Global Village", responses to this lecture, and reprints of some articles that played a central role in this discussion.

In this article I will restrict myself to the two first overlapping areas. The exegete's professional ethics involve a programme, or at least some overarching principles for scholarly praxis. It includes moral criticism but is much more comprehensive.[5]

Another distinction is between "moral criticism" and "ideological criticism". This distinction was made by Räisänen in his lecture, and I can make his understanding my own. Ideological criticism is the wider concept. Moral criticism can be seen as one aspect of ideological criticism, but the latter includes also analysis of social circumstances, group interests, etc. Moral criticism is thus something simpler and less sophisticated, a critique of texts and interpretations on the basis of universally recognised values such as justice, human rights, and life.[6] One should notice, however, that the term "moral/ethical criticism" is not always used by those who actually practise it.

There are many reasons why the practical consequences of biblical texts and interpretations and the question of scholarly responsibility have now become so vital issues. One reason is the emergence of new interpreting subjects in all fields of theological work, both in academic and church contexts. People from groups that have been, and still are, on the margins are increasingly taking part in interpretative work, and often direct their attention to the negative effects that biblical interpretation has had on them. Another contributing factor is the growing theoretical and methodical pluralism in exegetical study, and the awareness that there is no one and final interpretation of texts. As a consequence, we as exegetes have learned that there are always choices to be made between various methodological tools as well as between various interpretations and theological responses. And whatever you do, you are responsible for your choices.

Moreover, the new interpretative subject's criticism of texts and his/her interpretations and the enhanced awareness of the texts' many meanings, together contribute to the insight articulated by Joanna Dewey:

[5] See Elisabeth Schüssler Fiorenza, *Rhetoric and Ethic: The Politics of Biblical Studies*, (Minneapolis: Fortress Press, 1999) 195–98. Schüssler Fiorenza includes in her programme for an "ethics of interpretation" theoretical presuppositions concerning language and texts, and envisages a change not only of the individual exegete's praxis, but of the discipline's institutional structures and power relations. See also idem, "Defending the Center, Trivializing the Margins" in *Reading in Global Village*, 29–48, esp. pp. 47–48.

[6] Räisänen, "Etisk bibelkritik", 240.

> If meaning is not finally decidable; if there are no universal, valid standards for determining meaning, then it behooves us even more to pay explicit attention to how power functions in the texts, and how texts are used to affect people, all different groups and classes of people, to empower and/or oppress them. Meaning is indeed relative, but power is real, and abuse hurts.[7]

Dewey's observation underscores the necessity of moral and ethical criticism within and outside the exegetical and academic community. Today, all theological work, be it academic or church-related, should be done in the awareness that theology has its share in the exercise of power. To illustrate the point, let us just consider how the role of "grandmother" takes on new functions. The author of 2 Tim is the earliest Christian theologian to employ "grandmother" in his argumentation, as he has the fictional Paul say to the likewise fictional Timothy: "I am reminded of your sincere faith, a faith that lived first in your grandmother Lois and your mother Eunice and now, I am sure, lives in you." (2 Tim 1:5) This remark introduces a lengthy argument for keeping the faith. The author sharply distinguishes between those of the right faith and others. The "grandmother"—another fictional character—is employed to establish a clear institutional structure and a church dogmatics, in which power over defining the doctrine seems to go together with regulating the status of women.

But today, a growing number of scholars like myself recall the real "grandmothers"—in the widest sense—in order to write these marginal but flesh-and-blood people's subordination and protest into history, instead of uncritically continuing the rhetoric and historiography where women are exploited the way they are in 2 Tim and elsewhere in early Christian documents.[8] For us who identify ourselves as feminist scholars and theologians, it is a moral obligation not to carry on the Doctrine with the fictional Grandmother as its obedient helper. Neither do we want to repeat the clichés about women as warning examples, but employ our "grandmothers", and the consequences of the Doctrine for them, as tools for a critical

---

[7] Joanna Dewey, "Feminist Readings, Gospel Narrative and Critical Theory", *BTB* 22:4 (1992) 167–73, on p. 173.

[8] 2 Tim presents almost the whole spectrum. Here women appear as rhetorical figures or as silent Others who obey male authority. We are also introduced to dangerous seducers and their helpless victims, as in 2 Tim 3:6: "silly women, overwhelmed by their sins and swayed by all kinds of desires."

analysis of established truths. Our duty is to listen to the past and present voices of real-life women. Such voices serve as warning examples of the oppressive power of Christian faith and practices, but they also inspire us to constructive feminist theological projects. The constructive efforts, however, go beyond the strictly exegetical tasks and lead to normative theological reconstructions.

This brings me to the issue of the exegete's professional ethics. Useful contributions to this discussion are Elisabeth Schüssler Fiorenza's influential SBL Presidential Address, "The Ethics of Biblical Interpretation: Decentering Biblical Scholarship",[9] Daniel Patte's *Ethics of Biblical Interpretation*[10] and Schüssler Fiorenza's newest book, *Rhetoric and Ethic: The Politics of Biblical Studies.*

Daniel Patte points out that a professional ethics has always been there. Within the traditional paradigm, it has had the shape of what Patte, taking over a term from outside the exegetical discourse, calls "morality of knowledge".[11] The leading principle in this ethics is that the scholar apply the methodological tools in a proper way in a quest for the original meaning of the text and/or in order to solve historical or philological problems. Ethical questions and choices are in such a framework mostly connected with the right use of methods. The kind of ethics Patte sets up goes beyond historical-critical morality. In this effort to move beyond the morality of knowledge, Patte is in the company of feminist exegetes.

In the various formulations of an "ethics of biblical interpretation", two projects are often included. One is the critical reflection upon how exegesis has been done. Based on this critical project, there is a constructive project which seeks to give shape to the novel conception of professional ethics. A recent example of constructive work is the programme with 13 theses proposed by Schüssler Fiorenza in her *Rhetoric and Ethic.* The theses are prepared for and substantiated by a critical analysis of existing readings of New Testament texts.

In the critical part of *Rhetoric and Ethic*, Schüssler Fiorenza posits a very stark contrast between traditional historical-critical exegesis, with its claim to objectivity, and the engaged readings of which her

[9] Originally published in *JBL* 107 (1988) 3–17, reprinted in *Reading the Bible in the Global Village*, 107–123.

[10] Daniel Patte, *Ethics of Biblical Interpretation: A Reevaluation* (Louisville, Kentucky: Westminster/John Knox Press, 1995).

[11] Patte, *Ethics*, 17–18.

version of the feminist approach is offered as a prime example. Her critical remarks are representative of much feminist critique in general, and certainly capture something extremely important. At the same time, I do not think that her criticism always does justice to reality. For instance, in my opinion Schüssler Fiorenza ought to have taken account of those older forms of "engaged" exegesis, where it was realised that objectivity does not exist, instead of simply elaborating on the dichotomy between "objective" and "engaged" or "perspectival" research.

As for the critical task, my own reading of Rev 14:1–5 and of the female sexual imagery of the whole book of Revelation leads me to a critique that finds it virtually impossible to use this text in a feminist theology.[12] I then extensively studied both feminist and mainstream historical-critical interpretations of the analysed pericope. It was no surprise to observe that the traditional "morality of knowledge", as it was practised in this particular case, was so ignorant of the problems that become visible from a feminist perspective.[13]

However, I saw something else, too. Some representatives of mainstream exegesis recognised long ago the exclusion of women in Rev 14:4. The difference between my stance and traditional historical-critical exegesis did not lie in that observation. The crucial difference is rather that traditional exegesis is unable to view the androcentrism and the questionable attitude towards women in Revelation in a wider cultural setting. Due to this inability, mainstream exegesis leads either to frustration in front of the incomprehensible text, or to attempts to "explain" the text so as more or less to "explain away" its strangeness. Thus some would like to assume that the passage in question is a later gloss, whereby someone Other—the Gnostics, or a later ascetically-minded writer—is made responsible for an attitude that in a feminist analysis proves to be a very basic cultural model, one which would find its way into the church, Christian theology and the Western world quite apart from Gnostics and ascetics.[14]

I also observed—and I believe most of us who are familiar with exegetical works have noticed it—that many historical-critical scholars combine the ideal of a properly done, "objective" inquiry with

[12] Stenström, *Liberation or Backlash?* 65–110.
[13] Stenström, *Liberation or Backlash?* 120–49.
[14] For details, see my *Liberation or Backlash?* 123–41.

an aspiration to talk as a Christian theologian. It seems to be in the nature of many exegetical traditions that the scholar should as objectively and scientifically as possible uncover one or a few secured "then-meanings" in the texts, which are used as a basis for contemporary theology and preaching. In this way "objectivity" and Christian convictions are united.

I found several instances of exegetes trying to be accountable to the church and church-oriented common readers, who should be given an understandable and acceptable Bible. The question is whether these scholars really live up to the requirements of "the morality of knowledge", or rather whether, in trying to satisfy the Christian readers' need for a reasonable Bible, they betray their roles as historians who should expose the past in all its strangeness and oddity. The desire to make the biblical texts usable and acceptable for the common reader—which is conceived as a moral duty—hampers "moral criticism" and can also be an obstacle for consistent historical work.[15]

This understanding of biblical exegesis, which combines objective research with normative interpretation into a complex unity, does not I think find a place in the proposals for a new morality. Nor is the normative aspect of exegetical praxis always respected in anti-feminist exegetical rhetoric. Non-feminist scholars sometimes denigrate feminists as non-serious because we bring in value judgements in our work, but gladly accept Bultmann and Käsemann as serious scholars. Such conflict situations may have caused the critical and constructive work, both belonging to the exegete's professional ethics, to be discussed in terms of a dichotomy between objective and engaged or perspectival research. I doubt that we feminist exegetes should continue to use the same dichotomy.

Schüssler Fiorenza is among those who employ this dichotomy, and of the two opposite poles, objective vs. engaged scholarship, she tends to favour the latter. However, we should not forget that she also aspires to break the dichotomy; scholarly work ought not to overshadow the engaged interpretation, or vice versa. Schüssler Fiorenza is constantly putting new questions and speaking for the necessity of advancing novel theoretical models for producing knowledge. She also integrates classical methods, such as form and tradition history,

[15] Cf. Krister Stendahl's article "Biblical Theology, Contemporary", *IDB*, reprinted in *Reading in Global Village*, 67–106 with Stendahl's own comments, pp. 61–66.

in her feminist project. In the constructive proposal of *Rhetoric and Ethic*, she builds up the two-fold ethic sketched in "Decentering Biblical Scholarship". One thread in this ethic continues to be the kind of research we are used to label as "scientific" for its methodical, theoretical and intellectual strictness. The other thread is her concern for accountability and self-criticism; the individual scholar and the academic community must never cease to ask what values and human goals research is meant to advance.

This second thread in Schüssler Fiorenza's scholarly ethic is much the same as the second field I discuss in the present paper, and the one Räisänen took up in his lecture on "moral criticism".[16] It concerns the critical study and evaluation of the values expressed in the biblical texts, as well as of the interpretation of these texts throughout history. Such examination is necessarily based on ethical criteria. One asks whether the texts and interpretations express and have contributed to unacceptable values, e.g., antisemitism, or, if you prefer, how these have affected us women now, and our grandmothers. In his lecture, Räisänen also gave examples of traditional exegetes practising ethically based biblical criticism by, for instance, effective-historical surveys that illustrate how the saying on sinning against the Holy Spirit has nourished mental illness.[17]

I am convinced that even an exegete who does not apply a feminist approach, or one who is not personally affected by the way texts and interpretative traditions have furthered antisemitism, nevertheless ought to be aware of the consequences that the Bible and its history of interpretation have had in the real lives of many people. An exegete must be aware of his or her political role and the moral responsibility that comes with it. He or she must be consciously engaged in unravelling practices of injustice and oppression within his or her own discipline. Through one's scholarly efforts, one is obliged to contribute to the work for ethical ideals, be they justice, democracy or, as in Räisänen's project, the peaceful dialogue between people of different faiths.

Räisänen is right in pointing out that "moral criticism" has deep roots in the beginning of the exegetical discipline. As a child of

[16] Schüssler Fiorenza's second field includes Räisänen's "moral criticism", but also other tasks. See, e.g., her *Rhetoric and Ethic*, 193–198.

[17] Räisänen, "Etisk bibelkritik", 235–37; cf. idem, "Critics in Global Village", 24–25.

Enlightenment, historical-critical study of the Bible set off to expose and eradicate biblical texts that express fanaticism and intolerance. It was a means of liberating the scholar from what was experienced as oppression, namely the church's authority over faith and biblical interpretation.[18]

However, the Enlightenment was also the seedbed for the idea that the supreme exegetical value is value-free, objective research. As Schüssler Fiorenza maintains in her critical encounter with the tradition of historical-critical research, this ideal can, in some particular contexts, be emancipatory.[19] Räisänen's lecture described how this mode of *Sachkritik* for a number of reasons disappeared in the period between the two worldwars, to return more recently at the next paradigm shift when feminist critiques and other new scholarly trends questioned the objectivity of the historical-critical paradigm. Thus we see that an ideal which in one historical context is emancipatory, may turn conservative or even oppressive in another context.[20] There is a constant need of reformation, or, if you wish, revolution.

Räisänen has also provided examples of how an ethically alert biblical scholarship should be practised. His programme includes moral criticism of the Bible and its interpretations as well as a constructive project. The constructive project is a way of showing accountability and should meet high intellectual and scholarly standards. Among Räisänen's scholarly work, the prime example is his *Marcion, Muhammad and the Mahatma*.[21] The book aims at locating the scholar not so much in a church context or within the academy but in "the global village", that is, in the midst of our contemporary global and pluralistic society. Here Räisänen is realising the programme of his earlier book *Beyond New Testament Theology*.[22] The ethically responsible

[18] Räisänen tracks moral criticism down to Marcion, and further examples could be given from the history of biblical interpretation before the birth of historical-critical exegesis. See Räisänen, "Etisk bibelkritik", 234; cf. "Critics in Global Village", 20–23.

[19] I choose to refer here to Schüssler Fiorenza's article as it is published in Räisänen et al., *Bible in Global Village*. See also her "Decentering Biblical Scholarship", 107–8, 115.

[20] Schüssler Fiorenza, "Decentering Biblical Scholarship", 114–16.

[21] Heikki Räisänen, *Marcion, Muhammad and the Mahatma: Exegetical Perspectives on the Encounter of Cultures and Faiths* (London: SCM, 1997). See also the ten programmatic theses in "Etisk bibelkritik", 240–42.

[22] Heikki Räisänen, *Beyond New Testament Theology: A Story and a Programme* (London: SCM, 1990). In the second edition of the book (London: SCM, 2000), his programme is found on pp. 151–209.

study he advocates and exercises in *Marcion, Muhammad and the Mahatma* includes a measure of exegetical self-criticism. An important aim is to be in the service of peace between the contemporary religions, and to enhance sensitivity toward the positive value of non-Christian religions. As historians, exegetes can describe the encounters—both violent and peaceful—between different faiths in the past. Such information may improve our understanding of why things happened as they did, and thereby help us meet future challenges. The main bulk of the book is the attempt to read the Other's interpretation of the Bible in a compassionate and non-biased way. Marcion, Muhammed and Mahatma Gandhi (and a few others) are given a chance to be appreciated as they are, not as Arch Heretics, the Infidels, or Christians in Disguise. Räisänen allows their biblical interpretation to stand in their own right, without being measured according to Christian readings of the Bible. This is an exercise in, and a contribution to, dialogue and mutual understanding.

To this praise, I must add some critical reflections on Räisänen's programme for "moral criticism" and its practical application in *Marcion, Muhammad and the Mahatma.* Firstly, I have to say that the interpreter he depicts is a male. His study is not "In Memory of Her". It is not dedicated to Grandma, but aims at doing justice to Marcion, Muhammed and Mahatma Gandhi. These are all males; yet there are also marginalised women in the history of interpretation.

Furthermore, I would like to recall my earlier distinction between ideological criticism and ethical or moral criticism, which—from my feminist point of view—highlights some basic problems with "moral criticism" in Räisänen's sense.[23] The crucial thing here is the connection between ethics and politics. It is a telling fact that many ideological-critical exegetes employ the terms "politics" and "political" while addressing ethical issues in the Bible. Thus, for instance, Schüssler Fiorenza's *Rhetoric and Ethic* has the subtitle, *The Politics of Biblical Studies.* Schüssler Fiorenza argues that texts, interpretations as well as all forms of the oral and written outcome of professional exegetical study are rhetorical and therefore political acts—all this

[23] To be sure, Räisänen is well aware that his "moral criticism" lacks the critical analysis of power, but he seems not to regard it as problematic in the way I think it should be. Cf. Räisänen, "Etisk bibelkritik", 235, 240, and Schussler Fiorenza's critique of Räisänen in her "Defending the Center, Trivializing the Margins" in Räisänen et al., *Reading Bible in Global Village*, 29–48.

is oratory performed in the official sphere, in the *polis*. The aim of all these forms of public speech is to be effective, to persuade, to commend some practical models of behaviour while discarding others. With this goes responsibility for what the rhetorics does to people and the society. In her rhetorical analysis, Schüssler Fiorenza keeps reminding us of the question of power, as she asks who is speaking and whose interests are at stake. In this way the ethical and the political aspects are held together. As a feminist scholar I am worried whenever this tie seems broken.

In this respect, the examples Räisänen in his lecture gives of "moral criticism" leave me somewhat restless. There is an obvious risk that, in following that path, one cannot see the previous interpretations and one's own criticism in the framework of past and present power structures. Whether one's focus is on the individual or the collective, it is always human suffering that captuers one's interest.[24] Of course, such concern is in itself justified; but in effect it may cause the exegete to lose sight of the more difficult analysis of how oppression is related to group interests and power. This is probably why much of moral criticism is not so labelled, but only appears as the critical part of, for instance, post-colonial or feminist readings. Also Räisänen's *Marcion, Muhammad and the Mahatma* lacks analysis of power relations in the global village.

Here is an important project to continue, not for exegetes alone but in co-operation and in dialogue with feminists coming from other disciplines and working on various forms of power analysis. Some co-operation exists already, but much remains to be done. Even those who do not identify themselves as feminists should, in my opinion, be acquainted with some form of power analysis relevant in their own context, and define their "moral criticism" in relation to this.

In locating Räisänen's and his critics' positions—especially concerning the exegete's constructive role—on the hermeneutical and epistemological map, I find an article by Stephen Fowl[25] useful. Fowl's

[24] As examples, Räisänen mentions the Sachkritik of the early 1900's and the wirkungsgeschichtlich work of Ulrich Luz ("Etisk bibelkritik", 234–237). Some of the works Räisänen mentions in "Etisk bibelkritik" can include analysis of power, but this is not made quite clear. Räisänen even mentions more obviously political examples (post-colonial and feminist interpretation) in this article (pp. 227–228, 237–239); cf. his "Critics in Global Village", 18–22.

[25] Stephen Fowl, "The Ethics of Interpretation or What's Left Over After the

point of departure is that we now recognise that a text has many meanings. The very concept of "meaning" is difficult to define, and hence problematic to use. The question that interpreters have to pose, according to Fowl, is not how to attain the one "meaning" of the text, but "What particular interpretative interest should I adopt?"[26] In so asking, we approach the issue of our values and the rationale behind them.

The first position Fowl sketches is the "pluralistic" view. For a pluralist, a sufficient reason for doing something is that it is interesting. A pluralist is keen to create space in various milieus—universities, exegetical societies, academic press etc.—for as many diverging interpretative perspectives and methods as possible, so that others, too, might pursue what they for whatever reason find interesting. Pluralism is a goal in itself, but it must be actively created and supported. No one group or viewpoint can make claims to privilege of interpretation or knowledge.[27]

Another, in the present context more pertinent, position is what Fowl calls the "social responsibility position".[28] It shares with the feminist and liberationist exegetes the basic view that all interpretation, whether it is admitted or denied, is guided by interests and has a political role. An exegete who adopts this stance will actively take responsibility in the society for those who suffer or have suffered because of oppressive use of the Bible, and they motivate this with ethical and/or political principles. Here pluralism is not the only governing value. A desired goal may be "justice and well-being for all".[29] Certain ways of doing exegesis may be rejected on these premises as irreconcilable with social responsibility. No hermeneutical or epistemological privilege is accepted in this position, either.

Fowl defines himself as post-modern, and thereby criticises the social responsibility option on two crucial points.[30] First, this position implies that everybody is able to recognise oneself as a full member

Elimination of Meaning", in D.J.A. Clines, S.E. Fowl and S.E. Porter (eds.), *The Bible in Three Dimensions: Essays in Celebration of Forty Years of Biblical Studies in the University of Sheffield* (JSOTSup 87; Sheffield: Sheffield Academic Press, 1990) 379–98.

[26] Fowl, "Ethics of Interpretation", 388.

[27] Fowl, "Ethics of Interpretation", 389–390.

[28] Fowl, "Ethics of Interpretation", 391–92.

[29] Fowl, "Ethics of Interpretation", 391. In this formulation, Fowl quotes Schüssler Fiorenza, "Decentering Biblical Scholarship", 123.

[30] Fowl, "Ethics of Interpretation", 394.

of a global *polis*, toward which one has responsibility. Fowl doubts that the real world meets this ideal, so he is at least prepared for a more sophisticated analysis of power structures. Second, he holds that it is nowadays very hard to get all people united in a common understanding of "justice" or how "justice and well-being for all" can be realised. In a post-modern world, it is impossible to maintain that consensus on values which the social responsibility position presupposes.

Fowl's own choice, which he finds reasonable in a post-modern world, is a "communal or collective position."[31] The crucial insight in this position is that one has to take moral and political responsibility and, at the same time, to withhold universally valid definitions of, e.g., "justice". The choices one makes are manifested in one's belonging to a specific group, which is historically given and shaped and whose members share common convictions as to basic values, goals and means. In its own historical context, the community pronounces its understanding of justice and its exegetical practice for realising that justice. One is not a member of a global *polis*. Instead, communality is lived out in a "provisionally specified *polis* to which its life and practices are directed, to which its members are responsible by virtue of their communal commitments."[32] Obviously this position does not reckon with a privileged standpoint.

It is vital, according to Fowl, for such communities to live in a continuing dialogue with other groups in understanding and practising justice. "Pluralistic" institutions can be forums for such dialogue.[33] I am inclined to accept Fowl's position, and I readily admit the necessity of pluralistic institutions. These are not really alternative options, but rather complement each other in that striving for pluralism can mean striving for meeting-places and dialogues—provided that the power relations in the institutions in practice, for all talk of pluralism, do not silence or neglect the conflicting voices.

Fowl considers Schüssler Fiorenza's article "Decentering Biblical Scholarship" a representative of the "social responsibility position".[34] To anyone familiar with the main bulk of her feminist production, where she appears to be a standpoint feminist, this comes as

[31] Fowl, "Ethics of Interpretation", 395–97.
[32] Fowl, "Ethics of Interpretation", 395.
[33] Fowl, "Ethics of Interpretation", 396–97.
[34] Fowl, "Ethics of Interpretation", 391.

a surprise. I think, however, that precisely in this rhetorical situation, intent on persuading the whole of SBL and not a specific feminist or liberation-theologically minded audience, she had to adopt a more general and vague mode of speech. Schüssler Fiorenza's feminist and liberationist reading of Revelation[35]—particularly when interpreted in light of her feminist work—gives reason to identify a "standpoint" position in addition to the options described by Fowl.[36] A similar position is taken by the liberation theologian Pablo Richard.[37] In Schüssler Fiorenza's and Richard's interpretation of Revelation, "women's experience" or more generally "the experiences of the oppressed" are elevated to a standpoint from which the world is interpreted and transformed. The world-view that opens from this vantage point must be given some form of privilege before that of the rich and powerful ones.[38] Here, in the underside of history, are also found the interests that should govern the practice of interpretation. If Schüssler Fiorenza were asked what she means by "justice", I assume she would say that it is justice as it appears from the point of view of the oppressed.

Tina Pippin, another interpreter of Revelation,[39] defines herself as a post-modern feminist.[40] Therefore she provides an interesting point of comparison to standpoint feminism.[41] The two positions clearly

---

[35] See Elisabeth Schüssler Fiorenza, *Revelation: Vision of A Just World* (Proclamation Commentaries; Minneapolis: Fortress Press, 1991). My *Liberation or Backlash?*, 226–63, deals with Schüssler Fiorenza's reading of Rev especially as it appears in this book.

[36] Schüssler Fiorenza does not use "standpoint feminist" or the like as a self-description in her *Vision of A Just World*, but the position seems basic to her work. The standpoint feminist position is more clearly pronounced in her article, "Text and Reality—Reality as Text: The Problems of Feminist Historical and Social Reconstruction Based on Texts", *ST* 43, 19–34, esp. p. 19, and eadem, *But She Said: Feminist Practices of Biblical Interpretation* (Boston: Beacon Press, 1992) 88–92.

[37] Consult my *Liberation or Backlash?*, 158–73, for an exposition of Pablo Richard, *Apocalypse*: *The People's Commentary to the Book of Revelation* (The Bible and Liberation Series: Maryknoll, New York: Orbis Books, 1995).

[38] See, for instance, Schüssler Fiorenza, *Vision of A Just World*, 126, for a lucid example, as well as Richard, *People's Commentary*, 3.

[39] My *Liberation or Backlash?*, 264–85, examines Pippin's studies on Revelation, mainly in her *Death and Desire: The Rhetoric of Gender in the Apocalypse* (Literary Currents in Biblical Interpretation; Louisville, Kentucky: Westminster/John Knox Press, 1992). I was not able to include a discussion on her *Apocalyptic Bodies: The Biblical End of the World in Text and Image* (London and New York: Routledge, 1999).

[40] *Death and Desire*, 46.

[41] I cannot here enter into a detailed dicussion on these two positions or on "post-modernity". For definitions and discussion, see Sandra Harding, *The Science Question in Feminism* (Itaca, New York: Cornell University Press, 1986); Anne-Louise

relate to the question of the exegete's ethical task and political accountability. For the present discussion, it is relevant to note that the theoretical presuppositions for the concept of a specific "women's standpoint" (or "feminist standpoint") have been heavily questioned in recent years. Yet the various forms of standpoint feminism have a strong political appeal that the post-modern position may lack. Therefore, in my opinion, feminist exegesis that includes ethical criticism and aims to be politically relevant, must learn from those theorists and theologians who try to find viable ways between post-modern and standpoint feminism.

One of these mediating scholars is Sheila Greeve Davaney, whose ideas are to some extent akin to Fowl's.[42] Davaney wishes to formulate a feminist theology without postulating the essentialist conception of womanhood and women's experience that is often dangerously near at hand in feminist theologies. She also takes seriously that globally valid and universally accepted values cannot be taken for granted.[43] At the same time, she would not give up the possibility of formulating norms and values for a feminist theological praxis in society:

> ... feminist theologians need to return to women's experience, selfhood and identity, but in historicist terms. This means, to begin with, that we must elaborate notions of subjectivity that recognize the contextual, traditioned and hence concrete and particular character of our identity. In such an approach human subjectivity is a historical product, emerging within and dependent on the complex possibilities and limitations that have emerged within particular strands of history ...[44]

Here we have real women and men, who can only be understood in their particular, concrete historical contexts and the traditions that shape these contexts. These contexts and traditions are complex and changing, as places where negotiations and conflicts over power, meaning and values take place. This is also where concrete individuals

Eriksson, *The Meaning of Gender in Theology: Problems and Possibilities* (AUU, Uppsala Women's Studies A: Women in Religion 6; Uppsala, 1995); Rebecca S. Chopp and Sheila Greeve Davaney (eds.), *Horizons in Feminist Theology: Identity, Tradition and Norms* (Minneapolis: Fortress Press, 1997).

[42] Sheila Greeve Davaney, "Continuing the Story, But Departing the Text. A Historicist Interpretation of Feminist Norms in Theology", in Chopp and Davaney (eds.), *Horizons*, 198–214.

[43] Davaney, "Continuing the Story", 198–208.

[44] Davaney, "Continuing the Story", 209.

are being shaped, and take part in creating their contexts and traditions. Humans do not live in closed, static groups, but in open and integrating communities. In Davaney's model texts and interpretations are tried, not against essentially understood traditions, God's will or universal values, but against their concrete effects on the lives of women and men amidst a reality that is not simply good or bad but where we can participate in a continuous change of human conditions in history.[45]

I believe that such a model, in a refined form, can serve as a matrix for future work in the field of ethical biblical criticism. It will also be relevant to the historical study of the biblical documents themselves, since these are historical data. Thus, for instance, it is possible to view the female and sexual imagery of Revelation as impossible and irreconcilable with a vision of justice in one particular historical community, and yet not so in another community which also strives for justice.

Where can Räisänen's programme be located on the hermeneutical and epistemological map sketched above? I would think it is more or less representative of the "social responsibility position". While he does subscribe to the description of our time as "post-modern", Räisänen seems not to draw the full consequences of this. He seems to believe that there are some "basic, generally human principles."[46] The possibility of assuming such principles is precisely the problem exposed by the post-modern situation that Räisänen takes as his context. In discussion on ethical biblical criticism, loaded concepts such as "justice", "oppression" and "a good life" are used as if we all were agreed what these stand for—and the question today is whether we in fact agree.[47] But let me add that this critique in no lesser degree pertains to a theorist like Schüssler Fiorenza. She calls Revelation a vision of a "just world" but does not indicate, according to which feminist understanding of justice the world depicted at the end of

---

[45] Davaney, "Continuing the Story", 209–13.

[46] Räisänen, "Etisk bibelkritik", 240.

[47] In his review, "The Bible: Witness or Warrant: Reflections on Daniel Patte's *Ethics of Biblical Interpretation*", *BTB* 1996, 82–87, Bruce Malina criticises Patte for using vague concepts that are never definied. Part of the criticism levelled at Patte falls off the mark, since he does explain which ethical traditions guide him, mentioning above all Levinas; but this is done very briefly. See Patte, *Ethics*, 13–16. On the whole, Malina's review is very rude and indifferent to what Patte basically is trying to say, but it certainly illustrates the differences between various exegetical schools.

Revelation can be called just, or how she thinks values like "justice" can be defined or claimed today.

To summarise, I contend that future reflections on the ethical dimensions of interpretative practices, and on the ethical criticism of biblical texts and interpretations, must be exercised in a much closer dialogue with scholars of ethics and others who ask, e.g., how "justice" is to be understood and on what premises, if any, we may discuss "moral values" in a time of pluralism. Fowl's "communal collective position" and Sheila Greeve Davaney's attempts at finding a middle way between post-modern and standpoint feminism are useful contributions that deserve to be developed further. The task for feminist exegetes is to refine the concepts used. Feminist ethics today is such a vast field that I cannot quite see how a feminist scholar is able to talk about an ethical probing of texts and interpretations without saying which ethical tradition is meant.[48] In any case this will be

[48] In a recent Swedish dissertation, *Först när vi får ansikten—ett flerkulturellt samtal om feminism, etik och teologi* (Lund Studies in Ethics and Theology 9; Stockholm: Atlas Akademi, 1999), Karin Sporre deals with several concepts used by feminist theologians and scholars of ethics. Strikingly, none of the terms in Schüssler Fiorenza's book title *Revelation: Vision of A Just World* is unanimously defined even by feminist scholars. The conventional name of the last book in the New Testament canon is loaded with an extraordinary authority claim, which is discarded by an influential theological tradition (young Luther, for one). In like manner, every word of the sub-title is controversial. Karin Sporre describes various understandings of "vision". While Chung Hyun Kung, a Korean scholar now working in the USA, has an optimistic vision of justice as a possible or likely future, the womanist Katie Cannon is rather more pessimistic about the realisation of her vision. (Sporre, Ansikten, 238–52, 332–45.) "Justice" is another diffuse term. Schüssler Fiorenza does distinguish between "ethics of care" and "ethics of justice" and prefers the latter, but she does not indicate in her book which of the feminist theories of justice the vision of Revelation might match. Another feminist liberation theologian, Karen Lebacqz, in her entry "Justice" in Letty M. Russell & J. Shannon Clarkson (eds.), *Dictionary of Feminist Theologies* (Louisville: WJKP, 1996) 158–59, underscores that injustice is not merely a matter of personal relations and social structures, but manifests itself in "language, myth and narrative". This is also Schüssler Fiorenza's concern—but what can a "myth" or "narrative" about the victory over the Great Whore in Revelation possibly have to do with justice, considering everything we know of the connection between prostitution, poverty and oppression of women?

Finally, "world" and "earth" can be conceived in various ways which lead feminist theologians to diverging views of Revelation and apocalypticism in general. While Schüssler Fiorenza seems to think of "the world" as a term for the oppressive structures of the present order of things that must perish, a more ecofeminististally oriented theologian, like Rosemary Radford Ruether in her book *Gaia and God: An Ecofeminist Theology of Earth Healing* (San Francisco: HarperCollins, 1992) would rather see it as a reference to creation and material reality. On this understanding, longing for "a new earth" appears a dangerous, dualistic denial of the world.

necessary, if we wish to move beyond the most elemental recognition that the Bible and its interpretative history has produced many bad things, and if we really intend to stop reproducing such things.

If we admit that visions, too, are situated in an historical context so as to be provisional and subject to change, then it will not be necessary to "save" a biblical text such as Revelation for all those who now suffer oppression. We are freed to recognise that the text which Käsemann some half a century ago could read as an antidote to totalitarian regimes, and which in the 1980's inspired the anti-apartheid movement in South Africa, can no longer be a source of inspiration for Swedish feminist Christians in the beginning of the 21st century.

III

As I am now *(r)eading the Bible in the Global Village*, I find that many of the topics of my earlier lecture recur in the hot debate between Heikki Räisänen and Elisabeth Schüssler Fiorenza. Again, the question surfaces as to whether historical-critical analysis can ally "liberationist readings" (thus Räisänen) or not (thus Schüssler Fiorenza). Also, the question is raised whether the call for a more ethically aware exegetical work takes up something that was there in the beginning of modern biblical study but was lost (Räisänen), or whether the challenge from the margins really means a radical shift of paradigm (Schüssler Fiorenza).

In light of the debate, my suggestion above that Sheila Greeve Davaney's model be applied to analyse how exegetical research traditions and individual scholars shape their identity seems even more urgent. Such a project might help us transcend the rather static constructions of 'us and them', which Schüssler Fiorenza in particular tends to employ. At the same time, it should include an analysis of power structures which takes seriously, but need not accept *a priori* the details of Schüssler Fiorenza's critique of Räisänen.

Personally, I would like to take another angle to this debate. Schüssler Fiorenza's over-simplified contrast between her—our—identity and The Other follows the classical scheme, only this time The Other is located in the centre, not the periphery. I have tried to show above that the issue of values vs. objectivity, and engagement vs. history writing, is far more complex than that. Moreover, such simple contrasts fail to do justice to traditional biblical scholarship. In my view, the disagreement between Schüssler Fiorenza and Räisänen actually concerns another matter.

Räisänen may indeed have a point in his overview of the history of biblical research, as he connects the moral criticism of the early 1900's to that of our day. In my study of Revelation 14:1–5, I often felt a kind of relief when reading those earlier exegetes who let the text stand as it is, strange and alien to us, and do not try to make it acceptable for us at all costs. I am also convinced that the debate would have been more interesting if Schüssler Fiorenza had taken issue with older, theologically and politically engaged exegetes instead of positioning herself against a lightly caricatured "objective" scholar. I probably differ from both Schüssler Fiorenza and Räisänen in contending that feminist exegetes should acknowledge their comradeship with those older male scholars who already knew that there is no pure objectivity. This recognition would hardly render the feminist challenge less significant. It would only make clearer that the difference between feminist and malestream exegesis is not primarily that between a "new" value-based engagement and an "old" value-free scholarship. It would then appear that the difficulty in traditional biblical scholarship is not that exegetes have given up the ideal of objectivity and started mixing science with political engagement. Also, it would become clear, as also Schüssler Fiorenza emphasises, that feminist exegetes demand not less, but *more* and *better* historical research.

Hence my hypothesis: the real problem for the historical-critical "normal scholarship" is that *women* now practise it from a feminist perspective: "wrong" people take the right to do it on their own premises. The basic issue, thus, concerns power structures and inherited thought models rather than objectivity vs. values. In this light, we would see how blind even the enlightened and engaged have been for the truly difficult challenges. The necessity of the challenges from the margins appears all the more clearly, if we are serious about demanding responsible and self-conscious biblical scholarship.

Saying this, and placing myself as a female and feminist exegete in the dangerous margins, I am aware that many women and men who do not share the privileges I have as a white, Western academic would see in me the same blindness, and a compassion that does not really yield the good things in which I believe. Am I really able, for instance in criticising the female and sexual imagery in Revelation, to speak for women from other continents living in poverty? Or for that matter, how can a white Western academic, female or male, give a voice to the victims of the colonisation? So I stop here, and leave it for others to articulate that protest, and to teach me more about acting in responsible way as both a marginal and a privileged scholar.

Finally, I want to thank Heikki on his sixtieth birthday for the critical stimulus to think further and more profoundly about things that are our ultimate concerns. After all, the important thing is not that we should always agree with each other, but rather that we are concerned for the same things. And I think that we are. Therefore, just as I do not expect that the last word of this article will be my final word in these issues, I do look forward to continuing the dialogue with Heikki Räisänen.

POSTCOLONIAL THEORY AND BIBLICAL STUDIES

R.S. Sugirtharajah

We can't get nowhere until we settle accounts with history.

Earl Lovelace

This paper will have three parts. First, I will try to spell out what postcolonialism is about, and outline some of its theoretical and praxiological intentions and assumptions. Secondly, I will deal with the applicability of postcolonialism to biblical studies; and in the concluding part I will try to answer some of the questions constantly asked about postcolonialism, and end with my own cautionary support to the theory.

Briefly, let me try to spell out what postcolonialism is about. At the outset, I must admit that the task is not an easy one given the limited space, and, more importantly, because of the definitional ambiguity that surrounds the notion of postcolonialism.[1] To begin with, there is reluctance and shyness among the theorists to spell out the purpose and parameters of the discourse, electing to be freelance and thus making vagueness a cardinal virtue. Each scholar, depending on his or her academic speciality, subject status, and institutional connection, has come up with a different set of definitions, examples and emphases. Then there is the vexed issue of the positioning of the hapless hyphen. It has caused constant hermeneutical squabbles among the practitioners and their critics. In its hyphenated

[1] Recently, there have been a number of introductory texts that strive to wrestle with the aim and ambit of the discourse: A. Loomba, *Colonialism/Postcolonialism* (London: Routledge, 1998); L. Gandhi, *Postcolonial Theory: A Critical Introduction* (Edinburgh: Edinburgh University Press, 1998); B. Moore-Gilbert, *Postcolonial Theory: Contexts, Practices, Politics* (London: Verso, 1997); B. Ashcroft, G. Griffiths and H. Tiffin, *Key Concepts in Post-Colonial Studies* (London: Routledge, 1998); B. Moore-Gilbert, G. Stanton and W. Maley, *Postcolonial Criticism* (London: Longman, 1997); P. Childs and P. Williams, *An Inroduction to Post-Colonial Theory* (London: Prentice Hall, 1997); A. Quayson, *Postcolonialism: Theory, Practice or Process* (Cambridge: Polity Press, 2000); H. Schwarz and S. Ray (eds.), *A Companion to Postcolonial Studies* (Oxford: Blackwell Publishers, 2000); J. McLeod, *Beginning Postcolonialism* (Manchester: Manchester University Press, 2000).

form, post-colonialism, does it mark the end of colonization? Or the unseparated term, postcolonialism, does it indicate the continued messy and complicated history colonialism left in its awake? Then the whole discourse is torn between its use of mutually incompatible critical categories such as Marxism and poststructuralism. Added to this is the constant changing of frames of reference within the field.

Streams of Postcolonialism

There are three streams of postcolonialism at work. The first characterizes the notion of invasion and control; the second places enormous investment in recovering the cultural soul; and the third stresses mutual interdependence and transformation.

The first stream is about textual practices and resistance to colonial supremacy and management of other peoples' lives, territories and cultures. The focus of the discourse here is to expose colonial control and domination, with a view to gaining eventual independence and liberation. There are essayists, cultural critics and political activists ranging from Trinidadian C.L. James to Martiniquan Aime Cesaire, to Sri-Lankan Ananda Coomaraswamy, whose textual input is directed towards such a task. Here the hermeneutical engagement is locked into a battle between two unequal homogeneous entities—the invader and the occupied. Ironically, the debate is shaped by the language of resistance, and the epistemological assumptions of the occupier who supplied and informed anticolonial attitudes to class, culture, gender, subjectivity, and so forth.

The second stream concentrates on recovering the "cultural soul" from the intellectual and cultural grip of the master. Here we see two ploys at work. One is bent on recouping the pure essence of the native soul and culture which is momentarily debased and disgraced; the other is engaged in exposing the wiles of the master and the pitfalls of his claims to preeminence. The former is espoused by, among others, Ananda Coomaraswamy who emphasises the immense potentiality and perennial usefulness of indigenous cultural energies. The latter is exemplified by Fanon and Memmi whose distinguished work exposes the illegitimacies of the master culture. Both camps believe in the spiritual and theological superiority of African and Asian cultures which were undermined by the current Western supremacy. They tend to rely on the essentialist notions of a civilized native soul, and uncontaminated indigenous cultures, and thrived on utilizing polarizing categories.[2]

The third stream is about mutual interdependence and transformation. The emphasis here is on the construction of an identity based on the intertwined histories of the coloniser and the colonised. Its aim is to go beyond totalisms, essentialisms and dichotomies, and transcend the modernist notion of assimilating the marginalised and the minorities into one monolithic cultural whole. The key words here are hybridity and liminality, which denote an in-between-space. It is a space where one is equally committed and disturbed by the colonised and the colonizing cultures. In Homi Bhabha's words, it is the "Third Space"[3] which emerges from an analytical scrutiny of diverse cultures rather than from integrating them.

Though chronologically these streams emerge out of different contexts, they are neither linear nor monolithic; they sit side by side and interact constantly. More importantly, the protagonists, too, cannot be boxed into neat wholes.

Historical Background

The arrival of postcolonial discourse on the theoretical scene is crucial. Its advent was facilitated by three key events which occurred more or less simultaneously—the failure of the socialist experiment as practised in the Soviet bureaucracy; the rise of global capitalism and the market economy which resulted in the alteration of metropolitan and village economies; and the loss of political momentum among the Third World countries who covenanted to create a Non-Aligned movement in Bandung. Utilizing the space offered by the Western academy in the 80s, diasporic intellectuals of Third World origin reproblematized the understanding of colonialism formulated both by colonialists and nationalists. Though the critique emerged from different disciplinary needs, postcolonialism provided an interventionary impulse. And the text that played the most important part in opening up the debate and making the issue visible was Edward Said's *Orientalism*, published in 1978.

---

[2] For an introduction to and critique of the authors mentioned here, refer to one of the readers mentioned in n. 1 above.

[3] H.K. Bhabha, *The Location of Culture* (London: Routledge, 1994) 36–39, 218.

In spite of all these ambiguities, postcolonialism is a serviceable category because it conveys the historical phenomenon of European subjugation and colonialism and its attendant features, namely the rearrangement of power and the inter-mix of cultures within particular geographical locations. It is a convenient tool to unmask the past textual production of colonialism and to dislodge its legitimizing strategies. Positively, it provides a location for other voices, histories and experiences to be heard. The category is also useful in creating awareness of the colonial legacy as it continues to maintain a hold on people, communities and culture. It is also useful in signifying changing relations among these people, cultures, and communities in the postmodern world.

What postcolonial theory does is to offer a space for the once-colonised. It is an interpretative act of the descendants of those once subjugated. In effect it means a resurrection of the marginal, the indigene and the subaltern. It means engaging with the mass of knowledge which is produced on their behalf and which is in the domain of Euro-American interpretation. It is an act of reclamation, redemption and reaffirmation against the past colonial and current neo-colonising tendencies which continue to exert influence even after territorial and political independence has been accomplished. It is a tactic and a practice. It means finding ways of operating under a set of arduous and difficult conditions which jeopardise and dehumanise people.

Postcolonialism and Biblical Studies

Applied to biblical studies,[4] postcolonial criticism hopes to do the following:

First, scrutiny of biblical narratives for their colonial involvement. The Bible as a collection of documents which came out of various imperial contexts—Egyptian, Persian, Assyrian, Hellenistic and Roman—or were produced under courtly supervision of Davidic and Solomonic dynasties, needs to be reinvestigated again. It will recon-

[4] For recent attempts, see *Semeia* 75 (1996): "Postcolonialism and Scriptural Reading"; R. Sugirtharajah, *The Postcolonial Bible* (Sheffield: Sheffield Academic Press, 1998); idem, *Asian Biblical Hermeneutics and Postcolonialism: Contesting the Interpretations* (Sheffield: Sheffield Academic Press, 1999).

sider the biblical narratives, not as a series of divinely guided incidents or supernatural reports about divine-human encounters, but as emanating from colonial contacts. It will revalue the colonial ideology, stigmatization and negative portrayals embedded in the content, plot and characterization. It will scour the biblical pages for how colonial intentions and assumptions informed and influenced the production of the texts. It will attempt to resurrect lost voices and causes which are distorted or silenced in the canonized text.

The second task of postcolonial criticism is to engage in a reconstructive reading which will reread biblical texts from the perspective of postcolonial concerns such as liberation struggles of the past and present; it will be sensitive to subaltern and feminine elements embedded in the texts; it will interact with and reflect on postcolonial circumstances such as hybridity, fragmentation, deterritorialization, and/or hyphenated, double or multiple identities.[5]

The task of postcolonial criticism is to interrogate both colonial and metropolitan interpretations to draw attention to the inescapable effects of colonization and colonial ideals on interpretative works such as commentarial writings and historical and administrative records which helped to (re)inscribe the notion of a mystical, irrational, stagnant Orient pitched against a progressive, rational and secular Occident. It will also investigate interpretations which contested colonial interests and concerns. It will bring to the fore how the invadees, often caricatured as abused victims or grateful beneficiaries, transcended these images and wrested interpretation from the invaders, starting a process of self-discovery, appropriation and subversion.

Subjecting the Christian Bible to a postcolonial gaze is not in order to make the texts come alive and provide solace and comfort to those devout (in some case not so devout) readers who also have social and political perceptiveness. At a time when sacred texts may not be the only place to look for answers to abstract or existential problems, the purpose of postcolonial reading is not to invest texts with properties which no longer have relevance to our context, or with excessive and exclusive theological claims which invalidate other claims. It seeks to puncture the Christian Bible's Western protection

[5] For examples of diasporic hermeneutics, see F.F. Segovia (ed.), *Interpreting Beyond Borders* (Sheffield: Sheffield Academic Press, 2000).

and pretensions, and to help reposition it in relation to its oriental roots and Eastern heritage. The aim is not to rediscover the biblical texts as an alternative, or to search in its pages for a better world as a way of coping with the terrors of the colonial aftermath. The Bible is approached not for its intrinsic authoritativeness or distinctiveness, but because of the thematic presuppositions of postcolonialism, which are influenced by the cultural and psychological effects triggered by colonialism.

Postcolonialism's critical procedure is an amalgam of different methods ranging from the now unfashionable form-criticism to contemporary literary methods. It is interdisciplinary in nature and pluralistic in its outlook. It is an avenue of inquiry than a homogeneous project. One of the significant aspects of postcolonialism is its theoretical and intellectual catholicism. It thrives on inclusiveness, and it is attracted to all kinds of tools and disciplinary fields, as long as they probe injustices, produce new knowledge which problematises well-entrenched positions, and enhances the lives of the marginalised. Any theoretical work that straddles and finds hermeneutical home in different disciplines, is bound to suffer from certain eclectic theoretical discrimination. Such a selective bias, though unsafe, sometimes is necessary in order to press on with it for the sake of the task at hand.

Some Constantly asked Questions

Postmodernism and Postcolonialism—Are they same?

Postmodernism and postcolonialism embody an important impulse, an impulse to intervene and interrogate accepted knowledges, and to destabilize their complacencies. But what distinguishes postcolonialism from typically postmodern discourse is postmodernism's scepticism of history, its implicit privileging of present Western cultural norms, and its lack of any political agenda.

Unlike postmodernism which sees the end of grand narratives, postcolonialism views liberation as a meta story which still has to play out its full potential. Modernity itself is often regarded by postmodernists as an anachronism, but postcolonialism sees the less perverted forms of modernization as a very appealing and applicable option for Third World people, particularly as a vehicle of economic liberation. In its veneration of plurality, and its fear of replicating the modernistic sin of prescriptive and hegemonic tendencies, postmodernism is shy of making hard ethical and moral decisions. By contrast, postcolonial criticism argues for ethical practice even though it is suspicious of its universal applicability. Here I agree with Ato Quayson's plea for a proactive ethical involvement, notwithstanding the risk and danger involved in such an enterprise:

> Recognizing that there is much destitution, poverty and sheer despair in the world, it seems to me increasingly imperative that the risk of appearing prescriptive is worth taking if one is not to surrender completely to a debilitating anomie brought on by the apprehension of persistent social tragedies. Those who lose their limbs to landmines, are displaced through refugee crises or merely subsist in the intermittent but regularly frustrated hope that the world can become a better place, cannot wait for complete moral certitude before they take action to improve their existence. It is partly in the implicit (and often real) alliance with those who, to appropriate a phrase from Julian Murphet, "keep running all the time simply to keep pace with events" that we ought to take courage to make ethical judgements even in the full knowledge that we may be proved wrong. To this larger picture, and in service of this larger affirmation we ought to commit our critical enterprises.[6]

Is it Right to Subject Past Documents to the Current Notions of Racism, Sexism etc.?

Historians are often impatient if 20th century concerns are imported into ancient materials. Any attempt to read past documents from postcolonial and feminist perspectives are frowned upon. The real question is, as Gayatri Spivak puts it, "why structures of patriarchal dominations should be unquestionably recorded." She goes on to say that "historical sanctions for collective action toward social justice can only be developed if people outside of the discipline question the standards of 'objectivity' preserved as such by the hegemonic tradition."[7]

Another point is that, if these documents are historical phenomenon, then we should not claim any contemporary relevance for them be it the Bible or Shakespearan texts, and should leave them

[6] Quayson, *Postcolonialism: Theory, Practice or Process*, 155.
[7] G.C. Spivak, *A Critique of Postcolonial Reason: Toward a History of Vanishing Present* (Cambridge, MA: Harvard University Press, 1999) 301.

at that. More to the point, we revisit these texts not to be judgmental but to readjust our perceptions and prejudices and inform our present knowledge which often accepts the discriminatory practices as the norm.

Is Everything Postcolonial?

Increasingly one often hears today that, since most of the countries have gone through some kind of colonial experience, everything is postcolonial. There is a tendency to smooth out the different colonial experiences. Thus, 19th century British imperialists are equated with the 10th century Mongols who had the largest land empire, and the American invasion of Grenada is treated as equal to that of the Indonesian occupation of East Timor. It is this kind of thinking which would like to neutralize British colonialism in Hong Kong as a benevolent intrusion, and Chinese nationalism as native backwardness. Such a position, according to Rey Chow, flattens out past injustices and plays into the hands of global capitalism which views the past injustices as irksome and dispensable. For some postcolonials, whom Chow terms as postmodern hybridites, there is not much difference between the new globalism and cosmopolitanism. Such claims blur and obliterate complex histories, emphasizing on the "post" and reading the "post" as "after" and "over with" rather than putting the emphasis on the colonial. The significance of the post is not "after", rather it designates a space of cultural contest and change. Postcolonialism is not about a particular epoch, rather, it is about a set of measures undertaken by critics to infuse a new sense of destiny.[8]

Who Can Engage in Postcolonial Discourse?

There are two types of stories one hears. One is perpetuated by the former colonised who insist on the experience of oppression as a vital ingredient for holding on to a particular theoretical position. Their routine argument—"you don't know what it is like, because it never happened to you, and therefore you have no right to speak"—does not give room for a sober assessment. The colonial archives record instances of a missionary or a colonial civil servant, at the annoyance of the establishment, taking up the cause of the victims.

[8] R. Chow, *Ethics After Idealism: Theory—Culture—Ethnicity—Reading* (Bloomington: Indiana University Press, 1998) 155–56.

There are a number of righteous non-Jews, and anti-apartheid non-blacks who spoke out for what was right, irrespective of whoever they were. It will be lamentable if one resorts to personal experience as a hermeneutical trump card. In that case, one would have to be a Jew to resist anti-Semitism, a gay to support homosexual rights, and poor in order to advocate welfare reforms. If one extends this to its logical conclusion, then only animals could do animal theology and only trees could talk about deforestation. Personal experience, cultural affinities, and ideological closeness, important though they are, are poor surrogates for understanding and accountability in hermeneutics. Sensing and feeling what is right, is sufficient. One doesn't have to have lived it. To espouse a cause or plead for something because it concerns only you is far less impressive than championing it simply because it is fair.

The second story comes from mainstream intellectuals who wish to restrict the discipline to the former colonial victims, and to declare it as a no go area for First World people. This is a skilful way of restricting the discipline and ghettoising it. Segregation and setting up "we" against "them" are part of the colonial grand design. The point of postcolonial study is not only to question the unfairness meted out to certain groups of people and to their histories and cultures, but to study the involvement and incorporation of European and American institutional processes which facilitated, legitimatized and perpetuated such inequalities. The Chinese cultural critic Phebe Shih Chao, basing her argument on Fanon, charts a similar process which the coloniser, too, undergoes. The colonised passes through stages, from imitation of the master, to the desire to return to his or her roots, through to being an awakener of his or her people. Similarly, the coloniser, in his turn, moves from being a willing participant in colonialism, to a feeling of remorse, and finally to seeking to rectify past misdeeds and misperceptions. These processes may not coincide, and need not go hand in hand. Since both the colonised and the coloniser are inextricably involved, and have stake in unravelling race, gender and ethnicity, the whole exercise becomes pedagogically and critically ineffective if the field is restricted to one group of people.[9]

---

[9] P.S. Chao, "Reading The Letter in a Postcolonial World", in M. Bernstein and G. Studlar (eds.), *Visions of the East: Orientalism in Film* (London: I.B. Tauris Publishers, 1997) 292–93.

Comments, Concerns, Cautions

Like it or lump it, postcolonialism as a critical category will continue to exercise influence at least for some time to come, both in academic discourse and in general usage, since it signals an important new starting point and a significant shift. In its name significant work has already been done. The marginals and the natives have been rescued without fantasising and investing them with a venerable status; colonial configurations have been unmasked; established ideas and conventional discourse about representations set in place by colonialism have been dislodged. But this does not mean that everything is fine and that better days are here. The temptation is to be mesmerised by the recent kudos accorded by the academy, and to turn gamekeeper and superintend and police other discourses including the minority one. What is important is to employ postcolonial apparatus with caution and suspicion, and use it as an oppositional tool.

Anti-colonial reading is not new. It has gone on whenever a native put quill pen to paper to contest the production of knowledge by the invading power. Postcoloniality begins when subjects find themselves thinking and acting in certain ways. What is distinctive about the current enterprise, however, is that it is not locked into the colonial paradigm where the colonialists set the ground rules, but more importantly it concedes the complexity of contact between the invader and the invadees. It goes beyond the binary notions of colonised and coloniser and lays weighty emphasis on critical exchanges and mutual transformation between the two. Postcolonialism does not mean that the colonised are innocent, generous and principled, whereas the former colonisers, and now the neo-colonisers, are all innately culpable, greedy and responsible for all social evils. Such a notion is not only an inverted form of colonialism but it also absolves the Third World elite of their patriarchal and vassalising tendencies. What the current postcolonialism tries to do is to emphasise that this relationship between the ruler and the ruled is complex, full of cross-trading and mutual appropriation and confrontation.

Some of the hermeneutical and praxiological agenda that postcolonialism seeks to pursue coincide with other liberative movements such as feminism, etc. Though there is a shared intellectual and vocational mission, postcolonialism differs significantly from these critical undertakings in two ways. It combats the West's textualizing defamation of the colonised, and redresses cultural and political catastrophes caused by Western civilization. The other difference is that, unlike the dominant theoretical categories, postcolonialism did not begin its career as an answer to the West's intellectual and psychological dilemmas, but as meeting the needs of the colonised other. Interestingly, it is by them and about them, but has tremendous hermeneutical consequences for the West.

Unlike the other critical categories which are in vogue today, postcolonialism's incarnation was in the form of imaginative literature in the writings of Indians, Africans and Latin Americans. Theoretical fine-tuning followed later. In an era which is so paranoid about getting theoretical procedures correct, postcolonial critics may be enticed into spending their energy in a search for finer theoretical excellence, and so lose their ability to trigger off a new wave of imaginative hermeneutical renditions. If they persist in this they will forfeit their appeal and momentum, and are bound to become redundant. Such a pursuit would be then seen as an escapist activity, with inventive hermeneutical productions giving way to theoretical purity.

Any theory or discourse practice that does not have within itself an inbuilt mechanism for its own deconstruction will become a potent tool for theological and ideological propaganda. This applies to postcolonial theory as to any other.

The success of postcolonialism depends on its engagement with more than one constituency. It should be able to move freely in the academy and the world outside. It should involve both intellectual and popular discourse. Postcolonial theory as it is practised in certain circles has been perceived to be too complex and esoteric to have much influence outside the academy. While the academic community has produced incisive critiques of Orientalism, the popular media, and especially the ecumenical and denominational press continue to orientalise in their voracious portrayals of an exotic/demonic version of India/Africa through food, famine, films etc. One of the uses of postcolonial theory is to make readers and audience aware of the nature of representation.

The task of the postcolonial critic is not only to speak truth to the powerful, as Edward Said has been urging, but also to speak to the poor about the powerful, especially about the enormous power wielded by the media, multinationals and the institutionalized Church.

If postcolonial theory helps us to familiarise ourselves with the bylanes and pathways of Dickensian England, but acts as a diversion and fails to take note of today's inner cities and Third World problems, then the theory will not be worth employing. Textual reclamations and resistant reading practices will make sense only if they address the questions people face today. Eventually, the question is not whether our reading practice is seen as colonial or post colonial, modern or postmodern. Its usefulness will not be judged by its ability to offer a critique of the complex heritage that colonial occupation produced. Its critical relevance will be assessed when it has a bearing on the issues that cause concern to our people, such as housing, education, homeland, healthcare, social security, and the justice system. Its worth will be appraised in the light of the vital role it can play when the time comes for deciding these issues which affect people, rather than whether its theoretical base is modern or non-modern, colonial or anti-colonial. The task of postcolonialism is ensuring that the needs and aspirations of the exploited are catered to, rather than being merely an interesting and engaging avenue of inquiry.

This essay was written in appreciation of Heikki Räisänen's critical engagement with the interpretative voices that have emerged from outside the traditional Euro-American circles.

GLAUBE UND WISSEN:[1] EIN VORTRAG FÜR SOLCHE, DIE DEM CHRISTENTUM ENTWACHSEN SIND UND TROTZDEM WEITER NACH SEINER WAHRHEIT SUCHEN

Gerd Lüdemann

I

Wissen ist in der Alltagssprache ein ziemlich eindeutiges Wort, Glauben dagegen nicht. Wissen zielt auf Überprüfbarkeit, Allgemeingültigkeit, Rationalität und Objektivität. Griechische Philosophen waren die ersten, die wirkliches Wissen von blosser Meinung oder nur Glauben unterschieden. Glauben ist nämlich vieldeutig. Glauben kann etwa als blosse Meinung rein negativ verstanden werden. "Ich glaube" heisst dann so viel wie: "Ich weiss nicht genau". Ferner zeigt sich die Vieldeutigkeit des Begriffs Glauben dort, wo jemand einem anderen seinen Glauben lassen will, d.h. darauf verzichtet, ihn in einem konkreten Fall von dem an sich richtigen Gegenteil zu überzeugen. Hier hat Glauben den Beiklang von Illusion. Ähnliches kommt dort zum Ausdruck, wo jemand bedauert, er könne im Gegensatz zu einem anderen nicht mehr glauben. Hier ist Glaube etwas, das dem Sprecher nicht mehr zugänglich ist, offenbar weil die Realität ihm diesen Weg versperrt.

[1] Dieser Vortrag versucht die Ergebnisse historischer Forschung verständlich darzustellen und konstruktive Wege aus der damit gegebenen Glaubenskrise aufzuzeigen. Ich veröffentliche ihn bewusst in einer Festschrift für Heikki Räisänen, weil ich mich mit ihm in der rücksichtslosen Erforschung historischer Wahrheit verbunden weiss und ebenfalls mit ihm die Hochschätzung der Religionsgeschichtlichen Schule teile. Zu den im Vortrag vorausgesetzten historischen Einzelergebnissen sei verwiesen auf meine Bücher: G. Lüdemann, *Ketzer: Die andere Seite des frühen Christentums* (Stuttgart: Radius-Verlag, 1995); ders., *Jesus nach 2000 Jahren: Was er wirklich sagte und tat* (Lüneburg: zu Klampen, 2000) (mit Beiträgen von Frank Schleritt und Martina Janßen). Die Behandlung systematisch-theologischer Fragen und meine Kritik an Rudolf Bultmanns theologischem Ausweg aus der durch die historische Kritik hervorgerufenen Krise finden sich in meinem Büchlein *Im Würgegriff der Kirche. Für die Freiheit der theologischen Wissenschaft*, (Lüneburg: zu Klampen, 1998).—Frank Schleritt danke ich fürs Mitdenken und für seine Hilfe.

Die Relativierung der Gültigkeit des Glaubens in der Neuzeit ist eng mit der Abkehr der Wissenschaften von der Kirchenlehre verbunden. Wissen war fortan—wenigstens von seinem Anspruch her—rational begründet; Glauben wurde mit Irrationalität zusammen gesehen. Den irrationalen Beigeschmack des Glaubens gab der Massenpsychologe Gustav Le Bon vor einem Jahrhundert folgendermassen wieder: "Die religiösen Führer konnten in den Seelen jene furchtbare Macht erzeugen, die Glaube heisst und den Menschen zum völligen Sklaven seines Traumes machte."[2] Die Frage stellt sich hier allerdings, ob nicht in der Fähigkeit zum Glauben ein enormes, gegebenenfalls auch positiv zu wertendes Potential steckt und ob nicht zuweilen Wissen in sein gerades Gegenteil umschlagen kann. Das geschieht regelmässig dort, wo es seine eigenen Möglichkeiten überschätzt und ideologische, nicht mehr hinterfragbare Züge annimmt. Doch habe ich mit diesen Überlegungen schon vorgegriffen. Ich komme später darauf zurück.

II

Wenden wir uns zunächst wieder dem Glauben und seiner christlichen Interpretation zu. In den christlichen Gemeinschaften wird Glaube zumeist mit weiteren Bestimmungen verbunden. Hier ist das Objekt des Glaubens entscheidend: Vater, Sohn, Heiliger Geist, denn der Inhalt des Glaubens macht den Unterschied aus gegenüber rivalisierenden Bestimmungen. Innerchristliche Unterschiede werden dann durch weitere Glaubensobjekte wie Jungfrauengeburt, Auferstehung, Kirche usw. markiert.

Ein solches Verständnis von Glauben zieht sich durch die Kirchengeschichte der letzten 1700 Jahre hindurch. Es wird abgesichert durch zweierlei: *erstens* durch die Sammlung heiliger Schriften des Alten und des Neuen Testaments, in denen die Stimme Gottes durch den Mund auserwählter Menschen an die einzelnen Gemeinden in Vergangenheit und Gegenwart ergehen soll, und *zweitens* durch ein bestimmtes Geschichtsbild, das den Ursprüngen des christlichen Glaubens eine besondere Bedeutung beimisst. Wir können es kurz so wiedergeben: Jesus, der sündlose Gottessohn, offenbart seinen Aposteln die reine Lehre und stirbt für die Sünden der Welt. Er

[2] Gustav Le Bon, *Psychologie der Massen* (1911) 84.

wird am dritten Tage von den Toten erweckt, befestigt seine Kirche, die ein Herz und eine Seele ist, und beauftragt die Apostel, die frohe Botschaft allen Menschen zu verkündigen. Der Teufel, der in der Folgezeit Ketzer in die Welt schickt, um die rechtgläubigen Christen zu bekämpfen, kann den Lauf des Evangeliums nicht aufhalten.

Beides, die Auffassung von der Bibel als Gotteswort und die Idee der Jungfräulichkeit der frühen Kirche, ist bis in das 17. Jahrhundert unhinterfragbarer Ausgangspunkt des christlichen Dogmas geblieben. Dies änderte sich erst, als die Revolution des naturwissenschaftlichen Weltbildes und das Aufkommen der historisch-kritischen Methode zu einem grossen Dammbruch führten. Die historisch-kritische Methode beraubte die Bibel ihrer Göttlichkeit und das Urchristentum seiner Unschuld. Ja, sie führte zu einer völlig neuen Sicht auch derjenigen Welt, in der das frühe Christentum entstanden war. Alles geriet durcheinander: Die Verfasserangaben der meisten biblischen Schriften wurden widerlegt; man erkannte, dass die Bibel eine Schriftensammlung der siegreichen christlichen Partei im 2. Jahrhundert war; und das Bild der Urkirche als einer Jungfrau erwies sich als frommer Wunsch einer christlichen Gruppierung, die ihre eigene Sicht über wahre und falsche Lehre in die früheste Zeit zurückverlegte.

Die historisch-kritische Schriftforschung beschwor somit eine Krise herauf, die bis heute den Bibelausleger begleitet. War für den Reformator Martin Luther der Wortsinn der Schriften noch gleich mit ihrem historischen Gehalt, so rückte infolge der historisch-kritischen Methode beides auseinander: Das Bild der verschiedenen neutestamentlichen Verfasser von Jesus konnte hinfort nicht mehr als identisch mit dem tatsächlichen Hergang der Ereignisse gelten. Für den historischen Kritiker ist der geschichtliche Abstand jeder heute möglichen Theologie vom urchristlichen Zeitalter unübersehbar und zur Quelle des bis heute tobenden theologischen Kampfes geworden. Anders gesagt: Die Kluft zwischen historischem Faktum und seiner Bedeutung, zwischen Historie und Verkündigung, zwischen Geschichte Jesu und dem widersprüchlichen Bild von seiner Geschichte im Neuen Testament macht es unmöglich, die Bibel als Anrede an moderne Menschen anzusehen. Zudem ist der moderne Historiker der Bibel mit Recht davon überzeugt, dass er viele Dinge besser weiss als die Verfasser der von ihm untersuchten Quellen. Das gilt nicht nur für alle das antike Weltbild betreffenden Fragen, sondern erstreckt sich auf zahlreiche Punkte des harten Glaubenskern. Z.B. wurde Maria mit Sicherheit von einem Mann geschwängert. Denn die jungfräuliche Geburt ist dadurch als Deutung erkannt, dass nicht wenige grosse Männer der Antike, wie etwa Kaiser Augustus oder Alexander der Grosse, auch von einer Jungfrau geboren sein sollen. Ausserdem kennen die ältesten Quellen im frühen Christentum, die Paulusbriefe und das Markusevangelium, die Jungfrauengeburt gar nicht, so dass auch von hierher die Geburt aus der Jungfrau historisch als unzutreffend erwiesen wird.

Den geschichtlichen Gegebenheiten, unter denen sich die Wende zur Neuzeit vollzog, entspricht es, dass insbesondere Theologie und Kirche von dem Erwachen des historischen Bewusstsein getroffen wurden. Alsbald wurde der Kampf im Bereich der Schriftauslegung am heftigsten geführt. Die römisch-katholische Kirche schottete sich von dem Strudel der historischen Erforschung der Bibel von Anfang an ab: Der Papst stellte in zahlreichen Verlautbarungen amtlich in Abrede, dass es irgendeinen Widerspruch zwischen dem christlichen Glauben und der Geschichte geben könne. Abweichler hatten hier keine Möglichkeit, Gehör zu finden oder gar Einfluss auszuüben. So war die historische Erforschung der Bibel bis zum Anfang unseres Jahrhunderts hinein allein im evangelischen Bereich möglich. Doch wurde sie auch hier regelmässig Zielscheibe der Kritik, bis sie endlich wieder ein Zuhause im Raum der Kirche fand und sich dem Glauben unterordnete.[3]

Man sollte meinen, dass Kirche und Theologie angesichts der Springflut des säkularen historischen Bewusstseins längst aus der modernen Gesellschaft verschwunden oder zu Randgruppen geworden wären. Das Gegenteil ist der Fall. Die Ironie der Geschichte wollte es, dass beide Kirchen und die ihnen zugeordnete akademisch-kirchliche Theologie äusserlich unbeschädigt aus der Infragestellung durch die historische Kritik hervorgegangen sind. Sie haben in Deutschland einen nicht zu unterschätzenden Einfluss auf Staat und Gesellschaft und sind finanziell besser ausgestattet als je zuvor. Dies, obgleich sowohl unter Geistlichen als auch unter Kirchenmitgliedern eine

[3] Auch im evangelischen Bereich Deutschlands hat sich die Meinung durchgesetzt, dass ein evangelischer Theologieprofessor die Lehre der Kirche auf wissenschaftlicher Grundlage vertreten soll. Kommt er aufgrund seiner Forschungen zur Einsicht, dass das kirchliche Bekenntnis intellektueller Wahrhaftigkeit nicht entspricht, verliert er sein bekenntnisgebundenes Amt. Weiteres dazu in meinem Buch *Im Würgegriff der Kirche* (s. Anm. 1). Die entsprechenden Gerichtsbeschlüsse finden sich in meiner Homepage (www.gerdlvedemann.de) unter "Interviews".

schleichende Abkehr von traditionellen Inhalten des christlichen Glaubens zu beobachten ist.

Wie steht es aber wirklich mit dem Verhältnis von Glauben und Wissen im Lichte des allgemein anerkannten Tatsachenwissens zum frühen Christentum und zur Bibel? Wir erinnern uns: Der Glaube an die Jungfrauengeburt musste sich dem Wissen stellen, dass sie eine spätere Interpretation und kein historisches Faktum ist. Hinzu kommen weitere historische Ergebnisse, die den Glauben zu relativieren scheinen: Die meisten der für Jesus bezeugten Worte und Taten, wie sie in den Evangelien des Neuen Testaments beschrieben werden, gehen erst auf spätere Interpreten der Person Jesu zurück. Das geschah *erstens* im Rahmen der Auseinandersetzungen innerhalb der frühchristlichen Gemeinde. Man borgte sich die Autorität Jesu, um konkurrierende Mitchristen zum Schweigen zu bringen. Ein Beispiel ist das unechte Jesuswort Lk 16,17: "Es ist leichter, dass Himmel und Erde vergehen, als dass ein Häkchen vom Gesetz fällt."

Das Wort entstammt einer Gemeindesituation, in der ein Kampf zwischen liberalen und konservativen Christen entbrannt war. Die liberalen Christen sind wahrscheinlich Mitglieder von Gemeinden, denen auch der Apostel Paulus zuzuordnen ist. Er wurde von konservativen Christen des Abfalls vom Gesetz beschuldigt. Sie verbreiteten über ihn das Gerücht, er lehre alle Juden in der Diaspora, ihre Söhne nicht mehr zu beschneiden (vgl. Apg 21,21). Diese Christen gehörten der Gemeinde aus Jerusalem an, die unter der Führung des Jakobus, eines Bruders Jesu, zunehmend eine restaurative Haltung zum Gesetz einnahm. In diesen konservativen Kreisen dürfte Jesus ein so rigoroses Wort wie Lk 16,17 zugeschrieben worden sein: "Es ist leichter, dass Himmel und Erde vergehen, als dass ein Häkchen vom Gesetz fällt." Um die eigene Position im Kampf gegen andere Christen zu verteidigen, legte man Jesus dieses Wort einfach in den Mund.

Zweitens wurden Jesusworte aber auch im Kampf gegen ungläubige Juden erfunden. So schrieb der Evangelist Matthäus Jesus folgende Sätze zu:

> (34) Siehe, ich sende zu euch Propheten und Weise und Schriftgelehrte; und von ihnen werdet ihr einige töten und kreuzigen, und einige werdet ihr geisseln in euren Synagogen und werdet sie verfolgen von einer Stadt zur anderen, (35) damit über euch komme all das gerechte Blut, das vergossen ist auf Erden . . . (36) Wahrlich, ich sage euch: Das alles wird über dieses Geschlecht kommen. (37) Jerusalem, Jerusalem, die

> du tötest die Propheten und steinigst, die zu dir gesandt sind! Wie oft habe ich deine Kinder versammeln wollen, wie eine Henne ihre Küken versammelt unter ihre Flügel; und ihr habt nicht gewollt! (38) Siehe, euer Haus soll euch wüst gelassen werden. (Mt 23,34–38)

Die christlichen Propheten, Weisen und Schriftgelehrten in Mt 23, 34 zielen auf die Gegenwart des Matthäus. Sie werden das Schicksal der Tötung, Kreuzigung und Geisselung erleiden, und zwar durch die von Jesus der Heuchelei bezichtigten Pharisäer und Schriftgelehrten. Dabei denkt Matthäus an ein Gericht über ganz Israel. Die Klage über Jerusalem setzt die Strafe der Verwüstung Jerusalems im Jüdischen Krieg voraus, der erst 40 Jahre nach Jesu Tod stattfand. Denn die Verwüstung der Stadt wird hier nicht in Aussicht gestellt, sondern gilt als bereits geschehen: Die Stadt soll wüst (= in Trümmern) liegen bleiben.

Drittens wurden Jesusworte fingiert, um die besondere Würde des Gottessohnes auszudrücken. So entstammen zwei Worte, die Jesus am Kreuz gesprochen haben soll, der erbaulichen Lektüre der alttestamentlichen Psalmen. Der bekannte Verzweiflungsruf "Mein Gott, mein Gott, warum hast du mich verlassen?" aus Mk 15,34 ist ein Zitat aus Psalm 22,2. Und die versöhnliche Anrede "Vater, in deine Hände befehle ich meinen Geist" in Lk 23,46 entspricht wörtlich Psalm 31,6.

Hiermit noch nicht genug: Die Auffassung der neutestamentlichen Verfasser, Jesus selbst habe sein Leiden und seine Auferstehung vorhergesagt, ist durch historische Rekonstruktion ein für allemal widerlegt. Es handelt sich bei den diesbezüglichen Voraussagen ebenfalls um nachträgliche Rückdatierungen aus der Sicht des Glaubens.

Und um das Mass voll zu machen: Die Auferstehung Jesu fand so, wie sie in den neutestamentlichen Evangelien beschrieben bzw. vorausgesetzt wird, mit Sicherheit nicht statt. Die diesbezüglichen Texte vom leeren Grab stammen erst aus dem zweiten Stadium des Auferstehungsglaubens, als es darum ging, die Auferstehung Jesu von den Toten dingfest zu machen und den nachfragenden Juden auch aus den eigenen Reihen ein leeres Grab vorzuführen. Aber auch hierfür fanden die Christen wiederum einen Beleg aus den alttestamentlichen Psalmen. In Psalm 16,10 soll David alias Jesus prophezeit haben, Gott werde den Gottessohn nicht der Verwesung anheimfallen lassen. Also steigerte der Evangelist Lukas die Bedeutsamkeit Jesu dadurch, dass er diesen Psalm in Geschichte übersetzte und Jesus unverweslich werden liess. Das Grab *musste* leer gewesen sein.

Weitere Fakten kommen hinzu und stören das scheinbar harmonische Verhältnis von Glauben und Wissen empfindlich: Auch andere Weissagungen aus dem Alten Testament, die traditionell auf Jesus bezogen werden, haben mit diesem nichts zu tun. So sind sämtliche Voraussagen, die alljährlich im Weihnachts- und Karfreitagsgottesdienst erklingen, erst nachträglich mit Jesus in Verbindung gebracht worden. Weder hatte der Prophet Jesaja im achten vorchristlichen Jahrhundert Jesus im Sinn, als er dem König Ahas die Geburt eines Sohnes voraussagte (vgl. Jes 7,14), noch sind die alttestamentlichen Gottesknechtslieder Weissagungen über den gekreuzigten Gottessohn. Mit anderen Worten, die so eindringlichen Sätze: "Fürwahr, er trug unsere Krankheit und lud auf sich unsere Schmerzen. Wir aber hielten ihn für den, der von Gott geschlagen und gemartert wäre" (Jes 53,4)—diese Sätze haben mit Jesus nicht das Geringste zu tun, sondern beziehen sich auf jemand anderen, vielleicht sogar auf das Schicksal des Volkes Israel ein halbes Jahrtausend vorher.

Ich könnte hier die durch die historische Kritik unwiderleglich und ein für allemal herausgearbeiteten Widersprüche zwischen dem christlichen Glauben und dem tatsächlichen geschichtlichem Hergang noch lange fortsetzen. Die Schlacht ist aber inzwischen zu Ungunsten des Glaubens entschieden. Zwischen dogmatischer Sicht und historischer Rekonstruktion klafft ein Abgrund, den kein Interpretationsversuch der Welt überbrücken kann.

Doch haben moderne Theologen den Widerspruch zwischen Glauben und Wissen aufzulösen versucht. Sie wenden sich beispielsweise sogar entschieden gegen die Annahme, dass die Auferstehung Jesu eine geschichtliche Tatsache bzw. überhaupt ein Vorgang in Raum und Zeit sei. Sie sagen vielmehr: Sachlich bedeutsam an der Rede von der Auferstehung Jesu sei nur, dass der Gekreuzigte nicht vernichtet ist. Denn der Auferstandene sei der Gekreuzigte und nur als solcher für uns heute zu sehen. Doch scheint mir eine solche inhaltliche Bestimmung von Auferstehung sinnlos, da sie mit dem Wort "Auferstehung" und der in den biblischen Texten gemeinten Sache schlechterdings nichts mehr gemeinsam hat.

Unter dieses zugegebenermassen harteVerdikt fällt auch das Programm Rudolf Bultmanns, die Botschaft des Neuen Testaments zu "entmythologisieren". Bultmann wollte den Kern des christlichen Glaubens durch eine Interpretation bewahren, die sich mit dem heutigen Weltbild vereinbaren lässt. Jedoch ist der zur Rettung der Auferstehung herangezogene Gedanke, Jesus sei "in die Verkündigung auferstanden", eine so vollständige Entleerung der in der Bibel vorausgesetzten Sache der körperlichen Auferstehung Jesu, dass er mit keiner historischen Tatsache mehr zusammenprallen kann. Er bleibt, ohne dass ihm eine Spur von historischem Gehalt anhaftet, nur als Worthülse zurück.

Wir sagten, der Kampf um den christlichen Glauben sei durch das Aufkommen der historisch-kritischen Methode auf den Boden der Geschichtsforschung gestellt worden. Das letzte Wort über den Glauben musste also von der Geschichte und dem Wissen über sie gesprochen werden. Dann aber wurde die Entdeckung peinlich, dass sich die Verfälschung und Übermalung des Juden Jesus gegen seine eigenen Landsleute im Neuen Testament bereits in einem fortgeschrittenen Stadium befindet und dass die Schriften des Alten Testaments gegen ihren eigenen Wortsinn auf Jesus bezogen wurden.

Was aber ist gegenüber dem Versuch zu sagen, den christlichen Glauben unter Rückgang auf Jesus zu retten und Jesus etwa als Zeugen des Glaubens zu verstehen? Kann man so nicht guten Gewissens alles Sekundäre streichen, die Auferstehung als reine Interpretation auffassen und somit zu Jesus als dem ersten Christen in eine Beziehung treten? Die Antwort auf diese Frage muss ein entschiedenes "Nein" sein. Denn diesem Versuch gegenüber ist an das sicher verfügbare Wissen zu erinnern, dass Jesus der Religion des Judentums angehörte. Von hier zur christlichen Religion ist es ein weiter Weg. Die Entwicklung des christlichen Dogmas geschah nämlich auf Kosten Israels, gegen die Intention Jesu, der eine Kirche gar nicht erwartet hatte. Man kann Jesus daher nicht mit gutem historischen Gewissen für die christliche Religion in Beschlag nehmen. Jesus gehört Israel an.[4]

Angesichts dieses sicheren Befundes passt auf die weitere Verteidigung des christlichen Dogmas durch heutige Theologen wohl nur der Vorwurf "Betrug", wie ihn bereits jüdische Zeitgenossen im ersten Jahrhundert geäussert haben (vgl. Mt 27,64; 28,15).[5] Denn christliche Dogmatiker führen wiederum wider besseres Wissen eine Sicht

---

[4] Die gelegentlich zu hörende Meinung, Jesus gehöre zwei Religionen an, Israel *und* der Kirche, hat eine gute Intention, ist aber historisch unhaltbar.

[5] Vgl. mein Buch *Der große Betrug: Und was Jesus wirklich sagte und tat* (Lüneburg: Klampen, 1998), dessen Titel absichtlich den intellektuellen Skandal der Instrumentaliesierung eines erfundenen Jesus gegen ungläubige Juden und Abweichler in den eigenen Reihen aufs Korn nimmt.

Jesu ein, die mit Jesus, wie er wirklich war, nichts zu tun hat. Erinnert sei, neben dem bereits Gesagten, an die schlichte Tatsache, dass Jesus Mensch und nichts als Mensch war. Er hat sich durch seine Taufe zur Vergebung der Sünden ganz auf die Seite der sündigen Menschheit gestellt, so dass seine Erhöhung zum Weltenherrn und zum sündlosen Gottessohn nur als merkwürdiges Schauspiel anzusehen ist. Dieses Schauspiel, so sehr seine Glaubensnotwendigkeit betont werden mag, ist im Lichte des historischen Wissens ein für allemal unmöglich geworden.

III

Nun kennt das Wissen selbst seine Grenzen. Es kann z.B. im historischen Bereich immer nur Wahrscheinlichkeitsurteile fällen, und die von ihm angewandte Methode trägt das Mittel in sich, das Wissen immer wieder zu überholen und völlig umzustülpen. Echte Wissenschaft korrigiert sich unaufhörlich selbst. Gleichzeitig steht fest, dass der Mensch kein rein rationales Wesen ist, sondern andere Schichten besitzt, die sich beispielsweise in Kunst und Poesie widerspiegeln. Zu diesem Bereich der Person gehört aber auch die menschliche Fähigkeit und Kraft zum Glauben. Nur wenige Menschen sind imstande, diesen Teil ihrer Person durch Wissen oder Rationalität auch nur ansatzweise in den Griff zu bekommen. Dann aber verlangt das Wissen, die Rationalität selbst, nach einer Kraft, die diese irrationale Seite des Menschen bezeichnet. Ich nenne sie Glauben. Dieser Glaube kann freilich nie wieder Glaube an die Auferstehung oder an die Jungfrauengeburt oder gar an Gott oder an sonst etwas werden. Er ruht, vorläufig gesagt, in sich selbst und weiss sich von etwas getragen.

Eine Entsprechung findet sich vielleicht im Alten Testament, wo ebenfalls Glaube ohne Objekt gebraucht werden kann. Dort ist der absolut gebrauchte Begriff Glaube sprachlich verwandt mit den Begriffen Treue und Festigkeit.[6] Zu diesem sprachlichen Konzept gehört z.B. auch die Verwendung des Wortstamms *aemet*, um Gottes Treue auszusagen. "Amen" heisst dann so viel wie: Es hält, es gilt und darum ist es wahr, es geschieht, es wird Wirklichkeit. Wir begegnen dem absoluten Gebrauch von "glauben" im Alten Testament

[6] Man vgl. im Englischen das Verb "to trust" als Übersetzung von "glauben" oder entsprechend im Deutschen das Verb "trauen" als Äquivalent von "glauben",

an einer Stelle des Jesajabuches, wo der Prophet Jesaja den König Ahas zum Stillehalten angesichts einer politischen Bedrohung rät. Er sagt zu ihm: "Glaubt ihr nicht, so bleibt ihr nicht" (Jes 7,9).

Die Prägnanz dieses Satzes beruht darauf, dass sich im Hebräischen "glauben" und "bleiben" aus derselben sprachlichen Wurzel herleiten. In dieser absoluten Verwendung kann man einen besonders radikalen Ausdruck des alttestamentlichen Glaubensverständnisses sehen. Dass nicht hinzugefügt wird, an wen dieser Glaubende geglaubt hat, hat einen Grund, denn dessen Addition würde dem Glauben seinen eigentlichen Charakter nehmen oder doch abschwächen. Hier bei Jesaja hat der Glaube es zu tun mit dem, was dem Leben Bestand gibt. Wir befinden uns im Bereich des Seins oder Nichtseins. Im Glauben widerfährt dem Leben sein Gegründetsein. Glaube und Sein sind für Jesaja fast gleich, denn "Bestand haben" ist im Sinne des menschlichen Lebens nicht etwa als Lohn für den Glauben gedacht, sondern damit ist die Identität von Glauben und Bestand ausgesprochen. Die zwei verschiedenen Bedeutungen des Verbs im Wort Jesaja 7,9 gehen auf die eine, auf die ursprüngliche zurück: "standhalten".

An dieser Stelle sei betont, dass der Prophet Jesaja selbst mit seinem Wort "Glaubt ihr nicht, so bleibt ihr nicht" in erster Linie ein politisches Ziel verfolgte. Er wollte nämlich König Ahas von seinem Plan abbringen, sich freiwillig dem assyrischen Grossreich zu unterwerfen, um so der Bedrohung durch die Könige von Damaskus und Israel zu entgehen.

Ahas sollte vielmehr im Vertrauen auf Gottes Hilfe ruhig bleiben. Insofern dürfte Jesaja gegenüber dem gerade von mir entwickelten Verständnis von Glauben ziemlich entgeistert reagiert haben, da für ihn der Gott Israels ein sich in der Geschichte offenbarender Gott war. Doch setze ich voraus, dass jede sich an die Geschichte klammernde Theologie gescheitert und dass—damit zusammenhängend—jegliches direkte Reden von Gott fraglich geworden ist. Menschen produzieren menschliche Bilder von Gott. Könnten Ochsen ein Bild malen, so würde ihr Gott wie ein Ochse aussehen—so der griechische Philosoph Xenophanes im sechsten Jahrhundert v.Chr. All das schliesst aber nicht aus, die Rede vom Glauben im Alten Testament und in anderen Schriften aus der Antike, soweit sie die menschliche Ebene betreffen, für die heutige Zeit zu nutzen.

In der auf den Menschen bezogenen Rede vom Glauben im Alten Testament deutet sich eine heute mögliche Glaubensweise an, die ein tragbares Verhältnis von modernem Wissen und Glauben anbahnen kann. Im Untergrund des frühen Christentums, wie er sich in zahlreichen neugefundenen gnostischen Texten dokumentiert, vollzog sich nämlich bereits eine Wendung weg von dem dogmatischen Glaubensverständnis hin zu einem Glauben, der an Bestand und an Tiefe orientiert ist. Einige Mitglieder dieser ketzerischen christlichen Gruppen nannten sich "Angehörige des nicht wankenden Geschlechts".[7]

Ihr Glaube und der Glaube der meisten Gnostiker, der mit Erkenntnis gleichgesetzt werden kann, ist, modern verstanden, der Wille zur totalen Lebensvollendung angesichts des Schreckens der Schöpfung und des Absurden, das zu jeder Stunde den Erdenball durchzittert. In derselben rätselhaften Weise, wie im Laufe der Evolution das Leben auf dieser Erde gegeben wurde, drängt es nämlich auch nach der eigenen Erweiterung bis hin zum kosmischen Bewusstsein. Das so neu bestimmte Glaubensleben strebt nach Ausdehnung in eine unbekannte Richtung aus unbekannten Ursachen, schlicht aus der Tatsache seines Gegebenseins. Dieser Glaube bietet einen Weg, dass wir nämlich von dem festen Grund unseres im Glauben gewonnenen Selbst uns eintauchen lassen in den Strudel des Lebens. Glaube wird zur Macht, ja *ist* geradezu Anteilhabe an der Allmacht des Kosmos. Eine solche Formulierung mag Schrecken auslösen. Zugleich tut sich durch ihn hindurch ein Weg auf, das täglich neu hinzugewonnene Wissen mit dem vom Menschen her verstandenen Glauben in eine verträgliche Beziehung zu setzen.

IV

Ich blicke noch einmal zurück: Wir begannen mit einem Überblick über die umgangssprachliche Bedeutung von Glauben und Wissen und zeigten auf, wie stark der vorwiegend negativ besetzte Sinn von Glauben verursacht ist durch die Emanzipation der Wissenschaft von den Kirchenlehren. Anschliessend wurde aufgewiesen, wie durchgreifend der christliche Glaube als ein Glaube an bestimmte Inhalte wie "Auferstehung", "Jungfrauengeburt" und "Kirche" historisch endgültig widerlegt war. Am Schluss bemühten wir uns um eine tragfähige

[7] Zu den Einzelheiten vgl. Gerd Lüdemann und Martina Janßen, *Bibel der Häretiker: Die gnostischen Texte aus Nag Hammadi* (1997); dies. *Suppressed Prayers: Gnostic Spirituality in Early Christianity*, (London: SCM Press, 1998).

Verhältnisbestimmung von Wissen und Glauben. Sie wird dann möglich, wenn der dogmatische Glaubensinhalt restlos aufgegeben und ein ausschliesslich menschlich begründetes Glaubensverständnis gesucht und gefunden wird. Der so verstandene Glaube ist dann ein Teil des Menschen, dessen Drang nach Wissen sein Schicksal bleibt, dem aber täglich sein Gegründetsein im Kosmos widerfährt. Ob seine Träger jemals wieder ein christliches Haus bauen werden, ist eine Frage für die Zukunft.

INDEX OF ANCIENT SOURCES

Hebrew Bible

Apocrypha and Pseudepigrapha

Dead Sea Scrolls

Josephus

Philo

New Testament

Other Early Christian Literature

Rabbinic Literature

Other Ancient Literature

INDEX OF NAMES

SUPPLEMENTS TO NOVUM TESTAMENTUM

ISSN 0167-9732

2. Strobel, A. *Untersuchungen zum eschatologischen Verzögerungsproblem auf Grund der spätjüdische-urchristlichen Geschichte von Habakuk 2,2 ff.* 1961. ISBN 90 04 01582 5
16. Pfitzner, V.C. *Paul and the Agon Motif.* 1967. ISBN 90 04 01596 5
27. Mussies, G. *The Morphology of Koine Greek As Used in the Apocalypse of St. John.* A Study in Bilingualism. 1971. ISBN 90 04 02656 8
28. Aune, D.E. *The Cultic Setting of Realized Eschatology in Early Christianity.* 1972. ISBN 90 04 03341 6
29. Unnik, W.C. van. *Sparsa Collecta.* The Collected Essays of W.C. van Unnik Part 1. Evangelia, Paulina, Acta. 1973. ISBN 90 04 03660 1
31. Unnik, W.C. van. *Sparsa Collecta.* The Collected Essays of W.C. van Unnik Part 3. Patristica, Gnostica, Liturgica. 1983. ISBN 90 04 06262 9
34. Hagner, D.A. *The Use of the Old and New Testaments in Clement of Rome.* 1973. ISBN 90 04 03636 9
37. Reiling, J. *Hermas and Christian Prophecy.* A Study of The Eleventh Mandate. 1973. ISBN 90 04 03771 3
43. Clavier, H. *Les variétés de la pensée biblique et le problème de son unité.* Esquisse d'une théologie de la Bible sur les textes originaux et dans leur contexte historique. 1976. ISBN 90 04 04465 5
47. Baarda, T., A.F.J. Klijn & W.C. van Unnik (eds.) *Miscellanea Neotestamentica.* I. Studia ad Novum Testamentum Praesertim Pertinentia a Sociis Sodalicii Batavi c.n. Studiosorum Novi Testamenti Conventus Anno MCMLXXVI Quintum Lustrum Feliciter Complentis Suscepta. 1978. ISBN 90 04 05685 8
48. Baarda, T., A.F.J. Klijn & W.C. van Unnik (eds.) *Miscellanea Neotestamentica.* II. 1978. ISBN 90 04 05686 6
50. Bousset, D.W. *Religionsgeschichtliche Studien.* Aufsätze zur Religionsgeschichte des hellenistischen Zeitalters. Hrsg. von A.F. Verheule. 1979. ISBN 90 04 05845 1
52. Garland, D.E. *The Intention of Matthew 23.* 1979. ISBN 90 04 05912 1
53. Moxnes, H. *Theology in Conflict.* Studies in Paul's Understanding of God in Romans. 1980. ISBN 90 04 06140 1
56. Skarsaune, O. *The Proof From Prophecy.* A Study in Justin Martyr's Proof-Text Tradition: Text-type, Provenance, Theological Profile. 1987. ISBN 90 04 07468 6
59. Wilkins, M.J. *The Concept of Disciple in Matthew's Gospel, as Reflected in the Use of the Term 'Mathetes'.* 1988. ISBN 90 04 08689 7
64. Sterling, G.E. *Historiography and Self-Definition.* Josephos, Luke-Acts and Apologetic Historiography. 1992. ISBN 90 04 09501 2
65. Botha, J.E. *Jesus and the Samaritan Woman.* A Speech Act Reading of John 4:1-42. 1991. ISBN 90 04 09505 5
66. Kuck, D.W. *Judgment and Community Conflict.* Paul's Use of Apologetic Judgment Language in 1 Corinthians 3:5-4:5. 1992. ISBN 90 04 09510 1
67. Schneider, G. *Jesusüberlieferung und Christologie.* Neutestamentliche Aufsätze 1970-1990. 1992. ISBN 90 04 09555 1
68. Seifrid, M.A. *Justification by Faith.* The Origin and Development of a Central Pauline Theme. 1992. ISBN 90 04 09521 7

69. Newman, C.C. *Paul's Glory-Christology.* Tradition and Rhetoric. 1992. ISBN 90 04 09463 6
70. Ireland, D.J. *Stewardship and the Kingdom of God.* An Historical, Exegetical, and Contextual Study of the Parable of the Unjust Steward in Luke 16: 1-13. 1992. ISBN 90 04 09600 0
71. Elliott, J.K. *The Language and Style of the Gospel of Mark.* An Edition of C.H. Turner's "Notes on Marcan Usage" together with other comparable studies. 1993. ISBN 90 04 09767 8
72. Chilton, B. *A Feast of Meanings.* Eucharistic Theologies from Jesus through Johannine Circles. 1994. ISBN 90 04 09949 2
73. Guthrie, G.H. *The Structure of Hebrews.* A Text-Linguistic Analysis. 1994. ISBN 90 04 09866 6
74. Bormann, L., K. Del Tredici & A. Standhartinger (eds.) *Religious Propaganda and Missionary Competition in the New Testament World.* Essays Honoring Dieter Georgi.1994. ISBN 90 04 10049 0
75. Piper, R.A. (ed.) *The Gospel Behind the Gospels.* Current Studies on Q. 1995. ISBN 90 04 09737 6
76. Pedersen, S. (ed.) *New Directions in Biblical Theology.* Papers of the Aarhus Conference, 16-19 September 1992. 1994. ISBN 90 04 10120 9
77. Jefford, C.N. (ed.) *The* Didache *in Context.* Essays on Its Text, History and Transmission. 1995. ISBN 90 04 10045 8
78. Bormann, L. *Philippi – Stadt und Christengemeinde zur Zeit des Paulus.* 1995. ISBN 90 04 10232 9
79. Peterlin, D. *Paul's Letter to the Philippians in the Light of Disunity in the Church.* 1995. ISBN 90 04 10305 8
80. Jones, I.H. *The Matthean Parables.* A Literary and Historical Commentary. 1995. ISBN 90 04 10181 0
81. Glad, C.E. *Paul and Philodemus.* Adaptability in Epicurean and Early Christian Psychagogy. 1995 ISBN 90 04 10067 9
82. Fitzgerald, J.T. (ed.) *Friendship, Flattery, and Frankness of Speech.* Studies on Friendship in the New Testament World. 1996. ISBN 90 04 10454 2
83. Tilborg, S. van. *Reading John in Ephesus.* 1996. 90 04 10530 1
84. Holleman, J. *Resurrection and Parousia.* A Traditio-Historical Study of Paul's Eschatology in 1 Corinthians 15. 1996. ISBN 90 04 10597 2
85. Moritz, T. *A Profound Mystery.* The Use of the Old Testament in Ephesians. 1996. ISBN 90 04 10556 5
86. Borgen, P. *Philo of Alexandria - An Exegete for His Time.* 1997. ISBN 90 04 10388 0
87. Zwiep, A.W. *The Ascension of the Messiah in Lukan Christology.* 1997. ISBN 90 04 10897 1
88. Wilson, W.T. *The Hope of Glory.* Education and Exhortation in the Epistle to the Colossians. 1997. ISBN 90 04 10937 4
89. Peterson, W.L., J.S. Vos & H.J. de Jonge (eds.). *Sayings of Jesus: Canonical and Non-Canonical.* Essays in Honour of Tjitze Baarda. 1997. ISBN 90 04 10380 5
90. Malherbe, A.J., F.W. Norris & J.W. Thompson (eds.). *The Early Church in Its Context.* Essays in Honor of Everett Ferguson. 1998. ISBN 90 04 10832 7
91. Kirk, A. *The Composition of the Sayings Source.* Genre, Synchrony, and Wisdom Redaction in Q. 1998. ISBN 90 04 11085 2
92. Vorster, W.S. *Speaking of Jesus.* Essays on Biblical Language, Gospel Narrative and the Historical Jesus. Edited by J. E. Botha. 1999. ISBN 90 04 10779 7
93. Bauckham, R. *The Fate of Dead.* Studies on the Jewish and Christian Apocalypses. 1998. ISBN 90 04 11203 0

94. Standhartinger, A. *Studien zur Entstehungsgeschichte und Intention des Kolosserbriefs.* ISBN 90 04 11286 3 *(In preparation)*
95. Oegema, G.S. *Für Israel und die Völker.* Studien zum alttestamentlich-jüdischen Hintergrund der paulinischen Theologie. 1999. ISBN 90 04 11297 9
96. Albl, M.C. *"And Scripture Cannot Be Broken".* The Form and Function of the Early Christian *Testimonia* Collections. 1999. ISBN 90 04 11417 3
97. Ellis, E.E. *Christ and the Future in New Testament History.* 1999. ISBN 90 04 11533 1
98. Chilton, B. & C.A. Evans, (eds.) *James the Just and Christian Origins.* 1999. ISBN 90 04 11550 1
99. Horrell, D.G. & C.M. Tuckett (eds.) *Christology, Controversy and Community.* New Testament Essays in Honour of David R. Catchpole. 2000. ISBN 90 04 11679 6
100. Jackson-McCabe, M.A. *Logos and Law in the Letter of James.* The Law of Nature, the Law of Moses and the Law of Freedom. 2001. ISBN 90 04 11994 9
101. Wagner, J.R. *Herald of the Good News.* Isaiah and Paul "In Concert" in the Letter to the Romans 2001. ISBN 90 04 11691 5
102. Cousland, J.R.C. *The Crowds in the Gospel of Matthew.* 2002. ISBN 90 04 12177 3
103. Dunderberg, I., C. Tuckett and K. Syreeni. *Fair Play: Diversity and Conflicts.* Essays in Honour of Heikki Räisänen. 2002. ISBN 90 04 12359 8

94. Standhartinger, A. *Studien zur Entstehungsgeschichte und Intention des Kolosserbriefs.* ISBN 90 04 11286 3 *(In preparation)*
95. Oegema, G.S. *Für Israel und die Völker.* Studien zum alttestamentlich-jüdischen Hintergrund der paulinischen Theologie. 1999. ISBN 90 04 11297 9
96. Albl, M.C. *"And Scripture Cannot Be Broken".* The Form and Function of the Early Christian *Testimonia* Collections. 1999. ISBN 90 04 11417 3
97. Ellis, E.E. *Christ and the Future in New Testament History.* 1999. ISBN 90 04 11533 1
98. Chilton, B. & C.A. Evans, (eds.) *James the Just and Christian Origins.* 1999. ISBN 90 04 11550 1
99. Horrell, D.G. & C.M. Tuckett (eds.) *Christology, Controversy and Community.* New Testament Essays in Honour of David R. Catchpole. 2000. ISBN 90 04 11679 6
100. Jackson-McCabe, M.A. *Logos and Law in the Letter of James.* The Law of Nature, the Law of Moses and the Law of Freedom. 2001. ISBN 90 04 11994 9
101. Wagner, J.R. *Herald of the Good News.* Isaiah and Paul "In Concert" in the Letter to the Romans 2001. ISBN 90 04 11691 5
102. Cousland, J.R.C. *The Crowds in the Gospel of Matthew.* 2002. ISBN 90 04 12177 3
103. Dunderberg, I., C. Tuckett and K. Syreeni. *Fair Play: Diversity and Conflicts.* Essays in Honour of Heikki Räisänen. 2002. ISBN 90 04 12359 8